HARDPRESS.NET
HOME OF HARD-TO-FIND BOOKS

The Law of Injunctions
by Francis Hilliard

Address:
HardPress
8345 NW 66TH ST #2561
MIAMI FL 33166-2626
USA
Email: info@hardpress.net

LAW PUBLICATIONS

OF

KAY & BROTHER,

19 South Sixth Street, Philadelphia.

ACTS OF ASSEMBLY OF PENNSYLVANIA. The Complete Acts of the General Assembly of Pennsylvania, from the year 1801 down to the year 1865. 52 vols. 8vo. half sheep. (Exceedingly scarce.) $150 00.

ADDISON ON CONTRACTS. A Treatise on the Law of Contracts, and Rights and Liabilities, *ex contractu*, by C. G. Addison Esq., Barrister-at-Law. Third American from the fifth London edition, with copious Notes and References to American Cases, by Edward Ingersoll, Esq. (In preparation.)

ADDISON ON WRONGS. A Treatise on Wrongs and their Remedies. By C. G. Addison, author of "A Treatise on the Law of Contracts." With full American Notes. (In preparation.)

ALDEN'S CONDENSED REPORTS. The Reports of the Supreme Court of Pennsylvania, from the year 1754, to the year 1844. Condensed by T. J. Fox Alden, of the Pittsburgh Bar. 3 vols. 8vo. $12 00.

*** These volumes are furnished with an Index and Table of Cases, and are complete in themselves. They include the Reports of—

DALLAS	. . . 4 vols.	1754—1806	BINNEY	. . . 6 vols.	1799—1814
YEATES	. . . 4 "	1791—1808	ADDISON	. . . 1 vol.	1791—1799

BALDWIN'S CIRCUIT COURT REPORTS. Reports of Cases determined in the Circuit Court of the United States in and for the Third Circuit, comprising the Eastern District of Pennsylvania and the State of New Jersey, from 1828 to 1833. By Henry Baldwin, one of the judges of that court. 8vo. $6 00.

BALDWIN ON THE CONSTITUTION OF THE UNITED STATES. A General View of the Origin and Nature of the Constitution and Government of the United States, deduced from the political history and condition of the Colonies and States from 1774 to 1788, and the decisions of the Supreme Court of the United States; together with opinions in the cases decided at January Term, 1837, arising on the Restraints on the Powers of the States. By Henry Baldwin, one of the Associate Justices of the Supreme Court of the United States. 8vo. $1 75.

BALL & BEATTY'S REPORTS. Reports of Cases argued and determined in the High Court of Chancery, in Ireland, during the time of Lord Chancellor Manners. By T. Ball and F. Beatty, Esquires. Two vols. in one. 8vo. $5 00.

BELT'S SUPPLEMENT.   A Supplement to the Reports in Chancery
of Francis Vesey, Senior, during the time of Lord Chancellor Hardwicke, comprising
Corrections of Statements, and Extracts of the Decrees and Orders from the Registrar's Books, References to the Cases cited, subsequent determinations on the several
points, some Manuscript Cases, new Marginal Notes, and a copious Index.   By Robert
Belt, Esq.   8vo. $4 00.

BINNS'S JUSTICE.   A Treatife on the Office and Duties of Aldermen
and Justices of the Peace in the Commonwealth of Pennsylvania, including all the
required Forms of Process and Docket Entries, and embodying not only whatever
may be deemed valuable to Justices of the Peace, but to Landlords, Tenants, and
General Agents, and making the volume, what it purports to be, a Safe Legal Guide
for Business Men.   By John Binns, late Alderman in the City of Philadelphia.
Seventh edition, revised, corrected, and greatly enlarged, by F. C. Brightly, Esq.,
author of "Equity Jurisprudence," "Digest of the Laws of the United States," &c.
8vo. $5 50.

BISSET ON THE LAW OF PARTNERSHIP.   A Practical Treatife
on the Law of Partnership, including the Law Relating to Joint-Stock Companies.
With an Appendix of Precedents, Forms, and Statutes.   By Andrew Bisset, of Lincoln's Inn, Esq., Barrister-at-Law.   With very full Notes of American Cases.   8vo.
$2 50.

BLACKBURN ON THE CONTRACT OF SALE.   A Treatife on
the Effect of the Contract of Sale on the Legal Rights of Property and Possession in
Goods, Wares, and Merchandise.   By Colin Blackburn, of the Inner Temple, Esq.,
Barrister-at-Law.   8vo. $1 25.

BRIGHTLY'S DIGEST OF THE LAWS OF THE UNITED
STATES.   An Analytical Digest of the Laws of the United States, from the adoption
of the Constitution to the end of the Thirty-eighth Congress, 1789–1865.   By Frederick C. Brightly, Esq.   2 vols. imperial 8vo. $14 50.
₊ Either volume for sale separately.   The first, from 1789 to 1857, at $8 00.   The second, from
1857 to 1865, at $6 50.

BRIGHTLY'S DIGEST OF FEDERAL DECISIONS.   A Digeft of
the Decisions of the Federal Courts : comprising the Reports of the Supreme, Circuit,
and District Courts, and the Court of Claims, as reported in the regular Series ; and
also including the numerous Federal Cases contained in the State Reports and in the
Legal Periodicals.   (In preparation.)

BRIGHTLY'S EQUITY JURISPRUDENCE.   A Treatife on the
Equitable Jurisdiction of the Courts of Pennsylvania, with Notes of Pleading and
Practice in Equity, and an Appendix of Practical Forms.   By Frederick C. Brightly,
Esq., author of the "Law of Costs," "Nisi Prius Reports," &c. ; Editor of "Pur-
don's Digest," &c.   8vo. $5 50.

BRIGHTLY'S REPORTS.   Reports of Cafes decided by the Judges of
the Supreme Court of Pennsylvania, in the Court of Nisi Prius at Philadelphia, and
also in the Supreme Court, with Notes and References to recent Decisions.   By F. C.
Brightly.   8vo. $5 50.

BRIGHTLY ON THE LAW OF COSTS.   A Practical Treatife on
the Law of Costs in Pennsylvania ; with the Fee-Bill, and Decisions of the Courts
thereon ; and a View of the Remedies for taking illegal Fees.   By Frederick C
Brightly, Esq. Counsellor-at-Law.   8vo. $2 50.

BROWN'S FORUM.   The Forum ; or, Forty Years' Full Practice at the
Philadelphia Bar.   By David Paul Brown.   2 vols. 8vo. $6 00.

CASEY'S PENNSYLVANIA STATE REPORTS.   Pennfylvania State
Reports, containing Cases adjudged by the Supreme Court of Pennsylvania, from 1855
to 1860.   By Joseph Casey, Esq., State Reporter.   12 vols. 8vo. $54 00.

COKE UPON LITTLETON.   The firft part of the Inftitutes of the
Laws of England, or a Commentary upon Littleton, by Sir Edward Coke.   Revised
and corrected, with additions of Notes and proper Tables, by Francis Hargrave and
Charles Butler, Esqs., of Lincoln's Inn ; including also the Notes of Lord Chief
Justice Hale and Lord Chancellor Nottingham ; and an Analysis of Littleton, written
by an unknown hand, in 1658-9.   By Charles Butler, Esq., one of His Majesty's
Counsel.   First American, from the Nineteenth London Edition, corrected.   2 vols.
8vo. $13 00.

CORD ON THE RIGHTS OF MARRIED WOMEN. A Treatife on the Legal and Equitable Rights of Married Women; as well in respect to their Property and Persons as to their Children. With an Appendix of the recent American Statutes, and the Decisions under them. By Wm. H. Cord, Esq. 8vo. $6 50.

COVENTRY & HUGHES'S DIGEST. An Analytical Digefted Index to the English Common Law Reports, from the time of Henry III., to the commencement of the reign of George III., with a Table of Titles and Names of Cases. By T. Coventry, Esq., and S. Hughes, Esq. First American, from the last London Edition. 2 vols. 8vo. $9 00.

DEBATES IN THE CONSTITUTIONAL CONVENTION OF PENNSYLVANIA. Proceedings and Debates of the Convention of the Commonwealth of Pennsylvania, to propose Amendments to the Constitution, commenced and held at Harrisburg, on the 2d day of May, 1837. Reported by John Agg, Stenographer to the Convention. 14 vols. 8vo. $20 00.

DESAUSSURE'S REPORTS. Reports of Cafes Argued and Determined in the Court of Chancery of the State of South Carolina, and in the Court of Appeals in Equity. By Henry William Desaussure, Senior Judge of the Court of Equity, and President Judge of the Court of Appeals in Equity, in the said State. Second Edition. Revised and corrected. 4 vols. in 2, 8vo. $15 00.

DUANE ON THE LAW OF LANDLORD AND TENANT IN PENNSYLVANIA. A View of the Relation of Landlord and Tenant in Pennsylvania, as affected by Acts of Assembly and Judicial Decisions. By William Duane, Esq., author of "A Treatise on the Road Laws of Pennsylvania." 12mo. 75 cents.

DUANE ON THE ROAD LAWS OF PENNSYLVANIA. A View of the Law of Roads, Highways, Bridges, and Ferries in Pennsylvania. By William Duane, Esq., author of "A View of the Relation of Landlord and Tenant in Pennsylvania." 12mo. 75 cents.

DUNLAP'S BOOK OF FORMS. A Book of Forms, containing more than two thousand Forms for Practice in the Courts of Pennsylvania and of the United States, and for Conveyancing; also, for the use of Public Officers, and Men of Business generally. Adapted to the recent Acts of Assembly of Pennsylvania, with Explanatory Remarks, and numerous Precedents and References to Standard Authorities. By James D. Dunlap, Counsellor-at-Law, &c. Fourth edition, revised and greatly enlarged. 8vo. $5 50.

EDEN'S CHANCERY REPORTS. Reports of Cafes Argued and Determined in the High Court of Chancery, from 1757 to 1766, from the original manuscripts of Lord Chancellor Northington, collected and arranged with Notes and References to former and subsequent determinations, and to the Registrar's Books. By the Hon. R. H. Eden, Esq. First American, from the last London edition. 2 vols. in one. 8vo. 5 00.

EQUITY DRAFTSMAN, fee VAN HEYTHUYSEN.

EQUITY RULES. Rules of Equity Practice adopted by the Supreme Court of Pennsylvania, May 27th, 1865; with the Report of the Commissioners, and a full Index. 8vo. Pamph. 50 cents.

FEARNE ON REMAINDERS. An Effay on the Learning of Contingent Remainders and Executory Devises. By Charles Fearne, Esq., Barrister-at-Law. Fourth American, from the Tenth London Edition, containing the Notes, Cases, and other matter added to the former editions, by Charles Butler, Esq., with an original view of Executory Interests in Real and Personal Property, comprising the points deducible from the Cases stated in the Treatise of Fearne, as well as statements of, and the conclusions from, three hundred additional Modern Cases, together with References to numerous other Decisions, and so connected with the text of Fearne, as to form a body of notes thereto. By Josiah W. Smith, Esq. 2 vols. 8vo. $9 00.

FINLASON'S LEADING CASES ON PLEADING. A Selection of Leading Cases on Pleading and Parties to Actions, with Practical Notes elucidating the Principles of Pleading (as exemplified in cases of most frequent occurrence in Practice) by a Reference to the Earliest Authorities, and designed to assist both the Practitioner and the Student. By W. Finlason, Esq., of the Middle Temple, Special Pleader. 8vo. $1 50.

FORUM (The), fee BROWN.

GRAYDON'S FORMS OF CONVEYANCING AND PRACTICE.
Forms of Conveyancing, and of Practice in the Courts of Common Pleas, Quarter
Sessions, Oyer and Terminer, the Supreme and Orphans' Courts, and the Offices of the
various Civil Officers and Justices of the Peace, in Pennsylvania. By W. Graydon.
Fourth edition, revised, corrected, enlarged, and adapted to the present state of the
law; with copious Explanatory Notes and References, and also a new and very comprehensive Index. By Robert E. Wright, Esq. 8vo. $3 50.

GREENING'S FORMS. A collection of Forms of Declarations and
other Pleadings usually prepared in Attorneys' Offices. With Notes. By Henry
Greening, Special Pleader. With Notes and References, by R. E. Wright, Esq.,
adapting it to American Practice. 8vo. (In preparation.)

GRESLEY'S EQUITY EVIDENCE. A Treatife on the Law of Evi-
dence in the Courts of Equity. By the late Richard Newcombe Gresley, Esq., A. M.,
Barrister-at-Law. Second edition, with such Alterations and Additions as to render
it conformable to the Statutes, Decisions, and General Orders regulating the Law and
Practice as to Evidence in the High Court of Chancery; together with divers further
Illustrations, by reference to the Law and Practice, as to Evidence in the Courts of
Common Law and Civil Law. By Christopher Alderson Calvert, Esq., A. M., Bar-
rister-at-Law. 8vo. *Net*, $3 50.

HALE'S PLEAS OF THE CROWN. The Hiftory of the Pleas of
the Crown. By Sir Matthew Hale, Knt.: some time Lord Chief Justice of the King's
Bench. First published from his Lordship's original manuscript, and the several
references to the records examined by the originals: with Notes by Sollom Emlyn,
Esq., with a table of the principal matters. First American edition, with Notes and
References to later Cases, by W. A. Stokes and E. Ingersoll, Esqs. 2 vols. 8vo.
$11 00.

HARRIS'S PENNSYLVANIA STATE REPORTS. Pennsylvania
State Reports, containing Cases adjudged in the Supreme Court of Pennsylvania, from
1849 to 1855. By George W. Harris, State Reporter. 12 vols. 8vo. $54 00.

HARRISON'S DIGEST. An Analytical Digeft of all the Reported
Cases Determined in the House of Lords; the several Courts of Common Law in Banc
and at Nisi Prius, and the Court of Bankruptcy, from 1756 to 1852. Including the
Crown Cases Reserved, and a full selection of Equity Decisions; with the manuscript
cases cited in the best Modern Treatises not elsewhere reported. Second American,
from the third London edition. By R. T. Harrison, Esq. 7 vols. 8vo. *Net*, $50 00.
₊ Vols. 6 and 7 for sale separately, at $6 00 each, *net*.

HILDYARD ON MARINE INSURANCE. A Treatife on the Prin-
ciples of the Law of Marine Insurance. In two parts. I. On the Contract itself,
between the Assured and the Assurer. II. Of the causes which vacate that Contract;
in what cases the Assured is entitled to recover back the Consideration paid by him;
and lastly, what is the Remedy provided by the Law for either party against the other.
By Francis Hildyard, A. M., of the Inner Temple, Esq., Barrister-at-Law. 8vo.
$2 50.

HILLIARD ON INJUNCTIONS. The Law of Injunctions. By
Francis Hilliard, Esq., author of the "Law of Torts," "Law of Mortgages," &c. &c.
1 vol. 8vo. $6 50.

HINDMARCH ON PATENTS. A Treatise on the Law relative to
Patent Privileges for the Sole Use of Inventions, and the Practice of obtaining Letters
Patent for Inventions, with an Appendix of Forms and Entries. By W. M. Hind-
march, Esq., Barrister-at-Law. With an Appendix of, 1. The Acts of Congress; 2.
Decisions of the Courts of the United States, and 3. Forms for obtaining Letters
Patent. 8vo. $2 50.

HOOD ON EXECUTORS. A Practical Treatife on the Law relating
to Registers, Registers' Courts, Orphans' Courts, Auditors, Executors, Administrators,
Guardians, and Trustees in Pennsylvania. With Appendices of Acts of Assembly,
Forms, &c. &c., and an Index. By Samuel Hood, of the Philadelphia Bar. Second
edition. 8vo. (In preparation.)

KAY ON COMMERCIAL LAW. A Compendium of the Mercantile
Law of England. Intended as a Court and Circuit Companion. By Jos. Kay, M. A.,
of the Inner Temple, Esq., Barrister-at-Law. With full American Annotations. (In
preparation.)

LESTER'S LAND LAWS. Decisions of the Interior Department in the Public Land Cases, and Land Laws, passed by the Congress of the United States; together with the Regulations of the General Land Office. By W. W. Lester, Esq., of the Interior Department, Washington, D. C. $5 50.

LINN'S ANALYTICAL INDEX. An Analytical Index of Parallel Reference to the Cases adjudged in the several Courts of Pennsylvania; with an Appendix containing a collection of Cases overruled, denied, doubted, or limited in their application. By Samuel Linn, President Judge of the Twenty-fifth Judicial District. 8vo. $6 00.

MADDOCK'S CHANCERY REPORTS. Reports of Cases Argued and Determined in the Court of the Vice-Chancellor of England, during the time of the Right Hon. Sir Thomas Plumer, Knt. By H. Maddock, Esq. 6 vols. in 3. 8vo. $15 00.

MARSHALL'S CIRCUIT COURT DECISIONS. Reports of Cases Decided by the Honorable John Marshall, late Chief Justice of the United States, in the Circuit Court of the United States for the District of Virginia and North Carolina, from 1802 to 1833 inclusive. Edited by John W. Brockenbrough, Counsellor-at-Law. Vol. 2 only, the 1st vol. being out of print. $5 00.

MILES'S REPORTS. Reports of Cases determined in the District Court for the City and County of Philadelphia, from March, 1835 (with some previous cases), to December, 1840. By John Miles, Counsellor-at-Law. Vol. 2 only, the 1st vol. being out of print. $5 00.

MITCHELL'S PENNSYLVANIA CONSTABLE. A Manual for the Use of Constables in Pennsylvania, with the necessary Forms, &c. &c. By James T. Mitchell, Esq. 12mo. (In preparation.)

MORRIS ON THE LAW OF REPLEVIN. A Practical Treatise on the Law of Replevin in the United States; with an Appendix of Forms, and a Digest of Statutes. By P. Pemberton Morris, Esq., of the Philadelphia Bar. Second edition. 8vo. (In preparation.)

OPINIONS OF THE ATTORNEYS-GENERAL OF THE UNITED STATES. Official Opinions of the Attorneys-General of the United States, advising the President and Heads of Departments in relation to their Official Duties, and expounding the Constitution, Subsisting Treaties with Foreign Governments and with Indian Tribes, and the Public Laws of the Country; Embracing the Opinions of all the Attorneys-General from Randolph to Cushing; with Notes and References. The first 5 vols. by B. F. Hall, Esq.; vols. 6, 7, and 8, by C. C. Andrews, Esq. 8 vols. 8vo. $28 00.

PENNSYLVANIA REPORTS—

Sergeant & Rawle's Reports, 17 vols. Supreme Court.	. . .	$102 00.
Penrose & Watts's Reports, 3 vols. "	.	18 00.
Watts's Reports, 10 vols. "	.	60 00.
Watts's & Sergeant's Reports, 9 vols. "	.	54 00.
Harris's Pennsylvania State Reports, 12 vols. "	.	54 00.
Casey's Pennsylvania State Reports, 12 vols. "	.	54 00.
Wright's Pennsylvania State Reports, 12 vols. "	.	54 00.
Brightly's Reports, 1 vol.	.	5 50.
Miles's Reports, vol. 2 only (District Court of Philadelphia).	.	5 00.
Baldwin's Reports, 1 vol. (C. C. U. S. Eastern District of Pennsylvania).	.	6 00.

PENROSE & WATTS'S REPORTS. Reports of Cases adjudged in the Supreme Court of Pennsylvania, from September Term, 1829, to June Term, 1832. By William Rawle, Jr., Charles B. Penrose, and Frederick Watts, Counsellors at Law. Second Edition. 3 vols. 8vo. $18 00.

POTHIER ON OBLIGATIONS. A Treatise on the Law of Obligations and Contracts, by M. Pothier. Third American Edition. Translated from the French, with an Introduction, Appendix, and Notes, Illustrative of the English Law on the subject, by William David Evans, Esq., Barrister-at-Law. 2 vols. 8vo. $9 00.

PRICE ON LIMITATIONS AND LIENS. Of the Limitation of Actions and of Liens against Real Estate in Pennsylvania. By Eli K. Price. 8vo. $3 50.

PRITCHARD'S ADMIRALTY DIGEST.   An Analytical Digest of
all the Reported Cases determined by the High Court of Admiralty of England, the
Lords Commissioners of Appeal in Prize Causes, and (on Questions of Maritime and
International Law) by the Judicial Committee of the Privy Council ; also of the
Analogous Cases in the Common Law, Equity, and Ecclesiastical Courts, and of the
Statutes applicable to the Cases Reported ; with Notes from the Text Writers, and
other Authorities, on Maritime Law. and the Scotch, Irish, and American Reports.
By William Tarn Pritchard, Esq.   With an appendix containing the American Law
of Evidence in Equity Cases, being an Analytical Digest of Equity Cases decided in
the Courts of the United States and of the several States, from the earliest period
down to the date of the publication of this volume.   8vo. $3 50.

PURDON'S DIGEST, 1700–1861.   A Digeſt of the Laws of Pennſyl-
vania, from the Year One Thousand Seven Hundred to the Twenty-first day of May,
One Thousand Eight Hundred and Sixty-one.   Originally compiled by John Purdon,
Esq.   Ninth Edition.   Revised, with Marginal References ; Foot-notes to the Judi-
cial Decisions ; Analytical Contents ; a Digested Syllabus of each Title ; and a New,
Full, and Exhaustive Index.   By F. C. Brightly, Esq.   1 vol. Imperial 8vo. $7 50.

PURDON'S ANNUAL DIGEST, 1862–1865.   Annual Digeſt of the
Laws of Pennsylvania, for the years 1862 to 1865 : namely, from 21 May, 1861, to 21
June, 1865.   Together with some Laws of older date inadvertently omitted in Purdon's Digest ; completing Brightly's Purdon's Digest to the present time.   By Frederick C. Brightly, Esq., editor of Purdon's Digest, &c.   Imperial 8vo. pamph. $1 50.

ROBERTS'S DIGEST.   A Digeſt of Selećt Britiſh Statutes, compriſing
those which, according to the Report of the Judges of the Supreme Court made to
the Legislature, appear to be in force in Pennsylvania, with some others ; with
Notes and Illustrations.   By Samuel Roberts, President of the Court of Common
Pleas of the Fifth Judicial District of Pennsylvania.   Second Edition, with additional Notes and References to English and American Decisions, giving construction
to these Statutes, down to the present time ; and also, the Report made by the Judges
of the Supreme Court to the Legislature.   By Robert E. Wright, Counsellor-at-Law.
8vo. $2 50.

ROPER ON LEGACIES.   A Treatiſe on the Law of Legacies.   By the
late R. S. Donnison Roper, Esq., Barrister-at-Law ; and by Henry Hopley White,
Esq., Barrister-at-Law.   With References to American Cases.   Second American,
from the Fourth London Edition.   2 vols. 8vo. $11 00.

SANDERS ON USES AND TRUSTS.   An Eſſay on Uſes and Truſts,
and on the Nature and Operation of Conveyances at Common Law, and of those which
derive their Effect from the Statute of Uses.   By Francis Williams Sanders, Esq.
The Second American, from the last London Edition.   By George Williams Sanders,
Esq., and John Warner, Esq.   With References to later English and American Cases,
by a Member of the Philadelphia Bar.   Two volumes in one.   8vo. $5 00.

SAUNDERS ON PLEADING AND EVIDENCE.   The Law of
Pleading and Evidence in Civil Actions, arranged alphabetically, with Practical
Forms ; and the Pleadings and Evidence to support them.   By John Simcoe Saun-
ders, Esq.   The Second Edition by Robert Lush, Esq., Barrister-at-Law.   Sixth
American Edition.   With References by a member of the Philadelphia Bar.   (In
preparation.)

SELWYN'S NISI PRIUS.   An Abridgment of the Law of Nisi Prius.
By William Selwyn, Esq.   Seventh American, from the Eleventh London Edition ;
with the Notes of Messrs. Wheaton, Wharton and Law, and full References to the
late American authorities.   By Asa I. Fish, Esq.   2 vols. 8vo. $13 00.

SERGEANT ON THE MECHANICS' LIEN LAW OF PENNSYL-
VANIA.   A Treatise on the Lien of Mechanics and Material Men in Pennsylvania ;
with the Acts of Assembly relating thereto ; and various Forms of Claims.   By Henry
J. Sergeant, Esq.   Second Edition.   By E. Spencer Miller, Esq., Counsellor-at-Law
and Professor of the Law of Real Estate, Conveyancing, and Equity Jurisprudence in
the Law Department of the University of Pennsylvania. $3 50.

SERGEANT ON FOREIGN ATTACHMENT IN PENNSYLVA-
NIA.   A Treatise upon the Law of Pennsylvania relative to the Proceeding by
Foreign Attachment, with the Acts of Assembly now in force on the subject of Foreign
and Domestic Attachments.   Second Edition, with additions and improvements.   By
Thomas Sergeant, Esq.   8vo. $2 50.

SERGEANT ON THE LAND LAWS OF PENNSYLVANIA. A
view of the Land Laws of Pennsylvania, with Notices of its Early History and Legislation. By Thomas Sergeant, Esq., author of a " Treatise on the Law of Foreign Attachment, &c." 8vo. $2 50.

SERGEANT AND RAWLE'S REPORTS. Reports of Cases adjudged
in the Supreme Court of Pennsylvania, from June Term, 1814, to September Term, 1828. By Thomas Sergeant and William Rawle, Jr. 17 vols. 8vo. $102 00.

SMITH ON EXECUTORY INTERESTS. An Original View of
Executory Interests in Real and Personal Property, comprising the points deducible from the cases stated in the Treatise of Fearne, as well as Statements of, and Conclusions from, three hundred additional Modern Cases, together with References to numerous other Decisions, and so connected with the text of Fearne, as to form a body of notes thereto. By Josiah W. Smith, B. C. L. Esq., Barrister-at-Law. 8vo. $3 50.

SMITH'S FORMS. Forms of Procedure, in the Courts of Pennsylvania.
A complete and reliable Collection of Forms of Procedure, in the Courts of Quarter Sessions, Orphans' Court, Registers' Court ; before the Registers in the Court of Common Pleas, &c. &c. By P. Frazier Smith, Esq. 8vo. $5 50.

SMITH AND REED'S LAWS OF PENNSYLVANIA. Laws of the
Commonwealth of Pennsylvania, republished under the authority of the Legislature, with Notes and References. Commencing 14th October, 1700, and terminating 23d April, 1829. 10 vols. 8vo. $20 00.

₄ The 8th, 9th, and 10th volumes are sold separately, to complete sets, at $2 50 per vol.

STEPHEN ON PLEADING. A Treatise on the Principles of Pleading
in Civil Actions ; comprising a Summary View of the whole Proceedings in a Suit at Law. By Henry John Stephen, Sergeant at Law. Corrected in conformity with the rules of H. T., 1834, and otherwise improved. With notes and additions. By Francis J. Troubat, with additional notes by a member of the Philadelphia Bar. 8vo. $4 00.

TIDD'S PRACTICE. The Practice of the Courts of King's Bench, and
Common Pleas, in Personal Actions and Ejectment, to which are added the Law and Practice of Extents, and the Rules of Court and Modern Decisions, in the Exchequer of Pleas. By Wm. Tidd, Esq. Fourth American, from the ninth London edition, with Notes of Recent English Statutes and Decisions. By Francis J. Troubat, Esq., with additional Notes by A. I. Fish, Esq. 2 vols. 8vo. $13 00.

TROUBAT ON LIMITED PARTNERSHIP. A Treatise on the
Law of Limited Partnership in the United States. With a copious Appendix of Forms of Deeds of Limited Partnership, the Statutes of Limited Partnership enacted by the different States, and Reports of all the Decisions on this branch of the law which have been made in the American courts. By Francis J. Troubat, Esq., of the Philadelphia Bar. 8vo. $5 00.

TROUBAT AND HALY'S PENNSYLVANIA PRACTICE. New
Edition. The Practice in Civil Actions and Proceedings, in the Supreme Court of Pennsylvania, in the District Court and Court of Common Pleas for the City and County of Philadelphia, and in the Courts of the United States. By Francis J. Troubat and William W. Haly. Fourth Edition. 2 vols. 8vo., by A. I. Fish, Esq. (In preparation.)

UNITED STATES CIRCUIT COURT REPORTS—

Baldwin's C. C. Reports. Eastern District of Pennsylvania and New Jersey. 1 vol. 8vo. $6 00.

Marshall's C. C. Decisions. District of Virginia and North Carolina, vol. 2 only. The 1st vol. being out of print. $5 00.

VAN HEYTHUYSEN'S EQUITY DRAFTSMAN. The Equity
Draftsman. Being a Selection of Forms of Pleading in Suits in Equity. Originally compiled by F. Van Heythuysen, Esq. Revised and Enlarged, with numerous additional Forms and Notes, by Edward Hughes, Esq. Fourth American, from the last London edition, with copious Notes and References to American Cases, by a Member of the Philadelphia Bar. 8vo. $7 00.

WATTS'S REPORTS. Reports of Cases argued and determined in the
Supreme Court of Pennsylvania. from May Term, 1832, to September Term, 1840. By Frederick Watts, Counsellor-at-Law. Second Edition. 10 vols. 8vo. $60 00

WATTS AND SERGEANT'S REPORTS. Reports of Cafes adjudged in the Supreme Court of Pennsylvania, from May Term, 1841, to May Term, 1845. By Frederick Watts and Henry J. Sergeant. 9 vols. 8vo. $54 00.

WELFORD'S EQUITY PLEADINGS. A Practical Treatife on Equity Pleadings, with Observations on the New Orders of 1841, and an Appendix containing those Orders. By Richard Griffiths Welford, Esq., of the Inner Temple, Barrister-at-Law. 8vo. $1 50.

WHARTON'S AMERICAN CRIMINAL LAW. A Treatife on the Criminal Law of the United States: comprising a General View of the Criminal Jurisprudence of the Common and Civil Law. and a Digest of the Penal Statutes of the General Government, and of Massachusetts, New York, Pennsylvania, Virginia, and Ohio. By Francis Wharton, Esq., author of "Precedents of Indictments," &c. &c. Fifth and revised edition. 2 vols. 8vo. $14 00.

WHARTON'S PRECEDENTS OF INDICTMENTS AND PLEAS. Precedents of Indictments and Pleas, adapted to the use both of the Courts of the United States and those of the several States; together with Notes on Criminal Pleading and Practice, embracing the English and American Authorities generally. By Francis Wharton, Esq., author of a Treatise on "American Criminal Law," &c. Second and revised edition. 8vo. $7 50.

WHARTON ON THE AMERICAN LAW OF HOMICIDE. A Treatise on the Law of Homicide in the United States; to which is appended a Series of Leading Cases, now out of print, or existing only in manuscript. By Francis Wharton, author of a "Treatise on the Criminal Law of the United States," "Precedents of Indictments and Pleas," "State Trials of the United States," &c. 8vo. $4 50.

WHARTON'S LAW DICTIONARY. A Law Lexicon, or Dictionary of Jurisprudence; Explaining all the Technical Words and Phrases employed in the several Departments of English Law. Including also the various Legal Terms used in Commercial Transactions; together with an Explanatory as well as Literal Translation of the Latin Maxims contained in the writings of the Ancient and Modern Commentators. By J. J. S. Wharton, Esq., Barrister-at-Law, &c. Second American, from the second London edition, with additions. By Edward Hopper, Esq. 8vo. $7 50.

WHARTON AND STILLE'S MEDICAL JURISPRUDENCE. A Treatise on Medical Jurisprudence. By Francis Wharton, Esq., author of a "Treatise on American Criminal Law," &c., and Moreton Stillé, M. D., Lecturer on the Principles and Practice of Medicine in the Philadelphia Association for Medical Instruction. The Medical part Revised and Corrected with numerous additions, by Alfred Stillé, M. D., Prof. of the Practice of Medicine in the University of Pennsylvania. Second and revised edition. 8vo. $8 00.

WHEATON, fee SELWYN.

WILLIAMS ON EXECUTORS. A Treatife on the Law of Executors and Administrators. By Edward Vaughan Williams. (Now one of the Judges of Her Majesty's Court of Common Pleas.) Fifth American, from the last London edition. With Notes and References to American authorities, by Asa I. Fish, Esq. 2 vols. 8vo. $13 00.

WILLIAMS ON PLEADING. An Introduction to the Principles and Practice of Pleading in Civil Actions in the Superior Courts of Law at Westminster. Embracing an Outline of the Whole Proceedings in an Action at Law. By Watkin Williams, Esq., of the Inner Temple, Barrister-at-law. 2 vols. 8vo. With full Notes and References to American Authorities. (In preparation.)

WRIGHT'S PENNSYLVANIA STATE REPORTS. Pennfylvania State Reports, containing Cases adjudged by the Supreme Court of Pennsylvania. By Robert E. Wright, Esq., State Reporter. 12 vols. 8vo. $54 00.

THE

LAW OF INJUNCTIONS.

BY

FRANCIS HILLIARD,

AUTHOR OF "THE LAW OF TORTS," ETC.

PHILADELPHIA:
KAY & BROTHER, 19 SOUTH SIXTH STREET,
LAW BOOKSELLERS, PUBLISHERS, AND IMPORTERS.
1865.

PREFACE.

THE present work, as will be seen, is strictly confined to the subject expressed in the title, *Injunctions.* It is a very noticeable fault in a law treatise, as well as any other, if, while not wanting in *unity of plan*, it fail in *unity of execution;*—if, tempted by some casual association of other subjects with that of which it professes to treat, it fly off from the latter, and fill up its pages with the statement of cases and principles, which, however valuable in themselves, have no *scientific* connection with the main topic sought to be illustrated. Acknowledging its manifold other faults, I think it will be found that this book is not chargeable with the one in question. I may add, however, that, in treating of this single branch of the great *code* of *equity jurisprudence*, I have often been strongly tempted to wander into its other copious departments; with all of which, injunction has a direct connection. Equity is a portion of the law, with which no one can be brought even incidentally in contact, without becoming deeply interested, and inspired with the desire of a thorough and exhaustive exploration. A few remarks upon the general subject may be pardoned in the preface, as no departure from the rule above laid down with regard to the work itself.

Perhaps there is no feature in our American jurisprudence more full of encouragement, than the now prevalent disposition—supplanting a morbid and undefined fear of the shapeless evils which might result from such a policy—to incorporate into·our law the benign principles and the comprehensive and searching remedies of equity.(a) In one aspect, more especially, is this a most desirable tendency. I refer to the adoption of equity jurisprudence, as a substitute for attempts to soften, modify, and adapt the common law, by express statutory enactments. Had the rules and remedies of equity been introduced, with the common law, into our colonial and provincial jurisprudence; it may be doubted whether the statute books of the several United States would have so abounded with brief, positive, and abrupt changes upon some of the most vital subjects of municipal regulation. These changes have been with some truth, no doubt, deemed essential, in order that the law, the growth of less enlightened periods, might keep up with the progress of society. But, from the nature of the case, the remedy has often proved far worse than the disease. Unforeseen consequences have resulted, from the sudden abrogation of time-settled

---

(*c*) See the remarks of Mr. Chief Justice Gibson, on page 418.

rules and principles, far more disastrous than any occasional hardship or abuse in their practical application. As a single example, I need only mention the relation of *husband and wife*—in reference to which American legislation has been so sweeping, so fluctuating, so incoherently various, and, is it too much to say, so unqualifiedly discreditable. With regard to this and numerous other subjects which fall under equity jurisdiction, it would have been far better that the rigor of the common law should have been softened and *toned*, with exceptions and qualifications, like itself the gradual product of advancing ages; than that the same end should have been sought by a few lines of statutory provision, in a breath undoing the work of years and centuries, and often themselves furnishing the material for doubtful construction and interminable litigation.

The present work is designed to be *thoroughly American.* While the English cases have been cited, sufficiently to give a correct view of the English law, as the original foundation, and an existing constituent part, of our own jurisprudence; the process of *selection* has been more largely applied to them than to the decisions of the American courts, which last are designed to be fully and exhaustively stated. The subject of injunction involves so many points which are strictly points of *practice*, and the English differs so widely from the American practice, that many of the English cases would be of little

practical value in the United States.   It is believed,
however, that the leading English decisions, more
especially those of the most recent date, will be found
referred to, and often stated at considerable length.
At the present moment, when the indications are so
strong, of a prevailing desire to have the events of
the last four years treated as if they had never been,
it is perhaps hardly necessary to remark, that, in
citing the American cases, no distinction is made
between the Northern and Southern States.   It so
happens, that the decisions of Southern courts upon
the subject of injunction are comparatively very
numerous.   Every lawyer knows, that the judgments
of those tribunals often bear a favorable comparison
with those of any others in the land.   Upon the
one great subject, which now seems to have provi-
dentially disappeared from the broad surface of
American social and civil life, the remarks of a distinguished jurist are no exaggeration, even as applied
to Southern judges; •to whom, indeed, it would seem
they are almost exclusively applicable, not from want
of disposition, but of opportunity, in any others, to
illustrate them.   " As slavery is in derogation of
natural right, and exists only by positive institution,
the courts of this country, actuated by the spirit of
the common law, have always been disposed to apply
the maxim, *jura in omni casu libertati dant favorem.*"
" For the trial of the question of freedom—in all the
cases in the books it seems that a wide indulgence is

granted to the claimant, and the court will not suffer him to be defeated by an omission of formalities of procedure."(a)

If Southern courts and judges have thus humanely and manfully withstood those legislative and popular influences, which are very far from being entitled to the commendation just quoted; their integrity as well as ability may well entitle their adjudications upon any subject to be received everywhere with undiminished respect.

Injunction has been a subject of much statutory regulation. While, as I have already remarked, the prevailing tendency now is, to adopt equity into American jurisprudence; the distinction is very generally abrogated between *courts* of law and equity, and in some instances between *proceedings* in law and equity. The aphorism of Lord Bacon, to the practical wisdom of which, notwithstanding the *theoretical* absurdity of two codes of law, each administered by its own tribunal, in the same government, many will even now be disposed to assent, is pretty extensively set at nought in American legislation. "Apud nonnullos receptum est, ut jurisdictio, quæ discernit secundum æquum et bonum, atque illa altera, quæ procedit secundum jus strictum, iisdem curiis deputentur: apud alios autem, ut diversis; omnino placet curiarum separatio. Neque enim servabitur distinctio casuum,

---

(a) Parsons on Contracts (3d ed.), pp. 326, 328.

si fiat commixio jurisdictionum, sed arbitrium legem tandem trahet."(a)

The result has been, with reference to the subject of injunction, that in many of the States injunctions may be granted by the courts, or the judges thereof, miscellaneously. The same power is sometimes, though not often, conferred upon mere ministerial officers of the courts. From this consolidation of law and equity, other changes, also, have necessarily ensued, with reference to a proceeding which in its origin was so strictly *equitable*. In the *Appendix* will be found a summary statement of the statutory provisions in the several States; as also of some of the latest cases, which were not inserted in the body of the work.

With regard to the plan and arrangement of the present work, it will be seen that the first six chapters, as compared with those which follow, are of a general and comprehensive character. The succeeding chapters, relating to the *grounds*, *parties*, and *subjects* of injunction, are necessarily more brief and fragmentary, the same points and cases having been previously stated in some other connection. And this threefold division itself is unavoidably somewhat inaccurate; the respective questions, for what injury, by or against what person, and in reference to

---

(a) Bacon, de Aug. Scient., lib. 8, chap. 3, aph. 45.

what subject-matter, an injunction may issue, from the very nature of the case often running into each other.   The division adopted, whether good or bad, is my own.   It may follow, but has not been bor rowed from that of any other work.   F. H.

CONTENTS.

CHAPTER I.

CHAPTER II.

BOND OR OTHER SECURITY.

CHAPTER III.

DISSOLUTION OF INJUNCTIONS.

CHAPTER IV.

VIOLATION OF INJUNCTIONS . . . . 1⊣

CHAPTER V.

INJUNCTION OF JUDGMENTS AND EXECUTIONS . 15�

CHAPTER VI.

INJUNCTION OF SUITS OR ACTIONS . . . 220–260

2

CHAPTER VII.

CHAPTER VIII.

CHAPTER IX.

CHAPTER X.

CHAPTER XI.

CHAPTER XII.

CHAPTER XIII.

CHAPTER XIV.

CHAPTER XV.

CHAPTER XVI.

CHAPTER XVII.

CHAPTER XVIII.

CHAPTER XIX.

CHAPTER XX.

CHAPTER XXI.

CHAPTER XXII.

CHAPTER XXIII.

CHAPTER XXIV.

CHAPTER XXV.

CHAPTER XXVI.

CHAPTER XXVII.

CHAPTER XXVIII.

CHAPTER XXIX.

CHAPTER XXX.

CHAPTER XXXI.

TABLE OF CASES CITED.

3

THE

LAW OF INJUNCTIONS.

THE LAW OF INJUNCTIONS.

CHAPTER I.

DEFINITION, NATURE, AND PURPOSES OF AN INJUNCTION.

§ 1. AN injunction is defined as "a prohibitory writ, specially prayed for by a bill in which the plaintiff's title is set forth, restraining a person from committing or doing an act (other than criminal acts)(*a*) which appears to be against

---

(*a*) An early, and somewhat striking and *dramatic* case, would seem to negative this exception. The defendant and Sir William Russell,

equity and conscience."[1] If the subject of a bill in equity be "to quiet the possession of lands, to stay waste, or to stop proceedings at law, an injunction is also prayed, in the nature of an interdiction by the civil law, commanding the defendant to cease."[2]

§ 2. It is said "an injunction is extraneous to the cause and not a proceeding in it."[3] (See § 18.) So it is held that the injunction can issue only as *auxiliary* to some primary equity, except to stay waste or prevent irreparable injury.[4](a)

[1] Bouv. Law Dict.; Whart. Law Dict.
[2] 3 Bl. Comm. 441.
[3] Per Sir L. Shadwell, V. C.; Gooseman v. Dann, 10 Sim. 518.

[4] Stockton v. Briggs, 5 Jones Equ. 309; Schofield v. Bokkelen, Ib. 342; McRae v. Atlantic, &c., Ib. 395.

---

dining with the plaintiff at his house, after dinner fell into play with the plaintiff and won of him in ready money about 900l., which Brett brought away with him (though when they began to play the defendant and Sir William Russell had not above eight guineas between them), and Sir Bazil, being somewhat inflamed with wine, brought down a bag of guineas containing about 1500l., and Brett won that money also, and had it in his possession; but as he was going away with it out of the house, Firebrasse and his servants seized upon it and took it from him. Firebrasse had brought an information against Brett for playing with false dice, but Brett was acquitted; and Brett had brought an action of trespass against Firebrasse for taking from him, in a forcible manner, this bag of guineas; and thereupon Firebrasse exhibited his bill, charging many circumstances of fraud and circumvention, which were denied by the defendant's answer; and upon the plaintiff's motion the Lord Chancellor granted an injunction till the hearing of the cause, and said that he thought the sum very exorbitant for a man to lose at play in one night, and that if it was in his power he would prevent it, and cited the case of Sir Cecil Bishop and Sir John Staples, in the Lord Chief Justice Hale's time, about a wager upon a foot-race, and that the Chief Justice in that case said that those great wagers *proceeded from avarice, and were founded in corruption.* Firebrasse v. Brett, 1 Vern. 489.

(a) The Supreme Court of Maine can issue writs of injunction only in cases within its equity jurisdiction. Smith v. Ellis, 29 Maine, 422.

The 21st article of the charge against Cardinal Wolsey is, "that the said Lord Cardinal hath granted many injunctions by writ, and the parties never called thereunto, nor bill put in against them." See 1 Vern. 156, n., 4 Inst. 92.

§ 3. The following distinction is taken between an injunction and the somewhat analogous remedy of *prohibition :* (*a*)

§ 4. "A *prohibition* is a remedy against an encroachment of jurisdiction, issues only from a superior court, is granted on the suggestion that the court to which it is directed has not the legal cognizance of the cause, and is directed to the judge of the inferior court as well as to the parties in the cause. An injunction, on the other hand, where its object is to restrain proceedings in another court, is directed only to the parties, neither assumes any superiority over the court in which they are proceeding, nor denies its jurisdiction, but is granted on the sole ground that from certain equitable circumstances of which the court that issues it has cognizance, it is against conscience or the party to proceed in the cause."[1]

§ 5. Injunction is said to be wholly "a *preventive* remedy. (See § 14.) If the injury be already done, the writ can have no operation, for it cannot be applied correctively so as to remove it. It is not used for the purpose of punishment or to compel persons to do right, but simply to prevent them from doing wrong."[2] It is said: "The leading principle—the principle which I humbly conceive ought, generally speaking, to be the guide of the court, and to limit its discretion in granting injunctions, at least where no very special circumstances occur—is, that such a restraint should be imposed as may suffice to stop the mischief complained of, and where it is to stay injury, to keep things as they are for the present."[3] So it is held, that an injunction granted on an *ex*

---

[1] Waterman's Eden, Introd. 14.
[2] Atty. Gen. *v.* N. J., &c., 2 Green, 136.
[3] Per Lord Brougham, Blakemore *v.* Glamorganshire, &c., 1 My. & K. 185.

(*a*) The remedies of injunction and *certiorari* are sometimes compared. Thus. if a justice of the peace grants a new trial without notice, and the party does not appear at the second trial, he may elect between an injunction and a certiorari. Aycock *v.* Williams, 18 Tex. 392.

parte application, on filing the bill, does not require the defendant to do or undo anything, but simply restrains him from acting.[1] That its office is to restrain the acts of the defendant in the suit, and not to compel him to undo what he has already done, or to restore anything, further than this results from such restraint; unless issued after the decree, when it becomes a judicial process.[2]

§ 6. The lessee of an inn covenanted to use and keep it open as such, and not do any act to forfeit the licenses. He having threatened to act in violation of the former part of the covenant, the lessor obtained an *ex parte* injunction, restraining him from the discontinuance covenanted against, and from doing any act whereby the licenses might become forfeited or be refused. No intention appearing to violate the negative part of the covenant, and the court having no power to enforce the other part, which would be equivalent to ordering the defendant to keep an inn; held, the injunction should be dissolved.[3] So, upon motion for an injunction, the object was, to compel the party to put everything in the same state in which it was before, by filling up a ditch he had made, as well as to prevent digging farther. Lord Thurlow said: "I will not order him to fill up this ditch before answer. That would be a great deal too much to do. This ditch may be a mile long. Take an order that he shall do nothing more till answer or farther order."[4]

§ 7. From the nature of injunction as a preventive remedy it necessarily results, that, in order to justify its application, the injury in question must be likely to occur without it. Hence, where it appeared that there was no intention on the part of the defendants to do the alleged wrong, but they were attending to the plaintiff's objections, and endeavoring to ascertain what course was the best for them to pursue, the

[1] Bosley *v.* Susquehanna, &c., 3 Bland, 63.
[2] Murdock's Case, 2 Bland, 461 ;

Washington, &c. *v.* Green, 1 Maryland Ch. Decis. 97.
[3] Hooper *v.* Brodrick, 11 Sim. 47.
[4] 1 Ves. Jr. 140.

bill was dismissed with costs. The court remark : "If an injunction were granted in this case, it would be an injunction to restrain the defendants from doing acts, which they never had any intention of doing except in the performance of their duty, and which they have in pursuance of the plaintiff's suggestions formally resolved not to do at all."[1] And in a case relating to a water-course, it was remarked, with reference to the necessary conditions of granting an injunction : "One of those conditions is, that the injunction, by stopping the acts complained of, will restore or tend to restore the party complaining to the enjoyment of that right which he has established against the defendant. I say 'restore or tend to restore,' because I conceive it is no answer to an application of this sort for the defendant to say that other persons as well as he are polluting the stream, and, therefore, the injunction will not restore the plaintiff to the enjoyment of his legal right, inasmuch as it will not prevent those other persons from continuing to pollute the water ; for the plaintiff must sue each of the wrong doers separately, unless, indeed, they are acting in partnership or in concert together ; and the obtaining of an injunction against any one, though it may not actually restore, does tend to restore the plaintiff to the enjoyment of his right, as it is a step towards obtaining an injunction against each of them."[2] And in a subsequent part of the same judgment it is said : "But whenever human beings congregate in large numbers on the banks of a stream, the inevitable consequence is, that a great quantity of sewerage is discharged into the stream, which necessarily has the effect of polluting it. Therefore, to some considerable extent, the pollution of this stream is inevitable. Not all the courts of law and equity in the kingdom can prevent it. If this injunction were granted, it would not have the effect of restoring or tending to restore the plaintiffs to the position in which they originally stood."[3]

[1] Woodman v. Robinson, 15 Eng. L. & Equ. 150.

[2] Wood v. Sutcliffe, 2 Sim. N. S. 166.
[3] 2 Sim. N. S. 167.

§ 8. "Injunctions are either provisional or perpetual. *Provisional* injunctions are such as are to continue until the coming in of the defendant's answer, or until the hearing of the case, or until the Master has made his report(*a*). *Perpetual* are such as form part of the decree made at the hearing, upon the merits, whereby the defendant is perpetually inhibited from the assertion of a (pretended) right, or perpetually restrained from the commission of an act which would be contrary to equity and good conscience. Provisional injunctions are generally divided into two kinds, *common* and *special. Common injunctions*(*b*) are those which are granted as of course, upon a defendant being in default for not appearing, or for not answering within the time limited for that purpose by the orders of the court. *Special injunctions* are those which are granted upon special grounds arising out of the circumstances of the case. Injunctions of this description are issued sometimes on the merits disclosed by the answer, sometimes on affidavits before the answer is

---

(*a*) If a statute provides, that an injunction shall be granted only where the complaint shows that the party is entitled to the relief sought ; upon a motion for preliminary injunction, contrary to the usual practice, the court must inquire into its right to relieve. Hartt *v.* Harvey, 32 Barb. 55.

In reference to the granting of temporary injunctions in Massachusetts, the court remarks as follows : " Such (temporary) injunctions under the early practice of the court, as a court of equity, were granted with considerable facility, on the ground that being *ex parte*, it would not affect the merits on an ultimate hearing, and that if its operation were considerably injurious to the respondents, it was competent for them to move to dissolve it on affidavit, on application to any judge, upon short notice and cause shown. Somewhat more caution has been observed in this matter, latterly, on consideration that if such an injunction is not necessary to prevent irreparable injury, or render the purpose of the suit unavailing, it may operate injuriously to interrupt an important enterprise, and because after subpœna served, the respondent has notice of the suit, and proceeds, at the peril of all the consequences which may ensue." Per Shaw, C. J., Wing *v.* Fairhaven, 8 Cush. 363.

(*b*) The common injunction stays proceedings at law till answers or further order; the injunction in an interpleading suit stays them till further order. Moore *v.* Usher, 7 Sim. 383.

filed, and sometimes even without notice and before the defendant has appeared(a)."[1]   Although Lord Eldon remarked, " The party hears of the injunction before he hears of the bill. I do not like granting these injunctions on motion."[2]   And in a case in New York it is truly said : "There are many cases in which the complainant may be entitled to a perpetual injunction on the hearing, where it would be manifestly improper to grant an injunction *in limine.*   The final injunction is in many cases matter of strict right, and granted as a necessary consequence of the decree made in the cause.   On the contrary, the preliminary injunction before answer is a matter resting altogether in the discretion of the court, and ought not to be granted unless the injury is pressing and the delay dangerous."[3]

§ 9. The object of a preliminary injunction is to prevent some threatening irreparable mischief, until an opportunity for a full and deliberate investigation.[4]   It will not be granted when the main question in the case is being investigated by a court of law.   The right must be first settled.   So, although equity takes jurisdiction to restrain waste by injunction, and in some particular cases to obtain a discovery and account, and, having for these objects obtained jurisdiction, proceeds, in order to avoid multiplicity of suits, to compensate for damages done ; yet the jurisdiction itself must rest, in the first instance, on the necessity for an injunction, or discovery and account.[5]

[1] 3 Dan. Ch. Pl. (Perkins' Edn.) 1876.
[2] 1 Ves. Jr. 140.
[3] Per Walworth, Chanc., N. Y. Printing, &c. v. Fitch, 1 Paige, 98.

[4] Attorney General *v.* Paterson, 1 Stockt. 624.
[5] Lefforge *v.* West, 2 Cart. 514.

(a) " In 1 Hoffman's Chancery Practice, 78, it is said, there is nothing in our practice similar to this English practice, of issuing the writ upon the presumed admission of the defendant, by his default, of the plaintiff's right to it.   A special application is always made to the Chancellor, Vice-Chancellor, or Master, and the merits of the application are examined by him.   Thus a great number of the English rules become inapplicable."   3 Dan. 1877, n. 1.

§ 10. It is held that the complainant in a bill for an injunction should always be ready to prove the allegations in his bill.[1] And that an injunction will not be granted where the material allegations are only on information and belief.[2]

§ 11. All special injunctions must either stand or fall according to the merits which they possessed at the time when they were granted.[3]

§ 12. The following enumeration is given in an approved work, of the various cases in which this remedy may be applied.

§ 13. "To stay proceedings in the courts of law, in the spiritual courts, the courts of admiralty, or in some other court of equity; to restrain the indorsement or negotiation of notes and bills of exchange, the sale of land, the sailing of a ship, the transfer of stock or the alienation of a specific chattel; to prevent the wasting of assets or other property pending litigation; to restrain a trustee from assigning the legal estate, from setting up a term of years, or assignees from making a dividend; to prevent the removing out of the jurisdiction, marrying, or having any intercourse which the court disapproves of, with a ward; to restrain the commission of every species of waste to houses, mines, timber, or any other part of the inheritance; to prevent the infringement of patents, and the violation of copyright either by publication or theatrical representation; to suppress the continuance of public or private nuisances; and by the various modes of interpleader, restraint upon the multiplicity of suits, or quieting possession before the hearing, to stop the progress of vexatious litigation. These, however, are far from being all the instances in which this species of equitable interposition is obtained. It would indeed be diffi-

---

[1] Bradford v. Innes, 1 Hen. and M. 7.
[2] Waddell v. Bruen, 4 Edw. Ch. 671.
[3] Per V. C., India, &c., 17 Sim. 15.

cult to enumerate them all; for in the endless variety of cases in which a plaintiff is entitled to equitable relief, if that relief consists in restraining the commission or the continuance of some act of the defendant, a court of equity administers it by means of the *writ of injunction*."[1]   And by another writer it is said, "The extent to which the jurisdiction may be carried is not marked out by any adjudged case, and from the nature of things it must forever remained undefined."[2]   (See § 17.)

§ 14. The court will not grant an injunction, unless *real injury* is to be apprehended.[3] (See § 5.)   And an injury, not alleged to be *continuing*, is held no ground for an injunction.[4] Thus an injunction will not be granted to restrain a foreign corporation, against which the plaintiff has an attachment, judgment, and execution, from making a mortgage, unless it appears that the plaintiff will be thereby damnified; nor, consequently, from mortgaging property which the plaintiff, as a judgment creditor, could never reach.[5]   But, notwithstanding the *denial of title*, an injunction may issue to stay irreparable mischief or waste.[6] And *insolvency* in the defendant, in a bill for an injunction to prevent irreparable damage, should have influence with the court, according to its degree. So the allegation in a complaint, that the defendants justified under an adverse claim, will not, in any sense, prejudice the right to an injunction.[7]   For the purpose of quieting a possession, or preventing a multiplicity of actions, or where the value of the inheritance is in jeopardy, or irreparable mischief is threatened, in relation to either mines, quarries, or woodland, equity will interfere, by injunction, even against a person acting under a claim of right.[8]   Nor does an allegation, that the defendant claims some fictitious right, prejudice

[1] 1 Waterman's Eden, 10.
[2] Willard's Equity Juris. 408.
[3] Watrous *v.* Rodgers, 16 Tex. 410.
[4] Coker *v.* Simpson, 7 Cal. 340.
[5] Rogers *v.* Michigan, &c., 28 Barb. 539.
[6] United States *v.* Parrott, 1 McAll. C. C. (Cal.) 271.
[7] Mercea, &c. *v.* Fremont, 7 Cal. 317.
[8] Kerlin *v.* West, 3 Green, Ch. 448.

the plaintiff's right to an injunction.[1] And the *amount* of actual injury, where a right is involved, is held not to be material. Thus the defendants, owners of a mill upon a canal of the plaintiffs, were authorized by the canal charter to draw water for the purpose of condensing steam only. The water being used for other purposes, the plaintiffs brought an action and recovered nominal damages. The defendants attempted, unsuccessfully, to arrest the judgment, which was affirmed on error. The defendants still continuing to use the water as before, the plaintiffs apply for an injunction. The answer relied upon acquiescence on the part of the plaintiffs. Held, but for this defence an injunction should issue.[2]

§ 15. In the case of Campbell *v.* Scott,[3] Sir L. Shadwell, V. Chanc., remarked: " The only question is whether there has been such a *damnum* as will justify the party in applying to the court, because *injuria* there clearly has been. What has been done is against the right of the plaintiff. Now, in my opinion, he is the person best able to judge of that himself; and if the court does clearly see that there has been anything done which tends to an injury, I cannot but think that the safest rule is to follow the legal right and grant the injunction."

§ 16. In general, clear legal or equitable rights, free from reasonable doubt, must be satisfactorily shown, to authorize a preliminary injunction.[4] " It is an appeal to the extraordinary power of the court, and the plaintiffs are bound to make out a case showing a clear necessity for its exercise."[5] It is " the duty of the court rather to protect acknowledged rights than to establish new and doubtful ones."[6] At least,

[1] Tuolumne, &c. *v.* Chapman, 8 Cal. 392.
[2] The Rochdale, &c. *v.* King, 2 Sim. N. S. 78; M'Cord *v.* Iker, 12 Ohio, 387.
[3] 11 Sim. 39.
[4] Scott *v.* Burton, 2 Ashm. 312;

Snowden *v.* Noah, Hopk. 347 ; Steamboat, &c. *v.* Livingston, 3 Cow. 713.
[5] Per Johnson, J., Auburn, &c. *v.* Douglass, 12 Barb. 555.
[6] Per Sargent, J., Burnham *v.* Kempton, 44 N. H. 92; Booth *v.* Driscoll, 20 Conn. 555.

an injunction requires a strong *primâ facie* case of title.[1] Thus an injunction will not be granted to restrain the prosecution of a public work before the coming in of the answer, where it does not clearly appear that the complainant's rights have been violated.[2]

§ 17. But it is also held, that the granting and continuing of injunctions rest in the discretion of the court, to be governed by the nature of the case.[3] (See § 13.) "It is not usual, nor ordinarily is it proper, to inquire into the right of the court to grant relief, upon an application for an injunction; still less to refuse an injunction when the question of jurisdiction is doubtful and when refusing it may produce injury to the party applying." (But the general rule is modified by the express provisions of the New York Code.)[4] And, on the other hand, in the absence of special circumstances, equity will not interfere to control or limit the exercise of a discretionary power.[5]

§ 18. It is said, that an application to a court of chancery, for the exercise of its prohibitory powers or restrictive energies, must come recommended by *the dictates of conscience*, and be sanctioned by *the clearest principles of justice*.[6] And an injunction requested upon principles of equity and justice should never be refused in the first instance.[7] If there be no equity in the bill, there can be no injunction.[8] Either the want of an equitable title, or the establishment of a legal title, is a sufficient reason for denying equitable relief.[9] And the same general principle is further expressed in the propositions, that an action for damages is a matter of *right*, but

---

[1] Grey v. Ohio, &c., 1 Grant, 412.
[2] Elmalie v. Delaware, &c., 4 Whart. 424.
[3] Roberts v. Anderson, 2 John. Ch. 202; Tucker v. Carpenter, 1 Hemp. 440; Burchard v. Boyce, 21 Geo. 6; Jessel v. Chaplin, 37 Eng. L. and Eq. 472.
[4] Per Mullin, J., Ballard v. Fuller, 32 Barb. 68.

[5] Kekewich v. Marker, 5 Eng. L. and Eq. 129.
[6] Maryland, &c. v. Schroeder, 8 Gill & J. 93; Clayton v. Yarrington, 33 Barb. 144.
[7] Lee v. Montgomery, Walker, 109.
[8] Smith v. Lard, 28 Geo. 585.
[9] McAffee v. Lynch, 26 Miss. 257.

an injunction is of *grace*.[1] (See § 19.)   That the right to an injunction is not *ex debito justitiæ*, but the application is addressed to the sound conscience of the Chancellor acting upon all the circumstances belonging to each particular case.[2] That the Chancellor has the right to require a full and candid disclosure of all the facts, and, if there appears in the proceedings sufficient to show that this has not been made, he may properly refuse to grant an injunction.[3]   And that the process of injunction should be applied with the utmost caution.   The interference rests on the principle of a clear and certain right to the enjoyment of the subject in question, and an injurious interruption of that right, which on just and equitable grounds ought to be prevented.[4]   So an injunction is a secondary process (except it be for the prevention of torts), and must be asked in aid of some primary equity, which must be disclosed in the same bill that prays it.[5] (See § 2.)

§ 19.   In conformity with this general requisition of *equity* in the case presented, a bill of injunction may be dismissed on motion, without an answer, for the want of equity on its face.[6]   So where the answer denies all the equity, if any, of the bill, a preliminary injunction should not be granted.[7]   A familiar application of this principle is the case of *usury*. Thus, in New York, on a bill filed before the act of the 15th of May, 1837, to prevent usury, went into operation, to restrain a suit at law upon a usurious contract, a preliminary injunction was refused, the plaintiff not having offered to pay the amount equitably due upon the contract, with lawful interest.[8]   And it is held that the equity relied upon must relate *immediately* to the subject of complaint.   Thus it is no ground for restraining a railroad from the completion of their works, that they have violated a contract connected

[1] Grey v. Ohio, &c., 1 Grant, 412.
[2] Reddall v. Bryan, 14 Md. 444.
[3] Ib.
[4] Morse v. Machias, &c., 42 Maine, 119.

[5] Washington v. Emery, 4 Jones Eq. 29 ; Patterson v. Miller, ib. 451.
[6] Richardson v. Prevo, Breese, 167.
[7] Crandall v. Woods, 6 Cal. 449.
[8] Mitchell v. Oakley, 7 Paige, 68 ; Rogers v. Rathbun, 1 John. Ch. 367.

therewith.[1] So, that an injunction will be granted only to prevent the violation of a positive right. (See § 18.) Thus, where commissioners were appointed by statute to ascertain who were entitled under a preëmption law, the court refused to grant an injunction at the instance of one who claimed to be injured by their decision, as it was mere matter of favor, and not of right.[2] So an injunction will not be granted, in favor of a party claiming to exercise a right granted by an act of the legislature clearly unconstitutional.[3] And it has been held in Pennsylvania, that courts have chancery jurisdiction to enjoin such acts only as are *contrary to law*, and not merely contrary to equity.[4] But in a later case it is held, that, in Pennsylvania, equity is so much a part of the law, that the word law often means both, or either. Hence acts contrary to equity, as well as those contrary to law, may be enjoined.[5] So where a statute has made provision for all the circumstances of a particular case, no relief can be afforded by injunction, although the statute may conflict with the notions of natural justice and equity entertained by a court of chancery.[6] It is held that chancery will refuse an injunction, if the party propose to do equity in the presence of the court.[7]

§ 20. The *equity* of a claim, which justifies the summary remedy of injunction, necessarily precludes fault or wrong on the part of the plaintiff himself. Thus, upon an application for injunction against the use of a trade-mark, it was objected that the plaintiff falsely and fraudulently represented that the article was protected by a patent; and Wood, V. C., remarked: "It is very material that persons coming here for injunctions should be very careful what representations they have made. They must satisfy the court that in their own

[1] Gallagher *v.* Fayette, &c., 38 Penn. 102.
[2] Bell *v.* Payne, 2 Stew. 414.
[3] Moor *v.* Veazie, 31 Maine, 360.
[4] Hagner *v.* Heyberger, 7 Watts and Serg. 104.
[5] Stockdale *v.* Ullery, 37 Penn. 486.
[6] Glenn *v.* Fowler, 8 Gill & J. 340.
[7] Behn *v.* Young, 21 Geo. 207.

representations there has been nothing of fraud." And, in a case relating to the construction of a railroad, the court remark: "The case was one for compensation at law, and not to be remedied by injunction to enforce abatement of the road as a nuisance, or the perpetual restraint of its use. It was constructed under a contract with a stipulation to pay damages for consequent injury, and with a tribunal agreed upon for their assessment. To permit the party to construct their road under an amicable. contract, after a solicited withdrawal of compulsory proceedings, which would in all probability have resulted in giving the right, subject only to the condition of the payment of damages, and then ask to destroy the whole because of a non-compliance in some particulars, is a course so contrary to equity as to be a vain effort."[1]

§ 21. And the same consideration of equity is sometimes so applied as to include the rights and interests of third persons. Thus, in a case relating to a water-course, it was said: "In cases of such a nature as this, (the court) must have regard not only to the dry strict rights of the plaintiff and defendant, but also to the surrounding circumstances; to the rights or interests of other persons, which may be more or less involved."[2]

§ 21 a. The equity of the plaintiff's case may consist in the *mode* adopted by the defendant of exercising a certain right, rather than in the want of such a right itself; involving the necessity of this summary interference to reconcile the conflicting claims of the respective parties. Thus, where the defendant was entitled to a water-power supplied by a waste weir from a public canal, in a bill for injunction brought by the canal company, the court remark: "The defendants claim that during the time that business is suspended on the canal they have a right to have the water flow in its original channel; but they have not taken the right method of asserting

[1] Per Thompson, J., Pusey v. Wright, 31 Penn. 395–6.

[2] Wood v. Sutcliffe, 2 Sim. N. S. 164.

their right, if they have any. The plaintiffs are in possession of the water for the purpose of their canal, and the time during which they need it for the actual business, and the quantity which they need to keep in the canal during the winter season when business is suspended, are necessarily quite indefinite. It is impossible, therefore, that the defendants can be allowed to define for themselves the plaintiffs' right, and interfere with their possession. They insist on opening the weirs and helping themselves according to their own judgment; but this would be a lawless mode of vindicating their rights, and it cannot be allowed. If the defendants have any right to the water beyond what the plaintiffs are willing to concede to them, they must bring their bill or action to have those rights defined before they can be enforced."[1]

§ 22. And an injunction is sometimes refused upon the ground that it would cause great injury to the defendant.[2]

§ 23. Where a party has *a remedy at law*, he cannot come into equity, unless, from circumstances not within his control, he could not avail himself of his legal remedy;[(a)] nor for the assertion of a right, the existence or non-existence of which is properly determinable at law, and the exercise of which will do no injury to the party denying it;[4] nor where it is not essential to secure the party's rights, and the object can be effected by filing a notice of *lis pendens*;[5] nor where there is a remedy at law, and it does not appear but that damages at law would be realized, and there is no

---

[1] Per Lowrie, J., Erie, &c. v. Walker, 29 Penn. 173.
[2] Wood v. Sutcliffe, 2 Sim. N. S. 167.
[3] Nicolson v. Hancock, 4 Hen. & M. 491; Robinson v. Byson, 1 Bro. C. 588; Wallace v. McVey, 6 Ind. 300.
[4] Doughty v. Somerville, &c., 3 Halst. Ch. 51.
[5] Waddell v. Bruen, 4 Edw. Ch. 671.

(a) That full compensation can be had at law, "is the great rule for withholding the strong arm of the Chancellor." Per Thompson, J., Pusey v. Wright, 31 Penn. 396.

danger of irreparable injury.[1] More especially, where the matter of the bill itself shows that the plaintiff has an adequate remedy at law, an injunction on the bill cannot be sustained.[2] In such cases, an injunction will not at least be granted, until the petitioners have established their right to redress by an action at law.[3] Thus the principle upon which an equity court interferes by injunction, in cases both of public and private *nuisance*, is the inadequacy of the remedy at common law; and it is on the ground of injury to property that this jurisdiction rests.[4] So in case of devise to the widow of the testator, during her widowhood, or until their youngest child attained the age of twenty-one years, for the support of herself and their children, with remainder to the children, in fee, subject to dower; upon a bill filed by the widow and the children, charging against the defendant an unlawful and violent entry upon the land, taking the products thereof, and depriving the complainants of their means of support and maintenance, and praying that he might be compelled to surrender the land to them, and for an injunction and a receiver of the rents and profits, *pendente lite*, it was held, that the facts charged did not show that the defendant was committing irreparable damage to the property, to prevent which an injunction was necessary; that the remedy at law was ample and complete, either by action of trespass, ejectment, or, under the statutes, for a forcible entry.[5] So on a bill in equity, brought by the owner of a mill-dam, to restrain a town from opening certain sluiceways therein, on the ground that the dam, by raising the water over certain highways, is a nuisance, a temporary injunction will not be granted, or, if granted on application *ex parte*, will be dissolved; when it appears that the refusal to grant, or the dissolution of the injunction, cannot lead to any injury or cause any loss to the plaintiff which cannot be repaired in damages,

[1] Warne *v*. Morris, &c., 1 Halst. Ch. 410.
[2] Mallett *v*. Weybossett, &c., 1 Barb. 217.

[3] Arnold *v*. Klepper, 24 Mis. 273.
[4] Atty., &c. *v*. Sheffield, &c., 19 Eng. L. & Eq. 639.
[5] Pfeltz *v*. Pfeltz, 14 Md. 376.

or affect the merits of the controversy on a trial in due course.[1] So, in general, a purchaser of land, who has a full and complete remedy at law on the covenants in his deed, cannot have an injunction against his vendor to restrain him from collecting the purchase-money;[2] though a person who does not reside and has no property in the State may be restrained from collecting a note given for land to which he had no title, notwithstanding the remedy at law on a covenant of warranty.[3] (See *Title*.) So, in Georgia, the remedy for the opening of an old road by the superior courts is by *certiorari*, not by injunction against the commissioners who seek to execute the order.[4]

§ 23 *a*. The question has arisen, whether the remedy of injunction would lie in case of an agreed *penalty* or *forfeiture*. It has been held that the breach of a restrictive covenant in a lease may be enjoined, though secured by forfeiture of the lease and a penalty.[5] But where the plaintiff agreed with the defendants, a railroad company, that they might enter upon his land and build, and have the damages settled by award within a year, and that they should be paid within sixty days; if not, the license to cease, and all rights of the company, and its interest in the fixtures, to be as if it had entered in its own wrong: held, a case of forfeiture, not to be enforced by injunction against an entry upon the lands.[6] So in an early case the plaintiff let a farm to the defendant, at an annual rent, part of it pasture, the defendant covenanting not to break up or plough any part of it, and, if he did, to pay at the rate of twenty shillings per acre per annum. Injunction refused, because the parties had agreed the damage and set a price for ploughing. The court remarked that if the defendant was plaintiff against paying the twenty shil-

---

[1] Wing *v.* Fairhaven, 8 Cush. 363.
[2] Wilkins *v.* Hogue, 2 Jones Eq. 479.
[3] Green *v.* Campbell, 2 Jones Eq. 446.
[4] Nichols *v.* Sutton, 22 Geo. 369.

[5] Barret *v.* Blagrave, 5 Ves. 555. See Aylet *v.* Dodd, 2 Atk. 239; Benson *v.* Gibson, 3 ib. 396.
[6] Coe *v.* Columbus, &c., 10 Ohio N. S. 372.

2

lings, they would not relieve him.[1] And the general distinction is laid down, that breach of condition forfeits the estate. Breach of covenant is ground either of injunction or an action for damages.[2]

§ 24. A demand growing out of an illegal transaction, which cannot be recovered or enforced directly, cannot be made the foundation of a proceeding in chancery for an injunction against a legal demand.[3]

§ 25. The interference of a court of equity by injunction sometimes depends upon statutory provisions either for this or other remedies. Upon this point it is said : " The remedy by injunction is, notwithstanding the (statutory) provision for its exercise, only such in the absence of an adequate *legal remedy.*"[4]

§ 26. Where a statute provided a specific remedy against a plank-road for neglect to repair, it was held that equity would not enjoin the collection of tolls till the repairs were made.[5] So a bill for injunction was filed, alleging that the complainant made a contract with the defendants, a railroad company, by which he was to convey to them a right of way over his land, and a tract for a depôt; and that they had purchased other grounds and intended to use them for a depôt; and abandon those of the complainant. The defendants denied such abandonment. Held, the remedy of the complainant was by an action at common law, or under the railroad act.[6]

§ 27. The remedy by injunction does not preclude other remedies for the same injury. Thus, in California, a mort-

[1] Woodward v. Gyles, 2 Vern. 116. See Rolfe v. Peterson, 6 Bro. Parl. 470.
[2] Woodruff v. Water, &c., 2 Stockt. 489.
[3] Pond v. Smith, 4 Conn. 297.

[4] Per Thompson, J., Scheetz's, &c., 35 Penn. 95.
[5] Com. v. Wellsboro', &c., 35 Penn. 152.
[6] Gallagher v. Fayette, &c., 38 Penn. 102.

gagee may maintain replevin for fixtures, although the Prac
tice Act, s. 261, authorizes an injunction against their removal.[1]

§ 28. In Langton v. Horton,[2] a judge of the Court of
Queen's Bench had ordered an issue to try the title to property in the hands of a sheriff, by virtue of the Interpleader
Act, 1 & 2 W. 4, c. 58, and 1 & 2 Vict. c. 45. The plaintiffs,
claiming the property, apply for an injunction against these
proceedings. It appeared that the case involved the validity
of an assignment of a prospective cargo. Held, as this was
a matter peculiarly of equitable jurisdiction, an injunction
should be granted, the acts applying only to cases of strictly
legal rights.

§ 29. In the case of Baldwin v. Buffalo,[3] the distinction
is taken, that, where the proceedings in a street case are
illegal, and therefore inoperative and void, *certiorari* is the
proper remedy, unless the proceedings in the subordinate
tribunal, or the official acts of public officers, affecting the
title to real estate, lead, in their execution, to the commission of irreparable injury to the freehold, or to a multiplicity of suits; or unless the adverse claim to the land is
valid upon the face of the instrument or the proceedings
complained of, and extrinsic facts require to be proved to
establish the invalidity or illegality.

§ 30. Courts of equity have no *controlling, supervising,* or
superintending power over courts of law, and will neither
arrest nor interfere with their proceedings on the ground
that their decisions were *erroneous;* much less stay or interfere with them, in anticipation of such erroneous decisions.[4]
(See § 60.) Thus, if a city ordinance be in conflict with any
commercial regulation of Congress, a party prosecuted under

---

[1] Sands *v.* Pheiffer, 10 Cal. 258.
[2] 3 Beav. 464.
[3] 29 Barb. 399. See the Mayor,
&c. *v.* Meserole, 26 Wend. 132; Hey-
wood *v.* Buffalo, 14 N. Y. 534.

[4] Hood *v.* New York, &c., 23 Conn.
609; Richardson *v.* Baltimore, 8 Gill,
433.

it has an adequate remedy at law.   He may plead that fact in
defence in the city court, and, if the decision be against him,
he may appeal and then have a writ of error to the Supreme
Court of the United States.   Therefore the Circuit Court of
the United States would not grant relief by injunction even
if it had the power.[1]

§ 31. With more special reference to the character of the
injury in question, as *irreparable* by an action at law ; where
the injury is not susceptible of being adequately compensated in damages, or such as from its continuance or
permanent mischief must occasion a constantly recurring
grievance, which cannot be otherwise prevented, as where loss
of health, loss of trade or business, destruction of the means of
subsistence, or permanent ruin to property, may or will ensue
from the wrongful acts ; or where an easement or servitude
is annexed by grant, covenant, or otherwise to a private
estate ; equity will interfere by injunction in furtherance of
justice and the violated rights of the party, or to protect the
due and quiet enjoyment of the easement against encroach-
ments.[2]

§ 32. The omission of the charge of irreparable mischief
would not be a defect in a bill otherwise good, because the
court must be satisfied, from a statement of the grievances,
that the injury would be irreparable, and it is enough if the
court can discover this from the allegation of facts.[3] On the
other hand, mere allegation of danger of a great and irreparable injury is not enough ; facts must be stated, to satisfy
the court of the existence of such danger.[4]

§ 33. It is held, that, if the court interfere on the ground
that the complainant has not an adequate remedy at law, it
should do so by a direct decree to that effect, and not by
injunctions issued at a preliminary stage of the proceedings.[5]

[1] Rogers *v.* Cincinnati, 5 McL.
337.
[2] Webber *v.* Gage, 39 N. H. 182.
[3] Davis *v.* Reed, 14 Md. 152.
[4] Branch, &c. *v.* Yuba, 13 Cal.
190.
[5] Akrill *v.* Selden, 1 Barb. 316.

§ 34. In refusing to interfere by injunction, a court of equity takes notice of other remedies within the power of the party complaining, than that of an action at law.   Thus, in case of a bill by a part of the directors of an insurance company, constituted by deed, against another director, alleging misconduct, it appeared that the plaintiffs had not made use of the regulating authority given by the deed, and an injunction which had been granted was dissolved.[1]   So, in a case relating to a water-course, it appeared that other parties, who had polluted the stream in the same way, being threatened with suits, entered into an agreement with the plaintiffs to make a certain annual payment for the privilege of doing it; and the court held this to be sufficient proof that the plaintiffs had an adequate remedy at law, and were not entitled to an injunction.[2]

§ 35. It is said to be the general, though not universal rule, that an action at common law should be brought before an application is made for an injunction.[3]   So it is held, that, if the title of the complainant is denied, he must show former recoveries or long possession, in the case of patents; and, in case of waste and trespass, that there are no facts to warrant the denial; or the injunction will be refused till the disputed questions of title are settled at law.[4]   But the prevailing rule would seem to be, that a complainant, who has established his right at law, stands in no better position in respect to obtaining an injunction, than one whose right is not disputed.[5]

§ 36. While it is sufficient ground for refusing an injunction that the party has an adequate remedy at law, it is also held that there is no case, in which equity has granted a

[1] Ellison v. Bignold, 2 Jac. & W. 503.
[2] Wood v. Sutcliffe, 2 Sim. N. S. 163.
[3] United States v. Parrott, 1 McAll. C. C. (Cal.) 271. See Union, &c. v. Kerr, 2 Md. Ch. Dec. 460.
[4] Perry v. Parker, 1 W. & M. 280.
[5] Quackenbush v. Van Riper, 2 Green, Ch. 350.

perpetual injunction to a plaintiff to protect him in the enjoyment of a naked legal right, which he and those under whom he claims have stipulated by solemn deeds not to exercise. Legal rights must be asserted by legal means, and courts of equity never lend their aid where equity and justice do not imperiously demand it.[1]

§ 37. Notwithstanding the general rule that the party applying for an injunction must be remediless at law, the court of equity is not exceeding its functions, in deciding a purely legal question arising in a suit before it, either with or without legal assistance, but ought to decide such a question where the controversy and material facts are plain.[2] And an injunction may be granted where the defendant, against whom there is otherwise a good remedy at common law, is insolvent, or about to abscond.[3]

§ 38. As may be gathered from what has been already stated, with reference to the grounds which justify the interference of a court of equity by injunction; it is held, that, where a petition for an injunction does not show that the party applying for it is likely to be injured by the proceeding complained of, the injunction ought not to be granted; or, if granted, it ought to be dissolved, on motion.[4] Also that *past injuries* are not in themselves ground for an injunction; but when there is a continuance of an injury, and a right to continue it is claimed, an injunction may, in a proper case, be issued to restrain the continuance.[5]

§ 39. Another principle is, that, where either party may suffer by the granting or withholding an injunction, the rule in equity requires the court to balance the inconveniences likely to be incurred by the respective parties, by means of the action of the court, and to grant or withhold the injunc-

---

[1] Bosley v. McKim, 7 Har. & J. 468.
[2] Ponder v. Cox, 28 Geo. 305.
[4] Shrewsbury, &c. v. Stour, &c. 21 Eng. Law and Eq. 628.
[4] Cameron v. White, 3 Tex. 152.
[5] Society, &c. v. Morris Canal, Saxt. 157.

tion according to a sound discretion.[1] Where an injunction might cause irreparable damage to the defendant, in the event of the plaintiff's not being exclusively entitled, but the damage sustained by the plaintiff, in the event of establishing his title, allows of compensation, the injunction will be refused.[2]

§ 40. Equity may enjoin any act, from which irreparable injury to *public property* may result.[3]

§ 41. In cases of imminent danger of injury, a temporary injunction will be granted on filing amendments to a bill after appearance, but the injunction will be accompanied with an order to show cause why the bill should not be amended, and why the injunction should not be continued.[4]

§ 42. It is said that slight infringements of rights in respect of land, by *a large company of persons*, ought to be watched with a careful eye, and repressed with a strict hand, by a court of equity, where it can exercise jurisdiction.[5] (See *Corporations.*) But an injunction will not be granted for every wrongful or unconstitutional act of individuals *or corporations*.[6] Thus, where a city ordinance directed the plaintiff's lots to be filled and the expense assessed, an injunction was refused, on the ground that the injury was not shown to be irreparable, so that an action at law would not be an ample remedy, and that the assessment, if illegal, could not be collected.[7] So where the plaintiffs, for the purpose of preventing the defendants from laying their pipes from their gas-works into a city, purchased a lot of land so situated upon the highway, that it was necessary that the defendants' main pipe should pass through that part which lay within the limits of

---

[1] Grey v. Ohio, &c., 1 Grant, 412.
[2] Hartridge v. Rockwell, Charl. R. M. 260.
[3] Putnam v. Valentine, 5 Ham. 187.
[4] Hays v. Heyr, 4 Sandf. Ch. 485.

[5] [Per Sir J. L. Knight Bruce, L. J.] Atty, &c. v. Sheffield, &c., 19 Eng. L. and Eq. 639.
[6] Blake v. Brooklyn, 26 Bark. 301.
[7] Ib.

the highway, and the defendants laid their pipe across it, and avowed their determination to maintain it there; held, as the substantial controversy was in relation to the right to use the highway irrespective of any title to the soil, and as the defendants were liable in trespass for any damage done to the land, an injunction ought not to be granted.[1]

§ 43. To entitle the plaintiff to an injunction, he must not be guilty of any improper *delay* in applying for relief.[2] "If a party is guilty of laches or unreasonable delay in the enforcement of his rights, he thereby forfeits his claim to equitable relief—more especially where a party, being cognizant of his rights, does not take those steps to assert them which are open to him, but lies by, and suffers other parties to incur expenses and enter into engagements and contracts of a burdensome character."[3] *Acquiescence*, although not conferring a right on the opposite party, deprives the complainant of his right to the interference of a court of equity. Unless the applicant has acted promptly, he is held to have impliedly authorized what he now objects to.[4] Thus where a party applies to stay operations upon a large and costly work, it should appear that he applied for an injunction as soon as he became apprised of his rights and the extent of the threatened injury.[5] So where there has been great delay on the part of a vendor, the court will not enjoin an action against the auctioneer for the deposit.[6] So an injunction will not be granted to prevent back-flowage, where the party has suffered it to continue for nineteen years without objection, except a verbal notice when the dam was first built, and has seen it four times destroyed by floods and rebuilt.[7] So one owning the water of a creek cannot enjoin a canal company from using it, after they have used it for more than

---

[1] Norwich, &c. v. Norwich, &c., 25 Conn. 19.

[2] Grey v. Ohio, &c. 1 Grant, 412; Field v. Beaumont, 3 Madd. 61; Burden v. Stein, 27 Ala. 104; Long v. Cross, 5 Jones Eq. 323.

[3] Per Bigelow, J., Tash v. Adams, 10 Cush. 253.

[4] Binney's Case, 2 Bland, 99.

[5] Ib.

[6] Lloyd v. Collett, 4 Bro. Ch. 346, 469.

[7] Sheldon v. Rockwell, 9 Wis. 166.

twenty years, with the assent of the complainant and those under whom he claims, who were also compensated for such use.[1] So, on a bill by a legatee against the executor, a decree was rendered for the legacy against the executor by default, three years after the service of the *subpœna* on him ; whereupon the executor filed a bill to enjoin the decree, as obtained by surprise, alleging, that, at the time of the service of the *subpœna*, in the original suit, on the complaint, he was a non-resident of the State, and wrote to counsel practising in the court in which the suit was pending, to file his answer and attend to the suit; that such counsel neglected to answer, and died pending the suit ; that the notifications in the case did not come to complainant's knowledge ; and that he was in advance to the estate. Held, that the complainant had been guilty of laches, and was not entitled to relief.[2] So, a party cannot have an injunction against the execution of an award, if he has been injured by his own neglect to attend to his interests at the proper time.[3] So, in Texas, an unexcused delay of six months after judgment, in suing out an injunction, bars the right.[4] And on application made therefor by a surety, the fact, that the judgment was entered against his principal on an agreement for six months' stay of execution, and after the defendant's answers had been withdrawn, so that the surety could not obtain a reversal of the judgment, will not excuse the delay.[5] So, in Massachusetts, an injunction will not be granted under St. 1847, c. 37, to restrain the payment of money illegally voted by a town, if the petitioners have been guilty of gross laches, and knowingly have permitted others to incur liabilities in good faith, relying upon such appropriation for reimbursement.[6] Nor where the plaintiffs stood by while the defendants were constructing the works upon a stream, which caused the injury complained of, and suffered the use of them for five years without objec-

[1] Heilman *v.* Union, &c., 37 Penn. 100.

[2] Callaway *v.* Alexander, 8 Leigh, 114.

[3] Dulin *v.* Caldwell, 28 Geo. 117.

[4] (Hart. Dig. art. 1599.) Pillow *v.* Thompson, 20 Tex. 206.

[5] Ib.

[6] Tash *v.* Adams, 10 Cush. 252.

tion.[1] And the delay which precludes relief may apply to the right sought to be enforced, rather than the remedy. Thus where the plaintiff, who claimed under a preëmption right, prayed that he might be quieted in his title, and that the issue of a patent to the defendants might be enjoined; and more than three years had elapsed since his settlement, and the date of the preëmption act, and before the trial, though not before the suit was instituted : held, in order to entitle the plaintiff to relief, he ought to have shown that, within the three years prescribed by the statute, he had "covered the land with a valid certificate."[2] So it is only when the plaintiff in equity has exercised due precaution to prevent an injury, that he can be relieved by an injunction.[3]

§ 44. But it is held that mere delay will be no ground for refusing an injunction where the complainant's right is clear;[4] and that delay, if inadvertent, will not be ground for dissolution of an injunction.[5] And equity will not bar the claim of a bank against an indorser, because no action was brought for eleven years, and because of the loss of security of prior parties to the bill, if it appear that the indorser has used no diligence to protect himself against such loss of security.[6]

§ 45. To warrant an injunction, strong *primâ facie* evidence of the facts on which the complainant's equity rests must be presented to the court. The mere oath of the party as to the existence of a debt, of which he holds or is presumed to hold the written evidence, without producing it, should not be regarded as any proof of such debt. The instrument should be exhibited with the bill, or a satisfactory reason assigned for its non-production.[7] So in all cases of waste and nuisance it must appear clearly that the party has per-

---

[1] Wood *v.* Sutcliffe, 2 Sim. N. S. 168.
[2] Walters *v.* Wells, 8 Tex. 202.
[3] Russ *v.* Wilson, 22 Maine, 207.
[4] Burden *v.* Stein, 27 Ala. 104.

[5] Schermerhorn *v.* L'Espinasse, 2 Dall. 360.
[6] Malone *v.* Central Bank, 17 Geo. 111.
[7] Union, &c. *v.* Poultney, 8 Gill & J. 324.

sonal knowledge of the material facts charged, or he must produce supplemental proof.[1] So where the evidence introduced consists merely of the opinions of witnesses, a perpetual injunction is not to be decreed, unless the case is made out to the satisfaction of the court.[2]

§ 46. On a bill filed in one State, to enjoin a citizen thereof from prosecuting proceedings in another, an exhibit of the proceedings should be filed.[3]

§ 47. An injunction which depends on an indebtedness evidenced in writing will not be granted, unless such written evidence be submitted with the bill, or a satisfactory reason for its non-production be given.[4] (See § 55.)

§ 48. On a motion for an injunction, the denials made in the answer on personal knowledge, direct and responsive to the bill, are to receive the consideration due to them as if on the hearing, but matters set up by way of avoidance are to be received as affidavits.[5]

§ 49. On the hearing of an application for an injunction, where notice is given, affidavits taken *ex parte* and without notice may be read.[6](a) So, on a bill for an injunction, affidavits may be read on both sides, after answer made, if they do not refer to title.[7] So on a motion for an injunction the affidavit of the defendant is competent evidence against the oath of the plaintiffs.[8]

[1] Perkins *v.* Collins, 2 Green Ch. 482.
[2] Woodruff *v.* Lockerby, 8 Wis. 369.
[3] Buchanan *v.* Torrance, 11 Gill & J. 342.
[4] Nusbaum *v.* Stein, 12 Md. 315.
[5] United States *v.* Parrott, 1 McAll. C. C. (Cal.) 271.

[6] Hardenburg *v.* Farmers', &c., 2 Green Ch. 68. See 10 Sim. 50; Jackson *v.* Cassidy, 10 Sim. 326; Taylor *v.* Leigh, 2 Jac. & W. 387.
[7] Brooks *v.* Bicknell, 3 McLean, 250.
[8] Baker *v.* Taylor, 2 Blatch. 82.

(a) As in case of waste, in support of a motion for injunction on an *interpleading* bill, affidavits of the facts are admissible. Langston *v.* Boylston, 2 Ves. Jr. 101.

§ 50. Where an injunction will affect persons who have no opportunity to be heard, as an injunction to prevent the election of officers of a corporation, the plaintiff must, in addition to the allegation of his own information and belief, if he has no personal knowledge of the facts, annex the affidavit of a person who knows the facts, and from whom the information was derived.[1]

§ 51. It is held that the complainant cannot, on an application for an injunction against waste, read affidavits, on bill and answer, in support of his title.[2]

§ 52. In general, an injunction will not be granted upon mere information or belief; but if the particular allegations relied upon are stated positively in the complaint, and not on information and belief, a verification in the usual form is sufficient. A separate affidavit is unnecessary, if the cause for an injunction exists at the commencement of the suit.[3](a)

§ 53. In ordinary cases, an injunction may be granted upon the bill alone, supported by affidavit, before the *subpœna* has been served.[4]

§ 54. It is held unnecessary that an affidavit for an injunction, made by an agent, should set forth the absence of the

---

[1] Walker *v.* Devereaux, 4 Paige, 229 ; Southern, &c. *v.* Hixon, 5 Ind. 165.

[2] U. S. *v.* Parrott, McAll. C. C. (Cal.) 271.
[3] Woodruff *v.* Fisher, 17 Barb. 224.
[4] Jones *v.* Magill, 1 Bland, 177.

(a) An affidavit, which recites that "the facts and allegations set forth in the petition for an injunction are true," and that the facts, stated to be on his belief, he believes to be correct, is sufficient. Livingston *v.* Dick, 1 La. Ann. R. 323.

So an affidavit, that "the facts and allegations as set forth in the foregoing petition are true, as therein alleged, to the best of his (affiant's) knowledge and belief." Knox *v.* Coroner, 13 La. An. 88.

principal; it is sufficient to prove, on the trial, that he was absent when the affidavit was made.[1]

§ 55. The purpose of an affidavit is to obtain the confidence of the court, and this may be obtained by documentary evidence as well as by affidavit; as, for example, by an authenticated copy of the will under which the complainants claim their emancipation from slavery.[2] (See § 47.)

§ 56. Though a bill not sworn to does not entitle a party to an injunction in the first instance, yet if, at the close of the hearing, he shows himself entitled to it, it may then be granted.[3] So a petition or answer in a bill for an injunction, as a portion of the final relief, is not, for the want of an oath, to be regarded as a nullity, but is to be esteemed as sufficient for the purpose of admitting proof on the final hearing.[4]

§ 57. It is said, that, where an execution is sought to be enjoined, there is good reason why a petition should be under oath, as the defendant has rights which should not be disturbed, unless on real and substantial grounds. The reason why the answer should be under oath is not so manifest.[5] So, where the plaintiff, by bill sworn to, applies for an injunction to restrain the defendant from removing certain property, in which he claims an interest, and the defendant makes an insufficient answer, the court will allow the bill of the plaintiff to be read as an affidavit, and if, on the whole case, the matter is left in doubt, the injunction will be continued until the hearing.[6]

§ 58. An injunction to prevent the setting up of a fraudulent deed, embracing the whole estate of an old man, past the age of active labor, is a special one, and the bill of the plain-

---

[1] Wilson v. Curtis, 13 La. An. 601.
[2] Negro, &c. v. Sheriff, 12 Md. 274.
[3] Hawkins v. Hunt, 14 Ill. 42.
[4] Eccles v. Daniels, 16 Tex. 136.
[5] Ibid.
[6] Wilson v. Mace, 2 Jones Eq. 5.

tiff may be read as an affidavit in reply to the defendant's answer.[1]

§ 59. Where an affidavit was filed, and intituled in a cause in which there were three defendants, and the name of one was afterwards struck out, and an injunction granted on the affidavit as originally made; held, the injunction should stand. In answer to the argument of counsel, the Vice-Chancellor said, that the perjury, if any, was committed at the moment when the affidavit was filed.[2]

§ 60. The question is, of course, a very important one, what courts have jurisdiction to enjoin the proceedings of other courts, and on the other hand the proceedings of what tribunals are liable to be thus summarily interrupted. In this country, the subject is involved in peculiar complication, by reason of the concurrent authority of the United States and State courts, and the conflict liable to arise among the courts of different States.[3](a) (See § 30.)

[1] Peterson v. Matthis, 3 Jones Eq. 31.
[2] Hawes v. Bamford, 9 Sim. 653.
[3] See Martin v. O'Brien, 34 Miss. 21.

(a) In New York, an application by a party or privy to a suit in the Court of Chancery, to stay such suit, must be directly to the court, in the matter of the suit, not to an officer out of court. Ellsworth v. Cook, 8 Paige, 643. But, in Mississippi, where the case was such that an order would have been granted, and the objection was not taken on the argument, the injunction was allowed to stand for such order. Mason v. Payne, Walk. Ch. 459. On the other hand, judges, or any one of them, of the Court of Appeals of Virginia, out of court, but not the court itself, are authorized to grant an injunction, which has been refused by the judge of the Superior Court of Chancery. Mayo v. Haines, 2 Munf. 423. It has been held that one judge of the Supreme Court of Pennsylvania has not power to grant an injunction in any case; it can only be done by the court when sitting in banc. Riley v. Ellmaker, 6 Whart. 545. But, in a recent case, motion being made in Philadelphia that the court order a motion for a preliminary injunction to be argued before the court in *banc*, it was held, that such motions belong

§ 60 *a*. Some early cases best illustrate the nature of the remedy by injunction, as involving the authority of different courts.

---

properly to the judge at *nisi prius*, and the court will consent to hear them only when he regards them of such importance as to request it to sit with him for that purpose. Philadelphia, &c. *v.* Railway Co., 33 Penn. St. 82. Where a petition for leave to file a bill of review, under the act of 1795, c. 88, also praying an injunction, has been dismissed by the Court of Chancery, in Maryland, the Court of Appeals cannot grant the injunction, although the court below ought to have done so. Luckett *v.* White, 10 Gill & J. 480. In 1837, the Legislature of Maryland passed an act for laying out certain streets in Baltimore. If streets should be extended, certain owners of land should, in a certain court, be entitled to damages for one-half the bed of the street laid out in front of their land. In 1847, one of the streets was extended. The owners filed their bill, alleging that the damages, secured to them by act, had not been assessed to them, and praying an injunction against the collection of certain sums assessed on them as benefits, and for general relief. An injunction was granted. The answer of the mayor, &c., averred that the provisions of the act were specially brought to the attention of the jury, and deliberately considered by them ; and, thereupon, the chancellor dissolved the injunction, on the ground that a court of equity has no authority to stay the proceedings on the judgment of the Baltimore City Court. Richardson *v.* Baltimore, 8 Gill, 433. The several Superior Courts of Chancery, in Virginia, have jurisdiction to grant injunctions upon judgments at law rendered within their respective districts only. The place of the rendition of the judgment, and not the residence of the parties, determines the jurisdiction. Cocke *v.* Pellok, 1 H. & M. 499. In Texas, the judgment of a justice of the peace in a case in which he had no jurisdiction is a nullity, and may be perpetually enjoined ; and it is immaterial in such case whether the application for injunction is within ninety days or not. McFaddin *v.* Spencer, 18 Tex. 440. Where judgment has been rendered in the District Court upon a cause of action within the probate jurisdiction of the County Court, the defendant should appeal ; but, if he does not, he can have execution enjoined, for want of jurisdiction. Cunningham *v.* Taylor, 20 Tex. 126. The Circuit Courts of Mississippi have not jurisdiction to grant injunctions originating, and to operate, beyond their respective districts. Montgomery *v.* Commercial, 1 S. & M. Ch. 632. In Tennessee an injunction bill is a personal action, within the meaning of the statute requiring such actions to be brought in the county where the defendant resides. Childress *v.* Perkins, Cooke, 87. A bill to enjoin a judgment at law may be brought

§ 60 *b*. The defendant had obtained judgment in ejectment against the now plaintiff, and had execution awarded, but the under-sheriff refused to execute it; whereupon, by rule of court of the King's Bench, the under sheriff was ordered to attend, and for not attending an attachment was awarded against him.   After all this proceeding, the defendant in the ejectment exhibits his bill in this court, and Emerton praying a *dedimus* an injunction was granted of course.   I moved

---

in the county where the judgment was recovered, although the defendant may be found and served with process in another county.   Newman *v.* Stuart, Cooke, 339.   Where a court has jurisdiction only in case the amount in dispute exceeds $50, it has no jurisdiction to enjoin a judgment on account of an excess of $12 therein.   Rentfroe *v.* Dickinson, 1 Overton, 196.   If courts of law and equity have concurrent jurisdiction, a failure to make the defence at law, if the defendant answer to the merits, will not oust the jurisdiction of chancery; but if the defence set up was purely legal, and in its nature unfit for equity jurisdiction, the defendant may insist upon the want of jurisdiction at the hearing, though he may not have demurred.   Rice *v.* Railroad, &c., 7 Humph. 39.   In Georgia, a court in one county may enjoin an action pending in that county, though the plaintiff in such action resides in another; although it cannot further grant relief.   Key *v.* Rabison, 29 Geo. 34.   An injunction will not lie against the justices of the inferior court, and the only remedy, by which a contract can be enforced against them, is *mandamus.*   The Justices *v.* Croft, 18 Geo. 473.   In California, one court cannot interfere in proceedings before another of concurrent jurisdiction. All proceedings to enjoin judgments must issue from the court having the control of such judgments.   The rule is the same (§ 78) in an equity suit, when a bill is brought, and other parties joined, not included in the action at law sought to be enjoined.   The only case in which it will be allowed, is where the court, in which the action or proceeding is pending, is unable by reason of its jurisdiction to afford the relief sought. Where several fraudulent judgments are confessed in several courts, it would not be necessary for a creditor to sue in each.   So where the provisions of the court require the action to be tried in a particular county, there would be an exception.   Anthony *v.* Dunlap, 8 Cal. 26 ; Rickett *v.* Johnson, ib. 34; Revalk *v.* Kraemer, ib. 66; Chipman *v.* Hibbard, ib. 268; Phelan *v.* Smith, ib. 520 ; Gorham *v.* Toomey, 9 Cal. 77 ; Uhlfelder *v.* Levy, ib. 607.   A county judge may grant an injunction in a district court case.   Ruthrauff *v.* Kresz, 13 Cal. 639.

my lord that this injunction might not extend to stay proceedings against the under sheriff for his contempt to the Court of King's Bench for the contempt at the king's suit; and it was unnatural for the king, by his injunction, to stay his own suit in another court, the offence being committed before the bill exhibited; yet the motion was denied by my Lord Chancellor.[1]

§ 60 c. Upon a motion for an injunction to stop the sale of English Bibles, printed beyond sea, it was urged that the *Chancery* was a court of State, and therefore for the great mischief that might arise from these Bibles, if they should be suffered to be publicly sold, the sale ought to be prohibited by this court upon that politic account, as well as to quiet the king's patentees in their possession. Lord Keeper: I do not apprehend the *Chancery* to be in the least a court of State; neither can I grant an injunction in any case, but when a man has a plain right to be quieted in it; and, though the patent for law-books has been adjudged good in the *House of Lords*, yet that is not exactly the same case with this, though near it. Let there be a trial at law, and let the king's patentees be plaintiffs, and the defendants admit they have sold *twelve* Bibles, and when the trial is over come back again.[2]

§ 61. It was early held, that a court or a judge of a court of the United States cannot enjoin proceedings in a State court.[3] Hence, where cases are pending in a State court, in which property had been attached before any act of bankruptcy on the part of the defendant, and he had obtained and pleaded his discharge; the assignee and all claimants of the property may be enjoined from attempting to procure process from any court not acting under the authority of the State, with a view to prevent judgments or executions in such actions; and also from applying for or attempting to execute

[1] ——— v. Emerton, 1 Vern. 25.
[2] 1 Vern. 120.
[3] Diggs v. Wolcott, 4 Cranch, 179; Rogers v. Cincinnati, 5 McLean, 337.

3

any summary process, order, or decree of any court with the
view of taking from the creditors or their attorneys the fruits
of their judgments, on account of any supposed want of
right to render such judgments or their supposed invalidity,
while in force and unreversed. Also from making application or instituting proceedings, founded on any supposed
breach of an injunction or order, issued by any tribunal not
acting under State authority, by reason of any proceedings
in the State courts, arising after the discharge was pleaded (a).[1]
But a circuit court may grant an injunction to a judgment
at law, although a writ of error to the judgment is pending
in the Supreme Court.[2] And the fifth section of the Act of
March 2, 1793 (1 Sts. at Large, 334), which forbids the United
States Court to grant an injunction to stay proceedings in a
State court, does not restrain it from enjoining a sheriff from
levying on the property of A on a process against B.[3]

§ 62. A State court of chancery will not, by injunction,
restrain a suit or proceeding previously commenced in a
court of another State, or in any of the Federal courts.[4] In
a late case, being a bill to enjoin a judgment recovered in
the United States Court for infringement of a patent, it is
said : " We have not the power, if we had the inclination, to
enjoin proceedings in the courts of the United States; and
should hardly think of commencing so novel an enterprise
in a case for the infringement of a patent, which is expressly,
if not exclusively, confided by law to those courts. The

[1] Kittredge v. Emerson, 15 N. H. 227.
[2] Parker v. The Judges, 12 Wheat. 561.
[3] Cropper v. Coburn, 2 Curt. 465.

[4] Mead v. Merritt, 2 Paige, 402;
Schuyler v. Pelissier, 3 Edw. Ch. 191;
English v. Miller, 2 Rich. Equ. 320.
See Boyd v. Hawkins, 2 Dev. Ch.
329.

(a) This is one of a series of cases, involving a conflict of jurisdiction between the Circuit Court of the United States and the Supreme
Court of New Hampshire, with reference to proceedings under the late
bankrupt law. The State jurisdiction was finally vindicated by a judgment of the Supreme Court of the United States. See Peck v. Jen-
ness, 7 How. 612; Hilliard on Bankruptcy, &c. 123.

suggestion in the bill, that when this case was tried in the Circuit Court of the United States for this district, parties were not allowed, as now in our State courts, to be called, or to offer themselves as witnesses, affords not the slightest ground for our interference."[1]

§ 63. Application is sometimes made to enjoin proceedings in chancery.

§ 64. It is held that an injunction to restrain the execution of a decree in equity cannot be granted.[2] In Jackson v. Leaf,[3] Lord Eldon remarked: "I do not remember any instance where this court has enjoined a party from proceeding in another court of equity. In the same court of equity you do restrain them, when there are different suits for the same purpose." But a court of equity may withdraw its own process, in a proper case, or stay execution by *supersedeas*(a).[4]

§ 65. Where it was competent for the officer allowing an injunction to allow it either as injunction master or judge of the Court of Chancery, and where it does not appear clearly in which capacity he did act, it will be presumed that he acted as judge of the court.[5]

§ 66. It is held in New York, that, where an injunction has been granted by a judge at chambers, a motion for its dissolution may be made directly to the court, without having first applied to the judge who granted it.[6] But, in a recent case, section 324 of the Code is held to apply to injunction orders.

---

[1] Per Ames, C. J., Kendall v. Winsor, 6 R. I. 462.
[3] Greenlee v. McDowell, 4 Ired. Equ. 481.

[2] 1 Jac. & W. 232.
[4] 4 Ired. Equ. 481.
[5] Frost v. Myrick, 1 Barb. 362.
[6] Woodruff v. Fisher, 17 Barb. 224.

(a) The Supreme Court of Ohio cannot by injunction restrain a suit in chancery in the Court of Common Pleas, and take jurisdiction of the same subject matter, of which the courts have concurrent jurisdiction. Merrill v. Lake, 16 Ohio, 373.

Hence a judge of the Supreme or County Court may, on application *ex parte*, vacate or modify an injunction order made by him without notice. The power, however, should not be exercised, except to prevent serious loss by delay. And where the application had been delayed for a year, and all the defendants but one had appeared and answered; such an order was held to have issued improvidently.[1]

§ 67. In a case where a bottomry bond had been given for an amount grossly exceeding the value of the ship, an injunction was granted to restrain an admiralty suit upon such bond, nothing having been done towards determining the rights of the parties in the Admiralty Court before the filing of the bill, though money had been paid into court and bail given. The ground of decision was, that the matters could be more conveniently, directly, and effectually determined in equity than in admiralty.[2]

§ 67 *a*. In Ohio, it has been held that the power to grant an injunction, in a case pending in the Court of Common Pleas, cannot constitutionally be conferred upon the Supreme Court. The court remark, "that we can allow an injunction in a case pending in this court upon an appeal is very clear. An injunction may be the very object of the suit—the final decree sought—and so a provisional injunction, during the pendency of the suit, may be necessary for the purposes of justice. The power to allow these, is a part of the appellate jurisdiction, the grant of which is authorized by the constitution, and has been made by the law. But to allow an injunction in a case pending in another court, would be an exercise of original, and not of appellate jurisdiction. Now the original jurisdiction conferred upon this court by the Constitution, is limited to *quo warranto, mandamus, habeas corpus,* and *procedendo.* Art. 4, Sec. 2. It would be wholly inconsistent with, and in a great measure destructive of the judi-

[1] Peck *v.* Yorks, 41 Barb. 547.   [2] Duncan *v.* McCalmont, 3 Beav. 409.

cial system it ordains, to suppose that this original jurisdiction can be enlarged by law. It is true, there is no express prohibition against it, but none was necessary."[1]

§ 68. We shall have occasion in another connection to consider the question, whether and how far *foreign* proceedings may be restrained by injunction.(a) (See Chap. VI., *Suits*.) It may be here remarked, that, if the circumstances of a case are such as would make it the duty of one court in England to restrain a party from instituting proceedings in another court in England, they will also warrant it in imposing on him a similar restraint with regard to proceedings in a foreign court. The fact of a foreigner having property in England enables the court to make effectual an injunction issued to him; but, especially in the case of a foreigner who seeks no assistance from the English courts, the issuing of such injunction ought clearly to be shown to be required as conducive to justice.[2] So equity may entertain a bill respecting land, though the land is not within its jurisdiction, where its decree can be enforced by acting on the person of

---

[1] Per Thurman, J., Kent *v.* Mahaffy, 2 Ohio St. 498.   [2] Carron, &c. *v.* Maclaren, 35 Eng. Law and Eq. 37.

(a) In North Carolina, the court will not drive a party to seek redress in the courts of another State, when a less circuitous and better remedy can be given in the courts of North Carolina at less cost. Richardson *v.* Williams, 3 Jones, Eq. 116. A bill was filed by the plaintiffs, owners of a charter, from the State of South Carolina, of the Augusta Bridge over the Savannah River, which divides South Carolina from Georgia, against the City Council of Augusta, in Georgia, owners of a charter of the same bridge from the State of Georgia, for an account of tolls collected by the defendants, and for an injunction to restrain them from collecting more than one moiety of tolls, and also from collecting any tolls whatever at a new bridge which they had built in violation of the plaintiffs' charter. It was averred in the bill, that of so much of the Augusta Bridge as lay within the territorial limits of South Carolina, the plaintiffs were the owners, and it was incidentally stated that the defendants owned some lots in Hamburgh, in South Carolina. A plea to the jurisdiction, because the defendants were non-residents of South Carolina, was sustained. McKinne *v.* Augusta, 5 Rich. Eq. 55.

a party; and, in a proper case, the court will restrain the party from leaving the jurisdiction by a *ne exeat.*[1]

§ 69. With reference to the *pleadings* in applications for injunction,(a) an injunction will not ordinarily be granted under a prayer for general relief, but must be expressly prayed.[2]

§ 70. A complaint for an injunction need not disclose whether a bond is filed or not.[3]

§ 71. An injunction can only be granted when it appears by the complaint that the plaintiff is entitled to the relief demanded.[4]

§ 72. Where a bill is bad upon demurrer an injunction should not be granted, even if the defect is in point of form merely.[5] But where an action was commenced by the service of a summons, without complaint, and the motion for an injunction founded upon an affidavit, which, although commencing in form as a deposition, contained all the requisites of a complaint as prescribed by the (New York) Code; it was held, that the form of the paper furnished no sufficient ground of objection.[6]

[1] Enos v. Hunter, 4 Gilm. 211.
[2] Lefforge v. West, 2 Cart. 514. See Long v. Cross, 5 Jones, Eq. 323.
[3] Smith v. Chandler, 13 Ind. 513.
[4] Morgan v. Quackenbush, 22 Barb. 76.
[5] Rose v. Rose, 11 Paige, 166.
[6] Morgan v. Quackenbush, 22 Barb. 76.

(a) In New York, "the Code, Sec. 69, has expressly abolished the distinction between actions at law and suits in equity, and the forms of all such actions; and it declares that there shall be but one form of action for the enforcement or protection of private rights and the redress of private wrongs." Per Allen, P. J., Mallory v. Norton, 21 Barb. 436. In the same State, where a preliminary injunction is asked upon facts not alleged to be within the knowledge of the defendant, the bill must be sworn to positively, either by the plaintiff or by some person from whom information of the facts was derived. Paterson v. Bangs, 9 Paige, 627.

§ 73. Great strictness will be required, in proceedings for an injunction and the appointment of a receiver of a debtor's effects, under the Ohio act of February 25, 1848, amendatory of the act directing the mode of proceeding in chancery, especially in setting forth the matters required in the second section; and, if a bill be defective in this particular, it may be dismissed at any stage of the cause, unless particular circumstances take the case out of the general rule.[1]

§ 74. The mere allegation in a complaint, that the legal remedy is too tardy, or that irreparable mischief will ensue, is not sufficient; but the facts must be stated, to show that the apprehension of injury is well founded.[2]

§ 75. Allegations in a bill, that "a firm, or some of the members of said firm," had done certain acts, that "some of the firm had obtained control of certain executions by purchase, or otherwise," that said firm bought "the same either for R. or after his death," and that they had not done certain acts as "to some of these executions;" are too inaccurate, loose, and uncertain.[3]

§ 76. The complainant must disclose all the facts of his case, or it will be presumed that those not disclosed would make against him if known.[4]   Thus the averments in a petition, which seeks to enjoin the execution of a judgment on mere technical grounds, and without disclosing merits, must be taken most strongly against the complainant.   So, where one of two defendants, the other being dead, sought to enjoin, on technical grounds, an order of sale, and did not allege that the property, or any part of it, belonged to the petitioner; the court held that the injunction was properly dissolved.[5]   So where the complainant relies upon his own oath, the charges in the bill, and the affidavit to verify them, should be direct

---

[1] Gury v. Tannenwald, 18 Ohio, 481.
[2] Catching v. Terrell, 10 Geo. 576; De Witt v. Hays, 2 Cal. 463.
[3] Green v. Ingram, 16 Geo. 164.
[4] Sauvinet v. New Orleans, 1 La. Ann. 346.
[5] Gothard v. Reiley, 14 Tex. 461.

and positive, and not such as can only be made sufficient by the aid of presumption.[1]

§ 77. If an injunction is prayed in the bill, but omitted in the prayer for process, an injunction ought not to issue without an amendment.[2]

§ 78. The rule that, in injunction bills, the particular title of the complainant must be set forth, is more especially applicable in cases of waste; in cases of trespass and nuisance, it is sufficient to allege that the complainant is the owner in fee simple, and in possession.[3]   And, in a late case, where, in a bill for injunction the complainant alleged that he was "seized and possessed" of the land in question, but there was no demurrer or objection to evidence, but a special answer, putting in issue the question of ownership; held, even if the above words imported nothing more than possession, objection could not be taken by a motion in error.[4]

§ 79. An injunction bill will not be dismissed because the master has omitted to sign the *jurat*, if the bill has been actually sworn to.[5]

§ 80. An injunction of a sale of land, under a power in a mortgage, may be granted on a bill, which does not contain a sufficient description of the land to justify a writ of possession.[6]

§ 81. A bill for injunction need not contain a prayer for discovery.[7]

§ 82. An allegation of the *service* of an injunction means a service that is legal and sufficient in law.[8]

[1] Perkins v. Collins, 2 Green Ch. 482.
[2] Bailey v. Stiles, 2 Green Ch. 245.
[3] Van Winkle v. Curtis, 2 Green Ch. 422.
[4] Falls, &c. v. Tibbetts, 31 Conn. 166.
[5] Capner v. Flemington M. Co., 2 Green Ch. 467.
[6] Conant v. Warren, 6 Gray, 562.
[7] Laurence v. Bowman, 1 McAll. C. C. (Cal.) 419.
[8] Loomis v. Brown, 16 Barb. 325.

§ 83. On an *ex parte* application for an injunction upon bill alone, the injunction will not be refused for an apparent *misnomer* of the defendant, as he may not, on coming in, wish to avail himself of the objection.[1]

§ 84. A defendant cannot, after consenting to a decree against him, for an injunction and an account, object to the misjoinder of one of the plaintiffs.[2]

§ 85. Where a surety alleged, in his bill for relief against a judgment, that the creditor indulged the principal without the complainant's consent, and the respondent answered that such consent was given; held, the negative averment of the complainant was proper, but one which he was not bound to prove; that the denial of the defendant did not make his answer evidence; and that it was incumbent on him to prove such consent.[3]

§ 86. Where a bill asks for an injunction, to protect the complainants from apprehended danger, and the answer denies that the apprehensions are well grounded; the court will give the defendants the full benefit of their denial, and refuse the injunction, unless the complainants make out a very clear case in their bill and affidavits.[4]

§ 86 *a*. With reference to the pleadings subsequent to the bill, it is held that an injunction will not be granted before answer, unless some interest of the plaintiff will be injured or endangered by the proceedings of the defendant in the mean time.[5]   And, on a motion for a provisional injunction, the defendant may file and read his answer to the bill.[6]

§ 86 *b*. The (Maryland) acts of 1852, c. 133, and 1853, c. 344, do not apply to an answer, at the hearing of a motion

[1] Boeley *v.* Susquehanna, &c., 3 Bland, 63.
[2] Livingston *v.* Woodworth, 15 How. 546.
[3] Carpenter *v.* Devon. 6 Ala. 718.
[4] Rogers *v.* Danforth, 1 Stockt. 289.
[5] Osborn *v.* Taylor, 5 Paige, 515.
[6] Hulse *v.* Wright, Wright Ch. 61.

for the dissolution of the injunction, when such a hearing is not a final one.[1]

§ 86 c. A defendant may by a sufficient answer to the bill at once prevent an injunction;[2] as by an answer which would dissolve an injunction if granted.[3] But where the bill alleges fraud, forgery, and antedating, and the answer denies these allegations only on "information and belief," it is not sufficient to prevent the issue of an injunction.[4] And in the Circuit Court of the United States the practice is settled, that the denial of the plaintiff's title in an answer does not prevent the court from awarding a special temporary injunction.[5]

§ 87. With reference to the formal requisites of the injunction itself, it is held that an injunction should be clear and explicit, and apprise the defendant what he is restrained from doing, without the necessity of his resorting to the bill on file; and, if he does not in fact know to what the injunction applies, he will be justified in proceeding, notwithstanding the injunction.[6] (See Chap. IV.) Thus an injunction restraining a husband from annoying his wife is improper.[7] So an injunction must, upon its face, show clearly to what property it is intended to apply, or it cannot be enforced.[8] And an injunction should be restricted to the case made by the bill.[9] In Pennsylvania, it is said, "injunctions are frequently in the form of a *writ*, but these forms are not adapted to every case, and therefore the prohibition in numerous instances assumes the shape of an *order*, in the nature of an injunction. As the courts treat the disobedience of all orders as a contempt, and enforce the performance of them by imprisonment, the distinction between a *writ* of injunction and an *order* in the nature of one is disregarded in practice. Both are known by the

[1] Bouldin v. Baltimore, 15 Md. 18; Gellston v. Rullman, 15 Md. 260.
[2] Hall v. McPherson, 3 Bland, 529.
[3] Bell v. Purvis, 15 Md. 22.
[4] U. S. v. Parrott, 1 McAll. C. C. 271.
[5] Clum v. Brewer, 2 Curt. 506; Poor v. Carleton, 3 Sumn. 70.
[6] Sullivan v. Judah, 4 Paige, 444; 2 ib. 234.
[7] Lowrie v. Lowrie, 2 Paige, 234.
[8] Moat v. Halbein, 2 Edw. Ch. 188.
[9] 2 Paige, 234.

name of injunctions.   If the order be issued in mandatory language, it is substantially an injunction; if in terms of advice or caution, it is what has become known as an 'admonitory order.' "[1]

§ 88. An injunction may be granted upon a supplemental bill, though one founded upon the original bill has been dissolved upon its merits.[2] So a bill of injunction may be granted, after a former bill for the same cause has been dismissed for not having been served on the defendant in time; but there should be an affidavit of some particular hardship, and no omission on the part of the claimant.[3] So, in Georgia, by the act of 1842, the power of issuing a second injunction, when the first bill has been dismissed, is given to the Superior Court;[4] and in Virginia, though an injunction be refused by a judge of the Circuit Court, and also by a judge of the Supreme Court, such refusals are no objection to an injunction in the same case, granted by another judge of the latter court.[5]

§ 89. But a second injunction will not be granted for the same purpose, while the first is in force; and if the first has been withdrawn by the plaintiff, after it was served, that fact should be fully stated in the bill for a second.[6] And on an application to reinstate an injunction, if the newly-discovered equity could have been made available on the first trial, by the use of ordinary care and attention, the application should be refused.[7] So an *ex parte* injunction will not be granted on a new bill, or an amended bill, when a previous and similar injunction on the same parties was dissolved for want of equity.[8] So a second injunction in the same cause, upon new grounds, cannot be granted, if the new grounds existed

[1] Per Lewis, C. J., Erie, &c. v. Casey, 26 Penn. 292.
[2] Van Bergen v. Demarest, 4 John. Ch. 35.
[3] Mayfield v. Hawkins, Mar. 27.
[4] Cox v. Mayor, &c., 17 Geo. 249.
[5] Jaynes v. Brock, 10 Gratt. 211.
[6] Livingston v. Gibbons, 4 John. Ch. 571.
[7] Larson v. Moore, 1 Tex. 22.
[8] Hornor v. Leeds, 2 Stockt. 36.

when the first bill was filed.[1] Nor successive injunctions
upon different grounds, which might have been put at issue
in one proceeding.[2] So, in New York, after an injunction
has been refused by the chancellor or vice-chancellor before
whom the bill was filed, the plaintiff cannot, since the revised
statutes, apply to an injunction master, or vice-chancellor
acting as injunction master, for an injunction upon a new
bill upon substantially the same grounds.[3]

§ 90. It is the general rule, that an injunction cannot be
granted against a person who is not a party to the cause.[4]
And a complainant cannot avoid the necessity of making
particular persons parties, by waiving all claim against them
in his bill, where it is necessary to take an account against
the defendant, and where he has a right to have such persons
before the court, they being interested in the account, in
order to save the necessity of a future litigation with them.[5]
But an injunction inhibiting a defendant and all other persons from selling slaves, until a further order of the court,
prevents a valid sale of the slaves, on execution against the
defendant, although in favor of persons not parties to the
suit in chancery.[6]

§ 91. One owner of land over which a street is laid out
cannot enjoin the completion of such street for want of
notice to another.[7]

§ 91 a. Where a statute provided that no injunction should
issue without a bond, it was held to preclude the commonwealth from this remedy. The court say: "The words are
broad and general. They apply to all cases, and we cannot
see upon what principle we could except a case in which the
commonwealth is plaintiff. But the commonwealth can give

[1] United States Bank v. Schultz,
3 Ham. 61.
[2] Fluker v. Davis, 12 La. An. 613.
[3] Cummins v. Bennett, 8 Paige, 79.

[4] Fellows v. Fellows, 4 John. Ch.
25.
[5] Dart v. Palmer, 1 Barb. Ch. 92.
[6] West v. Belches, 5 Munf. 187.
[7] Nichols v. Salem, 14 Gray, 490.

no bond, there being no organ of the government authorized to execute it for her; and if she could give bond, she would not be suable on it.   The law which forbids an injunction to be granted without bond from the party can only be obeyed, in this case, by refusing the injunction altogether."[1]

§ 91 *b*. Though the court will not proceed against a member that has privilege of Parliament, yet, if a Parliament man sues at law, and a bill is brought to be relieved, the court will stay proceedings at law till answer or further order.[2]

§ 92. It is the prevailing rule that, in order to obtain an injunction, a party must show a particular injury distinct from that which he suffers in common with the public.[3] (See *Nuisance*.)   Thus an action, for the purpose of having the act of the board of supervisors, erecting a new town, declared null and void, and enjoining its organization, cannot be maintained by persons having no other interest than one in common with all the freeholders of the new town.   The only remedy is at the instance of the State or some officer.[4]

§ 93. But, on the contrary, it has been sometimes held that a private individual may obtain an injunction to prevent a public mischief by which he is affected in common with others.[5]   And where a public right appears, in a litigation between private individuals, the court is bound to protect it, though no one asserts the right in behalf of the State. Thus, where the matter in dispute was the right to charge wharfage for a wharf exclusively claimed by both parties, and the court found that neither had the right, and that the public were entitled to the free use of the wharf; both parties were enjoined from collecting such wharfage.[6]

[1] Per Black, C. J., Com. *v.* Franklin, &c., 21 Penn. 130.
[2] 1 Vern. 329.
[3] Falls, &c. *v.* Tibbetts, 31 Conn. 165.
[4] Doolittle *v.* Supervisors, &c., 18 N. Y. (4 Smith), 155.
[5] Whitfield *v.* Rogers, 26 Miss. 84.
[6] The Wharf Case, 3 Bland, 361.

§ 94. Where a contract is made for the sale of land, the vendee is a necessary party to a bill for an injunction to restrain a tenant from waste.[1]

§ 95. Where relief other than simply the quieting of possession is sought, and an account is to be stated between the warrantor and the party defendant, or on a bill by his grantee for the purpose of quieting possession, the warrantor is a necessary party.[2]   But if a warrantor bring his bill of complaint singly, asking, not for a bare injunction, but also for an account and general relief, and if no objection be taken in the early stage of the proceedings, nor any suggestion made that the interests of his grantee in possession require him to be made a party; it is not the duty of the court to delay the cause, for the reason that the grantee is not made a party.[3]

§ 96. Two or more persons, having separate and distinct tenements, injured or rendered uninhabitable by a common nuisance, or rendered less valuable by a private nuisance, which is a common injury to the tenants of both, may join in a suit to restrain such nuisance (a).[4]

§ 97. Where a bill was brought for an injunction by two parties, whose property was injured by the same nuisance, and one of the parties brought a suit at law on a declaration containing several counts, and recovered, and afterwards a supplemental bill was filed by both parties, setting up the verdict, and affidavits were offered in support of both bills and to determine the count on which the verdict was rendered; held, as the injunction was sought after order and

[1] Kidd v. Dennison, 6 Barb. 9.
[2] Brooks v. Fowle, 14 N. H. 248.
[3] Ibid.
[4] Murray v. Hay, 1 Barb. Ch. 59.

(a) The court exercises a sound discretion, without adhering to an inflexible rule, in determining whether there has been a misjoinder of parties in equity.

notice, the hearing should be had upon such affidavits as were pertinent to the issues, but that the injunction would follow the bill; that the parties were properly joined in the supplemental bill; that the injunction should be granted on the supplemental bill on the application of the party presenting the new matter; and that it was competent to show on which count the verdict was rendered.[1]

§ 98. Any one of several complainants, in a bill for injunction, may verify its statements, in order to authorize the sanction of the chancellor.[2]

§ 99. The proper allegation in a bill, by way of excuse for not making the representatives of a deceased person parties to the suit, is, that the decedent died insolvent, and without leaving any assets for the payment of his debts; an allegation that he died insolvent is not sufficient.[3]

§ 100. Where an injunction includes persons who were not parties to the proceeding in which it issued, the injunction is nevertheless valid as to parties to the proceeding.[4]

§ 101. The question of injunction often arises, in connection with some other ground of equitable jurisdiction, which constitutes the primary object of the bill.

§ 102. Upon a bill for *specific performance*, and for an injunction to protect the subject-matter of the contract, the latter will not be granted, unless the plaintiff is entitled to such performance.[5]

§ 103. In a suit for specific performance of a contract made by the agent of a state prison for the labor of the convicts, it seems that a preliminary injunction to restrain the

[1] Blunt v. Hay, 4 Sandf. Ch. 362.
[2] Hemphill v. Ruckersville, &c., 3 Kelly, 435.
[3] Dart v. Palmer, 1 Barb. Ch. 92.

[4] Tradesman's Bank v. Merritt, 1 Paige, 302.
[5] Geiger v. Green, 4 Gill, 472.

agent from making any other contract for such labor will not be granted, if it would prevent the employment of the convicts pursuant to the statute.[1]

§ 104. *Notice* is an important subject in connection with injunctions.

§ 105. Equity will not decree a *perpetual* injunction, which is to operate directly upon the parties in interest, without giving them an opportunity of being heard.[2]

§ 106. In New Jersey, it has been sometimes held, that notice of an application for an injunction should be given, where it can be done without risk of injury by the delay.[3] But in a later decision it is held, that notice is not necessary, unless specially ordered by the court, except where it is made after answer filed, and then it may be dispensed with by the court. And in such latter case, although it does not appear that notice was dispensed with, if it was a proper case for so doing, it will be presumed to have been done.[4]

§ 107. In Pennsylvania, an injunction cannot be granted, until the parties complained of have been served with a subpoena to appear and answer; until then, they are not in court.[5]

§ 108. In New York, on serving an injunction, the plaintiff should at the same time take out and serve such subpoena; but if the defendant voluntarily appears and answers, the objection for the irregularity is waived.[6] Under sect. 220 of the Code, requiring a copy of the affidavit to be served with the injunction, it is sufficient to serve a copy of the complaint, with its verification, upon which the injunction

---

[1] Jones v. Lynde, 7 Paige, 301.
[2] Marshall v. Beverley, 5 Wheat. 313.
[3] Ross v. Elizabethtown, &c. 1 Green, Ch. 422.
[4] Buckley v. Course, Saxton, 504.
[5] Blair v. Boggs, &c. 31 Penn. 274.
[6] Parker v. Williams, 4 Paige, 439; Seebor v. Hess, 5 Paige, 85; Marsh v. Bennett, 5 McLean, 117.

was issued.[1]   An injunction order may be allowed, signed and delivered to the officer, but cannot be served, before the defendant is summoned.[2]

§ 109. In Indiana, a court of chancery will not, where there is no emergency, grant an injunction, unless ten days' notice of the application has been given to the adverse party, or the application relates to a suit pending in the court. But where the court has granted an injunction in a case in which the adverse party was entitled to notice, and the transcript does not show whether notice was given or not, the Supreme Court will presume that the notice was given.[3]

§ 110. Injunctions cannot be granted in the courts of the United States without notice, and hence all of them are special.[4]

§ 111. It is not sufficient that *an order for publication* has been passed; the publication must be proved, in order to bring a respondent regularly before the court; and where this is not done, and a *pro confesso* taken, a decree perpetually enjoining a judgment at law will be reversed.[5]

§ 112. An injunction, affecting the rights of a party who has appeared, will not generally be granted on an *ex parte* application, on a supplemental bill, without regular notice; but a temporary injunction may, in the mean time, be granted, if necessary to prevent serious loss or injury.[6]

§ 113. It is said, although the practice in this country is to grant an injunction, on the filing of the bill, without notice to the defendant, yet the complainant must use due diligence

---

[1] Leffingwell *v.* Chave, 5 Bosw. 703.
[2] Ib.
[3] Vance *v.* Workman, 8 Blackf. 306.

[4] Perry *v.* Parker, 1 W. & M. 280.
[5] Moore *v.* Wright, 4 Stew. & Port. 84.
[6] Bloomfield *v.* Snowden, 2 Paige, 355.

4

in prosecuting his suit afterwards, or the bill will be dismissed. But where, at the time of granting the injunction, a *subpœna* was taken out, returnable at the next term of the court, which was returned, by the sheriff, *not found;* held, the want of service of the *subpœna* was not ground for dismissing the bill. In such case, the sheriff's return upon the subpœna is conclusive.[1]

§ 114. Upon injunctions to stay proceedings at law, the court may direct the *subpœnas* to be served on the law agents of the non-resident parties; but in cases of original bills it will not be permitted, as relief may be obtained in the Federal or State courts of the State or circuit where the party resides.[2]

§ 114 a. A bill for an injunction of a suit, commenced in a circuit court, is not an original suit, within the restrictions of the judiciary act of 1789, c. 20, § 11, and may be brought against one who is a resident in another State, without serving process upon him in the State where the suit is brought.[3]

§ 115. Notice to defendants that an injunction would be moved for, delivered to them six days before the commencement of the term, was held sufficient.[4]

§ 116. In New York, where an answer on oath is waived, and affidavits of disinterested witnesses in support of an injunction are annexed to, and filed and served with, the bill; the affidavits in support of the answer, and upon which the defendant relies in his application to dissolve the injunction, must either be served upon the complainant's solicitor with the answer, or must be served on him the usual length of time before the making of the motion to dissolve the injunction.[5]

---

[1] Corey *v.* Voorhies, 1 Green Ch. 5.
[2] Ward *v.* Sebring, 4 Wash. C. 472.
[3] Dunlap *v.* Stetson, 4 Mas. 349.
[4] New York *v.* Connecticut, 4 Dal. 1.
[5] Markham *v.* Markham, 1 Barb. Ch. 374.

§ 117. A bill of injunction is well served by leaving a copy at the residence of the defendant.[1]

§ 118. The defendant being in contempt for want of an appearance, the common injunction was extended to stay trial on a motion made without notice.[2]

§ 119. The following miscellaneous points have been settled in reference to injunctions.

§ 120. An injunction properly issued, in support of the *primâ facie* right or title of the party seeking it, does not affect or impair the right to a trial by jury.[3]

§ 121. Injunction is merely a remedial process, and, where the party obtaining it has also obtained judgment upon his cause, the court will not revise the propriety of granting the writ.[4]

§ 122. Writs of injunction, auxiliary to a suit pending, are returnable only to the county where such suit is pending.[5]

§ 123. An injunction in chancery is not equivalent to a release of errors in a suit at law.[6]

§ 123 *a.* Where no answer had been put in to an injunction bill, leave was granted to *amend,* so as to waive an answer under oath, on payment of costs.[7]

§ 123 *b.* A reference to a vice-chancellor of a motion to dissolve an injunction does not empower him to authorize an amendment of the bill.[8]

---

[1] Morris *v.* Bradford, 19 Geo. 527.
[2] Harrison *v.* Dixon, 11 Sim. 123.
[3] Woodworth *v.* Rogers, 3 W. & M. 135.
[4] Hicks *v.* Davis, 4 Cal. 67.
[5] Allen *v.* Menard, 5 Tex. 378.
[6] Prodot *v.* Doe, 24 Miss. 169.
[7] Bronson *v.* Green, Walk. Ch. 486.
[8] Cowman *v.* Lovett, 10 Paige, 559.

§ 123 *c.* The amendment of an injunction bill, unless allowed by the chancellor without prejudice to the injunction, displaces the injunction ; and the allowance of an amendment by the court, which the complainant could have made as of right, does not necessarily operate a continuance of the injunction until answer.[1]

§ 123 *d.* For an error in a bill which is amendable, a preliminary injunction will not be refused, although the amendment has not been actually made.[2]

§ 123 *e.* An injunction is not affected by an *appeal* from it.[3]

§ 124. On application for an injunction, the court may go into the merits, and may dismiss the bill, before answer filed ; but the defendant cannot introduce extraneous matter of proof.[4]

§ 125. Injunctions in certain cases may be granted without the filing of a bill.[5](*a*)   The fact, that the bill was not filed until after the injunction was ordered, is at most but a mere irregularity, which cannot operate a reversal of the order granting it.[6]   No particular form is necessary to the writ.[7]   The substantial thing is an authentic notification to the defendants of the mandate of the judge, which they must then at their peril obey.[8]

[1] Semmes *v.* Mayor, &c., 19 Geo. 471.
[2] Packer *v.* Sunbury, &c., 19 Penn. 211.
[3] Merced Mining Co. *v.* Fremont, 7 Cal. 130.
[4] Rose *v.* Hamilton, 1 Desau. 137.
[5] Peck *v.* Crane, 25 Vt. 146.
[6] Davis *v.* Reed, 14 Md. 152.
[7] Summers *v.* Farish, 10 Cal. 345.
[8] Ibid.

(*a*) In Maryland, no injunction to stay a sale, under the act of 1826, c. 192, can be granted, unless the bill be filed by the party, and contain the allegations required by ¿ 8 of that act.   Gayle *v.* Fattle, 14 Md. 69. In California, an injunction is ordinarily to be asked for before the complaint is filed, so that it can issue with the summons, though it does not take effect until the filing of the complaint.   Heyman *v.* Landers, 12 Cal. 107.   The provisions of the Revised Statutes of New York, prohibiting the issuing of an injunction before the bill is filed, do not relate to cases where the court have in another way obtained jurisdiction. Matter of Hemiup, 2 Paige, 316.

§ 126. Where a bill prays for relief, by way of injunction, and does not pray for the process of injunction, the process cannot be granted.[1]

§ 127. In some cases of injunction, a *receiver* will be appointed. Thus, there was a devise of a house and lot to trustees, for the use of B. for his life, then of B.'s wife, if she survive him; the trustees to convey the same, after the death of B. and his wife, to their children. Also to B. a legacy for $2,000. With a part of this $2,000, B. built another house on the land, and was in the receipt of the proceeds. C. obtained judgment at law, and issued execution, but failed to obtain payment for want of property subject to execution at law. On bill filed by C. the court appointed a receiver of the rents of the latter house to be applied to the judgments, and enjoined the trustees from receiving the rents.[2] But where a bill was filed by the purchaser of land at a sheriff's sale, praying an injunction to restrain one who entered under the former owner from cultivating turpentine trees, on the allegation of irreparable mischief from the defendant's insolvency; and it appeared that the defendant entered by virtue of a lease of the trees for making turpentine, made before the sheriff's sale: held, it would be inconsistent with the relief sought by the bill, to decree the appointment of a receiver of the rent to secure its payment to the reversioner.[3]

§ 128. Under a bill praying for an injunction and a receiver, the receiver may be appointed before answer.[4]

§ 129. An injunction may prohibit any further interference by executors with the estate devised, even before the acceptance of the receiver appointed, if there is no danger of injury to the estate.[5]

[1] Union Bank *v.* Kerr, 2 Md. Ch. Decis. 460.
[2] Johnson *v.* Woodruff, 4 Halst. Ch. 120.
[3] Burns *v.* Campbell, 3 Jones, Eq. 410.
[4] Johns *v.* Johns, 23 Geo. 31.
[5] Ibid.

§ 130. The court in England will grant the common injunction on any day, although out of term, and not a *seal* day or a continuation of the seal.[1]

§ 131. An injunction does not operate upon proceedings subsequent to its allowance, but before its service.[2]

§ 132. In reference to the *statutory* provision for the remedy by injunction, it is said by the court in Massachusetts: "Where the legislature have the power to provide redress for either a public or private wrong, the remedy or mode of redress is wholly a subject of legislative discretion. If an injunction is better adapted to accomplish the objects proposed, than any other form of judicial process, there seems no reason why the legislature should not have power to direct it."[3](a)

[1] Reece v. Humble, 10 Sim. 117.
[2] Ramsdell v. Craighill, 9 Ham. 197.
[3] Per Shaw, C. J., Com. v. Farmers, &c., 21 Pick. 552.

(a) The Supreme Court of Alabama has power to grant an injunction in a proper case. Davis v. Tuscumbia, &c., 4 Stew. & Port. 421. In Texas, the act of 1846, Hart. Dig. Art. 1599, does not apply to injunctions sought for causes arising subsequent to the judgment. Clegg v. Varnell, 18 Texas, 294. As to the county jurisdiction in Indiana, see State v. Michaels, 8 Blackf. 436. See also Roshell v. Maxwell, 1 Hemp. 25. In New York the *Code* has not, by the union of equitable and legal powers, enlarged in any respect the previous powers of the court to grant perpetual injunctions. New York, &c. v. Supervisors, &c., 4 Duer, 192. The discretion of the commissioner in granting a specific injunction is not restrained, in South Carolina, by the statute of 1840. It continues in force until dissolved by order of the chancellor. Ellis v. Commander, 1 Strobh. Eq. 188. The provision of the statute of Georgia of 1811, that " in all cases of injunction, they shall be disposed of, and a decision made, at the second term of said court, held in and for said county where such suit originated," means the second term after the parties are served and the cause set down for trial. Johnson v. Holt, 3 Kelly, 117.

CHAPTER II.

BOND OR OTHER SECURITY.

§ 1. Injunction *bonds* are an ordinary though not an invariable accompaniment of this form of equitable interposition.(a)　And an injunction order is not operative until the

---

(a) The practice on this subject is various in the different States. In Pennsylvania, courts are bound to require the security provided for in the act of May 6th, 1844, before issuing any injunction, or an order in the nature thereof. Erie, &c. *v.* Casey, 26 Penn. 287. In South Carolina, except where the application for an injunction is for stay of proceedings in an action, a commissioner has no authority to require a bond or other security. Fant *v.* Martin, 10 Rich. 428. In Maryland, where, upon a suit in equity for an injunction, the answers have come in, and they show on their face a case for a perpetual injunction, and the continuance of the injunction is not dependent upon a question of law or fact to be subsequently established, it is unnecessary to require an injunction bond. Alexander *v.* Ghiselin, 5 Gill, 138. Under the Georgia amendatory act of 1842, an injunction may be granted by the judges of the superior courts upon such terms as in their discretion the case may require. They may dispense with security altogether, provided the party, against whom the injunction is to operate, do not need it for his protection. Guerry *v.* Durham, 11 Geo. 9. In Louisiana, where executory proceedings are enjoined on the allegations of fraud and payment, supported by affidavit, an injunction bond is not required. Cordier *v.* Zuntz, 14 La. An., 861.

written undertaking, required by statute, is given.[1] One restrained by an injunction from doing a lawful act may recover damages for any injury that he has suffered, in a suit on the injunction bond, if in the usual form.[2]

§ 2. Where a void injunction has been obtained, the bond given to obtain it is not void.[3] But a bond is void for want of authority in the commissioner.[4]

§ 3. Where the judge, in an order granting an injunction, neglects to state the amount of the bond as required by statute, he may amend his *fiat*, either before or after the execution of the bond, and it is error to dissolve the injunction for that cause.[5]

§ 4. Security in other form than that of a bond is sometimes required as the condition of an injunction. In a late case in Vermont, the court remarks: " It was formerly the practice in England, and perhaps is at the present time, to order the party on whose application an injunction is granted, when the court require the damages to be paid, if any are sustained, to order such party to pay a sum of money into court, out of which the damages will be paid if in the course of the subsequent proceeding the orator shall be adjudged liable therefor, but in such case before payment can be made out of such fund, the court must proceed to ascertain the

[1] Elliott v. Osborne, 1 Cal. 396.
[2] Cain v. McGuire, 13 B. Mon. 340.
[3] Stevenson v. Miller, 2 Litt. 306.
[4] Fant v. Martin, 10 Rich. 428.
[5] Dickenson v. McDermott, 13 Tex. 248.

But the court has no power, upon granting an interlocutory injunction to stay proceedings at law for a money demand, to dispense with the security required by the statute. Hunt v. Smith, 1 Rich. Ch. 277. In California, whether or not the statute gives the chancellor power to require a bond on the issuance of a temporary injunction, yet he has power to order one as a matter in furtherance of the objects of the litigation and the protection of the subject matter thereof. If there was a suit pending, the chancellor had authority to order the injunction and the bond. Prader v. Purkett, 13 Cal. 588.

amount of the damage which the party is to pay, and order its payment."[1]

§ 5. In New York, upon a bill for an injunction to restrain a sale of the property of the plaintiff, taken on execution against a stranger, a *deposit* or *security* by the plaintiff is not required by the statute, though the injunction master may require it in a proper case; and, if a deposit is made, the defendant, the execution creditor, cannot take it out of court, upon giving security for repayment in case the plaintiff should succeed in the suit.[2] In the same State, upon application for an injunction against a judgment on the ground of usury, the applicant will not be allowed to give bond, instead of bringing the amount of the judgment into court, as directed by the statute, unless he will consent to waive the forfeiture, and pay the amount justly due.[3] The provisions of the Revised Statutes on this subject were not repealed by the Code of 1848. An injunction to stay an execution will be set aside, where it was issued without a deposit and bond, or an order of court prescribing a bond in lieu of the deposit to be given. To authorize the court in dispensing with the deposit and bond, there must have been, on the part of the plaintiff, such a fraud as the substitution of one paper for another, a false statement, &c.[4]

§ 5 a. In Wisconsin, the Rev. Sts., c. 84, by their true construction, require in all cases where an injunction is granted, to stay proceedings at law in personal actions, a deposit of the sum for which judgment was rendered, and the execution of a bond to the plaintiff in such sum as the officer allowing the injunction shall direct, conditioned for the payment of such damages and costs as may be awarded at the final hearing of the cause, or a bond in lieu of the deposit in addition to the one last above mentioned,

[1] Per Pierpoint, J., Sturgis v. Knapp, 33 Verm. 520.
[2] Hegeman v. Wilson, 8 Paige, 29.
[3] Gee v. Southworth, 10 Paige, 297.
[4] Cook v. Dickerson, 2 Sandf. 691.

or a bond conditioned for the payment of the judgment, and also for the payment of the damages and costs.[1]

§ 6. In Maryland, where a party applying for an injunction against a suit at law admits that he owes a balance, the court may require such balance to be brought into court, to be paid accordingly.[2] So an injunction, to restrain a suit upon promissory notes given for the purchase-money of land, will not be granted without an injunction bond; and, if injunction be claimed upon the ground that the vendee has paid taxes on the land which the vendor was bound to pay, the bill should state how much will remain due after deducting the taxes, and the balance should be brought into court to be paid to the vendor.[3]

§ 7. By the practice of the third (United States) Circuit, no money penalty is inserted in an injunction.[4]

§ 8. Where the security given for obtaining an injunction is not sufficient, further security will be ordered.[5] And, in general, where an injunction issues without bond, the defendants may petition for an order of court requiring a bond to be given by a reasonable period, or, on default, to have the injunction dissolved.[6] So, in New York, if the officer granting an injunction neglects to take the bond required by the rules, application may be made to the court for relief.[7] But a failure to give bond and security, prior to the granting of an injunction, is no cause for dismissing a bill.[8]

§ 9. In Maryland, the mere delivery to the clerk of an injunction bond does not import its acceptance and approval by the court. If, however, the bond remains where it should be if accepted, and the parties act under it, these circumstances are evidence of its acceptance by the proper authority.

[1] Cooper v. Tappan, 4 Wis. 362. See Dungey v. Angove, 3 Bro. Ch. 36.
[2] Flickinger v. Hull, 5 Gill, 60.
[3] Reynolds v. Howard, 3 Md. Ch. Decis. 331.
[4] Low v. Hauel, Wallace, Jr. 345.
[5] Moredock v. Williams, 1 Overton, 325.
[6] Alexander v. Ghiselin, 5 Gill, 138.
[7] Cayuga, &c. v. Magee, 2 Paige, 116.
[8] Querry v. Durham, 11 Geo. 9.

After overruling a prayer, affirming that acceptance by the court was necessary to an injunction bond, it is error in the court to rule, that signing, sealing, and delivery were sufficient for such bond. Otherwise, if the latter ruling stood alone, since then counsel might have asked the court to rule that delivery included acceptance. Under the act of 1723, ch. 8, § 5, application for an injunction bond must be made to the county court, and that court must approve the bond. But it does not appear what is then to be done with such bond, nor is there any provision for recording it. It would seem, however, that it was intended to remain in the clerk's office as a supersedeas to further proceedings.[1] It is not necessary to an injunction that a bond be filed with the bill. Such a bond need not be filed till ordered by the court.[2]

§ 10. In New York, it is irregular to file an injunction bond before it is proved and acknowledged.[3]

§ 11. The filing of an injunction bond, and consequent issue of the writ on the same day, are regarded as concurrent acts, and a recital in the bond, that the obligors " have obtained" such writ, will be interpreted in the present tense, and held to refer to the writ actually issued.[4]

§ 12. In Kentucky, an injunction awarded to enjoin a judgment at law, with a direction that the bond shall be as the law directs, is sufficiently explicit; but in other cases the order itself ought to direct what kind of a bond shall be taken.[5] (See § 19.)

§ 13. Conditions in an injunction bond, not required by statute, or broader than those provided by statute, and rendering the bond insensible, are held to be surplusage.[6] Thus, in a recent case, a statute provided that writs of injunction might be issued upon filing a bond " to respond to all dam-

---

[1] Burgess v. Lloyd, 7 Md. 178.
[2] Negro Charles v. Sheriff, 12 Md. 274.
[3] Harrington v. American Life Ins. Co., 1 Barb. 244.
[4] Wallis v. Dilley, 7 Md. 237.
[5] Stevenson v. Miller, 2 Litt. 306.
[6] Johnson v. Vaughan, 9 B. Mon. 217; Gully v. Gully, 1 Hawks, 23.

ages and costs." A bond was given to pay "all such damages and costs as shall be sustained and *awarded*" by reason of the injunction. Held, the words "and awarded" might be rejected as surplusage, and the bond enforced.[1] But when the conditions are not such as are prescribed by statute, the bond cannot have the force of a judgment.[2]

§ 14. The following points are settled in reference to injunction bonds in New York. The undertaking, required on the making of an injunction order, must be approved and filed with the clerk of the court. In general, an undertaking will be required on an order restraining the defendant temporarily, in connection with an order to show cause. The plaintiff's own undertaking will not be received, unless he can justify as being a freeholder or householder, and worth double the sum specified over and above all his debts and liabilities. A surety, when one is required, must justify in like manner. And a plaintiff, residing out of the State, must give a resident surety.[3]

§ 14 a. The Circuit Court of the United States for the Eastern District of Louisiana, on a bill in equity brought to stay an execution sale, directed an injunction, upon the complainant's giving a bond in the form in common use in courts of chancery, conditioned " to answer all damages which the defendant might sustain in consequence of the injunction being granted, should the same be afterwards dissolved." The condition of the bond filed was "to pay all such damages as the defendant should recover against him, in case it should be decided that the injunction was wrongfully obtained,"— the form used in the State courts, under the law of the State (judgment being rendered on the bond for the debt, interest, and damages, and upon dissolution of the injunction); and the injunction was thereupon issued. Held, the United States Court, acting according to the established

[1] Proprs., &c. v. Mussey, 48 Maine, 307.

[2] Hanks v. Horton, 5 Tex. 103.
[3] Sheldon v. Allerton, 1 Sandf. 700.

principles of equity, the acts of Congress, and the practice of the High Court of Chancery in England, and not according to the State laws, could not give judgment on the bond upon dissolving the injunction; and the defendant could not enforce the bond till he had recovered a judgment at law.[1]

§ 15. When an action is brought on an injunction bond, the law court may look into the proceedings in equity which led to giving the bond, in order to determine its validity.[2] So a reference to the record in a bond makes the record a part of the bond, and where the description and the proceeding described are both before the court, the latter will control the former.[3]

§ 16. With reference to the *parties* to an injunction bond, a bond made to A. and B., on suing out an injunction to enjoin a judgment in favor of H., for the use of B., is a bond to the "adverse party" within the meaning of a statute.[4] So where a statute required the bond of a person applying for a stay of execution by injunction to be taken in the name of the plaintiff, and a master, on granting an injunction, took a bond payable to himself and his successors in office, and then assigned the bond to the plaintiff; held, the bond was good, and the assignee could sue on it.[5] In Alabama, a bond to A. B., register, appearing on its face to be an obligation taken by him in his official capacity, is good under the Code, § 2973.[6] In Iowa, the fact that a bond for an injunction, to restrain a county officer from committing a public wrong, is executed to the county judge in his official capacity, instead of the county itself, affords no grounds for dissolving the injunction.[7] In Louisiana, an injunction bond to all the obligees by name creates a liability to each, from its essential nature and purpose, though not so expressed, and therefore the party

[1] Bein *v.* Heath, 12 How. 168.
[2] Norris *v.* Cobb, 8 Rich. Eq. 58.
[3] Williamson *v.* Hall, 1 Ohio St. 190.

[4] Scott *v.* Fowler, 2 Eng. 299.
[5] Cay *v.* Galliot, 4 Strobh. 282.
[6] Buckner *v.* Stewart, 34 Ala. 529.
[7] Collins *v.* Ripley, 8 Clarke, 129.

really injured has, under the practice of the State, a separate right of action, and must not join the other obligees.[1]　(See § 26.)

§ 17. So much of an order granting an injunction, as directed a particular person to be taken as security, was held to be surplusage, it being the duty of the clerk to approve and accept the security in injunction bonds.[2]

§ 18. Where the principal in an injunction bond, given on an injunction to stay an execution, at the time of its dissolution is not an inhabitant of the State, absolute notice of such dissolution, or a waiver thereof, must be brought home to such principal to charge him, in an action for the amount of the judgment and costs paid by the surety, though the parties were residents of the same State at the time the bond was given.[3]

§ 19. With regard to the terms of the condition in an injunction bond; it is held in New York, that a penal bond with sureties, conditioned to pay such damages as the defendant may sustain by reason of the injunction, is a sufficient compliance with § 222 of the Code.[4]　(See § 12.)

§ 20. A bond, restraining execution creditors from selling certain articles, is merely security to the obligees for any damage they may receive, and not for the amount of the debt; and if such bond gives the obligees greater security, equity will relieve against it.[5]

§ 21. Where an injunction bond does not bind the obligors to pay costs, this is not a defect of which they can complain.[6]

§ 22. Injunction bonds by *executors* should secure to the creditor all the rights and legal consequences, resulting from

[1] Connor v. Zuntz, 14 La. An. 861.
[2] Greathouse v. Hord, 1 Dana, 105.
[3] Iglehart v. Moore, 16 Ark. 46.
[4] St. Peter v. Varian, 28 Barb. 644.
[5] Hanley v. Wallace, 3 B. Monr. 184.
[6] Gillespie v. Thompson, 5 Gratt. 132.

an unsuccessful prosecution of the injunction, which existed at the time it was obtained, or which followed its dissolution, to the extent of assets at the time of obtaining it; and to that extent the surety is bound also.[1]

§ 23. In reference to the *construction* of injunction bonds; the general principle is held applicable, that the construction of bonds, taken under the provisions of law, is more rigorous than of bonds taken voluntarily.[2] But, as against the surety in a bond, while general and doubtful phrases are to be construed in view of what was sought to be enjoined,[3] the contract of the surety is within the statute of frauds, and is to be strictly construed, and no parol evidence is admissible to add to, vary, or contradict it in any of its terms. Though a misrecital in the condition, as to the amount of the judgment enjoined, may be corrected by the bill, where the bond contains a plain reference to it; on the principle that that is certain which can be made certain.[4] The securities in an injunction bond, in the usual form, are not only bound for the performance of any final decree against their principal; but, where he dies before final hearing, and the cause is revived in the name of his administrator, for the satisfaction of the decree rendered against him, costs included.[5] The securities are estopped from denying that the injunction, recited in the bond, was granted and ordered.[6] To an action on such bond, the securities cannot plead, that an execution was sued out on the judgment at law, and satisfied by a levy on property, before the final decree in the bill for injunction.[7]

§ 24. The order for the injunction is to be taken in connection with the bond, and, when so taken, sufficiently expresses the *consideration* within the statute of frauds.[8] So

[1] Mahan *v.* Tydings, 10 B. Mon. 351.
[2] Hanks *v.* Horton, 5 Tex. 103.
[3] Weatherby *v.* Shackleford, 37 Miss. 559.
[4] Williamson *v.* Hall, 1 Ohio St. 190.
[5] Fowler *v.* Scott, 6 Eng. 675.
[6] Ib.
[7] Ib.
[8] Prader *v.* Purkett, 13 Cal. 588.

the suspension and delay to be produced by the injunction are *primâ facie* evidence of consideration. And a plea, alleging merely the want of consideration, is bad; it must show that these were not sufficient considerations.[1]

§ 25. In Alabama a bond which operates to supersede a judgment at law has the force and effect of a judgment, on a dissolution of the injunction, without an order of the chancellor.[2] A statute, requiring the register to certify to the law court the dissolution of an injunction, is mandatory only, and not necessary to an execution on the bond.[3]

§ 26. It is held that the suit on an injunction bond is properly brought in the name of the party alone interested, though there are several obligees.[4] But, on the other hand, debt may be maintained on a bond executed to several jointly in the name of all, for an injury to either by a failure to perform the condition.[5] (See § 16.)

§ 27. It is sometimes held, that an action of debt on an injunction bond cannot be maintained to recover damages occasioned by the suing out of the writ, unless vexatiously done;[6] upon which point the record of the suit in which the injunction was sued out is admissible, but not conclusive, evidence. But on the other hand it is held, that, in an action on the bond, the existence or non-existence of probable cause for the injunction is immaterial.[7] And the action may be maintained without a previous action on the case, to ascertain the damages occasioned by the vexatious suing out of the writ.[8](a)

[1] Mahan *v.* Tydings, 10 B. Mon. 351.
[2] Wiswell *v.* Munroe, 4 Ala. 9.
[3] Ib.
[4] Prader *v.* Purkett, 13 Cal. 588.

[5] Watts *v.* Sanders, 10 B. Mon. 372.
[6] Garrett *v.* Logan, 19 Ala. 344.
[7] Cox *v.* Taylor, 10 B. Mon. 17.
[8] Garrett *v.* Logan, 19 Ala. 344.

(a) The Alabama statute of 1826, "to provide a speedy remedy against the obligors in injunction bonds," applies to bonds executed in cases in which the judgment shall have been enjoined. Dunn *v.* Bank,

§ 28. The defendant in an injunction suit may plead the damages he has sustained by it, in *reconvention*, or have an action on the bond.[1] But where a defendant sues and obtains judgment at law upon the bond, he cannot afterwards have execution out of the Court of Chancery upon it.[2]

§ 29. It is a good defence for sureties in the bond, that the complainant was corruptly induced to dismiss his bill, so that the sureties might become liable.[3]

§ 30. An injunction against a judgment, on the ground of usury, having been properly dissolved, usury cannot be set up as a defence to a suit in chancery to set up the lost bond.[4]

§ 31. After parties have obtained an injunction, it is too late for them to set up, as a defence to the suit on the bond, a want of jurisdiction to grant the injunction.[5]

§ 32. With reference to the *pleadings* in an action upon an injunction bond; the bond declared on must be described with such precision, certainty, and clearness, as fully to apprise the defendants of the cause of action which they are required to answer. It is sufficient to set forth such facts as constitute a breach. The extent of the damages is

---

[1] Carlin *v.* Hudson, 12 Tex. 202.
[2] Harrison *v.* Casey, 1 Dev. & Bat. Ch. 322.
[3] Boynton *v.* Robb, 22 Ill. 625.
[4] Clark *v.* Young, 2 B. Monr. 57.
[5] Loomis *v.* Brown, 16 Barb. 325.

&c., 2 Ala. 153. In Texas, when the damages sustained by the defendant, by the issuing of an injunction, grow out of other matters than the collection of money, and present questions of difficulty; inasmuch as the statute does not imperatively require them to be settled in the main action, a separate suit may be brought therefor on the injunction bond. Hammonds *v.* Belcher, 10 Tex. 271. A *scire facias* will lie upon an injunction bond, in North Carolina, it being made part of the record by statute of 1810. Bozman *v.* Armistead, 2 Taylor, 183. So, though the bond was made before that statute was passed. Bozman *v.* Armistead, 2 Taylor, 264.

matter of proof for the jury.[1]   Thus, when the condition is
to pay the balance due upon a certain judgment specifically
mentioned and set forth in a decretal order of the court,
bearing a particular date, and ten per cent. thereon ; the precise amount of such judgment need not be stated in the declaration, that being a matter of proof, on trial.[2]

§ 32 a. Where, in an action on an injunction bond, the
recitals and condition of which mentioned a judgment, the
defendant pleaded a general performance, the plaintiff assigned a breach, the defendant rejoined *nul tiel record*, and
the plaintiff surrejoined, traversing the rejoinder, and issue
was joined to the court, who found that there was such record; and the plaintiff afterwards introduced a record as
evidence to the jury, to support the issue joined on the plea
of *nul tiel record*, to which the defendant objected : held, the
defendant's rejoinder would have been held bad if demurred
to ; that the issue was correctly tried by the court; and that
the defendant, having admitted, by his pleading, every fact
which the record could establish, could not complain of its
admission as evidence, whether competent or not, and although such evidence might be unnecessary.[3]

§ 33. The obligor in an injunction bond cannot, in a suit
upon the bond, plead that he did not obtain any injunction.[4]

§ 34. The *summary judgments* on bonds taken for injunctions under the statute of 1841, in Texas, after the conditions
are forfeited, are not in derogation of the right of trial by
jury, or of other constitutional rights.[5]

§ 35. Where a bond was taken, which did not in any way
comply with the statute, but bound the obligors absolutely
to pay the penalty, if the injunction should be dissolved, and

---

[1] Tallahassee v. Hayward, 4 Flori. 411.
[2] Ibid.
[3] Hardey v. Coe, 5 Gill, 189.
[4] Lloyd v. Burgess, 4 Gill, 187.
[5] Janes v. Reynolds, 2 Tex. 250.

not to pay the amount of judgment and costs; held, summary judgment could not be rendered.[1]

§ 36. In reference to what constitutes a *breach* of an injunction bond; if the plaintiff dismisses his bill, the defendant has an immediate right of action on the bond, and need not wait till the order of dismissal is confirmed at the next term of court.[2] But an injunction bond is not broken so long as the injunction remains in force; nor when an injunction has been dissolved and then reinstated.[3]

§ 37. A bond conditioned, that, if the defendant shall cause certain property (specified) "to be forthcoming, to be subject to the final order of the court," &c., and "shall abide by and perform such orders and decrees as the said court shall make in the said cause," &c., was construed, *ut res magis valeat quam pereat*, to require the defendant to abide by and perform such orders and decrees as the court shall make touching the property specified, which was to be forthcoming, &c., and not to require the performance of any decree which the court might make.[4] (See § 39.)

§ 38. A suit was brought upon an injunction bond, after the injunction had been dissolved by the Circuit Court, but while an appeal was pending in the Supreme Court, and an order was in force staying all further proceedings therein until further order by the court. The defendant pleaded in bar that no cause of action had accrued at the time the suit was commenced. The plaintiff filed a replication, that, at a day subsequent to the commencement of the suit, the decree of the Circuit Court was affirmed. Held, the replication was not responsive to the plea, and was insufficient.[5]

§ 39. The *surety* in an injunction bond is liable only ac-

---

[1] Janes v. Reynolds, 2 Tex. 250.
[2] Roach v. Gardner, 9 Gratt. 89. See Spevey v. M'Gehee, 24 Ala. 476.
[3] Bentley v. Joslin, 1 Hemp. 218.

[4] Aldrich v. Kirkland, 8 Rich. Eq. 349.
[5] Scott v. Fowler, 14 Ark. 427.

cording to the strict terms of his undertaking.[1] Thus suit
was brought against a surety on a bond, which described the
judgment enjoined as being for $2,300 and costs. Held, a
judgment for $2,346, and costs, though answering the de-
scription in other respects, could not be shown. Also, as
the bond undertook to describe the judgment fully, the petition for injunction could not be referred to for another description of it.[2] So an injunction bond, conditioned to cause
certain property " to be forthcoming, to be subject to the
final order of the Court of Equity in a certain cause," &c., and
to " abide by and perform such orders and decrees as the
said court shall make in the said cause," was construed, in
an action thereon against the surety, not to require the principal debtor to pay, absolutely, any money decree which the
court might pronounce. It was held that, before the recovery could be had, the plaintiff must show a failure to produce the property specified, and the damage sustained by
reason of such failure.[3] (See § 37.)

§ 40. In an action on a bond given on obtaining an injunction to stay a suit at law, it may be alleged and shown,
that, by reason of the delay in obtaining judgment and execution, occasioned by the injunction, the property of the defendant in the suit was so wasted, sold, incumbered, and disposed of, that the plaintiff at law lost his debt.[4]

§ 41. Damages may be recovered on an injunction bond,
when the injunction has been improperly sued out.[5] As to
the mode of recovery, the practice is not uniform. It is
held that, upon the removal of an injunction prohibiting the
collection of money, the court should render judgment for the
sum enjoined, and the damages assessed, against the principal
and his sureties.[6] While, on the other hand, the obligors in

[1] Hall v. Williamson, 9 Ohio
(N. S.), 17.
[2] Ibid.
[3] Aldrich v. Kirkland, 6 Rich. 334.

[4] Tryon v. Robinson, 10 Rich. 160.
[5] Gelston v. Whitesides, 3 Cal. 309.
[6] Cook v. Garza, 13 Tex. 431 ; Burr
v. Burton, 18 Ark. 214.

the bond, given on enjoining a judgment, are, on dissolution of the injunction, liable to pay the judgment, though no damages are awarded against the complainant.[1] In a late English case, one claiming copyright in the work of a foreigner assigned to him obtained an injunction, on giving an undertaking to abide by any order of the court respecting damages the defendant might sustain by reason of the injunction. The House of Lords (after conflicting decisions in the courts of law) decided that the plaintiff had no title to copyright, and the injunction was dissolved without opposition. The defendant moved for an inquiry as to damage, but one of the vice-chancellors refused it, and merely dismissed the bill with costs, refusing the plaintiff's motion to dismiss without costs. Held, upon appeal, that the defendant was entitled to an inquiry what, if any, damage he had sustained.[2]

§ 42. But in the United States Court it is held, that a court of equity cannot order the complainant and his sureties on an injunction bond to pay the damages sustained by reason of the injunction. The defendant must resort to an action on the bond. And it is doubted whether Congress could confer such a power.[3] So in Illinois, except in cases of injunctions to restrain actions at law, damages cannot be awarded on the dismissal of an injunction bill.[4] And, in California, when an injunction is dissolved, and the suit dismissed by the plaintiff's action, this constitutes no admission that it was improperly sued out, which must be proved before damages can be recovered.[5]

§ 43. Where a bond is conditioned for the payment of such damages as may be sustained from the suing out of the injunction, "should the same be dissolved," a recovery can

[1] Hunt v. Scobie, 6 B. Mon. 469.
[2] Novello v. James, 31 Eng. Law and Eq. 280.
[3] Merryfield v. Jones, 2 Curt. 306.
[4] Phelps v. Foster, 18 Ill. 309.
[5] Gelston v. Whitesides, 3 Cal. 309.

only be had for the actual damages.[1] So in a suit on an injunction bond, which stipulates that the complainant should pay to the defendant the damages, not exceeding $500, which he might sustain by reason of the injunction; the only damages the plaintiff can recover were such as resulted to him individually from the operation of the injunction itself.[2] So where the injunction sought to restrain the collection of certain notes given to a trustee in consideration of the hire of slaves, and the bond was conditioned for the payment of only the actual damages; a recovery cannot be had for the trouble and expense of a rescission of the contract alleged to have been caused by the pendency of the injunction, nor for the privations and physical hardships to which the beneficiaries of the trust estate were subjected, in consequence of the inability of the trustee to collect and pay over to them the enjoined debts.[3]

§ 44. In Louisiana, the plaintiff and his surety on the injunction bond are bound *in solido* to the defendant for damages, only on the amount for which the injunction is dissolved.[4]

§ 45. On dissolution of the injunction, and failure of the obligors to perform the conditions, the bond becomes forfeited, and a right of action accrues for the *penalty*, for which penalty, as well as for such damages as the jury may assess, the court is bound to give judgment.[5] But, in an action of covenant on a bond against the surety, it was held that he was only liable to the extent of the penalty, with interest thereon from the time of forfeiture, although the actual damages exceeded it.[6]

§ 46. Where the bond provided for payment of such dam-

[1] Bullock v. Ferguson, 30 Ala. 227.
[2] Burgen v. Sharer, 14 B. Mon. 497.
[3] Bullock v. Ferguson, 30 Ala. 227.

[4] Perry v. Kearney, 14 La. An. 400.
[5] Tallahassee, &c. v. Hayward, 4 Florida, 411.
[6] Hughes v. Wickliffe, 11 B. Mon. 202.

ages as should be awarded by any competent court, held, in an action against the sureties, the award must be alleged and proved.[1] So a bond, to pay such damages as may be awarded, generally, secures only such as may be awarded in the injunction suit, and, in a suit thereon, the declaration must allege such award.(a)[2] And where no clause is inserted in the condition of bond, consenting that the defendant's damages shall be summarily ascertained upon a reference, the court has no jurisdiction to direct a reference for that purpose.[3]

§ 47. In Virginia, one not party to a judgment, who procures it to be enjoined, is liable to the statutory ten per cent. damages on its dissolution, as much as one who is a party.[4]

§ 48. The right to recover interest on a judgment is a legal incident to the judgment; hence a surety on a bond given to enjoin a judgment is bound for interest to accrue on the judgment.[5] (See § 53.)

§ 49. An injunction was obtained to stay the collection of a judgment at law. The plaintiff in equity gave a bond to the defendant, who was the plaintiff at law, conditioned to "abide the decision which should be made on the bill, and pay all sums of money, damages, and costs that should be adjudged against him." The injunction was dissolved and the bill dismissed, and the obligor was decreed to pay the costs in the chancery suit. In a suit against the sureties, held, they were not liable for the amount of the judgment

---

[1] Tarpey v. Shillenberger, 10 Cal. 390.
[2] Anderson v. Falconer, 34 Miss. 257.
[3] Garcie v. Sheldon, 3 Barb. 232.
[4] Clayton v. Anthony, 15 Gratt. 518.
[5] Weatherby v. Shackleford, 37 Miss. 559.

(a) In Virginia, the bond provides in terms for the payment of such damages as may be awarded by the court upon dissolution. The ten per cent. damages given by statute are to be deemed awarded, unless expressly remitted by the court. Clayton v. Anthony, 15 Gratt. 518.

enjoined, nor for the costs of the chancery suit, unless the defendant had first paid them to the officers entitled to them.[1]

§ 50. A. obtained two judgments against B., and levied executions on land as belonging to B. C., claiming the land, enjoined the sale, and gave D. as surety in the bond. The injunction was dissolved, and A. brought an action of covenant on the bond. Held, the damages which might accrue by reason of the injunction were the measure of damages, and not the amount of the judgments.[2]

§ 51. Where an injunction was obtained upon the sale of certain property, the complainant giving bond to pay all damages; in a suit on the bond, held, the rule as to damages was the difference between the cash value of the property when the bond was given and what it produced when sold, and the interest on the difference.[3]

§ 52. Where, on an application for an injunction to stay the erection of a mill-dam, the chancellor exacted a bond to pay all damages that might result to the defendant from the injunction, in case the suit was not successful; in a suit on the bond, held, the chancellor had the discretionary power to take such a bond; and if the complainant failed to prosecute his suit successfully, the defendant was entitled to recover all the damages he had sustained by reason of the injunction.[4]

§ 53. In an action on an injunction bond, where the injunction forbade the payment of money, interest is recoverable thereon up to the day the money is paid into court, and an offer to invest the amount, less costs and expenses thereon, is not admissible in evidence to reduce the interest.[5] So where a debtor is enjoined from paying over the money to his creditor, but not from using it in any other manner, he can only discharge himself from interest by paying the

---

[1] Corder v. Martin, 17 Mis. 41.
[2] Hord v. Trimble, 1 Litt. 413.
[3] Rubon v. Stephan, 25 Miss. 253.
[4] Newell v. Partee, 10 Humph. 325.
[5] Wallis v. Dilley, 7 Md. 237.

money into court; consequently, in an action on the bond, a recovery cannot be had for interest, by way of damages, for the period intervening between the dissolution of the injunction by the chancellor and the affirmance of his decree on error, no *supersedeas* bond having been given.[1] (See § 48.)

§ 54. Counsel fees, necessarily incurred in the defence of an injunction suit, not consequential on other injuries, but direct and immediate, may be recovered in an action of debt on the bond, though they may not be actually paid.[2] It is said in a late case, that the expression *all costs and damages* includes counsel fees. " It was in contemplation of the defendant to institute legal proceedings, thereby subjecting the plaintiff to costs, and the employment of counsel. He would be necessarily damnified in consequence thereof to the amount he should be compelled to pay such counsel. It was a damage clearly within the contemplation of the act, and of the parties."[3] So a restraining order continues until the hearing on the rule to show cause why the injunction should not issue, though it be postponed from the day first fixed ; and therefore the bond covers damages during such a continuance. Counsel fees for dissolving the order are recoverable, though paid after that day, provided a retainer was paid before.[4]

§ 55. The defendant obtained an injunction to restrain the plaintiff from cleaning out a race-way through his premises to the plaintiff's mills, or from drawing water through them from the Miami Canal, and thereupon he gave a bond, conditioned to pay " all moneys and costs due and to become due from him, and all moneys and costs which shall be decreed against him in case said injunction shall be dissolved." Held, in a suit on the bond, for damages sustained by the plaintiff in the stoppage of his mills, that such a

[1] Bullock *v.* Ferguson, 30 Ala. 227.
[2] Garrett *v.* Logan, 19 Ala. 344 ; Thaie *v.* Quan, 3 Cal. 216.
[3] Per Davies, J., Corcoran *v.* Judson, 10 Smith N. Y. 107.
[4] Prader *v.* Grim, 13 Cal. 585.

loss was included in the bond, although the decree of the court, dissolving the injunction, was for the costs of suit only.[1]

§ 55 a. But where B. filed a bill, to enjoin the sheriff from paying over to G. a certain fund in his hands claimed by G. under an execution; and an interlocutory order for an injunction was granted, the condition being that B. should give bond with surety to "save harmless the said G. from all damage which he may sustain by reason of the making of said order, and the issuing of said writ in accordance therewith": in a suit on the bond, held, G. could not recover, as damages, either a counsel fee and other expenses paid (not including costs), of the suit in equity, and a counsel fee incurred in the suit at law on the bond, or interest on the fund during the time it was enjoined in the sheriff's hands.[2] So in an action on an injunction bond, a recovery cannot be had for counsel fees in the Supreme Court, to which the injunction suit was removed by the plaintiff below, after the dismissal of his bill by the chancellor.[3] So costs imposed on the plaintiff in an action on an injunction bond, as the condition of a continuance, are not recoverable as a part of the actual damages.[4] And the recovery is limited, in regard to costs and expenses, to such as may have accrued from the time of the issuing of injunction down to the affirmance of the order for its dissolution.[5]

§ 56. In an action on an undertaking executed on suing out an injunction, it is no defence that the business enjoined was a public nuisance;[6] nor, in mitigation of damages or otherwise, in an action against the securities, that the principal is solvent, and able to pay his own debts.[7]

§ 57. Where the common law gives a remedy for maliciously suing out an injunction without probable cause, such

[1] Roberts v. Dust, 4 Ohio (N. S.), 502.
[2] Gadsden v. Bank, &c., 5 Rich. 336. Aco. Wallis v. Dilley, 7 Md. 237.
[5] Bullock v. Ferguson, 30 Ala. 227.
[4] Ibid.
[5] Wallis v. Dilley, 7 Md. 237.
[6] Cunningham v. Breed, 4 Cal. 384.
[7] Hunt v. Burton, 18 Ark. 188.

remedy is not merged in the remedy upon an injunction bond.[1]   But the injunction must be charged in the declaration as an abuse of the process of the court, through malice and without probable cause, otherwise the remedy is on the bond.[2]

§ 58. Damages were refused to a builder against whom an injunction had been sued out, where his whole ground of action was a supposed hindrance thrown in his way in execution of a building contract, which confessedly required for its execution the use of a sidewalk erected by the plaintiff in the injunction, and for which he had not been compensated.[3]

§ 59. An action does not lie for the malicious suing out of an injunction against the plaintiff, until the injunction is finally disposed of, or the suit in which it was sued out is terminated.[4]

[1] Cox v. Taylor, 10 B. Mon. 17.
[2] Robinson v. Kellnm, 6 Cal. 399.
[3] Jamison v. Duncan, 12 La. An. 785.
[4] Tatum v. Morris, 18 Ala. 302.

CHAPTER III.

DISSOLUTION OF INJUNCTIONS.

§ 1. The nature of a temporary and preliminary, as distinguished from a perpetual and final injunction, has been already explained. (See Chap. I.) A necessary incident to injunctions of the former description, is a liability to be terminated or *dissolved* before the termination of the suits in equity, of which they were made a part; and the nature and grounds of a dissolution of temporary injunctions constitute a very copious and important part of the general subject treated in this book.[1]

§ 2. If the grounds for a provisional injunction be removed, it will be dissolved.[2]

§ 3. It is held that a decree, authorizing the payment of money in the hands of a party to the suit, enjoined from paying it out, is a dissolution of the injunction.[3]

§ 4. An injunction may be *discharged* for irregularity, but can be *dissolved* only for want of equity.[4]

§ 5. A temporary injunction issued when the bill is filed is granted to protect *primâ facie* right or title. Motions to dissolve it must be heard on new evidence. When the answer is filed (in a patent case) denying the validity of the patent, and *primâ facie* evidence offered in support of the answer, the injunction will be dissolved, unless the opposite party support the validity of the patent by evidence in rebuttal. The court must weigh the evidence, and retain or dissolve the injunction according to its preponderance.[5]

§ 6. The power of dissolving as well as granting injunctions must necessarily rest much in the discretion of the court, and should be exercised so as to prevent injustice.[6]

§ 7. When the complainant had due notice of a motion to dissolve an injunction, and he neglected to appear and oppose the motion, the defendant was permitted to take his order dissolving the injunction, with costs.[7]

[1] See M'Brayer *v.* Hardin, 7 Ired. Eq. 1.
[2] Lowe *v.* Warren, &c., Wright, 616.
[3] Crook *v.* Turpin, 10 B. Mon. 243.
[4] Judah *v.* Chiles, 3 J. J. Marsh, 302.
[5] Woodworth *v.* Rogers, 3 W. & M. 135.
[6] Cammack *v.* Johnson, 1 Green Ch. 163.
[7] Kellogg *v.* Barnes, Harring. Ch. 258.

§ 8. It is the general rule that an injunction will be dissolved, when the plaintiff's legal title is doubtful, and the continuance of the injunction unnecessary for the protection of the plaintiffs and injurious to the defendants.[1]   Or, where the bill shows no necessity for the desired protection, even if the injunction might do no harm.   The court will not restrain a person in the exercise of any legal right unless justice requires it.[2]   Thus A., in pursuance of an agreement with B., received a deed of certain property from B., and took possession of the same, and delivered to B. a deed of certain other property, of which B. took possession.   B. afterwards refused to pay the sum which he had agreed to pay for the exchange, and the property which he conveyed to A. was found to be incumbered to a greater extent than was stated by him.   A. thereupon filed a bill, praying that B. might be decreed to pay him the sum stipulated, and to reduce the incumbrances to the amount stated.   He further obtained an injunction, enjoining B. from entering or interfering with the property conveyed to A., or from exercising any act of ownership over it, and from disposing of the property conveyed by A. to B., or from selling, incumbering, or in any way impairing the value of any other property in B.'s possession, or under his control, in the mortgages referred to. On motion to dissolve the injunction, held, as the defendant was not alleged to be insolvent, or unable to pay any amount the court might decree, the injunction was too broad, and must be dissolved.[3]   So the court will not deny a defendant the benefit of his answer, when a complainant has not been diligent in prosecuting his suit, and where no great mischief can be done by dissolving the injunction.[4]   And an injunction will be dissolved if obtained through *misrepresentation*, whether caused by carelessness, misinformation, or otherwise.   As where an injunction upon an action of ejectment was dissolved, on the ground that the equity of the bill

---

[1] Shrewsbury, &c. v. London, &c., 1 Eng. Law and Eq. 122; 12 Geo. 5.
[2] Mullen v. Jennings, 1 Stockt. 192.
[3] Ibid.
[4] Greenin v. Hoey, 1 Stockt. 137.

was fully answered, and another bill, got up by the same party, and similar in all material respects to the former, with the substitution of a different complainant, was filed, and an injunction obtained thereon through a misrepresentation of facts, no reason appearing or being suggested for instituting another suit. It was held, that to countenance such proceedings would encourage litigation and the multiplication of suits, and by the injunction powers of the court to embarrass and retard instead of promoting justice.[1]

§ 9. But in a late case, where, on appeal, the court thought the questions not entirely free from doubt, and the case being one of great importance, in which both parties desired a hearing, they refused to reverse the order of the chancellor retaining the injunction until the final hearing.[2] And, upon a motion to dissolve an injunction, the chancellor confines himself exclusively to the consideration of the case or combination of facts set forth in the bill out of which the equity of the injunction arose, and to the answer of the defendant to those facts; and the best test as to what are properly averments of facts in the bill or answer is, whether they are such matters as a witness might properly be called on to prove, or the truth of which must be established by evidence; if not, they are either sheer principles of equity, or some of those public and established facts of which the court is bound to take judicial notice without any proof.[3]

§ 10. Whether or not an injunction should be dissolved, rests in the discretion of the court.[4] So also to continue an injunction, where the nature and circumstances of a case require it, and where justice will be attained by that course.[5] And therefore the dissolution of an injunction is not to be interfered with without strong reason.[6]

[1] Endicott v. Mathis, 1 Stockt. 110.
[2] Morris, &c. v. Jersey, &c., 1 Beasl. 227; Jersey, &c. v. Morris, &c., Ib. 542.
[3] Canal, &c. v. Railroad, &c., 4 Gill & J. 1.
[4] Cox v. Mayor, &c., 18 Geo. 728; Semmes v. Mayor, &c., 19 Geo. 471; Fleischman v. Young, 1 Stockt. 620.
[5] Nelson v. Robinson, 1 Hemp. 464.
[6] Buchanan v. Ford, 29 Geo. 490.

§ 11. An injunction granted upon bill, answer, and evidence, taken by commission, will not be dissolved, if the bill shows sufficient equity, not denied by the answer, to support it.[1] So, when dissolution of an injunction is calculated to work an irreparable injury, by depriving members of a corporation of privileges, the value of which cannot be pecuniarily estimated, the injunction cannot be set aside upon giving bond.[2] Nor will the court dissolve an injunction where the cause would be virtually thereby decided, and the complainants deprived of their remedy, and the answers do not disclose the true nature of the transaction.[3]

§ 12. A motion to dismiss a petition for an injunction is in the nature of a demurrer, and in deciding upon it the court can only look to the statements in the petition.[4]

§ 13. Where a judgment has been enjoined, and a new trial at law ordered, the court may afterwards, although no verdict has been certified, if it becomes satisfied that a new trial ought not to have been granted, set aside the order and dissolve the injunction.[5]

§ 14. A special injunction was dissolved, with costs, where office copies of the affidavits in support of it were not obtained upon moving for it.[6] So a petition for an injunction, with a defective jurat, was granted. Motion was made to dissolve it for that cause. Motion was also made to amend, with an affidavit that the petitioner had sworn to it, when the fiat was issued, before the same judge. Held, that the judge might have amended by signing the jurat himself, but that it was a personal matter within his discretion, and, as he would not do so, it was presumed to be for good reason, and the injunction was held to be rightly dissolved.[7] But it

---

[1] Hamilton v. Whitridge, 11 Md. 128.

[2] Knabe v. Fernot, 14 La. An. 847.

[3] Fleischman v. Young, 1 Stockt. 620.

[4] Floyd v. Turner, 23 Tex. 292.

[5] Vass v. Magee, 1 Hen. & M. 2.

[6] Jackson v. Cassiday, 10 Sim. 326.

[7] Sims v. Redding, 20 Tex. 386.

is not proper to absolutely dismiss a bill or dissolve an injunction, for a deficient injunction bond, or for want of notice; in such cases, an amendment should be allowed.[1] So the fact, that a bond for an injunction, to restrain a county officer from committing a public wrong, is executed to the county judge in his official capacity, instead of the county itself, affords no grounds for dissolving the injunction.[2]

§ 15. The question of dissolving an injunction may arise in an appellate court. An order dissolving an injunction is appealable, certainly where it affects the merits of, or involves an adjudication upon, any of the material questions in the principal controversy. And in case of an order dissolving an injunction, which restrained a city from opening a street over certain lands, until an appeal from the verdict which condemned the land and allowed no damages could be determined; the owners were held entitled to an injunction, until the time thus fixed.[3] So, in Louisiana, an appeal will lie from an *ex parte* order, setting aside an injunction, upon giving bond according to law,[4] and the necessary consequence of maintaining the appeal is to reverse the order.[5] But where an injunction against a judgment was dissolved and the case continued; held, the order dissolving the injunction was not a final order, from which an appeal would lie.[6] And, as we have seen, the granting and continuing of an injunction rest in the sound discretion of the court below, governed by the circumstances of the case. (See § 35.) Hence a court above will not control that discretion, unless its exercise has been manifestly improper.[7] And where, on an appeal from such order, the chancellor granted an order staying the proceedings, to restrain which the injunction had issued, until the next sitting of the

---

[1] Gamble *v.* Campbell, 6 Florida, 347.
[2] Collins *v.* Ripley, 8 Clarke, 129.
[3] Iowa College *v.* Davenport, 7 Clarke, 213.
[4] Knabe *v.* Pernot, 14 La. An. 847.

[5] Trufant *v.* Cazenave, 14 La. An. 57.
[6] Rodman *v.* Fortine, 2 Met. 325.
[7] Dent *v.* Summerlin, 12 Geo. 5; Loyless *v.* Howell, 15 Geo. 554.

6

court of errors and appeals; and a motion was made in that court, at its next sitting, for an order extending the stay until the hearing on the appeal : held, the court had power to make such an order; but the granting or refusing it rested in the sound discretion of the court.[1]   So, if the answer admits the equity in the bill, and alleges such matter as, if proved, would defeat the complainant's equity, although this matter be not strictly responsive to the bill; the Supreme Court will not control the discretion of the chancellor below in retaining the injunction.[2]   And, in Alabama, the Supreme Court will not interfere, by *mandamus* or otherwise, to compel the dissolution of an injunction on the filing of an answer.[3]   So where A. had petitioned for a *mandamus* against the commissioner of the land-office, to compel him to issue patents to the petitioner for certain lands; and B. obtained a temporary injunction to restrain the petition and the issuing of the patents, claiming some of the lots : on a motion to dissolve the injunction, held, as all the questions could be tried on the petition, and as B. and all other parties interested had notice thereof and were bound to come into court and defend their interests, the injunction must be dissolved, though it was doubtful whether on B.'s bill and A.'s answer the injunction should be dissolved; and, the time of the injunction having expired before the hearing in the appellate court, though it had not when the motion was heard in the court below, that the injunction should be dissolved.[4]

§ 16. On motion to dissolve an injunction, it is held, in Missouri, that the plaintiff is entitled to a trial on the merits, and after it is dissolved, to a jury to assess the damages.[5]

§ 17. Where an injunction is granted until the coming in of the answer, it will not be thereby dissolved, but will remain to await the order of the court.[6]   So when, on motion

[1] Doughty *v.* Somerville, 3 Halst. Ch. 629 and 51.
[2] Hargraves *v.* Jones, 27 Geo. 233.
[3] Montgomery, 24 Ala. 98.
[4] Smith *v.* Power, 2 Tex. 57.
[5] Home, &c. *v.* Bauman, 14 Mis. 74.
[6] Turner *v.* Scott, 5 Rand. 332.

to dissolve an injunction, it appears from the answer, that the complainant was entitled to an injunction at the time of obtaining it; it will continue until final hearing or further order, unless the defendant admits everything alleged in the bill, upon which the injunction rests. When that admission is made, and the injunction has been to stay execution at law, the injunction may be dissolved, with a proviso that no more be levied than remains due after allowing everything claimed by the complainant; but when a proper ground for the injunction is admitted by the answer, and there still remains a dispute between the parties, the injunction is always continued until final hearing or further order.[1]

§ 18. On the dissolution of an injunction, it is of course to order the money to be retained in the office, on affidavit showing a danger of its loss if it goes into the hands of the defendant.[2]

§ 19. It is irregular to dissolve an injunction in court with direction that the order shall not go out, and then in vacation to direct that the order shall go out.[3]

§ 20. A motion to dissolve an injunction before answer, and without notice to the complainant, is regular, if made on the ground, that, admitting the allegations of the bill to be true, it contains no equity; but it is irregular to dismiss the bill by motion on that ground.[4] So where it is shown, by a special plea, that there is no equity in the bill, it is held to be the same, so far as regards the motion to dissolve, as though the equity of the bill was fully denied by the answer.[5] (See § 34.) So an injunction will be dissolved, on motion, at the return term of process, if the complainant has taken no steps to have process served, without an answer of the defendant, although he has appeared by attorney.[6]

[1] Lynch v. Colegate, 2 Har. & J. 34.
[2] Lane v. Brown, 2 Hay. 215.
[3] Randolph v. Randolph, 6 Rand. 194.
[4] Beard v. Geran, Hardin, 12; Harring. Ch. 162.
[5] Eldred v. Camp, Harring. Ch. 162.
[6] Hightour v. Rush, 2 Hay. 361.

§ 21. Where an injunction has been granted by a judge at chambers, a motion for its dissolution may be made directly to the court, without having first applied to him.[1]

§ 22. General notice of a motion to dissolve an injunction for want of equity is sufficient; but, any special ground, not touching the equity, should be stated.[2] A notice to dissolve an injunction "for irregularity in the proceedings" is not sufficiently specific. The irregularity should be pointed out.[3]

§ 23. A motion to dissolve the injunction on the matter of the bill only must be viewed as if it were an original application for an injunction, and opposed by the defendant.[4]

§ 24. A motion to dissolve an injunction for want of equity on the face of the bill, in the absence of a rule of court to the contrary, will be heard before answer filed, and at any time, unless for special cause shown.[5]

§ 25. On a motion to dissolve an injunction, the parties stand before the court as to all those facts and circumstances of which it is bound to take notice, as where a dissolution is asked for on the ground that the facts set forth in the bill give rise to no equity for an injunction; and where the facts, as stated in the bill, give rise to no such equity, the injunction will be dissolved, whether the defendant has answered or not, or however imperfectly he has answered.[6]

§ 26. A judge of the Superior Court of Georgia may dissolve an injunction in vacation; and under the rule of court,

---

[1] Woodruff v. Fisher, 17 Barb. 224.
[2] Morris, &c. v. Bartlett, 2 Green Ch. 9.
[3] Miller v. Traphagan, 2 Halst. Ch. 200.
[4] New York, &c. v. Fitch, 1 Paige, 97.

[5] Morris, &c. v. Biddle, 3 Green Ch. 222; Woodhull v. Neafie, 1 Green Ch. 409; Jones v. Commercial, &c., 5 How. Miss. 43; Minturn v. Seymour, 4 John. Ch. 173.
[6] Canal, &c. v. Railroad, &c., 4 Gill & J. 1.

directing injunctions to be granted "until further order," an injunction may be dissolved before answer, on affidavit denying the equity of the bill.   But where the defendants had established their right at law, it was held, that the injunction should be dissolved, on their giving a forthcoming bond, and, on application of other parties interested in the judgments, that the complainants should be compelled to amend their bill by making them defendants, without prejudice to the injunction, and that, on their refusal, the injunction should be dissolved.[1]

§ 27. An injunction granted by a justice of the Supreme Court, in Michigan, in cases where the statute authorizes it, stands upon the same footing as if granted by the chancellor; and in either case it is competent for the defendants, in vacation, and before they put in their answer, to move to dissolve the injunction for want of equity in the bill.[2]

§ 28. But a motion to dissolve an injunction for want of equity cannot be heard before the return of process.[3] So, after an injunction has been ordered to stand to the hearing, it seems to be irregular to dissolve it, on motion, before the hearing;[4] while, on the other hand, though an order for dissolving an injunction, on terms, might be discharged on motion or petition, the proper course is to discuss the merits of the order, upon a rehearing.[5] So a motion to dissolve an injunction before answer is irregular; at all events, it ought not to be entertained, after a general demurrer has been set down for argument, and before argument.[6] In Kentucky, the chancellor has no right, at the appearance term, and before the filing of an answer, to dissolve an injunction or dismiss a bill, if the bill contains equity.[7] So, in Tennessee, a

[1] Read v. Dewes, Charl. R. M. 358.
[2] Cooper v. Alden, Harring. Ch. 72.
[3] Barton v. Lytle, Cooke, 89.
[4] Smith v. Harkins, 4 Ired. Eq. 486.

[5] Van Bergen v. Demarest, 4 John. Ch. 35.
[6] Ransom v. Shuler, 8 Ired. Eq. 304.
[7] Judah v. Chiles, 3 J. J. Marsh. 302.

motion to dissolve an injunction will not be heard until after answer filed, or its equivalent.[1] So where, after five years from the filing of a bill, an injunction was granted for want of an answer; held, the injunction should not be dissolved until the answer came in, though the defendant lived abroad. And, on the other hand, where it appeared that copies of the bill had been sent to the defendant, by his attorney (upon whom service of the *subpœna* had been made at the time of filing the bill, and held sufficient by the court), and also by the complainant, and that a sufficient time had elapsed for the answer to have been transmitted to the court, but it did not appear that an appearance had been entered by the attorney, or that a *pro formâ* attachment had been served upon him; it was held, that the bill should not be taken *pro confesso*.[2]

§ 29. A defect in the bond may be a good cause for dissolving the injunction on motion, but is no ground for dismissing the bill, which prays other relief.[3]

§ 30. On notice of a motion to dissolve an injunction given before answer, an answer filed after the motion, though before the day fixed by the notice for the hearing of the motion, cannot be read in support of it.[4]

§ 31. On a motion to dissolve an injunction before answer, the allegations in the bill are to be taken for true.[5]

§ 32. Before the plaintiff can oppose the dissolution of an injunction, on the ground that one of the defendants has not answered, he must have taken the proper steps to compel an answer, or must show a sufficient excuse for the omission.[6]

§ 33. Where a bill of injunction has been taken for con-

[1] Rentfore *v.* Dickinson, 1 Overton, 196.
[2] Read *v.* Consequa, 4 Wash. C. 174.
[3] Boswell *v.* Wheat, 37 Miss. 610; Pillow *v.* Thompson, 20 Tex. 206.
[4] Cattell *v.* Nelson, 3 Halst. Ch. 122.
[5] Schwarz *v.* Sears, Harring. Ch. 440.
[6] Ward *v.* Van Bokkelen, 1 Paige, 100.

fessed, for want of an answer, a motion to dissolve the injunction by the defendant in contempt, on the ground that it was improvidently granted, will not be entertained.[1]

§ 34. The usual method of obtaining a dissolution of injunctions is by *answer*. But it is held that an order *nisi* for dissolution cannot be obtained on putting in a *plea*. The Vice-Chancellor says: "It cannot stand for a moment. The order *nisi* begins with a recital that the defendant has put in a full answer, and thereby denied the plaintiff's equity."[2] (See § 20.)

§ 35. And although the ordinary mode of dissolving injunctions is by the answer of the defendant;(a) yet an application to dissolve an injunction upon the answer alone, as in case of mesne motion, rests in the sound discretion of the court.[3] (See § 15.) And an injunction may be continued to the hearing, though the equity of the bill is fully answered by the defendant. Where its dissolution would work a greater injury than its continuance, the question of continuance must rest in discretion, though controlled by rules.[4]

§ 36. An irregularity in an injunction bill and affidavit is not waived by putting in an answer, where the answer is not relied on in the motion to dissolve. But an insufficiency in

[1] Turpin v. Jefferson, 4 Hen. & M. 483.
[2] Wroe v. Clayton, 10 Sim. 185.
[3] James v. Lemly, 2 Ired. Ch. 278; 9 N. H. 230; 2 Geo. Dec. 15; Swift v. Swift, 13 Geo. 140.
[4] Chetwood v. Brittain, 1 Green Ch. 439.

(a) It seems to be irregular to grant an injunction until the coming in of the answer, and then to stand dissolved, without a rule *nisi*. Ross v. Woodville, 4 Munf. 324. The course of practice on this subject is thus described. Injunction causes, upon motions to dissolve, are usually heard on bill and answer. Allegations in the answer, not responsive to the bill, without proof, do not affect the injunction. At a final hearing, the defendant need not prove his allegations in avoidance in the first instance. The complainant must then establish his case, and all his allegations then not proved are taken against him. Hutchins v. Hope, 7 Gill, 119.

the affidavit is error, and cannot be waived, nor amended, at the hearing of the motion to dissolve.[1]

§ 37. Notwithstanding the discretionary power on the subject (see §§ 13, 35) it is the general rule, that an injunction will be dissolved, at the hearing of a motion to dissolve it on bill and answer, if the answer fully, fairly, plainly, distinctly, and positively denies the allegations in the bill, on which the injunction was granted.[2] And if the bill is not supported by proof.[3] Or where the answer denies *the equity charged in the bill*.[4] In such case the injunction cannot be sustained unless there be some special reasons to authorize it.[5] Thus in case of a naked claim of property and for damages, denied by the answer; the court dissolved the injunction.[6] So where a bill was filed to rectify a written agreement, and all the matters charged outside of the agreement were denied in the answer.[7] So where every material allegation of a bill to stay waste is expressly and plainly denied in the answer.[8] So where a bill to enjoin a trespass upon real estate, together with the answer responsive to the bill, showed a lease in the defendant older than the complainant's title.[9] So an injunction was granted, and a receiver appointed before answer, upon a bill by a judgment creditor, who, after exhausting his remedies at law, was seeking to enforce, by bill in equity, his judgment lien against personal property covered by a mortgage. The only allegations of the bill, authorizing this equitable interference, were, that the mortgagor, the judgment debtor,

---

[1] Perkins v. Collins, 2 Green Ch. 482.

[2] Harris v. Sangston, 4 Md. Ch. Decis. 394.

[3] Doolittle v. Jones, 2 Cart. 21.

[4] Lindsay v. Etheridge, 1 Dev. & Bat. Ch. 36.

[5] West v. Rouse, 14 Geo. 715; Gardner v. Perkins, 9 Cal. 553; Hemphill v. Ruckersville, &c., 3 Kelly, 435; Sharpe v. King, 3 Ired. Ch. 402; Smith v. Harkins, 3 Ired. Ch. 613; Radcliffe v. Alpress, 3 Ired. Ch. 556; Wooden v. Wooden, 2 Green Ch. 429; Moore v. Ferrell, 1 Kelly, 7; Jones v. Joyner, 8 Geo. 562; Green v. Phillips, 6 Ired. Eq. 223; Boring v. Rollins, 20 Geo. 623; Miller v. Maddox, 21 Geo. 327; Lively v. Bristow, 12 Tex. 60; Greenin v. Hoey, 1 Stockt. 137; Cowles v. Carter, 4 Ired. Eq. 105; Alexander v. Markham, 25 Geo. 148; Weaver v. Garner, 28 Geo. 503; Gravely v. Southerland, 29 Geo. 335; Clark v. Cleghorn, 6 Geo. 220; Perkins v. Hollowell, 5 Ired. Eq. 24.

[6] Burnett v. Whitesides, 13 Cal. 156.

[7] Edmondson v. Jones, 19 Geo 19.

[8] Wright v. Grist, 1 Busb. Eq. 203.

[9] Field v. Howell, 6 Geo. 423.

was in possession of the property, selling and converting the same to his own use, that he was insolvent, and that the complainant was thereby in danger of losing his debt. These charges were denied by the answer, but the court below, without proof on either side, refused to dissolve the injunction, and discharge the receiver. Upon appeal, it was held, that the injunction should have been dissolved, and the receiver discharged.[1] So a bill alleged that a certificate for a pre-emption claim was obtained by false swearing. The purchaser and grantee under the certificate answered, that he purchased for value and without knowledge of the alleged perjury. Held, that an injunction, to restrain such purchaser from taking possession under a recovery in ejectment founded on his grant, must be dissolved.[2] So an injunction, to restrain the enforcement of a judgment upon a note in favor of an assignee, was granted, upon a bill alleging that the note had been paid and agreed to be surrendered, and that nevertheless it had been assigned to the judgment plaintiff, who had full knowledge of the equity of the complainant. From the answer it appeared that a new agreement was in the hands of the plaintiff, which was to stand in lieu of the note, unless the maker could obtain it from the assignee and surrender it, which he could not do. Held, that the injunction must be dissolved.[3] So a complainant alleged that he was the owner of four shares in an estate represented by the respondent, administrator *de bonis non ;* that he became the purchaser of the property belonging to the estate, for which he gave his notes, with an understanding with the then executrix, that they should be paid by allowing his shares; that suit had been instituted against him upon the notes, and was proceeding to judgment; and prayed that the judgment might be enjoined and the agreement enforced. Held, upon the coming in of the answer distinctly denying that the estate owed the complainant anything, and stating that the four

[1] Furlong *v.* Edwards, 3 Md. 99.   [3] Woodfin *v.* Johnston, 1 Jones
[2] Evans *v.* Lovengood, 1 Jones   Eq. 317.
Eq. 298.

shares claimed had been paid him, the injunction **was** properly dissolved.[1]

§ 38. The distinction is made, that, where a motion to dissolve an injunction is submitted on bill and answer, and the bill contains equity on its face, the material allegations of which are denied by the answer; the injunction should be dissolved, and, if desired, the cause should be set for hearing on bill, answer, and proofs; otherwise, at once dismissed. But where the bill does not contain sufficient equity on its face to authorize relief, the injunction may be dissolved, and the bill dismissed, without consulting the complainant.[2]

§ 39. But, as already suggested, where the answer to a bill for an injunction does not respond to a material allegation, the court will not dissolve the injunction on the coming in of the answer, but will order it to be continued to the hearing.[3] (See § 55.) So where the *gravamen* of a bill is not fully answered, and the answer is otherwise vague, general, and indefinite, an injunction will not be dissolved.[4] So where the denial consists of matter of opinion only.[5] And the further general rule, to which we have already adverted, is laid down, that, where the answer has denied the equity of a bill, a dissolution does not necessarily follow, but rests in the discretion of the court.[6] So, where a strong presumption appears in the bill that the complainant may be entitled to relief upon the final hearing, and in the mean time might suffer irremediable injury, the court will not dissolve an injunction, although the general equities of the bill are denied in the answer.[7] So, upon the hearing of the answer, if the statements are such as to leave in the mind of the court a reasonable doubt whether the plaintiff's equity is sufficiently

[1] Ford *v.* Tison, 8 Geo. 466.
[2] Williams *v.* Berry, 3 Stew. & Port. 285.
[3] Rich *v.* Thomas, 4 Jones Eq. 71.
[4] Horn *v.* Thomas, 19 Geo. 270; Pledger *v.* M'Cauley, 25 Geo. 46.

[5] Callaway *v.* Jones, 19 Geo. 277.
[6] Crutchfield *v.* Danilly, 16 Geo. 432; Nelson *v.* Robinson, 1 Hemp. 464.
[7] Linton *v.* Denham, 6 Florida, 533.

answered, the injunction will not be dissolved, but will be continued to the hearing.[1] In a leading case it is remarked: "It is true that it was said by Lord Eldon in Clapham *v.* White (8 Ves. R. 36, 37) that, 'if the answer denies all the circumstances upon which the equity is founded, the universal practice, as to the purpose of dissolving or not reviving the injunction, is, to give credit to the answer; and that is carried so far that, except in the few excepted cases, though five hundred affidavits were filed, not only by the plaintiff but his many witnesses, not one could be read as to this purpose.' This is strong language, but many qualifications must be engrafted on it, as will be manifest from the learned chancellor's own decision in Peacock *v.* Peacock (16 Ves. R. 49), and Norway *v.* Rowe (19 Ves. R. 144), and indeed as his own exceptive words clearly import."[2] In breaking the general rule, the court will take into consideration the consequences to follow upon the dissolution, and the conduct of the complainant in prosecuting his suit.[3] Where a special injunction is granted on the allegation by the plaintiff that irreparable injury to him will result from the contemplated act of the defendant, and the defendant in his answer, sworn to, denies that such injury will result, the court will not dissolve the injunction, but continue it to the hearing.[4] Thus, where the prayer of the bill was for an injunction to restrain a suit at law, in which the defendant in equity sought to recover of the plaintiff the value of work performed by the latter, and the bill alleged that this work was performed for the benefit of a partnership existing between the parties, and ought to be taken into the partnership account, and the answer denied all the equity of the bill; the court held that there was nothing in the circumstances of this case to take it out of the general rule, and that the only effect of dissolving the injunction would be to permit the question to be tried in regular course

---

[1] Monroe *v.* McIntyre, 6 Ired. Eq. 65.

[2] Per Story, J., Poor *v.* Carleton, 3 Sumn. 75.

[3] Greenin *v.* Hoey, 1 Stockt. 137.

[4] Troy *v.* Norment, 2 Jones Eq. 318.

in a suit at law.[1] While on the other hand, if in the answer
the facts on which the complainant grounds his equity are
positively denied, or the truth of them is greatly impaired by
the facts and circumstances stated in the answer, and the defendant swears that he has no knowledge of the truth of the
complainant's allegations, and that he disbelieves them; if
from the facts and circumstances so set forth and sworn to
the complainant's equity is rendered doubtful, the court will
dissolve the injunction.[2]

§ 40. The question, as to dissolving an injunction upon
the answer, sometimes depends in part upon accompanying
evidence offered by one or both of the parties. Where an
injunction is granted, and the answer denies all the material
allegations of the bill, which are supported only by several
ex parte affidavits; the injunction must be dissolved; no
weight will be given to such affidavits.[3](a) (See § 69.) But a
motion to dissolve an injunction cannot be sustained merely
upon affidavits, when the answer does not sufficiently deny
the equity of the bill.[4] And an injunction granted on notice,
and after hearing upon affidavits on both sides, and especially upon the affidavits of the defendants themselves, going
to the merits, will not be dissolved on the answer of the defendants.[5] In cases of the common injunction, issued for not
answering at the prescribed time, it is of course to dissolve
the injunction, if the answer denies the whole merits; and
the plaintiff will not be permitted to read affidavits contradicting the answer, upon the motion to dissolve.[6]

---

[1] Hollister *v.* Barkley, 9 N. H. 230; Cornwise *v.* Bourgum, 2 Geo. Decis. 15.
[2] McFarland *v.* McDowell, 1 Car. L. R. 110.
[3] Withers *v.* Dickey, 1 Stew. 190.
[4] Bouldiu *v.* Baltimore, 15 Md. 18.
[5] Sinniokson *v.* Johnson, 2 Green Ch. 374.
[6] Poor *v.* Carleton, 3 Sumn. 70.

(a) In Maryland, where the material allegations of a bill are denied
by the answer, the motion to dissolve must prevail, unless the bill can
be supported by testimony taken under the act of 1835, c. 380, § 8.
Washington, &c. *v.* Green, 1 Maryland Ch. Decis. 97.

§ 41. The frequent, and perhaps general language of the cases upon this subject, speaks of the *equity of the bill.* As already suggested, an injunction will not be dissolved as of course, though the equity of the bill is denied by the answer. If by such dissolution the complainant is likely to be deprived of all the benefits of the suit, it will not be dissolved.[1]

§ 42. Nor, in general, in case of irreparable mischief,[2] or where fraud is the *gravamen* of the bill set up.[3]

§ 43. And it remains to be more fully explained, that an injunction will not be dissolved, when the answer does not deny clearly, explicitly, positively, and satisfactorily the equity of the bill.[4]   More especially, where an answer did not deny the allegation in the bill, and there seemed to be some equity in the complainant's claim to have the fund in litigation applied as prayed for, which claim might be enforced at the hearing, an injunction was retained by the court until the hearing.[5]   So an answer founded upon hearsay is not sufficient to remove the complainant's equity, though, resting upon the information derived from others, it denies the facts out of which that equity arose.   Credit can only be given to the answer, in so far as it speaks of responsive matters, within the personal knowledge of the defendant, and unless, so speaking, the equity of the bill is sworn away, the injunction cannot be dissolved.[6]   Nor if an answer does not deny the averments in which the equity of the bill consists, but only states, " that respondent does not believe, and cannot admit, that the said attorney made any such arrangement or contract as set forth in the bill."[7]   Nor where the equity of

[1] Attorney, &c. v. Oakland, &c., Walk. Ch. 90.
[2] Poor v. Carleton, 3 Sumn. 70; Cornwise v. Bourgum, 2 Geo. Decis. 15.
[3] Dent v. Summerlin, 12 Geo. 5.
[4] Thomas v. Horn, 24 Geo. 481; 1 Md. Ch. Dec. 127; Atty., &c. v. Oak-land, &c., Walk. Ch. 90; Schermerhorn v. Merrill, 1 Barb. 511; Thompson v. Adams, 2 Cart. 151.
[5] Clark v. Martin, 4 Edw. Ch. 424.
[6] Doub v. Barnes, 1 Md. Ch. Dec. 127.
[7] Kent v. Ricards, 3 Md. Ch. Dec. 392.

the bill is not charged to be within the knowledge of the defendant, and he merely denies all knowledge and belief of the facts alleged.[1]   Thus the answer of an executor, that he was not privy to the fraud charged against his testator, and that he disbelieved the facts alleged, from his confidence in his integrity, is not sufficient to dissolve an injunction to restrain proceedings at law in favor of the estate.[2]   So, while any material allegation of an injunction bill remains un-answered, the equity is not all sworn off, and the injunction will not be dissolved;[3] and the allegations not denied are taken to be true.[4]   The distinction is made, that, if the allegations be weakly made in the bill, as upon belief merely, and strongly denied in the answer, the injunction should be dissolved.[5]   But in order to warrant a dissolution, it is necessary that the answer should deny any material allegations, with the same clearness and certainty as they are charged.[6] It must appear that the answer fully meets the plaintiff's equity.   It must not be deficient in frankness, candor, or precision, nor must it be illusory.[7]

§ 44. And the answer can be regarded only so far as it is *responsive to the bill*.[8]   So 'an injunction should not be dissolved if the answer is evasive or uncertain, or if the case made by it does not show clearly that the complainant is not entitled to relief.[9]   And the facts stated in the answer are alone to be taken as true, and not the arguments and inferences drawn and made by the defendant on and from these facts.[10]   Thus, where the bill alleged that the notes sought to be enjoined were given in consideration that the defendants

[1] Coffee v. Newsom, 8 Geo. 444.
[2] Ib.
[3] Jackson v. Jones, 25 Geo. 93; Wooten v. Smith, 27 Geo. 216; Farmers', &c. v. Ruse, ib. 391; Lawrence v. Philpot, ib. 585.
[4] Cronise v. Clark, 4 Md. Ch. Decis. 403.

[5] Williams v. Garrison, 29 Geo. 503.
[6] Buckner v. Bierne, 9 S. & M. 304.
[7] Little v. Marsh, 2 Ired. Eq. 18; Mitter v. Washburn, 3 Ired. Eq. 161; Deaver v. Eller, 7 Ired. Eq. 24.
[8] Rembert v. Brown, 17 Ala. 667.
[9] Ibid.
[10] Chase v. Manhardt, 1 Bland, 333.

would procure and make to the plaintiff a fee-simple title to a tract of land, in which they then had only an estate *pur autre vie*, which they denied, and that, in fact, they were unable to procure and make such title, and the plaintiff's allegation was corroborated by the terms of a deed, which they did make; and the defendants answered evasively, insisting upon an unequal and improbable version of the transaction: the court ordered the injunction to be continued to the hearing.[1] So where an injunction issues to restrain suits at law upon a deed alleged in the bill to be fraudulent, and the answer avers that the defendant has no knowledge of the fraud, and disbelieves the existence of it.[2]

§ 45. It is more especially held, that, on a charge involving *fraud*, either actual or constructive, especially where direct interrogatories are put in relation to particular facts, the court cannot be satisfied with a general answer, or one in any way evasive, as a ground for dissolving an injunction.[3] Thus an injunction issued on a bill to stay proceedings in an ejectment, charging fraud in the deeds on which the defendants' title rests, will not be dissolved on the coming in of the answer, unless the answer be full and satisfactory upon the merits. Stating the ignorance of the defendants of any fraud, that they believe their title to be good, and that they are *bonâ fide* purchasers, is not sufficient.[4] So the answer of a defendant, who knows nothing concerning the transaction charged in the bill as fraudulent, denying the fraud, is not such a denial as will authorize the dissolution of an injunction.[5]

§ 46. To entitle the defendant to a dissolution, an answer to the several charges of the bill, *literally*, is not sufficient;

[1] Jones *v.* Edwards, 4 Jones Eq. 257.
[2] Apthorpe *v.* Comstock, Hopk. 143; S. C. 8 Cow. 386.
[3] Scull *v.* Reeves, 2 Green Ch. 84.
[4] Roberts *v.* Anderson, 2 John. Ch. 202.
[5] Ward *v.* Van Bokkelen, 1 Paige, 100.

it must traverse *the substance* of the charges.[1] Thus, where
a judgment on a covenant to pay certain costs was enjoined,
the complainant alleging that no costs had been incurred;
held, an answer, alleging that the defendant had expended
large sums of money, but not particularizing them, was insufficient to dissolve the injunction.[2] So where the equity of
a bill is denied in terms, but at the same time circumstances
are shown which raise strong equities for the complainant, it
lies in the option of the court to dissolve or continue an
injunction.[3] But where the subject-matter of an injunction
was certain actions between the parties for slander and false
imprisonment, and the bill alleged insolvency of the defendant; the defendant answered, admitting the pendency of the
suits, but denying, generally, that he was guilty of the
charges therein, also denying his insolvency, and alleging
an assignment of one-half of his judgment before the injunction bill was filed: on exception to the answer, held, a
denial of the particular facts alleged was not necessary, but
a general denial, that the defendant was not guilty, was sufficient.[4]

§ 47. A. filed a bill in chancery, to enjoin a judgment at
law, in favor of B., on the ground of newly discovered evidence. The bill stated, that A. could fully prove the payment
of the debt on which the judgment was founded, by several
witnesses, whose names were inserted in the bill, which was
verified by positive affidavit, and the injunction was granted.
B. stated in his answer, that A. filed an affidavit, for the continuance of the suit at law, on account of the absence of two
of his witnesses (other than those named in the bill), and
denied the diligence set forth, as the evidence of said two
witnesses was not brought before the court, though B. offered
to take their testimony, without notice. B., on the bill and

[1] Everly v. Rice, 3 Green Ch. 553.
[2] Tooley v. Jasper, 2 Hay. 383.
[3] Allen v. Hawley, 6 Florida, 142;

Carter v. Bennett, ib. 214; Linton v.
Denham, ib. 533.
[4] Parkinson v. Trousdale, 3 Scam.
367.

answer, moved the court to dissolve the injunction, and dismiss the bill, which was done. Held, that the word "as," in B.'s denial, was a qualified one, and did not authorize the motion to dissolve.[1] So an injunction to restrain a trespass to land will not be dissolved, where the answer merely questions the title of the complainant.[2] So where husband and wife, claiming under a marriage settlement, joined with the trustee in a bill of injunction, to restrain creditors of the husband from selling property conveyed by the marriage settlement, which, on its face, and by the oaths of the complainants, including the trustee, who did not appear to have any interest in the property, appeared to have been executed before the marriage, and was recorded on the acknowledgment of the parties without having been attested; and the defendants in their answer did not allege that the deed was antedated, but only that it was acknowledged after the marriage: held, the injunction ought not to be dissolved.[3]

§ 48. If the whole equity of the bill is denied, the injunction may be dissolved, though the answer contain other matters which are scandalous or impertinent.[4]

§ 49. An injunction granted upon a mere *bill of discovery*, in aid of a defence at law, will be dissolved of course as soon as the answer is perfected, whether the charges in the bill are admitted or denied.[5]

§ 50. On a motion to dissolve an injunction, before the plaintiff has had an opportunity to examine his witness, every allegation positively sworn to in the bill, which is not substantially denied in the answer upon the defendant's own knowledge, must be taken as true.[6] So if the answer neither admits nor denies the allegations of the bill, they are to be taken as true.[7] If the defendant might have answered directly.[8]

---

[1] Thompson v. Adams, 2 Cart. 151.
[2] Moore v. Ferrell, 1 Kelly, 7.
[3] Scott v. Loraine, 6 Munf. 117.
[4] Livingston v. Livingston, 4 Paige, 111.
[5] King v. Clark, 3 Paige, 76.

[6] Grimstone v. Carter, 3 Paige, 421.
[7] Young v. Grundy, 6 Cranch, 51 ; 3 Ired. Ch. 153 ; Randolph v. Randolph, 6 Rand. 194 ; Wilson v. Hendricks, 1 Jones Eq. 295.
[8] Parks v. Spurgin, 3 Ired. Ch. 153.

7

§ 51. Where the answer admits that there remains a dispute between the parties, the injunction will be continued until the final hearing.[1] So where an injunction had been obtained against a trustee, forbidding him to sell slaves, which were part of the trust fund, on the allegation that the purposes of the trust had been fulfilled; and on the coming in of the answer it was left doubtful whether the allegation was true.[2] So the answer to a bill for specific performance and to enjoin a trespass admitted the trespass, and, in words, denied the agreement set out in the bill. It admitted, however, the facts, in part, which made up the agreement, and the facts, in part, which showed that it was entered into. Upon a motion to dissolve upon the coming in of the answer, it was held that enough was admitted to retain the injunction.[3] But an injunction upon executions, obtained upon notes given for the consideration of a contract charged in the bill of the complainants to be by fraud or mistake for too large a sum, cannot be sustained, if the answer, denying fraud, admits the mistake, and avers that the overcharge has been credited upon the executions.[4]

§ 52. As has been already intimated, an injunction granted upon a bill which contains equity on its face and is positively sworn to by the plaintiff, as being based on matters within his own knowledge, will not be dissolved upon a denial by the defendant on his *information and belief*, such matters not being within his personal knowledge.[5] Especially if the dissolution might work irremediable mischief.[6] Thus the denial of facts positively charged, and constituting a strong equity, by an executor, who answers on information and belief only, and whose representative character in most cases shows that he can have no knowledge, will not entitle him to a dissolution.[7] Nor a mere denial, in an answer by

[1] Chase v. Manhardt, 1 Bland, 333.
[2] McNeely v. Steele, 1 Busb. Eq. 240.
[3] The Justices, &c. v. The Griffin, &c., 11 Geo. 246.
[4] Rodaban v. Driver, 23 Geo. 352.

[5] Norton v. Woods, 5 Paige, 249; Everly v. Rice, 3 Green Ch. 553; Nelson v. Robinson, 1 Hemp. 464.
[6] Holmes v. George, 24 Geo. 636.
[7] Powell v. Brown, 22 Geo. 275.

an administrator, of his personal knowledge of a transaction between his intestate and a complainant.[1] So where to a bill for an injunction, which did not charge that the matters stated in the bill were within the knowledge of the defendant, the defendant answered, denying all knowledge or belief as to the principal facts stated ; held, the injunction could not be discharged.[2] And where a bill for an injunction is not properly verified by affidavits, and its allegations are denied by the answer on information and belief only ; the injunction should not be unconditionally dissolved, but the chancellor should direct that the complainant, or some one acquainted with the facts, verify the bill within a reasonable time, and in default thereof that the injunction be dissolved.[3]

§ 53. There are, however, exceptions to this general rule. Thus, contrary to the cases already cited, an answer by an executor or administrator, stating facts "as he is informed and verily believes," is held sufficient for a dissolution.[4] So where an administrator answers, that he is ignorant of the facts charged, but has understood and believes that they are altogether different, and his answer is confirmed by several statements in the bill.[5] So on a bill brought by A. for specific performance of an alleged agreement by B. for a sale of land to A., an injunction was issued to restrain C., a subsequent purchaser, from proceeding in an action to recover possession from A. The answer of B. denied such agreement, and the answer of C. denied any knowledge, information, or belief thereof. The injunction was dissolved.[6] So where the allegations of the bill are made upon information and belief, an injunction granted thereon will be dissolved, if they are denied by the answer in the same manner ; especially if it does not appear that the complainant enjoyed superior means of acquiring information.[7]

[1] Williams v. Stevens, 1 Halst. Ch. 119.
[2] Rodgers v. Rodgers, 1 Paige, 426.
[3] Calhoun v. Cozens, 3 Ala. 498.
[4] Coale v. Chase, 1 Bland, 136.
[5] Clayton v. Lyle, 2 Jones Eq. 188.
[6] Rockwell v. Lawrence, 1 Halst. Ch. 20.
[7] Hogan v. Branch, &c., 10 Ala. 485.

§ 54. It is not error to refuse to dissolve an injunction, when the insolvency of a party, on which the equity of the case largely depends, is charged positively upon knowledge and belief in the bill, and positively denied in the answer.[1]

§ 55. In conformity with the rule already referred to, that, upon a motion to dissolve, the defendant can rely only upon so much of the answer as is *responsive to the bill* (see § 39); an injunction will not be dissolved, except in special cases, on an answer admitting the equity of the bill, and setting up *new matter* as a defence.[2] Nor where the equity of the bill is admitted or not denied, but a new equity is introduced to rebut it.[3] *Matter in avoidance* is not evidence on a motion to dissolve an injunction on bill and answer.[4] Though the answer sets up a complete defence to the bill, but fails to deny the allegations on which the injunction was granted.[5] If replied to, the defendant in the trial is as much bound to establish the allegations, so made, by independent testimony, as the complainant is to sustain his bill.[6]

§ 56. The statute of limitations set up in an answer is not sufficient ground for dissolving the injunction.[7] Nor the plea of limitations, though insisted upon in the answer.[8]

§ 57. But, it is said, in regard to new matter, introduced by a defendant in his answer to a bill for an injunction, there seems to be this distinction. Where the bill charges the receipt of money, and a general accountability, and the

[1] Powell v. Brown, 22 Geo. 275.

[2] Att'y, &c. v. Oakland, &c., Walk. Ch. 90; Wilson v. Mace, 2 Jones Eq. 5; Drury v. Roberts, 2 Md. Ch. Dec. 157; Morris, &c. v. Jersey, &c., 1 Beasl. 227; Green v. Pallas, ib. 267; Wooten v. Smith, 27 Geo. 216; Cornelius v. Post, 1 Stockt. 169; M'Namara v. Irwin, 2 Dev. & Bat. Ch. 13; Kerns v. Chambers, 3 Ired. Ch. 576.

[3] Lyerly v. Wheeler, 3 Ired. Ch. 170; Nelson v. Owen, 3 Ired. Ch. 175; Hutchins v. Hope, 12 Gill & J. 244; 3 Bland, 125; Yonge v.

McCormick, 6 Flori. 368; Wilson v. Mace, 2 Jones Eq. 5; Strong v. Menzies, 6 Ired. Eq. 544; Cornelius v. Post, 1 Stockt. 196; M'Namara v. Irwin, 2 Dev. & Bat. Ch. 13; Kerns v. Chambers, 3 Ired. Ch. 576.

[4] Ferriday v. Selcer, 1 Freem. Ch. 258; Hutchins v. Hope, 12 Gill & J. 244; Bellona, &c., 8 Bland, 442.

[5] Salmon v. Clagett, 3 Bland, 125.

[6] Lewis v. Leak, 9 Geo. 95.

[7] Hutchins v. Hope, 12 Gill & J. 244.

[8] White v. Flannigain, 1 Md. 525.

answer admits the receipt, and seeks to accouut ·for the money by alleging its application to some particular ·purpose, the injunction will not be dissolved. But when the bill charges a payment on a particular account, and the answer denies that any payment was made on that account, and accompanies the denial with an admission that a certain sum was received, as a payment on some other account, the injunction will be dissolved; for there is no confession and avoidance by new matter, but a positive denial of the allegation, together with an explanation of a circumstance, relied on to give color to the allegation.[1]

§ 58. An injunction may be dissolved on bill and answer, though a *replication* has been filed. But if proofs have been taken, the court will not investigate the merits, unless there are particular reasons against any delay.[2] .

§ 59. In determining whether an injunction was properly dissolved, impertinent matter, which, if stricken out, would not affect the merits, cannot be considered.[3]

§ 60. The dissolution of a temporary injunction is not a decision upon the merits, and will not preclude a final hearing upon the bill and a perpetual injunction.[4] The bill should not be dismissed.[5] The complainant has the right to continue it as an original bill and to proceed to a final hearing of the cause.[6] Thus it is error to dismiss a petition asking an injunction, and containing a prayer for general relief, on the dissolution of the injunction, if it contain averments sufficient to maintain an action of trespass to try title.[7] So when the allegations of the bill do not warrant an injunction, the injunction may properly be dissolved, and the bill retained for other relief.[8] So where, in a bill for injunction

---

[1] Deaver v. Erwin, 7 Ired. Eq. 250.
[2] Grandin v. Le Roy, 2 Paige, 509.
[3] Barney v. Earle, 13 Ala. 106.
[4] Barnes v. Racine, 4 Wis. 454; Thompson v. Adams, 2 Cart. 151; Allen v. Smitherman, 6 Ired. Eq. 341.

[5] Beams v. Denham, 2 Scam. 58.
[6] Blow v. Taylor, 4 Hen. & M. 159; Johnston v. Alexander, 1 Eng. 302.
[7] Burnley v. Cook, 13 Tex. 586.
[8] Norris v. Norris, 27 Ala. 519.

and relief, that part is not sworn to, which sets forth the facts justifying such interference; the injunction should be dissolved, but the bill should not be dismissed.[1] So where a petition, which shows a good cause of action against the plaintiff, and also prays for an injunction restraining the defendant from collecting an execution against him, which is granted, is met by an answer, denying the equities of the petition; it is proper to dissolve the injunction; but, unless the plaintiff rests his cause upon the evidence contained in the answer, it is error to dismiss the petition.[2] So if an injunction be granted in vacation on a valid bill, and it be shown to the court, at the next term, that the injunction had been irregularly granted; the injunction may be dissolved, but the bill should not be dismissed.[3]

§ 61. Where the principles of a cause are adjudicated, in an order rejecting a motion to dissolve an injunction; the cause may be continued to the hearing; or, if an appeal has been allowed, it may be dismissed, as having been prematurely allowed.[4]

§ 62. A bill in chancery for an injunction, &c., was filed, and the writ issued in vacation. It did not appear from the record that the summons was ever served, or returned into court. One of the defendants appeared, and filed his answer, to which there was no replication. A bond for costs was filed, and the case continued to the next term, but no steps were taken to bring the other defendant into court. At the second term, the case was called in its order; the defendant again appearing, and no one appearing for the complainant, the bill was dismissed, and the injunction dissolved, for want of prosecution, but without prejudice. Held, that the dismissal of the bill and the dissolution of the injunction were proper.[5]

---

[1] Porter v. Moffett, 1 Morris, 108.
[2] Fulgham v. Chevallier, 10 Tex. 518.
[3] Gray v. Baldwin, 8 Blackf. 164.
[4] Baltimore, &c. v. Wheeling, 13 Gratt. 40.
[5] Duncan v. Finch, 5 Gilm. 296.

§ 63. A preliminary injunction to restrain an alleged trespass was dissolved at the hearing. Held, on appeal, that this amounted to a nonsuit, and was not a bar to other proceedings.[1]

§ 64. A dismissal of an injunction bill, on the final hearing, is a determination that the party was not entitled to an injunction.[2](a)

§ 65. A bill remains in court, after dissolution of the injunction, of course, and without motion.[3]

§ 66. A. having obtained a judgment at law against B., B. obtained an injunction, which was subsequently dissolved, and the bill dismissed. B. appealed. A. obtained an order of court for an execution. On error, it was held that the appeal suspended the order dissolving the injunction, as well as that dismissing the bill, and that the execution was irregular.[4]

§ 67. But upon the coming in of the answers to a bill for discovery, the injunction granted upon the filing of the bill

[1] Zugenbuhler v. Gilliam, 3 Clarke, 391.
[2] Loomis v. Brown, 16 Barb. 325.
[3] Cole v. Sands, 1 Overton, 183.
[4] Yocom v. Moore, 4 Bibb, 221.

(a) Before a bill can be dismissed, in Illinois, there must be an issue made up as prescribed by the statute; and to justify a hearing upon bill and answer, it must appear that the complainant has not filed his replication within the time prescribed. Beams v. Denham, 2 Scam. 58. The third section of the Virginia statute of 1804, concerning proceedings in chancery, which provides for the dismissal of a bill on dissolving an injunction, does not apply to bills for injunction and other and further specific relief. Hough v. Shreeve, 4 Munf. 490. In North Carolina, where a preliminary injunction has been dissolved upon the coming in of the answer, the bill will be dismissed for want of prosecution, if the plaintiff takes no step in the suit for two terms after the dissolution of the injunction. Avery v. Brunce, 1 Hay. 369. But not in case of an application, for a *dedimus* to take evidence, by the complainant, after a dissolution of the injunction. Dawson v. ———, 2 Hay. 296.

having been dissolved, it is practically an end of the suit. It is erroneous to continue the bill for discovery, or to allow a supplemental and amendatory bill.[1]   So, where a perpetual injunction is the only proper relief, on dissolving the injunction the bill should be dismissed.[2]

§ 68. The answer may entitle the defendant to a *partial* dissolution of the injunction.   Thus it is erroneous to dissolve an injunction for more than the amount claimed in the answer.[3]   So where a temporary injunction has been granted upon a judgment at law, and upon further proceedings the defendant appears entitled to a sum less than the amount of such judgment, the injunction should be dissolved as to that amount and perpetuated as to the residue.[4]   And where enough of the bill remains unanswered to raise a probability of the plaintiff's sustaining his claim, an injunction will not be dissolved before the hearing, if such a dissolution might render a decree for the plaintiff unavailing.[5]

§ 69. We have already (§ 40) referred to the effect of *affidavits*, when accompanying or following a denial by answer.   It remains to be stated, as the general rule, that an injunction can be dissolved only on the answer of the defendant.   Upon a motion, on the coming in of the answer, to dissolve an injunction, the question must be decided upon the answer, and the exhibits filed and admitted by the answer.   Affidavits are not admissible to sustain or oppose the motion.[6]   Thus the *ex parte* affidavit of a person not party to the bill is not sufficient ground.[7]   Nor the affidavit of a person interested, but party to the suit, without the answer of the defendant.[8]   But the exception is sometimes

[1] Yates *v.* Monroe, 13 Ill. 212.
[2] Edwards *v.* Pope, 3 Scam. 465.
[3] Vandyke *v.* Hardin, 6 J. J. Marsh, 122.
[4] Lyles *v.* Hatton, 6 Gill & J. 122 ; Pillow *v.* Thompson, 20 Tex. 206.

[5] Sherill *v.* Harrell, 1 Ired. Ch. 194.
[6] Moore *v.* Reed, 1 Ired. Ch. 418 ; Thompson *v.* Allen, 2 Hay. 150; Bellona, &c., 8 Bland, 442.
[7] Christmas *v.* Campbell, 1 Hay. 123.
[8] Thompson *v.* Allen, 2 Hay. 150.

made, that an injunction will not be dissolved on affidavits, except in cases of waste and partnership.[1] And, on a motion to dissolve an injunction of a special nature, as to stay waste and the like, where the injury would be irreparable, the bill will be read as an affidavit to contradict the answer.[2] So where the plaintiff, by bill sworn to, applies for an injunction against removing property, and the defendant makes an insufficient answer, the court will allow the bill of the plaintiff to be read as an affidavit, and if, on the whole case, the matter is left in doubt, the injunction will be continued until the hearing.[3]

§ 70. With regard to the nature, weight, and legal admissibility of testimony upon applications of this nature, it is held that an injunction will not be dissolved, as a matter of course, on the coming in of the answer denying the equity of the bill, if the complainant has adduced auxiliary evidence of his right.[4] And that on a motion to dissolve an injunction, the defendant ought not to be required to invalidate, by full proof, the allegations of the bill; the burden is on the plaintiff to support them; and the defendant is required only to show that the evidence on which the injunction was granted is not entitled to credit.[5] It is not expected that a party shall come as fully prepared with proofs as he might do on a final hearing.[6] The bill can only be read as an affidavit.[7]

§ 71. *Depositions* are sometimes offered as evidence. And where depositions were taken under an order of a county court in Maryland, to be used on the hearing of such motion, and the case was removed to the chancery court, the chancellor refused to exclude them on the hearing.[8]

§ 72. We have already spoken of the insufficiency of affida-

---

[1] Sackett v. Hill, 2 Mich. 182.
[2] Lloyd v. Heath, 1 Busb. Eq. 39.
[3] Wilson v. Mace, 2 Jones Eq. 5.
[4] Orr v. Littlefield, 1 W. & M. 13.
[5] North v. Perrow, 4 Rand. 1.
[6] Bibb v. Prather, Kentuck. Decis. 158.
[7] Airs v. Billops, 4 Jones Eq. 17.
[8] Bellona, &c., 3 Bland, 442.

vits, without an answer of the defendant.   Affidavits, however, are often admitted in evidence.(a)   Thus an affidavit
is admissible, which goes to show that the injunction was
irregularly issued, or that the officer allowing it was misled,
and induced to grant it contrary to law.[1]   And, on the other
hand, where a special injunction has been obtained on affidavits, and, on the answer coming in, the defendant moves
to dissolve; such affidavits may be used against the answer.[2]

§ 73. Where an injunction is prayed for to prevent irreparable injury, and the case, as it appears on the bill, is a
proper one for the interference of the court; if any of the
material facts are denied in the answer, the court will not
dissolve the injunction-upon the bill and answer alone, but
hold it over until proofs are taken, or the matters in dispute,
if questions at law, are decided by a court of law.[3]

§ 74. The distinction is made, that affidavits taken by the
complainant in a bill for an injunction, before the coming in
of the answer, may be read in support of the allegations of
the bill, on a motion to dissolve the injunction; but affidavits filed after the coming in of the answer cannot be read.[4]
The general rule is, however, that, upon a motion to dissolve

[1] Carroll v. Farmers', &c., Harring.
Ch. 197.
[2] Custance   v.   Cunningham,   17
Eng. L. & Eq. 501.

[3] Purnell v. Daniel, 8 Ired. Eq. 9.
[4] Kinsler v. Clarke, 2 Hill Ch. 617.

(a) In New York, where a preliminary injunction is granted absolutely
in the first instance, and the defendant seeks a dissolution thereof upon
the ground that the whole equity of the bill is denied by the answer; it is
not the practice to allow him to read affidavits in support of the answer,
except where the answer is not conclusive under the 27th rule.   Village,
&c. v. Matthews, 9 Paige, 504.
But where the plaintiff is directed to give notice of his application
for an injunction, or the defendant is required to show cause why the
injunction should not be granted, whether a temporary injunction is
allowed or. not in the mean time, the defendant may produce his own
affidavit, or those of any other persons, to show that the injunction
should not be granted.   Ib.

an injunction upon the coming in of the answer, the plaintiff cannot, except in a few cases, introduce affidavits to contradict the answer.[1]   The exceptions are held to be in the case of an injunction to stay waste;[2] or where, in case of a dissolution of the injunction, the parties will not remain *in statu quo* at the hearing;[3] or where irreparable mischief would ensue on the dissolution of the injunction.[4]   In New York, where the defendant moves to dissolve an injunction, upon the answer and the affidavits attached thereto, the plaintiff may oppose the motion by affidavits other than those attached to the complaint on which the injunction was granted.[5]

§ 75. Where new matter is contained in the answer, not responsive to the bill, which is relied upon in any way as a foundation for setting aside the injunction, the complainant may read affidavits in contradiction of the new matter.[6]

§ 75 a. Where a bill was filed for an injunction, an injunction issued, and an answer on oath waived, but answer was made and affidavits read in its support, and a conflict of evidence produced, the injunction was not dissolved as of course, but was retained until a full hearing.[7]

§ 76. Where the plaintiff relies upon the affidavits of third persons, annexed to the bill, to sustain an injunction, in opposition to an answer under oath, though the oath has been waived by the plaintiff, the defendant will be permitted to read the affidavits of third persons, in support of his answer.[8]

[1] Gentry v. Hamilton, 3 Ired. Ch. 376.
[2] Long v. Brown, 4 Ala. 622. See West v. Coke, 1 Mur. 191 ; Merwin v. Smith, 1 Green Ch. 182.
[3] Davis v. Fulton, 1 Overton, 121.
[4] Moredock v. Williams, 1 Overton, 325 ; Swindall v. Bradley, 3 Jones Eq. 353.
[5] Hascall v. The Madison, &c., 8 Barb. 174.
[6] Merwin v. Smith, 1 Green Ch. 182.
[7] Mead v. Richards, 4 Edw. Ch. 667.
[8] Haight v. Case, 4 Paige, 525.

§ 77. In New York, on motion to dissolve an injunction, the defendant may introduce evidence, in support of his answer, to rebut the affidavits annexed to the bill under the rule (37).[1]

§ 78. There are various miscellaneous points of *practice* connected with the dissolving of injunctions.(a)

§ 79. After an injunction has been dissolved on the merits, the complainant may *amend*, and obtain an injunction on the amended bill.[2]

§ 80. A cross bill, formal in other respects, but which omits the prayer, that it be allowed as such, and heard with the original bill, is amendable, and on application to the chancellor, in vacation, to dissolve the injunction, should be regarded by him, *pro hac vice*, as amended. Such bills are treated with greater indulgence than original bills.[3]

§ 81. Where a defendant moves to dissolve an injunction, and the motion is refused, and afterwards, by permission, he amends his answer, he is at liberty again to move the dissolution.[4]

§ 82. If an amendment to a bill presents no new case, and changes no equities, the defendant may move a dissolution of an injunction, without answering such amendment.[5]

§ 84. If the original bill, on which an injunction was granted, be sworn to, the addition of an unsworn amendment, not needed to continue the injunction, is no cause for a dissolution.[6]

[1] Brown v. Haff. 5 Paige, 235.
[2] Buckley v. Corse, Saxton, 504; Arnold v. Kreissler, 22 Tex. 580.
[3] Nelson v. Dunn, 15 Ala. 501.
[4] Edney v. Motz, 5 Ired. Eq. 233; Thomas v. Horn, 21 Geo. 177.
[5] Mahone v. Central Bank, 17 Geo. 111.
[6] Maddox v. Rowe, 28 Geo. 61.

(a) As to *costs*, see Cyrus v. Hicks, 20 Tex. 483.

§ 85. In case of *appeal* from a verdict for the defendant in an equity cause, a final verdict only dissolves a previous injunction.[1]

§ 86. It is a sufficient answer to an application to dissolve an injunction, that the equity of the bill on which the injunction rests is not denied by the answer, although no *exceptions* have been filed.[2] And, on the hearing of a motion to dissolve, objections of every kind to the answer may be made, and are then in order.[3]

§ 87. On motion to dissolve an injunction upon answer, exceptions filed are no objection to the motion, unless they affect the answer in points relating to the grounds of the injunction.[4](a)

§ 88. Nothing in answer to a bill of discovery can be deemed impertinent, which tends to disprove the existence of such defence as is stated in the bill; and to entitle the

[1] Neisler *v.* Smith, 2 Kelly, 265; see White *v.* Cazenave, 14 La. An. 57; Albright *v.* Mallory, 19 Tex. 106.
[2] Wakeman *v.* Gillespy, 5 Paige, 112.
[3] Gibson *v.* Tilton, 1 Bland, 352.

[4] Lewis *v.* Leak, 9 Geo. 95; Smith *v.* Thomas, 2 Dev. & B. Ch. 126; Bainey *v.* Earle, 13 Ala. 106; Wyckoff *v.* Cockran, 3 Green Ch. 420; Doe *v.* Roe, Hopk. 276.

(a) In New York, an order by an injunction master, or vice-chancellor, at chambers, under Rule 125, allowing the plaintiff further time to except, does not enlarge the time within which exceptions must be filed to prevent the dissolution of an injunction, upon bill and answer. Wakeman *v.* Gillespy, 5 Paige, 112. Where an answer has been excepted to for insufficiency within the time prescribed by the rules of court, the defendant cannot move to dissolve the preliminary injunction, on bill and answer, until the time for procuring the master's report has expired. Parker *v.* Williams, 4 Paige, 439. An application to dissolve an injunction, and to discharge a *ne exeat*, upon bill and answer, cannot be heard until the expiration of the time (10 days) allowed the plaintiff to except. Satterlee *v.* Bargy, 3 Paige, 142. In North Carolina, contrary to the English practice, where exceptions are filed to an answer to an injunction bill, the exceptions and the motion to dissolve the injunction will be heard together. Edney *v.* Motz, 5 Ired. Eq. 233.

complainant to retain his injunction until his exceptions are disposed of, he must show some actual injury from the alleged impertinent matter.[1]

§ 89. On a motion to dissolve an injunction after answer, the court will not examine exceptions, as to their merits, further than to ascertain that they are not frivolous.[2]

§ 89 *a*. Where on a motion to dissolve the parties actually appear, and do not object the insufficiency of notice, the objection is waived.[3]

§ 90. *Laches*, neglect or delay will be ground for the dissolving of an injunction.[4] Thus, under peculiar circumstances, and after a lapse of sixteen years, an injunction to stay proceedings at law will be dissolved, irrespective of the merits of the questions at issue.[5] So, in a patent case, a temporary injunction will be dissolved at the next term, if the law case, directed by the court to try the validity of the complainant's patent, is not brought before that time.[6] So an agreement was made, and a large part of the property embraced in it was conveyed. Three years afterwards, the vendees filed a bill for a conveyance of the rest, and a year after that the vendor prayed for an injunction to restrain the vendees from conveying, on the ground that the agreement was obtained by fraud, which it appeared he knew of at the time. The answer denied the equity of the vendor's bill. Held, the vendor was guilty of great laches, and so the injunction was dissolved with costs to the respondent.[7] So an injunction will be dissolved on motion, if a copy of the bill on which it was obtained is not served upon the defendant within a reasonable time after his appearance.[8] On the other hand, delay may prevent the dissolving of an injunction. The

[1] Jemett *v.* Belden, 11 Paige, 608; Doe *v.* Roe, Hopk. 276.
[2] Hopk. 276.
[3] Penrice *v.* Wallis, 37 Miss. 172.
[4] See Hightour *v.* Rush, 2 Hay. 361.
[5] Hunt *v.* Smith, 3 Rich. Eq. 465.
[6] Woodworth *v.* Edwards, 3 W. & M. 120.
[7] Trustees, &c. *v.* Gilbert, 1 Beasl. 78.
[8] Furgison *v.* Robinson, Hopk. 8.

court will not dissolve an injunction on enforcement of an important right, unless the party enjoined use due diligence in getting the question before the court.[1]

§ 90 a. The neglect of the plaintiff, on serving an injunction, to serve a *subpœna* to appear and answer on some of the defendants, is no ground for an application, by a defendant on whom the *subpœna* has been served, to dissolve the injunction.[2](a) And the rule of dissolving does not apply, where process is regularly sued out, but irregularly served, and the complainant uses due diligence in suing out new process.[3]

§ 91. Where a plaintiff, upon obtaining an injunction, neglected to serve that and the *subpœna* upon one of the defendants, such defendant may nevertheless enter an appearance, and join with the other in an application to dissolve the injunction.[4]

§ 92. An injunction may be dissolved, though all the defendants, who could and ought to answer, have not done so, if the plaintiff does not proceed in his cause with reasonable diligence. As where an injunction had been granted to stay a suit at law, and some of the defendants had answered, but the plaintiff had neglected for nine months to take any steps to compel the others to appear and answer, or to have the bill taken *pro confesso* against them ; or if the *subpœna* is not served and returned at the term to which it is made returnable, or at least an attempt made to have it served ; and this, although the suit is against the sheriff, and there is no coroner in the county. In such case it may be served by

[1] Baird *v.* Moses, 21 Geo. 249.
[2] Seebor *v.* Hess, 5 Paige, 85.
[3] Payne *v.* Cowan, 1 S. & M. Ch. 26.
[4] Waffle *v.* Vanderheyden, 8 Paige, 45.

(a) In Kentucky, upon an injunction being dissolved, and the bill continued as an original, if the complainant neglects to take out commissions or *subpœna* witnesses, the suit is discontinued at the second term after the injunction is dissolved. Bizzel *v.* Binke, Mar. 61.

any one; but the return must be made under oath, and rule taken upon the defendant to answer, &c.[1]

§ 93. But where the situation of the cause is such that the plaintiff cannot proceed in it, delay is no cause for dissolving an injunction.(a)[2] And an injunction will not be dissolved for laches in prosecution, when the cause has been set down by the opposite party to be heard the next term.[3]

§ 94. An injunction ought not to be dissolved upon an answer not made *under oath*, and where evidence of the truth of the facts was not furnished.[4] Though the plaintiff has waived an answer on oath, the answer must still be sworn to in order to dissolve an injunction.[5] And the defendant may answer under oath for that purpose, with the same effect as in case of other sworn answers.[6] If the plaintiff waives an answer on oath from all the defendants, and one of them answers on oath, denying the whole equity of the bill; he may move to dissolve the injunction upon his answer, though the other has put in an answer not under oath.[7]

§ 95. An injunction should not be dissolved for the reason that the bill was not sworn to, where the effect of the dissolution would be to put the property out of the power of the court.[8]

§ 96. A motion to dissolve an injunction may be taken and disposed of at any time before the cause is regularly

---

[1] Depeyster v. Graves, 2 John. Ch. 148; West v. Smith, 1 Green Ch. 309; Hightour v. Rush, 2 Hay. 361.
[2] Schermerhorn v. Merrill, 1 Barb. 511.
[3] Smith v. Cooper, 21 Geo. 359.
[4] Gray v. McCance, 11 Ill. 325.

[5] Dougrey v. Topping, 4 Paige, 94.
[6] Manchester v. Dey, 6 Paige, 295.
[7] Schermerhorn v. Merrill, 1 Barb. 511.
[8] Schermerhorn v. L'Espenasse, 2 Dal. 360.

(a) An injunction will not be dissolved, because it was obtained more than five months after the judgment enjoined was rendered. Pugh v. Maer, 4 Hawks, 362.

—

reached on the docket, or called for trial,[1] more especially after answer.[2] And, if a bill is wanting in equity, the Chancellor may dissolve the injunction in vacation, after the coming in of the answer, notwithstanding all its allegations are therein admitted.[3] A party moving to dissolve an injunction in vacation need not wait to file his answer in court, or at the rules, but may put in his answer and have the benefit of it at the hearing of the motion.[4](a)

§ 97. It is error to *perpetuate* an injunction against a party without having him before the court.[5] And upon a motion to dissolve an injunction, upon the coming in of the answer, it is not proper to decree that the injunction be made perpetual, in whole or in part.[6] So an injunction will only be perpetuated as issued for some legal cause stated in the petition.[7]

§ 98. Injunctions are sometimes *revived* after dissolution on the merits. Or awarded afresh on special motion, or new facts stated in an amended or supplemental bill, or on proof taken.[8] A court of chancery is always open to reinstate, as well as to grant, an injunction.[9] If the dissolution of an injunction be improperly obtained, it will be revived.[10] And where an injunction is awarded until the coming in of the

---

[1] Huston *v.* Berry, 3 Tex. 235.
[2] Deklyn *v.* Davis, Hopk. 135.
[3] Nelson *v.* Dunn, 15 Ala. 501.
[4] Goddin *v.* Vaughn, 14 Gratt. 102.
[5] Chapman *v.* Harrison, 4 Rand. 336.
[6] McReynolds *v.* Harshaw, 2 Ired. Ch. 29.

[7] Pitman *v.* Robicheau, 14 La. An. 108.
[8] Tucker *v.* Carpenter, Hemp. 440.
[9] Radford *v.* Innes, 1 Hen. & M. 7.
[10] Billingslea *v.* Gilbert, 1 Bland, 566.

(a) Under the statute of Alabama, authorizing a motion to dissolve an injunction in vacation, upon the coming in of the answer, the Chancellor may hear the motion and make the decree at a place out of his division. The course of practice, in appealing from such a decree, is precisely the same as if the decree were made in term time. Griffin *v.* Branch, &c., 9 Ala. 201.

8

answer, though dissolved of course on the answer's being filed, without motion, the plaintiff may move to reinstate it.[1](a)

§ 99. It is no ground to dissolve an injunction in one State, that an injunction has issued from a court of another, and that the defendant has given security to perform the decree.[2](b)

§ 100. If a party, who has unsuccessfully applied for an injunction, afterwards apply to another court of concurrent jurisdiction, for the same purpose, upon the same grounds, without disclosing his former application, relief may be extended to the other party in a summary way upon his petition; but where the equities of the two applications are different, the temporary injunction should not be dissolved without answer from the defendant, or, at least, notice to the complainant; and where the defendant had neglected to answer for a long time, during which, in the ordinary course of practice, proceedings pending in a court of common law would have been settled, and the matter out of which the proceedings in equity arose, determined in favor of one of the parties, it was held an additional reason for refusing to interfere before answer.[3]

[1] Beal v. Gibson, 4 Hen. & M. 481.   [3] Wood v. Bruce, 9 Gill & J. 215;
[2] McKim v. Fulton, 1 Overton, Lowry v. McGee, 5 Yerg. 238.
238.

(a) In such case, in Virginia, the bill is to be dismissed, unless the injunction be reinstated, or unless cause be shown against it at the term ensuing the coming in of the answer. 4 Hen. & M. 481. After an injunction has been dissolved, a motion to have it reinstated, on new evidence, is in the nature of an original application, and, if refused, the complainant may apply to one of the judges of the Court of Appeals. Gilliam v. Allen, 1 Rand. 414.

(b) The pendency of a bill in the County Court of Virginia, after the dissolution of the injunction, is no bar to the complainant's obtaining another injunction in the Superior Court of Chancery. Roberts v. Jordans, 3 Munf. 488.

§ 100 *a*. Where an injunction against a judgment was dissolved, and another obtained on a new claim, this was also dissolved.[1] So where an injunction has been dissolved on answer, the court will not hear a motion for renewal on testimony taken afterwards in the case.[2] And where an appeal from an order dissolving an injunction has been withdrawn, the propriety of such order cannot be drawn in question, upon a subsequent petition in the same cause, for an injunction or order for the same purpose as the first. So after an order of the Vice-Chancellor, dissolving an injunction, had been affirmed on appeal to the Chancellor, and an appeal taken to the Court of Errors; the Vice-Chancellor refused an order in effect reviving the injunction, upon proofs merely cumulative in support of the facts in issue upon the dissolution of the injunction, and before the closing of proofs in the cause.[3] So where an injunction has been voluntarily dissolved by the plaintiff, or the dissolution of it, without his consent, has been ratified by being made the ground of other proceedings, the plaintiff cannot, on petition, renew the injunction, without new and special reasons.[4] And a regular order dissolving an injunction will not be vacated, merely to admit a formal objection to the application to dissolve.[5]

§ 101. An injunction will not be dissolved until the equity of a supplemental bill be sworn off.[6]

§ 102. Where the common injunction has been dissolved on the merits in the answer, and the bill is afterwards amended, a like injunction cannot be obtained, as of course, for want of appearance to the amended bill.[7]

[1] Grubbs *v.* Lipscomb, 1 Bibb, 145.
[2] France *v.* France, 4 Halst. Ch. 619.
[3] Jewett *v.* Albany, &c., 1 Clarke (N. Y.), 241; Tone *v.* Brace, 1 Clarke (N. Y.), 503.
[4] Livingston *v.* Gibbons, 5 John. Ch. 250.
[5] Champlin *r.* The Mayor, &c., 3 Paige, 573.
[6] Rogers *v.* Solomons, 17 Geo. 598.
[7] Zulueta *v.* Vincent, 7 Eng. Law and Eq. 185.

§ 103. Where the right to an injunction is apparent upon the answer, a preliminary injunction will not be dissolved, though improvidently issued.[1]

§ 104. An injunction to restrain the defendant from selling under a mortgage was retained, after the grounds on which it was granted were removed, until the decision of an action at law, brought by the plaintiff against the defendant on the covenant of seizin in a deed.[2]

§ 105. It has been already stated, in connection with the subject of *denial* by the answer, that an injunction may be dissolved *in part*. It may be here added, as a general rule of *practice*, that an injunction may be partially dissolved in accordance with the case made out by the answer.[3] Thus a bill in equity, filed by a surety in a bond to try the right of property, against whom judgment on the bond had been rendered, charged that there had not been a fair trial, and that he could prove that the slaves in dispute had been conveyed away by deed of trust before they were levied on; and an injunction was granted. The answer denied the identity of one of the slaves named in the deed with that levied on, and there was no proof in the case. The injunction was dissolved by the court below, as to that particular slave, and such a decree was affirmed.[4]

§ 106. Where a part only of the defendants apply to dissolve an injunction, it can be dissolved as to them only.[5] And if the plaintiff has used due diligence to obtain the answers, exceptions to the answers of some of the defendants, submitted to, or allowed by the Master, are sufficient to defeat a motion to dissolve the injunction.[6] The answers of all the

---

[1] Smith v. McLeod, 3 Ired. Ch. 390.
[2] Tillou v. Sharpsteen, 5 John. Ch. 260.
[3] Edwards v. Perryman, 18 Geo. 374.
[4] Pass v. Dykes, 8 S. & M. 92.

[5] Teller v. Van Deusen, 3 Paige, 33.
[6] Noble v. Wilson, 1 Paige, 164; Wisham v. Lippincott, 1 Stockt. 353; Stautenberg v. Peck, 3 Green Ch. 446; Jones v. Magill, 1 Bland, 177; Cape, &c., 3 Ib. 606; Reynolds v. Mitchell, Bre. 135.

defendants implicated must be perfected before the injunction can be dissolved. So where the defendant, who has been restrained, denies the equity, but the others most interested in the subject matter admit all the material allegations, the injunction must stand.[1] So on a bill for an injunction against two, and an answer by one only, that he is ignorant of the facts charged, the injunction will not be dissolved until the answer of the other is put in.[2] If the answering defendants are unable, from want of knowledge, to deny material allegations of the bill, the injunction is retained, and this although the only defendant who can answer such allegations is absent from the State.[3] (See § 109.)

§ 107. But a motion to dissolve an injunction may be granted, though one of the defendants has not answered, if his answer would not affect the rights of the party enjoined.[4] Or, upon the answer of those defendants within whose knowledge the facts charged in the bill must be, if they exist at all, although there are others who have not answered.[5] Or, upon the answer of the defendant who alone is interested, denying all the facts and circumstances charged in the bill, upon which its equity is based.[6] Or, where the defendants have not an identity of interest, and the act of one will not affect the other.[7] And in general, though an injunction upon parties jointly implicated will not be dissolved, without the answer of the defendant on whom the *gravamen* of the bill rests; it is otherwise, if the defendant who answers is able to lay the facts before the court, which show that the complainant has no equity.[8] Or, if the plaintiff has not taken the requisite steps to compel an answer from all.[9] And where the defendants,

---

[1] Zabriskie v. Vreeland, 1 Beasl. 179.
[2] Councill v. Walton, 4 Ired. Eq. 155.
[3] Lines v. Spear, 4 Halst. Ch. 154.
[4] Wilson v. Hendricks, 1 Jones Eq. 295; Evans v. Lovengood, 1 Jones Eq. 298.
[5] Dunlap v. Clements, 7 Ala. 539;

Long v. Brown, 4 Ala. 622; Schermerhorn v. Merrill, 1 Barb. 511.
[6] Dennis v. Green, 8 Geo. 197.
[7] M'Vickar v. Wolcott, 4 John. 509; Goodwin v. State, &c., 1 Des.
[8] Gregory v. Stillwell, 2 Halst. Ch. 51.
[9] Mallet v. Weybossett Bank, 1 Barb. 217.

on whom the *gravamen* rests, have fully answered, they may apply to have the injunction dissolved as to them, although a co-defendant has not answered.   Nor is the general rule (§ 106) applicable where the injunction has not been properly granted.[1]   In such cases, the cause will be placed in a situation to obtain a dissolution, without the answer.[2] More especially will the answer of one be sufficient, where the party not answering is not charged in the bill with any particular knowledge of the facts alleged, and the parties who have answered were so charged.[3]   Or if all have answered, against whom the complainants claim an equity.[4]   Or if the defendant, on whom the *gravamen* of the charges is made, has fully answered.[5]

§ 108. A bill was filed to restrain proceedings at law brought by three of the defendants, and the common injunction was obtained against the three.   Two, A. and B., answered, and obtained an order to dissolve the injunction, generally, which was made absolute.   C., the third party, not having answered, A. and B. then issued execution against the plaintiff.   Held, that they were not thereby guilty of contempt of court, but that the orders *nisi* and *absolute* for dissolving the injunction ought to have been confined to A. and B.[6]

§ 109. The answer of a *corporation*, denying the allegations of the bill, but verified by its corporate seal only, is held insufficient to authorize a dissolution of the injunction.[7]   But, on the other hand, the cashier of a bank is not necessarily one of the corporators, and is not a party to a bill against the bank, unless made so by the bill, and his answer will not be sufficient to dissolve an injunction.[8]   So where the president

[1] Depeyster *v.* Graves, 2 John. Ch. 148 ; Price *v.* Cleavanger, 2 Green Ch. 207 ; Wiett *v.* Tommasson, 1 Green Ch. 404.
[2] Jones *v.* Magill, 1 Bland, 177.
[3] Ashe *v.* Hale, 5 Ired. Eq. 55.
[4] Semmes *v.* Mayor, &c., 19 Geo. 471.

[5] Fowler *v.* Williams, 20 Ark. 641.
[6] Money *v.* Jorden, 1 Eng. Law & Eq. 146.
[7] Griffin *v.* The State Bank, 17 Ala. 258, overruling Hogan *v.* The Branch, &c., 10 Ala. 485.
[8] McGuffie *v.* Planters', &c., 1 Freem. Ch. 383.

of a bank was alleged to be implicated with the bank in the fraud charged in the bill, and was made party thereto, the court refused to dissolve an injunction, issued against the bank alone, upon the oath of the cashier, before the other parties had answered; though the answer of the bank, sworn to by the cashier, was, if true, sufficient ground for dissolving the injunction.[1]

§ 110. The following distinctions are made upon this subject. A corporation may answer a bill for an injunction under its corporate seal, but the injunction will not be dissolved without the oath of some agent or member acquainted with the facts stated in the answer.[2] But upon a bill for discovery, and to enjoin an action brought by a corporation, the officers being joined; the corporation having answered, held, the injunction should be dissolved.[3] And the general rule that an injunction, properly granted, will not be dissolved until all the defendants have answered, does not apply where one of the defendants is a foreign corporation, which cannot be compelled to answer.[4] (See § 106.)

§ 111. A bill prayed an injunction against a judgment at law in ejectment, &c. Several of the defendants were *infants*. The parties appeared by counsel. There was no guardian *ad litem* appointed for the infants; there were no answers; there was no decree *pro confesso;* nor was there any evidence by any of the parties. Held, the injunction was properly dissolved.[5]

§ 112. A *misjoinder* of plaintiffs is not ground to dissolve an injunction, but only of demurrer.[6] More especially where it is mere form.[7]

---

[1] Vandervoort *v.* Williams, 1 Clarke (N. Y.), 377.
[2] Hemphill *v.* Ruckersville, &c., 3 Kelly. 435.
[3] Klapcott *v.* Copper, &c., 11 Sum. 314.
[4] Baltimore, &c. *v.* Wheeling, 13 Gratt. 40.

[5] Stephens *v.* Hornbrook, 2 Cart. 666.
[6] Abraham *v.* Plestoro, 3 Wend. 538.
[7] Tradesman's, &c. *v.* Merritt, 1 Paige, 302.

§ 113. Where the complainant, after a statutory foreclosure, filed his bill to foreclose the same mortgage, alleging that the statutory foreclosure was invalid, and obtained an injunction; it was dissolved, on the ground that he had no longer any interest in the mortgage or mortgaged premises, and that the purchaser at the sale, or his grantees, should have filed the bill.[1]

§ 114. Where a member of Assembly, in Virginia, before its session, obtained an injunction to stay proceedings in execution against his property; held, that he could not object his privilege as a member, to prevent the hearing of a motion to dissolve the injunction during the session.[2]

§ 115. *Intervenors* in an injunction suit can oppose the dissolution of an injunction, only by making out a case which would entitle them to an injunction.[3]

§ 116. Where the defendants answer that they have no substantial interest in the subject matter of the bill, but that a third person, not a party, is alone interested, the court will not dissolve the injunction at their instance, for his benefit.[4]

§ 117. An injunction against two defendants will not be dissolved, if, construing their answers and the bill together, the allegations of the bill are *primâ facie* maintained.[2]

§ 118. Where an injunction has been issued against a party against whom there is no equity, the court may order it *conditionally dissolved.*[5]

§ 119. The bill, filed in 1848, stated that, in 1817, the complainant's mother agreed with him that he might take

---

[1] Gilbert *v.* Cooley, Walk. Ch. 494.
[2] Botts *v.* Tabb, 10 Leigh, 616.
[3] Taylor *v.* Gillean, 23 Tex. 508.
[4] James *v.* Norris, 4 Jones Eq. 225.

[5] Hammett *v.* Christie, 21 Geo. 251.
[6] Cabiness *v.* Crawford, 21 Geo. 312.

possession of certain land and make improvements, and in consideration of so doing might take the rents and profits during his life ; that he accordingly took possession, and has hitherto continued to cultivate the same ; has built a dwelling-house and other buildings thereon, and has always since been in the occupancy thereof, and taken to his own use the rents and profits ; that in September, 1846, she conveyed the tract to the defendant N., wife of the defendant W., her heirs and assigns, for the consideration of natural love and affection ; that the deed was made and accepted with full knowledge of the rights and interests of the complainant ; and the bill prayed that the deed may be corrected in conformity with the alleged agreement, and an injunction issued restraining the defendants from prosecuting an ejectment, &c.   The answer denied all knowledge or information of the agreement, and stated that the defendants are informed and believe no such agreement was ever made, &c.   The mother was not made a party.   Held, the mother should have been made a party defendant, and, as she was not, the answer was sufficient to dissolve the injunction.[1]

§ 120. Where, after injunction, the defendant *dies*, and the complainant has not revived the suit, the proper mode of proceeding is by order that he revive within a specified time after service of the order, or that the injunction be dissolved.[2] So, *mutatis mutandis*, where, after answer, the complainant dies.[3]

§ 121. Where there is a motion to continue an injunction, and at the same time the death of the defendant is suggested, the question of the death will be tried *instanter*.[4]

§ 122. Where the answer of the defendant is made and

[1] De Groot *v.* Wright, 3 Halst. Ch. 516.
[2] Cummins *v.* Cummins, 4 Halst. Ch. 173.
[3] White *v.* Fitzhugh, 1 Hen. & M. 1 ; Carter *v.* Washington, 1 Hen. & M. 203.
[4] Thompson *v.* Allen, 2 Hay, 237.

sworn to, before his death, it may be used on a motion to dissolve the injunction, though filed subsequently.[1]

§ 123. A motion to dissolve an injunction, on the coming in of the answer after the death of the complainant, administration not having been granted on his estate, will not be heard.[2]

§ 124. It is no objection to the dissolution of an injunction, that the representatives of a deceased party have not put in their answer, where the foundation of the injunction is a fraud charged against them jointly with the other defendants.[3]

§ 125. Where four plaintiffs united in the same bill for an injunction to stay four several judgments at law against them respectively, on grounds common to all, against five defendants, and the injunction was granted; and, pending the suit, two of the plaintiffs and three of the defendants died; an order, that unless the living plaintiffs, and the representatives of the deceased plaintiffs, should revive the injunction in the name of the representatives of the deceased plaintiffs, against those of the deceased defendants, on or before a certain day, the injunction should stand dissolved, was held irregular and erroneous.[4]

§ 126. Where a *receiver* has been appointed in a creditor's suit, it is not a matter of course to dissolve the injunction, upon a full denial of the equity of the bill, if there is good reason for retaining the property in the hands of the receiver.[5]

§ 127. Where a defendant is restrained by injunction from collecting his debts, and preserving or disposing of perish-

[1] Dennis v. Green, 8 Geo. 197.
[2] Hill v. Jones, 1 Mur. 211.
[3] Wakeman v. Gillespy, 5 Paige, 112.
[4] McKays v. Hite, 2 Leigh, 145.
[5] Bank, &c. v. Schermerhorn, 1 Clarke (N. Y.), 303.

able property, the complainant should apply for the appointment of a receiver; and, if he neglects to do so, the court will dissolve the injunction, so far as to enable the defendant to preserve it himself.[1]

§ 128. Although it is a good objection to an application for the appointment of a receiver in a creditor's suit, that no execution has been issued to the county in which the judgment debtor resided; yet, when the complainant has sworn, in his bill, that an execution has been so issued, an injunction will not be dissolved upon a simple affidavit contradicting that fact, but the defendant must put in his answer, denying the allegation, and then move to dissolve the injunction on bill and answer.[2]

§ 129. An injunction issued on a bill filed in the old Chancery Court of New York, in June, 1847, was ordered to be dissolved, unless the plaintiff gave the injunction bond required within thirty days. He failed to give the bond, and before the expiration of the thirty days, and after the new Constitution went into effect, dismissed his bill, and filed a new bill, substantially the same, in the Supreme Court, on which he applied to a judge at chambers, and the injunction was granted. Held, the proceeding was irregular, and, if there were grounds for an injunction on the new bill, he should have applied for a temporary injunction, and had an order to show cause why it should not be continued until the hearing.[3]

§ 130. Service of the rule *nisi* for dissolving an injunction in vacation, under the rules in equity, in Georgia, may be made on the complainant's solicitor, after appearance by the defendant's solicitor.[4]

§ 131. The injunction meant by the Alabama statute

[1] Osborn *v.* Heyer, 2 Paige, 342.
[2] Strange *v.* Longley, 3 Barb. Ch. 650.
[3] Harrington *v.* American, &c., 1 Barb. 244.
[4] Moore *v.* Ferrell, 1 Kelly, 7.

(Clay's Digest, 357, § 79), upon the dissolution of which the bond is to have the force and effect of a judgment, is the writ of injunction, and, unless such writ issues, there is nothing to support the statutory judgment.[1]

§ 132. In New York, a voluntary dismissal of an injunction bill, after answer, is *primâ facie* evidence that the complainant was not entitled equitably to an injunction, and the defendant may therefore have a reference to ascertain his damage by reason of the injunction. Such dismissal takes the cause from the calendar, but does not prevent consequential proceedings, and motions may still be made in the suit. A notice of hearing, after a dismissal of the suit, is irregular, but not such a proceeding as will be set aside on motion.[2]

§ 133. Where an injunction is wholly dissolved in a county or corporation court, in Virginia, the bill is not to stand dismissed until two terms succeeding have been held in such county or corporation; and the appellate court will not presume, from lapse of time, that two such terms have been held; but this must expressly appear in the transcript.[3] It is doubted, whether the neglect of the clerk to enter the dismissal after the lapse of two terms can have the effect to keep the cause on the docket.[4]

§ 134. A bill for an injunction and other specified relief ought not to be dismissed at the next term after a dissolution of the injunction, under the statute of Virginia of 1804.[5] The statute does not apply to causes instituted before the statute went into operation.[6]

§ 185. In California, an injunction granted *ex parte* may be dissolved without notice.[7]

[1] Shorter v. Mims, 18 Ala. 655.
[2] Mutual, &c. v. Roberts, 4 Sandf. Ch. 592.
[3] Pitts v. Tidwell, 3 Munf. 88.
[4] Ib.
[5] Singleton v. Lewis, 6 Munf. 397.
[6] Callego v. Quesnall, 1 Hen. & M. 205.
[7] Borland v. Thornton, 12 Cal. 440.

§ 136. In California, a county judge, in granting an injunction, acts in the place of the district judge, and therefore the latter may dissolve the injunction as if granted by himself.[1]

§ 137. In Texas, a motion to dissolve an injunction may be determined at any time, even pending a motion for continuance to obtain testimony.[2]

§ 138. Parties may be called out of the county where their cause is pending, to argue a motion to dissolve an injunction.[3]

§ 139. The argument of a motion to dissolve an injunction may be heard in chambers; it is no more a trial of the case than the hearing of an application for injunction.[4]

§ 140. In Kentucky, the remedy for the improper dissolution of an injunction is by prayer for stay thereof, and application in the mean time to a judge of the Court of Appeals, under §§ 326, 327 of the Code.[5]

§ 141. On overruling a motion to dissolve an injunction, before final decree, the parties should be heard on the merits of the bill, if a default has not been taken.[6]

§ 142. When an interlocutory order is made, that a motion to dissolve an injunction should stand as part of the answer, it cannot cause irreparable injury, and, consequently, cannot be appealed from. And when the motion puts at issue the truth of the allegations of the petition for injunction, it is proper that such an order should be made.[7]

§ 143. Pending an injunction, granted upon the authority

---

[1] Borland v. Thornton, 12 Cal. 440.
[2] Smith v. Ryan, 20 Tex. 661.
[3] Semmes v. Mayor, &c. 19 Geo. 471.
[4] Ibid.
[5] Rodman v. Forline, 2 Met. (Ky.) 325.
[6] Ottawa v. Walker, 21 Ill. 605.
[7] Denson v. Stewart, 14 La. An. 703.

of a case that was ultimately overruled, the defendant acquired a statutory right as against the plaintiff. Held, that, upon dissolving the injunction, the court would not impose terms upon the defendant which would have the effect of depriving him of his right so acquired.[1]

§ 144. On the dissolution of an injunction, either surety may at once pay the amount and claim contribution from the co-surety, and that though the principal be solvent.[2]

§ 145. Where a motion is not made to dissolve an injunction until the cause is regularly set for hearing on the court docket, the hearing shall be final.[3]

§ 146. A motion to dissolve an injunction ought not to be continued, unless from some very great necessity.[4]

§ 147. It is the practice in Maryland, where a doubt is entertained as to the propriety of granting an injunction, or where, when granted, it operates in restraint of public commissioners for the opening of a road or the like, or stops or embarrasses the operation of a large manufacturing establishment, or restrains a public ferry, and in other cases of a peculiar character, to appoint a very early day for hearing the motion for a dissolution, and that, too, with or without answer. But where the injunction, by the defendant's own showing, operates in restraint of a right recently acquired, or not long decidedly and exclusively enjoyed, and there is nothing peculiar in the case, it must, as in other cases where individuals only are restrained, take the course of the court.[5]

§ 148. We shall hereafter consider at length the application of the remedy of injunction to restrain proceedings upon *judgments at law.* (See Chap. V.)   Numerous points arise

[1] South Staffordshire, &c. *v.* Hall, 8 Eng. Law and Eq. 229.
[3] Buckner *v.* Stewart, 34 Ala. 529.
[2] Byrne *v.* Lyle, 1 Hen. & M. 7.
[4] Radford *v.* Innes, 1 Hen. & M. 7.
[5] Williamson *v.* Carvan, 1 Gill & J. 184.

in this class of cases, with particular reference to the *dissolving* of injunctions.

§ 149. The plaintiff had obtained the common injunction to stay execution in an action on the same day that the action was tried, but before verdict. Held, upon motion by the defendant, before answer, the plaintiff must pay the amount of the judgment into court within a specified time, or the injunction must be dissolved.[1] So, upon a bill for an injunction upon a judgment at law, and to have the benefit of a set-off, in the answer to which, the defendant consented to make a certain allowance; the plaintiff failed to prove his claim, and obtained an order upon the basis, and for the amount, of the defendant's admission. Held, the injunction could not be continued.[2] And on a bill to enjoin a judgment, if it appear, on final hearing, that the judgment ought not to be enjoined, and that the complainant was allowed a credit at law which should not have been allowed; the injunction should not only be dissolved, but the amount of that credit should be decreed against him.[3] So an injunction to stay a judgment was granted more than six months after it was rendered, and the grounds for the injunction appeared to have existed and been known to the party when the judgment was rendered. Held, the injunction ought to be dissolved.[4]

§ 150. An injunction staying judgment will be dissolved, unless the equity of the bill is confessed by the answer, or unless the answer is unfair, evasive, and so defective as to be subject to exception.[5] Or where the answer has so far denied the allegations of the bill as to leave it without equity as respects the remaining facts not denied.[6] It makes no difference that the bill is sworn to by several plaintiffs. And giving bond to secure the amount of the judgment does not

---

[1] Anderson v. Noble, 13 Eng. L. and Eq. 45.
[2] McClure v. Miller, 1 Bail. Ch. 107.
[3] Todd v. Bowyer, 1 Munf. 447.
[4] Doss v. Miller, 6 Tex. 338.
[5] Capehart v. Mhoon, 1 Busb. Eq. 30.
[6] Rogers v. Bradford, 29 Ala. 474.

entitle the plaintiff to retain the injunction, after a full denial of the equity of the bill.[1] But where a bill for relief against a judgment stated, that the judgment was recovered for the price which the plaintiff in the bill had promised to pay for certain work to be performed by the defendant, after the contract for the work had been abandoned in consequence of his inability to complete it, and the answer denied the facts charged, but alleged that the damages to the defendant, by breach of the contract, were equal to the amount of the judgment; held, this was not such a denial of the equity stated in the bill as to justify the dissolution of an injunction.[2]

§ 151. Where an injunction to a judgment is dissolved, a decree for the amount of the judgment ought not to be made against the complainant, but the creditor should be left to his remedy on the judgment; and so, though the judgment creditor has deceased, and a revival of the judgment will be necessary.[3]

§ 152. An injunction to a judgment for the purchase-money of land, obtained by the vendee on the ground of a defect of the vendor's title, being dissolved, he obtained another injunction, on the ground, which he sustained, that he was entitled to compensation for a deficiency in the quantity of the land, equal to the amount of unpaid purchase-money. Held, he was entitled to relief against the damages which accrued on the dissolution of the former injunction, as well as the judgment itself.[4]

§ 152 a. A decree against the surety in the injunction bond for the amount of the judgment at law and costs, and interest thereon at six per cent., damages, and costs in equity, is erroneous.[5] And, on dissolving an injunction upon a judgment, it is not competent for the court to

---

[1] Manchester v. Dey, 6 Paige, 295.
[2] Skinner v. White, 17 John. 357.
[3] Medley v. Pannill, 1 Rob. (Va.) 63; Duncan v. Morrison, Bre. 113.
[4] Crawford v. McDaniel, 1 Rob. (Va.) 448.
[5] Hubbard v. Hobson, Bre. 147; Richardson v. Prevo, Bre. 167; Duncan v. Ingles, Bre. 215.

decree that execution shall issue against any person except the defendant in the judgment or his administrator.[1]

§ 153. Upon application for an injunction to restrain the execution of a judgment at law, on the ground of errors in the account on which the judgment was founded, and which were pointed out in the bill, the preliminary injunction was dissolved upon the answer, as to so much of the bill as was therein denied.[2] So, when payments have been made on a judgment after an injunction upon it has been dissolved, and the bill continued; the decree, at the dismissal of the bill, should be for the balance due at the time, and the legal penalty on that balance.[3] So where, in a suit in chancery for land, the complainant has recovered a part of the land, and there has been an injunction as to the balance; the court, in their final decree, should dissolve such injunction, and permit the plaintiff in ejectment to recover his full costs at law.[4]

§ 154. Similar questions arise, having more particular reference to the *execution* upon a judgment at law.

§ 155. Where an injunction to stay the sale of any particular property, by virtue of certain levies, has been dissolved as to a part of the property only, and continued as to the balance, and the property released, not diminished in value in consequence of the injunction, has been sold, and the proceeds of the sale applied to the judgments under which the levies had been made; no decree against the complainant should be rendered, on account of the dissolution of the injunction, for the amount of the judgment, penalty, &c.[5] So where a stranger to the record obtains an injunction against the sale of property on execution, and it is dissolved; judgment cannot be rendered against him and his sureties for the amount of the original judgment.[6] And where an injunction to set

---

[1] Harris *v.* Carter, 3 Stew. 233.
[2] Martin *v.* Spier, 1 Hay. 369.
[3] Lewis *v.* Sutliff, 8 Ham. 60.

[4] Bradford *v.* Allen, Hardin, 1.
[5] Teaff *v.* Hewett, 1 Ohio St. 511.
[6] Carlin *v.* Hudson, 12 Tex. 202.

9

aside an execution sale is dissolved, equity cannot render judgment against the complainant for the amount of a judgment at law in his favor.[1] So, where an execution has been properly enjoined, it is an error for the court, upon dissolving the injunction for causes arising subsequent to its issue, to render judgment against the defendant in execution and his sureties in the injunction bond, for the amount of the original judgment, interest, and costs.[2](a)

§ 156. Where an execution was returned by the officer more than a month before the return day, and a judgment creditor's bill was filed after the return day, the injunction was dissolved.[3]

§ 157. By an award between two partners, A. was to pay B. a certain sum, and B. was to pay certain debts of the partnership. Afterwards two executions for such debts were levied on the goods and lands of both A. and B., and A. obtained an injunction against the sale of his lands before those of B. should be sold. It appeared that A. had not paid to B. the sum awarded. On motion to dissolve the injunction, an order was made that A. pay that sum on the executions within thirty days, or that otherwise the injunction should be dissolved.[4]

§ 158. Where an injunction has been dissolved, and the money collected by an execution at law, and paid into the court of law, equity will, upon proper affidavits, direct the

[1] McDonald v. Cook, 11 Mis. 632.
[2] Bryan v. Bridge, 10 Tex. 149.
[3] Stafford v. Hulbert, Harring Ch. 435.
[4] Runyon v. Brokaw, 1 Halst. Ch. 340.

(a) It is the practice of the courts in Texas, on the dissolution of an injunction restraining the collection of an execution, to enter up judgment against the principal and sureties in the injunction bond, for the amount of the execution, under Articles 1602 and 1603 of the statute.—Fall v. Ratliff, 10 Texas, 291.

money to be paid into the office of the clerk and master of
the court; and when the interests of the plaintiffs at law are
several, the court will direct that the parts belonging to those
who are insolvent, or removed out of the State, shall not be
paid to them, until they have given bond and security, respectively, that they will refund the money, if the court of
equity shall ultimately make a decree in favor of the plaintiffs in equity.   And if such bonds shall not be given, after
due notice, the clerk and master shall lend out the money
upon bond and good security, to be subject to the future
orders of the court.[1]

§ 159. Where judgments at law, upon which executions
have issued, and been levied upon lands, are enjoined; after
the dissolution of the injunction, nothing more is necessary
to authorize the sheriff to sell, than writs of *venditioni ex-
ponas*; the lands are to be regarded as *in custodiâ legis*, and
the death of the defendant in the judgments, after execution
had issued and been levied, does not render a *scire facias*
necessary against his heirs or terre-tenants.[2]

§ 160. In February, 1841, A. recovered a judgment against
B., and issued an execution thereon, which was levied on a
house and lot as the property of B.   C., his son, for himself,
and as guardian of his infant children, filed a bill, stating
that B., in July, 1773, sold and conveyed the land to him,
and in December, 1837, sold and conveyed the lot to his
wards, and that both deeds were recorded in 1846, and
stating facts tending to show the validity of the deeds, and
praying an injunction to restrain A. from proceeding with
his execution.   The injunction was allowed.   An answer
denied the validity of the deeds, stated facts to sustain the
denial, and insisted they were not valid against the judgment, because not recorded in season.   Held, that both questions were properly triable at law, on ejectment, by the pur-

[1] McDowell v. Simms, 7 Ired. Eq.
50.

[2] Boyd v. Harris, 1 Maryland Ch.
Decis. 466.

chaser under the execution; and that the judgment creditor should be permitted to proceed. The injunction was dissolved.[1]

§ 161. Analogous to the case of judgments and executions as the subject-matter of injunction, is that of *suits at law*, prior to judgment, which will also be considered at length. (See Chap. VI.)

§ 162. An injunction, staying proceedings in sixty-seven suits, commenced in one day against the county commissioners, before justices of the peace, on county orders, was, on motion, dissolved, on the ground that their defence was at law.[2]

§ 163. If a case is retained in a court of equity for final relief, and the complainant is the defendant in an action at law in regard to the same subject-matter at the same time, an injunction granted to stay the proceedings at law will be continued till the case is settled in equity.[3]

§ 164. Where an injunction restraining proceedings at law before judgment is dissolved, it is erroneous for the court to decree judgment for the debt; the court, as a court of chancery, has nothing to do with the case, after dissolving the injunction, and awarding damages.[4]

§ 165. An injunction was granted to restrain a suit at law, but with liberty to proceed to judgment. On motion to dissolve the injunction, it appeared by the answer, and affidavits in support thereof, that the same persons, upon whose affidavits the injunction was granted, were witnesses in the suit at law, and that the jury found a verdict in opposition to their testimony, and that the plaintiff had no personal know-

[1] Freeman v. Elmendorf, 3 Halst. Ch. 475, 655.
[2] Lapeer County v. Hart, Harring. Ch. 157.
[3] Mulford v. Bowen, 1 Stockt. 797
[4] Powers v. Waters, 8 Mis. 299.

ledge of the facts stated in his bill.   The injunction was thereupon dissolved.[1]

§ 166. A suit at law was brought in favor of A. and B., against C., on a draft.   C. filed a bill of discovery against A. and B., to discover whether they ever were the owners of the draft, or paid any money for it, and obtained an injunction.   The answer by A. (B. being dead) disclosed all the facts within the knowledge of A., and left the legal consequences of these facts to the court.   Held, that A. had answered fairly and properly, and the injunction was dissolved.[2]

§ 167. An order of injunction for restraining the commencement of a suit may be reversed, although an injunction bond has been given.[3]

§ 168. An injunction, to stay proceedings in one suit until the determination of another, may be dissolved after judgment in the latter in the (Texas) District Court, though notice of appeal has been given.[4]

§ 169. An injunction to a suit at law, upon a bill praying for relief as well as discovery, will not be dissolved, on the ground that the equity of the bill had been fully answered.[5]

§ 170. An injunction, to restrain the sale of goods pending an action at law, is necessarily dissolved, on dismissal of the action.[6]

§ 171. The question, of a defendant's right to bring an action of trespass *quare clausum* against the plaintiff, is exclusively a legal one, and cannot be considered in discussing the propriety of dissolving an injunction.[7]

[1] Brown v. Haff, 5 Paige, 235.
[2] Adams v. Whiteford, 9 Gill, 501.
[3] King v. Hall, 5 Cal. 82.
[4] Wolf v. Durst, 10 Tex. 425.
[5] Brown v. Edsall, 1 Stockt. 256.
[6] Phelps v. Foster, 18 Ill. 309.
[7] Wright v. Grift, 11 Busb. 203.

§ 172. Where, on examining the plaintiff's claim of title to timber land from which the defendant has been restrained from cutting, the court is fully satisfied that the plaintiff has no title; the injunction will be dissolved, though an action of trespass is still pending.[1]

§ 173. The subject of *damages* is an important one, in connection with the dissolving of injunctions; governed, however, to some extent, by express statute and local practice.(a)

§ 174. Where no injunction is obtained, though a bill is filed, a decree for damages and dissolution of the supposed injunction is erroneous.[2] So where an injunction is prayed for, but not granted, and the bill is dismissed, damages cannot be given.[3] Nor upon the dissolution of injunctions not granted by competent authority.[4] So, where a bill is filed by the vendee of land to perfect his title under the purchase, before the title is made or tendered, and an injunction ordered to restrain collection of the purchase money, and the title is made complete before the hearing; the dissolution of the injunction should be without damages.[5] So, where an in-

[1] Westcott v. Gifford, 1 Halst. Ch. 24.
[2] Harlan v. Wingate, 2 J. J. Marsh. 138.
[3] Garner v. Strode, 5 Litt. 314.
[4] Montgomery v. Houston, 4 J. J. Marsh. 488.
[5] Lampton v. Usher, 7 B. Mon. 57.

(a) Upon dissolution of an injunction, it is not error to *enter up judgment* against the principal and his sureties in the injunction bond. Western v. Woods, 1 Tex. 1. On dissolution, judgment may be rendered on the bond, and execution issue thereon as of course. Where the petition is continued for trial, a refunding bond may be required, as a condition of issuing execution, but where the injunction is dismissed for want of equity in the bill, the suit is thereby determined, and there need be no continuance nor refunding bond. Pryor v. Emerson, 22 Tex. 162. In this case the motion to dissolve was sustained, and judgment and execution ordered on the bond, disposing of the whole subject-matter, and no motion was made to continue for trial. Held, that the judgment, though not in form, was yet in substance *final*, within the meaning of the above-mentioned rule. Ib.

junction has been granted without requiring any bond, and the bill has been prosecuted in good faith, damages will not be awarded on dissolving it.[1] So where an injunction was rightfully awarded, but afterwards properly dissolved upon matters done or arising afterwards.[2] So an injunction was obtained by a surety in a bond, restraining a levy on his property, until land of the principal had been first levied on. Held, the plaintiff's judgment having been satisfied from the estate of the principal, the plaintiff was entitled to no damages, on the injunction's being dissolved.[3]

§ 175. The damages of six per cent., authorized to be imposed in Alabama, where an injunction is obtained for delay, cannot be allowed, unless the facts stated in the bill are shown to be untrue or evasive, nor where the bill is dismissed for want of equity.[4]

§ 176. Where an injunction is dissolved upon the matter of the bill only, it is a final decision that the plaintiff was not entitled to the injunction; and the defendant may proceed at once to ascertain his damages under the rules of court. But where the injunction is dissolved upon bill and answer, the final decision is not deemed to be made until the final hearing of the cause.[5](a) The general rule, however, seems to

---

[1] Lexington, &c. v. Applegate, 8 Dana, 289.
[2] Taylor v. Bush, 5 Monr. 84.
[3] Kilpatrick v. Tunstall, 5 J. J. Marsh. 80.
[4] Crawford v. Bank, &c., 5 Ala. 55.
[5] Dunkin v. Lawrence, 1 Barb. 447.

(a) In Alabama, where a cause for injunction against a judgment is submitted on bill and answer, and the defendant denies the equity of the bill, and alleges that it was filed for delay; six per cent. damages may be allowed on the judgment. Weissinger v. Johnson, 13 Ala. 93. In Kentucky, ten per cent. damages were held to have been properly awarded on dissolving an injunction, obtained on filing a bill of review against enforcing a decree, where the decree had been replevied. Williamson v. Williamson, 6 B. Mon. 307. Where an injunction was granted, in Arkansas, under the territorial laws, and the injunction was dissolved and damages assessed after the State laws went into force, it

be that the court, upon dissolving an injunction, must fix the amount of damages.[1] In a late case it is held, that no damages can be recovered by a party, against whom an injunction has been granted, unless either an order was passed for that purpose in connection with the injunction, or a bond taken for the damages. But, in case of such order or bond, the court, independently of statute or the chancery rules of the State, may, upon dissolution of the injunction, ascertain through a master or otherwise the amount of damages, and decree that they be paid. The bond can only be enforced at law. But the damages cannot exceed the penalty of the bond.[2]

§ 176 a. With regard to the *measure* of damages in various cases, it is held that, in dissolving an injunction upon a judgment, damages should be awarded only on so much of the judgment as the plaintiff has a right to collect.[3]

§ 177. Where an injunction has been sued out on grave charges of fraud and simulation, and the plaintiff offers no

---

[1] Dawson v. Stratton, 2 J. J. Marsh. 551; Cook v. Edmonson, 3 J. J. Marsh. 423; Wilson v. M'Cullough, 5 J. J. Marsh. 363; Griffin v. Pickett, 6 J. J. Marsh. 388.

[2] Sturgis v. Knapp, 33 Verm. 486.
[3] Ward v. Davidson, 2 J. J. Marsh. 443; Southerland v. Crawford, 2 J. J. Marsh. 369.

---

was held, that the court had no power to assess greater damages than were authorized by the State laws. Miller v. Hemphill, 4 Eng. 488. In Mississippi, where the court is of opinion that an injunction was sued out for delay, damages may be awarded on its dissolution, but not otherwise. Tyler v. McCardle, 9 S. & M. 230. In Missouri, by statute (Sess. Acts, 1849, p. 85, § 12), upon the dissolution of an injunction, damages shall be assessed by the court or jury; but, if money shall have been enjoined, the damages shall not exceed ten per cent. on the amount released, exclusive of legal interest and costs. This restriction does not apply to the case where the sale of trust property has been enjoined. City, &c. v. Alexander, 23 Mis. 483. In Texas, upon dissolution of an injunction, the defendant is not entitled to either special or vindictive damages, unless upon evidence showing him entitled thereto. Jordan v. David, 20 Tex. 712.

evidence whatever to sustain them; the maximum of damages allowed by law should be awarded.[1]

§ 178. Taxable costs and reasonable counsel fees, on the application to dissolve the injunction, are properly allowed as damages.[2] And the fee of counsel need not have been actually paid.[3] So counsel fees, for defending the suit, and moving to dissolve the injunction, may, under the New York Code, be included in the damages allowed by a referee to the party enjoined.[4] (See Chap. II., § 54.)

§ 179. In Louisiana, the judge may allow damages to the amount of twenty per cent. on the judgment enjoined, without proof.[5] But when counsel fees are proved and allowed, exceeding twenty per cent., the judge cannot, in addition to such allowance, award twenty per cent. as damages. And counsel fees will not be allowed as special damages, where an injunction is maintained against a seizure of property, and the case is not a proper one for vindictive damages.[6](a)

§ 180. Where an injunction to restrain a sale of lots advertised for sale was dissolved, and the complainant's bill dismissed, the answer of the defendant showing that he would be obliged to advertise the lots again, and incur the additional expense; it was held, that a decree to the defendant of the cost of advertising them was proper.[7]

§ 181. Upon a reference to a master, to ascertain the damages which the defendants had sustained, by reason of an injunction restraining them from selling mortgaged pre-

[1] Oulliber v. Joublanc, 12 La. An. 237.
[2] Edwards v. Bodine, 11 Paige, 223. But see Sturgis v. Knapp, 33 Verm. 486.
[3] McRae v. Brown, 12 La. An. 181.
[4] Coates v. Coates, 1 Duer, 664.
[5] Williams v. Close, 14 La. An. 737.
[6] Neven v. Voorhies, 14 La. An. 738.
[7] Edwards v. Pope, 3 Scam. 465.

(a) The *plaintiff* in an injunction suit cannot claim from the defendant the amount of fees paid his counsel. Dyke v. Dyer, 14 La. An. 701.

mises, under a decree of foreclosure, in another suit, after the premises had been advertised for sale under such decree; held, the master's fees for services which had been performed a second time, after the dissolution of the injunction, and the expense of re-advertising the sale, were properly allowed.[1]

§ 182. After the dissolution of an injunction in restraint of a suit at law, the plaintiff in the suit obtained a verdict, and thereupon moved for payment of his costs in the suit, which were occasioned by the injunction, out of the deposit made by the plaintiff on obtaining the injunction. Held, that the right to the deposit must abide the event of the cause.[2]

§ 183. Where the complainant's property is taken and sold to satisfy an execution against another person, he cannot on that ground have relief in equity; and (in Kentucky) ten per cent. damages should be given, on dissolving an injunction obtained by the complainant to stay proceedings on a sale bond in such a case.[3]

§ 184. It is proper, in dismissing a bill, not to award damages on a judgment at law, when the order enjoining the judgment was signed by only two justices, the act then in force requiring the concurrence of three justices.[4]

§ 185. In Kentucky, ten per cent. damages should not be decreed, on dissolving an injunction to restrain a proceeding under a deed of trust from the plaintiff to secure a debt due the *cestui que trust*.[5]

§ 186. On dissolving an injunction, damages should be given only where the defendant to the judgment enjoined is the complainant.[6]

[1] Edwards v. Bodine, 11 Paige, 223.
[2] Leggett v. Dubois, 1 Paige, 574.
[3] Fawcet v. Pendleton, 5 Litt. 136.
[4] Wilkins v. Owings, 5 Litt. 239.
[5] Johnson v. Blackford, 6 Litt. 187.
[6] Thomas v. Brashear, 4 Monr. 65.

§ 187. No damages should be decreed on dissolving injunctions of decrees in chancery.[1]

§ 188. Where a final decree awarding a perpetual injunction against a judgment at law is reversed in the appellate court, the damages are recoverable, though no injunction bond has been entered into, and no original injunction, at the commencement of the cause, has ever issued.[2]

§ 189. The court above will not, in general, revise the judgment of the court below in giving or refusing damages on the dissolution of an injunction, unless for manifest error or mistake of law.[3]

§ 190. When an injunction restrains proceedings by a judgment debtor against certain property claimed by a third party, without interfering with the creditor's remedy against other property or the person of the debtor, who is not made a party to the bill, and the injunction is subsequently dissolved, and the bill dismissed; the court will not decree, on motion, against such third party, for the amount of the judgment.[4]

§ 191. A. bought land of B., but, finding after he had made one payment that there were other claims to the land, refused to pay the balance, and obtained a judgment at law, and brought his bill to cause the right to be determined. On the injunction being dissolved, A. was decreed to pay damages, but, on appeal, the decree was reversed, with costs.[5]

§ 192. It is erroneous to dissolve an injunction twice, and give two distinct and separate decrees for damages, when there was but one order for an injunction in the case.[6]

§ 193. On dissolution of an injunction to a judgment in

[1] Martin v. Wade, 5 Monr. 77; Head v. Perry, 1 Monr. 253.
[2] Davis v. Ballard, 7 Monr. 603.
[3] Ross v. Lister, 14 Tex. 469.
[4] Portsmouth, &c. v. Byington, 12 Ohio, 114.
[5] Massie v. Sebastian, 4 Bibb, 433.
[6] Mullvoy v. Same, 4 Dana, 289.

detinue, for a slave, damages should be decreed only on the costs of the action and on the damages for detention, but not on the value of the slave.[1] When a bill asks for an injunction against part of a judgment only, it is erroneous to decree damages on dissolving the injunction on the whole amount.[2] On dissolving an injunction against a judgment at law, damages should be given on the amount of the judgment alone.[3]

§ 194. Where an injunction of the enforcement of a replevin bond is dissolved on bill and answer, the complainant (in Kentucky) should be decreed to pay ten per cent. damages on the amount enjoined.[4]

§ 195. The statute, directing damages to be given on decreeing the dissolution of an injunction against a judgment, applies to the case of a replevin bond, given on satisfaction of a decree for money, which is enjoined.[5]

§ 196. Where, after the granting of an injunction, the parties agree, that, after testimony has been taken, a *pro forma* decree shall be made by the Chancellor, for the purpose of an appeal and a speedy decision; upon dissolution of the injunction, the defendant may recover damages as well for the time subsequent as prior to such agreement.[6]

§ 196 *a.* A. and B., as trustees of the bondholders of a railroad, leased it to a railroad company. The orators, owning one-quarter of the bond, brought a bill, for themselves and all other bondholders who should choose to come in and prosecute, against A. and B. and the lessees, to set aside the lease. An injunction was granted against the use and occupation of the road by the defendants, the orators giving a bond for damages. The bill being dismissed, held, the relation of the

---

[1] Elliott *v.* Krimbough, 6 J. J. Marsh. 834.
[2] Mitcherson *v.* Dozier, 7 J. J. Marsh. 53.
[3] Patterson *v.* Hobbs, 1 Litt. 275.
[4] Yantis *v.* Lyon, 3 J. J. Marsh. 152.
[5] McIlvoy *v.* McIlvoy, 4 Dana, 289.
[6] Sturgis *v.* Knapp, 33 Verm. 486.

trustees and the orators was such as to excuse the lessees from paying rent to the trustees pending the injunction, and therefore the trustees were entitled, as damages, to that proportion of the rent, pending the injunction, which belonged to the bondholders, not parties.[1]

§ 197. In case of an injunction against bondholders of a railroad, to restrain the use of the road, upon dismissal of the bill, the defendants may have damages, a bond having been given, although at the time of the injunction a receiver was appointed and took possession of the road; deducting, however, the net receipts of the receiver.[2]

[1] Sturgis v. Knapp, 33 Verm. 486.   [2] Ib.

CHAPTER IV.

VIOLATION OF INJUNCTIONS.

§ 1. THE *violation*, as well as dissolution, of injunctions gives rise to numerous and important questions.

§ 2. It is sometimes held, that a defendant is not enjoined by so much of an injunction as goes beyond the prayer of the bill.[1] But it is also held, that, while an injunction is in force, it must be obeyed, though broader than is authorized by the bill. That the remedy of the defendant is to apply for a modification of the injunction.[2] On the other hand, the defendant should not be referred to the bill to learn the matter enjoined. But, if he has knowledge of the matter *dehors* the injunction, an infringement will not be excused, because he is so referred.[3]

§ 3. If the defendant be informed of the issuance of an injunction, he will be bound thereby, as if it had been actually served, and will be committed for the breach of it. So,

[1] Freeman *v.* Deming, 4 Edw. Ch. 598.
[3] Richards *v.* West, 2 Green Ch. 456.
[2] Byam *v.* Stevens, 4 Edw. Ch. 119.

also, if he is informed that an injunction has been granted, and its issue has not been unnecessarily delayed.[1]   A party is in contempt of court, who knows that an injunction has issued, or is about to issue, against him, and yet commits the act prohibited, before the injunction can be formally issued and served upon him.[2]

§ 4. So far as the rights of the plaintiff are affected by the breach of an injunction, it is no defence to the party violating the injunction that he acted with the advice of counsel, though, if he has acted in good faith, he may be protected from punishment as for a criminal contempt.[3]

§ 5. Defendants duly served with an injunction are personally responsible for a violation of it, in whatever capacity they acted, and from whatever motives.[4]

§ 6. *Pragmatic trespassers*, pending an injunction, may be compelled to remove all erections made by them in breach of the injunction at their own cost.[5]

§ 7. Property attached cannot be sold by the officer, if an injunction not to sell has been issued; and, if sold, the attaching plaintiff is liable.   So an injunction upon a creditor is violated by a sale by the officer, in his presence, without objection, the officer being so far his agent.[6]

§ 8. An injunction against several defendants is binding upon so many as have actual notice of it, though neither the injunction nor *subpœna* has been served upon them.[7]

§ 9. An injunction, issued in a suit by one partner, pro-

---

[1] Foster *v.* Farnsworth, 1 Swan. 1.
[2] Endicott *v.* Mathis, 1 Stockt. 110; Waffle *v.* Vanderheyden, 8 Paige, 45.
[3] Hawley *v.* Bennett, 4 Paige, 163.
[4] Quackenbush *v.* Van Riper, 2 Green Ch. 350.
[5] Murdock's Case, 2 Bland, 461.
[6] Blood *v.* Martin, 21 Geo. 127.
[7] Waffle *v.* Vanderheyden, 8 Paige, 45.

bibiting the other from meddling with the partnership property, will not prevent creditors of the firm from proceeding
at law to recover their debts : nor any member of the firm
from confessing a judgment to such creditors, so as to give
them preference in payment.[1]

§ 10. On application to the court, in the nature of a civil
remedy, to punish for breach of an injunction, the plaintiff
must show that he has an interest in the subject-matter or a
right to prosecute for the breach, except in the case of infants,
lunatics, &c., who are incapable of protecting their own
rights.[2]

§ 11. If parties violate an injunction, an attachment will
issue against them for contempt.[3]

§ 12. Slight evidence will justify a judgment *nisi*, to show
cause why a party should not be fined, &c., for violating an
injunction.[4]

§ 13. It was held, that the value of property, sold in violation of an injunction, should be paid by the party selling to the receiver, the court having assessed it as a fine for
contempt.[5]

§ 14. But where a railroad had been enjoined from giving
certain undue preference in carriage to a particular line of
transportation, the court refused to grant an attachment
against the company for disobedience of the order, their affidavit showing *bonâ fide* endeavor to comply with it.[6] And
while an injunction, though improperly issued, must be re-
spected so long as it remains in force ; after dissolution, a
motion for an attachment, for a violation of the injunction

[1] M'Credie v. Senior, 4 Paige, 378.   [5] Ib.
[2] Hawley v. Bennett, 4 Paige, 163.   [6] Ransome v. Eastern, 4 C. B. N. S.
[3] Newark v. Elmer, 1 Stockt. 754.   135.
[4] Blood v. Martin, 21 Geo. 127.

while in force, cannot be sustained.[1]   So, where a case has been removed from a State Court to the Circuit Court of the United States, under § 12 of the Judiciary act (1789), it stands as if originally brought in the Circuit Court; and therefore an injunction, allowed by the State Court, falls by the removal, so that the Circuit Court has no power to grant an attachment against the defendant, for a violation of the injunction before the case was removed.   But a motion for an injunction on the face of the bill may be heard in the Circuit Court, as if it had been originally filed there.[2]

§ 15. If the damages, caused by a constructive infringement of an injunction, cannot be calculated, an attachment will be refused, and the damages will be left to be embraced in the decree.[3]

§ 16. Where, on a motion for attachment for alleged violation of an injunction, it appeared that there had been no violation; and further, that the plaintiff had induced the defendant to do the acts which constituted the alleged violation; held, the plaintiff must pay the costs of the motion.[4]

§ 17. A motion for an attachment, for contempt of court in not obeying an injunction, should state, in the proofs on which the application is founded, the specific acts of omission or commission which constitute the alleged contempt.[5]

§ 18. Where the defendant in this proceeding was ordered to answer certain interrogatories; held, the interrogatories must be limited to the particular offences specifically alleged in such proofs, and he could not be required to answer as to particulars charged on information and belief, and not on direct evidence.[6]

[1] Moat v. Halbein, 2 Edw. Ch. 188.
[2] McLeod v. Duncan, 5 McL. 342.
[3] Byam v. Stevens, 4 Edw. Ch. 119.
[4] Sparkman v. Higgins, 2 Blatch. 29.
[5] Parkhurst v. Kinsman, 2 Blatch. 78.
[6] Ib.

10

§ 19. Where interrogatories, unauthorized in law and bad in substance, were demurred to; held, the defendant was entitled to costs on the demurrer; but, the defendant having answered other interrogatories, taking issue upon them, that the enforcement of the costs should be stayed until the issues were disposed of.[1]

§ 20. The proper mode of proof on such issues is by testimony taken orally before a Master.[2]

§ 21. A party who, after notice of a writ of injunction awarded against him, is guilty of a breach of it, may be committed without production of such writ.[3]

§ 21 *a*. The defendants having taken out execution in breach of an injunction, and some of the bailiffs, who served the execution, having found out a place in a wall in the plaintiff's house, that was made up again with bricks, wherein was hid 150*l.*, and having taken away the money, and done great spoil to the plaintiff's goods, an order was made and affirmed, that the defendants should make good this money to the plaintiff, and should satisfy all other damage which the plaintiff would swear he had sustained. The Lord Keeper "thought it an idle practice in the court to put a thief to his oath to accuse himself, for he that has stolen will not stick to forswear it; and therefore in *odium spoliatoris* the oath of the party injured should be a good charge upon him that has done the wrong."[4]

§ 21 *b*. An act done by a party, in violation of an injunction issued against him, will be deemed ineffectual, as to the purpose intended by him; therefore, if he take possession of premises under a writ of possession, which he had been enjoined from procuring, his possession is unlawful; and the party injured will be relieved as well by a writ of forcible

[1] Parkhurst *v.* Kinsman, 2 Blatch. 78.
[2] Ib.
[3] McNeil *v.* Garrett, 1 Cr. & Ph. 98.
[4] Childrens *v.* Saxby, 1 Vern. 206.

entry and detainer at law, as in chancery.[1] So where, after an injunction against proceedings under an execution, the officer sells property levied upon before the injunction, he becomes a trespasser *ab initio.*[2]

§ 22. In case of disobedience of an order to deliver possession, under a decree of sale, containing no direction of that kind, an injunction issues, and, on proof of a refusal to comply with the injunction, a writ of assistance issues to the sheriff, of course. Where the order to deliver possession is made part of the decree of sale, the proper remedy, in case of disobedience, is a writ of execution of the decree.[3]

§ 23. Where a dam had been erected upon a stream, in violation of an injunction issued in a cause then pending, the court, on motion, ordered the dam to be removed.[4]

§ 24. While a party is in contempt for disobedience to an injunction, he cannot properly have a hearing on a motion for its dissolution. Otherwise, where the nature and extent of the punishment to be inflicted for such contempt depend on the question whether the injunction shall be continued or not.[5]

§ 25. The benefit of an injunction is not waived by delaying for three years to proceed for a violation of it.[6]

§ 25 a. We now proceed to illustrate more particularly by examples, what does or does not constitute a violation of an injunction.

§ 26. Notice of trial is a breach of injunction to stay proceedings in an action at law.[7]

§ 27. An injunction, restraining a party from navigating

[1] Fowler *v.* Farnsworth, 1 Swan, 1.
[2] Turner *v.* Gatewood, 8 B. Mon. 613.
[3] Kershaw *v.* Thompson, 4 John. Ch. 609.
[4] Hammond *v.* Fuller, 1 Paige, 197.

[5] Williamson *v.* Carnan, 1 Gill & J. 184.
[6] Dale *v.* Rosevelt, 1 Paige, 35.
[7] Clark *v.* Wood, 2 Halst. Ch. 458. See Jamison *v.* Knotts, 12 Rich. 190.

the Bay of New York, applies to the waters between Staten Island and Whitehall Landing in New York city.[1] And where an injunction was granted, restraining a party from running a steamboat between two points (New York and Elizabethtown), and the defendant proceeded to carry passengers a portion of the distance, when they were transferred to a boat belonging to another person, in which they completed the passage; and he also carried passengers from one *terminus* of the route to a point out of the direct course, and, after a stop of a few minutes, proceeded to the end of the route: held, either course of proceeding was a violation of the injunction.[2]

§ 28. Where an injunction was imposed in general terms, without any reference to previous judicial proceedings, from which the defendant claimed to derive his authority; held, the act enjoined was prohibited while the injunction remained undissolved, although a new authority was obtained by the defendant from a similar source.[3]

§ 29. Where a defendant was enjoined against "selling, pledging, or disposing of" any goods belonging to the plaintiff, a mere offer by him to sell some of the plaintiff's goods was held to be a violation, sufficient to authorize the appointment of a receiver, though not for an attachment.[4]

§ 30. Upon a bill filed in the (Maryland) High Court of Chancery, an injunction was granted, restraining the defendant, A., from giving, and the defendants, B. and wife, from receiving from A., a preference over his other creditors. Held, that proceedings subsequently instituted by B. and wife in the County Court as a court of equity, and a decree thereby obtained, giving them such preference, were violations of the injunction, and that the former court had a right to prohibit, by injunction, the execution of such decree, and to treat it, with the proceedings by which it was obtained, as a nullity.[5]

[1] Vanderbilt, 4 John. Ch. 57.
[2] Ogden v. Gibbons, 4 John. Ch. 174.
[3] Williamson v. Carnan, 1 Gill & J. 184.
[4] Tyler v. Pope, 4 Edw. Ch. 430.
[5] Winn v. Albert, 2 Md. Ch. Decis. 42.

§ 31. An injunction prohibited an assignee for the benefit of creditors from "intermeddling with, receiving, or collecting" any of the assignor's property. Held, the bringing of an action of trespass against a sheriff, who assumed to take such property out of the possession of the assignee, would not be a violation of the injunction, and therefore the failure to bring it was not excused by the injunction, under the statute of limitations.[1]

§ 32. We have already seen (Sec. 8), that an injunction may take effect without any technical formality, where the party has notice. In connection with the point now under consideration, what constitutes a breach of an injunction, it may be here added, that a person is held not bound to obey an injunction, until after due service thereof on him. And that verbal notice that an order has been made is not sufficient.[2](a)

§ 32 a. Want of notice must be distinctly alleged in the answer. Thus, where the petition prays for an injunction to restrain the defendant from paying over money held by him as trustee, and also for a decree that it be paid to the plaintiff; it is not sufficient to allege in the answer that the money had been paid to the *cestui que trust*, but it must be stated that it was so paid before notice of the injunction.[3]

§ 33. A defendant and his clerk in court will not be committed for breach of an injunction, notice of which was given to the clerk. He is not an agent for this purpose.[4] But where notice of the order for an injunction against waste was

---

[1] McQueen v. Babcock, 41 Barb. 337.
[2] Elliott v. Osborne, 1 Cal. 396.
[3] Hollis v. Border, 10 Tex. 360.
[4] Gooseman v. Dann, 10 Sim. 518.

(a) In reference to notice to the *plaintiff;* violation of an original injunction granted *ex parte*, modified on motion of the defendant, without notice to the plaintiff, on bond by the defendant, is no contempt, as the judge had a right to modify the order by § 334 of the (California) Practice act. If he erred in so doing, the remedy of the plaintiff is by appeal; he cannot have a mandamus to compel an attachment for contempt. Fremont v. Merced Mining Co., 9 Cal. 18.

personally served on the defendant the morning after it was obtained, and it was fully explained to him, and he was insolvent, he was committed for proceeding with the waste. The Lord Chancellor remarked, that if the party is in court at the time that the injunction is granted, that is enough; or even if he is on the outside of the court, and informed by one on the inside.[1]

§ 34. Where a husband had been enjoined from *annoying* his wife, it was held that sending her a letter, at the suggestion of her next friend, which was delivered to him unsealed, informing her of the transmission of certain articles for her use, was not a breach of the injunction, though it contained animadversions upon her conduct.[2] And the mere expression of a wish to the wife, to have his children back, was held not to be *claiming* them, within the terms of the injunction, prohibiting him from making such claim.[3]

§ 35. Where an injunction had been granted, enjoining the defendant from interfering with or incumbering certain lands and premises, and the defendant, at and previous to the granting of the injunction, being in possession of and claiming title to a mill on the land, forcibly put out the agents of the complainant, who came into the mill after the injunction had been served, and refused to leave when requested; it was held to be no violation of the injunction, which was not intended to dispossess the defendant.[4]

§ 36. Where the proprietors of a canal were enjoined from obstructing the use of the towing path, which the public had a right to use as such; it was held, that obstructions by the defendants to the use of the path for other purposes were not a breach of the injunction, though they had no legal right to make them.[5]

§ 37. Mere notice to the sheriff of the injunction is suffi-

---

[1] Vawsandan *v.* Rose, 2 Jac. & W. 264; acc. 1 Cal. 396.
[2] Lourie *v.* Lourie, 9 Paige, 234.
[3] Ibid.
[4] Hemmingway *v.* Preston, Walk. (Mich.) 528.
[5] Bosley *v.* Susquehanna, &c., 3 Bland, 63.

cient, and if he afterwards proceeds it is a contempt.[1]   And to a bill, to enjoin execution creditors from proceeding to enforce their executions, the sheriff is not a necessary party. Notice to him of the order for an injunction is sufficient.[2] So an injunction, restraining the levy of an execution, precludes the creditor from placing it in the officer's hands, though no sale is made.[3]   So, after the first proclamation under a writ of *exigi facias*, a common injunction was issued.   The sheriff applied to the judgment creditor's solicitor for instructions, but the solicitor declined to give any.   The sheriff then made three of the remaining proclamations.   Held, the creditor was guilty of a contempt, punishable by costs, though not by a commitment.[4]

§ 38. After service of the ordinary injunction in a creditor's suit, the defendant is not guilty of contempt, by proceeding to judgment in a suit previously commenced.[5] So it is not a violation of an injunction, restraining a party from suing the executors, or other representatives of the testator, to sue the heirs.[6]   But a judgment debtor, after the issuing of an injunction in a creditor's suit upon the judgment, will incur a contempt, by applying money previously earned, or in his possession at the time of the service of the injunction, to the payment of other debts, though small, and contracted for family supplies.[7]

§ 39. Where a party, against whom judgment had been rendered, was enjoined against interfering with or disposing of his property until a receiver was appointed, and confessed judgment in another case begun after the first, and with intent to delay the payment to the plaintiff in the first suit, and made an assignment to the receiver appointed in the second suit; he was held to be guilty of contempt, and was fined to the amount of the first plaintiff's costs and judgment.[8]

[1] Edney v. King, 4 Ired. Eq. 465.
[2] Hext v. Walker, 5 Rich. Eq. 5.
[3] Sugg v. Thrasher, 30 Miss. 135.
[4] Woodley v. Bodington, 9 Sim. 214.
[5] Parker v. Wakeman, 10 Paige, 485.
[6] Dale v. Rosevelt, 1 Paige, 35.
[7] Taggard v. Talcott, 2 Edw. Ch. 628.
[8] Ross v. Clussman, 3 Sandf. 676.

CHAPTER V.

INJUNCTION OF JUDGMENTS AND EXECUTIONS.

§ 1. JUDGE STORY remarks: "Injunctions *to stay proceedings at law* are sometimes granted to stay trial ; or, after verdict, to stay judgment ; or, after judgment, to stay execution ; or, if the execution has been effected, to stay the money in the hands of the sheriff; or, if part only of the judgment debt has been levied by a *fieri facias*, to restrain the suing out of another *fi. fa.*, or a *ca. sa.*, according to the exigency of the particular case. The common mode, in which this relief was granted, was after a judgment at law by enjoining the plaintiff not to sue out execution upon the judgment. This was supposed to trench upon the jurisdiction of the courts of common law from its tendency to destroy the conclusiveness, and to make nullities of their judgments ; since an execution is properly said to be *fructus, finis, et effectus legis ;* and, therefore, is the life of the law. The exercise of this jurisdiction, however, can be distinctly traced back to the beginning of the reign of Henry the Seventh, and although it was constantly struggled against, and even constituted one of the articles of impeachment against Cardinal Wolsey in the reign of Henry the Eighth, yet it was constantly upheld by the Chancellors, and was finally and conclusively established in the reign of King James in the manner already mentioned."[1]

§ 1 *a*. Another late work gives the following account of the interference of a court of equity with the *judgment* only.

§ 1 *b*. "This subject was the cause of a warm contention between Lord Ellesmere and Lord Chief Justice Coke ; the former insisting that courts of equity had jurisdiction, not indeed to overrule the judgments of courts of law, but to prevent a person who had obtained a judgment at law, contrary to equity, from making the courts of law instruments of injustice ; the latter contending, on the other hand, that an injunction to stay proceedings in the courts of common law was an encroachment upon their jurisdiction, and a violation of the statute law of the land. The following is the account given by Mr. Hallam of the dispute between Lord Ellesmere and Lord Coke. 'It happened,' he relates, 'that an action was tried before Coke, the precise circumstances of which do not appear wherein the plaintiff lost the verdict in consequence of one of his witnesses being artfully kept away. He had recourse to the Court of Chancery, filing a bill against the defendant to make him answer upon oath, which he refused to do, and was committed for contempt. Indictments were upon this preferred at Coke's instigation against the parties who had filed the bill in chancery, their counsel and solicitors for suing in another court after judgment obtained at law, which was alleged to be contrary to the statute of Premunire. But the grand jury, though pressed, it is said, by one of the judges, threw out these indictments. The

---

[1] Story's Eq., 3d Ed., Sect. 874. See Coit *v.* Haven, 30 Conn. 190.

king, already incensed with Coke, and stimulated by Bacon, thought this too great an insult upon his Chancellor to be passed over. He first directed Bacon and others to search for precedents of cases where relief had been given in chancery after judgment at law. They reported that there was a series of such precedents from the time of Henry VIII., and somewhere the Chancellor had entertained suits even after execution. The Attorney-General was directed to prosecute in the Star Chamber those who had preferred the indictments, and as Coke had not been ostensibly implicated in the business, the king contented himself with making an order in the Council Book, declaring the Chancellor not to have exceeded his jurisdiction.' "[1]

§ 1 c. In the present chapter we propose to consider injunctions of *judgments* and *executions*.

§ 2. It is said, in an old case: " When a judgment is obtained by oppression, wrong, and a hard conscience, the Chancellor will frustrate it and set it aside, not for any error or defect in the judgment, but for the hard conscience of the party."[2] And the general rule is laid down, that equity will grant relief against a judgment, which is against conscience, or the justice of which can be impeached by facts, or on grounds of which the party could not avail himself at law, or of which he was prevented from availing himself by fraud, accident, mistake, or the act of the opposite party, without any negligence or fraud on his own part.[3](a) So equity will prevent the inequitable use of a good judgment.[4]

[1] 1 Hall. Const. Hist. 472; 3 Lead. Cas. in Eq. 160.
[2] Per Lord Ellesmere, Oxford's Case, 1 Ch. Rep. 1 ; Toth. 126.
[3] Kent v. Ricards, 3 Md. Ch. Decis. 392 ; Marine, &c. v. Hodgson, 7 Cranch, 332 ; Jarvis v. Chandler, 1 Turn. & R. 319 ; Lamb v. Anderson, 1 Chand. 224 ; Rowan v. Runnels, 5 How. 134 ; Moore v. Gamble, 1 Stockt. 246 ; Pollock v. Gilbert, 16 Geo. 398 ; Little v. Price, 1 Md. Ch. Decis. 182.
[4] Garlick v. McArthur, 6 Wis. 450.

(a) It is said, equity cannot set aside the judgment of a court of law, and grant a *new trial*. (See § 4.) It cannot act upon the *case*, but may upon the *person*, and so might well decree that, unless he consents to

§ 3. But, on the other hand, it is said : " The general rule is, that this court will not relieve against a judgment at law on the ground of its being contrary to equity, unless the defendant below was ignorant of the fact in question, pending the suit, or it could not have been received as a defence. There may be cases, perhaps, in which this general rule would be subject to some modification."[1] And the general doctrine is laid down, that courts of equity reluctantly interfere to restrain proceedings had in courts of law, and especially after judgment.[2] That a court of chancery will not

[1] Lansing v. Eddy, 1 John. Ch. 50; Dunham v. Downer, 31 Verm. 249.

[2] Marsh v. Edgerton, 1 Chand. 198.

have the judgment set aside and a new trial awarded, he shall be perpetually enjoined from executing it. Pelham v. Moreland, 6 Eng. 443. See Pickins v. Yarborough, 30 Ala. 408. But, on the other hand, it is held competent to a court of chancery to grant a new trial in an action at law, and to restrain the prevailing party from enforcing his judgment, where it is against conscience to enforce it, and where the other party had no opportunity to make defence, or was prevented by accident, fraud, or improper management, and without any fault on his own part. Carrington v. Holabird, 19 Conn. 84. Though, it is said, "Applications to this court for a new trial, after a verdict at law, are very rare in modern times, since courts of law exercise the same jurisdiction and to the same liberal extent." Smith v. Lowry, 1 John. Ch. 223. Where a party's remedy is *purely equitable*, he loses nothing by suffering judgment at law to go against him. Clifton v. Livor, 24 Geo. 91. The Chancellor has power, on a bill filed for that purpose, to enjoin proceedings at law *before a justice of the peace*, and compel a discovery of facts, to be used upon the trial at law before the justice. Semple v. Murphy, 8 B. Mon. 271. Equity will relieve against a judgment at law upon a void contract, although the defence might have been made at law. Lucas v. Waul, 12 S. & M. 157. Where a case has been determined at law, that a party is without redress at law, and that the time to petition for a new trial has elapsed, forms no substantive ground for relief in equity. Burton v. Wiley, 26 Vt. 430. Where it was left at the choice of counsel, in a court at law, to take judgment for nominal damages, or have the case sent back for a new trial, and from a misapprehension of the facts the judgment was taken, and would be liable to do the party injustice, and the time to petition for a new trial had elapsed; held, a bill in chancery for a new trial would not be sustained. Ibid.

interfere with a judgment at law, unless some special ground for relief is shown.[1]   More especially where the relief sought is predicated on a defence equally available at law.[2]   That, where a party is sued in a court of law, having exclusive jurisdiction of the subject-matter, he must make his defence there, and cannot resort to equity for relief, unless he is hindered or prevented from making such defence.[3]   And that, before equity will grant relief, three things must concur: ignorance of the defence when the judgment was rendered, diligence on the part of the complainant, and that adequate relief cannot be had at law.[4]   So it is held that equity will not relieve against a judgment at law, except for fraud, accident, surprise, or manifest injustice, unmixed with fault or negligence on the complainant's part.[5]   A party seeking to enjoin a judgment must show that the plaintiff had no cause of action.[6] That a defence which he failed to make would have been available.[7]   That the judgment is clearly contrary to equity and good conscience.[8]   Equity will not enjoin a judgment merely on the ground of *error*.[9]   (See § 4.)   So it is held, that a judgment at law cannot be impeached *collaterally* in equity.[10] A court of chancery cannot enter into a case which has been already investigated in a court of law, according to the ordinary rules of investigation in such courts, merely on the ground that injustice has been done.   Or that the judgment was obtained through the erroneous statement of witnesses. Or on the ground of error in law, committed by the law court.   Or that the complainant was deprived of his defence at law by the court's admitting parol proof of a judgment.[11]

[1] Lockard v. Lockard, 16 Ala. 423; 17 Ibid. 672.
[2] Foster v. The State Bank, 17 Ala. 672.
[3] Jamison v. May, 8 Eng. 600; White v. Cabal, 2 Swan, 550.
[4] Taylor v. Sutton, 15 Geo. 103; Hendrickson v. Hinchley, 17 How. 443.
[5] Pearce v. Chastain, 3 Kelly, 226; Phelps v. Peabody, 7 Cal. 50; Rice v. Railroad Bank, 7 Humph. 39.
[6] Huebschman v. Baker, 7. Wis. 542.
[7] 23 Verm. 720.
[8] Wright v. Eaton, 7 Wis. 595; 1 Stockt. 246; Bradley v. Richardson, 23 Verm. 720.
[9] Dann v. Fish, 8 Blackf. 407.
[10] Redwine v. Brown, 10 Geo. 311.
[11] Vaughn v. Johnson, 1 Stockt. 173. See Ellis v. Gosney, & J. J. Mar. 346; Bantly v. Dillard, 1 Eng. 79; Hempstead v. Watkins, Ibid. 317.

And a party has no right to enjoin the execution of a judgment, absolute and unconditional as to the matters it professed to decide, during a litigation as to other matters in controversy reserved by the judgment.[1] Thus a bill in equity brought to enjoin a judgment upon a promissory note, where there is no allegation that adequate relief could not be had at law, or that by the contrivance or unfairness of the defendant a remedy was not had at law, and nothing from which the court can infer that a discovery is necessary; contains no averments authorizing relief in equity.[2] So equity cannot relieve against a verdict for being contrary to equity, unless the former plaintiff knew the fact to be different from what the jury have found it, and the defendant was ignorant of it at the time of trial; or where effectual cognizance cannot be taken at law; or where a verdict is obtained by fraud. But not where the party omitted to avail himself of a legal defence.[3] So to an action upon promissory notes, the defendant pleaded failure of consideration. Judgment having been rendered against him, he filed a bill in chancery, praying, upon the same ground, that the judgment be enjoined. Held, the contract having been entered into with a full knowledge of all the circumstances, there being no misrepresentation or concealment, which could affect its validity, the petitioner not being a loser by any omission on the part of the payee, and there being other equitable circumstances in the case, the court would not interfere.[4] Also, that the petitioner should have averred that he made no defence at law, or have shown such facts as would excuse him for coming into chancery, notwithstanding such defence.[5] So where property of a debtor, subject to attachment in a suit pending at law, is sold in trust for creditors, and a judgment rendered in the suit, and the creditors institute proceedings in equity to be relieved against the judgment, alleging that it was unduly obtained, and for too large an amount; the court will not

[1] Hereford v. Babin, 14 La. An. 333.
[2] Hungerford v. Sigerson, 20 How. 156.
[3] Gatlin v. Kilpatrick, 1 Car. L. R. 534.
[4] Dickson v. Richardson, 16 Ark. 114.
[5] Ibid.

inquire merely whether the judgment was just and equitable, as between the parties to it, but only whether it includes claims or demands, not covered by the action, or not due and payable at the commencement of the action, or which, by a proper application of payments, or credits, will appear to have been paid and satisfied, and were not therefore existing legal claims.[1]

§ 4. The restriction upon courts of equity, as to their interference with judgments at law, is sometimes expressed in the proposition, that, unless a necessity exists for it, and a manifest injury would otherwise be done, no court, *other than that rendering the judgment*, has jurisdiction over the execution.[2] Relief against an *erroneous* judgment at law cannot be granted by the Chancellor.[3] (See § 3.) If a defendant wishes to avoid the effect of a judgment improperly rendered against him, he should apply to the court in which it was rendered; and if he does not so apply, it seems a court of chancery will not inquire beyond the record, into the means by which the judgment was obtained.[4] So, as we have already seen, (§ 2, n.) it is held, with some qualifications, that a court of equity cannot set aside the judgment of a court of law, and grant a party a *new trial;* it cannot act upon the *case*, but may upon the *person*, and so might well decree that, unless he consents to have the judgment set aside and a new trial awarded, he shall be perpetually enjoined from executing it.[5]

§ 5. Where there is a judgment, and also a *decree* for the same demand, the collection of the money under the decree cannot be enjoined, unless the complainant allege in his bill that the judgment has been satisfied.[6] So, to entitle a party to an injunction on the execution of a decree, pending a re-

---

[1] Bradley v. Richardson, 23 Vt. 720.
[2] Donnell v. Parrott, 13 La. An. 251.
[3] Reynolds v. Horine, 13 B. Mon. 234; Methodist, &c. v. Mayor, &c., 6 Gill, 391.
[4] Hone v. Woolsey, 2 Edw. Ch. 289.
[5] Pelham v. Moreland, 6 Eng. 443.
[6] Dunham v. Collier, 1 Iowa, 54.

bearing, he must present such a state of facts as, if true, would entitle him to a reversal of the decree.[1] And the proper course to stay proceedings, under a decree for irregularity, is not by a bill of injunction, but by petition to the court.[2] An original bill for an injunction by the parties to a former suit, or their privies, will not lie to restrain proceedings under the decree in such suit.[3] But an injunction, commanding and enjoining one to cease from all proceedings on his judgments recovered at law, was held to operate to restrain him from proceeding in equity.[4]

§ 5 a. A case, involving some departure from the strict rules upon this subject, early arose between two States of the Union, as respectively parties to the suit. The Governor of Georgia brought a bill, on behalf of the State, against A., alleging that B., a subject of Great Britain, whose property had been confiscated by the State, was indebted on a bond to A., who had recovered judgment on the bond, on which execution had issued, and prayed for an injunction. Held, if Georgia had a right to the debt, it was a right to be pursued at common law, but, as the bill was founded in the highest equity, the injunction should be granted, and continued till the next term, and then dissolved, if Georgia had not then instituted her action at law.[5]

§ 6. In reference to the *amount* of a judgment, as bearing upon the right to an injunction; equity will enjoin a judgment by mistake excessive in amount, though the land of the debtor, upon which execution is levied, was previously conveyed, fraudulently, to defeat the judgment.[6]

§ 7. For the sums of two dollars and ten dollars chancery will not allow a judgment to be stayed, unless in cases of the grossest fraud.[7]

[1] Luckett v. White, 10 Gill & J. 480.
[2] Dyckman v. Kernochan, 2 Paige, 26.
[3] Ibid.
[4] Little v. Price, 1 Md. Ch. Dec. 182.
[5] Georgia v. Brailsford, 2 Dal. 402, 415.
[6] Williamson v. Johnson, 1 Halst. Ch. 537.
[7] Yantes v. Burdett, 3 Mis. 457.

§ 8. Interest and sheriffs' commissions, on a part of a debt which is enjoined, should be included in the injunction.[1]

§ 9. Where an injunction is granted on a judgment, and afterwards dissolved, and the judgment is collected pending the bill, the court, on final decree perpetually enjoining the judgment, may decree the money to be refunded, though there is only a prayer for general relief.[2]

§ 10. An injunction may issue against a judgment recovered in one State, on a prior judgment recovered in another State, for cause affecting the judgment of the other State.[3] So it is held in Illinois, that a bill may be filed to enjoin proceedings upon a judgment of one of the courts of the State, recovered upon a judgment in the courts of another State, if the party applying has not been guilty of any laches in the assertion of his rights, and the judgment of the foreign court has been reversed.[4] So equity will restrain the use of an advantage gained in a court of ordinary jurisdiction of another State by fraud, accident or mistake.[5] Thus A., a manufacturing company in the State of Connecticut, having had dealings with B., a dealer in New York; C., as the agent of A., purchased a quantity of iron of B., B. knowing that A. was the party with whom he was contracting. Afterwards B. brought a suit for this iron, against C. individually, in the Superior Court of the city of New York, and process was duly served on C., by arresting his body. Soon after the suit was instituted, C. called on D., the attorney of B., and explained to him the circumstances under which the contract was made, and the mistake in suing him individually, instead of A., his principal. D. said to C., that he would see him again on the subject. This D. did not do; but he, shortly after, wrote C. a letter, informing him, that nothing would be done in relation to that suit, until further notice should

[1] Greathouse v. Hord, 1 Dana, 105.
[2] Bryan v. Primm, Breese, 33.
[3] Wilson v. Robertson, 1 Overton, 266.
[4] McJilton v. Love, 13 Ill. 486.
[5] Pearce v. Olney, 20 Conn. 544.

be given him.   C., relying on this communication, and hearing nothing further from D. or B., did not appear, in person or by attorney, before the court to which the process was returnable; but D. appeared, and obtained a judgment against C. without his knowledge.   The record stated, that on the first Monday of April, 1846, came, as well the plaintiff, by his attorney, as the defendant, in his proper person ; and the defendant defends the wrong and injury, and says nothing in bar or preclusion of said action ; wherein the plaintiff remains therein undefended against the defendant.   In November, 1848, B. brought, in Connecticut, an action of debt on the judgment, during the pendency of which, C. filed his bill to restrain B. from enforcing his judgment.   Held, 1. That the taking of judgment operated as a surprise upon C., tantamount to a fraud, and justly called for the interposition of a court of equity, unless prevented on the ground of some technical objection; 2. That the "full faith and credit" required by the Constitution of the United States, and the law of Congress, to be given to the judicial proceedings of other States, did not preclude such interposition, inasmuch as a court of equity here does not impugn the New York judgment, but considers the equities subsisting between the parties and acts upon them personally, restraining the one from pursuing a judgment so obtained, and protecting the other; 3. That the record of the New York judgment, finding that the defendant "appeared, in his proper person, and said nothing in bar or preclusion of said action," does not necessarily conflict with the facts above stated, inasmuch as the plaintiff in that suit might, under the laws of New York, have obtained a judgment and had a record made, like the judgment and record in question, without any actual appearance of the defendant.[1](b)

----

[1] Pearce v. Olney, 20 Conn. 544.

(b) Different *local* rules prevail in different States, with reference to the enjoining of judgments.   In Texas, an injunction to stay execution should be directed to the District Court of the county in which judgment was

11

§ 11. With regard to the *terms* upon which a judgment will be enjoined ; it is held that, where a judgment debtor comes into equity for protection, on the ground that he has satisfied the judgment, the door is fully open for the court to modify or grant his prayer, upon such conditions as justice demands.[1]

§ 12. An injunction to a judgment at law will, in general, be at the cost of the complainant.[2]

§ 13. Unless in aid of a suit at law, it is held that no injunction should be granted, where the applicant for it does not submit to a judgment at law, as he cannot contend at law and in chancery at the same time.[3]

§ 14. An order for injunction to a sale under execution is not effectual, until the execution of the bond required by the order.[4]

§ 15. In North Carolina, under the statute of 1800, before a judgment will be enjoined, the amount of it must be paid to the clerk of the court.[5]

§ 16. The statute of New Jersey (Rev. Laws, 704, § 6),

[1] Mechanics', &c. v. Lynn, 1 Pet. 376.
[2] Mosby v. Haskins, 4 Hen. & M. 427.
[3] Conway v. Ellison, 14 Ark. 360.
[4] Pell v. Lander, 8 B. Mon. 554.
[5] Pugh v. Maer, 4 Hawks, 362.

rendered. Hendrick v. Cannon, 2 Tex. 259. In Kentucky, where A. and B. obtained judgments against each other in different counties ; held, the Chancellor of the county in which the defendant lived might enjoin one judgment, and set it off against the other. Mitchell v. Stewart, 4 J. J. Marsh. 551. But a judgment in the Circuit Court of one county cannot be enjoined by the Circuit Court of another. Lamaster v. Lair, 1 Dana, 109. In Ohio, an injunction cannot be issued by the Court of Common Pleas, to restrain an execution of the Supreme Court, upon a decree of alimony. The remedy is by application to the Supreme Court on return of the execution. Sample v. Ross, 16 Ohio, 419.

which directs an injunction to stay proceedings in a personal action at law, after verdict and judgment, on application of the defendant, unless the money be first paid into court, applies to bills of interpleader.[1] The statute is not confined to proceedings in the suit in which the judgment is recovered.[2] So it applies, where an injunction is prayed by the defendant in a judgment, to restrain proceedings by foreign attachment to enforce the judgment.[3]

§ 17. In Maryland, an injunction may be granted to stay execution, in some cases, without bond.[4]

§ 18. In New York, on a bill to restrain proceedings at law upon a judgment, the plaintiff will not be ordered to pay the amount of the judgment into court, unless there is danger of his insolvency.[5] And where a creditor's bill charged that the defendant, pending a suit at law by the plaintiff, confessed judgment to another person, for a debt not due, and which was fully secured; an injunction to stay proceedings upon the judgment was granted, without a deposit of security by the plaintiff.[6]

§ 19. A purchaser, who shows no sufficient reason for not making his defence at law, and seeks equity for relief, must be governed by the general rule on this subject, to submit to take a title at the hearing, and complete his purchase.[7]

§ 20. In a suit to enjoin the collection of a judgment, the complainant gave a bond for the exact amount of the judgment, conditioned to pay when ordered by the Superior Court. Held, the sureties were bound only for that sum.[8]

§ 21. To obtain an injunction against a judgment, on the

---

[1] Morris, &c. v. Bartlett, 2 Green Ch. 9.
[2] Kinney v. Ogden, 2 Green Ch. 168.
[3] Ib.
[4] Cape, &c., 3 Bland, 606.
[5] Rodgers v. Rodgers, 1 Paige, 426.
[6] Burns v. Morse, 6 Paige, 108.
[7] McLaurin v. Parker, 24 Miss. 509.
[8] Dickerson v. Cook, 3 Duer, 324.

ground that the complainant cannot safely pay it, there being several claimants, he should file a bill of interpleader, and pay the debt into court for the party showing himself entitled thereto.[1]

§ 22. In some cases there may be *successive injunctions* to the same judgment. Thus, after the dissolution of one injunction, another was granted to the same judgment, and made perpetual, it appearing that the contract in question, though not tainted with fraud, was founded in a mistake of both parties in relation to the existence of a fact of which both parties were ignorant, and which was not known to the complainant until after the first injunction was dissolved.[2]

§ 23. The question of *time* often becomes material in cases of this nature.

§ 24. Delay in an application for relief against a judgment furnishes a presumption against the equity of the proposed defence.[3]

§ 25. Thus, after a verdict for the plaintiff on a bond, equity will not order an account of transactions which are old and stale, although occurring, in part, subsequently to the making of the bond, for the purpose of obtaining a discount.[4] So equity will not disturb a judgment by default, upwards of twenty years old, and an execution title to real estate vested under it, for want of notice of a writ attaching the defendant's real estate, when he was openly at large within the State; the facts having come to his knowledge about seventeen years before the filing of his bill for relief; the sole excuse for the delay to proceed being, that the complainant had no evidence of the facts upon which he relied for relief, until the passage of a recent statute enabling parties to be witnesses for themselves in civil cases; and the

---

[1] Fowler *v*. Lee, 10 Gill & J. 358.
[2] Armstrong *v*. Hickman, 6 Munf. 287.
[3] Bartlett *v*. Glendy, 3 Mis. 345.
[4] Randolph *v*. Randolph, 1 Hen. & M. 181.

purchaser under the execution having, in the mean time, built upon and improved the estate.[1]

§ 26. In a suit to stay proceedings at law, a defendant obtained time to answer, and then pressed on the action and obtained judgment. After a very considerable delay, he again applied for further time to answer; but it was held, that, as he came for an indulgence, it could only be granted upon the terms of staying execution in the action.[2]

§ 27. In North Carolina, the statute, providing that an injunction upon a judgment at law shall not issue more than four months after the rendition of judgment, does not apply, where the ground of the application did not exist when the judgment was rendered.[3]

§ 28. As has been already suggested, a judgment, erroneous simply because the defendant or his attorney neglected to make a defence which he could have made, in the absence of surprise, accident, mistake or fraud, will not be enjoined. And it is even held sufficient ground of refusal that the bill itself shows a good defence.[4] (See §§ 29, 31.) So where the defendant might have had all the relief he was entitled to, upon an application in the original action, which he neglected

[1] Briggs v. Smith, 5 R. I. 213.
[2] Zulueta v. Vinent, 21 Eng. Law and Eq. 581.
[3] Kerns v. Chambers, 3 Ired. Ch. 576.
[4] Jordan v. Thomas, 34 Miss. 72; Todd v. Fish, 14 La. An. 13; Gibson v. Moore, 22 Tex. 611; Kriechbaum v. Bridges, 1 Clarke, 14; Champion v. Miller, 2 Jones Eq. 194; Vaughn v. Fuller, 23 Geo. 366; 2 Fairf. 218; Rogers v. Kingsbury, 22 Geo. 60; Carter v. Bennett, 6 Florida, 214; Jones v. Kilgore, 2 Rich. Eq. 63; Pearce v. Chastain, 3 Kelly, 226; Brandon v. Green, 7 Humph. 130; Meek v. Howard, 10 S. & M. 502; Methodist, &c. v. Mayor, &c., 6 Gill, 391; Conway v. Ellison, 14 Ark. 360; Little v. Price, 1 Md. Ch. Dec. 182; Williams v. Jones, 10 S. & M. 108; Semple v. McGatagan, 10 S. & M. 98; Brandon v. Green, 7 Humph. 130; Faulkner v. Campbell, 1 Morris, 148; Miller v. McGuire, 1 Morris, 150; Paynter v. Evans, 7 B. Mon. 420; 12 Tex. 4; Shipp v. Wheeless, 33 Miss. 646; Donnell v. Parrott, 13 La. An. 251; Walker v. Robbins, 14 How. 584; Bellamy v. Woodson, 4 Geo. 175; Duncan v. Lyon, 3 John. Ch. 351; Trevor v. McKay, 15 Geo. 550; Skinner v. Deming, 2 Cart. 558; Bruner v. Planters' Bank, 23 Miss. 406; Scroggins v. Howorth, 23 Miss. 514; Basye v. Beard, 12 B. Mon. 581; Prewitt v. Perry, 6 Tex. 260.

to make, he cannot have an injunction.[1] Thus if he could have
had the judgment opened; even though the claim was unconscientious.[2] So where a party moved for a new trial on the
ground of surprise, and for other causes examinable at law, the
motion being denied and no exceptions taken; the Court of
Chancery has no jurisdiction to grant relief.[3] Thus it is no
sufficient excuse for not making a defence at law, so as to give
chancery jurisdiction, that a creek, which had to be crossed to
get to the court-house, was so swollen by rains, on the first
day of the court, that it could not be crossed, and so continued
for three days; it not being shown on what day the court ad-
journed, or when the judgment was rendered, and no effort
having been made to get to the court-house after the flood sub-
sided.[4] So equity will not relieve against a judgment at law,
because the attorney who conducted the defence, through ignorance or design, managed the case unskilfully. Nor because the
complainant was deprived of the benefit of a defence, pleaded
by him in the suit at law, in consequence of another plea
subsequently filed by his counsel.[5] So a garnishee, who had
discharged the judgment, being sued on the original debt, for
the use of another, employed, as counsel to defend the suit,
the same attorneys who had obtained the judgment against
him as garnishee, but did not inform them of his defence, in
consequence of which a second judgment was rendered
against him for the same debt. Held, this was gross negligence, and chancery could not relieve him.[6] So A., a garnishee, appeared and answered, and was charged. He was
afterwards garnished again on the same account, and paid
the amount due to the plaintiffs in the second suit. Bill in
equity to enjoin a suit on the former judgment, on the ground
that A. did not know of the first suit, when he paid the other
judgment, and that he supposed the proceedings would have
been returned to the District Court for final action. It ap-

[1] Borland v. Thornton, 12 Cal.
440.
[2] Ibid.
[3] Hendrickson v. Hinkley, 5 Mc-
Lean, 211; Champion v. Miller, 2
Jones, Eq. 194.
[4] English v. Savage, 14 Ala. 342.
[5] Burton v. Hynson, 14 Ark. 32.
[6] Sanders v. Fisher, 11 Ala. 812.

peared that the agent of A., in his absence, was informed of the judgment by the justice.   Held, A. was guilty of negligence in not attending to the suit, and the injunction was refused.[1] And an injunction will not be granted, where a defendant has not used due diligence in applying to chancery for a *discovery* to assist his defence at law.[2]   Or where he neglected to prosecute a *certiorari* in season.[3]   Or where he has a perfect remedy by a cross-action, for breach of warranty of the article, for the price of which the original suit was brought; or has any other adequate remedy.[4]   He must show that he has a good defence, of which he had no knowledge until after judgment, or that he was prevented from using it by fraud or accident, or the act of the adverse party, unmixed with negligence or fault on his part.[5]   So any defence, which might be interposed at law to defeat a recovery upon a contract, *or a portion of it*, must be so interposed, or it is concluded by the judgment.[6]

§ 29. The same general principle is adopted in reference to the *pleadings*. (See § 28.) Thus, though the bill states, that the complainant was ignorant of facts which would constitute a perfect defence to an action at law against him, until after judgment; yet equity will not restrain the collection of the judgment, unless it be further stated, that the complainant had, before the rendition of the judgment, used due diligence to ascertain the facts necessary to his defence.[7]   So it is not sufficient for the complainant to allege, that he was ignorant of the facts on which he relies for defence until long after the rendition of the judgment.[8]

§ 30. But it is held, that the same certainty of proof is not required to establish an excuse for not making a defence at

---

[1] Houston *v.* Wolcott, 7 Clarke, 173.

[2] Titcomb *v.* Potter, 2 Fairf. 218.

[3] Musgrove *v.* Chambers, 12 Tex. 32.

[4] Ponder *v.* Cox, 26 Geo. 485; Fitzhugh *v.* Orton, 12 Tex. 4.

[5] Robbins *v.* Mount, 3 Kelly, 74; Brandon *v.* Green, 7 Humph. 130; Meek *v.* Howard, 10 S. & M. 502.

[6] Day *v.* Cummings, 19 Vt. 496.

[7] Slack *v.* Wood, 9 Gratt. 40; Taliaferro *v.* Branch Bank, 23 Ala. 755.

[8] 23 Ala. 755.

law, which would be required to establish the existence of
that defence.[1]   And the general rule above stated does not
apply, if the defendant in an action at law, who seeks relief
in equity, had a good defence, but his neglect to make it was
the result of fraud or accident, or the action of the plaintiff.[2]
As where he was not served with process, had no notice of
the suit, and neither appeared, nor authorized any one to
appear for him.[3]

§ 30 a. It is another technical form of expressing the same
rule already stated, that a bill of injunction will lie to restrain
proceedings on a decree obtained by *surprise*.[4] If a defendant
in a judgment did not, when it was rendered, know of certain
facts which would have been a valid defence, he is entitled to
relief against the judgment.[5] So it is ground for relief against
a judgment on a note, that a written contract, without which
the maker could not make his defence at law, had been lost.[6]
Or that a party failed, because of sickness, to file his defence.[7]   So if the defendant, in an action on a promise, is
surprised at the trial, and there are a verdict and judgment
against him, he may have relief in equity, though he made
no effort to obtain a new trial in the common law court.[8] So,
A. and B. being partners, A. made a loan and took a note in
the name of the firm, which was afterwards put in suit by
B., who had no knowledge of usury in the note; and it
appeared by the declaration that A. had parted with all his
interest in the note. A., on being called by the defendant
at the trial to prove the usury, declined to testify, on the
ground that he was still interested in the note. Held, a surprise, which entitled the defendant to relief against the verdict.[9] So where one defendant required the testimony of
another, he may be relieved in chancery after a judgment at
law against him.[10] So an injunction will be granted, to restrain

[1] Rice v. Railroad, &c., 7 Humph.
39.
[2] Watt v. Cobb, 32 Ala. 530 ; Farmers', &c. v. Ruse, 27 Geo. 391.
[3] Stubbs v. Leavitt, 30 Ala. 352.
[4] Gallaway v. Alexander, 8 Leigh,
114.

[5] Meem v. Rucker, 10 Gratt. 506.
[6] Vathir v. Zane, 6 Gratt. 246.
[7] Clifton v. Livor, 24 Geo. 91.
[8] White v. Washington, 5 Gratt.
645.
[9] Post v. Boardman, 1 Clark, 523.
[10] Jordan v. Loftin, 12 Ala. 547.

a landlord from enforcing a judgment for possession for non-payment of rent, if the judgment has been obtained by surprise, upon payment into court of the rent claimed as due.[1] So where a sheriff made a false return of service, and judgment was rendered without notice or appearance, chancery will enjoin the judgment.[2] So where a general return of "executed" is made, and the service was by copy, left at the residence of the defendant, in his absence, of which he did not receive notice in time to defend at law; equity will grant a new trial.[3]

§ 31. But an injunction will not be granted against a judgment, for a fact or cause which existed, and was known to the party, before trial.[4] (See § 28.) And where an injunction to stay a judgment was granted more than six months after it was rendered; and the facts, stated as the ground for an injunction, appeared to have existed and been known to the party when the judgment was rendered: held, the injunction ought to be dissolved.[5] So a party seeking relief in equity against a judgment at law, on the ground that he was ignorant of his defence until after the rendition of the judgment, must show the exercise of ordinary diligence to discover it, or that he was prevented from employing such diligence by fraud, accident, or the act of the opposite party, unmixed with fault or negligence on his own part.[6] So where the plaintiff in an action at law fails, for want of evidence, as to the identity of the slaves sued for, this is matter to be considered on a motion for a new trial, but is no ground for relief in equity.[7] Nor that the complainant was sick at the time of the court; that the witnesses had been directed to be summoned by his counsel, but the subpoena was issued so late that the sheriff could not execute it, and the complainant, by reason of his sickness, could not be present to file an affidavit for a continuance; nor

[1] Forrester v. Wilson, 1 Duer. 624.
[2] Ridgeway v. The Bank, &c., 11 Humph. 523.
[3] Lapiece v. Hughes, 24 Miss. 69.
[4] Prewitt v. Perry, 6 Tex. 260.
[5] Doss v. Miller, 6 Tex. 338.
[6] Perrine v. Carlisle, 19 Ala. 686.
[7] Pickens v. Yarborough, 30 Ala. 408.

that the contract on which the judgment was founded was usurious; nor that the complainant was an infant when the contract was made.[1] Nor the death of the original counsel employed in the defence, and the want of familiarity, on the part of the counsel who succeeds him, with the grounds of defence.[2] So the refusal of the judge to continue a cause upon motion, supported by affidavit, presents no sufficient reason, upon an application to the same court, for enjoining the judgment, but the party should apply, if at all, to the appellate court.[3] So chancery will not relieve from a judgment rendered against one as trustee, on the ground that through forgetfulness he failed to attend court and make his disclosure, even though he would have been discharged upon making such disclosure, no fraud being imputable to the other party. Even if, in case of fraud, equity would relieve, except by bill of discovery, while the party could have an *audita querela*.[4] So a bill to set aside a judgment, on the ground that service of process was not made upon the defendant, and that an appearance and plea were entered without his authority, was held to have been properly dismissed; where the appearance and plea were entered at the direction of a co-defendant, there was a trial on the merits, no fraud was shown, and the bill did not allege that the attorneys appearing were irresponsible, nor show any defence to the suit at law.[5] So where process of attachment was in fact served, the execution will not be enjoined, on the ground of surprise in obtaining the judgment of condemnation.[6] So equity will not relieve against a judgment, on the ground that a witness for the defendant did not testify on the trial to material facts within his knowledge, and as to which he was not examined, when, by proper diligence, the defendant could have ascertained what the witness knew in reference to the matters in controversy.[7] And it is doubted whether equity will interfere in a case at law, upon the allegation that the verdict was obtained

---

[1] Robb v. Halsey, 11 S. & M. 140.
[2] Powell v. Stewart, 17 Ala. 719.
[3] Western v. Woods, 1 Tex. 1.
[4] Warner v. Conant, 24 Vt. 351.
[5] Harris v. Gwin, 10 S. & M. 563.
[6] Peters v. League, 13 Md. 58.
[7] Powell v. Stewart, 17 Ala. 719.

by the testimony of a witness, which was known to be false by the party using it, and which the opposite party had no means of contradicting at the trial, or in time to support a rule for a new trial, and without any allegation that the false witness had been presented for perjury, or has absconded so as not to be answerable to the process of the law.[1] So equity will not interfere against a judgment at law because a witness, introduced to prove a cash payment, stated that the payment was made in jury certificates. Nor because a witness, offered voluntarily, was intoxicated.[2]

§ 32. Where, through *accident, or mistake* (as well as fraud), a judgment has been entered for an amount, or in terms, not as intended, equity will, on clear proof, give relief.[3] But not where the party was prevented from making his defence at law, by a mistake of law, although a mutual mistake of both parties.[4] Nor on the ground that his counsel mistook the facts of his defence, if he was present at the trial.[5] Nor that the party has mistaken his rights, and so failed to make a defence, which it was competent for him to make at law.[6] So where a judgment was obtained by default, in consequence of a letter's not being received in season, which was sent by mail by the party to his attorney; this was held not to be such an accident as would warrant the interference of a court of equity, since common prudence would have guarded against it by sending an agent.[7]

§ 33. *Fraud* is another ground of injunction.[8](a) And

[1] Dyche v. Patton, 8 Ired. Eq. 295.
[2] Governor v. Barrow, 13 Ala. 540.
[3] Katz v. Moore, 13 Md. 566.
[4] Richmond, &c. v. Shippen, 2 P. & H. (Va.) 327.
[5] Jamison v. May, 8 Eng. 600.
[6] Dickerson v. Board, &c., 6 Ind. 128.
[7] Essex v. Berry, 2 Verm. 161.
[8] See Munn v. Matlock, 17 Ark. 512; Wingate v. Haywood, 40 N. H. 437.

(a) It is said, in a proceeding to set aside a judgment for *fraud*, the province of equity is to test the conscience of parties, not the legality of the judgment, or to correct the errors of a court of law. Clapp v. Ely, 2 Stockt. 178. The *plaintiff* in a former judgment may sometimes be

this, although the party might find a remedy in a court of law; or though he had notice of the judgment in time to appeal, and made an abortive attempt to do so.[1] A former recovery, pleaded in bar to a bill for relief against a judgment at law, alleged to have been obtained by fraud, will not avail the defendant.[2] Thus equity will enjoin a judgment, on the ground that there was a good defence, of which the defendant did not know at the time the judgment was rendered, and that he was entitled to pay the debt in depreciated notes, of which privilege it had been sought to deprive him by fraud and collusion.[3] And where, after a judgment for A., a nominal party, a fraud is discovered, by which a bill for the enforcement of the judgment by A. for B. is successfully resisted; this is binding on A. and B., and a suit for cancelling the judgment and for perpetual injunction will be sustained. The last suit may be brought by the defendant in the original cause, or his assignees as representing his property, that the cloud upon the property may be dispelled.[4] So where a party, having a good defence to an action, is prevented, by the gross fraud of the plaintiff in the suit, and others, from setting up that defence, and a judgment is obtained against him, without any negligence or fault on his part; it is a proper case for relief in equity against the judgment; and the persons guilty of the fraud, although not parties to the suit at law, are proper parties to the bill in equity.[5] So where an owner of personal property, incumbered by liens for more than its value, sold it, under a representation that it was unincumbered, and then obtained a judgment for the purchase-money, the collection of the judgment was enjoined till the incumbrances were removed.[6](a)

---

[1] Nelson v. Rockwell, 14 Ill. 375.
[2] Easton v. Collier, 3 Mis. 379.
[3] Davis v. Tileston, 6 How. 114.
[4] Monroe v. Delavan, 26 Barb. 16.
[5] Huggins v. King, 3 Barb. 616.
[6] Poe v. Decker, 5 Ind. 150.

relieved by injunction from the fraud of a third party. Thus, in case of a suit brought by an attorney who is poor and irresponsible, without authority, if the defendant recovers a judgment for costs, such judgment will be perpetually enjoined. Smyth v. Balch, 40 N. H. 363.

(a) It seems, a decree of the House of Lords, obtained by the fraudu-

§ 34. A bill, to enjoin a judgment at law for fraud in the contract on which it is founded, must show that the defence was not made at law, and that the omission to make it occurred without any neglect of the complainant.[1] Thus a temporary injunction will not be granted, against a judgment rendered on a promissory note by default, the complainant alleging that the plaintiff and the defendants were relatives, and that the note had been due for a long time, and that this was done to defraud the other creditors; no defence having been made, because no valid defence existed, and the note being for a valid and valuable consideration.[2] So A. and B., brothers, not being indebted to each other, and for a nominal consideration, mutually agreed that A. should convey certain personal property to B. B., by another agreement, stipulated to reconvey the property to A., or to him in trust for his wife and children. A. then agreed to confess a judgment to B., who further agreed to sue out execution, levy it upon the whole estate of A., make purchases to the amount of the judgment, and then convey it to A., or to him in trust for his wife and children. This judgment was confessed, and B. died. It was then revived by his administrators. It appeared in fact, and by the answers to a bill filed by A. to vacate the agreements and judgment, and procure a reconveyance of the property to himself, that their object, known to both parties, was to hinder, delay, and defraud the credi-

[1] Parker v. Morton, 5 Blackf. 1.   [2] Sohier v. Merril, 3 W. & M. 179.

lent collusion of both parties, in order to defeat the objects of public justice, or the rights of one of the nominal parties, being an infant, may be questioned even in an inferior court, and an original suit for relief there instituted. Per Lord Cranworth, L. C., Shedden v. Patrick, 28 Eng. Law and Eq. 56. It seems, such decree may even be treated as a nullity in the inferior court, and the question will simply be, was it a real judgment or not? Per Lord Brougham, ib. It seems, though such decree might perhaps be treated by the inferior court indirectly as a nullity, if the case shows manifest gross direct fraud, yet the relief should be sought for in the House in the first instance. Per Lord St. Leonards, ib.

tors of A.   Held, the complainant was not entitled to relief in equity.[1]

§ 35. In reference to the question of *consideration*, it is held to be against conscience to collect the amount due on a note, when nothing has been received for it.[2]

§ 36. Equity will restrain an innocent *bonâ fide* assignee, for value, of a security given for money lost in gaming, from enforcing his claim, even upon a judgment already obtained.[3] So on a bill filed to enjoin a judgment, because the debt was for money won at cards, the evidence leaving it doubtful whether this was the consideration, or, if it was, whether the judgment creditor, an assignee of the debt, had not taken it under a false representation or concealment of the debtor as to the consideration; held, the bill should not be dismissed, but that the injunction should be continued, and an issue had to determine the facts.[4]

§ 37. But relief will not be granted against a judgment upon a note, given solely for the purpose of testing, by a collusive action, whether the maker had any title in property held in trust for his wife.[5]

§ 38. In reference to *formal errors* as a ground for equitable interference; the fact, that an error in the docketing of a judgment was the error of the clerk, and not the fault of the judgment creditor or his attorney, will not authorize the Court of Chancery to interfere, to deprive another judgment creditor of his legal priority thereby obtained.[6] Judgments of a court of record cannot be falsified by proof *aliunde.* Thus where a judgment was entered by the clerk as upon a verdict, the error cannot be corrected by a court of chancery,

---

[1] Freeman v. Sedwick, 6 Gill, 28.
[2] Richardson v. Williams, 3 Jones Eq. 116.
[3] Gough v. Pratt, 9 Md. 526.
[4] Nelson v. Armstrong, 5 Gratt. 354.
[5] Wells v. Smith, 13 Gray, 207.
[6] Buchan v. Sumner, 2 Barb. Ch. 165.

upon parol proof that the judgment, by agreement, should have been entered *nil dicit* for a less sum.[1] So A. commenced a suit against B. on a valid debt, and attached a large amount of property; the writ being issued by a clerk who had usually issued such writs, but, as was afterwards decided, without authority. B. brought an action of trespass against A. and obtained judgment. A. filed a bill to enjoin the judgment. Held, he was not entitled to relief.[2]

§ 39. A defendant in chancery, who resists the complainant's injunction, on the ground of a judgment against the complainant at law, must exhibit the record, that the court may see that the form of action prosecuted admitted the defence.[3]

§ 40. Equity will not perpetually enjoin a judgment, upon the ground that the officer's return as to the service was false.[4](a) So a bill for an injunction did not allege fraud on the part of the plaintiff in the judgment, but merely that the deputy sheriff served the summons out of his bailiwick, and, being informed of the defendant's residence out of his bailiwick, failed to make the return of *non est* as he had promised to do. The bill also admitted indebtedness for a part of the amount, but did not state how much, nor offer to pay it. Held, no sufficient ground of injunction.[5] So (in California) a judgment by default will not be enjoined, on the ground that the sheriff's return on the summons does not show the place in which service was made, where it is proved on the hearing, that the defendant was served in a certain county in the State more than forty days before the entry

[1] Bank of Tennessee *v.* Patterson, 8 Humph. 363.
[2] Stetson *v.* Goldsmith, 31 Ala. 649.
[3] Wiliams *v.* Caplinger, 6 Humph. 257.
[4] Walker *v.* Robbins, 14 How. 584.
[5] Gardner *v.* Jenkins, 14 Md. 58.

(a) As to the evidence on which it was held that service must be considered good, and such as to preclude relief from the judgment, see Windwart *v.* Allen, 13 Md. 196.

of his default.[1] But equity will enjoin the judgment in a suit where the plaintiff is a sheriff and serves his own writ.[2] So, where no process was executed upon a defendant in an action at law, and he did not appear or make defence, and judgment went against him, of which he had no notice until long after its rendition; held, he was entitled to an injunction against the judgment, whether he could have made a valid defence or not.[3] And a judgment obtained by means of a false return, and without any notice to the defendant, may be relieved against. Thus where it was uncertain whether the notice was served at all, and, if it was, it appeared to have been served in such a manner, by reading it to the defendant, who was a laboring man and unacquainted with such matters, and at the same time handing to him the declaration in another suit, as would naturally mislead him; and it appeared that he had a good defence to the action: an injunction against the judgment was ordered.[4]

§ 41. That a debt was divided, and suit brought on each portion in a justice's court, which would have no jurisdiction over one suit for the whole amount; is no reason for enjoining the judgment in one suit, unless it also appears that by means of the division the defendant was deprived of some right or remedy, and that he had not consented to the division.[5]

§ 42. Questions often arise, in reference to *the precise mode* in which the judgment sought to be enjoined was rendered.

§ 42 *a.* Equity will relieve against a judgment obtained on *default*, by the fraud of the plaintiff.[6] So, where there is no service and a default, the judgment will be relieved against in equity, if the merits require it.[7] So where, by

---

[1] Pico *v.* Sunol, 6 Cal. 294.
[2] Knott *v.* Jarboe, 1 Met. (Ky.) 504.
[3] Bell *v.* Williams, 1 Head, 229.

[4] Owens *v.* Ranstead, 22 Ill. 161.
[5] Pryor *v.* Emerson, 22 Tex. 162.
[6] Porter *v.* Moffet, 1 Morris, 108.
[7] Lucas *v.* Waller, 1 Morris, 303.

the neglect of an attorney of good reputation, a party has been defaulted; if he, immediately upon discovering the default, apply for redress, he is not guilty of laches, and (certainly where the attorney is insolvent) he will be relieved from the default.[1]   But where a defendant, whose counsel was elected to the bench, heard the court announce at the next term, that no case in which he had been employed would be heard, and went away and was defaulted; held, in the absence of any substantial defence, he was not entitled to an injunction.[2]   So a party, against whom a judgment at law is rendered by default, cannot obtain relief against it in equity, upon the ground that his attorney failed to appear for him, and appeared for the opposite party; when he had only requested the attorney to attend to any and all business for him, and had not mentioned any particular case.[3]   Nor where a defendant misnamed in the process is in court when judgment is rendered against him by default, and fails to defend by advice of his counsel.[4]   Nor where one, not duly served with process, suffers judgment by default, and, on the execution of a writ of inquiry at a subsequent term, appears, defends, submits evidence to the jury, makes various motions, files a bill of exceptions, and appeals, but makes no proper attempt to have the judgment by default set aside.   His remedy was perfect at law.[5]

§ 43. A judgment may also have been rendered by *confession.*

§ 44. In order to induce a court of equity to declare a judgment confessed for a certain amount to be merely collateral security for whatever sum might be found due, they must be satisfied beyond a reasonable doubt that such was the agreement; but they will then enjoin the judgment, on

---

[1] Huebsch v. Baker, 7 Wis. 542.
[2] Cardin v. Jones, 23 Geo. 175.
[3] Watts v. Gayle, 20 Ala. 817.

[4] Graham v. Roberts, 1 Head, 56.
[5] Ibid.

12

the ground that to enforce it would be a fraud[1] So A. held a note against B., and signed the following indorsement: "If B. does not bring a suit against C., I am not to demand the within." B. confessed judgment at law, reserving equity, and in his bill charged, that the note was given for services to be rendered in prosecuting a *caveat*, and prayed discovery. A. answered that he did not remember for what suit the note was given. A perpetual injunction was decreed.[2] So, in August, 1844, B. recovered a judgment against A., who was then seized of certain lands. On the 6th of January, 1845, A. conveyed an undivided half of the lands to C. On the 14th of January, 1845, A. confessed a judgment to D., upon which execution was immediately issued, and levied on all the rights of A. On the 19th of August, 1845, execution was issued on B.'s judgment, and levied on all the lands. An injunction was allowed, restraining the sheriff from selling, under the judgment confessed to D., the undivided half which had been conveyed to C. prior to the entry of his judgment. The bill further charged, that the judgment to D. was collusively confessed, and taken for the purpose of defeating the prior judgment, and of protecting A.'s property from his creditors; and prayed that B.'s judgment might be declared the prior lien on all the lands. A demurrer to the bill was overruled.[3] So a *scire facias* on a dormant judgment, obtained during the sickness of the defendant and in the absence of his attorney, by an unauthorized confession of judgment by an inexperienced attorney, upon a note outlawed by the statute of limitations, which had been duly pleaded, is properly restrained by injunction until the complainant can establish the facts alleged in his bill, in which case either the judgment should be decreed satisfied, or the suit to revive it perpetually enjoined.[4]

§ 45. But it will require a very strong case to justify an

[1] Heighler *v.* Savage, &c., 12 Md. 383.
[2] Daveiss *v.* M'Kee, 1 Bibb, 331.
[3] Oakley *v.* Young, 2 Halst. Ch. 453.
[4] Cheek *v.* Taylor, 22 Geo. 127.

injunction upon a judgment rendered by confession on a debt due for more than thirty years, from which no appeal has been taken.[1] So where judgments were rendered on confession before a justice of the peace, no warrants having been issued or served on the defendants; on a bill for injunction to restrain executions, it was held, that relief should be sought at law, by appeal, and not in equity.[2]

§ 46. Where contractors on a railroad agreed with the company to refer all disputes and differences to the engineer of the company, whose decision should be conclusive and without appeal; and the engineer was a stockholder to the amount of ten thousand dollars, which was unknown to the contractors at the time of making the agreement; held, on a bill filed by the contractors, equity might set aside the award, and order an account for their damages by breach of the contract.[3] So where a defendant agreed that the justice should render a conditional judgment against him, and the justice entered an absolute judgment, by confession; held, chancery had jurisdiction to relieve against the judgment.[4]

§ 47. Equity will not grant relief against a decree of the Probate Court, because it was rendered without notice to the parties, when the rendition of the decree was suspended by consent, until the opinion of the Supreme Court in another case between the same parties "could be had," and the decree was not rendered until after such opinion had been obtained.[5]

§ 48. Where an illegal contract has been partially performed, and the party who has received the benefit of such performance gives a judgment for the value, equity will not relieve him from the judgment, although the amount could

[1] Gravely v. Southerland, 29 Geo. 335.
[2] Brumbaugh v. Schnebly, 2 Md. 320.
[3] Milnor v. Georgia, &c., 4 Geo. 385.
[4] Gwinn v. Newton, 1 Humph. 710.
[5] Stein v. Burden, 30 Ala. 270.

not have been recovered at law, on account of the illegality.[1]

§ 49. An equitable jurisdiction is exercised over judgments entered by confession, upon *bonds and warrants of attorney*, by courts of law.[2] But where a debtor who is under arrest gives to the creditor, as·the consideration for his discharge, a warrant of attorney for the whole amount of the debt, together with the sums due on other accounts; his being under arrest will not be a ground for relief, if the arrangement has been entered into by him deliberately, advisedly, and with full knowledge of the circumstances. So, although one of the debts is barred by the statute of limitations.[3]

§ 50. A bill for relief against a judgment at law, rendered by default, alleging that the writ was not served upon the complainant, that an attorney *entered his appearance* for him without his knowledge, and that judgment was rendered without the knowledge of the attorney, and showing a good defence at law, the allegations being wholly unsupported by proof, was dismissed, and the injunction dissolved.[4] So where a regular attorney of the court appears and answers for the defendant in a suit at law, a judgment recovered by the plaintiff will not be vacated nor execution enjoined, though the attorney appeared without authority, unless it is shown that the attorney is not of sufficient ability to answer for the damages caused by his unauthorized appearance, or there has been collusion between him and the plaintiff in the suit at law.[5]

§ 51. Equity will not relieve against a judgment, where the plaintiff has given a *forthcoming bond* which was forfeited,

[1] Young v. Beardsley, 11 Paige, 93.
[2] Lake v. Cooke, 15 Ill. 353.
[3] Richards v. Curlewis, 31 Eng. Law and Eq. 419.

[4] Prather v. Prather, 11 Gill & J. 110. See Cayce v. Powell, 20 Tex. 767.
[5] Bunton r. Lyford, 37 N. H. 512.

although the judgment on the bond was erroneous, the party having a remedy for the error at law.[1]

§ 52. Equity will not re-examine and readjust settlements made by *compromise* judgments in courts of law having jurisdiction of the subject-matter, unless in case of fraud, accident, or mistake.[2]

§ 53. A bill will not lie to enjoin a judgment upon an *award*, upon the ground that the arbitrators received hearsay evidence, and committed other irregularities at the hearing.[3]

§ 54. After a verdict in an inferior court, which has no power to grant a new trial, chancery will grant relief on the ground of *newly discovered evidence*, where the sum in controversy is sufficiently large to bear the expense.[4] And where a bill in equity alleged, that an important fact had been discovered since a former decree, without the negligence of the complainant, that by this fact the decree would be changed, and prayed for general relief and for an injunction against part of the former decree; held, the bill should be considered as one of review, though the record of the former case was not made part of it; and that on the prayer relief would be granted, as in a bill of review.[5]

§ 55. A part of certain property conveyed by a deed in trust was sold on execution against the grantor, the sheriff taking a bond of indemnity from the judgment creditor. Suit was afterwards brought upon the bond, in the name of the sheriff, for the benefit of the trustee in the bond. The defence was set up, of fraud in the deed, but a verdict was recovered and judgment rendered for the plaintiff. The defendant then files a bill in equity, on the ground of newly-

---

[1] Robb v. Halsey, 11 S. & M. 140.
[2] Hahn v. Hart, 12 B. Mon. 426.
[3] Hunt v. Coachman, 6 Rich. Eq. 286.
[4] Floyd v. Jayne, 6 John. Ch. 479.
[5] Basye v. Beard, 12 B. Mon. 581.

discovered evidence, proving the fraud as to some of the debts secured, but not disputing the others, and prays for an injunction to the judgment, a new trial, and general relief. Held, not a ground of new trial, which would not probably afford the proper relief, but that the court would retain the cause, and allow the plaintiff to impeach the deed, notwithstanding the defence at law; that he was entitled to an account of the trust subject, and to have it properly disposed of among the parties in interest; and that, as the deed purported to indemnify one of the parties, as to whom the deed was alleged to be fraudulent, as surety of the grantor for certain debts due to specified creditors, these creditors, as well as those directly secured, and whose debts were not questioned, were necessary parties.[1]

§ 56. In a bill to enjoin a judgment on the ground of newly-discovered evidence, such evidence should be set forth.[2] It must not be *cumulative*.[3] And it has been sometimes held that equity will not interfere, except in a case of fraud, in behalf of either party, upon the ground of testimony being discovered since the trial, which was unknown to the party at the time of the trial, and which would have materially varied the result.[4] Such relief will not be granted for newly-discovered evidence of payment, where the plaintiff neglected to plead the payment, and to produce witnesses of admissions, by the defendant, of the payment; though the full extent of their testimony was not known to the plaintiff, who, it appeared, had made no inquiry.[5]

§ 57. Where the execution of a judgment has been enjoined, and the defendant admits, upon being interrogated, a *partial payment*, the injunction should be perpetuated for this amount, and dissolved for the remainder.[6] So where

[1] Billups v. Sears, 5 Gratt. 31.
[2] Miller v. McGuire, 1 Morris, 150.
[3] Pemberton v. Kirk, 4 Ired. Eq. 178.
[4] Powell v. Watson, 6 Ired. Eq. 94.
[5] Floyd v. Jayne, 6 John. Ch. 479.
[6] Perry v. Kearney, 14 La. An. 400; Tapp v. Beverley, 1 Leigh, 80.

part of the judgment appears from the petition to be just, an injunction as to the whole should be reversed.[1] So where, in reducing to writing a contract for the sale of land and the crops thereon, valued at $100 in the contract, the undertaking of the seller to put the purchaser in possession of the crops was omitted by mistake, and he did not thus put him in possession, but recovered judgment for the whole amount of the purchase-money; held, the judgment should be enjoined for $100.[2] So where foreigners were sued, in an action which gave them no notice of the particular claim, and new counts were filed at the trial, covering a claim not before embraced in the declaration, and a verdict was given for the plaintiff, which could not have been obtained upon facts, which the defendants would have supplied on having notice; held, a case of surprise, and that an injunction should issue as to so much of the verdict as was clearly wrong, and which would not have been given but for the surprise.[3] So where the parties to a suit submit to arbitration, and an award is made that the defendant pay a certain sum, with costs, which he does, for the debt, by note with security, but fails to pay the costs, and the plaintiff recovers judgment for the whole debt, the defendant not appearing and pleading; equity will relieve on the ground of surprise.[4] So A., having a judgment against B., agreed to receive from the trustee of B. the amount of the judgment, without interest, in satisfaction, and a part was accordingly paid. A. afterward took out execution for the whole amount. Held, on a bill by the trustee, that he might have the interest enjoined, or his obligation to pay the judgment cancelled.[5] So in an action at law on accounts, the defendants applied for an injunction to the judgment. Held, that a mistake and miscalculation on the part of the jury, which, if discovered in time, would have furnished good grounds for a new trial, entitled the appellant to relief in equity, when ascer-

---

[1] Crisswell v. Bledsoe, 22 Tex. 658.
[2] Booth v. Kesler, 6 Gratt. 350.
[3] Bell v. Cunningham, 1 Sumn. 89.
[4] Sneed v. Town, 4 Eng. 535.
[5] Thomas v. Brashear, 4 Monr. 65.

tained by after-discovered testimony.[1] Held, also, that the
relief should be by reference to a commissioner to ascertain
the real amount due.[2] So where a judgment debtor delivered
to the creditor a bill of exchange, to be credited on the judgment when collected; on a bill to enjoin the judgment, held,
the creditor must credit the bill upon the judgment, or
deliver it back to the debtor.[3] So where a justice's judgment was enjoined upon proof that it was had without service; upon admission of the debt, the court, having acquired
jurisdiction, continued the injunction as to the justice's costs,
but gave judgment to the respondent for the debt.[4] But
where one ground of injunction against a judgment was, that
the plaintiff in the suit enjoined had received payment of a
large part of the debt, in consideration of which he had
agreed to dismiss the suit at his own cost, and that he had
not done so, but had taken judgment for the whole amount;
held, it did not appear that he was seeking to enforce payment without giving the proper credits, and, if he was, the
complainant could not enjoin the whole judgment because of
the payment of a part.[5]

§ 58. When the amount of the *fi. fa.* exceeds that of the
judgment, the right to enjoin is limited to the excess.[6]

§ 59. Equity will grant relief against a judgment obtained
by fraud, to the extent of the injury, and, if it applies only
to part of the land, relief will be granted to that extent.[7]

§ 60. Where, on relieving against a judgment, there is no
means of ascertaining how far it is correct, but only that
it is unconscionable to some extent, it will be set aside *in
toto.*[8]

[1] Rust v. Ware, 6 Gratt. 50.
[2] Ibid.
[3] Newman v. Meek, 1 S. & M. Ch.
331.
[4] Willis v. Gordon, 22 Tex. 241.
[5] Alexander v. Baylor, 20 Tex.
560.

[6] Barrow v. Robichaux, 14 La. An.
207.
[7] Dunlap v. Stetson, 4 Mas. 349.
[8] McRae v. Woods, 2 Wash. Va.
80.

§ 61. Equity has, under ordinary circumstances, no power to reduce an assessment of damages by a jury in an action of covenant, or to enjoin the collection of any part thereof.[1]

§ 62. A bill, to enjoin a judgment on account of usury, must tender the amount equitably due.[2] And an injunction, on the ground that the defendant is entitled to a credit for part of the judgment, should be with a proviso, that the plaintiff may proceed by execution to collect the balance.[3]

§ 63. *Payment* may be set up as the ground for an injunction. As where a payment is made in confidence that it will be credited, and the credit is not given, but judgment taken for the whole amount.[4] So, where prior judgments have been paid, and yet the holder threatens to levy on land, the holder of a junior judgment may have this cloud on the title removed by injunction.[5] Judge Story says: "One of the plainest cases, which can be put, of the propriety of granting an injunction to a judgment at law, is, where it has been in fact satisfied, and yet the judgment creditor attempts to set it up, and enforce it, either against the judgment debtor or against some person claiming under him who is thereby injured in property or rights. In such cases a court of law would often be exceedingly embarrassed in giving the proper redress if it could give it at all. But courts of equity deal with it at once, and apply the most complete remedial relief.[6] Suppose a party is sued at law for a debt of long standing; and a judgment is obtained against him for the amount although he has actually paid it, but he is unable, after due search, to find a receipt or release which would establish the fact; and then, after judgment, the paper is unexpectedly found, either in his own possession or in that of a third person. At law there would be no redress under such circumstances. The judgment would be conclusive. But a

[1] Reed v. Clarke, 4 Monr. 18.
[2] Shelton v. Gill, 11 Ohio, 417.
[3] Hodges v. Planters', &c., 7 Gill & J. 306.
[4] Dickenson v. M'Dermott, 13 Tex. 248.
[5] Shaw v. Dwight, 16 Barb. 536.
[6] 2 Story's Eq. 194, sect. 876.

court of equity would in such a case afford relief by a perpetual injunction of the judgment."[1]   Thus, after a mandate
from the Supreme Court of the United States, ordering the
Circuit Court to enter judgment for the plaintiff, the defendant moved the Circuit Court for leave to file a plea *puis
darrein continuance* that he had paid the whole amount in
question under process from the State courts, but the court
refused, on the ground that they could do nothing but carry
out the mandate of the Supreme Court.   Held, such defendant was entitled to an injunction to stay proceedings at law
under the judgment of the Circuit Court.[2]   So (in Maryland)
when a decree of the Court of Appeals has been satisfied,
either by a payment in money, or money's equivalent, but
the party is proceeding to enforce it by execution; equity
may and is bound to prevent it by injunction.[3]

§ 64. But it is no ground for relief from a judgment, that
a payment on a bond was not indorsed on the bond. Such
defence might have been made at law.[4]   Nor that the party
did not prove, on the trial, payments which he alleges he
had made, unless he shows some fraud or circumvention, to
prevent his making the proof.[5]   So, it is held, the defendant
in a judgment has a full and complete remedy at law, by
supersedeas, to obtain credit for a part payment of the judgment, and consequently such payment constitutes no ground
for equitable relief.[6]   So equity will not interfere with a
judgment, recovered after a settlement between the parties,
prior to the commencement of suit. The remedy is by
appeal or error.[7]   So, in Texas, the statute (Hart. Digest,
Art. 1599) manifestly has no application to an injunction
to stay execution, for causes which have arisen subsequent
to rendition of the judgment. As that the debtor had placed
claims in the hands of the creditor's attorney, to be collected

[1] 2 Story's Eq. 196, sect. 879.
[2] Humphreys v. Leggett, 9 How.
297.
[3] M'Clellan v. Crook, 4 Md. Ch.
Decis. 398.

[4] Harnsbarger v. Kinney, 13 Gratt.
511.
[5] Deaver v. Erwin, 7 Ired. Eq. 250.
[6] Perrine v. Carlisle, 19 Ala. 686.
[7] Dunn v. Fish, 8 Black. 407.

and applied on the execution, and that large sums had been collected on these claims. These facts do not show payment.[1]

§ 65. Where the defendant in a judgment pays the amount to the plaintiff, after notice of an assignment of the judgment, equity will not relieve him from an execution thereon for the benefit of the assignee.[2] But where an agent prosecuted a suit in favor of his principal to judgment, and indorsed upon the execution that a part of it was for his own benefit; and, before the execution was placed in the hands of the sheriff, the defendant paid the whole amount to the principal, and took his receipt in full discharge: held, equity would enjoin all further proceedings on the execution.[3]

§ 66. On a bill, filed by sureties in a bond given for the purchase-money of land, to have a judgment thereon against them entered satisfied, or perpetually enjoined; in granting the prayer of the bill, the court must vacate the sale of the land; and, to do this, the purchaser or his heirs must be parties to the bill.[4]

§ 66 a. Where the plaintiff has enjoined the execution of a judgment, alleging that it had been paid, and praying that it should be decreed to have been satisfied; it is error to render a final judgment, on overruling the defendant's motion to dissolve the injunction. The conservatory process of injunction, in such a case, is separate from the principal demand, which should be put at issue regularly, before final judgment.[5]

§ 67. Where the petitioner avers that an execution had been issued "for the amount of the judgment and costs," and that certain payments had been made thereon, but not, dis-

---

[1] Williams v. Bradbury, 9 Tex. 487.
[2] Holland v. Dale, Minor, 265.
[3] Crawford v. Thurmond, 3 Leigh, 85.
[4] Buchanan v. Torrance, 11 Gill & J. 342.
[5] Knox v. Coroner, 13 La. An. 88.

tinctly, that they had not been credited, a general demurrer cannot be sustained.[1]

§ 68. Where creditors, after the debt has been paid to them, seek to enforce a judgment against a receiptor of the property attached, equity, to prevent circuity of action, will enjoin the suit. The judgment against the receiptor, being merely collateral to the debt, is in the nature of a penalty; and if payments were made prior to that judgment, and not allowed for in making it up, equity will restrict the creditor to the collection of the balance. Where it is obvious that the creditors, after having obtained judgment against the receiptor for the full amount of the debt, making no allowance for payments, received from the receiptor the balance actually due to them upon the debt, and, by words and actions, gave him to understand that they considered the judgment against him paid, with a mere view of keeping him along until his remedy by petition for a new trial should be gone by lapse of time, and then pursuing him for the balance appearing due upon the judgment against him; there can be little doubt that equity may enjoin the judgment, upon the mere ground of fraud.[2]

§ 69. Equity will relieve against the suing out or levy of execution upon a judgment enjoined, which has been discharged by proceedings in bankruptcy.[3] (See *Bankruptcy*.) But where a defendant filed a bill in equity to set aside a judgment, alleging that the plaintiff, after a default at the first term, fraudulently permitted the case to be continued to the second, third, and fourth terms, and at the fifth term took his judgment, the defendant having filed no plea or answer, notwithstanding he had obtained a discharge in bankruptcy, subsequent to the first term, supposing judgment had been rendered at that term; held, on demurrer to the bill, that the demurrer only admitted the facts alleged,

[1] Williams *v.* Bradbury, 9 Tex. 487.
[2] Paddock *v.* Palmer, 19 Vt. 581.
[3] Peatross *v.* McLaughlin, 6 Gratt. 64.

and not the fraud; and that those facts did not constitute a fraud in the procurement of the judgment, so as to authorize a court of equity to set it aside.[1]

§ 69 *a.* Analogous to payment, as a defence, is that of *set-off.*

§ 70. The allegations in a bill in equity, for an injunction against a judgment, that the defendant is indebted to the complainant, that he is insolvent, and that the demand sought to be enforced at law is satisfied, are sufficient to give the court jurisdiction.[2] So A. obtained two judgments against the administrators of B., which were unsatisfied. Commissioners were appointed to sell the real estate of B. on credit, and to pay over the proceeds to the administrators. A. purchased at the sale, giving his notes in payment. Held, that A. might enjoin a judgment on the notes, and set off the judgments held by him against it, if it did not appear by the answer that there were any demands against the estate entitled to precedence; and that it was not necessary for A. to aver that fact in his bill.[3]

§ 71. Where G., and L. his wife, who was executrix of a will by which she was required to educate and support the wife of M. during her minority, boarded M.'s wife under an agreement not to charge her for such board, and afterwards obtained judgment in attachment for such board, and at the time of the attachment had funds in their hands belonging to M. in the right of his wife, more than enough to satisfy the judgment; it was held that M. was entitled to be relieved against the judgment; and that, independent of the agreement, if G. and his wife had funds enough in their hands to pay the board of M.'s wife, which could properly be applied to such payment, the court would compel such an appropriation in satisfaction of the judgment.[4]

[1] Bellamy v. Woodson, 4 Geo. 175.
[2] Bettison v. Jennings, 3 Eng. 287.
[3] Dickinson v. Chism, 2 Monr. 144.
[4] Moore v. Gamble, 1 Stockt. 246.

§ 72. But a party going into equity to enjoin a judgment on the ground of offsets, must show as strong a claim to be paid the offsets as if he were suing on them in law or equity.[1] And a defendant in an action at law, having a set-off available either at law or in equity, but neglecting to plead it, cannot afterwards make it a ground of relief in equity from the judgment against him in such action, without showing sufficient excuse for his neglect. That he was advised the law court had no jurisdiction of the set-off, is no such excuse.[2] So where an answer admitted, that the jury did not allow a credit to which the complainant was entitled, but it appeared upon calculation, upon the data on which the verdict was made, that the credit was allowed, a decree enjoining the amount was reversed.[3] So an injunction was refused, where a party was guilty of negligence in omitting to file a set-off, though he alleged sickness in his family and the absence of his counsel; there having been no motion for a continuance, nor affidavit of grounds therefor.[4] And where, in an action at law, the defendant was prevented by unavoidable accident from setting up independent offsets liable to be enforced at law, he cannot enjoin the judgment and set up his offsets against it, but must pursue his remedy at law. And if his offsets are only recoverable in equity, he cannot enjoin the judgment and avail himself of his claims against it.[5] So where a bill was filed to have an execution enjoined, on the ground that the plaintiff in execution was insolvent, and, at the time he recovered his judgment, was indebted to the defendant in execution, and the complainant sought to have this indebtedness set off against the execution; held, the bill must be dismissed for want of equity.[6] So A. obtained a judgment against B. for $1,200, and subsequently B. purchased and took a written assignment of two judgments against A. for $1,384, and filed his bill to have them set off

[1] Walker v. Ayres, 1 Clarke, 449.
[2] Pearce v. Winter, &c., 32 Ala. 68.
[3] Pogue v. Shotwell, 2 Dana, 281.
[4] Griffith v. Thompson, 4 Gratt. 147.
[5] Hudson v. Kline, 9 Gratt. 379.
[6] Rives v. Rives, 7 Rich. Eq. 353.

as a satisfaction of A.'s judgment. Held, according to the Georgia judiciary act of 1799, it should affirmatively appear that there were no other judgment liens upon the defendant's property, before equity would interfere and decree satisfaction of a particular judgment therefrom; and that the complainant had an ample and adequate remedy at law, to obtain satisfaction of his judgments out of the property of the defendant.[1] So A. recovered a judgment against B., in a justice's court, on a store account for $75. B., alleging that A. was indebted to him in the sum of $180 on a promissory note, which he could not have pleaded in offset, in a justice's court, applied for an injunction to restrain him from levying his execution until he could recover a judgment on the note, when it could be set off. Held, the petition did not state sufficient cause for an injunction, but insolvency or special circumstances of hardship should appear. Also, that the petitioner should have brought suit on the note, and in his petition have prayed an injunction. One suit then would have sufficed.[2]

§ 73. So equity cannot restrain the execution of a judgment recovered by a non-resident plaintiff, merely because the defendant has a cross action at law growing out of the same transaction, but which he cannot prosecute in the courts of the State as long as the plaintiff keeps out of it.[3]

§ 74. Where a judgment at law is enjoined, and an account directed to be taken, the commissioner ought not to give the plaintiff at law credit for claims not exhibited to the jury, nor mentioned in the answer, and which are prior in date to the commencement of the suit at law.[4]

§ 75. It has already been stated, that a trial at law and a judgment founded thereon cannot be revised by a court of

[1] Wellborn v. Bonner, 9 Geo. 82.
[2] Brady v. Hancock, 17 Tex. 361.
[3] Beall v. Brown, 7 Md. 393.
[4] Lipscomb v. Winston, 1 Hen. & M. 453.

equity, unless there are special equitable reasons for such interference. The general rule is applied, of *res judicata* and *estoppel*. It is said, "There are cases cognizable at law, and also in equity, and of which cognizance cannot be effectually taken at law, and therefore equity does sometimes interfere; so, where a verdict has been obtained by fraud, or where a party has possessed himself, improperly, of something, by means of which he has an unconscientious advantage at law, which equity will either put out of the way or restrain him from using: but without circumstances of that kind, I do not know that equity ever does interfere to grant a trial of a matter which has already been discussed in a court of law, a matter capable of being discussed there, and one which the court of law had full jurisdiction."[1] And, in conformity with these views, an injunction will not be maintained in arrest of an execution, on grounds that might have been pleaded in defence before judgment.[2] Where a defence has been made to a suit at law, the defendant has elected his tribunal; and, from that time, he must make his entire defence in that court, if such as may be heard by it.[3] Thus, in case of a bill for an injunction against a judgment and a new trial, alleging the same facts pleaded in answer to the suit at law; held, the judgment was conclusive, and the bill was dismissed.[4] So when a cause, exclusively of legal jurisdiction, has been tried at law, and a judgment rendered against the defendant, and there was no fraud or concealment by the plaintiff at law, chancery has no jurisdiction to interfere.[4] So, as we have already seen in another connection, the execution of a judgment cannot be enjoined on grounds which *might have been* urged as a defence to the original action.[6] So where a party first submits to try at law, with a knowledge of the facts upon which he rests in support of his title, and a verdict is rendered against him; he cannot come into

[1] Per Lord Redesdale, Bateman v. Willoe, 1 Sch. & Lef. 201.
[2] McRae v. Purvis, 12 La. An. 85.
[3] Dickson v. Richardson, 15 Ark. 114.
[4] Forsythe v. McCreight, 10 Rich. Eq. 308; Yongue v. Billups, 23 Miss. 407.
[5] White v. Cahal, 2 Swan, 550.
[6] Minor v. Stone, 1 La. An. 283.

equity and file his bill for discovery and relief, and enjoin the operation of the verdict, until he can have another trial in equity in attempting to perfect his title.[1]

§ 76. Of four obligors, joint and several, A. and B. were sued separately at law. They defended the actions on the ground of fraud and misrepresentation, but judgments were recovered against them. The four then paid up the amount; and C. and D. assigned their interest to A. and B., who then filed their bill against the obligee, seeking relief on the same ground on which the actions at law had been defended, and at the trial used C. as a witness. Held, they were not entitled to relief.[2] So equity will not restrain the execution of a judgment upon a contract, the consideration of which was illegal, when the plaintiff knew of the illegality, and might have set it up in defence; and, after the recovery, executed a bond for the payment of the judgment, which operated as a second judgment against him.[3] So where a defendant sets up a former recovery in defence, and succeeds, he is estopped afterwards, in an action against him upon the former judgment, to deny its validity; and, on a bill by him to enjoin the judgment rendered upon the former judgment, he cannot deny the validity of the judgments in his favor. And it makes no difference, that the plaintiffs replied *nul tiel record*, as the reply was appropriate, and necessary to elicit the opinion of the court on the effect of the record. Nor that the former recovery was had in a different State from that in which the subsequent suit is brought.[4]

§ 77. So *mutual accounts*, if not complicated, do not furnish ground for overhauling a judgment at law, more especially when they have been submitted to, and passed upon by the court.[5] So a defendant, who has demurred to the

---

[1] Donaldson *v.* Kendall, 2 Geo. Decis. 227.
[2] Campbell *v.* Briggs, 4 Rich. Eq. 370.
[3] Sample *v.* Barnes, 14 How. 70.
[4] Lucas *v.* Bank, &c., 2 Stew. 280.
[5] Powell *v.* Stewart, 17 Ala. 719.

13

declaration, will be regarded as having elected to defend at law, and will be precluded from coming into equity for relief, in reference to any matter of defence of which he might have availed himself in a court of law.[1] So, if a defendant at law makes an equitable defence, if it be such as courts of law take cognizance of, he cannot come into chancery for relief, unless unavoidable accident, ignorance of facts, surprise, or fraud, have prevented him from making his defence at law.[2] And a defence cannot be set up in equity which has been fully and fairly tried at law, although it may be the opinion of the court that the defence ought to have been sustained at law.   Thus the allegation, that the judgment was obtained by fraud, was denied by the answer, and not established by proof.   The bill contained no allegation that the complainant was defeated at law by accident or surprise, nor that the proof he offered, upon the question there decided, came to his knowledge after the trial.   Held, a court of law would have refused a new trial, and there was certainly no ground for claiming the interposition of a court of equity.[3]

§ 78. But a matter which could not have been determined at law, in which the interposition of equity is asked, is not within the estoppel of the legal decision.[4]

§ 79. After judgment at law upon a security given for a gaming debt, the defendant may have relief in equity, although he did not resist the suit at law on that ground.[5]

§ 80. The doctrine of estoppel, growing out of concealment or implied fraud, may be applied to invalidate the judgment against which relief is sought.   Thus the complainant in his bill stated, that in January, 1842, A. and B. in consideration of $10,000 conveyed to him a farm; that at the delivery of

---

[1] Arrington v. Washington, 14 Ark. 218.
[2] Burton v. Hynson, 14 Ark. 32; 7 Gill, 189.
[3] Briesch v. McCauley, 7 Gill, 189.
[4] White v. Crew, 16 Geo. 416.
[5] Gough v. Pratt, 9 Md. 526.

the deed he was ignorant that C., the defendant, had a judgment in his favor against A. and B., or that he had a judgment bond against them; that the object of A. and B. in selling the farm was to raise money to pay their creditors, of whom C. was one, and that the money was thus duly applied; that, during the negotiation, C. was acquainted with the whole matter, advised the sale, and knew that the plaintiff was buying, supposing there was no judgment in C.'s favor; but that C., after the agreement, and on the 19th of January, 1842, had a judgment entered upon a judgment bond against A. and B.; that A. and B. had ample real estate remaining after sale to satisfy the judgment, but that C. released the same or large portions thereof from the lien of the judgment; that C. before the sale held two judgments against A. and B., which had been assigned to him, and that, on the 7th of December, 1842, they transferred to him a draft for $6,000, drawn and accepted as collateral security for the payment of such judgments, amounting to about $5,000, C. agreeing under his hand and seal to apply what he should receive on the second draft, first to his two last-mentioned judgments, and to account for the surplus; that C. received on the draft $5,287.52, and did not so apply the same, but raised the amount of the judgment by sales on execution, and now insists on appropriating the money to the judgment entered since the deed to the complainant; and which C. holds against A. and B, leaving older judgments unpaid, and thereby charging the complainant's farm with the amount thereof; and that C. has caused an execution, issued on his said judgment of January 19, 1842, to be levied on the complainant's farm. The bill prayed relief, and an injunction restraining sale on the last-mentioned execution; and the injunction was allowed.[1] So A., while a *feme sole*, became the owner of a bond and warrant of attorney, upon which judgment had been entered up, which the plaintiff, B., had given to secure £1,200, and she repeatedly

---

[1] Van Mater v. Holmes, 2 Halst. Ch. 575.

promised not to enforce them, upon which promise B. contracted irrevocable engagements. A., after her marriage, jointly with her husband, took proceedings at law to enforce these securities. Upon a bill filed by him, the court granted a perpetual injunction, and directed satisfaction to be entered upon the judgment, with costs.[1]

§ 81. With reference to the *pleadings* in cases of this nature; chancery will not restrain a judgment upon a bill in which all the material facts are charged upon information and belief only, without any allegation as to whence the information was derived, or any affidavit connected with the bill.[2] Nor will equity enjoin a judgment at law and grant a new trial, unless the complainant's bill sets forth distinctly his causes of grievance.[3] The plaintiff must state the cause of his not defending at law, where he had a legal defence,[4] more especially in a case which is, in general, exclusively cognizable at law.[5] And a court of chancery will not grant relief so readily against a judgment in attachment to an *absconding*, as to an *absent* or *non-resident* debtor; a bill should therefore state in which of these characters the attachment was taken out against the defendant.[6] So in a bill for relief against a judgment, on the ground that the defendant was prevented from defending at law by fraud or accident, the matter of fraud or accident must be set forth with certainty and precision, and it must also be alleged, that the fraud or accident is unmixed with any negligence on the part of the complainant.[7] And allegations, that a judgment was obtained *through fraud and other ill practices*, are too general to authorize the arrest of its execution.[8]

[1] Money v. Jordan, 11 Eng. Law and Eq. 182.
[2] Williams v. Lockwood, 1 Clark, 172.
[3] Gamble v. Campbell, 6 Florida, 347.
[4] Yancy v. Fenwick, 4 Hen. & M. 423.
[5] Dilly v. Barnard, 8 Gill & J. 170.
[6] Moore v. Gamble, 1 Stockt. 246.
[7] French v. Garner, 7 Port. 549.
[8] Brooks v. Williams, 13 La. An. 374.

§ 82. An injunction cannot stand based on a written agreement alleged to be lost, where the bill does not allege that the party in whose custody it was placed has been asked to produce it, nor that its contents can be proved, and where it appears that the party who executed it is dead, and its existence and all transactions concerning it are fully denied by the answer.[1]

§ 83. If a bill of injunction, to stay proceedings on a judgment, charge the plaintiff at law with having failed to do an act on which the equity of his claim depends, and in his answer he take no notice of that allegation; the court, on the hearing, will consider this an admission that he has not done the act in question, and will decree against him without any exception to the answer, or any interlocutory order, taking the bill for confessed in part.[2]

§ 84. On a bill for injunction against a judgment on a bond given in payment for a mare, alleging the warranty to be false, and an agreement for delay, the answer contained a positive denial, and was disproved by but one witness. Held, that the complainant's remedy was properly at law, and that the bill must be dismissed.[3]

§ 85. Where a bill for relief from a judgment at law alleged, as a reason for not making a defence, that the plaintiff was deceived by his attorney as to the time of trial; held, this fact must be proved, although not answered, or denied by the answer.[4]

§ 86. All the *parties* to a decree, the execution of which is sought to be enjoined, must be made parties to the injunction bill.[5] The plaintiff in the judgment enjoined is a neces-

---

[1] Kent v. De Baun, 1 Beasl. 220.
[2] Page v. Winston, 2 Munf. 298.
[3] Hardwick v. Forbes, 1 Bibb, 212.
[4] Cowan v. Price, 1 Bibb, 173.
[5] Hendrick v. Robinson, 7 Dana, 165.

sary party.'(a)   So, to a bill by a purchaser of land from a
judgment debtor, to enjoin the judgment creditor from subjecting the land to his judgment, the debtor is a necessary
party.[2]   So, to a bill for relief, from a judgment on a note
against the maker, in favor of an assignee of the note, the
payee is a necessary party.[3]   So the assignee of a judgment
is a necessary party to a bill, to perpetually stay proceedings
thereon for equities existing between the parties previous to
the assignment.[4]   But a surety need not be made party to a
bill by the principal, for an injunction against a judgment.[5]
Nor a sheriff, to a bill brought to enjoin the execution of
legal process.[6]   The clerk and sheriff are not proper parties to a bill for an injunction to stay execution.[7]

§ 87.   The distinction is made, that no person can enjoin a
judgment at law, to which he is not a party ; but, if he is
aggrieved by the proceedings thereon, he should pray for
an injunction to the execution.[8]   Thus A. bought railroad
ties of B., and sold them to C., who mixed them with other
ties used on the track.   B. gave notice to C. that the ties were
his, and then C. refused to pay A. for them.   A. brought a
suit against C., and recovered judgment for the value of the
ties.   B. then brought a suit in chancery, and alleged fraud
in A., and the court enjoined C. from paying the judgment
in favor of A., and ordered the sheriff to collect it for the

[1] Daniel v. Hannegan, 5 J. J.
Marsh. 48.
[2] Scott v. Bennett, 1 Gilm, 646.
[3] Elston v. Blanchard, 2 Scam.
420.
[4] Mumford v. Sprague, 11 Paige,
438.

[5] Bentley v. Gregory, 7 Monr. 368.
[6] Olin v. Hungerford, 10 Ohio,
268.
[7] Edney v. King, 4 Ired. Eq. 465.
[8] Jordan v. Williams, 3 Rand.
501.

(a). A. offers for probate a paper as the will of B., in which he is made
executor and a legatee.   Verdict against the will.   A bill in equity is filed
by C., to set aside this verdict, and to be allowed to prove, as the will of
B., all that part of the paper in which A. has no interest, alleging that
the verdict was fraudulent and void.   A. was not made a party.   Held,
there was no equity in the bill.   Barksdale v. Brown, 16 Geo. 95.

benefit of B. Held, that it is not a proper exercise of chancery powers, to interfere with the collection of a judgment, fairly obtained as between the parties to it.[1]

§ 88. It is held that, where property of one is levied on to satisfy the debt of another, a bill of injunction may be maintained by him to restrain the sale, notwithstanding he has also remedies at law, and although the sheriff, by reason of his doubts as to the title to the property, takes an indemnifying bond.[2] But it is also held, that a sale of personal property will not be enjoined at the suit of a third person, claiming the property, but he will be left to his legal remedy.[3] Thus where slaves are levied on, and are claimed by a third person, under a prior sale from the debtor, equity will not restrain the sale, unless the slaves seem to possess some peculiar value, which cannot be recompensed in damages.[4] So (in Louisiana) the vendor cannot enjoin the seizure and sale of the property of his vendee, when it is seized under execution as the property of a third person, on the ground that his obligation in warranty may attach. In such a suit the question of title to property is involved, and it therefore partakes of the nature of a petitory action, which can only be maintained by the party in whom the legal title is vested.[5]

§ 89. An execution in ejectment will not be restrained at the instance of a stranger holding a paramount title; for if his title is good, the judgment does not affect him. It makes no difference, that after judgment the defendant attorned to that title and received possession under it.[6]

§ 90. Where, in a suit between A. and B., judgment was rendered that A. recover against B. a certain sum, and that certain land be sold to satisfy the judgment; another claimant

1 Scott v. Whitlow, 20 Ill. 310.
2 Wilson v. Butler, 3 Munf. 559.
3 Poage v. Bell, 3 Rand. 586. See Bowyer v. Creigh, 3 Rand. 25.
4 Allen v. Freeland, 3 Rand. 170.
5 Kelly v. Wiseman, 14 La. An. 661.
6 Harper v. Hill, 35 Miss. 63.

of the land, in order to obtain an injunction against the sale, must show by what title he claims, or that B. had no title; must state facts showing that the judgment was obtained by fraud and collusion between A. and B.; and must allege that he is in possession, or that he will suffer loss or damage by the sale, and that he was ignorant of the pendency of the suit.[1]

§ 91. A perpetual injunction may be granted to stay proceedings on a judgment at law, obtained in a suit brought in the name of a person not interested, for the purpose of preventing a defence, which the defendant had against the real plaintiff.[2]

§ 92. A judgment debtor who has been garnished may compel the creditor and the garnishee to interplead, and may have the execution enjoined until the interpleader is determined.[3]

§ 93. A defendant in replevin, who has given a forthcoming bond and holds the property, may have an injunction against a sale of the property on an execution against the plaintiff, without alleging that the property is his.[4]

§ 94. One of two co-obligors filed his bill for relief from a judgment, on the ground that the bond was usurious. Held, the other ought to have been made a party, or good reason suggested why he was not.[5]

§ 95. A. and B. confessed a judgment in favor of C. for the amount of a usurious note. A., who was only surety, afterwards filed his bill in his own name alone against C., to be relieved from the judgment on the ground of usury. Held, B. had a common interest with A. in the subject matter of

---

[1] Henderson v. Morrill, 12 Tex. 1.
[2] Greenleaf v. Maher, 2 Wash. C. 44, 393.
[3] Henderson v. Garrett, 35 Miss. 554.

[4] Cooper v. Newell, 36 Miss. 316.
[5] Macey v. Brooks, 4 Bibb. 238.
See Kendrick v. Rice, 16 Tex. 254.

the bill, and should have been made a co-complainant with him, unless some sufficient excuse for not doing so was stated; and if there were a sufficient excuse, he should have been made a party defendant; and no reason being stated in the bill for the non-joinder of B., the bill was dismissed with costs.[1]

§ 96. When several complainants join in a bill, asking relief against a judgment at law, against which some of them show no ground for equitable relief, the bill is demurrable.[2]

§ 97. When an injunction to a judgment is made perpetual at the instance of one defendant, who has been required to give a forthcoming bond, and it appears that there is no equity in favor of the other defendant, on whom the execution was not served; the court should so extend the decree, as to enjoin such defendant from availing himself of the return of the execution and forthcoming bond, to prevent proceedings against him on the original judgment.[3]

§ 98. Equity will not interfere at the suit of one of the defendants in a judgment at law, to compel the plaintiff to collect his judgment out of another defendant, who, by agreement with his co-defendant, had bound himself to pay it.[4]

§ 99. A bill, to restrain a judgment against a co-tenant in common, should expressly charge the insolvency of the defendant.[5]

§ 100. An injunction upon a judgment on a bill of exchange against the acceptor does not enjoin suits against the other parties to the bill.[6]

[1] Boughton v. Allen, 11 Paige, 321.
[2] Tucker v. Holley. 20 Ala. 426.
[3] Poindexter v. Waddy, 6 Munf. 418.
[4] Skinner v. Barney, 19 Ala. 698.
[5] McLendon v. Hooks, 15 Geo. 533.
[6] Bohannon v. Combs, 12 B. Mon. 563.

§ 101. Where there has been a dismissal of a bill for an injunction against a judgment and an *appeal*, it is irregular to apply in the appellate court, pending the appeal, for a new injunction to stay proceedings on the same judgment.[1]

§ 102. When application is made for relief against a judgment, upon facts in relation to which the proof is contradictory, it is in the discretion of the Court of Equity to decide the facts, or to send an issue to a jury.[2] And where an injunction to a judgment was granted, on the ground of improper practices by the plaintiff with the jury, an issue was directed to ascertain the justice of the plaintiff's demand.[3]

§ 103. On a bill to enjoin a judgment, with a prayer for an account, where the defendant goes into the account, it is too late, after the testimony is closed, for the complainant to object that the court has not jurisdiction of the subject matter of the account.[4]

§ 104. Where a creditor has obtained a decree against the estate of his deceased debtor, authorizing a levy upon the estate in whoseever hands it might be, he will not be enjoined from proceeding against a part of the estate in the hands of specific legatees, on the ground that the testator set apart a portion of his estate for payment of his creditors.[5]

§ 105. Where a sheriff levied a *fi. fa.* upon the lands of a deceased debtor, founded on a judgment recovered during the life of the debtor, without a *sci. fa.;* the court refused to relieve, on the ground that there was a remedy at law.[6]

§ 106. A judgment suspended by an injunction may be revived on the death of either party; and the injunction

---

[1] Graves *v.* Graves, 2 Hen. & M. 22.
[2] Key *v.* Knott, 9 Gill & J. 342.
[3] Humphries *v.* Blevins, 1 Overton, 36.
[4] Head *v.* Gervais, Walker, 431.
[5] Maxwell *v.* Maxwell, Charl. R. M. 462.
[6] Perkins *v.* Bullinger, 1 Hay. 367.

operates on the judgment or *scire facias*, prohibiting the issue of execution thereon.[1]

§ 107. One of the most frequent occasions for enjoining a judgment arises in connection with *title to lands*. Thus an order of seizure and sale, to enforce payment of the purchase-money, may be enjoined, on the ground of a deficiency in the quantity of the land sold, which would entitle the vendee to a diminution of the price.[2] So a vendee, with covenants of warranty, against whom a judgment is recovered on the notes given for the purchase-money, and who is afterwards evicted through title paramount, may enjoin the judgment when his vendor is insolvent, and the defence could not have been made at law.[3] More especially upon alleging the vendor's fraudulent representations of title.[4] And a statutory remedy, by *motion*, to supersede an execution, does not deprive the Chancery Court of its original jurisdiction to remove a cloud upon the title to land. Therefore a vendee, whose land has been sold under execution (issued on a judgment recovered against his vendor before his purchase), and bought in by himself, may come into equity to enjoin the collection of his bid, and all further proceedings under the judgment, upon an allegation that the judgment had been paid and satisfied before the issue of the execution.[5] So A. and B., brothers, and owners of adjacent tracts, agreed upon a marked line, transferring twelve acres to B., and afterwards sold the land, with reference to this line, to C., who had previously occupied the twelve acres. C. made improvements, and sold to D., who also made improvements, of all which A. had notice. E., a purchaser with notice from A., who conveyed without legal title, files a bill against the heirs of A.'s vendor, obtains a conveyance, including the twelve acres, and sells to F., who brings a writ

[1] Richardson v. Prince George, 11 Gratt. 190.
[2] Davis v. Millandon, 14 La. An. 868.
[3] Wray v. Furniss, 27 Ala. 471.
[4] Walton v. Bonham, 24 Ala. 513.
[5] Brewer v. The Branch, &c., 24 Ala. 439.

of right against D. for the twelve acres, and recovers judgment. Held, D. was entitled to an injunction against this
judgment.[1] So an elder patentee in possession brought his
bill against the junior patentee, for an injunction to the execution of a writ of *hab. fac.* against his tenants, upon whom
there had been no service of notice, and for a release of the
claim. Held, that the bill might be sustained under the
statute authorizing the holder of the elder grant to try the
merits of the junior patent, though there could be no injunction to such an execution.[2] But an injunction was refused
in the following case: A., who was the equitable owner,
under articles of agreement, of a tract of land, on which a
balance of purchase-money was due to B., his vendor, contracted to sell it to C., and to give him a clear and unincumbered title. For the purpose of carrying out his agreement,
A. procured from B. a deed of the land, and gave his bond
and warrant for the balance of purchase-money, and B., with
knowledge of the contract between A. and C., took from A.
an assignment of a contract between C. and a third person,
as collateral security for the payment of B's. bond. Held,
that these facts gave C. no equity, as against B., to restrain
him from levying on the lands, by virtue of the judgment
entered on the bond.[3] And equity will not relieve against
a judgment for the purchase-money of land, on the ground
that the vendor had not title, where, at the time of sale, the
vendor gave notice that there were doubts as to the validity
of the title, but gave his warranty deed of the land, he being
of undoubted ability to answer the warranty.[4]

§ 108. Equity has jurisdiction to enjoin a sale of land on
execution, on the application of the owner of an equitable
lien prior to the lien of the judgment; and having thus obtained jurisdiction, the court will adjust the rights of all the
parties.[5]

---

[1] Stafford v. Carter, 4 Gratt. 63.
[2] Jones v. Chiles, 3 Monr. 340.
[3] Dent v. Ross, 35 Penn. 337.
[4] Merritt v. Hunt, 4 Ired. Eq. 406.
[5] Parker v. Kelly, 10 S. & M. 184.

§ 109. The withdrawal of a claim to real estate does not affect the right of the claimant subsequently to file a bill, praying for a perpetual injunction against the levy of executions on such estate.[1]

§ 110. Equity cannot restrain a plaintiff, who has obtained judgment, on a writ of forcible entry and detainer, from having restitution of the possession, notwithstanding he is insolvent, and the complainant holds the undisputed legal title.[2]

§ 111. Similar questions arise in connection with the obligation of *suretyship*. Thus equity will, in favor of a surety, enjoin a judgment, suffered by him on the promise of the creditor, that it shall only be used to enforce a settlement with the principal, and will give him relief if the judgment is too large.[3] So where, in consequence of representations made to him by the holder of a note, the surety upon it ceases to maintain a valid ground of defence, proceedings under a judgment so obtained will be enjoined.[4] But in the following case equity refused to interpose: The State Bank held a promissory note against A., upon which B. was surety. A. died insolvent, and, at the time of his death, the State, who owned the State Bank, was indebted to A. as a member of the Senate, and otherwise. The General Assembly appointed an agent to receive the money due to A., and, after defraying his expenses, to pay over the balance to A.'s administrator. The surety notified the auditor to retain in his hands a sufficient sum to pay the note, which he did not do. A judgment was recovered against the surety in an action on the note, and thereupon he filed his bill in equity, praying that the judgment might be perpetually enjoined. Held, that the bill could not be sustained; that the assets of the bank were a fund for the payment of its creditors, and, however it might be in respect to the power of the Legislature to

[1] Cox *v.* Mayor, &c., 17 Geo. 249.
[2] Hamilton *v.* Adams, 15 Ala. 596.
[3] Cage *v.* Cassidy, 23 How. 109.
[4] Dew *v.* Hamilton, 23 Geo. 414.

authorize the agent to receive the money and to apply it to the debts of the deceased before they were judicially determined, it had no right to retain any part of the money due to A., and apply it to the note, although the State was the real owner of the note.[1]

§ 112. The same remedy is applied in cases of *trust*. Thus a bill was filed for an injunction, alleging that A. made a deed of property in trust for himself and wife, remainder in trust for their children; that he was possessed, at the time of making such deed, of property far greater than the amount of his liabilities; that the defendant took a note from A., executed after the enrolment of the deed (of the existence of which deed the defendant was well aware), and has since taken out execution on a judgment on such note, and caused a levy to be made on the property conveyed in trust, alleging that such conveyance was void as to creditors, intending thereby to injure the sale of such property on the execution, to the irreparable injury of the complainants, the wife and child of the grantor. Held, the bill disclosed sufficient ground for injunction. Held, further, that, on appeal from the order granting such injunction, the case must be decided on the bill alone, without reference to the answer.[2]

§ 113. Various points of miscellaneous practice arise in connection with the injunction of judgments.

§ 114. An injunction to stay execution of a judgment at law is a release of errors in the judgment, by the Tennessee Statute of 1801, c. 6; and so, though the complainant afterwards dismiss his bill.[3]

§ 115. Where a statute provides, that a party filing a bill, and obtaining an injunction to stay proceedings upon a judgment, shall release all errors in the judgment, and that

[1] Pike v. The State, &c., 14 Ark. 403.

[2] McCann v. Taylor, 10 Md. 418.
[3] Henly v. Robertson, 4 Yerg. 172.

no injunction shall be granted without such release ; a party obtaining such injunction is estopped to deny his release of errors, the effect of such denial being to work a fraud on the opposite party.[1] In Kentucky, it is irregular to grant an injunction to stay proceedings on a judgment at law without a release of errors, and such injunction may be discharged on motion ; but it is no cause for reversing a decree making an injunction perpetual.[2] But it is held that an injunction, to stay proceedings on a judgment in violation of law, does not operate as a release of errors.[3] And where a bill is filed to enjoin a judgment without release of errors, the Chancellor can do no more than dissolve the injunction on that account; he cannot dismiss the bill for that reason.[4]

§ 116. Where, on a bill to stay proceedings on a judgment, it appears from the report of the commissioner, that the complainant is entitled to a credit which the defendant had not given him, the bill ought not to be dismissed because the complainant had neglected to carry into effect a previous order of the court, referring, by consent, the account to a different commissioner; but, the last order being made on the defendant's motion, and the report being excepted to for want of notice to the complainant, a new account ought to be ordered.[5]

§ 117. In Texas, an application for an injunction, to stay proceedings on a judgment, must be made to the court in which the judgment was rendered, unless made by one who was not a party to the judgment, and whose residence is in a different county.[6]

§ 118. In Missouri, the County Court having jurisdiction to enter a judgment sought to be enjoined, there is no authority to enter into an examination of its merits. An in-

[1] McFarland v. Rogers, 1 Wis. 452. See Dickerson v. Board, &c., 6 Ind. 128.
[2] Bradley v. Lamb, Hardin, 527.
[3] Burge v. Burns, 1 Morris, 287.
[4] Paulding v. Watson, 21 Ala. 279.
[5] Roberts v. Jordans, 4 Munf. 488.
[6] Winnie v. Grayson, 3 Tex. 429.

junction is a release of errors at law, and the proceedings on it are not appellate in their nature.[1]

§ 119. Though the petition prays for an injunction, yet if the matter was neither passed upon by the court below, nor in any way brought to its notice, the Supreme Court will not interfere.[2]

§ 120. Mere mistakes, in a bill of exceptions in chancery, are no ground for enjoining from the prosecution of a writ of error.[3]

§ 121. In a suit brought to enjoin the collection of a justice's judgment, after demurrer, for want of verification of the complaint and of bond filed, overruled, trial by the court, and motion for new trial, overruled; it is not error to allow the affidavit to be made and the bond to be filed, where no steps have been taken by the defendant to obtain a stay of proceedings or to have the complaint set aside.[4]

§ 122. The precept of injunction is often applied directly to *executions* upon judgments at law; and in what has been said with reference to judgments, it has not been found practicable to omit some cases which would seem equally applicable to executions.[5] Thus if a valid judgment at law be iniquitously used, equity will annul what has been improperly done under it.[6] So chancery will grant an injunction to prevent a party's making use of a legal writ of execution for the purpose of vexation and injustice.[7] Or restrain the sale of property illegally taken in execution.[8] So the sheriff may be enjoined from paying over money received from the sale of an estate under executions issued by

---

[1] Price v. Johnson County, 15 Mis. 433.
[2] Barada v. Carondelet, 16 Mis. 323.
[3] Ford v. Weir, 24 Miss. 563.
[4] Denny v. Moore, 13 Ind. 418.
[5] See Strong v. Daniel, 5 Ind. 348;

Shiff v. Carpreth, 14 La. An. 801; Sowle v. Pollard, 14 La. An. 287; Gleises v. McHatton, 14 La. An. 560.
[6] Bissell v. Bozman, 2 Dev. Ch. 160.
[7] Colt v. Cornwell, 2 Root, 109.
[8] Kenyon v. Clarke, 2 R. I. 67.

individual creditors, where it appears that the complainants had a specific lien on the estate, and a preference over individual creditors, and that the claim was pending and undetermined.[1] And it seems an injunction will be granted to stay a sale on execution, though the plaintiff would have a perfect defence at law against the purchaser at such sale.[2] So, in New Hampshire, the Superior Court, or a judge thereof in vacation, may grant an injunction to stay the collection of an execution, either before or after the issuing of a writ of error.[3] So an execution issued on a judgment, the record of which has been destroyed, there being no renewal by substitution, will be restrained by injunction.[4] So an order of seizure and sale, to enforce payment of the purchase-money, may be enjoined for deficiency in the quantity of the land sold, which would entitle the vendee to a diminution of the price.[5] So equity will enjoin the delivery of a deed, where different lots of land have been sold on execution *en masse* at a great sacrifice, though previously offered separately.[6] So, where an insolvent plaintiff was endeavoring, by execution regular on its face, to enforce a judgment recovered in due form in a justice's court, which judgment had been paid and satisfied, and, from the want of a transcript of the record, the county court had no jurisdiction of a motion for relief, or power to issue a judge's order, and the defendant, if compelled to pay, would have no adequate remedy, and no action against the officer; held, equity might on an action in the nature of a bill in equity enjoin further proceedings, set aside the execution, and decree the judgment satisfied.[7] So A., having the legal title to land in trust for B., conveyed to C. in trust for D.; but these trusts did not appear in either A.'s or C.'s deed. When A. conveyed to C., E. had a judgment against C. and D., and there were other judgments against D. C. and D., by writing, reciting the sale to C. and 'the levy of C.'s execution on the land, pro-

---

[1] Read *v.* Dews, Charl. R. M. 355.
[2] Petitt *v.* Shepherd, 5 Paige, 493.
[3] Grant *v.* Lathrop, 3 Fost. 67.
[4] Cyrus *v.* Hicks, 20 Tex. 483.

[5] Davis *v.* Millaudon, 14 La. An. 808.
[6] Ballance *v.* Loomis, 22 Ill. 82.
[7] Mallory *v.* Norton, 21 Barb. 424.

14

mised to pay A. $5000 if they did not return the land to them free from incumbrance ; and it was agreed between B. and D., that one F. should sign this writing, but he did not. The land being about to be sold on E.'s execution, A. and B. filed their bill to enjoin the sale, and for a cancelment of A.'s deed to C. It appeared by the answer and evidence, that the conveyance by A. to C. was for the purpose of having E. levy on the land, and enable C. and D. to take the benefit of the valuation law in order to gain time. D. testified that the conveyance was made to C. because there were other judgments against D. Held, it was not sufficiently proved, that the conveyance to C. was made in order to delay E., and the deed to C. should be cancelled, the title re-vested in A., and E. perpetually enjoined from levying on the land.[1] So A. purchased slaves of B. An execution against B. had been returned fully satisfied ; but shortly after the purchase the return was set aside, and, without notice to A., another execution issued and levied on the property. The court granted a perpetual injunction against proceeding further with the levy.[2] So A., as sheriff, and B., his successor, under subsequent levies of other executions, sold the land of the defendant, of which C. became the purchaser, at the sale made by A., and D. at that made by B. D. paid no money on his bid, but received a deed from B., and D. commenced an action against C. to recover possession. C. and D. compromised the suit, by D.'s executing to C. a quitclaim to the land, and by C.'s confessing a judgment to D. for the amount of his bid at the sale made by B., with the understanding that this judgment was not to be enforced, unless B. should be compelled to pay the amount of the bid to some creditor whose execution was in the hands of B. at the time of the sale, and should call on D. for reimbursement. C. then procured an assignment to himself of the only operative judgment and execution which could claim the money arising from sales, and D. afterwards settled with B. the amount of the bid, by

[1] Taylor v. Strong, 10 S. & M. 63.   [2] Sevier v. McWhorter, 27 Miss. 442.

delivering up to him evidences of debt which he held against him, and caused execution to be issued on the judgment confessed by C., and levied on his property. Held, equity had jurisdiction of a bill filed by C. to restrain D. from enforcing the judgment, and the answer of D., which merely denied that the judgment was confessed "upon the distinct agreement" alleged, was insufficient to authorize a dissolution of the injunction.[1] So a bill in equity will lie to enjoin a sale on an execution, obtained by the creditor of A., a son of the owner of the estate, and levied upon what was claimed to be his interest in the estate of his father, who had died intestate, leaving real estate, but who before his decease had made an advancement to A., exceeding what would have been his portion of his father's estate.[2]

§ 123. But equity does not, as of course, take executions upon judgments at law into its own hands, as such power would be oppressive both to the debtor and the court.[3] And the presumption is, that the court which renders a judgment is competent to enforce it by its own process, and it is only in special cases that chancery interferes.[4] So a debtor cannot resort to equity to enjoin an execution against him, if he has had an opportunity to apply to the court from which it issued for redress.[5] And it is held, that it would take a very strong case of fraud, mistake, surprise, or accident, to induce equity to interfere with the completion of a sale upon an execution at law.[6] Thus the claimant of personal property, taken on several executions against the same person, cannot maintain a bill to enjoin the proceedings; his proper remedy is at law.[7] So an injunction will not be granted, to stay a sale under an execution, on the ground of usury, that being a good defence at law.[8] Nor upon the

[1] Moore v. Barclay, 16 Ala. 158.
[2] Dyer v. Armstrong, 5 Ind. 437.
[3] Macon. &c. v. Parker, 9 Geo. 377.
[4] Ibid.
[5] Beckley v. Palmer, 11 Gratt, 625.

[6] Skillman v. Holcomb, 1 Beasl. 131.
[7] Henderson v. Bates, 3 Blackf. 460.
[8] Lansing v. Eddy, 1 John. Ch. 49.

allegation that the judgment has been satisfied, the remedy at law, in such case, being prompt and adequate.[1] So a bill for an injunction was brought against the sheriff, to stop the sale of slaves on execution, alleging a *bonâ fide* purchase on the part of the complainant, previous to the execution. The bill was dismissed, on the ground that the remedy was at law.[2] So an agreement, by a third person, with the defendant in the execution, to pay it off, is no ground for an injunction against the enforcement of the execution.[3] So equity has no jurisdiction to enjoin the sale of. property seized on execution, on the application of a third party, claiming it as his own, though he is a trustee of the property.[4] And where a statutory writ of possession has been awarded by a court of law, to enjoin the issuing of such writ in favor of a purchaser of lands, at a sale under an execution against a party in possession, where there is no allegation or pretence that waste may be committed, or irreparable mischief done, is held to be a clear abuse of the writ of injunction.[4] So, where the object of a bill will be answered by restraining the proceeds of a sheriff's sale in his hands, the sale of the property ought not to be enjoined.[6] Nor merely on the ground that the validity of the execution or the justice of the judgment is denied by the party who applies for the injunction.[7] So, where the plaintiffs sought to restrain the defendants from taking and selling on execution specific articles of property, on the ground that they consisted of family relics, family pictures, and gifts from deceased friends, of great interest and value to the plaintiffs; and the only articles within that description, which had been levied upon, were four ottomans, four vases, a solar lamp, and a china tea-set, given, in the lifetime of the testator, to his wife (now his widow), by friends and relatives, as family presents;

[1] Lansing *v.* Eddy, 1 John. Ch. 49.
[2] Kendrick *v.* Arnold, 4 Bibb, 235.
[3] Triplett *v.* Turner, 2 J. J. Marsh, 475.
[4] Watkins *v.* Logan, 3 Monr. 20.
[5] Blakeney *v.* Ferguson, 14 Ark. 641.
[6] Receivers, &c., 3 Green Ch. 222.
[7] Williams *v.* Wright, 9 Humph. 493.

and she was not a party to the suit; and the plaintiffs did
not offer to pay the value of the articles which they sought
to protect: held, the court would not interfere.   In such case
it would not strengthen the plaintiff's claim, that the execution debtor had more than sufficient to pay all her debts, other
than the property in question.   And where the plaintiffs in
such bill alleged, that the defendants threatened and were
about to levy their execution upon the real estate of the
deceased; and that such levy would not only be illegal, but
would greatly embarrass the settlement of the estate; and it
appeared, that the time limited for the settlement of the estate
had long since expired, without any manifestation of a desire,
by the plaintiffs, to complete the settlement: it was held, 1.
That the interference of the court, in the manner claimed,
would enable the plaintiffs, by their delay, effectually to shield
the property of the debtor from the claims of her creditors;
2. The levy of an execution upon her life-estate in the realty
would not affect proceedings in relation to the settlement of
the estate concerning the personalty.[1]

§ 124. Where, pending an issue to try the right to personal property taken on execution, other executions are issued
on the same judgments, and levied on the same property, an
injunction will be granted to restrain proceedings on the
latter.[2] So an injunction will issue, at the instance of an
execution creditor, to restrain the debtor and a prior execution creditor, from selling or removing any of the personal
property levied on, unless by sale under the execution, until
the second execution is satisfied.[3] So A. and B. had severally attached certain personal property of C., the attachment
of A. having precedence, and both had obtained judgment,
the property being, however, insufficient to satisfy either
judgment.   On a petition brought by B. against A., praying

---

[1] Johnson v. The Connecticut, &c.,
21 Conn. 148.
[2] Huntington v. Bell, 2 Porter, 51.

[3] Edgar v. Clevenger, 1 Green
Ch. 258.

that A. be enjoined against levying his execution on the
property, it having been found by the court that B.'s judgment was based on a just and legal claim, but that A.'s
judgment, though nominally based on a payment of money
for C., was yet founded wholly on a liability of A. as maker
of a note indorsed by C. and by one F., and which C. had
agreed but had failed to pay; held, the judgment of A. ought
to be postponed, and the injunction was granted.[1]   So,
between 1832 and 1839, judgments were rendered against
A. and his sureties.   In October, 1839, the defendants A., B.,
and C., conveyed their property in trust, to sell and pay judgment and other creditors, according to their legal priorities.
In 1840 and 1841, the trustees sold parcel of the estate to E.,
and the purchase-money was applied by him in discharge of
elder judgments, which were thereupon assigned to the purchaser.   A full and fair value was paid for the land.   In
1838, F. and G. obtained judgments against A. and others,
and, in 1844, revived them by *scire facias* against A. and his
terre-tenants, of whom E. was one.   The judgment of F. and
G. was junior to those paid off by E.   The purchaser, when
the *sci. fa.* issued, was a non-resident, and not returned *summoned* under that writ.   The judgment being revived, F.
and G. were proceeding to a sale of the land, under the lien
of their judgments of 1838.   It appearing that the amount
of the judgments, prior to 1838, was more than the value of
the whole estate; it was held that an injunction obtained by
E. should be continued until final hearing, unless F. and G.
would bring into court the sum paid by E. in discharge of
the senior judgments.   That the defendants, F. and G., not
having assented to, nor participated in, the formation of the
trust created by A., B., and C., nor having ratified it, were
not bound by it.   That the complainant, E., having no
defence at law, could not have successfully pleaded to the
scire facias, or have maintained payment, satisfaction, or

[1] Norton *v.* Hickok, 25 Conn. 356.

release of the judgment of F. and G. at law, or that A. was not seized at the rendition of the judgment. But, that in equity, as no combination, fraud, or unfairness, appeared in the purchase of the land, as it was sold for its full, utmost value, as the whole purchase-money had been applied by the purchaser to the judgments prior in date, and preferred liens on the land, as there then remained due on judgments a large amount against A., prior in point of date to the judgment of F. and G., and as the payment of the judgment of F. and G. out of this land was hopeless; the purchaser was entitled to relief by injunction, as against such revived judgment, and execution thereon.[1] But on a bill to enjoin an execution against particular property, the allegation, that a prior execution in favor of another plaintiff against a part of the same defendants had been enjoined, is not ground for equitable relief, it not appearing but that the ground for the prior injunction had reference to the judgment or process itself, and not to the property.[2] And two executions of the same kind may be issued upon the same judgment, and, as courts of law have authority to prevent abuse of their own processes, equity will not interfere for that purpose.[3]

§ 125. To sustain a bill to enjoin the sale of a slave, the title of the complainant must appear to be clear and uncontrovertible.[4] So to entitle a party, who has purchased slaves of a judgment debtor a short time before the judgments, to an injunction to restrain the levy of execution on the slaves, he must make out a clear and undisputed title, or a purchase for a *bonâ fide* consideration, above suspicion or doubt in relation to its fairness.[5] So the vendor cannot enjoin the seizure and sale of the property of his vendee, when

[1] Barnes *v.* Dodge, 7 Gill, 109.
[2] Dunn *v.* Bank, &c., 2 Ala. 152.
[3] Elliott *v.* Elmore, 16 Ohio, 27.
[4] Pope *v.* Eakin, 3 Humph. 413; 6 Yerg. 24. Wood *v.* Cruisman, 6 Humph. 279; Saunders *v.* Woods, 5 Yerg. 142.
[5] Warwick *v.* Michael, 11 Gill & J. 153.

it is seized under execution as the property of a third person, on the ground that his obligation in warranty may attach. In such a suit, the question of title to property is involved, and it therefore partakes of the nature of a *petitory* action, which can only be maintained by the party in whom the legal title is vested.[1] So where personal property is improperly levied on, the party claiming it cannot enjoin the creditor from proceeding at law, on the ground that another person has interposed a claim to it by mistake. The true owner has an adequate remedy at law, by suit or interposing a claim, under the statute (of Alabama).[2] So where one seeks to enjoin an execution, on the ground that the property seized does not belong to the judgment debtor, but to him, no other issue can be made but that of ownership. An affidavit that the sheriff had "seized" the individual property of the defendant, without any description of the property, or statement of its value, is too vague to authorize an injunction, and a petition not sworn to cannot supply the defect.[3] But where the title of a claimant to slaves is clear and unquestionable, chancery will enjoin the sale of them under an execution against a stranger.[4]

§ 126. A. obtained a judgment against B., levied execution on lands with notice of a superior equitable title in C. to a part, and purchased at the sale. Held, that he took as trustee for C., that he might be enjoined from proceeding on the judgment against C.'s share, and required to release such share to him.[5]

§ 127. Where an injunction to stay the sale of particular property on execution, but not in any way affecting the judgment or the collection of it out of other property, is

---

[1] Kelly v. Wiseman, 14 La. An. 661.
[2] Marriot v. Givens. 8 Ala. 694.
[3] McRae v. Brown, 12 La. An. 181.
[4] Capertown v. Huddleston, 7 Humph. 452.
[5] Gutshall v. Salsberry, Wright, 127.

dissolved, no decree ought to be rendered against the complainant.[1]

§ 128. Where slaves, in possession of a debtor under a
parol loan, for more than five years, were levied on for his
debt; on a bill to enjoin the sale by the owner, an issue was
granted to try the question whether the claim of the execution creditor was fair or fictitious.[2]

§ 129. Where a sheriff, with full knowledge of the facts,
neglects to levy an execution upon the property of the principal, and proceeds first upon the property of a co-defendant
who is only a surety, it seems that the Court of Chancery,
upon a bill filed for that purpose, will relieve the surety, if
the surety cannot obtain satisfaction for the injury by an
action upon the case against the sheriff.[3]

§ 130. Where an injunction has been issued to prevent
the completion of a levy against one charged as trustee
upon default, the case will be retained, after a new trial has
been granted the trustee, for the purpose of controlling
the injunction and of determining the ultimate question of
costs.[4]

§ 131. An injunction will not be granted upon an execution issued against the complainants, as securities on a twelve
months' bond, given under the 17th section of the (Texas)
execution law of 1840, for a purchase of land sold under *fieri
facias*, and admitted by them to have been forfeited; on the
ground that the execution had been issued without the authority of any court of justice, and without the sanction of the
judicial tribunals of the land; nor upon an allegation that

---

[1] Hammond *v.* St. John, 4 Yerg. 107.
[2] Beale *v.* Digges, 6 Gratt. 582.
[3] Boughton *v.* Bank, &c., 2 Barb. Ch. 458.
[4] Nashua, &c. *v.* Stimpson, 35 N. H. 286.

the complainants "are informed and believe that the bond on which said execution was issued was not taken in conformity with law, and is not such a one as execution could issue on."[1]

§ 132. A bill to stay proceedings upon an execution is addressed to the execution creditor, instead of the officer, and such creditor should be a party to the bill.[2]

§ 183. Where a sheriff, who had levied upon perishable personal property, was restrained by injunction from selling; the injunction was so modified, as to permit the sheriff to sell, and pay the proceeds into court, to abide the event of the suit.[3]

§ 134. A bill to enjoin an execution, on the ground that a previous execution on the same judgment had been levied on the property of another defendant, must be filed in the county where the judgment was recovered. Objection to the jurisdiction may be taken at the hearing.[4]

§ 135. Where there is no equity in a bill to enjoin a sale on execution, it is not proper to decree a sale under the execution; the bill should be dismissed and the injunction dissolved.[5]

§ 136. Where a sheriff's sale would not pass any title to the purchaser, such sale will not be enjoined, on the ground merely that it would cast a cloud on the title.[6]

§ 137. In a suit to enjoin an execution (in Texas), on the ground that the judgment has become dormant, the defendant may plead the judgment in *reconvention.*[7]

[1] Bryan *v.* Knight, 1 Tex. 180.
[2] Bean *v.* Blanton, 3 Ired. Ch. 59.
[3] Heath *v.* Hand, 1 Paige, 329.
[4] Beckley *v.* Palmer, 11 Gratt. 625.
[5] Lovett *v.* Longmire, 14 Ark. 339.
[6] Drake *v.* Jones, 27 Mis. 428.
[7] Oldham *v.* Erhart, 18 Tex. 147.

§ 138. After a sheriff had sold property on an execution, and received the money therefor, an injunction was issued to stay further proceedings "until the further order of the court." Subsequently the County Court passed an order to the sheriff, to pay the money over to the owner of the property. Held, this order was erroneous, because the injunction had not been made perpetual.[1]

[1] Dail v. Traverse, 8 Gill, 41.

CHAPTER VI.

INJUNCTION OF SUITS OR ACTIONS.

§ 1. THE injunction of *suits before judgment* is as common and familiar a head of equity jurisdiction as that of judgments.[1]

§ 1 a. It is held, that the great purpose of a court of equity, in assuming jurisdiction to restrain proceedings at law, is to afford a more plain, adequate, and complete remedy for the wrong complained of than the party can have at law.[2](a) Thus it will interpose, to correct or prevent the abuse of the

[1] See Ragatz v. Dubuque, 4 Iowa, 343.

[2] Glenn v. Fowler, 8 Gill & J. 340.

(a) The remedy of injunction is sometimes applied to criminal prosecutions. Thus the agents of a receiver in a cause, acting under leave of the court, took forcible possession of a house occupied by a servant of one of the defendants. An order was made, restraining that defendant from prosecuting an *indictment* against the agents. Turner v. Turner, 2 Eng. Law and Eq. 130. In New York, equity may restrain a creditor from proceeding, under the act abolishing imprisonment for debt, and to punish fraudulent debtors, against the person and equitable interests of his debtor. Frost v. Myrick, 1 Barb. 362.

process of common law courts.[1] But in general equity will
not interfere with other courts.[2] And equity will restrain proceedings at law when necessary to the attainment of justice,
not by assuming jurisdiction over the courts in which the
proceedings are pending, but by controlling the parties to
such proceedings by injunction.[3] In an approved work
upon this subject, it is said : " It frequently happens that a
person, in consequence of some circumstances of which judicial notice can only be taken in a court of equity, has an
advantage in proceeding in a court of ordinary jurisdiction,
which must make that court an instrument of injustice.
There are also many cases in which the legal defence to a
claim set up at law rests either exclusively or in a great
degree within the knowledge of the party advancing the
claim, by which means that defence can only be obtained
through the assistance of a court of equity. As it is against
conscience, therefore, that the party should in the one case
make any use of the advantage of which he is thus inequitably possessed, or that he should in the other proceed in
the assertion of his claim, without communicating the
information, it has become one of the most ordinary modes
of equitable interposition to afford relief by *injunctions to
stay proceedings at law*."[4] So it is said, in a late case,
" Injunction to restrain proceedings at law is one of the
most common heads of equity jurisprudence. It is a preventive remedy. It is not used for the purpose of punishment,
or to compel persons to do right, but simply to prevent them
from doing wrong. Where the right of the plaintiff is doubtful,
or where he has an adequate remedy at law, injunction will
not be granted ; but where the right is clear, and the danger
probable that the right will be defeated without this special
interposition of the court, it will in general be granted."[5]

[1] Morris *v.* Thomas, 17 Ill. 112.
[2] Bank, &c. *v.* Rutland, &c., 28
Verm. 470.
[3] Burpee *v.* Smith, Walker, Ch.
327.

[4] 1 Eden (Amn. Edn.) 14.
[5] Per Woodward, J., Miller *v.*
Gorman, 38 Penn. 312–3.

§ 2. The restraining of suits at law is a power inseparably incident to courts of equity, but will not be exercised by a court of law, invested by statute with specific and limited equity jurisdiction. Thus the court in Massachusetts remark : " We have no power in chancery, except by statute ; and the general authority to issue injunctions has not been given. The exercise of such a power exists only when the subject matter falls within the jurisdiction granted by the legislature. Injunctions against proceeding at law, are within the general jurisdiction of chancery, which we are not authorized to assume."[1]

§ 3. We have already considered the remedy of injunction, as applied to *judgments*. This is said to be the form in which equity commonly interferes with proceedings at law. It is held to be the ordinary course to restrain the *execution*, but allow the plaintiff to proceed to a trial and judgment : and that it is only upon an averment in the bill, that the plaintiff in equity believes the answer will afford discovery material to his defence at law, that an injunction to stay the trial ought to be granted.[2]

§ 4. With regard to the circumstances under which equity will interfere to restrain a suit at law ; it is held that an injunction will never be granted to stay a suit before judgment, merely because the plaintiff has *no cause of action*.[3] So an injunction to stay proceedings at law, because another bill was pending, which embraced the same cause of action as that asserted in the suit at law, was held to have been improvidently issued, and to be properly dissolved on motion. The proper course would have been, to file a petition, or make a motion, for the injunction, in the suit already pending.[4] So equity will not restrain a creditor from prosecuting

---

[1] Per Parker, C. J., Stone *v.* Hobart, 8 Pick. 466.
[2] Williams *v.* Sadler, 4 Jones Eq. 378.
[3] Chadoin *v.* Magee, 20 Tex. 476.
[4] Washington *v.* Emery, 4 Jones Eq. 29.

his legal remedy against the personal representatives of his debtor, unless there is a decree under which the creditor has a right to go in and prove his debt.[1]

§ 5. Where the equity of a bill is fully met and distinctly denied, proceedings at law will not be restrained, unless under special circumstances.[2] Nor if an application for an injunction, *pendente lite*, leaves the plaintiff's case in great doubt.[3]

§ 6. The jurisdiction of a court of equity, to enjoin proceedings of a special nature in other tribunals, is sometimes very liberally construed. Thus a statute provided, that no order of the poor law commissioners should be removed by *certiorari* into any court of record except the King's Bench, and that every order removed into that court should, until declared illegal, continue in force and be obeyed. Held, equity might still restrain the commissioner and the guardians of a union from acting upon an order, pending a *certiorari*. That the effect of the statute was, merely that the removal of an order by *certiorari* should not of itself be conclusive of its illegality, leaving to an individual his right to an action of trespass or any other legal remedy.[4]

§ 7. But, on the other hand, a more strict construction has been given to the power of a court of equity in this respect. Thus chancery has no jurisdiction, to restrain *quasi* criminal proceedings on the part of the municipal authorities of a city, for repeated violation of an alleged invalid ordinance.[5] And in a suit to set aside, as irregular, proceedings in progress under authority of law, which may affect the title to property; the complainant must point out and establish the defects in the proceedings; otherwise, the court

---

[1] Ellicott *v.* The United States, 7 Gill. 307.
[4] Brett *v.* Sellers, 27 Geo. 185.

[3] Fredericks *v.* Mayer, 1 Bosw. 227.
[4] Frewin *v.* Lewis, 9 Sim. 66.
[5] Burnett *v.* Craig, 30 Ala. 135.

will leave him to his remedy at law. Such proceedings will not be arrested, nor will a corporation be required to show their regularity, upon a mere suggestion or general allegation of illegality or irregularity.[1] And where the defendant in an alternative mandamus exhibited a bill in equity, alleging an equitable defence to the demands of the plaintiff, and praying for an injunction, and that the bill might be received as a return to the writ; the injunction was refused, and a return ordered.[2]

§ 8. A suit to recover a debt will not be enjoined, merely because the plaintiff in such suit has *security for the debt*. Thus a debtor sold his creditor certain goods, which were to be a satisfaction of the debt, unless they were taken from him by superior liens. Held, the debtor could not enjoin the creditor from proceeding to judgment on his claim, without showing that there were no superior liens outstanding, as the creditor had a right to reduce his claim to judgment, though he could not collect it so long as he held the goods.[3] So equity will not enjoin proceedings at law on a mortgage, before hearing the party against whom the injunction is prayed.[4] So, although equity has undoubted authority to compel a creditor to satisfy his debt out of a particular fund, to which he alone can resort; yet it will never do so to the injury of such creditor, or where that course will work injustice to other parties. The protection of the creditors in their just rights, and also the rights of others, is the primary duty of the court.[5] So, on a motion by the defendants for a new trial, in an action upon a special contract, the Supreme Court of Errors decided, that the Superior Court had erred, in instructing the jury that the defendants were estopped, by the facts proved by the plaintiff, from alleging that they had no power to make the contract declared on, and advised a

[1] Williams v. Detroit, 2 Mich. 560.
[2] Neuse, &c. v. Commissioners, 6 Jones, 204.
[3] Camp v. Matheson, 29 Geo. 351.
[4] Todd v. Pratt, 1 Har. & J. 465.
[5] Morrison v. Kurtz, 15 Ill. 193. See Dewey v. Bulkley, 1 Gray, 416; Hilliard on Mortgages (3d Ed., Chap. XIII).

new trial. The plaintiff brings his bill to restrain the defendants from further prosecuting such motion for a new trial, on the ground, that the defendants by their representations had induced the plaintiff to enter into the contract and alter his condition, and therefore that the defence was inequitable and unconscientious. Held, 1. That the question whether, upon the facts proved on the trial, it was competent for the defendants, and consequently would be, on another trial, to set up that defence, was not involved in the bill. 2. That the defendants would not be estopped in equity, any more than at law, from setting up the defence. 3. That, inasmuch as the plaintiff could have adequate protection at law on such new trial, if he was entitled to it anywhere, there was no occasion for him to come into equity for that purpose, and consequently such bill was not maintainable.[1]

§ 9. In reference to the restraint of *a suit in chancery*, it is held that proceedings in the Court of Chancery will not be restrained by injunction upon an original bill, whether filed by a party, privy or stranger to such bill; but the proper course is to apply by petition in the original suit.[2] So an injunction will not be granted, to restrain a party from instituting proceedings in equity for an account, &c., where the complainant has an equitable defence to such proceedings, which he can set up in his answer.[3] But the court by which a receiver is appointed will restrain him from prosecuting an unjust and vexatious suit at law, although the complainant is not a party to the suit in which the receiver was appointed.[4] So, where a bill has been filed and decree made for an account, and a creditor comes in before the Master, but afterwards brings an action; such action will be enjoined, but without costs, if he has not applied in the first instance.[5] And a plaintiff is bound to put under the control

[1] Hood v. New York, &c., 23 Conn. 609.

[2] Smith v. American, &c., 1 Clarke, 307; Lane v. Clark, 1 Clarke, 309.

[3] Hall v. Fisher, 1 Barb. Ch. 53.

[4] Matter of Merritt, 5 Paige, 125.

[5] Hardcastle v. Chettle, 4 Bro. Ch. 119, 163.

15

of the court his legal rights relating to the subject-matter of litigation. Therefore, where a party brought a suit for specific performance, and, after obtaining a decree, an action for damages, an injunction was granted.[1](a)

§ 10. No injunction lies against a suit, if the bill shows a good defence to such suit; or if it otherwise appears that there was such a defence. As, by a creditor, who has received payment from his insolvent debtor, to enjoin the prosecution of a suit against the creditor to recover the amount of such payment; the bill alleging that the payment was not an unlawful preference.[2] And where the present plaintiff has a good defence at law, the mere neglect of the defendant in chancery to object to the jurisdiction of the court on this ground will not entitle the complainant to a preliminary injunction, and thus make it the duty of the Court of Chancery to assume the exclusive jurisdiction of the subject matter of the suit. But, after a final decree, the court will restrain, by injunction, any proceedings at law inconsistent with such decree, and a clause to that effect will be inserted in the decree.[3] More especially, if a defendant has a legal defence to a suit, and ample means of proving it, chancery will not interfere by injunction.[4] Nor where the petitioner, if, as alleged, he is defrauded in such suit, has a remedy by *certiorari*.[5] As in case of an action of forcible entry and detainer brought before a justice of the peace, although the land is

---

[1] Prothero v. Phelps, 35 Eng. Law and Eq. 518.
[2] Fuller v. Cadwell, 6 Allen, 503; Hood v. New York, &c., 23 Conn. 609; 26 Geo. 167; New York, &c. v. American, &c., 11 Paige, 384; 20 Tex. 661.
[3] 11 Paige, 384.
[4] Chambless v. Taber, 26 Geo. 167.
[5] Smith v. Ryan, 20 Tex. 661.

(a) The expression "equitable grounds," in St. 17 and 18 Vict. c. 125, § 83, means grounds depending on *equitable principles*, not merely on the *practice of courts of equity*. Held, therefore, in the above case, that a plea of the decree in equity was not such a plea as the statute contemplated, and that its being overruled by a court of law did not preclude a court of equity from granting an injunction. 35 Eng. Law and Eq. 518.

worth more than $100.[1] And, in cases of doubt, an injunction *pendente lite* ought not to be granted, unless there is reason to believe that, during the necessary delay before trial, the plaintiff may sustain injury which the court will be unable fully to redress, or that acts may be committed which will prevent the full relief which the plaintiff seeks by his action.[2] Thus, pending a suit on a note, though the defendant was not served and has not appeared, he cannot have an injunction against the collection of the note, merely on the ground that he has a good defence.[3] So one injured by the worthlessness of a patent assignment, delivered as good, has a remedy at law against his vendor, and therefore equity will not enjoin a suit on the notes for the purchase-money, in the absence of some equitable ground, such as insolvency.[4] So an injunction will not be granted, to stay a suit at law for breach of warranty of seisin, upon the ground of the loss of an unrecorded deed, it not appearing that such loss will endanger the complainant's defence.[5] So, in suits by creditors, a receiver was appointed of certain property of the debtor. The debtor afterwards made an assignment for creditors, and the assignee claimed the property. Held, the dispute, whether the receiver or the assignee should have the property, was a pure question of law, not free from difficulty, and of the construction of the statute, and a judgment in a suit brought by either would be conclusive in a suit by the other; and therefore the assignee could not maintain a bill to restrain the receiver from prosecuting an action against him for the property. Though all the parties submitted to the jurisdiction, the bill was not retained.[6]

§ 11. Equity will not by injunction enable a party to try in equity a case the defendant has begun to try, and which can and should most properly be tried at law.[7]

[1] Smith v. Ryan, 20 Tex. 661.
[2] Spring v. Strauss, 3 Bosw. 607.
[3] Smith v. Sparrow, 13 Cal. 596. See McGregor v. Axe, 10 Ind. 362; Maxwell v. Mullis, 12 Ind. 99.
[4] Black v. Stone, 33 Ala. 327.
[5] Rogers v. Cross, 3 Chand. 34
[6] Newkirk v. Morris, 1 Beasl. 62.
[7] Reeves v. Cooper, 1 Beasl. 223, 498.

§ 12. Where a debt is justly due, proceedings under the (New Jersey) act of 1855 are not to be restrained, on the ground that the statute is unconstitutional or has been repealed, or that the attachment was not properly executed by the sheriff, or that the property is not liable to attachment; as the complainant cannot ask the aid of equity to escape payment of his just debts, and the questions should be tried in a court of law.[1]

§ 13. In New York, a defendant who has an equitable defence, being authorized under the present rules of practice to interpose it by answer, is bound to do so, and cannot bring a separate action, merely to restrain another action pending in the same court.[2] Nor can one court enjoin a suit in another court of the State, having equal power to grant the relief sought by the complaint.

§ 14. The limitations to the rule, that an injunction will not lie to restrain a suit at law, where the plaintiff in equity has a good legal defence to such suit, are well illustrated in a late case in Connecticut. In an application for injunction against a suit at law, founded upon an alleged discharge or satisfaction of the claim sued on, the court remarked as follows: "Even if this settlement was not founded on a good pecuniary consideration, as it certainly is, it might be received as a family settlement, and as such it should be sustained and upheld in a court of equity, and viewed in that character, if one part of it is good, every other part is equally so, as there is the same general consideration for the whole. But it is said that if we hold that the petitioner is released from the debt, there is a good defence of the action at law, and for that reason a court of equity should not interfere by injunction. This may possibly be so. A plea could perhaps be so framed in that action, as to present this discharge as a sufficient answer to the plaintiff's declaration, still the

---

[1] Reeves v. Cooper, 1 Beasl. 223, 498.   [2] Winfield v. Bacon, 24 Barb. 154.

writing is not a technical discharge, and we think that the remedy is not so clear, certain, and adequate, as that, in the exercise of a sound discretion, we ought on that account to dismiss the bill, and hand the case over for further investigation elsewhere; nor would such a course be of the least benefit to the respondents. The effect of the writing is a question of law and not of fact, and a trial by jury or in a court of law, would not enable the administrators to escape the legal construction which the court in any case will give it."[1]

§ 15. Equity will restrain by injunction, not only the suit at law itself, but also the introduction of evidence in such suit, which, though perhaps legally admissible, is manifestly contrary to right and justice. Thus, where the defendants took land of the complainant under a charter, and the appraisers, in his absence, being misled as to some material facts, appraised the damage at one dollar when it really amounted to five thousand dollars; held, equity would enjoin the use of the appraisers' record by the defendants in an action at law for the damages. The formal regularity of the proceedings was held no objection to this interposition, but rather an additional ground, as depriving the party of any remedy at law. Held, also, that a new appraisement should be made under the direction of the court, and the injunction should stand until the damages thus awarded were paid.[2] So, although payment discharges a bond or judgment at law; equity may enjoin a party from setting up such payment.[3]

§ 16. Equity will sometimes aid as well as restrain a suit at law by injunction.(a) Thus an injunction will be granted

[1] Per Ellsworth, J., Hurlbut v. Phelps, 30 Conn. 50.
[2] Wells v. Bridgport, &c., 31 Conn. 316.
[3] M'Cormick v. Irwin, 35 Penn. 111.

(a) In Texas, writs of injunction, *ancillary* to a suit pending, are returnable only to the county where such suit is pending. Allen v. Menard, 5 Tex. 378.

to restrain the assignor of an equitable claim from dismissing a suit for such claim, brought in his name by the assignee.[1] So where suits had been brought before a magistrate against the drawers of prizes in a lottery, for the purpose of a forfeiture to the State under the statute, held, the district courts might enjoin the owner of the lottery from disposing of such prizes until the suits should be decided.[2] So, in case of necessity, the court will interfere to prevent the defendant from affecting property in litigation by contracts, conveyances, or other acts; or order security therefor.[3] Thus A. sued B. and C., in trespass, for malicious injury to his property. He then filed a bill in equity, alleging the facts of the trespass, and that B. and C. were engaged in it, and that they were disposing of their property to avoid its being taken to satisfy his judgment. He also prayed for a discovery. Held, the ancillary jurisdiction of a court of equity was properly invoked, though the defendants need not answer anything tending to criminate them.[4] But it is sometimes held, that the court has no jurisdiction to restrain the defendant in a suit at law from alienating his property, for the purpose of defeating the impending judgment.[5] Nor to compel parties to hold goods, pending a trial at law, to satisfy a possible judgment.[6](a)

§ 17. An injunction will not be granted in aid of an illegal

[1] Deaver v. Eller, 7 Ired. Eq. 24.
[2] People v. Kent, 6 Cal. 89.
[3] Shrewsbury, &c. v. Same, 4 Eng. L. and Eq. 171; 8 Rich. 349; Miller v. Washburn, 3 Ired. Ch. 161.
[4] Cottrell v. Moody, 12 B. Mon. 500.
[5] Moran v. Dawes, Hopk. 365.
[6] Phelps v. Foster, 18 Ill. 309.

(a) It is doubted whether equity will, by injunction, restrain the defendant, in an action of trover, from disposing of the property, pending the suit. Robertson v. Bingley, 1 McC. Ch. 333. A special injunction, ordering security for the forthcoming of property in litigation, is within the powers of the Court of Equity, and in South Carolina may be granted by a Master or Commissioner, under the 8th section of the act of 1840. Aldrich v. Kirkland, 8 Rich. 349.

proceeding at law.[1]　Nor to protect a legal right which may be tried at law, unless under special circumstances.[2]

§ 18. An injunction upon a bill of discovery in aid of an action at law may be dissolved, though the complainant has excepted to the answer for impertinence merely, where the bill has been fully answered.[3]

§ 19. In reference to the *parties* in cases of this nature; it is held that *the government* cannot be sued, except by its own consent, given by statute; and, consequently, an injunction to stay proceedings at law cannot be allowed against the United States.[4]

§ 20. The State of Connecticut having commenced several ejectments, the State of New York brought a bill, alleging title to the soil and jurisdiction of the land in dispute, and prayed a discovery, relief, and an injunction. Held, as New York was not a party to the suits below, nor interested in those decisions, an injunction should not be granted. And as the State of Connecticut did not appear, and a *subpœna* had not been served sixty days before the return day, as required in suits in equity, the complainant should not be at liberty to proceed *ex parte* on the first day of the ensuing term, if the State did not appear, but an *alias subpœna* should be awarded.[5]

§ 21. Separate purchasers of different parcels of the same lot of land cannot join in a bill against the former owner, to enjoin the prosecution of separate ejectment suits commenced by him against them.[6]

§ 22. Where a creditor held several securities for a debt, the court refused to enjoin him from proceeding to enforce

---

[1] Haight *v.* Bergh, 2 Green Ch. 386.
[2] Wooden *v.* Wooden, 2 Green Ch. 429.
[3] Jewett *v.* Belden, 11 Paige, 618.

[4] Hill *v.* The United States, 9 How. 386.
[5] New York *v.* Connecticut, 4 Dal. 3.
[6] Wood *v.* Perry, 1 Barb. 114.

one of them, in order that the debtors might have opportunity to settle among themselves a question of priority as to their liabilities.[1]

§ 23. Where a creditor, on receiving a judgment bond, agreed to collect the debt secured by it, ratably, against the obligors and others, he was enjoined from proceeding to collect the debt of the obligors in the bond only.[2]

§ 24. With regard to the *terms* on which a suit at law will be enjoined; it is the prevailing rule, that where a defendant at law, before judgment, files his bill for relief on equitable grounds, and for an injunction, the injunction should be granted only on condition that he confess or agree to confess judgment, though he may have grounds of defence at law distinct from his equitable defence.[3] In such case, where the injunction is dissolved because the complainant refused to confess judgment, and there is an appeal, the appellate court will not examine the merits of the case, though at the time the order was made the cause stood for hearing.[4] So on a bill filed by a defendant at law, on the ground that the subject is a trust, and proper for equitable cognizance, an injunction ought not to be granted, staying the trial at law, but only execution on the judgment which may be recovered.[5] So where a defendant at law transfers the case to a court of equity, upon an allegation that his defence is equitable, the plaintiff at law should be allowed to proceed to judgment, that there may be no delay of execution, if the defendant does not succeed in his defence.[6] So it is held, that a party applying for an injunction, to stay proceedings at law upon a money bond, must be bound, by order, to bring no writ of error.[7] Upon this ground, in New York,

---

[1] Goodwin v. State Bank, 4 Desau. 389.

[2] Briggs v. Low, 4 John. 22.

[3] Warwick v. Norwall, 1 Leigh, 96 ; Matthews v. Douglass, Cooke, 136 ; 3 Ired. Ch. 178. *Contra*, Lawrence v. Bowman, 1 McAll. C. C. (Cal.) 419.

[4] 1 Leigh, 96.

[5] Justice v. Scott, 4 Ired. Eq. 108.

[6] Anderson v. Walton, 1 Freem. Ch. 347.

[7] 3 Ired. Ch. 178.

a bill, for an injunction to stay a suit at law, must state whether issue has been joined; for, if it has, a provision must be inserted in the injunction, allowing the suit to proceed to judgment; and if not, the master has no authority to issue an injunction, without the security required by statute.[1] So the complainant must show in his bill the state of the pleadings, and the court in which the suit is pending, in order to enable the officer, to whom the application is made for the injunction, to judge of the propriety of its allowance, and to prescribe the terms.[2]

§ 25. The terms of granting an injunction in this class of cases often depend upon the statutory law. Thus it is held, that the statute of Michigan (R. S. 374, § 91) is peremptory, that no injunction shall be granted to restrain proceedings at law, when a cause is at issue, without filing a bond in such sum as the officer allowing the injunction shall prescribe.[3] So, in Indiana, upon a bill for discovery in aid of a defence to an action at law, also praying a stay of proceedings till such discovery; held, the latter prayer should not be granted, without a statutory bond.[4]

§ 26. Injunction is often connected with *discovery*, another important and leading head of equity jurisdiction. In New York, an injunction master cannot stay proceedings in a suit, in which issue has not been joined, except in case of a mere bill of discovery in aid of the defence, or where the only relief prayed is merely in aid of the defence.[5] The Master, if no issue has been joined, should direct a provision in the injunction, permitting the party to proceed to judgment, unless the bill was for a discovery merely.[6] In the same State it is held, that, upon a bill of discovery in aid of a suit at law, an *ex parte* injunction to prevent the defendant

[1] Teller v. Van Deusen, 3 Paige, 33.
[2] Carroll v. Farmers, &c., Harring. Ch. 197.
[3] Ibid.
[4] Lemon v. Morehead, 8 Blackf. 561.
[5] Melick v. Drake, 6 Paige, 470.
[6] Jenkins v. Wilde, 2 Paige, 394.

from proceeding to trial should not be granted, where no fact is positively sworn to as being within the knowledge of the defendant, which, if proved, would defeat the defence, and enable the plaintiff to recover.[1]

§ 27. Where the defendant, in an action of trover, filed a bill for a discovery and an injunction, but failed to obtain a discovery, the court refused to grant the injunction, and dismissed the bill.[2] So, where a bill is filed to restrain a suit at law, on the ground that the complainant has a legal defence, but that it cannot be established without the evidence of the defendants to the bill; this is a bill of discovery merely, and, on the coming in of the answer, denying the equity of the bill, it should be dismissed on dissolving the injunction.[3]

§ 28. When an action at law is brought on a penal bond, conditioned for the payment of money on performance of a condition precedent, and the defendant files a bill to obtain a discovery as to the execution of the trust which constituted the condition; if the answer of the obligee discloses that the trust has not been fully executed, the court may enjoin the action at law, without compelling the obligor to account for the benefit received from the partial performance.[4]

§ 29. A very important point of inquiry, in reference to the injunction of suits at law, arises from the conflicting authority of the State or the tribunal, with which the court of equity, whose aid is invoked, is called upon to interfere. Upon this subject, in a late English case, it is said, " Even though no decree has been obtained in this country, yet if a suit instituted abroad appears ill calculated to answer the ends of justice, the Court of Chancery has restrained the foreign action, imposing, however, terms which it has considered

[1] Burgess v. Smith, 2 Barb. Ch. 276.
[2] Brown v. Dickinson, 10 Rich. Eq. 408.
[3] Steele v. Lowry, 6 Ala. 124.
[4] Rives v. Toulmin, 25 Ala. 45 2.

reasonable for protecting the party who was suing abroad."[1] " Where, pending a litigation here, in which complete relief may be had, a party to the suit institutes proceedings abroad, the Court of Chancery in general considers that act as a vexatious harassing of the opposite party, and restrains the foreign proceedings."[2] So the court in Massachusetts, in a very recent case, remarks as follows: " The authority of this court, as a court of chancery, upon a proper case being made, to restrain persons within its jurisdiction from prosecuting suits either in the courts of this State and of other States, or foreign countries, is clear and indisputable. In the exercise of this power, courts of equity proceed, not upon any claim of right to interfere with or control the course of proceedings in other tribunals. But the jurisdiction is founded on the clear authority vested in courts of equity over persons within the limits of their jurisdiction and amenable to process, to restrain them from doing acts which will work wrong and injury to others. As the decree of the court in such cases is pointed solely at the party, and does not extend to the tribunal where the suit or proceeding is pending, it is wholly immaterial that the party is prosecuting his action in the courts of a foreign State or country."[3](a)

[1] Per Lord Cranworth, The Carron, &c. v. Maclaren, 35 Eng. Law and Eq. 50.

[2] Per Lord Cranworth, The Carron, &c. v. Maclaren, 35 Eng. Law and Eq. 49.

[3] Per Bigelow, C. J., Dehon v. Foster, 4 Allen, 550.

(a) So it is said by the court in New Hampshire: " It would be a great defect in the administration of the law, if the mere fact, that the property was out of the State, could deprive the court of the power to act. As much injustice may be perpetrated in a given case, against the citizens of this State, by going out of the jurisdiction and committing a wrong, as by staying here and doing it. As the Legislature has conferred upon the court the power to issue injunctions whenever it is necessary to prevent injustice, it is the duty of the court to exercise that power upon the presentation of a proper case, and when it can be done consistently with the acknowledged practice in courts of equity. As the principle which is sought to be applied here, has been recognized for nearly two hundred years, we have no hesitation in holding that the court has jurisdiction." Per Gilchrist, C. J., Great Falls, &c. v. Wors-

§ 30. In the case, with reference to which these remarks were made, a citizen of Massachusetts attached in Pennsylvania personal property of an insolvent debtor residing in Massachusetts. Held, the assignees of such debtor, under the insolvent laws of Massachusetts, might maintain a bill for an injunction, though the suit was commenced before the institution of insolvency proceedings, more especially if done with notice that they were about to be instituted, and in order to obtain a preference.[1](a)

§ 31. Some of the leading cases, which fully justify these views, are as follows:—

§ 32. In Portarlington v. Soulby,[2] Lord Brougham restrained the indorsee of a bill from suing the plaintiff in the Irish courts on such bill, upon certain equitable grounds, which would have warranted a similar injunction against any action in the English courts. So where a decree had been obtained for the execution of the trusts of a deed for the benefit of creditors, and a receiver of real estates in England and Ireland appointed, and some of the trustees afterwards filed a bill in Ireland for executing the trusts; Lord Eldon restrained them from prosecuting that suit, on the ground that it sought the same relief as might be had under the decree obtained in England. But his lordship said that

---

[1] Dehon v. Foster, 4 Allen, 545; [2] 3 My. & K. 104.
7 Ib. 57.

---

ter, 3 Fost. 470. See Penn v. Baltimore, 1 Ves. 444; Arglasse v. Muschamp, 1 Vern. 75; Toller v. Carteret, 2 Vern. 494; Cranstown v. Johnson, 3 Ves. 170; Portarlington v. Soulby, 3 M. & K. 104; Massie v. Watts, 6 Cranch, 148; Mitchell v. Bunch, 2 Paige, 606; Mead v. Merritt, 2 Paige, 404; Hawley v. James, 7 Paige, 213.

(a) It was intimated that the decision might be different if it appeared that there were foreign creditors, who would by the injunction of the suit acquire a preference. With regard to *costs*, it was ordered that the defendant should be identified for the costs of his action, up to notice of the bill in equity; and the plaintiff have his costs in equity after the filing of the bill. Dehon v. Foster, 7 Allen, 57.

he would not prevent them from filing a bill in Ireland for the mere purpose of calling on the receiver there to account for his receipts and payments, without making it a general suit for administering the trusts of the deed.[1] So, after a decree in England for an account on a bill to redeem a West India mortgage, Sir John Leach would not suffer the mortgagee to prosecute a suit in Jamaica for foreclosing the same mortgage, on the ground that full relief might be obtained under the decree in England.[2] So where a bill was filed by the obligor in a bond, against the obligee and a person claiming under him by assignment, to have the bond delivered up and cancelled, the court would not permit the assignee, who was a Scotchman and had real estates in Scotland, to prosecute an action on the bond, which action he had raised in the Court of Sessions, even though the Scotch proceedings had been commenced two months before the bill to restrain them was filed. The bond was alleged to have been given in England for a gaming debt, as was known to the assignee, and the question to be decided in any form was, whether by the law of England the assignee was entitled to recover. Sir John Leach thought, first, that this question could be better decided in England, where the courts judicially know the law, than in Scotland, where the courts could only know the law as a matter of fact, to be communicated as evidence; and, secondly, that the remedy in England, if the obligor should make out his title to relief, would be more complete than could be had in Scotland. He therefore restrained the defendant, the assignee, from going on with the Scotch action, putting the plaintiff on terms as to giving a judgment for security to the holder of the bond.[3]

§ 33. In another recent case, a distributee in Mississippi procured the administrator's accounts to be settled in the Probate Court in that State, and a large balance was found due thereon. He then sued the surety on the bond, and

[1] Harrison v. Gurney, 2 Jac. & W. 563.

[2] Beckford v. Kemble, 1 Sim. & St. 7.

[3] Bushby v. Munday, 5 Madd. 297.

persuaded him to make no defence, by telling him that he should not be molested, but that the judgment was wanted only to bring the administrator to a settlement. The surety gave his note for the judgment, and, not procuring a settlement with his principals, obtained an injunction in Tennessee to stay suit on the note, notwithstanding which, the payee sued the note in the Circuit Court. Pending that suit, the probate decree in Mississippi was reversed, on appeal, and a very small balance decreed to be due. Thereupon the maker applied for an injunction in the Circuit Court in that State to stay the suit on the note. Meantime the Tennessee court, upon sufficient evidence, had decreed that the payee should cease his suit upon payment of a small balance. Held, thereupon, that the injunction should issue from the Circuit Court in Mississippi.[1]

§ 34. But it will not be the duty of the court to restrain foreign proceedings, if substantial justice is likely to be promoted by allowing them to take their course. Thus, where the plaintiff, who was heir of *tailzie* under a Scotch settlement, filed a bill to have his estate exonerated from an heritable bond by means of the personal estate; Sir John Leach declined to restrain proceedings in Scotland, where the question as to the right claimed would be more conveniently discussed; and ordered the cause in England to stand over, till the result of the Scotch proceedings should have been determined.[2] And in a late case in Vermont it is held, that a suit in one State will be enjoined to parties in another, only when the ends of justice, and not the mere convenience of parties, require it.[3] So, in late cases in England, from one of which the remarks of the court have been already cited, the general propositions were laid down, that where it would be the duty of one domestic court to restrain a party from instituting proceedings in another, it may also restrain proceedings in a foreign court. Also, that where

[1] Cage *v.* Cassidy, 23 How. U. S. 109.

[2] Elliott *v.* Minto, 6 Madd. 16.

[3] Bank, &c. *v.* Rutland, 2 Wms. 470.

there is a plain equity in favor of an injunction, and the representatives of the real and personal property, who seek it, are in this country, the court will grant it, and restrain proceedings in the courts of a foreign country. In such a case, the court will decide upon a consideration of all the circumstances, and require parties here to take or omit such steps in a foreign court as the ends of justice may require. The particular provisions of the foreign law, applicable to a transaction, proceedings as to which in a foreign court are thus restrained, must not be disregarded. But still, under the circumstances of the case, an injunction was refused. The facts of this case, as successively reported, were as follows: A company was chartered in Scotland for the manufacture of iron. Its manufactory and chief office of management were there; it had agents for the sale of the goods in different parts of Scotland and England; and possessed real estate in both countries. A., a large shareholder in the company, and possessed of real and personal property in England and Scotland, was the company's agent for the sale of goods, and was domiciled, in London. When he died, he made a will in the English form, and appointed as his executors persons who were resident in both countries; his heir was one of these persons, and was also the person who succeeded him in the London agency for the company. Probate of the will was taken out in England, and such of the executors as thought fit to apply to the Scotch court were according to the Scotch law confirmed in the execution of the will. An administration suit was instituted in the Court of Chancery, and the usual order for a general account of the debts and assets made. After the date of this order, the iron company took proceedings in the Scotch courts against the real and personal estate of the testator in Scotland. Notice of an injunction, at the suit of the executors, was served on the company's agent in London, and on the company's manager in Scotland; the company did not appear, and the injunction was issued. The company then moved to dissolve the injunction. No order was made. Held (Lord St. Leonards dissenting), that the injunction should not be maintained. In another case, growing out of the same transactions, a bill was brought by the executors and trustees of A., who had large estates, both real and personal, in England and in Scotland, for the administration of his estate, in which there was the ordinary decree. Suit in Scotland by a Scotch company, whose agent in London A. had been, claiming a large balance on the accounts between them and A. The Master of the Rolls, on motion by the plaintiffs, restrained the Scotch company from proceeding in this suit; but on appeal to the House of Lords that order was reversed, Lord St. Leonards dissenting. A second bill was then filed in this country against the Scotch company, for discovery of the dealings and transactions between the company and the testator. There was conflicting evidence as to whether it would be more convenient to take the accounts in this country or in Scotland. Motion in both suits to restrain the Scotch company from proceeding in their suit refused with costs.[1] In this case, heard in the House of Lords, the whole subject of restraining foreign suits by injunction is fully gone into, and elaborate and learned opinions are delivered by Lords Cranworth, Brougham, and St. Leonards.

§ 35. It was held, that, where there has been a final decree in a suit in India, upon motion by the defendant in a similar suit in England, between the same parties and for the same purpose, the court in England will make an order staying all proceedings in the English suit, without prejudice to any proceedings which the plaintiff may be advised to adopt with reference to the decree and proceedings in India. That an administrator *de bonis non*, &c., in India, appointed by the authority of the plaintiff, administrator in England, is substantially the same party for this purpose. That such administrator in India is authorized to assent to a compromise, under the authority of the court in India, and a decree adopt-

---

[1] Maclaren *v.* Stanton, 35 Eng. Law and Eq. 384; 15 Eng. Law and Eq. 500; Carron *v.* Maclaren, 35 Eng. Law and Eq. 37.

ing that compromise is a final decree.   And that, after such
decree, the plaintiff in England cannot, by supplemental bill
or amendment under the new practice, continue the English
suit, in order to obtain discovery of facts which would enable
him to set aside the decree in India.[1]   But in the same case
it was subsequently decided, that before equity interposes,
upon an interlocutory application, to stay proceedings in a
suit, by reason of a decree or judgment in a foreign country,
it must be satisfied that the foreign decree or judgment does
justice, and covers the whole subject of the suit.[2]

§ 36. In reference to the right of one court to restrain proceedings in another, and the question of conflicting jurisdiction; in a late English case, brewing utensils, hops, &c.,
having been seized under execution from a county court
against the goods of A., were claimed by B.   On the 5th
of October, the bailiff caused an interpleader summons
to be issued, calling on the parties to appear on the 18th,
when the claim would be adjudicated upon.   The county
court judge decided that the goods were the property of
B.   The goods having been given up, B. commenced an
action against the execution creditor for damages, for wrongfully depriving him of the possession of the goods, by means
whereof he was prevented from carrying on his trade as a
brewer, alleging special damage.   The court refused to interfere to stay the proceedings at the instance of the defendant.
It seems that, if the proceedings on the interpleader summons
constituted a defence to the action, it should have been
pleaded.[3]

§ 37. In England, a court of common law cannot grant
an injunction in an action of ejectment, under § 82 of the
common-law procedure act, 1854, 17 and 18 Vict. c. 125.[4]

---

[1] Ostell v. Lepage, 17 Eng. Law
and Eq. 57.
[2] Ibid., 21 Eng. Law and Eq. 640.

[3] Jones v. Williams, 4 Hurl. &
Nor. 706.
[4] Baylis v. Legros, 40 Eng. Law
and Eq. 272.

16

§ 38. A court of equity will not enjoin a suitor in that court from moving for relief in the same court.[1] And the court will not enjoin its own proceedings, though it may suspend its own order.[2]

§ 39. Where executors applied for leave to amend a bill filed by their testators, and for an injunction against suits begun in the United States Circuit Court, or to reinstate an injunction against suits in a State court, which had been dissolved; held the bill could be amended by adding new matter, without excuse for its being originally omitted, and notwithstanding the denial of the matter proposed to be added by affidavits. The injunction against the suits in the Circuit Court was denied, and the petitioners left to apply there for a stay of proceedings, until the matter of equitable relief was finally heard in the State court. The other injunction was refused by the Vice-Chancellor, as the case had been appealed, and the Chancellor had control of the appellate proceedings.[3]

§ 40. Where the defendant in an ejectment suit brought on the law side of the Circuit Court of the United States, by one claiming under a patent of the United States, filed a bill on the equity side of the court, for an injunction upon the plaintiff in ejectment, alleging that the patent was fraudulently obtained, and on the hearing no fraud was proved; held, the bill must be dismissed, and the merits of the case left to be settled in the trial at law.[4](a)

---

[1] McReynolds v. Harshaw, 2 Ired. Ch. 195.
[2] Medlock v. Cogburn, 1 Rich. Ch. 477.
[3] Coster v. Griswold, 4 Edw. Ch. 364.
[4] Gaines v. Nicholson, 9 How. 356.

(a) The practice, in reference to the particular court with whose proceedings equity will interfere by injunction, depends in this country, to some extent, upon local usage. It is held that the Court of Chancery of New York will not grant an injunction to stay the proceedings in a suit commenced in a court of competent jurisdiction in another State,

§ 41. Equity often interferes with suits at law by injunction, for the purpose of preventing or stopping *useless or vexatious litigation.*[1] So in a recent case it was held, that, where land has been laid out in town lots, or otherwise divided among many occupants, who are threatened with numerous suits, a bill in equity lies to quiet the title, and enjoin a suit at law for a particular fractional part, although the complainants have a legal title, and therefore an adequate remedy at law in each particular case. The object of such bill is to relieve the title from the embarrassment of the adverse claims, and also to restrain a multiplicity of suits.[2] So on a bill for injunction against a fifth ejectment, threatened by the defendant after two dismissals and two judgments for the complainant, one of which was affirmed in the appellate court, the bill should be sustained, and an answer directed, according to the rules of equity.[3] And injunction is a suitable process, to prevent a party who has commenced proceedings in one court from proceeding in the same matter in another; more especially where the former court has made a decision against him.[4] So a court of chancery may compel

[1] Woodruff v. Fisher, 17 Barb. 224.
[2] Crews v. Burcham, 1 Black, 352. See Woodruff v. Fisher, 17 Barb. 224.

[3] Dedman v. Chiles, 3 Monr. 426.
[4] Conover v. Mayor, &c., 25 Barb. 513.

except in a very special case. Burgess v. Smith, 2 Barb. Ch. 276. And by a later case the rule seems to be established without any exception. Williams v. Ayrault, 31 Barb. 364. The court will not grant an injunction to stay proceedings in a court having the same power to grant relief. Grant v. Quick, 5 Sandf. 612. In Michigan, courts of chancery will not sustain an injunction bill to restrain a suit or proceeding previously commenced in a court of a sister State, or in any of the Federal courts. Carroll v. Farmers, &c., Harring. Ch. 197. In Tennessee, suits in courts of law, on notes executed for the purchase-money of estates sold at a chancery sale, are improper, and may be enjoined, but not in any other court than that in which the original chancery suit is pending. Deaderick v. Smith, 6 Humph. 138. The Supreme Court cannot issue an injunction to restrain proceedings in a cause in the Circuit Court. Barry v. Green, 5 Hey. 67.

a party, who is prosecuting two suits for the same thing, to abandon one or the other, and select in which tribunal he will continue to prosecute.   But this rule only applies, where a recovery in one would be a bar to a judgment or decree in the other.[1]   So equity will enjoin suits which are in substance if not literally violations of a former order.   Thus a perpetual injunction was granted, restraining the defendant from interfering with the navigation of the plaintiffs' canal. He afterwards brought fifteen actions against the plaintiffs for the passage of that number of barges over the land claimed by him.   Held a violation of the spirit of the former decree, and the actions were enjoined.[2]   And a bill in equity, to enjoin several lawsuits, will be retained, to settle the whole controversy, especially where the legal rights of the parties have already been settled by a decree in the suit.[3]

§ 42. But where the ground, on which a party seeks relief in the court against the operation of a city ordinance, would be equally valid as a defence to a suit at law for a breach of such ordinance, the court will not grant an injunction to prevent a multiplicity of suits for such breaches, until the invalidity of the ordinance has been settled in a suit at law.[4] So a bill to enjoin proceedings in some, out of a large number of, actions of ejectment, and to permit the plaintiffs at law to proceed in as many as might be deemed necessary to try the title to the lands in question, the parties, title, and testimony being the same in each suit, was dismissed, on the grounds that the relief sought, if proper at all, could be afforded as well at law as in equity, and that the application was premature, before several verdicts had been rendered.[5] So where A., pending a suit at law in the Supreme Court against B., for obstruction of a water-course, commenced a new suit before a justice of the peace, every week, for the continuance of the obstruction; it was held that B., not

[1] Laraussini v. Carquette, 24 Miss. 151.
[2] The Grand, &c., v. Dimes, 17 Sim. 38.
[3] Dwelle v. Roath, 29 Geo. 733.
[4] West v. Mayor, &c., 10 Paige, 539.
[5] Peters v. Prevost, 1 Paine, 64.

having established his title at law, was not entitled, on a bill of peace, to an injunction upon A. to prevent litigation.[1] So, in a case of two creditor's bills, the first alleged that the defendant—the widow and personal representative of the debtor—had carried on his trade, and prayed for an account of the profits. The second prayed only for the common relief, and a decree was rendered in the second. Held, the first suit had an advantage over the second, and should not be enjoined.[2] And, in general, in order to entitle a party to maintain a bill of peace to restrain ejectment on the ground of preventing vexatious litigation; it must appear that the title has been fully and satisfactorily established at law; it is not enough that suits have been instituted and abandoned before trial.[3]

§ 43. The interference of the court in this mode may sometimes be affected by the question of *amount*. Thus the court refused to stay by injunction an action to recover certain instalments due for work, in order that the amount might be ascertained by a reference, or issue of *quantum damnificatus;* the amount of the instalments sued for appearing, by the answer, not to exceed an adequate compensation for the materials found and work done.[4]

§ 43 a. On a bill by one in possession of land, for the specific performance of an alleged agreement by the defendant to purchase the land at sheriff"s sale, on execution against the complainant, and take a mortgage for the amount advanced by him to pay incumbrances; an injunction to stay proceedings to recover possession from the complainant will not be retained until the hearing, if the amount due is large in proportion to the value of the land, and the responsibility of the complainant is comparatively limited.[5]

[1] Eldridge v. Hill, 2 John. Ch. 281.
[2] Underwood v. Jee, 17 Sim. 119.
[3] Patterson v. McCamant, 28 Mis. 210.
[4] Skinner v. Dayton, 2 John. Ch. 526.
[5] Clark v. Wood, 2 Halst. Ch. 458.

§ 44. The following remarks of Lord Loughborough, though immediately applicable to the equitable remedy of *interpleader*, have a bearing upon the subject of injunction: "A party claiming no right in the subject, is doubly vexed by having two legal processes in the names of different persons going on against him at the same time. He comes upon the most obvious equity to insist, that those persons claiming that to which he makes no claim, should settle that contest among themselves, and not with him. It may be said in all cases of interpleader—'stand the action.' If A. proceeds first, and you have a good defence against him, that puts an end to his claim; if not, that is a defence against the claim of B. That is precisely the situation in which the plaintiffs ought not to be placed."[1] And where one of the defendants to a bill of interpleader is suing the plaintiff in equity, and another at law, the court will enjoin both suits.[2]

§ 45. Suits relating to *real property* are perhaps more frequently than any others the subjects of applications for injunction, whether brought directly to recover the land itself, or growing out of incidental and collateral contracts and liabilities connected therewith.[3] (See Chap. XXVIII.) Where one has obtained a patent for land, with knowledge of a prior equitable title, of which the legal title is outstanding in a third person, and has brought a writ of right for the land; equity will stay the proceedings at law for a reasonable time, to afford the tenant an opportunity to get in the legal title.[4] So it is held that equity will restrain an ejectment against the owner of an entry, to give him an opportunity of obtaining a grant.[5] So where one has a legal as well as an equitable title, equity will enjoin an ejectment brought against him by a party who, if successful in the action, would be a trustee for him.[6] So a bill for an injunc-

---

[1] Langston *v.* Boylston, 2 Ves., Jr., 108.
[2] Crawford *v.* Fisher, 10 Sim. 479.
[3] See the State *v.* Murphy, 8 Blackf. 493.

[4] Goodwin *v.* McCluer, 3 Gratt. 291.
[5] Hendrick *v.* Dallum, Cooke, 220; 1 Overt. App. 489.
[6] Crofts *v.* Middleton, 35 Eng. Law and Eq. 466.

tion lies to restrain an ejectment, and for other relief, where the original parties actually hold and possess as tenants in common, and the complainants have made valuable improvements.[1] So a claimant, resting on an equitable title, depending on a deed and a bond for title, both lost, may go into equity and obtain an injunction to stop suits at law for the premises, and also obtain full relief.[2]

§ 46. An ejectment for land may sometimes be restrained upon the ground of *equitable estoppel* or *implied trust.* Thus the route of a raceway of an incorporated company was located over certain lots of A.'s. The company appointed a committee to negotiate with the land-owners for the purchase of the land over which the route was located. B. was president, and also an acting manager, of the company, and offered to negotiate for the committee the purchase of A.'s land for the company, and the committee thereupon intrusted the negotiation to B. B. bought A.'s lots for fifty dollars a lot, and took a deed in his own name, the deed stating the amount paid as one hundred dollars per lot. The company offered B. what he had paid for the lots, and went on and constructed their raceway over the land. B. was perpetually enjoined from bringing ejectment to recover possession.[3] In the same case, B. owned another lot over which the raceway was located and constructed, and was president and acting manager of the company at the time of such location and construction, and made no objection, but was active in the direction and proceedings of the company in locating and constructing the raceway on and over the lot. He was perpetually enjoined from bringing ejectment to recover possession. An issue was ordered to ascertain the value of the lots.[4] So a colliery proprietor constructed a railroad from the colliery across the lands of several other persons, by agreement, and his solicitors wrote a letter to the defendant, whose lands he

[1] Jackson *v.* Jones, 25 Geo. 93.
[2] Frith *v.* Roe, 23 Geo. 139.
[3] Trenton, &c. *v.* McKelway, 4 Halst. Ch. 84.
[4] Ibid.

wished to cross, in which he referred to an act of Parliament, as authorizing him to take lands, and offered to pay for the land at a fair valuation. Some time afterwards, the plaintiff and defendant met, but did not agree as to the price. The road having been made, three or four years afterwards, the defendant brings ejectment. Held, an injunction should be granted against the suit, upon the plaintiff's giving judgment therein, and paying into court a sum equal to the utmost valuation of the land.[1]

§ 47. The same remedy is sometimes applied, to relieve from the consequences of failure in *the strict performance of a condition or contract.* Thus A. conveyed land to B., with condition that, if B. should pay one hundred dollars to C., and certain other sums to certain other persons, in one year from the decease of A., the deed should be good and valid, otherwise null and void. On the 14th of February, 1841, A. died; and within one year B. paid the sums, except the one hundred dollars to C. On the 7th of March, 1842, B. tendered that sum, with interest, to C., which C. did not accept. On a bill in chancery, brought by B. against C. and the heirs at law of A., praying for a confirmation of B.'s title, and an injunction against the further prosecution of an action at law then pending, brought by D., one of the heirs at law of A., to recover possession of the land; held, B. was entitled to the relief sought.[2]

§ 48. But it is held that a party, whose right to land has not been established at law, will not be protected by injunction against a suit to recover the land.[3] So where no final verdict in ejectment has been obtained by the complainant, equity cannot enjoin the bringing of an ejectment; and this objection may be taken after the filing of the answer, and even when the court is charging the jury.[4] And equity will

---

[1] Powell v. Thomas, 6 Hare, 300.
[2] Bowen v. Bowen, 20 Conn. 127.
[3] Thompson v. Engle, 3 Green Ch. 271.
[4] Brown v. Redwyne, 16 Geo. 67.

not enjoin such suit, on the ground of any claim arising under the statute of limitations, that being a matter peculiarly proper for the consideration of a court of law.[1] So an injunction to restrain heirs from prosecuting an ejectment, to recover property of inheritance sold by a trustee, to whom their mother, who had a life-estate in the premises, had conveyed it in trust for the use of her minor children, or an order to execute releases thereof, will not be granted, where there is no evidence of consent to, or consideration received for, the sale by them after their majority.[2] So it is a rule of practice in the Circuit Court of the United States, not to allow an injunction to stay an ejectment, until it can be investigated in equity, unless judgment be entered therein.[3] So (in England) the common-law procedure act of 1854 does not authorize a writ of injunction in an action of ejectment.[4] And where it is plain that the deed, under which the plaintiff in ejectment claims, is invalid in law, the defendants will be left to make their defence in the action, and cannot have it enjoined.[5]

§ 49. Where a note, given for the purchase-money of land, to which the payee has given bond to make title, has been assigned to a third party, and suit instituted upon it, and the payee is unable to make title to the land, the vendee is entitled to relief in equity.[6] So where there is a defect in the title to land sold, and the solvency of the vendor is doubtful, the collection of the purchase-money will be restrained, until the purchaser is indemnified.[7] And, on the other hand, where a vendee of land had purchased a prior incumbrance, and had set up this new title in an action on the note for the purchase-money, brought by his vendor, as showing a total failure of consideration; held, on a bill in

[1] Caldwell v. Williams, 1 Bail. Ch. 175.
[2] Farley v. Woodburn, 2 Stockt. 96.
[3] Turner v. American, &c., 5 McLean, 344.
[4] Baylis v. Le Gros, 2 C. B. (N. S.) 316.
[5] Morris Canal, &c. Co. v. Dennis, 1 Beasl. 249.
[6] Black v. Bowman, 4 Eng. 501.
[7] Jones v. Stanton, 11 Mis. 433.

equity for an injunction against such defence, the remedy in equity was more certain and complete than that at law, and the grantee was enjoined from setting up his new title as a defence beyond the amount which he had paid for it.[1] But the mere claim by a third person of a paramount title, not alleged by the bill to be valid, and bringing suit upon that claim against the purchaser, are not sufficient to authorize a court of equity to stay, by injunction, the vendor who has warranted the title, from proceeding either at law or in equity to collect the unpaid purchase-money.[2] So an injunction should not be granted to restrain a suit for the purchase-money of land, upon the ground that there were prior liens due, and that the complainant gave more for the land than he otherwise would have done, in consequence of misrepresentations made by the vendor or his agent at the time of the sale, unless the plaintiff sets forth in his bill, as nearly as he can, the amount of such liens, and what he believes to be the amount of the injury sustained. And where the purchaser is entitled to compensation merely, he cannot enjoin the vendor from collecting the purchase-money; or, at most, he can only enjoin him for the sum which he alleges distinctly in his bill to be due to him for such compensation.[3] So where a purchaser had remained ten years in the undisturbed enjoyment of the property, it was held to be no ground of injunction to stay proceedings for the recovery of the purchase-money, that the original purchase was void by the laws of the State, but that he had neglected to urge that defence at law; or that he had heard that some persons unknown might possibly, at some future time, assert a title to the property; and such an injunction, if granted, must be dissolved.[4]

§ 50. A. sold land to a company of which B. was a member, and took B.'s individual guaranty on bonds given for the purchase-money. At the same time A. made an

---

[1] Champlin v. Dotson, 13 S. & M. 553.
[2] Gayle v. Fattle, 14 Md. 69.
[3] Ashe v. Hale, 5 Ired. Eq. 55.
[4] Truly v. Warner, 5 How. 141.

indenture with the purchasers, covenanting that the lands in five years would sell for a certain price, and pledged therefor his stock in the company. Shortly after the sale, A. deposited the bonds as collateral security for a loan to him, with the United States Bank. The bank sold the bonds to C. and others. A. became insolvent, the land depreciated greatly in value, and he was wholly unable to indemnify the purchasers. The holders of the bonds brought suits on them against B., who filed a bill for an injunction against the suits, and prayed also that the lands might be sold and the proceeds applied on the bonds. Held, that while the bonds were in the hands of A., even before the expiration of the five years, B. would have been entitled, on a well-founded apprehension of loss, to a bill, *quia timet*, for an injunction restraining A. from selling the bonds. But as he had parted with them before his insolvency, that the rights of third parties had intervened, and they must be protected against loss through equities existing between the original parties.[1]

§ 51. Where a bill was filed to restrain the defendant from proceeding at law to obtain possession of the land in question, but an ejectment suit, commenced by the defendant after the bill was sworn to, but before it was filed, was not noticed in the bill; held, an injunction, which did not permit the defendant to proceed to judgment in the ejectment, was irregular, though the commencement of that suit was unknown to the plaintiff at the time of filing the bill.[2]

§ 52. In ejectment cases, where no discovery is sought, and the title at law is admitted, an injunction will be granted upon terms only, so as to leave the party to proceed to trial and judgment at law.[3]

§ 53. A. brought ejectment against B. B.'s wife and another, joining B. as a necessary party, and alleging title in

[1] Coster *v.* Griswold, 4 Edw. Ch. 364.
[2] Carroll *v.* Sand, 10 Paige, 298.
[3] Ham *v.* Schuyler, 2 John. Ch. 140.

the wife, obtained an injunction against A. from setting up any claim under his deeds, alleged to be a cloud on the wife's title, but making no reference to the pending ejectment.   Thereupon judgment was given for A. in the ejectionment suit, without a trial by jury.   Held erroneous, but also that the injunction did not in terms restrain the writ, and, if it did, the plaintiff could not proceed in violation of it, but must have leave under it to proceed at law.[1]

§ 54. To obtain an injunction of an action at law on account of *confusion of boundaries*, the complainant must allege such confusion, and set forth the circumstances which produce it.[2]

§ 55. Upon petition for an injunction to restrain proceedings at law, affecting real estate, until a decision upon a bill in equity for title to such real estate, if the bill upon demurrer be insufficient to sustain a decree, it is error to perpetuate the injunction.[3]

§ 56. A bill for enjoining a suit, brought to recover land, is not prevented by the plaintiff's assigning his title to the land, even to a resident of another State.   The right is not an estate in the land, but a personal claim for relief, which does not pass by a conveyance of the plaintiff's title to the land, and which, it seems, is not assignable.[4]

§ 57. In Maryland, chancery will not grant an injunction to prevent the execution of a writ of *replevin*.[5]

§ 58. The question of *set-off* or discount often arises in this class of cases.   Thus an action on a forthcoming bond was enjoined at the instance of the surety therein, on the ground that he had a debt of larger amount against the

[1] Wildy v. Bonney, 35 Miss. 77.
[2] Foster, 6 Eng. 304.
[3] Blakeney v. Ferguson, 4 Eng. 487.

[4] Dunlap v. Stetson, 4 Mas. 349.
[5] Glenn v. Fowler, 8 Gill & J. 340.

plaintiff, and that the latter was insolvent.[1] So where covenants, in form independent, are in fact part of the same
transaction, and mutual, equity will restrain the collection
of one, upon the failure of the other.[2] So the insolvency of
the vendor of a diseased slave is sufficient ground to enjoin
the payment of a note of a third party, assigned by the
vendee to the vendor, the note being at the time unpaid.[3]
But where a lessee, entitled to away-going crops, was evicted
by a prior mortgagee, during the term, and while the crops
remained upon the land; the court refused to stay a suit for
the rent, to enable the lessee to offset the damages for the
loss of his crop, the allegations in the bill, that the plaintiff
was out of the jurisdiction, and insolvent, being fully denied
in the answer.[4]

§ 59. The doctrine of *estoppel* furnishes ground for injunction against suits at law. (See *Estoppel*.) The court
will restrain a party from enforcing a legal claim, where
promises have been made to the person legally liable not
to enforce it, upon the faith of which obligations have been
entered into.[5] Thus it is held that, where a note was
signed and delivered with an understanding that it should
not be enforced, chancery will enjoin its enforcement.[6] So
a garnishee may enjoin the plaintiff, where his defence is,
that for a consideration the plaintiff promised to pay the
debt garnished.[7] So where one accepts land devised to him,
on condition of ratifying a previous sale by the testator, and
sells portions thereof; he may be perpetually enjoined from
proceeding at law to avoid the sale by the testator.[8] So
where the plaintiff sent the defendant a draft, telling him
he might use it, if he would extend a certain overdue
mortgage, which the plaintiff was under no personal liability
to pay; and the defendant kept the draft but declined to

[1] McClellan *v.* Kinnaird, 6 Gratt.
352.
[2] King *v.* Lindsay, 3 Ired. Ch. 77.
[3] Brownston *v.* Cropper, 1 Litt. 173.
[4] Tone *v.* Brace, 1 Clarke, 291.
[5] Money *v.* Jorden, 11 Eng. Law
and Eq. 182.

[6] Bell *v.* Gamble, 9 Humph. 117.
[7] Matthews *v.* Robinson, 33 Ala.
320.
[8] Leonard *v.* Crommelin, 1 Edw.
Ch. 206.

stay his foreclosure suit unless he received more money on account of the mortgage: held, the defendant must accept the money on the terms offered, or not at all, and must return it or be bound by the condition. Also, that the plaintiff was not to be driven to his remedy at law, but might enjoin the foreclosure suit.[1] So where money has been expended, or improvements have been made, and buildings erected, on the faith of a parol license; equity will interpose, so far, at least, as to restrain the licenser from appropriating to his own use the money and labor thus expended, without placing the licensee in the same situation he was in before making the expenditures.[2]

§ 60. And in the present connection it may be stated, though not precisely applicable to the subject of the present chapter, that, on the other hand, one may be debarred by estoppel from maintaining an injunction. Where one lies by and permits another to erect works at great expense, and to use them for several years without objection, he cannot come into equity for an injunction to restrain the use of such works in the same manner as they have been before used.[3] Thus where the complainants had agreed to allow the defendants to draw water, for running a mill, from a certain lake, the outlet of which flowed through the complainants' lands, and had suffered them to go on and construct a mill and race, at an expense of $3,000, before informing them that they did not intend to abide by their promise; an injunction, which had been granted to restrain the taking of the water of the lake for the mill, was dissolved.[4] So where the complainant had stood by without objecting, and allowed the defendant to go on and expend a considerable amount of money in the erection of a mill, in violation of the terms of a grant made by the complainant, in consideration of the erection of the mill, and of the right to use the water of a creek in a particular manner; held, by his

[1] Grinnan v. Platt, 31 Barb. 328.
[2] Hazelton v. Putnam, 3 Chand. 117.
[3] Southard v. Morris, &c., Saxt. 518.
[4] Payne v. Paddock, Walk. Ch. 487. See Mitchell v. Leavitt, 30 Conn. 587.

silence, he had waived all right to an injunction against diverting the water.[1](a)

§ 61. *Fraud* is another ground of interference. (See *Fraud.*) Thus A., very soon after coming of age, was induced by B., his superior officer, to accept bills for 3,000*l.* at two months, for his accommodation, which were handed by B. to C., a money-lender, in payment of a debt of 2,590*l.* C., who was privy to the transaction, afterwards agreed to arrange a renewal of these, and another bill for 500*l.* for twelve months, in consideration of A.'s note for 2,500*l.* payable in three years, which sum C. charged for his expenses and trouble. An injunction was granted against C. to restrain a suit for the 2,500*l.*, there being reason to suppose, upon investigation, and evidence offered, that A. might have been induced to give the note by misrepresentation as to the extent of his previous liability and the nature and extent of C.'s services.[2] So where, by misrepresentation, an act of Assembly had been obtained, whereby lands previously sold in accordance with a former act were included in a new grant; it was decreed that the second grantee should release such land to the State, by deed, and an ejectment against the claimant under the first act was enjoined.[3]

[1] Jacox *v.* Clark, Walk. Ch. 249.   [3] The State *v.* Reed, 4 Har. & [2] Lloyd *v.* Clark, 6 Beav. 309.   M'Hen. 6.

(a) The court below having held, that a party, who by representations had induced another to enter into irrevocable engagements, must be restrained from taking proceedings to enforce obligations and promises, the abandonment of all intention to enforce which was the subject of those representations; the decree granting a perpetual injunction to restrain such proceedings was on appeal confirmed. Lord Justice Cranworth dissenting, first, because this case was not within the principle of the cases on which the decree below was professed to be grounded, there being no misrepresentation of fact; and secondly, because the promise alleged by the plaintiff was supported by the evidence of one witness only, who had since died, and which was not, in his lordship's opinion, supported by the surrounding circumstances, and was positively denied by the answer. Money *v.* Jorden, 13 Eng. Law and Eq. 245.

§ 62. Where A. conveyed to B. a piece of land, representing it to contain a coal mine, for which B. promised to pay a certain sum, and an annuity, on condition that, in case the mine, after being faithfully and scientifically wrought, should not yield a certain quantity of coal, the annuity should cease; held, the judgment of reasonable men, who had examined the spot, and had actually worked upon it, that an attempt to work the mine would be useless, or attended with great expense and hazard, was sufficient to satisfy the condition; and A. was enjoined from prosecuting any suit for recovering the annuity, or any part thereof.[1]   So, A. having sued B. on a promissory note, it appeared that the consideration for the note was an undertaking, on the part of A., that C. should convey land to B., which A. alleged that C. owned, and for which, on the conveyance being made, B. made to A. a cash payment in addition to the note, fully covering the value of all C.'s interest in the land, which was but three-fifths of what A. had represented it to be.   Held, the suit should be enjoined, without any offer on the part of B. to rescind the sale.[2]   So where a creditor fraudulently aids and assists the principal debtor to remove from the county, with the intent to hinder and delay the surety in his remedy against the principal, equity will enjoin the creditor from enforcing his claim against the surety.[3]   But where a decree in chancery had been reversed, on the ground of fraud practised in obtaining it, and the party was restored to his former situation, and an action at law had been brought for the fraud; held, chancery would not grant an injunction against the suit.[4]   So a creditor, having brought an action, with an accompanying attachment, cannot bring a second action in the Supreme Court, for the recovery of his debt, to set aside an alleged fraudulent judgment previously recovered against the debtor, and for an injunction to restrain the paying over of the proceeds of a sale of property levied upon by virtue

[1] Dale v. Roosevelt, 5 John. Ch. 174.
[2] Warren v. Carey, 5 Ind. 319.
[3] Smith v. Hays, 1 Jones Eq. 321.
[4] Peck v. Woodbridge, 3 Day, 508.

of an execution issued on such judgment. In such cases, the creditor must wait until he has established his debt by judgment, before he will be entitled to an injunction, or other equitable relief, against the judgment alleged to be fraudulent. And, *it seems*, he has a complete remedy at law, by proceeding with the attachment suit, obtaining a judgment therein, and selling the property under it.[1]

§ 63. A. and B. were creditors of C. C. confessed judgment in favor of A., and B. obtained an injunction to stay proceedings by A. upon his judgment, on the ground of fraud. While the injunction continued in force, B. brought an action at law to enforce his debt, and, on petition by A., was put to his election to stay proceedings at law, or to dissolve the injunction.[2]

§ 64. *Mistake* is another ground of injunction against suits. (See Chap. VIII.) Thus, in a case of bastardy, a warrant was issued for the arrest of A., by virtue of which he was arrested and taken before a justice. A. denied the charge, and offered to give security for his appearance at court. The justice, being told to do so by the constable, prepared a bond to indemnify the township, which A. and his security signed, supposing it to be an instrument of security for appearance. On the hearing, the court made no order of bastardy against A., yet the overseers of the township brought an action on the bond of indemnity. On bill filed, praying an injunction against further proceedings, and that the bond may be cancelled, the injunction was at once granted, and subsequently a decree was entered for the complainants.[3]

§ 65. But in the following case this relief was refused.

§ 66. A. purchased of B., by bond, part of a lot of land,

<hr>

[1] Mills *v.* Block, 30 Barb. 549.
[2] Livingston *v.* Kane, 3 John. Ch. 224.
[3] Field *v.* Cory, 3 Halst. Ch. 574.

subject to the legal title of B., and to C.'s claim for the price of the whole lot. He gave C. a bond for the amount of his claim, and took from him, in return, a bond to convey. The consideration of B.'s bond was the payment of this claim, but it was not expressed, and, by mistake, the bond was given for a conveyance of the whole lot, although C. knew the dimensions of the part purchased, and that the possession of the residue was in another person. The mistake and the consideration of B.'s bond were proved by his answer, and by parol evidence. A. brought a bill to enjoin a suit on his bond, and for specific performance of C.'s. An injunction granted was finally dissolved, and it was decreed that C. should convey the land originally purchased of B., on payment of his claim and his costs in both suits.[1]

§ 67. The court will interfere by injunction, to prevent, in all cases, the jurisdiction of the court, the validity of its process or orders, or the title of its *officers*, from being drawn in question in another court, by a suit against the officers or persons acting under the authority of the court. But where process has been irregularly issued, and set aside by the court on that account, or where an officer has transcended his authority; it is not a matter of course to stay proceedings against the wrong-doer in all other courts. And where process has been set aside for irregularity, the officer, or party, desiring the protection of the court for acts performed under such process, must apply promptly; and the application comes too late after judgment against him for such acts.[2]

§ 68. Where an *executor*, residing out of the State, and being insolvent, is seeking to obtain a fund belonging to the estate, which it is feared may be wasted; equity may and ought to restrain him by injunction from prosecuting his proceedings at law, until he submits himself to the jurisdiction of the court.[3] (See *Executors*.)

[1] Bickham *v.* Gough, 4 Har. & McHen. 17.

[3] Dougherty *v.* Walker, 15 Geo. 442.

[2] Mackay *v.* Bluckett, 9 Paige, 437.

§ 69. Where a perpetual injunction was decreed by the Vice-Chancellor against a suit at law, which decree was *appealed from*, the Chancellor refused to modify the injunction so as to let the suit at law proceed to judgment without prejudice, pending the appeal; no particular necessity appearing for so doing.[1]

§ 70. A few miscellaneous points of practice remain to be stated.

§ 71. After a preliminary injunction, restraining a suit at law, had been dissolved, the plaintiff in such suit, before final decree in the court, had compelled the bail to pay the debt. Held, that these facts should have been brought before the court, by supplemental bill, without which they could not be taken into consideration, upon making the final decree.[2]

§ 72. When a court of equity has issued an order for an injunction restraining a party from bringing an action, the higher court will enforce such order by staying proceedings under the common law procedure act, 1852, 15 and 16 Vict. c. 76, § 226, although no writ of injunction has been actually issued.[3]

§ 73. A statute, requiring a release of errors on filing a bill for an injunction to stay proceedings at law, applies only to the defendant in the law proceedings, and not to third persons.[4]

§ 74. Where a bill in equity was brought to restrain a suit at law in another court, the parties filed an agreement, requesting that, if the court were of opinion they had not jurisdiction to grant the injunction, but that the facts

[1] Fulton, &c. v. New York, &c., 3 Paige, 31.
[2] Griswold v. Baker, 2 Edw. Ch. 461.
[3] Cobbett v. Ludlam, 33 Eng. Law and Eq. 418.
[4] Sevier v. Ross, 1 Freem. Ch. 519.

stated in the bill would be a defence to the action at law, they would decide accordingly; and they agreed that the decision should bind the parties as if that suit were pending in the court in which the bill was filed. But the court declined to determine the point.[1]

§ 75. It is no sufficient reason for disregarding an injunction to restrain a suit, that, in the writ of injunction served, the suit restrained is described as one in which A. B. alone is a party, when in reality A. B. and wife are concerned; there being sufficient identification of the suit.[2]

[1] Stone v. Hobart, 8 Pick. 464.   [2] Endicott v. Mathis, 1 Stockt. 110.

CHAPTER VII.

GROUNDS OF INJUNCTION—FRAUD.

§ 1. HAVING now completed our view of those general topics in the law of injunction which apply alike to all the grounds for that equitable remedy; we proceed to consider the particular wrongs or injuries which may be thus prevented or redressed. We shall next treat of the *parties*, and then of the *subject-matters*, in this form of proceeding. It is to be remarked, however, that each of these several topics has been often referred to, and sometimes considered at length, in the several preliminary chapters, relating, respectively, to the general nature of injunction, the dissolving of injunctions, judgments and executions, and suits at law. Consequently, some of the succeeding chapters of the book will be found comparatively brief and fragmentary; their omissions, however, being readily supplied, with the aid of a copious Table of Contents and Index, by reference to the more full chapters which precede them.

§ 2. Prominent among the *wrongs*, to which the remedy of injunction is applied, is *fraud;* which is alike the subject matter of general equitable relief, as peculiarly liable to the want of any adequate remedy at law, and also of injunction, as one of the most effective intruments of such relief.[1]

§ 3. Injunction is often resorted to in case of alleged fraud

---

[1] See Wingate *v.* Haywood, 40 N. H. 437.

upon creditors.(a) Thus where a creditor's bill alleges the fraudulent execution of a bond by the defendant, upon which he is about to confess a judgment in fraud of creditors; an action on the bond will be enjoined. But the claim must be distinctly stated, and proper exhibits must accompany the bill.[1](b) So attaching creditors of an insolvent may, before judgment, enjoin an execution against the property attached under a judgment alleged to be fraudulent; all the material allegations, except the fraud, being admitted.[2]

§ 4. In New York, it was formerly held, that only after judgment (and perhaps execution) at law against a debtor, will the court, in a proper case, grant an injunction to restrain him from disposing of his property.[3] Also, that the 219th section of the code applies only to the single case, where, pending a judgment about to be recovered, the defendant manifests an intent to place his property beyond the reach of an execution. And that a simple contract creditor, having acquired no lien on his debtor's property, cannot restrain the debtor and his assignee from further proceedings in a fraudulent assignment made before the commencement of the action.[4] But, as the law now stands, an injunction may be issued, and a receiver (in the person of the sheriff) appointed, before judgment, at the instance of any creditor,

---

[1] Mahaney v. Lazier, 16 Md. 69.
[2] Heyneman v. Dannenberg, 6 Cal. 376.

[3] Candler v. Pettit, 1 Paige, 168; Wiggins v. Armstrong, 2 John. Ch. 144.
[4] Reubens v. Joel, 3 Kern. 488.

(a) Mere *misrepresentation* will not always prevent the interference by injunction, even against the party injured by such misrepresentation. Thus an injunction was granted to stay an action against an auctioneer for the deposit, though the estate sold was represented as freehold with leasehold adjoining, and turned out nearly all leasehold, and though there had been great delay in making out the plaintiff's title. Fordyce v. Ford, 4 Bro. Ch. 370, 495.

(b) On the other hand, equity will assist a grantee from a trustee under a deed made in fraud of creditors, against those who are not creditors. Gridley v. Wynant, 23 How. 500.

and against any debtor, to prevent a fraudulent disposition of property, and as a security for the satisfaction of such judgment as the plaintiff may recover.[1]   So A., being insolvent, transferred his entire property to B., his brother and clerk, who was young, without family, experience, or property, for $20,000, secured only by the notes of B., and payable in one year with interest.   The same day A. assigned the notes to C. for benefit of creditors, with preferences. Held, the two transfers constituted in law but one transaction, and there was sufficient evidence of fraud to justify an injunction.[2]   So where creditors of an absent debtor had obtained an attachment against his goods, and a brother of the debtor, to whom the property had been fraudulently conveyed, was disposing of it and preventing the creditors from seizing it; held, the creditors had a lien under the attachment, which could be enforced by injunction, restraining the brother from disposing of the property, and removing it out of the jurisdiction of the court.[3]

§ 5. But on a bill by creditors, to enjoin an administrator from confessing judgment on a bond, alleged to have been given by the intestate in fraud of creditors; a perpetual injunction cannot be decreed, without proof or an admission in the answer that the complainants are in fact creditors. The silence of the answer, in this respect, is not an admission of the fact.[4] (See *Executors*.) So the alleged fraudulent transfer of his property by a debtor charged to be insolvent is no ground for injunction and the appointment of a receiver, without clear proof of fraud, and of imminent danger unless such relief is granted. It is not sufficient for the bill to charge positively that the defendant is indebted to the plaintiff, and to state, upon information and belief (but not the sources of information), a series of facts tending to show a

---

[1] Mitchell *v.* Bettman, 25 Barb. 408.
[2] Litchfield *v.* Pelton, 6 Barb. 187.
[3] Falconer *v.* Freeman, 4 Sandf. Ch. 565.
[4] Holliday *v.* Potter, 3 Hawks, 198.

fraudulent conveyance of all the defendant's property.[1] So where an assignment by a debtor, as set forth in a bill to set it aside as fraudulent, contained no provision which was illegal, or the necessary effect of which would be to defraud creditors, and the bill was not under oath; held, there was no ground for a preliminary injunction.[2] So where a bill alleged that the defendant was indebted to the complainants; that he was disposing of his property, collecting and secreting the debts due him, and, with intent and purpose to defraud his creditors, and before judgment could be recovered against him, after completing his sales and collections, to abscond: held, under the laws of Maryland, the bill disclosed no ground for an injunction, or appointment of receivers. Such a case is not within the act of 1835, c. 380, § 2.[3]

§ 6. Fraud *between the parties* may also furnish ground of injunction. Thus A. obtained from B. a deed of land, through fraud, in which C. was concerned, and afterwards confessed a judgment to C., who assigned it to D. for valuable consideration, without notice of the fraud. Held, the judgment created no valid lien upon the land, and a conveyance to B. of the land must be decreed, discharged of the judgment, and a perpetual injunction awarded against its execution upon that land.[4] But a decree for an injunction, upon evidence that a mare was unsound at the time of the sale, the *scienter* and fraudulent concealment not being proved, is erroneous.[5]

§ 7. Where a steam-mill property and land are subject to dower and judgments to an amount exceeding their value; it is fraud on the part of the owner to sever and remove the engine or other machinery, in order that they may be seized on a subsequent execution as chattels; and equity will restrain such removal by injunction, on application of a judgment

[1] Blondheim v. Moore, 11 Md. 365.
[2] Bogert v. Haight, 9 Paige, 297.
[3] Uhl v. Dillon, 10 Md. 500; Hubbard v. Hubbard, 14 Md. 356.

[4] Livingston v. Hubbs, 2 John. Ch. 512.
[5] Howell v. Freeman, 1 J. J. Marsh. 54.

creditor. The point, whether such interference would be justified on the mere ground of *waste* is left undecided.[1]

§ 8. An action was brought by A. against B., to recover the proceeds of sale of a ship, owned by them jointly, which sale B. made as agent. The ship was sold twice, in California and in China. It was alleged that the sale in California was fraudulent; that she was bid in for B.; that B., as agent for the nominal purchaser, sold her in China for a much larger sum, and that A. was entitled to share in the proceeds of the last sale. The complaint prayed an injunction to prevent the disposal by B., during the pendency of the suit, of the proceeds of the last sale, they being identified as specie drafts and credits in his hands. An order of injunction was granted. On a subsequent application the injunction was continued, though the allegations in relation to the California sale were denied by B. in his answer and affidavit, it not appearing to the court that the plaintiff's case was thus overborne.[2]

§ 9. Where, in a suit in equity, facts are admitted, from which the court or jury may properly infer a fraudulent intent; a general denial of fraud will not prevent an injunction, and it should continue till final judgment.[3]

[1] Witmer's, &c., 45 Penn. 455.
[2] Merritt v. Thompson, 3 E. D. Smith, 283.
[3] Litchfield v. Pelton, 6 Barb. 187.

CHAPTER VIII.

ACCIDENT AND MISTAKE.

§ 1. ANOTHER ground of injunction is *accident and mistake.*
(See p. 257.)   The distinction between accident and mistake
is thus pointed out by approved writers.   Accident is "an
occurrence in relation to a contract, which was not antici-
pated by the parties, when the same was entered into, and
which gives an undue advantage to one of them over the
other, in a court of law."[1]   Accident is "not merely inevitable
casualty, or the act of Providence, or what is technically
called *vis major*, or irresistible force; but such unforeseen
events, misfortunes, losses, acts, or omissions, as are not the
result of any negligence or misconduct in the party."[2]   Mistake is "that result of ignorance of law, or of fact, which has
led a person to commit that which, if he had not been in
error, he would not have done."[3]

§ 2. Where a party, with a full knowledge of all the facts,
pays or executes his note for money, voluntarily, under a
mistake of law, he cannot recover back the money, or enjoin
the collection of the note, on the ground of mistake.[4]   So it
is no ground for continuing an injunction upon a judgment
at law, that there is a mistake in a title bond of the description of the land, without showing that the other party, on
request, refused to correct the mistake.[5]   But where A., being
in possession of land owned by the State, as a settler, conveyed one acre to B. ; and C. afterwards obtained A.'s title,

---

[1] Jeremy, Eq. Juris. 358.
[2] 1 Story, Eq. sect. 78.
[3] Jeremy, Eq. Juris. 385.

[4] Hubbard *v.* Martin, 8 Yerg. 498.
[5] Long *v.* Brown, 4 Ala. 622.

the deeds all excepting B.'s acre, and the State conveyed the whole of the land to C.: held, B. was entitled to relief against this conveyance, and a judgment founded thereon.[1] And, on the other hand, equity will not enjoin proceedings to correct a mistake in reference to lands. Thus a corporation empowered by special acts, which embodied the act of 8 & 9 Vict. c. 18, to construct waterworks, and to take certain lands, required lands belonging to A. and B., the boundary between which was improperly described in their plans and books of reference. In consideration of B.'s withdrawing his opposition to their bill in committee, they agreed to settle the value of the land required from and the compensation due to him, by arbitration under the above act, and to fix the exact quantity of land within six months after the passing of the bill. In the proceedings under the reference to arbitration, the mistake of the boundary was pointed out; but the award fixed a value, in terms, only for the land within the boundary so inaccurately delineated, and the corporation took that land accordingly, leaving between it and the true boundary line a narrow strip of land belonging to B., but which the corporation had agreed to purchase from A. as part of this land, and for which they paid a sum of money to A., and of which they took possession as part of the land purchased from A. B. recovered the strip of land afterwards from the corporation in ejectment, and a rule for a new trial was refused. The corporation thereupon proceed, within six months from such refusal, to make themselves legal owners of the strip of land in question, under the compulsory powers given in case of mistake by the 124th section of the lands clauses consolidation act above mentioned. B. filed a bill for an injunction to restrain them from so doing, which, upon motion, was refused with costs. Held, that the circumstances amounted to mistake, within the meaning of the 124th section. Also, that this section applied to land altogether omitted to be purchased by mistake,

---

[1] Dunlap v. Stetson, 4 Mas. 349.

as well as an outstanding interest therein so omitted to be purchased.[1]   So, at a certain time, the ordinary method of removing a case from a justice's court was by *certiorari*, grantable by a judge, to be applied for within ninety days after judgment.   An act was passed, authorizing the clerks of the district courts to issue writs of *certiorari*, and a party obtained one from the clerk; but the law was decided to be unconstitutional.   Held, the mistake of the law was sufficient excuse of the party for not having obtained a *certiorari* in due time from the district judge, and, on a showing of merits, he was entitled to an injunction.[2]

[1] Hyde *v.* Manchester, 10 Eng.   [2] Cobbs *v.* Coleman, 14 Tex. 594.
Law and Eq. Rep. 42.

CHAPTER IX.

NUISANCE.

1. General jurisdiction.
2. Restrictions.

3. Public nuisance.
15. *Abatement.*

§ 1. A VERY frequent ground of injunction is *nuisance.* The established rule on this subject is, that chancery has power to interpose in behalf of one who is injured by a continuing, permanent, or recurring private nuisance, unless the injury be such as may be compensated in damages.[1] So when a nuisance is likely to occasion a special injury to one individual, which cannot well be compensated in damages, equity will entertain jurisdiction of the case at his suit.[2] In a case in Massachusetts, the court remarked, "It was contended, in argument, that the court would take jurisdiction of nuisances only in urgent cases, where the prompt interposition of the court is necessary, by immediate injunction, and where the proceedings at law would be too slow. But we think this no test of the superior efficacy and completeness of the remedy in equity, although it is one of its advantages. We think it sufficient that the remedy in equity is more adequate, and better adapted to meet the justice of the case, and more complete by being at once more comprehensive and effectual."[3] And in a recent case in Pennsylvania, the court give a concise and comprehensive view of the general grounds for an injunction, in the remark—" The loss of *health and sleep,* the enjoyment of *quiet and repose,*

[1] Norris *v.* Hill, 1 Mann. 202; Clack *v.* White, 2 Swan, 540; 1 Gill & J. 184.

[2] Milhau *v.* Sharp, 28 Barb. 228.
[3] Per Shaw, C. J., Bemis *v.* Upham, 13 Pick. 171.

and the *comforts of home*, cannot be restored or compensated in money."[1] So equity may enjoin the owner of land, adjoining the plaintiff's premises, from removing any soil, in such manner as to cause the plaintiff's land, by reason of the withdrawal of its lateral support, to fall away or subside.[2] (See Chap. XXVII.) So an ordinance of the city council, ordering a blacksmith's shop to be closed, as a nuisance, is authorized by law, and may be carried into effect by an injunction restraining the owner from continuing it.[3] So an injunction was granted, after a trial at law, against the ringing of the bells of a Roman Catholic Church, so as to annoy or disturb the plaintiff who lived very near the church.[4] So the defendants, a railroad corporation, bound by their charter to fence their road, for the purpose of constructing a permanent fence along their track through the meadow of the orator, which was subject to overflow, began to plant willows upon each side of the track, upon the land used by them, and within three feet of A.'s line, with the expectation that they would grow, and that boards might be attached to them, forming a fence, which, in the opinion of the officers, would be more permanent, useful, and economical than any other kind of fence. It appeared that the land of A. would be seriously injured by the roots and branches of the trees, and that there was no absolute necessity for thus making a fence. Held, the planting of the trees might be enjoined.[5] (See Chap. XXVI.)

§ 2. But, it is said, ordinarily equity interferes in case of nuisance, only to restrain irreparable mischief, suppress interminable litigation, or prevent a multiplicity of suits. And in these cases equity will not ordinarily decide that such nuisance exists, if controverted, but will require that the

---

[1] Per Thompson, J., Dennis v. Echardt, (Pennsylvania) Law Reg. Jan. 1863, p. 169.
[2] Farrand v. Marshall, 21 Barb. 409.
[3] New Orleans v. Lambert, 14 La. An. 247.
[4] Soltau v. De Held, 2 Sim. N. S. 132.
[5] Brock v. Connecticut, &c., 35 Verm. 273.

complainant first establish his right at law, except where he has been in the long, quiet, and uninterrupted enjoyment of the right, in which case the other party may be enjoined until he proves his own title.[1]   "It is not every violation of the rights of another which may be ranked under the general head of nuisance which will authorize the interposition of this court by means of an injunction. It must be a case of strong and imperious necessity, or the right must have been previously established at law, or it must have been long enjoyed without interruption."[2] So, in a recent English case, it is said, "The jurisdiction of this court over nuisance by injunction at all is of recent growth, has not till very lately been much exercised, and has at various times found great reluctance on the part of the learned judges to use it even in cases where the thing or the act complained of was admitted to be directly and immediately hurtful to the complainant."[3]   Conformably with these views, where a matter complained of is not, in itself, a nuisance, but may be so according to circumstances, those circumstances must be ascertained by the verdict of a jury, before chancery will interfere by injunction.[4] So where, upon the bill and answer, the structure complained of is not *primâ facie* a nuisance, the injunction will not be continued, but the defendant will proceed with his acts at his peril.[5] So where damages will compensate, either the benefit derived, or the loss suffered, from a nuisance, equity will not interfere.[6] Nor if the evidence is conflicting, and the injury doubtful, eventual, or contingent.[7] More especially where an issue at law thereon has been twice found in favor of the defendants.[8] So a bill in equity, praying for an injunction to suppress a nuisance to the plaintiff's land, will be dismissed on general demurrer, for want of equity, unless

---

[1] Bean v. Coleman, 44 N. H. 539.
[2] Per Appleton, J., Jordan v. Woodward, 38 Maine, 424.
[3] Per Lord Brougham, Ripon v. Hobart, 3 My. & K. 169.
[4] Kirkman v. Handy, 11 Humph. 406 ; 1 Grant, 412.
[5] Cunningham v. Rice, 28 Geo. 30 ; Muggatt v. Goetchins, 20 Ibid. 350.
[6] Grey v. Ohio, &c., 1 Grant's Cas. 412.
[7] Laughlin v. President, &c., 6 Ind. 223 ; Butler v. Rogers, 1 Stockt. 487.
[8] Davidson v. Isham, 1 Stockt. 186.

it appears, from the subject-matter affected by the alleged nuisance, and the extent and nature of the injury to be apprehended from it, that there is danger of irreparable mischief, or of an injury such that it cannot be adequately compensated in a suit at law, or that the right of the plaintiff to enjoy the land, free from the molestation complained of, has been established in a suit at law.[1] And the *amount* of injury is sometimes a material consideration. Thus a gas company was incorporated by act of Parliament, for the purpose of supplying the town of S. with gas. Some years afterwards, another company was formed, and registered under the joint-stock companies registration act, for a like purpose, and commenced opening up the streets and highways of S. to lay down their pipes, &c., some of the inhabitants approving, and some disapproving, of the works. Upon an information and bill by the incorporated company, the court (Sir J. L. Knight Bruce, L. J., *dissentiente*) refused an injunction to restrain the new company from continuing their works, the nuisance or damage being trivial.[2] So an injunction was refused, against the burning of bricks upon ground, of which the defendant had taken a building lease to build New Bond Street, and near to the plaintiff's houses; for the reasons that, if a final injunction were denied, the defendant would be irremediably injured by non-fulfilment of contracts; that burning brick-kilns were standing in all parts, and some almost in the heart of some of the principal streets; and that there was a sufficient remedy at law, unlike the case of cutting down avenues or the like.[3] And in the case of a bill for an injunction, to stay building a hospital for people infected with the smallpox in "Cold Bath Fields," very near the houses of several tenants of the plaintiff; Lord Hardwicke said, "I cannot make any order in this matter; I am of opinion it is a charity like to prove of great advantage to mankind. Such an hospital must not be far from a town, because those

---

[1] Coe v. Lake Co., 37 N. H. 254. [3] Duke, &c. v. Hilliard, 18 Ves.
[2] Attorney-General v. Sheffield 219; 1 Ambl. 159.
Gas Co., 19 Eng. Law and Eq. 639.

that are attacked with that disorder in a natural way may not be in a condition to be carried far."[1]

§ 3. The question has often been held material, whether an alleged nuisance is *private* or *public*. Upon this subject Judge Story remarks: "Nuisances may be of two sorts: 1. Such as are injurious to the public at large, or to public rights; 2. Such as are injurious to the rights and interests of private persons. In regard to public nuisances, the jurisdiction of courts of equity seems to be of a very ancient date, and has been distinctly traced back to the reign of Queen Elizabeth. The instances of the interposition of the court, however, are, it is said, rare, and principally confined to informations seeking preventive relief. Thus, informations in equity have been maintained against a public nuisance by stopping a highway. Analogous to that, there have been many cases in the Court of Exchequer of nuisances to harbors, which are a species of highway; but the question of nuisance or not must, in cases of doubt, be tried by a jury; and the injunction will be granted or not, as that fact is decided. And the court, in the exercise of its jurisdiction, will direct the matter to be tried upon an indictment, and reserve its decree accordingly.—In the first place, they can interpose, where the courts of law cannot, to restrain and prevent such nuisances which are threatened or are in progress, as well as to abate those already existing. In the next place by a perpetual injunction the remedy is made complete through all future time; whereas, an information or indictment at the common law can only dispose of the present nuisance, and for future acts new prosecutions must be brought. In the next place, the remedial justice in equity may be prompt and immediate before irreparable mischief is done; whereas, at law, nothing can be done, except after a trial, and upon the award of judgment. In the next place, a court of equity will not only interfere upon the in-

[1] Baines *v.* Baker, 1 Ambl. 158.

18

formation of the Attorney-General, but also upon the application of private parties, directly affected by the nuisance;
whereas, at law, in many cases the remedy is, or may be,
solely through the instrumentality of the Attorney-General.
But, in all cases of this sort, courts of equity will grant an
injunction to restrain a public nuisance only in cases where
the fact is clearly made out upon determinate and satisfactory
evidence."[1]

§ 4. Upon the same subject, the somewhat unsettled state
of the law may be best illustrated by citing the observations
of eminent judges in some leading cases.

§ 5. "If the subject were represented as a mere public
nuisance I could not interfere, as the Attorney-General is not
a party; and if he were a party, the complaint must not be
of a public nuisance merely, but which, being so in its nature,
is attended with extreme probability of irreparable injury,
nor could the court interfere with it after a trial by law."[2]

§ 6. "Where the bill is filed by the Attorney-General,
and the right is clear, and the threatened injury irreparable,
an injunction will be awarded although the right has not
been established at law."[3]

§ 7. In the case of Attorney-General v. Forbes,[4] Lord Cottenham remarked "it was broadly asserted, that an application to this court to prevent a nuisance to a public road,
was never heard of. A little research, however, would have
found many such instances. Many cases might have been
produced in which the court has interfered to prevent
nuisances to public rivers and to public harbors.—Those
commissioners possess a jurisdiction founded on acts of Parliament, and they have a right, within the due limits of

[1] 2 Story Eq. §§ 920—924a, pp.
232—6.
[2] Cowder v. Tinckler, 19 Ves. 617.
[3] Per Hepburn, J., Com. v. Rush,
14 Penn. 195.
[4] 2 My. and Cr., 133.

their authority, to do all necessary acts in the execution of their functions.   Nevertheless, if they so execute what they conceive to be their duty, as to create or occasion a public nuisance, this court has an undoubted right to interpose."

§ 8. In another case, it is said : " It does not follow because a thing is a nuisance to several individuals, that, therefore, it is a public nuisance.   One may illustrate that very simply by supposing the case of a man building up a wall which has the effect of darkening the ancient lights of half a dozen different dwelling-houses.   It does not follow, that, therefore, it is a public nuisance which can be indicted, or for which the Attorney-General can file an information in this court."[1]

§ 9. " To constitute a public nuisance, the thing must be such as, in its nature or its consequence, is a nuisance—an injury or a damage to all persons who come within the sphere of its operation, though it may be so in a greater degree to some than it is to others.   For example, take the case of the operations of a manufactory, in the course of which operations volumes of noxious smoke or of poisonous effluvia are emitted.   To all persons who are at all within the reach of those operations it is more or less objectionable, more or less a nuisance in the popular sense of the term.   It is true that, to those who are nearer to it, it may be a greater nuisance than it is to those who are more remote ; but still, to all who are at all within the reach of it, it is more or less a nuisance.   Take another ordinary case—the stopping of the king's highway.   This is a nuisance to all who may have occasion to travel that highway.   It may be a much greater nuisance to a person who has to travel the road every day of his life, than it is to a person who has to travel it only once a year, or once in five years.   If, however, the thing complained of is such that it is a great nuisance to those who are more immediately within the sphere of its operations,

<hr>

[1] Per V. Chanc., Soltan v. De Held, 2 Sim. N. S. 144.

but is no nuisance or inconvenience, or is even advantageous or pleasurable to those who are more removed from it, there, I conceive, it does not come within the meaning of the term public nuisance. The case before me is a case in point. A peal of bells may be, and no doubt is, an extreme nuisance, and, perhaps, an intolerable nuisance to a person who lives within a very few feet or yards of them; but to a person who lives at a distance from them, although he is within the reach of their sound, so far from its being a nuisance or an inconvenience, it may be a positive pleasure."[1]

§ 10. Motion for an injunction to stay the building of a house in which to inoculate for the smallpox. The Chancellor intimated that the Attorney-General could at his discretion file an information as for a public nuisance, but, as it had not been settled that the house would be a nuisance, the injunction was denied.[2]

§ 11. Information on the relation of the Scotch Hospital, to enjoin the obstruction and darkening of the ancient lights of the hospital. The injunction having been granted, a dissolution was moved, but the jurisdiction was held undoubted, though an indictment would also lie.[3]

§ 12. It is held, in recent American cases, that chancery may grant an injunction against an act threatened, which, if committed, would be punishable under the criminal laws as a nuisance.[4] Where the complainant shows that acts about to be done by the defendant, amounting to a public nuisance, will also cause special damage to himself.[5] So chancery will restrain a party from doing an act injurious to an individual, or which may be prejudicial as a public nuisance, pending judicial proceedings before those tribunals, by which

---

[1] Per V. Chanc., Soltan v. De Held, 2 Sim. N. S. 143.
[2] Baines v. Baker, Amb. 158; 3 Atk. 750.
[3] Atty.-Gen. v. Nichol, 16 Ves. 338.

[4] The People v. St. Louis, 5 Gilm. 351.
[5] Walker v. Shepardson, 2 Wis. 384.

the authority to do the act, or its lawfulness, is to be determined.[1]

§ 13. In one of the cases already cited it is held, that one specially injured by a public nuisance may enjoin it, without making the Attorney-General party to the bill.[2] And, in another case, it is said, "In informations and proceedings for the purpose of preventing public nuisances, the ordinary course is for the Attorney-General to take it on himself to sue, as representing the public; but it is equally certain that individuals, who conceive themselves aggrieved, may come forward and ask the assistance of the court to prevent a public nuisance from which they have individually sustained damage."[3]

§ 14. We shall hereafter (Chap. XXVI.) consider the remedy of injunction, as applied specially to *railroads.* In the present connection, it may be remarked that a steam railroad in a city is not necessarily a nuisance, nor subject to injunction as such.[4](a)

[1] Williamson v. Carnan, 1 Gill & J. 184.
[2] Soltan v. De Held, 2 Sim. N. S. 132.
[3] Per Lord Cottenham, Atty.-Gen. v. Forbes, 2 My. & Cr. 131.
[4] New Albany, &c. v. O'Daily, 12 Ind. 551.

(a) In deciding the same point, the following remarks were made by a learned judge in New York, which, for their rhetorical animation and vivid metaphor, may be quoted as a happy departure from the ordinary tameness and dryness of judicial language: "To protest against this power of adaptation, inherent in the common law, to cases as they arise in our onward progress, is to restrain and impede, not develop and improve. It would be quite as wise to insist that the maritime law, which was sufficient to regulate the commerce of the world when a Roman galley swept timidly and cautiously along the shore and was deemed hopelessly lost in a starless night, shall now constitute our entire code, when every ocean is whitened with our canvas, every sea 'vexed with our fisheries,' and the keels of our adventurous navigators plough as well the regions of equatorial heat as of eternal frost, visit all climes, and exact tribute from all lands." Per Bacon, J., Williams v. N. Y. Central, &c., 18 Barb. 248.

§ 15. The remedy of injunction does not supersede that of *abatement.* It is said, in a case in Massachusetts, "The plaintiffs' right being fully established, they are entitled not only to the abatement of the nuisance, but to a perpetual injunction to prevent its renewal, and thereby to prevent multiplicity of suits and oppressive litigation; especially as the defendants have undertaken to maintain their supposed right by force, whereby the plaintiffs have been for a long time disturbed in the enjoyment of their just right of property."[1]

[1] Per Wilde, J., Stevens v. Stevens, 11 Met. 257.

CHAPTER X.

TRESPASS.

1. General rule.   4. Dissolving of injunction.
3. Irreparable injury.

§ 1. AN injunction will not be granted to restrain a *tres-pass*,(a) unless the trespasser is insolvent, or the injury irreparable and destructive to the plaintiff's estate—to its very nature and substance; and such as calls for immediate relief.[1] There must be something particular or special in the case, for which a court of law cannot afford adequate redress, and for which, either from difficulty of proof or some other cause, the party cannot obtain adequate satisfaction in the ordinary course of law.[2] "Lord Eldon said that there was no instance of an injunction in trespass, until a case before Lord Thurlow, relative to a mine (Fleming's case), and which was a case approaching very nearly to waste (the defendant having worked from his own land into the coal-mine of the plaintiff), and where there was no dispute about the right. (The case rested upon the principle of irremediable mischief to the mine.) Lord Thurlow had great difficulty as to injunction for trespass; and though Lord Eldon thought it surprising that the jurisdiction by injunction was taken so freely in waste, and not in trespass, yet he proceeded with

[1] James *v.* Dixon, 20 Mis. 79; Foster, 6 Eng. 304; Wilson *v.* Hughell, 1 Morr. 461; Catching *v.* Terrell, 10 Geo. 576; Shipley *v.* Ritter, 7 Md. 408; 5 Geo. 576; 26 Miss. 84; Centreville, &c. *v.* Barnett, 2 Cart. 536; Brooks *v.* Diaz, 35 Ala. 599.

[2] Bethune *v.* Wilkins, 8 Geo. 118; The Justices, &c. *v.* The Griffin, &c., 11 Geo. 246; Anthony *v.* Brooks, 5 Geo. 576; 10 Geo. 576; The Justices, &c. *v.* The Griffin, &c., 11 Geo. 246; 26 Miss. 84.

(a) More especially if without color of right. Sutherland *v.* Maschop, 2 Stockt. 57.

the utmost caution and diffidence, and only allowed the writ
in solitary cases of a special nature, and where irreparable
damage might be the consequence, if the act continued.   It
has also been allowed in cases where the trespass had grown
into a nuisance, or where the principle of multiplicity of
suits among numerous claimants was applicable."[1](a)   So it
is said, in a very recent case, "The interference of a court of
equity by injunction, in a case of trespass to land, and where
an action at law will lie, is of modern origin, and an exercise
of power to be justified only in a case of great and irreparable injury.   Doubtless, too, the petitioner who invokes
it, in conformity with principle and precedent, should show
at least a strong *primâ facie* case of *right*."[2]   But the court
may grant an injunction, if the trespass should continue so
long as to become a nuisance or a constant grievance.[3]   Or
in case of repeated acts and trespasses.[4]   Though the fact,
that a trespasser is insolvent, will not give chancery jurisdiction to enjoin his acts, where the other circumstances of
the case preclude it.[5]

§ 2. Thus the plaintiff complained, that the defendant was
accustomed to land his steamboat at a dock of great value
belonging to the plaintiff, pretending that the dock was
public; but, as no serious damage was to be apprehended

---

[1] Stevens *v.* Beekman, 1 John.
Ch. 319 ; Will. Eq. 382.
[2] Per Butler, J., Falls, &c. *v.* Tibbetts, 31 Conn. 168.
[3] Whitfield *v.* Rogers, 26 Miss. 48 ;

7 Md. 408 ; Moore *v.* Ferrell, 1 Kelly, 7.
[4] Schetz's, &c., 35 Penn. 88.
[5] Centreville, &c. *v.* Barnett, 2
Cart. 536.

(a) "On the same ground, the injunction is granted against the taking of stones of peculiar make, or stones from a quarry. The mischief
reaches the very substance and value of the estate. The practice is
now more liberal. For the purpose of quieting a possession, or preventing a multiplicity of actions, or where the nature of the inheritance
is in jeopardy, or irreparable mischief is threatened, the court will interfere by injunction, even against a person acting under a claim of right.
When the right of a party is doubtful, the court will not grant an injunction, until the right is established at law." Will. Eq. 382.

from the continuance of the act, the court refused to grant an injunction *in limine*.[1] So also to restrain a stranger from taking rails from the owner's land, and for an account, &c.[2] So for cutting and carrying away timber, however wilful, an injunction will not be granted.[3] So, although damages are recoverable from one who, in building a house, has inserted the ends of the joists into his neighbor's wall without license; an injunction to remove the joists will not be granted, unless special facts are shown requiring it.[4] Nor for placing earth or other materials on another's land; the proper remedy is an action for trespass.[5] Nor for throwing down fences, and letting in cattle upon a growing crop; the injury being susceptible of perfect pecuniary compensation.[6] Nor for a tenant illegally dispossessed by a sheriff, under a sale made by him.[7] So a bill for injunction alleged, that the defendant, without authority, and against the wishes of the justices in whom the title was vested, seized on a public square, and was proceeding to erect a building for a court-house, insufficient for that purpose, and that injury would be thereby caused, either irreparable or to be repaired only after great delay and at great expense. Injunction refused.[8]

§ 3. A prayer for an injunction, to restrain a trespass which does not appear to cause irreparable injury, is fatally defective.[9] And whether the damage is irreparable or not, is a conclusion of law, which the court draws from the facts and circumstances in regard to the trespass, as set forth in the bill.[10](a)

---

[1] N. Y. Printing, &c. v. Fitch, 1 Paige, 97.
[2] Cooper v. Hamilton, 8 Blackf. 377.
[3] Cowles v. Shaw, 2 Clarke, 496.
[4] Rankin v. Charless, 19 Mis. 490.
[5] Mulvany v. Kennedy, 26 Penn. 44.
[6] Catching v. Terrell, 10 Geo. 576.
[7] Sullivan v. Hearnden, 11 Geo. 294.
[8] Justices v. Cosby, 5 Jones Eq. 254.
[9] Bolster v. Catterlin, 10 Ind. 117.
[10] The Justices, &c. v. The Griffin, &c., 11 Geo. 246.

(a) So an injunction ought not to be granted *in aid* of an action of trespass, unless it appear that the injury will be irreparable and cannot be compensated in damages. It is not sufficient that the affidavit alleges

§ 4. It is held that an injunction to restrain a trespass will be dissolved, on the coming in of the answer, denying the right of the complainant, unless it appears that there is a suit at law pending to try the title.[1]

[1] Stewart v. Chew, 3 Bland, 440.

irreparable injury; it must be shown to the court how and why it would be so; especially where no action has ever settled the plaintiff's rights. Waldron v. Marsh, 5 Cal. 119.

CHAPTER XI.

WASTE.

§ 1. *Waste* is a familiar ground for injunction; and perhaps an injury better entitled to be termed *irremediable* than any other.[1]

§ 2. The history of the common law in reference to waste is thus stated by Lord Chief Justice Eyre in Jefferson *v.* Durham,[2] termed by Judge Story "a celebrated case:"[3] "At common law the proceeding in waste was by writ of prohibition from the Court of Chancery, which was considered as the foundation of a suit between the party, suffering by the waste, and the party committing it. If that writ was obeyed, the ends of justice were answered. But, if that was not obeyed, and an *alias* and *pluries* produced no effect, then came the original writ of attachment out of chancery, returnable in a court of common law, which was considered as the original writ of the court. The form of that writ shows the nature of it. It was the same original writ of attachment which was and is the foundation of all proceedings in prohibition, and of many other proceedings in this court. It has been said, and truly so, I think, so far as can be collected from the text writers, that, at the common law, this proceeding lay only against tenant in dower, tenant by the curtesy, and guardian in chivalry. It was extended by different statutes to farmers, &c. That, which these statutes gave by way of remedy, was not so properly the

---

[1] See Walker *v.* Sherman, 20 Wend. 638.

[2] 1 B. & P. 120.
[3] 2 Story Eq. 223, § 909.

introduction of a new law, as the extension of an old one to a new description of persons. The first act, which introduced anything substantially new, was that which gave a writ of waste or estrepement, pending the suit. But, except for the purpose of staying proceedings pending a suit, there is no intimation in any of our text writers, that any prohibition could issue from those courts." Judge Story remarks, however, that "courts of equity have, by no means, limited themselves to an interference in cases of this sort (*estrepement* in real actions). They have, indeed, often interfered in restraining waste by persons having limited interests in property, on the mere ground of the common law rights of the parties, and the difficulty of attaining the immediate preservation of the property from destruction or irreparable injury, by the process of the common law. But they have also extended this statutory relief to cases, where the remedies provided in the courts of common law cannot be made to apply; and where the titles of the parties are purely of an equitable nature."[1] So it is remarked, that the interference of equity in case of waste "is a wholesome jurisdiction, to be liberally exercised; the prevention of irreparable injury, and depends on much latitude of discretion in the court."[2] And that "the jurisdiction of English equity in cases of waste began with the injunction *pendente lite,* but has long since extended itself to cases where no action at law was pending, but where it was needed for the protection of trust estates and estates in reversion and remainder, and has now become one of the well-defined branches of equity jurisprudence."[3] So also, that an injunction to stay waste has become almost a matter of course.[4]

§ 3. Conformably with these views, "equity will, in many cases, restrain waste, though the lease contain the clause *without impeachment of waste,* which takes away the remedy

---

[1] 2 Story Eq. 227, § 912.
[2] Kane *v.* Vanderburgh, 1 John. Ch. 11.
[3] Per Woodward, J., Denny *v.* Brunson, 29 Penn. 384.
[4] Smith *v.* City, &c., 19 Geo. 89.

at law; as where this power is exercised in an unreasonable manner, and against conscience."[1] So an intermediate
tenant for life may enjoin the tenant for years against waste.[2]
So where there is a tenant for life subject to waste, remainder
for life dispunishable for waste, remainder in fee ; the court
will not suffer an agreement between the two tenants for life
to commit waste to take place against the remainder-man,
before the time when the term of the second tenant for life
commences.[3] And a bill in equity against waste lies for any
remainder-man who is injured ; though an action at law can
be maintained only by the owner of the first estate of inheritance.[4] So equity will by injunction protect a mortgagee
of personal as well as real property, against waste or destruction by the mortgagor in possession, whether a default
have been made or not.[5] (See Chap. XXVIII.) So, in a proper
case, the assignee of a tenant for life, without impeachment
for waste, may be restrained from committing waste; though
he may exercise the same rights as his assignor might have
exercised.[6] So A. granted lands to the use of trustees for a
term *sans* waste, and, subject thereto, to the use of herself for
life *sans* waste, with remainder to the use of B. for life *sans*
waste, with remainder over, with remainder to B. in fee.
The trusts of the term were, by cutting and selling timber,
or by demising, mortgaging, and selling the premises, to
raise three sums, the first of which was to be raised forthwith and paid to A. A. died before any money had been
raised. Six years after the date of the grant, B., as tenant
for life in possession, advertised a sale of timber. Held, on
a bill by the trustees for an injunction agaist B., that by the
terms of the grant the trustees had, as to the mode of raising
the moneys, a discretion with which the court could not interfere, and therefore a right to enter and cut timber, to
which right B.'s estate, though *sans* waste, was subordinate;

[1] Kane *v.* Vanderburgh, 1 John.
Ch. 11.
[2] Roswell's Case, 1 Rolle's Abr.
377.
[3] Robinson *v.* Litton, 3 Atk. 210.

[4] Dennett *v.* Dennett, 43 N. H.
503.
[5] Parsons *v.* Hughes, 12 Md. 1.
[6] Clement *v.* Wheeler, 5 Fost. 361.

and B. was restrained from cutting or selling the timber while the moneys remained to be raised.[1]

§ 4. Equity will grant an injunction, to prevent the destruction of timber, ornamental, or fruit trees, whether such trees were planted for shade and ornament, or grew naturally in the position which renders them thus valuable to the owner. And the jurisdiction does not depend on their value as wood or timber, but on their location as part of an estate, rendering it more valuable by the use to which they are or may be devoted.[2] So acts which would result in the destruction of all the timber on a man's home plantation, where wood and timber are necessary to the enjoyment of the property in that character, are sufficient to authorize an injunction.[3] So, on the ground of irreparable damage, and if done without authority of law, digging deep holes, and planting therein large stone pillars or abutments, digging and carrying away large banks of valuable clay, and constructing an aqueduct by ditches and embankments through, and thus permanently dividing, the complainant's land.[4] So insolvent persons, who threaten to enter upon land owned and possessed by the complainant, and to dig thereon, whereby the streams and springs would be greatly injured, may be enjoined.[5] But an injunction will not be granted against cutting trees merely alleged to be ornamental. It must appear that they were planted or left standing for ornament.[6] Nor is it a sufficient averment, that they "contribute to ornament."[7]

§ 5. But it was held in an early American case, though somewhat too broadly in the light of subsequent decisions, that an injunction to stay waste is never granted against a

[1] Kekewich v. Marker, 5 Eng. Law and Eq. 129.
[2] Shipley v. Ritter, 7 Md. 408.
[3] Davis v. Reed, 14 Md. 152.
[4] Reddall v. Bryan, 14 Md. 444.
[5] Bensley v. Mountain, &c., 13 Cal. 306.

[6] Coffin v. Coffin, Jac. 70; Marquis, &c. v. Sandys, 6 Ves. 110. See Lord Tamworth v. Lord Ferris, 6 Ves. 419; Day v. Merry, 16 Ves. 375; Williams v. McNamara, 8 Ib. 70; Newdegate v. Newdegate, 1 Sim. 131.
[7] Williams v. McNamara, 8 Ves. 70.

defendant in possession, *and claiming by title adverse to that of the plaintiff*.[1] And Lord Eldon remarked: "It was always surprising to me, that the jurisdiction by injunction was taken so freely in waste and not in trespass; for there is a writ at common law after action to restrain waste. But a trespass after one action may be repeated."[2](a) And he decided in the same case, that no injunction lies against waste in case of a disputed title between heir and devisee.[3] And it is held that a bill for injunction to stay destructive waste cannot be sustained against one in exclusive possession, claiming colorably the absolute estate, where no action at law has been brought and none contemplated.[4] And that a party is not to be restrained from cutting timber on land in his possession, when the weight of the evidence is rather in favor of his right and title.[5] Thus A., claiming title to a cedar swamp, complained that B. had cut a part of the cedar, and moved it to lands of a third person, where it had been sold at auction; and he prayed an injunction against B. and the bidders, restraining them from carrying it away, and B. from farther cutting. The injunction was allowed. After answer of B.,

---

[1] Per Kent, Chanc., Lansing *v.* North, &c., 7 John. Ch. 164; Pillsworth *v.* Hopton, 6 Ves. 51 ; Storm *v.* Mann, 4 John. Ch. 21.

[2] Per Lord Eldon, Smith *v.* Collyer, 8 Ves. 90.
[3] Smith *v.* Collyer, 8 Ves. 89.
[4] Bogey *v.* Shute, 4 Jones Eq. 174.
[5] Smith *v.* Wilson, 10 Cal. 528.

(a) In an earlier case, Hanson *v.* Gardiner (7 Ves. 306), Lord Eldon remarks upon the caution with which equity had interfered by injunction in cases of trespass or even of waste, citing the authority of Hardwicke, Thurlow, Buller, and Kenyon. And Lord Hardwicke remarks: "There is no such thing as an injunction until hearing being of course. There cannot be a stronger instance—than the case of waste. After answer come in and affidavits read—the court will, according to their discretion, continue the injunction until hearing or not, and yet the plaintiff may go on with the cause, and finally have a decree to stay waste." Potter *v.* Chapman, 1 Ambl. 98.

Plaintiff, being a termor at ground-rent, brought a bill against his lessee to stay waste, and moved at the Rolls for an injunction, *but was denied;* and it was now moved again before *Lord Chancellor,* and granted. Farrant *v.* Lee, 1 Ambl. 105.

claiming title to the swamp, and proof that B. was able to respond, the court dissolved the injunction.[1] But it has been held in a late case, that chancery will interpose to prevent the destruction of the inheritance, even where both title and possession are in dispute.[2] And the following remarks of the court in New York show a much more liberal adoption of the remedy than was sanctioned by the earlier cases. "The defendant insists that as he is in possession, claiming adversely to the plaintiff, and as the title is in dispute, an injunction bill to stay waste cannot be sustained. *Storms* (Storm) v. *Mann*[3] is cited in support of this proposition. In that case, the defendant had been in possession of the premises a long time, and was in possession at the time of the filing of the bill; the plaintiff had commenced an ejectment at law, and the defendant had joined issue with him on the question of title, and the action was pending undetermined. But in the bill in that case there was no allegation of the insolvency of the defendant, or that the waste which he was committing would be an irreparable injury to the premises."[4]

§ 5 *a*. Lord Eldon said: "I never would grant an injunction upon an affidavit, stating, that the deponent verily believes the defendant is about to cut timber."[5] So an injunction was refused where the bill stated that the defendants had commenced cutting, and that the complainants "believed" that the defendants had threatened and then intended to cut down and carry away "large quantities of the wood," &c.[6]

§ 5 *b*. On account of the great expense incident to *mining*, an injunction will not be readily granted in such case; nor in case of *laches*.[7] And in the case of Haigh v. Jagger,[8]

[1] Brown v. Folwell, 3 Halst. Ch. 593.
[2] Cornelius v. Post, 1 Stockt. 196.
[3] 4 John. Ch. 21.
[4] Per Paige, J., Spear v. Cutter, 5 Barb. 487.

[5] Etches v. Lance, 7 Ves. 416.
[6] Cornelius v. Post, 1 Stockt. 196.
[7] Grey v. Northumberland, 17 Ves. 281; Birmingham, &c. v. Lloyd, 18 Ib. 515.
[8] 2 Coll. 238.

the Vice-Chancellor remarked : " The defendants, who claim a right to do what they are doing, are, it is true, by working the coal, taking the very substance of the property, which may in a sense be perhaps called in this case, and might in others most certainly be, waste or destruction; but, on the other hand, it is the only mode in which the property in question can be usefully enjoyed or made available, and may, therefore, in a sense perhaps be deemed not more than taking the ordinary use of the thing in dispute; nor is an unskilful or unworkmanlike working established against the defendants, nor are they said to be insolvent."

§ 6. A bill alleging that a trespasser is about to commit irreparable injury by boxing and working turpentine trees, and by cutting timber and making staves on land, fit only to be cultivated for these products, without an averment of the defendant's insolvency, will be dismissed on motion.[1]

§ 7. An injunction will not lie to prevent the commission or repetition of a trespass, in entering and cutting down timber on land of which the plaintiff is in possession as owner, he having an adequate remedy at law for the trespass, and nothing appearing in the case so special or peculiar as to call for that particular relief. But where the complainant is a married woman, and the lands are her separate estate, by deed appointing her husband trustee, who, contrary to her wishes and to his duty, enters into an agreement for the submission to arbitration of an unfounded claim by one of the respondents to cut timber on the land; and an award is made in favor of the claimant: upon a bill alleging that the respondents, armed with the award, are cutting the timber, and assert the right to do so, "and will continue to do so, unless restrained" by the order of the court, an injunction will be granted.[2]

[1] Gause v. Perkins, 3 Jones Eq. 177.   [2] Thomas v. James, 32 Ala. 723.

19

§ 8. An injunction to stay waste, pending an ejectment suit, will not be continued, where the defendant is in possession claiming adversely, especially if there has been needless delay in the prosecution of the ejectment.[1]

§ 9. "In cases of waste, the account goes merely upon the injunction."[2] "The right to an account for waste already committed is incidental to the right to file a bill to prevent further waste, though no bill will lie merely for an account for waste done, because the plaintiff has an ample remedy at law."[3] So equity may forbid by injunction the removal of what has been obtained by past waste.[4] So, although equity will not sustain a bill filed solely to prevent removal of timber wrongfully cut, or for an account of past waste, there being a complete remedy at law; yet when the bill is also filed to prevent future waste, to avoid multiplicity of suits, the court will allow an account of and satisfaction for what has been done, and, to prevent irreparable mischief, will enjoin removal of the timber.[4]

§ 10. A party praying for an injunction against a lessee for waste, alleging himself to be a purchaser from the lessor by deed, must exhibit his deed, and prove its execution, in order to obtain an injunction.[6]

§ 11. A bill for a special injunction, to restrain a party in possession, and claiming adversely, from cutting timber, must not only set forth that the threatened injury would be irreparable, but must also state how it would be so, that the court may see clearly that such would be the result.[7](a)

---

[1] Higgins v. Woodward, Hopk. 342.
[2] Per Lord Eldon, Grierson v. Eyre, 9 Ves. 346.
[3] Per Bell, C. J., Dennett v. Dennett, 43 N. H. 503.
[4] United States v. Parrott, 1 McAll. C. C. 271.

[5] Spear v. Cutter, 5 Barb. 486.
[6] Loudon v. Warfield, 5 J. J. Marsh. 196.
[7] Thompson v. Williams, 1 Jones Eq. 176; Bogey v. Shute, 1 Jones Eq. 180.

(a) A bill being filed for an injunction to restrain waste, pending an action of ejectment brought to try the title, the ejectment being successful, the injunction submitted to, and the defendant having quietly permitted the plaintiff, after a verdict at law, to sell the estate, and not alleging that he intended to take any steps to disturb the verdict at law, and the defendant being a pauper, and having recently changed his solicitor; it was held, that the special circumstances took the case out of the general rule, on a motion to dismiss for want of prosecution. Pinfold v. Pinfold, 15 Eng. Law and Eq. 10.

CHAPTER XII.

USURY.

§ 1. USURY is sometimes set up as a ground of injunction.[1] Thus a creditor is not allowed to make it a condition of a loan, that be shall receive a compensation for his services in procuring the money; and if such compensation is included in the security given for the loan, the court will, on the debtor's paying into court the sum reported to be due by a master, after deducting the sum charged for such services, grant an injunction to stay proceedings upon a mortgage by which the loan is secured.[2]   The court remarks: "This court is always jealous of collateral demands and advantages claimed by a creditor as a *condition* of the loan of money. The actual expenses of the writings ought to be paid; but to allow the creditor to make it a condition of the loan, that he shall receive a *compensation for his services*, in procuring the money, and to include that compensation in the security, is against sound principle, and tends most manifestly to oppression and usury, if it is not usury in itself."[3]

§ 2. In cases of concurrent jurisdiction, a preliminary injunction to restrain a suit at law upon a usurious contract will not be granted, unless the plaintiff shows that he would be deprived of some legal or equitable right, if the adverse party should be permitted to proceed.[4]   Thus the court will not stay a suit at law upon a note not negotiable, on the ground of usury, of which the lender is the only witness; be having, under the statute, a complete defence, by exam-

[1] See Spann *v.* Sterns, 18 Tex. 556.
[2] Hine *v.* Handy, 1 John, Ch. 6.
[3] Per Kent, Chanc. Hine *v.* Handy, 1 John. Ch. 6.
[4] Mitchell *v.* Oakley, 7 Paige, 68.

ining the plaintiff in the suit.[1] Nor will an injunction be granted on the ground of usury, which the party neglected to set up after notice.[2]

[1] Perrin v. Striker, 7 Paige, 598.   [2] Chinn v. Mitchell, 2 Met. Ky. 92.

CHAPTER XIII.

POSSESSION AND REMOVAL.

§ 1. EQUITY sometimes interposes by injunction to give *possession* of property.   It is said, " Courts of equity interfere and effectuate their own decrees in many cases by injunctions, in the nature of a judicial writ or execution for possession of the property in controversy ; as, for example, by injunctions to yield up, deliver, quiet, or continue the possession, followed up by a writ of assistance.   Injunctions of this sort are older than the time of Lord Bacon, since, in his ordinances, they are treated as a well-known process.   Indeed, they have been distinctly traced back to the reign of Elizabeth and Edward the Sixth, and even of Henry the Eighth."[1](a) Thus where a court of equity decrees a conveyance, and the defendant refuses to obey the decrée, a writ of injunction, to compel delivery of the possession, may be issued, and, if that be not obeyed, an *habere facias possessionem.*[2]

§ 1 *a.*   In a case often cited, the plaintiff claimed, as *treasure-trove* upon his manor, an ancient silver altar-piece,

[1] 2 Story Eq. 268, § 959.   [2] Garretson *v.* Coale, 1 Har. & J. 370.

(a) Where a complainant obtains an injunction to restrain the sale of property, which remains in his possession, he giving bond and security to have it forthcoming to answer the decree of the court, and the bill is dismissed upon appeal, the defendant cannot obtain possession of the property upon application by petition to the chancery court, by virtue of a writ of restitution.   He must resort to his remedy upon the injunction bond, or to an original suit to obtain possession.   In practice, the writ of restitution appears to be unknown in the chancery court.   Starke *v.* Lewis, 23 Miss. 151.

having a Greek inscription and dedicated to Hercules, which came into the defendant's hands with notice of his title. The plaintiff brings a bill to enforce his title to the article, and also to prevent the defendant from defacing the altar-piece. Held, from the peculiar nature of the thing, as an article of curiosity, in consequence of which an action at law might afford inadequate compensation, an injunction should be granted.[1] So, in Pennsylvania, a bill for an injunction was maintained in behalf of a surveyor, who had left in the hands of the defendant, a former pupil, certain plans and surveys of lands and streets, and also furniture and instruments used in the business of surveying. Mr. Justice Bell, in his elaborate opinion, refers to the several English cases where this remedy was applied to restore possession of title-deeds, valuable paintings, an antique silver altar-piece, an ancient horn, the symbol of tenure, heirlooms, and a finely-carved cherry stone. "Such articles as these are commonly esteemed not altogether, or perhaps at all, for their intrinsic value, but as being objects of attachment or curiosity, and, therefore, not to be measured in damages by a jury who cannot enter into the feelings of the owner; so, too, the impossibility, or even great difficulty of supplying their loss, may put damages out of the question as a medium of redress. But these are not the exclusive reasons why chancery interferes." But also "where, from the nature of the subject, or the immediate object of the parties, no convenient measure of damages can be ascertained, or where nothing could answer the justice of the case but the performance of a contract in specie." The court proceed to justify the jurisdiction upon these grounds, in reference to the plans, surveys, &c., and in regard to the other articles remark: "If the jurisdiction once attaches from the nature of one of the subjects of contest, it may embrace all of them, for equity abhors multiplicity of suits. Where a person is found wrongfully in possession of a farm, over which the court had undoubted power, and also in possession of the stock upon it, at the

[1] Duke, &c. v. Cookson, 3 P. Wms. 390.

same time and under the effect of the same wrong, the court will undoubtedly make him account for and deliver back the whole. The surveying instruments and office furniture stand in the same category with the maps, &c., were delivered at the same time, and are withheld by an exertion of the same wrong." The jurisdiction was also maintained upon the ground of the inadequacy of a writ of replevin, and of trust.[1] So although equity will not seek to enforce a doubtful right by injunction, yet it will thus interpose in favor of one who has had long, undisturbed, and exclusive possession of land under a deed really invalid, but which was recorded, and which the grantee and others holding under him supposed to convey a title, the party disputing such title being a trespasser without color of right.[2] So a bill alleges that certain buildings were used for medical instruction, and as an infirmary for the sick, by the professors composing the medical faculty of a corporation, and prays that the defendant shall be restrained from so acting as to interfere with their possession and use for that purpose; and that he be commanded to forbear from the repetition of the acts which impeded the enjoyment of the rights, and the discharge of the duties, on the part of the professors. Held, an injunction of this description could not be regarded as going beyond the legitimate office of the process, or as possessing the character of a judicial writ.[3]

§ 2. But, on the other hand, it is held that the only ground on which injunctions are granted, against third persons in possession of personal property, and ostensibly its rightful owners, upon an *ex parte* application, is for the protection of the fund or property, when shown to be in danger without this interposition.[4] Some of the leading cases on the general subject of possession are as follows.

[1] McGowin v. Remington, 12 Penn. 56, 61, 62, 63.
[2] Falls, &c. v. Tibbetts, 31 Conn. 165.
[3] Washington, &c. v. Green, 1 Md. Ch. Dec. 97.
[4] Thayer v. Smith, Harring. Ch. 430. See Martin v. Broadus, 1 Freem. Ch. 35.

§ 3. In an early English case, the Lady Poines's trustee having contracted to sell her estate to one person, she herself having actually sold it to another, this trustee disturbed the purchaser in his possession; and it was now moved for an injunction to quiet the possession of the purchaser. But it was answered that such a motion never was made to have an injunction to quiet the possession for a defendant, who had no bill in court, and that before the cause was heard. An injunction for quieting the possession is only grantable when the plaintiff has been in possession for the space of three years before the bill exhibited, upon a title yet undetermined, or in case the cause hath been heard, and judgment passed upon the merits of the cause by the court, and therefore the Lord Keeper denied the motion.[1] So equity will not enjoin the sailing of a vessel, containing goods sold to an insolvent person, where the right of *stoppage in. transitu* still continues. The Lord Chancellor remarked: " If a ship contains a cargo belonging to twenty-four persons, and A. B. has a right to part of it, am I to stop the ship from sailing with the goods of the other twenty-three? There is no instance, that I recollect, of stopping in *transitu*, by a bill in equity."[2] So one in actual possession of an exclusive privilege, claiming title, will not be restrained by injunction from its exercise, until the establishment of a better, adverse right at law, especially at the suit of a party who merely denies right, without setting up any in himself.[3] In a leading case in New York, the court remarked substantially as follows: " The defendants claim and exercise the right of exclusively navigating the Hudson River, with vessels propelled by fire and steam, under certain acts of the legislature. The defendants, and those from whom they claim to have derived title, have been, ever since the year 1807, in the actual possession and enjoyment of such exclusive privilege. The plaintiffs assert no right peculiar to themselves, but only a

---

[1] The Lady Poines's Case, 1 Vern. 156.

[2] Goodhart *v.* Lowe, 2 Jac. & W. 349-50-51.

[3] Lansing *v.* North, &c. 7 John. Ch. 162.

right common to every citizen, nor do they allege any actual infringement in their particular case, of that common right. An injunction would be unprecedented. The common right must be first legally established, and the defendants must be first duly ousted of their pretension and possession, by due course of law. The plaintiffs insist that the exclusive right has expired. It is sufficient that the defendants claim such an exclusive privilege, and that they are in the actual possession and enjoyment of it, by color of law."[1] And in another case in the same State it is held, that, where possession is the principal object of the suit, and would give a very important advantage to either party, it cannot be transferred by an *ex parte* preliminary injunction. The facts were as follows: A bill was filed by the complainants, as members of an association for raising out of the water the British frigate "the Hussar," which during the revolutionary war had sunk in the East River, near Morisania, in sixty or seventy feet of water, and was stated in the bill to be abandoned and derelict. The defendants by their answer claimed, that, before the association of the plaintiffs was formed, a similar enterprise had been undertaken by them, of which the plaintiffs had notice. In giving their opinion upon the case, the court remarked: "The right claimed by each of the contending parties, is the right of occupancy. Both parties have prepared means and have taken measures to raise the sunken frigate; neither party has yet effected that object, and neither party has yet obtained any actual or exclusive possession. The whole case stated in this bill, is that which would be presented to a court of law, in an action of trespass. The peculiar situation of this sunken vessel affords no ground of equitable jurisdiction. It is not alleged that the defendants are insolvent; that any contract exists between the parties; that there is in the case any fraud, trust, or other ground of equitable jurisdiction; or that there is any impediment to the ordinary remedies of the law.—The right is disputed, the possession of either party is

[1] 7 John. Ch. 164-5.

very incomplete. To award possession to either party would be to determine the main question of rightful possession, in a summary manner. The writ of injunction would be greatly misapplied, should it be used to transfer the possession from one party to the other, in this case, in which possession must give a most important advantage." The injunction was accordingly dissolved.[1] So the hirer of a house and land, furniture and effects, being in possession, cannot enjoin the levy of an execution thereupon under a judgment against the owner. The court remarked: "The party has a possessory right. If his possession is intruded upon, he has a remedy at law. The right to take in execution is a question of law. Injunctions would be applied for every day, where executions were improperly issued, if the court were to assume a jurisdiction."[2]

§ 4. The possession of vendees, under a bond for a deed, is a sufficient possession of the vendor to enable him to maintain a bill *quia timet*.[3]

§ 5. A statute, which provides that "any person having the possession and legal title to land may institute a suit against any other person setting up a claim thereto," &c., does not give courts of equity power to disregard the settled rules of law governing their proceedings; but was intended to authorize a person in possession of land to institute a suit in equity, in a proper case, against one claiming title to the land, though no attempt had been made to disturb the complainant in his possession.[4]

§ 6. Equity sometimes interposes by injunction to prevent the unlawful *removal* of property.

§ 7. To justify an injunction against the removal of property by a tenant for life, or an order compelling him to

[1] Deklyn *v.* Daveis, 1 Hopk. 135; Per Sanford, Chanc., Ib. 141, 142, 143.
[2] Garstin *v.* Asplin, 1 Madd. 90–1.
[3] Thomas *v.* White, 2 Ohio (N. S.) 540.
[4] Clark *v.* Drake, 3 Chand. 253.

give security for its forthcoming, it must be shown that there is danger of such removal beyond the jurisdiction of the court.[1]

§ 8. Equity will interfere, at the instance of a remainder-man in slaves, to prevent the owner of the life-estate from removing them out of the State; but not after such removal has taken place—especially before a right of partition has accrued.[2]

§ 9. Where slaves are taken from the owner for life, under an order of sequestration, to prevent a removal, and are hired out, equity will order the hires to be paid to such owner.[3]

§ 10. Where an amended bill alleged, that, since the original bill was filed, the defendant had sold three slaves claimed as partnership property, and that the complainant had good cause to believe that he was about to sell or remove beyond the jurisdiction of the court the remaining negroes belonging to the co-partnership; and the answer admitted the sale, and did not deny the intention to remove the residue: held, an injunction was proper, and an order made by the commissioner to restrain the defendant from selling or removing, and to compel him to give a bond for the forthcoming of the property to abide the final order of the court.[4] So, in a bill for an injunction to prevent slaves from being taken out of the State, an allegation that the defendant is about to sell his perishable property, and that it is rumored he is about to remove, and that the plaintiff believes, if he does so, he will carry off the slaves, which he holds for life only; is sufficient ground for an injunction, and, not being met by the answer, though it denies the intention of removing, the injunction will be continued.[5]

[1] Clagon v. Vesey, 7 Ired. Eq. 175; Cross v. Cramp, Ib. 193.
[2] Bowling v. Bowling, 6 B. Mon. 31.
[3] Rowland v. Partin, 1 Jones Eq. 257.
[4] Ellis v. Commander, 1 Strobh. Eq. 188.
[5] Swindall v. Bradley, 3 Jones Eq. 353.

§ 11. Where a debtor, pending a suit against him, removed with his property (slaves) from the State; and after recovery of judgment, and after the plaintiff's execution had lost its active energy, the slaves were brought back, it was held that he could sustain a bill to prevent their removal until he could revive his execution.[1]

§ 12. When a party is surety on a bond given by a deputy-sheriff to his principal, and has taken a mortgage on personal property for his indemnity, and the sheriff and the deputy have collected money for which the sheriff is sued, and the deputy has departed the jurisdiction, and a third person has got possession of the mortgage property on a pretended claim of right, and is charged with intending to remove it beyond the jurisdiction of the courts; equity will restrain him by injunction, and require bond and security for its forthcoming, to respond to the mortgage.[2]

§ 13. The effect of a temporary injunction, granted under the New York Code, § 219, is not to restrain any removal or disposition of the property of the debtor, but only a removal or disposition with intent to defraud creditors.[3]

§ 14. Under the head of *removal* may be noticed the *unlawful transfer of stock*, which is often mentioned as a proper subject of injunction. Thus an injunction was granted until answer, against the transfer of stock, standing in the name of the defendant, a steward of the plaintiff, upon affidavits, tending strongly to show that the stock was the produce of the plaintiff's property, consisting of rents and profits received for many years without account. But the injunction was refused in reference to money standing in the name of the defendant at his banker's, the last payment having been made two years before, and the law not justifying a presumption that the money remained the same. Lord Eldon

---

[1] Abrahams *v.* Cole, 5 Rich. Eq. 335.

[2] Outlaw *v.* Reddick, 11 Geo. 669.

[3] Brewster *v.* Hodges, 1 Duer, 609.

spoke of the case as one of "astonishing improvidence in the plaintiff, not demanding any account, but taking such sums as the defendant pleases to feed his occasions with." His Lordship further remarks: "The question then is, whether, if this stock and money are by his wrongful act confounded with his own, there is not a fair ground to say, that he having mixed them shall not be permitted to dispose of them until he shall have satisfactorily distinguished by an answer put in here that, which in conscience he never ought to have mixed. I do less mischief by fixing the injunction upon the whole till he informs me what is his master's, than by not fixing the injunction upon any part, giving him an opportunity of doing the enormous injustice, of which from these affidavits he appears capable."[1]

[1] Lord Chedworth v. Edwards, 8 Ves. 46, 48, 50.

CHAPTER XIV.

TITLE AND EVICTION.

§ 1. An injunction will not lie, to restrain a party in possession who claims title, and who expressly denies all title on the part of the complainant, either legal or equitable. Where title is in dispute, a temporary injunction is sometimes granted to preserve it until answer filed; but this is never done (in Maryland) unless the damage complained of is intolerable, and the mischief irreparable, or where the trespass goes to the destruction of the thing. Even where irreparable damage is apprehended, an averment to that effect is not sufficient; the facts must be stated, to show that the apprehension is well founded. The proper course, when an injunction is applied for, and the legal title is doubtful, is to send the complainant to a court of law, to have his title first established.[1] Lord Eldon remarked: "I remember when, if a plaintiff stated, that the defendant claimed by an adverse title, he stated himself out of court."[2] And, in a case relating to a mill, the Lord Chancellor said: "In this case it has been put upon this ground, that it is within the equity of this court to take *ex ab origine* a question whether or not a right is violated. It struck me immediately, from a general recollection of the cases, that the court has exercised no such jurisdiction. There are two ways in which applications to this court have been made in this kind of case: first, in order to compel the party to try the right— secondly, to prevent a multiplicity of suits."[3] But although equity has no authority, in general, to try questions of title

---

[1] Chesapeake, &c. *v.* Young, 3 Md. 480.

[2] Per Lord Eldon, Smith *v.* Collyer, 8 Ves. 90.

[3] Weller *v.* Smeaton, 1 Cox, 103.

to lands, it is otherwise where the whole dispute is on the construction of a will or other written instrument, under which both parties claim.[1] So equity may interfere by injunction in favor of one who owns and has possession of the land, but upon whose title a cloud rests in consequence of an adverse claim.[2]

§ 2. Equity may restrain by injunction a citizen of the State from injuring real estate out of the State.[3] So where a non-resident vendor of land is unable to make title, an averment, in a bill filed by the vendee, that the vendor is in very "slender circumstances," and unable to respond in damages on her covenant of warranty, is sufficient to authorize the vendee to come into equity, to enjoin the collection of the purchase-money.[4]

§ 3. It is a general rule, that a party seeking an injunction, to protect him in the enjoyment of real property, must show a right, such as the court, upon his own showing, will feel bound to protect against the defendant. In respect to applications for injunctions to stay waste, such rule is strict. But where the *gravamen* of the case is an alleged fraudulent purchase by the defendant of the complainant, if the latter states his right so as to authorize him to complain of the fraud, and to entitle him to relief against it, this is sufficient.[4]

§ 4. A vendee, who has not acquired the legal title, cannot sustain a *bill of peace*. Thus equity will not enjoin an action of ejectment brought against a purchaser of real estate at a guardian's sale, the sale not having been reported to or approved by the Circuit Court, though he paid for the land, supposing his title perfect.[5] Nor, at the instance of a party claiming the legal title to land, a sale of the land by an ad-

---

[1] Gibbes *v.* Elliott, 5 Rich. Eq. 327.
[2] Eldridge *v.* Smith, 34 Verm. 484.
[3] Great Falls, &c. *v.* Worster, 3 Fost. 462.

[4] Graham *v.* Tankersley, 15 Ala. 634.
[5] Outcalt *v.* Disborough, 2 Green Ch. 214.
[6] Young *v.* Dowling, 15 Ill. 481.

verse claimant.[1] So where A. conveyed to B. a piece of ground, on condition that B. should be restricted to the privilege of erecting or running a saw-mill or saw-mills thereon; held, equity would not enjoin B. from using the building on the land for other purposes, after he had incurred considerable expense in the construction thereof, or compel him to stop the machinery already in motion, where no sufficient excuse was rendered by A. for his failure or neglect to apply for an injunction sooner.[2]

§ 5. Eviction from real estate purchased with warranty is sometimes a ground of injunction. (See Chap. XXVIII.) Thus, where A. agrees to convey to B. by warranty deed, but conveys only his "right, title, and interest," or with a warranty to defend "the aforesaid premises," and the land is subject to mortgage; B. may enjoin a suit on the note given for the purchase-money, till the mortgage is discharged and a proper deed given.[3] So in a late case A. purchases land of B., giving a mortgage back for the price, and then contracts to sell to C., who has no notice of the mortgage. B. then records the mortgage, after which C. receives a warranty deed from A., taking possession, paying part of the price, and giving two negotiable notes for the balance, which A. delivers to D. and E. severally, as collateral security, but without indorsement, and afterwards dies insolvent. B. files a petition for foreclosure of his mortgage and a sale of the land, making C. a party, as being in possession and claiming title. C. files a cross petition. All parties in interest being before the court, held, C. was entitled to enjoin the collection of so much of the notes last falling due as would cover the mortgage. The court remark as follows: "It is further contended in behalf of James Thompson, that Weller ought not to be allowed to avoid the payment of the remaining note, but ought to be turned over to such remedy as he may hereafter have on the

[1] Overseers,&c. v. Hart, 3 Leigh, 1.　　[3] Bowen v. Thrall, 28 Verm. 382.
[2] Water Lot Co. v. Bucks, 5 Geo.
315.

20

covenants of warranty, and this for the reason that he has not yet been evicted. And Picket v. Picket, 6 Ohio St. Rep. 525, is cited in support of this position. In that case it was held, that 'a purchaser of land, who has received a deed containing a covenant of warranty, cannot plead in bar to an action on the note given for the purchase-money, defect of title, unless he has been evicted by title paramount.' Without questioning the authority of that case, we may say that it was an action at law in assumpsit, in which principles governing courts of law were rigidly applied, and which evidently ought not to be extended. The case before us is in the nature of a proceeding in equity, and the parties in interest are all in court, and their rights are open to consideration and adjustment. There it did not appear but that the warrantor was, or would be, fully able to respond to an action on his covenant when it should mature; here, the warrantor is dead, and his estate insolvent; in that case there was no eviction, and *non constat* that there ever would be; in this the decree we are about to render establishes a constructive eviction to the extent of the mortgage incumbrance. There will be a judgment for plaintiffs for the sale of the mortgaged premises, unless the amount remaining due on the mortgage is paid by a day to be named, and an order perpetually enjoining," as above.[1]

[1] Kyle v. Thompson, 11 Ohio St. 616–22–3, per Brinkerhoff, J. Acc. Wiley v. Howard, 15 Ind. 169. Yonge v. McCormick, 6 Flori. 368.

CHAPTER XV.

PARTIES—CORPORATIONS.

§ 1. HAVING considered the *grounds* for interference of a court of equity by way of injunction, we now proceed to an inquiry as to the *parties* who may avail themselves of this relief.

§ 2. No class of parties is more frequent, in the present period of numerous and varied companies for the accomplishment of public undertakings and improvements, than that of *corporations*. And in reference to corporations it is held, that, although the operations of large companies ought not ordinarily to be arrested by injunction without notice, yet it is a matter resting in the sound discretion of the court; and if a Master allows such an injunction without notice, the Chancellor will not of course dissolve it, though he might have exercised the discretionary power differently.[1] That where a corporation employs its powers and funds for purposes not within the scope of its charter, a stockholder may have a remedy by injunction. But, independently of its thus exceeding its powers, the will of a majority, properly expressed at a legal meeting, must control.[2]

[1] Perkins *v.* Collins, 2 Green Ch. 482. See Capner *v.* Flemington, &c., 2 Green Ch. 467.

[2] Gifford *v.* New Jersey, &c., 2 Stockt. 171.

§ 3. Equity has jurisdiction against a corporation, when the money which should be divided among the stockholders has been applied contrary to the charter or articles of agreement. Such misapplication is held a breach of trust and a fraud on the part of the majority towards the minority, who may have a remedy by injunction. Intentional wrong or actual fraud is not necessary to sustain such bill.[1]

§ 4. Questions have arisen, in case of proposed applications, on the part of corporate bodies, to the legislative power, for some change in their chartered privileges. Thus where shareholders of a company had resolved to use its funds and pledge its credit, and make contracts, for the purpose of applying to Parliament to vary the original object contemplated by the original charter, an injunction was granted to other shareholders.[2] So an injunction was granted to restrain the corporation of Norwich from soliciting, at the expense of the borough fund, a bill in Parliament, to enable them to improve the navigation of the river flowing through that town to Yarmouth.[3]

§ 5. But, on the other hand, the plaintiff agreed with the defendants, a railway company, to withdraw his opposition to their bill in Parliament, in consideration of their completing their line in a certain way. The defendants afterwards found themselves unable to go on, and gave notice of their intention to apply to Parliament for authority to abandon their road. Held, an injunction would not lie, to restrain such application. Lord Cottenham remarked: "It has been suggested that this court could not interfere with infringing upon the privileges of Parliament; so the courts of common law thought at one time; and there is as much foundation for the one as for the other supposition. In both cases this court acts upon the person, and not upon the jurisdiction.

[1] March v. Eastern, &c., 43 N. H. 515.
[2] The Great, &c. v. Rushout, 5 De Gex & Sm. 290.
[3] Atty. Gen. v. Norwich, 16 Sim. 225. See Simpson v. Denison, 10 Hare, 51.

In a proper case, therefore, I have said here and elsewhere, that I should not hesitate to exercise the jurisdiction of this court by injunction, touching proceedings in Parliament for a private bill or a bill respecting property ; but what would be a proper case for that purpose it may be very difficult to conceive. The case of Parliament differs widely from that of the courts of common law ; the province of the latter is to enforce legal rights, and the object of the injunction is to prevent an inequitable use of such legal right, but the ordinary province of Parliament in such bills is to abrogate existing rights, and to create new rights. To hold, therefore, that no application should be made to Parliament, because the object of the application was to interfere with some right or interest of some other party, would be in effect to hold that this court should by its injunction deprive the subject of the benefit of parliamentary interference in such cases. The injunction, therefore, cannot be granted, upon the ground that the act applied for would interfere with existing rights, it being the very object of it to do so. What difference, then, can it make, whether such pre-existing right exists by the tenure of property or by virtue of contracts. In both cases Parliament has the same power of destroying, altering, or affecting such pre-existing rights, providing, as it always does or intends to do, compensation to the party affected ; and in neither has this court a right to interfere by injunction to deprive the subject of the right of applying to Parliament for a special law to supersede the rules of property by which he finds himself bound, whether arising from contract or otherwise."[1]

§ 6. An injunction will issue to restrain a city from taking private property without legal right.[2] (See *Railroads*.) And, in general, except where the public necessity admits no delay, equity will enjoin the taking of private property, without

---

[1] Heathcote *v.* The North, &c., 2 Mac. & G. 100.

[2] Lumsden *v.* Milwaukee, 8 Wis. 485.

first making compensation.[1] So an injunction lies against taking land, till security is given for the value, although the party has not petitioned for damages.[2] Though not where the appraisers have returned that no damages be paid. The remedy in such case is by *appeal*.[3] So if the power of taxation in a municipal corporation is so limited, as not to be adequate to pay, within any reasonable time, the damages caused by the opening of a public street; a court of equity will prohibit such opening by injunction, until security for payment be given.[4] So a harbor improvement company, in the prosecution of their works, under the authority of a special act of Parliament, obstructed access to a wharf from the place of business of A., by which he was put to expense in loading and unloading ships. A., claiming compensation, gave a notice and proceeded to appoint an arbitrator, under the 68th section of the 8 Vict. c. 18 (the lands clauses consolidation act, 1845). Upon a bill filed by the company, an injunction was granted to restrain the further proceedings of A. until he established his right at law, but on appeal it was dissolved.[5] While, on the other hand, an injunction, to restrain an appropriation of public property to private purposes, will not be dissolved upon the coming in of the answer, admitting the acts charged, but denying that the public interest will be thereby prejudiced.[6] So a municipal corporation may be restrained by perpetual injunction from entering upon and taking possession of land, and opening and grading a street thereon, by virtue of proceedings regular in form, where it appears by an extrinsic fact that the commissioners have awarded the owner of the land only one dollar for land worth twelve dollars. In such case, it seems that *certiorari* is not an adequate remedy.[7]

[1] Penrice v. Wallis, 37 Miss. 172. See Standish v. Liverpool, 15 Eng. Law and Eq. 255.
[2] Somer v. Philadelphia, 35 Penn. 231.
[3] McCrory v. Griswold, 7 Clarke, 248 ; Connolly v. Same. ib. 416.
[4] Keene v. Bristol, 26 Penn. 46.

[5] Sutton, &c. v. Hitchins, 1 Eng. Law and Eq. 202 ; 9 Ib. 41.
[6] Atty., &c. v. Cohoes Co., 6 Paige, 133.
[7] Baldwin v. Buffalo, 29 Barb. 396. See Betts v. Williamsburg, 15 Barb. 255.

§ 7. But although a city cannot occupy or appropriate private property without compensation, or do direct, incidental, wanton damage to private property, the exercise of its discretion within proper limits cannot be enjoined.[1]   So, although persons obtaining from the legislature power to interfere with the rights of property are bound strictly to adhere to such powers, to do no more than the legislature has sanctioned, and to proceed only in the mode which the legislature has pointed out; yet (except in a proceeding at the instance of the Attorney-General) any one seeking the assistance of a court of equity, to restrain the violation of such a contract with the legislature, is bound to show that he has a private interest in the matter.   Therefore, where a water-works act empowered a company to divert the water of a stream (without limit as to quantity), by means of an open channel filled with loose stones, and they were diverting it by means of a culvert; it was held that another company, who were entitled to the water of a stream into which the diverted stream had flowed, were not entitled to an injunction to restrain a violation of the terms of the act, as to the mode of diversion.[2]

§ 8. An injunction will be granted to prevent the franchise of a corporation from being destroyed, as well as to restrain a party from violating it by attempting to participate in its exclusive privileges.[3]   It is foreign from the plan of the present work, even to refer to the numerous and important cases, in which the questions have been discussed, how far the grant of a franchise is a *contract*, and the franchise itself *private property*, the former of which, by fundamental constitutional provisions, cannot be impaired, nor the latter appropriated without compensation to public uses; or under what circumstances a subsequent grant of a similar or rival

---

[1] Plum *v.* Morris, &c., 2 Stockt. 256.
[2] The Mayor, &c. *v.* Corley, &c., 21 Eng. Law and Eq. 620.

[3] Osborn *v.* Bank of the U. S., 9 Wheat. 738.

franchise interfering with the former one is, upon the grounds mentioned, unconstitutional and void. (See *Railroads*, *Bridges*, *Ferries*.) In a late and important case in Pennsylvania, the prevailing doctrine on the subject is thus explained: "All acts of incorporation and acts extending the privileges of incorporated bodies, are to be taken most strongly against the companies. Whatever is not expressly and unequivocally granted in such acts is taken to have been withheld.[1] The same rule was laid down in very clear terms by Chief Justice Marshall in Billings v. The Providence Bank.[2] In the Charles River Bridge v. The Warren Bridge,[3] it was placed on grounds so impregnable by the present Chief Justice of the Supreme Court of the United States, that it is not probable we will ever hear it questioned again."[4] On the same subject it is said: "Where a party claims a franchise under a statute, and is in the possession and enjoyment of such franchise, equity will interpose to protect and secure the enjoyment of such franchise, because it affords the only plain and adequate remedy. In the present case, certain rights and franchises were granted to the plaintiffs, by the legislature, upon the ground that the enjoyment and exercise of them would not only be a benefit to the persons incorporated, but would also contribute to the public benefit. Another ground is, where the party complained against professes to act by public authority, to enter upon, and to a certain extent to use the land of third persons, and exceeds his authority, it is held to be a peculiarly proper case for the interposition of a court of equity. It is also another ground that what the defendants propose to do, and claim a right to do, is the erection of a work, which is in its nature permanent and perpetual. It is not like the case of a single or temporary disturbance, the injury arising from which can be measured and estimated and compensated in damages in a

[1] 11 East, 685; 4 Bingham, 452; 2 Barn. & Adol. 635.
[2] 4 Peters, 514.
[3] 11 Peters, 521.
[4] Per Black, C. J. Packer v. Sunbury, &c., 19 Penn. 211.

single suit; the plaintiffs would be compelled to bring successive suits from time to time. This is more especially a ground of interference, where the party complained against professes to exercise a public authority, and where the claim is to appropriate the property or franchises of the complainant, to a purpose claimed to be public, and where the plaintiff denies and contests the right of the defendant to exercise such power."[1]

§ 9. One interested in a trading corporation may enjoin the directors from mismanaging the business or wasting the funds.[2] (See § 11.) But, in New Jersey, the court will not grant an injunction and receivers on an incorporated company, under "the act to prevent frauds by incorporated companies," unless the protection of the public or the interest of the stockholders require it.[3] So a motion to restrain and enjoin will be refused, where, upon pleadings and proof, the court would not be warranted in declaring a corporation insolvent, and subjecting it to the provisions of the act.[4] Chancery will interfere to prevent a disposition of the property of a corporation for other than corporate purposes, upon a proper case made out; but as to what is a proper case, the court will be guided by the general principles upon which it usually exercises its powers.[5] So, in New York, under the act to prevent frauds by incorporated companies, where it is proved that an insurance company is insolvent, the Chancellor is not bound, as of course, to issue an injunction, but must use his discretion, and take such course as will inure to the benefit of all concerned.[6]

§ 10. Where the rules of a friendly society were framed

---

[1] Per Shaw, C. J., Boston Water, &c. v. Boston, &c. R. R., 16 Pick. 525.
[2] Sears v. Hotchkiss, 25 Conn. 171.
[3] Rawnsley v. Trenton, &c., 1 Stockt. 347.

[4] Rawnsley v. Trenton, &c., 1 Stockt. 95.
[5] Kean v. Johnson, 1 Stockt. 401.
[6] Farrand v. Marshall, 21 Barb. 409.

on erroneous principles, and the annuities chargeable on the funds had in consequence become so numerous as to be likely to exhaust the whole; upon a bill filed against the committee and trustees for the purpose of a dissolution, an injunction was granted to restrain further payments, and the selling of the stock.[1](a)

§ 10 a. A corporation proposing illegally to lease an important ferry for ten years may be enjoined.[2]

§ 11. A stockholder may enjoin the directors of a corporation.[3] (See § 9.) So where a suit was brought against a corporation, in Massachusetts, on a judgment rendered in New York, and no defence had been made by the company in New York; a temporary injunction was granted, restraining the suit, on a bill filed by an individual stockholder.[4]

§ 12. A preliminary injunction should not issue upon the complaint of a minority of the directors, to restrain a person from voting on an alleged excess of stock, which the company have taken no steps to declare void, where it does not appear that his voting would produce irreparable and permanent injury, or any great and imminent danger.[5]

§ 13. In Wisconsin, an injunction, to restrain an alleged stockholder from voting for directors, does not suspend the

---

[1] Reeve v. Parkins, 2 Jac. & W. 389. But see India, &c., 17 Sim. 15.
[2] People v. New York, 32 Barb. 102.
[3] Mississippi, &c. v. Cross, 20 Ark. 443.
[4] Sumner v. Marcy, 3 W. & M. 105.
[5] Reed v. Jones, 6 Wis. 680.

(a) In Ellison v. Bignold, 2 Jac. & W. 511, Lord Eldon speaks of "those very distressing cases, where persons who have been expecting a provision for their old age from benefit societies, have found themselves at last disappointed, from the societies being founded on erroneous principles. The court has there been obliged to consider the whole as originating in a blunder, and to put an end to them by a dissolution."

general and ordinary business of the corporation ; and there-fore, under Code § 132, may be granted by the court com-missioner.[1]

§ 14. Unless there has been tardiness in the organization of an incorporated company, it may have relief by injunc-tion, against wrongs done and threatened between the act of incorporation and the issuing of letters patent.[2]

§ 15. Where there is a mortgage upon the capital stock of a corporation, and the treasurer is one of the mortgagees, an injunction will be granted to stay a sale under a power in the mortgage, until the treasurer shall furnish to the mortgagor any information relative to the condition of the corporation, and affecting the value of the stock, which the treasurer may have obtained by virtue of his office, beyond what appears from the books of the corporation.[3]

§ 16. *Cities and towns* constitute a class of corporations or *quasi* corporations, with reference to which the process of injunction is often invoked.(a)   Thus, in Massachusetts, a

---

[1] Reed *v.* Jones, 6 Wis. 680.
[2] Packer *v.* The Sunbury, &c., 19 Penn. 211.
[3] Frieze *v.* Chapin, 2 R. I. 429.

(a) As to the remedy of injunction in the case of a *county*, see County, &c., *v.* Hunt, 5 Ohio, N. S. 488. It is laid down, as the general rule, that only the people can prosecute for violations of public trust. Municipal corporators and tax payers, unless individually injured, cannot enjoin a public wrong. Ketchum *v.* Buffalo, 4 Kern. 356 ; Davis *v.* Mayor, &c., ib. 506. Equity will not interfere in behalf of a *monopoly.* Thus the amendment of a city charter provided, that a right given by the city to lay gas-pipes through the streets and public grounds should be exclusive, except as against any persons or corporations that might receive similar authority from the legislature. The plaintiffs were purchasers of the gas-works and business. After such amendment, the defendants, organ-ized under the statute relating to joint stock corporations, commenced opening the streets to lay their pipes. Upon a bill praying an injunc-tion, held, such amendment, so far as it restricted the free manufacture

town voted to loan its portion of the surplus revenue, received under St. 1837, c. 85, "to the inhabitants of the town, as the population of the town was, on the head and the heads of families, to give their securities for themselves and minor children, guardians for children they are guardians for, and the selectmen for town paupers, and that the trustees of the surplus revenue in behalf of the town accept the securities of minor children, who have no parents or guardians." At a subsequent meeting the town voted that "the trustees of the surplus revenue loan the same in equal sums to each and every inhabitant of the town, and that each inhabitant give two sureties which should be acceptable to the trustees; that the loan be made according to a census to be taken, and that the trustees need not require one of the sureties to be a freeholder." Held, such votes were in violation of the act concerning the deposit of the surplus revenue passed March 24, 1837, and were illegal and void; and that compliance with such votes on the part of the trustees should be prohibited by injunction.[1] So where the city of New London appropriated money for the celebration of the anniversary of independence; a bill was sustained on behalf of certain tax-payers to restrain the payment of such appropriation. The court remarked: "The city corporation was in the nature of a trustee of the money in its treasury, for the corporators, the inhabitants of the city, for the purposes for which they were incorporated, and here was a meditated misappropriation of the trust fund; and, secondly, it is extremely doubtful, whether the plaintiffs could have any other remedy. The amount appropriated by this vote, was in the city treasury, and, if abstracted, must, when wanted for other and legitimate purposes, be

---

[1] Pope v. Halifax, 12 Cush. 410. See Hood v. Lynn, 1 Allen, 103.

---

and sale of gas, was a monopoly, unconstitutional and void, and the injunction was refused. Norwich, &c. v. Norwich, &c., 25 Conn. 19, (containing a learned and elaborate discussion of the law of franchises and monopolies).

supplied, by a tax on the inhabitants. It is suggested that the plaintiffs should bring an action against the city, for a misappropriation of its funds, or that, when such a tax is laid, they should, by a proper action, resist its collection. We are, by no means, prepared to say, that an action could be maintained, on either of these grounds, and are strongly inclined to think it could not. But, however this may be, we are clearly of opinion, that the plaintiffs are not bound to wait until the money is misspent, nor until such tax shall be levied, and attempted to be collected, but that they may call on a court of equity to interpose, by way of preventing the injury."[1] But where an action was commenced against the selectmen of a town for illegally refusing a vote, and the town voted to pay the expenses already incurred in defending the suit, and that it would be the duty of the town to refund any sum which the selectmen should be compelled to pay, and a minority of the legal voters, who were liable to pay more than half the taxes of the town, filed a bill against the selectmen and treasurer, praying for an injunction to restrain them from carrying such vote into effect; held, before the passage of (Massachusetts) stat. 1847, c. 37, the court had no jurisdiction in the case.[2]

§ 17. Chancery has power by injunction to restrain the trustees of a village from transcending their powers under the act of incorporation, where the act complained of would injuriously affect the value of property in the village.[3]

§ 18. To authorize a preliminary injunction to stay the proceedings of the corporation of a city, in the alteration of streets, on the ground of fraud, the plaintiff should be able to point out some particular act of fraud, or *primâ facie* evidence of corruption, on the part of the members of the corporation who voted for the ordinance.[4]

---

[1] New London v. Brainard, 22 Conn 552–6.
[2] Hall v. Cushman, 6 Met. 425.
[3] Oakley v. Trustees, &c., 6 Paige, 262.
[4] Champlin v. Corporation, &c., 3 Paige, 573.

§ 19. It is held, that equity will enjoin the use of a district school-house for religious meetings and Sunday-schools by vote of the district, on the application of any tax-payer, however slightly injured.[1]

§ 20. The court will not restrain the mere act of voting on a resolution or ordinance, proposed in either board of the common council of a city, unless, on the mere voting or formal passage thereof, such ordinance or resolution would instantly, and without any action or attempt to enforce any right or privilege under it, effect an irremediable injury.[2] And a *legislative act* cannot be enjoined; as, for instance, an order of a city common council to a department, to give an individual a particular contract. But the execution of such order by the city, after its passage, may be enjoined.[3] And the like distinction is made, that although, generally, equity will not interfere with the ordinances of a municipal corporation, yet, where questions arose, as to the effect of a dedication of lands under water, and of letting the land lie unreclaimed fifty years by the public, and where the ordinance, based upon one view of the above questions, was about to do irreparable injury to the complainants, and the defendants did not object to the jurisdiction in their answer, an injunction was granted.[4]

§ 21. Where an injunction issues against a city, and all its members, officers, and agents, restraining them from making a certain grant; a member of the city council, who votes for the grant, violates the injunction, though the resolve, in favor of the grant, is conditioned on the grantee's acceptance of its terms.[5]

§ 22. The question of property and right of possession,

[1] Schofield v. Eighth, &c., 27 Conn. 499. See Sheldon v. Centre, &c., 25 Conn. 224.
[2] Whitney v. Mayor, &c., 28 Barb. 233.
[3] People v. New York, 32 Barb. 35.
[4] Morris, &c. v. Jersey, &c., 1 Beasl. 252.
[5] People v. Sturtevant, 5 Seld. 263.

between two bodies, each claiming to be the trustees of an incorporated *religious society*, is a question to be determined at law. Thus a part of a religious society, which owned a house of public worship and burial-ground, built a new house, in another place, and elected a board of trustees. A part continued to worship in the old building. The trustees of those who worshipped at the old house refused to permit the new party to enter and use the burying-ground; and the latter, on several occasions, broke open the gates for the purpose of burying therein. On bill filed, injunction was granted, restraining such forcible entry. On answer and argument, the court held that a forcible entry for such a purpose was not such an injury as called for injunction.[1] So an injunction will not be granted, at the suit of a pew-holder, to prevent the trustees of a church from pulling down the old church, where it has become dilapidated, for the purpose of erecting a new one, but will leave the pew-holders to their remedies at law.[2] So on a bill filed by pew-holders in a church, an injunction was granted, restraining the authorities of the church from pulling it down, as they were proposing to use the materials in the erection of a new church on a different site. On answer, the injunction was dissolved, on the ground that, if the complainants had rights which would be violated, there was a remedy at law, and that the nature and extent of the injury were not such as called for an injunction.[3]

§ 23. The process of injunction is very frequently applied in connection with *banking corporations;* which, from the peculiar nature of their relations with the community at large, and the unforeseen fluctuations incident to them, often call for judicial interference more prompt and summary than could otherwise be afforded. In reference to a statutory

---

[1] Miller *v.* English, 2 Halst. Ch. 304. See Scott *v.* Stipe, 12 Ind. 74.
[2] Heeney *v.* St. Peter's Church, 2 Edw. Ch. 608.

[3] Van Horn *v.* Tallmadge, 4 Halst. Ch. 108.

provision for the issuing of an injunction against a bank upon
the application of bank commissioners, Chief Justice Shaw
remarks: "An injunction is often issued in other cases, upon
affidavit before hearing or notice.   But such a complaint,
from responsible officers is fully as much entitled to credit
as an affidavit.   It is in some measure like an inquisition,
somewhat like an indictment, but perhaps still more like an
information, all of which are known forms of proceeding to
put a party on trial.   Again, here is room for the exercise
of judicial powers.   The judge is judicially to inquire and
ascertain that the complainants are such bank commissioners;
that they have examined the bank complained against in the
manner required by the statute; that they have come to the
opinion, that the bank is insolvent, and that its condition is
such, that its further proceeding is dangerous to the public,
and that it has violated its charter, and also, that they have
made application in such form and manner as the law requires.   There is also room for the exercise of judicial discretion, in determining upon the complaint, to what extent
such injunction shall go, whether to prevent their issuing
bills only, or to prevent their paying bills, or deposits, or
other debts; in short, whether it shall be a total suspension
of all their operations, or a slight interference with them."[1]
And in a very recent similar case it is said, the authority of
this court to issue an injunction against a bank on the application of the bank commissioners, and to make such injunction perpetual, as set forth in Gen. Sts. c. 57, s. 7, is very
broad and comprehensive.   It is not limited to cases where
the corporation is insolvent, or its further continuance in
business will be hazardous to its creditors, but extends to all
cases where a bank has exceeded the powers conferred on it,
or has failed to comply with any of the rules, restrictions,
or conditions, provided by law for its regulation and management; nor is the nature of the injunction defined or limited
by any legislative restriction.   This is left to be determined

Com. v. Farmers, &c., 21 Pick. 552.

by a sound judicial discretion. The object of conferring this very extensive jurisdiction in equity over this class of corporations is obvious. The nature of the important powers and duties with which they are intrusted renders it expedient and necessary that they should be subjected to careful supervision, and that any irregularity or illegality in their mode of conducting business should be promptly checked and prevented.[1] Accordingly it was held, that there should be an injunction against a bank, for not keeping on hand an amount of specie equal to fifteen per cent. of its liability for circulation and deposits, under Gen. Sts. c. 57, s. 19. But it was further held, that, if a bank has violated the provisions of a statute under a mistake or misapprehension of the law, and with no wilful intent of violation, and it is not alleged that any other or further like acts are threatened or intended, a temporary injunction may be dissolved on payment of costs.[2] So, by the charter of a bank, a majority of the directors, the president being one, were to form a board or quorum for the transaction of any business, " but ordinary discounts may be made by the president and four directors." " The rate of discount shall not exceed one-half of one per centum for thirty days." The cashier and president discounted paper without four directors, and paper was discounted at a higher rate than that above stated. Held, a temporary injunction should be granted against the bank.[3]

§ 24. In Pennsylvania, the commonwealth filed a bill against a bank, alleging that the bank held funds of the commonwealth in trust, and had misapplied large portions thereof, and praying an injunction against a further misapplication. An injunction was granted after notice and without objection. Afterwards the bank was allowed to pay the funds to the use of the complainant, and the current expenses of the bank, without prejudice. The respondents answered, deny-

---

[1] Per Bigelow, C. J., Com. v. Bank, &c., 4 Allen, 8, 9.
[2] Com. v. Bank, &c., 4 Allen, 1.
[3] Manderson v. Commercial, &c., 28 Penn. 379.

21

ing that they were trustees, and that they received the funds otherwise than as ordinary deposits; answering the residue of the bill; and praying that the injunction might be dissolved.   A statute was then passed, authorizing the bank to make an assignment, the assignment to be approved by the stockholders, with a proviso that the commonwealth should have the right to vote in the choice of assignees, according to the number of shares held by her.   The statute also prescribed the powers and duties of the assignees, and that the assignment should not be made until the debt due the commonwealth had been paid.   The stockholders voted to assign, and chose assignees; but the election was declared void by the Supreme Court for defects in the proviso as to the number of votes by the commonwealth.   Held, that the residue of the statute was valid and in full force, by which the priority of the commonwealth was secured, and that the injunction ought not to be dissolved.[1]   But an injunction to restrain persons from carrying on the business of banking, in contravention of a statute of New York, on an information by the Attorney-General, was refused by the court.[2]   And an affidavit of information and belief of the insolvency of a bank, in contradiction of its official reports, and its suspension of specie payments, in common with other banks, are not sufficient grounds for a temporary injunction, on the charge of insolvency.[3]

§ 25.   Where a lien and power of sale upon and over the shares are given by charter to a bank, for debts due from the stockholders to the bank, equity will enjoin a sale, or, under equitable circumstances, set aside a conveyance, of shares, attempted or made by the bank against the will of an insolvent stockholder, for a debt really due to a director, under color that it is due to the bank; such sale being a

[1] Com. v. Bank, &c., 3 Watts & Serg. 184.
[2] Attorney., &c. v. Utica, &c., 2 John. Ch. 371.
[3] Livingston v. Bank, &c., 26 Barb. 304.

fraudulent abuse of a statute power, and a fraudulent attempt without the authority of the stockholder to give preference amongst his creditors.[1]

§ 26. In a proceeding against a bank, its attorneys, &c., to enjoin the collection of a judgment in its favor, service was had on the attorney of the bank who had obtained the judgment and was endeavoring to collect it. Held, not to be sufficient to give the court jurisdiction to order a perpetual injunction; and this notwithstanding the bank was a foreign corporation, there being at the time other legal means by which jurisdiction over the defendants for the purposes required could be obtained.[2]

§ 27. A stockholder of a bank having filed a bill, to compel the president and directors to re-transfer to the bank certain shares, which the bank itself had owned, and which the defendants had sold and purchased at less, as was alleged, than the market value; held, the corporation should have been made a party to the bill.[3]

§ 28. A board of freeholders in New Jersey being authorized by statute to build a *bridge* over a certain river, chancery cannot interfere in respect to their acts in relation to the bridge, on the ground that they are arbitrary, or that the complainants have been denied a fair hearing. The remedy is by application to the Supreme Court for a *certiorari*.[4]

§ 29. On application for a preliminary injunction, to stay the first election of officers under an act of incorporation, on the ground that the apportionment of stock by the commissioners was void; it appearing that an injunction would affect the interests of many who had purchased stock in

[1] Seagraves *v.* Railroad Bank, 4 R. I. 372.
[2] Death *v.* Bank, &c., 1 Clarke, 382.
[3] Charleston, &c. *v.* Sebring, 5 Rich. Eq. 342.
[4] Tucker *v.* Freeholders, &c., Saxt. 282.

good faith, and it being doubtful whether the commissioners could fix upon another day for the election, if not held at the time appointed, the injunction was denied.[1]

§ 30. A corporation may recover the amount of a subscription to its stock, notwithstanding a temporary injunction against proceeding with its works.[2]

§ 31. Service of the notice of motion at the office in London is, for the purposes of the corporation, a good service where it is admitted that at the head office in Scotland the corporation had notice.[3]

§ 32. The Supreme Court of Pennsylvania has not jurisdiction to grant an injunction against a corporation situated in Montgomery County; their supervision of corporations is among that class of cases in which their jurisdiction is limited to the city and county of Philadelphia.[4](a)

---

[1] Walker v. Devereaux, 4 Paige, 229.
[2] Crossman v. Penrose, &c. 26 Penn. 69.
[3] McLairon v. Stainton, 15 Eng. Law and Eq. 500.
[4] Cassel v. Jones, 6 Watts & Serg. 552.

(a) We have already—Chapter III.—referred to the rights and duties of corporations in regard to the dissolution of an injunction. The following remarks of eminent judges, expressing the judgments of courts of alike high authority, may properly be cited, as directly opposite views of an important point of practice. "I am strongly of opinion, upon principle, that such an answer (an answer under the corporate seal) is sufficient to produce either of the consequences which have been mentioned. The corporate body is called upon, and is compellable, to answer all the allegations of the bill, but can do so under no higher sanction than its common seal. A peer of the realm in England answers upon his honor, the oath being dispensed with. In like manner, the plaintiff may, in ordinary cases, dispense with the oath to an answer; and, if he do so, the court will order the answer to be taken without oath. Now if, in these cases, the answer, denying the equity of the bill, cannot avail the defendant as an answer under oath would do, to prevent the granting of an injunction, or to dissolve it when granted, the legal impossibility to take an oath in the first case, the privilege of the peer in the second, and the dispensation extended to the defendant in the last, would place each of those defendants in a situation infinitely more disadvantageous than that of the other defendants, whose answers cannot be received otherwise than upon oath. Such then cannot be the practice of a court of equity." Per Washington, J., Haight v. Proprs., &c., 4 Wash. C. 601. On the other hand, in a case in New York the Chancellor remarked as follows : "The case of a corporation defendant is an anomaly in the practice in relation to the dissolution of an injunction. In most cases the injunction is dissolved as a matter of course, if the answer is perfect, and denies all the equity of the bill in the points upon which the injunction rests. It is not, however, a matter of course, to dissolve the injunction where the defendant acts in a representative character, and founds his denial of the equity of the bill upon information and belief only. Corporations answer under their seal and without oath. They are therefore at liberty to deny everything contained in the bill, whether true or false. Neither can any discovery be compelled, except through the medium of their agents and officers, and by making them parties defendants. But no dissolution of the injunction can be obtained upon the answer of a corporation, which is not duly verified by the oath of some officer of the corporation, or other person who is acquainted with the facts contained therein. There can be no hardship in this rule as applied to corporations, as it only puts them in the same situation with other parties. Other defendants can only make positive denial as to facts within their own knowledge. In relation to every other matter, they must answer as to information and belief. If the agents of the institution, under whose direction the answer is put in, are acquainted with the facts, so as to justify a positive denial in the answer, they can verify its truth by a positive affidavit ; and if none of the officers are acquainted with the facts, their information and belief can have no greater effect than that of ordinary defendants, however positive the answer in the denial may be. In this case, the officer of the institution, who was such at the time referred to in the claimant's bill, has studiously avoided saying anything as to the truth of the answer, leaving it to the secretary, who knows nothing of its truth or falsehood, to express his belief on the subject." Fulton, &c. v. New York, &c., 1 Paige, 311.

CHAPTER XVI.

EXECUTORS AND ADMINISTRATORS.

1. General administration, &c., of assets.
2. Injunction against an executor, &c.
4. Injunction in favor of an executor, &c.
9. Miscellaneous cases as to estates of persons deceased.

§ 1. THE interference of equity " in the *administration and marshalling of assets*" is said to rest " upon principles almost purely of an equitable and conscientious nature. In most of the cases of this nature, there is no pretence to assert the jurisdiction upon any of the ordinary grounds of accident,(a)

(a) Accident, however, may furnish additional and special ground for the interference of equity in this class of cases. The same learned writer elsewhere says : "Suppose an executor or administrator should be in possession of abundant assets to pay all the debts of the deceased, and by an accidental fire a great portion of them should be destroyed, so that the estate should be deeply insolvent. In such a case he might be sued by a creditor at law, and the loss of the assets by accident would be no defence ; for when he once becomes chargeable with the assets at law, he is forever chargeable, notwithstanding any intervening casualties. But courts of equity will enjoin proceedings at law in cases of this sort upon the purest principles of justice." 2 Story's Eq. 196, § 878. Accordingly, in an early case, an administrator, who had committed a *devastavit* at law by paying legacies, was relieved against a bond which unexpectedly started up, the assets having been originally sufficient, but the greatest part of them, consisting of houses, having been burned in the fire of London. Croft *v.* Lindsey, 2 Freem. 1. It is truly remarked, "The jurisdiction of courts of equity in cases of this kind arises from their general jurisdiction over trusts, which cannot be taken away but by express legislation. The special power given to surrogates' courts, in these cases, is merely auxiliary to that of the Supreme Court," now (in New York) having full chancery jurisdiction.

mistake, fraud, or confidence.   It stands upon the more enlarged principles of general justice, and was probably derived
from that great reservoir of general principles, the Roman
Civil Law.'"(a)   Thus equity will restrain the Orphans'
Court from proceeding in the final settlement of an estate,
where matters of purely equitable cognizance are to be adjudicated, or where a discovery is necessary to ascertain facts,
which cannot be established otherwise.[2]

§ 2. A suit brought by an administrator, for the sole benefit
of persons neither parties nor privies, and having no title
themselves, in order to enable them to use the intestate's title
against the tenant in possession, will be enjoined.[3] So an
injunction lies against an executor, to prevent his paying a
distributive share, on the application of a creditor of the
distributee (even though no judgment has been obtained)
who is hopelessly insolvent.[4] So where an administrator
sells at auction a slave, as the property of his intestate, and
recovers judgment on the bond given for his purchase-
money; and the son of the intestate, claiming the slave by
gift, threatens to sue for it: equity will prevent the suit by
injunction, as the parties are now all before the court, and
full justice can be done them; and it will also prevent the
administrator from taking out execution, until the title is
ascertained, or the purchaser indemnified.[5] So where A., an

---

[1] 2 Story Eq. 199, § 884. See At-
kinson v. Henshaw, 2 Ves. & B. 85;
Ball v. Oliver, ib. 96; King v. King,
6 Ves. 172; Goate v. Fryer, 3 Bro.
Ch. 23.

[2] Horton v. Moseley, 17 Ala. 794.
[3] Pierce v. Jones, 23 Geo. 374.
[4] Lawson v. Virgin, 21 Geo. 356.
[5] Curtis v. Hartsfield, 1 Car. L. R.
501.

Will. Eq. 368.   The Court of Common Pleas (in Pennsylvania) cannot
enjoin an executor from selling real estate under an order of the
Orphans' Court. "The Orphans' Court is, of itself, a court of equity.
It sits as a court of equity, and, in a rude way, uses the forms of a court
of equity when it orders land to be sold for the payment of debts."
Loomis v. Loomis, 27 Penn. 233, 236, per Lowrie, J.

(a) Equity will not enjoin an execution, issued after the death of the
plaintiff in the name of his administrator, without a scire facias.   Am-
mous v. Whitehead, 31 Miss. 99.

administrator, permitted two slaves to go into possession of
B., a distributee, before all the debts were paid, upon condition that he should give a refunding bond; and the latter
sold them to C. without giving the bond; and trover was
brought by A. against C., and recovery had for the value of
the slaves: in a bill by C., to enjoin the collection of this
judgment for all beyond B.'s share of the unpaid debts,
held, his liability was that which would have existed against
B. on his bond, had he given one, and A. should be restrained
by injunction from collecting anything beyond that sum.[1]
So where a party claimed to be executor and universal
legatee under a will, proved the will, took possession of a
considerable part of the effects, and threatened to take the
whole; A., one of the executors, under a shortly subsequent
and revoking will, with B. and C., filed a bill in equity to
enjoin such taking possession, and to stay the trial of actions
brought by the defendant against debtors to the estate, including A., B., and C. Per Vice-Chancellor: "As you state
the defendant is insolvent, you have shown a case where
irreparable mischief may ensue, and, under the circumstances,
take your motion, upon paying into court the money sought
to be recovered by the actions."[2] So where the testator devised to his executors for the payment of debts; on a bill by
some of the creditors, stating that the executor refused to
execute the trust, and that he threatened to prefer certain of
the creditors, having no claim to such preference, he was
enjoined from selling, except under the direction of the court.[3]
So an insolvent gave to A. and B., his sureties in a guardian's
bond, a note for the amount of a deficiency in his guardian's
account. They sued the note, and obtained judgment and
execution, which was satisfied in part by a levy upon real
estate, set off to them jointly. B. having paid the deficiency,
and continued in possession of the whole estate, in person,
or by his grantee; held, he was entitled to an injunction

[1] Johnston v. Howell, 4 Jones Eq.
87.

[2] Mansfield v. Shaw, 3 Madd. 60.
[3] Depan v. Moses, 3 John. Ch. 349.

against the executors of A., to restrain them from selling their testator's legal estate in the premises, unless they shall have accounted with B. on such terms as the court may direct.[1] So where an administrator in one State, without settlement of his administration, brings the property, or a part of it, into another, in fraud of the rights of creditors and distributees; chancery will hold him to account as a trustee, and compel him, at the instance of either creditor or distributee, to surrender the trust estate.[2] So A., an administrator, recovered a judgment against B., a distributee, for $3,000. B. filed a bill to enjoin the sale of his property under the judgment, in which it was averred that there were funds in the hands of A. coming to him, amounting to $5,000; that A. had held possession of the estate six or seven years, and was believed to be insolvent; but not that the securities to the administration bond were involved. Held, the bill could not be dismissed upon demurrer, but the injunction must be retained till a hearing thereon.[3]

§ 3. But on a bill charging executors with having converted a part of the estate to their own use, with being insolvent, and being about to sell real estate in a manner forbidden by the will, &c., an injunction was granted restraining the sale. The executors answered, explaining their conduct, and moved that the injunction be dissolved; and it was dissolved.[4] So where a creditor, in a suit at law against the administrator of his debtor, relied upon the account of sales of the administrator as evidence of the assets, and a fair trial was had; held, he was bound by the verdict, unless he could show that the administrator had deceived him by fraudulent representations, and that he could not come into equity to avoid a sale by the administrator, on the ground that he was himself the beneficial purchaser, and that he purchased at an under price.[5] So a bill for an injunction, to prevent an exe-

[1] Brooks v. Fowle, 14 N. H. 248.
[2] Patton v. Overton, 8 Humph. 192.
[3] Carter v. McMichael, 20 Geo. 96.
[4] Schanck v. Schanck, 3 Halst. Ch. 140.
[5] Wilson v. Leigh, 4 Ired. Eq. 97.

cutor from interfering in any way with a trust estate, containing no prayer for the appointment of a receiver, cannot be sustained.[1]   And the allegations, that the complainants have just cause to fear, and do fear, the defendants will remove certain property bequeathed by a will alleged to be void, will not confer jurisdiction on a court of equity, in the absence of allegations that the complainants have applied, or intend to apply for administration.[2]   So where a temporary injunction had been granted, and a perpetual injunction was prayed for, against executors, who had failed to file an inventory of personal property, and were wasting the estate: but the surrogate had obliged them to give security, until the inventory should be filed, and against wasting the estate: held, the surrogate had full power to prevent waste, and, as he had exercised it as far as he thought proper, equity would not interfere. The temporary injunction was dissolved.[3] So where a slave was sold by an administrator, by order of court, to effect division of an estate; it was held that chancery would not enjoin against the collection of the purchase-money, notwithstanding the seller said he believed the girl was sound, and it appeared in evidence that she had been sick for a year before the sale, and died about a year after the sale, having been under the influence of a fatal disease the whole time.[4]   So the laches of an executor is no ground for injunction.[5] So where the defendant, against whom a decree is rendered in favor of an administrator, for money due his intestate, is notified by the representatives, that the complainant has ceased to be administrator, and has no right to collect the money; if the defendant has good ground to believe that it would be unsafe to pay it over to him, his proper course is to file a bill in the nature of a bill of interpleader, and bring the money into court; but, if he file a bill to enjoin the execution of the decree, retain the money in his own hands, and upon final hearing produce no evidence

[1] Boyd v. Murray, 3 John. Ch. 48.
[2] Watson v. Rothwell, 11 Ala. 650.
[3] Whitney v. Munro, 4 Edw. Ch. 5.
[4] Williams   v.   M'Cormack,   7 Humph. 308.
[5] Furlow v. Tillman, 21 Geo. 150.

to sustain the material allegations of his bill, and they are denied by the answer, the court must, under the statute, award damages on the dissolution of the injunction.[1] So an administratrix loaned money belonging to the estate, for which a judgment was obtained against the borrower, and made a final settlement of her administration. Subsequently, she assigned the judgment to A., as security for a note given for money borrowed. The note not being paid, A. was proceeding to collect the judgment, when B., sole heir of the estate, filed a bill to enjoin A. from proceeding to collect it. The bill, not charging fraud, alleged that the complainant was entitled to a share of the judgment, as heir, and that the administratrix was insolvent. Held, the rights of third persons could not be prejudiced in this state of facts, until B., the heir, had ascertained and established his right.[2] So where an administrator brings a suit for land for the benefit of the heirs, more than seven years after the death of the intestate, one of the heirs having been ever since *non compos*, and the other a *feme covert*, and abandoned by her husband, who would not bring a suit; equity will not enjoin the suit.[3]

§ 4. An administrator, who had failed to plead because advised that his plea would not avail, and had afterwards discovered facts, which made his plea good, was held to be entitled to relief against judgment on default, as he was obliged, from the nature of his office, to rely upon information.[4] So, after publication of his will, the testator gave certain property, thereby bequeathed, to those of his children to whom he had not previously made advancement. The executor by mistake included the property in the inventory; and those who had been advanced procured a decree for distribution, having joined the other children in their petition without their consent. Held, the joining them was a

---

[1] Fowler v. Williams, 20 Ark. 641.

[2] Grayson v. Williams, 27 Miss. 553.

[3] Fleming v. Collins, 27 Geo. 494.

[4] Hewlett v. Hewlett, 4 Edw. Ch. 7.

fraud on the court, and the executor was entitled to an injunction to stay proceedings under the decree.[1] So an injunction will be granted, on the application of an administrator, upon the suits of creditors of his deceased, where the affairs in administration are involved, complicated, and difficult.[2] So after a general decree against an executor to account and distribute, a creditor may be enjoined even from proceeding to a trial at law, though with the right of proving costs. The Lord Chancellor remarked: "The decree gives every creditor who carries in a claim equal to that of a creditor by judgment. The court does not take away from a creditor the benefit of such a judgment, if prior to the decree; but it only supports the decree as equal in point of rank to a judgment, and then follows the rule of law in giving preference to the prior debt in point of time."[3] So where equity has taken jurisdiction over the estate of a deceased person, for the purposes of settlement, it will restrain by injunction an action against the administrator on his bond for an alleged breach of duty. If the suit was commenced before the decree for an account was entered, the order will be to stay its further prosecution, but if commenced afterwards, the suit may be dismissed.[4] So averments of an irregular sale of land by administrators, and of acquiescence by the party in interest, will sustain a bill for an injunction against interference by one claiming under the acquiescing party.[5] So an action was brought by a creditor of a testator against the executors. Plea, the decree in a suit for administration. The plea was adjudged bad, and judgment given for the plaintiff. On a motion for an injunction by the executors, held, the creditor should be enjoined from enforcing his judgment against the assets, but not against the executors personally.[6](a)

[1] Fairly v. Thompson, 34 Miss. 101.
[2] Berrs v. Strobecker, 21 Geo. 442.
[3] Goate v. Fryer, 2 Cox, 201.
[4] Washington v. Emery, 4 Jones Eq. 32.
[5] Beckham v. Newton, 21 Geo. 187.
[6] Burles v. Popplewell, 10 Sim. 383.

(a) In South Carolina, where the creditors of an insolvent estate are numerous, the executor may file a bill to enjoin them from proceeding

§ 5. Where executors, claiming property, resorted to the Court of Chancery to restrain certain creditors from taking it, on the ground that it was needed for the payment of debts; and it was not shown that it was in fact so needed, but the reverse appeared: held, they were not entitled to the relief sought; and, if the fact were otherwise, still, in the absence of insolvency, the remedy would be at law.[1] So a suit by a creditor against executors will not be restrained, because an order for preliminary accounts and inquiries has been obtained in such suit.[2] So equity cannot enjoin the sale of a slave belonging to an estate under a levy, where an indemnity by bond has been given to the sheriff, on a bill by the administrator, alleging that the assets were insufficient to pay debts in full; for in such case the plaintiff claims merely as an incumbrancer, whose remedy is at law, upon the bond, or by a suit to recover the property.[3] So an administrator *de bonis non* recovered a decree, on final settlement, against the administrator in chief; the money was collected of the surety of the latter; the decree was afterwards reversed; and the surety sued at law to recover the money which he had paid. The defendant, alleging that he had paid over the money to the distributees, some of whom were insolvent, and that the surety had been indemnified by his principal,

[1] Johnson *v.* The Connecticut Bank, 21 Conn. 148.
[2] Teague *v.* Richards, 11 Sim. 46.
[3] Jarrell *v.* Eddins, 2 P. & H. (Va.) 579.

---

at law, and to have the estate administered in equity. And it seems that he may, in the same bill, make his heirs and devisees defendants, in order to compel a sale of real estate in aid of assets. In such case, the practice is, to make only one or two of the principal creditors defendants, and bring in the others by order. None of them need answer, except when specially required to do so by the court, but may appear and litigate orally. But all are enjoined, by order or injunction issued in conformity to an order, from suing elsewhere. In such case, the funds in the hands of the executor should be placed in the possession of the court to be administered; and it seems that a sale of real or personal estate should be by a Master. Thompson *v.* Palmer, 2 Rich Eq. 32.

prayed for an injunction against the plaintiff and the suit at law, and for general relief. Held, the defendant was not entitled to an injunction.[1] So where a claim was allowed by an administrator, and approved by the probate judge, and it was subsequently discovered that the claim was statute-run at the time it was allowed, though the claimant had in his possession a written promise of the intestate, amounting to a renewal of the debt, which promise he did not present; held, an injunction could not be granted to stay action on the claim, as the mistake was made by all parties, and, before a wholly new action could be begun, the new promise itself would become statute-run.[2] And an injunction in favor of an administrator, on the ground of a deficiency of assets, should not be made perpetual, but only until assets shall come into his hands, reserving to the creditors to show assets by *sci. fa.* at law.[3]

§ 6. Where administrators filed a bill, praying for an injunction, upon the ground that more money was due on a previous judgment revived in their favor against the defendants, than was due on the judgment for which the plaintiffs were then pressed for payment; held, equity would not interpose by injunction, to prevent circuity of action, the remedy being peculiarly a common law remedy.[4]

§ 7. An administrator, who wishes an injunction against a judgment at law against his intestate, must give the bond required by statute in case of applications for injunction.[5]

§ 8. Under the Tennessee statutes of 1829 and 1831, a judgment against an administrator or executor within six months after qualification, and an execution issued within less than twelve months, cannot be enjoined in chancery.[6]

[1] Simmons *v.* Williams, 27 Ala. 507.
[2] Jones *v.* Underwood, 11 Tex. 116.
[3] Haydon *v.* Goode, 4 Hen. & M. 460.
[4] Clay *v.* Sheftall, T. U. P. Charlton, 263.
[5] Osborn *v.* Ellis, 1 Cart. 451.
[6] Roche *v.* Washington, 7 Humph. 142.

§ 9. A few miscellaneous cases may properly here be stated, where the remedy of injunction has been invoked in reference to the estates of persons deceased.

§ 10. Where a judge of an orphans' court is advised that an injunction has been granted at the instance of an executor, to restrain the heirs and distributees from proceeding with a settlement begun in such court; he should suspend all further proceeding, as long as the injunction continues in force.[1]

§ 11. Where suits are enjoined before judgment, and a bond for the debt given by the administrator, he becomes personally liable, if the injunction is dissolved and the suits are prosecuted to judgment.[2]

§ 12. The power of the Court of Chancery of Maryland, to grant injunctions to restrain creditors from proceeding at law, after a decree for an account, is not confined to cases in which the application is made by the executor or administrator, but extends to applications made by the heir, or by another creditor, or a common legatee, or by a residuary legatee.[3]

§ 13. A., an infant, died intestate, possessed of a slave, and leaving B., an infant brother, her sole distributee. There being no debts, no administration was taken out, but the slave passed into the hands of the father of B., and was levied on under an execution against him. Held, equity would restrain a sale.[4]

§ 14. Where two administrators make a sale, but only one executes the deed; equity will enjoin an ejectment brought by the heirs on this ground.[5]

---

[1] The State v. The Judge, 15 Ala. 740.
[2] Brown v. Speight, 30 Miss. 45.
[3] Boyd v. Harris, 1 Maryland Ch. Decis. 466. See Jackson v. Leaf, 1 Jac. & W. 229.
[4] Gould v. Hill, 18 Ala. 457.
[5] Wortman v. Skinner, 1 Beasl. 358.

§ 15. One distributee, who makes a fraudulent representation as to property of the estate offered for sale, without the
knowledge of the others, does not thereby affect their rights.
The purchaser has his remedy against him; and he cannot
enjoin the purchase-money.[1]

[1] Williams *v.* McCormack, 7 Humph. 308.

CHAPTER XVII.

BANKRUPTS AND INSOLVENTS.

§ 1. INJUNCTION is a remedy often resorted to with reference to proceedings in bankruptcy and insolvency.

§ 2. In a previous chapter—Chap. VI.—we have referred to an important controversy which arose between the United States Court and the Supreme Court of New Hampshire, with reference to the effect of an *attachment* of property, prior to the institution of bankruptcy proceedings, and the claim of the State Court to enforce and perfect such attachment, notwithstanding the subsequent assignment. In the present connection it may be added, that, under the late bankrupt law, the District Court, pending bankruptcy proceedings therein, was held to have the power of enjoining the enforcement of debts due from the bankrupt in a State court; and it was also held that an officer would be liable for selling property after such injunction.[1]   And, in general, the comprehensive jurisdiction given to the courts of the United States, under the bankrupt law, was held to involve to a certain extent a control over those of the States.   Judge Story, who may be regarded as emphatically the champion of the most enlarged jurisdiction of the former tribunals, remarked: " Under the provisions of the sixth section of the act, the District Court does possess full jurisdiction to suspend or control such proceedings in the State courts, not by acting on the courts, over which it possesses no authority, but by acting on the parties through the instrumentality of an injunction or other remedial proceedings

---

[1] Stinson *v.* M'Murray, 6 Humph. 339.

22

in equity upon due application made by the assignee, and a proper case being laid before the court requiring such interference.   Such a course is very familiar in courts of chancery, in cases where a creditor's bill is filed for the administration of the estate of a deceased person, and it becomes necessary or proper to take the whole assets into the hands of the courts, for the purpose of collecting and marshalling the assets, ascertaining and adjusting conflicting priorities and claims, and accomplishing a due and equitable distribution among all the parties in interest in the estate.   Similar proceedings have been instituted in England in cases of bankruptcy, and they were, without doubt, in the contemplation of Congress, as indispensable to the practical working of the bankrupt system."[1]

§ 3. In Massachusetts, the remedy of a party whose rights are affected by an assignment under the insolvent laws, when the preliminary proceedings are irregular, is by application in equity to arrest the proceedings, and set aside the assignment. This may be done, on petition, by any party aggrieved, and the assignment will thereupon be adjudged, once for all, to be valid or invalid.[2]   And insolvency proceedings, commenced before a judge having no jurisdiction, will be set aside on a bill filed under statute 1838, c. 163, s. 18, more than a year after. "Lapse of time could only be evidence of acquiescence and consequent assent; and in a case like the present, affecting a great variety of persons and interests, consent cannot give jurisdiction."[3] So, in Maryland, a bill was filed in chancery on the 14th September, 1846, by the creditors of A., alleging his insolvent condition, and that he designed to give an undue preference to certain of his creditors, especially B. and wife.   Upon this bill an injunction was

---

[1] Christy, 3 How. 318. See Regina v. Law, 40 Eng. Law and Eq. 64; Moore v. Jones, 23 Verm. 739.

[2] Hawson v. Paige, 3 Gray, 239; Partridge v. Hannum, 2 Met. 569;
Wheelock v. Hastings, 4 Met. 504. See Cheshire, &c. v. Gay, 3 Gray, 531.

[3] Grafton, &c. v. Bickford; per Shaw, C. J., 15 Gray, 564, 574.

granted, restraining A. from giving, and B. and wife from taking, any such preference.   On the 29th of the same month, B. and wife filed a bill on the equity side of the Baltimore County Court, alleging A.'s indebtedness to them on account of his misapplication of certain trust funds belonging to the wife, and his promise to secure them by a conveyance of certain real estate, which he had failed to do, and praying that he might be decreed to pay them the sum thus due under the trust.   A. answered this bill, admitting its averments, and, on the 31st of October following, a decree was passed by the Baltimore County Court, directing A. to bring into court the amount ascertained and admitted to be due to the complainants.   Held, that the original bill of September 14th drew to the Court of Chancery the whole litigation in regard to the distribution of A.'s estate; that the proceedings of B. and wife, in the Baltimore County Court, were in violation of the Chancellor's injunction; and that it was competent for the Court of Chancery to restrain, by injunction, the execution of this decree, and treat the whole proceeding in the county court as a nullity.   Also, that the appropriate remedy for B. and wife was in chancery, on the original bill, that court having ample power to afford them the relief which they sought in another form, in another court of concurrent jurisdiction.[1]

§ 4. The plaintiff, an insolvent, agreed upon a certain composition with his creditors.   The defendant, a creditor, refused to come in unless the plaintiff would give his note for the balance, which he did; and the defendant brought an action upon the note, having received the agreed percentage. Held, such suit should be enjoined.[2]

[1] Albert v. Winn, 7 Gill, 446.   [2] Constantein v. Blache, 1 Cox, 287.

CHAPTER XVIII.

PRINCIPAL AND AGENT.

§ 1. IN general, an injunction will not be allowed, nor a decree rendered, against an agent, where the principal is not made a party. Thus, to a bill for enjoining collection of the purchase-money for land, though sold by an agent, who took a bond to himself, the principal is an indispensable party.[1] So one for whose use an action at law is brought, which fact is apparent from the record, should be made a party to a bill enjoining the judgment.[2]

§ 2. Where the principal is not subject to the jurisdiction of the court (as in the case of a sovereign State) the rule may be dispensed with.[3] But an injunction does not lie against the agent of a foreign government, charged only with the settlement of certain claims upon such government, and acting wholly under the control of its resident ambassador. The defendant was said "to be in much the same situation as an inferior servant, who is bound to take the directions of an upper servant, while both are bound to take directions from the same mistress;" and held to have all the immunities from this process, provided either by the common or statute law, which the ambassador himself would have.[4] So it is erroneous to make a mere agent party to a suit for specific performance of a contract; and, if he is made a party, the

[1] Sweets v. Biggs, 5 Litt. 17; 9 Wheat. 738.
[2] Turner v. Cox, 5 Litt. 175.
[3] Osborn v. Bank, &c., 9 Wheat. 738.
[4] Service v. Castaneda, 2 Coll. 56.

complainant will not be entitled even to a decree for costs against him, although he suffers the bill to be taken as confessed for want of an answer.[1](a)

§ 3. The defendant, holding certain chattels as agent of the plaintiff, in breach of his duty, contracted to sell them. Upon the ground that by such sale the plaintiff's title would be embarrassed, he was allowed to maintain a bill for an injunction.[2] So a bank recovered a judgment against A. for $59,000. B., assuming to act as agent and attorney of the bank, effected a compromise with A. to pay $20,000, and A. assigned and delivered over to B., as agent and attorney, property and securities to that amount. The bank denied the authority of B. to make the compromise. A. assigned the property and securities to C., and B. refused to redeliver them and was proceeding to collect and dispose of them. Upon bill filed by C., an injunction was granted, to restrain the collection and disposition of the property and securities, and the Chancellor refused to dissolve the injunction, on motion to dissolve for want of equity in the bill.[3]

§ 4. Where the payee of a note deposits it in the hands of an agent, to be collected, who causes a suit to be instituted thereon in the payee's name, for his own use, and, upon a judgment being obtained, refuses to yield the control thereof, but insists upon collecting and appropriating the proceeds to himself; equity may enjoin the agent from all further interference, and the defendants in the judgment from paying, until the matters shall be there heard and adjudicated.[4]

[1] Boyd v. Vanderkemp, 1 Barb. Ch. 273.
[2] Wood v. Bowcliffe, 3 Hare, 308.
[3] Pratt v. Campbell, Harring. Ch. 236.
[4] Dunn v. Dunn, 8 Ala. 784.

(a) It is doubted whether service of notice of an injunction on an agent, when the principal is out of the jurisdiction, is good, especially when the former is merely an agent for the sale of the goods of the latter. Carron, &c. v. Maclaren, 35 Eng. Law and Eq. 37.

§ 5. Under a contract of hiring and service, containing stipulations of such a nature that specific performance could not be enforced, equity will not restrain the employer from excluding, or enjoin him to retain, a servant, agent, or manager; it seems, even if there has been no breach of covenant by the latter.[1]

---

[1] Stocker v. Brockelbank, 5 Eng. Law and Eq. 67.

CHAPTER XIX.

HUSBAND AND WIFE; INFANT; GUARDIAN; REMAINDER.

§ 1. "AT the common law the *husband and wife* are treated, for most purposes, as one person.—A man cannot grant anything to his wife, or enter into a covenant with her.—It is also generally true that contracts, made between husband and wife, when single, are avoided by the intermarriage. Upon the same ground it is, that if the wife be injured in her person or property during the marriage, she can bring no action for redress without the concurrence of her husband ; neither can she be sued, without making her husband also a party. All this is very different in the civil law. Courts of equity, for many purposes, treat the husband and wife as the civil law treats them, as distinct persons, capable (in a similar sense) of contracting with each other, of suing each other, and of having separate estates, debts, and interests."[1]

§ 2. Where the separate estate of a wife is levied on for the debt of her husband, an injunction may be obtained to stay the sale, in default of any other remedy.[2] Thus in the case of Lady Arundell v. Phipps, Lord Eldon interfered by injunction in favor of a married woman to protect ancient family pictures, furniture, and other articles of peculiar nature and value, taken on execution by creditors of the husband.[3] So a bequest to an unmarried woman was made for her separate use. She afterwards married, and the property was seized upon an execution against the husband. Held,

[1] 2 Story Eq. 734, §§ 1367—8. See Cayce v. Powell, 20 Tex. 757.
[2] Calhoun v. Cozens, 3 Ala. 498.
[3] 10 Ves. 139.

although the husband was at law entitled to the property, it was only as trustee, and an injunction was granted to restrain a sale.[1] So, although courts of equity usually refuse to restrain a trespass by injunction, yet, where property was bequeathed to the separate use of a feme covert without any trustee, and was about to be sold under an execution against the husband for his debt; held, the legal estate being in the husband, and therefore there being no one to sue for the trespass, the court would interfere by injunction.[2] So A. made a deed of slaves to B. in trust for his daughter, which was not recorded. The slaves went into possession of the daughter's husband, and they were levied on and sold under an execution against him, and were bought by C. B. obtained a verdict against C., which C. never paid. The daughter filed her bill for an injunction against B. and C., for the specific delivery of the slaves, and for an account of their hire. Held, as C. had acquired no title under the execution sale, and the verdict had never been paid, he had neither the legal nor equitable title, and the complainant was entitled to the relief prayed for; and B. was enjoined against enforcing the verdict against C.[3] So A. married B., the sister of his deceased wife, in 1821. Previous to the marriage, she being a minor, they executed a marriage settlement, by which her property was conveyed to a trustee, in trust for her separate use during her life. In 1824, they were indicted for their marriage and cohabiting as man and wife, and appeared by attorney and pleaded guilty, and the court thereupon adjudged the marriage null and void. They, however, continued to live and cohabit together as man and wife; and two, at least, of their four children were born after the judgment. B., however, dealt and was dealt with, as to her property, as a *feme sole*. She died in 1833, having given all her property by will to be equally divided among her four children, and having appointed A. their guardian. A. qualified as guar-

[1] Newlands *v.* Painter, 4 My. & Cr. 408.

[2] Smith *v.* Bank, &c., 4 Jones Eq. 303.

[3] Bush *v.* Bush, 3 Strobh. Eq. 131.

dian, and, as such, took possession of the property. A creditor of A., having recovered a judgment against him, levied his execution upon certain of the slaves, so left by B.'s will. The four children, by their next friend, brought a bill in equity against the creditor for an injunction, which was granted, and, upon a hearing, perpetuated.[1] So a wife may enjoin execution of the deed upon the sale of a homestead under an execution against her husband.[2]

§ 3. It is held that, where the claimants of a husband's interest in his wife's slaves cannot effect a division without the aid of a court of equity, a sale of the property will be enjoined till she is suitably provided for.[3] So equity will, on application by the wife, restrain her husband from proceeding at law to obtain possession of a legacy or portion in personal estate, which comes to her by will or inheritance, without providing for her support, unless she is residing apart from him, without his consent, and without sufficient cause.[4]

§ 4. A. borrowed money from B., arising from the sale of his wife's real estate, and gave a bond therefor payable to the wife. On the husband's death, the wife brought suit on the bond against A., who filed an account of set-offs, consisting of the dealings of B. with A.'s firm, and alleged an agreement that such dealings should be set off against the bond. This plea was waived, and judgment had for the plaintiff. The defendant then filed a bill, praying an injunction against the judgment. Held, if the defendant had any defence, it was a legal one, which having failed to make, with no excuse, he could have no relief in equity. And this although A. was also B.'s executor, and in that capacity was not a party to the previous suit.[5]

§ 5. Where trustees under a deed from the wife, who was

[1] Kelly v. Scott, 5 Gratt. 479.
[2] Dunn v. Tozer, 10 Cal. 167; Alverson v. Jones, 10 Cal. 9.
[3] Corley v. Corley, 22 Geo. 178.
[4] Fry v. Fry, 7 Paige, 461.
[5] Perkins v. Clements, 1 P. & H. (Va.) 141.

deceased, undertook to sell, to satisfy debts according to the terms of the deed; an injunction to restrain the sale was refused to the husband, who had paid or tendered only part of the debts.[1] And to maintain an injunction against the sale of lands of a deceased wife under a trust deed from her, as her administrator, the husband must show that he inherited some interest in the land.[2]

§ 6. French stock, belonging to a bankrupt, was transferred by him to his wife, who afterwards transferred it to her sisters; and the wife, having a general power of appointment over moneys standing in the name of trustees in the English funds, made a will, by which she exercised the power, and died, leaving the husband. One of the sisters, being an appointee and residuary legatee, and usually residing in France, took out administration upon her estate, with the will annexed. Held, the assignee of the husband might enjoin the trustees from transferring any of the stocks in the English funds, over which the power of appointment of the wife extended.[3] So where the husband of an executrix was abroad, and an irresponsible person; held, a party interested in the estate might by injunction restrain her from getting possession of the assets, and have a receiver appointed, with authority to bring actions in her name.[4]

§ 7. In a suit for separation of husband and wife, an injunction master has no power to grant an injunction, which will deprive the husband of the custody of his children; and such an injunction will not be granted, *ex parte*, by the court itself, except in a case of necessity, as to prevent the children from being carried out of the jurisdiction.[5]

§ 8. Where a suit at law is brought against the husband and wife, for the purpose of affecting her interest, she is a necessary party to a bill in chancery, by the husband, for an

[1] Stringham v. Brown, 7 Clarke, 33.
[2] Ibid.
[3] Stead v. Clay, 4 Russ. 550.
[4] Taylor v. Allen, 2 Atk. 213.
[5] Laurie v. Laurie, 9 Paige, 234.

injunction to restrain proceedings in the suit.[1]   But in a bill in equity to set aside a will, securing to the testator's daughter, who is a married woman, and to her issue, a share of the testator's property, for her separate use during coverture; the husband and wife should not join as complainants, their interests being in conflict; but the wife should be made a defendant.[2]

§ 9. Judge Story remarks, that "the origin of chancery jurisdiction over *infants* is very obscure, and has been a matter of much juridical discussion. The prevailing theory is, that the king is bound to protect all his subjects, and is represented in this particular by the Court of Chancery. Another explanation is that guardianship is in the nature of a *trust*, which is a peculiar subject of equity jurisdiction.—But, whatever may be the true origin of the jurisdiction—it is now conceded, on all sides, to be firmly established, and beyond the reach of controversy.   Indeed, it is a settled maxim, that the king is the universal guardian to infants, and ought, in the Court of Chancery, to take care of their fortunes."[3] The prevailing, and almost universal, practice in the United States has vested the special jurisdiction of the subject in the *Courts of Probate*, and thus rendered the English doctrines and decisions comparatively unimportant.(a)

---

[1] Booth v. Albertson, 2 Barb. Ch. 313.
[2] Alston v. Jones, 3 Barb. Ch. 397.
[3] 2 Story's Eq. pp. 692–705, §§ 1328–1337. See Wellesley v. Beaufort, an interesting and important case.

(a) Equity may restrain a father from moving his infant child out of the country. De Manneville v. De Manneville, 10 Ves. 64.   In cases of gross drunkenness and blasphemy, the father's right to the control of his children is subordinate to the power of the court to take his child from him.   10 Ves. 62.   Where an infant ward is about to marry without the consent of the court, an injunction lies, to restrain the marriage, and all verbal or written communication with the infant; and if the guardian connives at the marriage, he may be enjoined against consenting without leave of court.   Eden, 349; Pearce v. Crutchfield, 14 Ves. 206; Water v. Yorke, 19 ib. 451.   A minor entered into partnership in

§ 10. A *guardian*, by request of the ward, changed the ward's personal into real estate, and some of her real into personal estate, for the purpose of reinvesting in other real estate. The ward having married, her husband assented to these proceedings, but brought a suit upon a note taken for the real estate sold. The guardian brings a bill to enjoin a suit against himself, brought by the husband as administrator of his wife for the moneys thus invested. The husband, by cross-bill, offers to make a valid title to the purchaser of the land. Held, the suit against the guardian should be enjoined.[1]

§ 11. Where there is a *tenant for life* of slaves, and a *remainder-man*, and the tenant for life sells the slaves to a third person, who threatens to convey them out of the State, the remainder-man is entitled to an injunction.[2] But, to induce a court of equity to interfere with a tenant for life, in the enjoyment of his property, by an injunction or sequestration, it is necessary for the remainder-man to allege and prove facts and circumstances, showing reasonable ground to apprehend that such tenant will commit a fraud and defeat the ulterior estate, by destroying the property, or removing it to parts unknown.[3] Thus equity will not restrain the

[1] Singleton v. Love, 1 Head, 357.
[2] Brown v. Wilson, 6 Ired. Eq. 558.
[3] Mercer v. Byrd, 4 Jones Eq. 358. See Cross v. De Valle, 1 Wall. (U. S.), 1.

Sussex County, New Jersey, with two others, and put in $1,000. Before he came of age the partnership was dissolved, the minor receiving his $1,000. After the dissolution, he removed to Huntington County, and A. recovered a judgment against the members of the firm, including the minor, without his knowledge. A. transferred the judgment to B. Three years afterwards, B. brought an action on the judgment, and recovered a second judgment, no process being served on the minor. B. caused an execution to be issued to the sheriff of Huntington County, and to be levied on the property of the minor there. The minor filed a bill, stating the foregoing facts, charging fraud, &c., and obtained an injunction to stay proceedings on the execution. On motion, made to dissolve the injunction, it was ordered that it be continued to the hearing. Vansyckle v. Rorback, 2 Halst. Ch. 234.

owner of a determinable estate in the enjoyment of his rights, on proof of an isolated conversation between him and the ulterior claimant, in which the former, under the excitement of spirits and of an angry quarrel, made a threat to run the property off and defeat the expectancy.[1]

[1] Airs v. Billops, 4 Jones Eq. 17.

CHAPTER XX.

SURETIES.

§ 1. "WHENEVER a creditor, in pursuance of a valid agreement for such a purpose, gives time for payment to the principal debtor on a bond or other security, without the consent of the surety, the latter will be held discharged in equity, although he might still be held bound at law—whether the surety has sustained any actual damage or not," or though "the arrangement may be for his benefit.—Under such circumstances, the surety has a right to restrain the creditor from proceeding at law against him to recover the debt; and a perpetual injunction constitutes the true and effectual remedy."[1] Thus where a creditor recovered judgment against the principal and surety, levied his execution on property of the principal, and, on payment of part of the execution, directed the sheriff to restore the property, and gave further time to pay the residue, without the assent of the surety; held, the judgment was thereby discharged as to the surety; and, if these facts had been returned on the execution, he might have been relieved at law; but, they not having been returned, equity would enjoin any subsequent execution.[2] So A. and B. signed a note with C., as his sureties, to D. D. recovered judgment upon the note, and assigned it to E., who, with notice of the facts, agreed by parol with C. to extend the time of payment, and did so. E. afterwards sued A., B., and C., upon the judgment, and A. and B. unsuccessfully set up the extension of time in defence. A. and B. then

---

[1] 2 Story Eq. 199, § 183. See Tysor v. Sutterloh, 4 Jones Eq. 247; Armistead v. Ward, 2 P. & H. 504.

[2] Baird v. Rice, 1 Call, 18.

filed a bill for injunction. Held, the defence was good in equity, though not at law, and a perpetual injunction was ordered.[1]

§ 2. And there are numerous other cases, where equity interposes by injunction for the relief of a surety.(a) Thus where execution issues on a judgment against principal and surety, and a part of the money is made by a levy on the estate of the principal, but the execution is returned "no money made," and an *alias* issued against the surety for the whole amount of the judgment; the sheriff having absconded, the surety is entitled to relief in equity, and the court may enjoin the execution for the amount made.[2] So where the surety on a note had a good defence thereto, of which the principal debtor was the only witness, a bill by the surety, to restrain a suit at law upon the note, against himself and the principal jointly, and for relief against the note, was sustained.[3] So W. recovered judgment against S. as principal, and J. as surety, on a simple contract debt. Before execution issued W. sued out a garnishment upon the judgment against F., and recovered judgment thereon. Before this judgment, full satisfaction of the debt was made by J. Upon proceedings in equity to compel F. to pay the amount due to J., it was decreed: That when J. paid the original judgment to W., the judgment was extinguished at law, as between W. and S. and J., and that if the judgment upon the garnishment against F. had been finally rendered at the time of the payment of the original judgment, it would also have been extinguished at law, so far as W. was concerned. That, J. having paid the original judgment before final judgment upon the garnishment, had F. known the fact, and interposed it as a defence, the court of law could have rendered

---

[1] Dunham *v.* Downer, 31 Verm. 249.

[2] Fryer *v.* Anstell, 2 Stew. 119.
[3] Miller *v.* McCan, 7 Paige, 457.

(a) As to the same interposition *against* a surety, see Isler *v.* Turner, 7 Humph. 116.

no judgment against him in favor of W. for the debt which he owed to S. That on payment of the original judgment, W. having failed to enter satisfaction thereof in the manner prescribed by statute, and F. being thereby deprived of the legal mode of deriving a knowledge of such satisfaction, and having no actual notice of the payment in any other manner, and judgment having been rendered against him upon the garnishment after such payment; he might in equity enjoin the execution of the judgment, so far as W. was concerned. That though the payment of the original judgment by J. extinguished it, and extinguished the right of W. to proceed upon and enforce the garnishment against F. at law, yet such payment did not extinguish the debt which F. owed S.; and had F. filed his bill to be relieved from the judgment against himself exclusively, upon the ground of the payment of the original judgment by J., having made J. a party, equity would hardly have granted him such relief, without his paying to J. the debt which he owed to S., in the absence of any showing on his part of an equitable right, to withhold such payment. That as the judgment against F., in favor of W., was at law extinguished by the payment of the original judgment against S. and J., and as the execution of the judgment against F. by W., in whose favor it stood upon the record of the law court, was perpetually enjoined; the right of the surety to be subrogated to the rights of W. must be enforced by a decree of a court of equity, upon a proper case made for its interposition by parties claiming such rights. That, as judgment at law was recovered against F., as surety for S., by another creditor, before judgment was recovered against him in the garnishee suit in favor of W.; the claim of F. to indemnity in equity was hardly cut off by the proceedings at law in the garnishment suit, where he was not permitted to interpose an equitable defence.[1]

§ 5. The sureties upon a note cannot maintain a suit in

---

[1] Newton v. Field, 16 Ark. 216.

equity to be relieved against a judgment at law upon the note, on the ground that the note was given for a usurious loan, and that the payee, who had indorsed the note to the nominal plaintiff in the suit at law, testified on the *voir dire* that he was the owner of the note and the plaintiff in interest, and the court excused him thereupon from testifying; the defendants having given notice of the defence of usury, but not having verified the notice according to law so as to entitle them to examine the plaintiff as a witness. Nor can they sustain the bill upon any ground which might have been set up as a defence in the action at law, unless prevented from setting it up by fraud or accident, or by the act of the opposite party.[1] So, where judgments were recovered against sureties by default, and suit was afterwards brought against the administrator of the principal, in which the defence of usury was successfully made, he having accidentally discovered the evidence of it among the papers of the principal, and judgment therein was rendered for the sum loaned only, which he paid; held, this was a satisfaction of the judgments against the sureties only *pro tanto*, and that they could be relieved from the judgments, on the ground of usury, only on paying the sum loaned and legal interest.[2]

§ 4. Where a surety receives a mortgage of slaves from his principal to indemnify him, and afterwards they are levied on for the debt of the principal, while it is uncertain whether the surety will sustain a loss by his suretyship; the surety may have an injunction to restrain the sale.[3] But upon a bill, by a surety, to be discharged from his liability, the court, having denied the prayer of the bill, refused to grant an injunction, restraining the creditor from enforcing the debt, to give the surety an opportunity to avail himself of collateral security.[4] And where A., as surety of B., received two negroes from him as indemnity; and C. afterwards re-

---

[1] Vilas v. Jones, 1 Comst. 274.
[2] Jones v. Kilgore, 2 Rich. Eq. 63.
[3] Marshall v. Colvert, 5 Leigh, 146.
[4] Rutledge v. Greenwood, 2 Desau. 389.

23

covered a judgment against A., and levied the execution on the negroes, and A. then brought an action of trespass against C., and recovered judgment, which C. enjoined by bill against A. alone: held, B. should have been made a party, and the bill was dismissed without prejudice.[1]

§ 4 *a*. On the other hand, an action against a surety may be enjoined, where equity requires that the debt should be first satisfied from securities of the principal debtor held by the creditor as a primary fund; more especially in case of doubt as to their validity. Equity holds that this question should be first settled in an action, and at the expense of the creditor.[2]

§ 5. Equity will not enjoin a judgment against the surety upon a note, on the ground that the note was procured through misrepresentation as to its purpose by the principal, unless the payee were also guilty of such misrepresentation.[3]

§ 6. If sureties neglect, when judgment is rendered, to cause the entry to be made that they are sureties, as required by statute (of Ohio), chancery will not compel the judgment creditor to exhaust first the property of the principal.[4]

§ 7. M., a stockholder in a manufacturing corporation, with L., another stockholder, indorsed notes of the company, upon the other stockholders' executing a bond to save them harmless; M. and L. to bear any loss only in proportion to the stock held by them. The company afterwards failed, leaving several of the notes outstanding. M. conveyed away his real estate, and removed from the State, and had never paid anything on the notes. L. and the other stockholders, having paid sundry debts of the company on which they were severally holden as sureties, procured suits to be brought on the notes, and the real estate to be attached, in

[1] King *v.* Harper, 4 Bibb, 570.
[2] Hays *v.* Ward, 4 John. Ch. 134.
[3] Griffith *v.* Reynolds, 4 Gratt. 46.
[4] Elliott *v.* Elmore, 16 Ohio, 27.

order to compel M. to contribute his *pro rata* share of the loss. M. then brought a bill in equity against L. and the obligors of the bond, praying for an account of the loss, a disclosure, and an injunction against the suits, and alleging that some of the notes had been in fact paid, and were put in suit in bad faith by the respondents. Held, in dismissing the bill, that, so far as the bond was concerned, the plaintiff had no cause of complaint, since it was only a bond of indemnity, and he had not been damnified, having paid nothing on his liabilities for the company; that the remedy at law was sufficient. Also as the plaintiff was in any event to bear a portion of the loss on the liabilities, the suits were not inequitable.[1]

§ 8. A bill cannot be maintained, by the sureties of a purchaser under the decree of a court having jurisdiction, and after confirmation of the report of commissioners for the sale, for relief against a judgment on the bond given for the purchase-money, upon the ground of error in the decree or the proceedings under it.[2]

§ 9. A., being one of several defendants, prosecuted a writ of error, and the Supreme Court affirmed the judgment. They also rendered judgment against the principal and sureties in the writ of error bond. Held, the sureties could not enjoin execution upon the latter judgment, on the ground that the original co-defendants of their principal were not joined in it, nor that a levy had been made on their property, notwithstanding their principal and his co-defendants had sufficient property to satisfy the execution.[3]

[1] Monson *v.* Lawrence, 27 Conn. 579.

[2] Worsham *v.* Hardaway, 5 Gratt. 60.

[3] Turner *v.* Smith, 9 Tex. 626.

CHAPTER XXI.

PARTNERS AND OTHERS JOINTLY INTERESTED.

§ 1. PARTNERSHIP is a relation, which in various ways calls for the action of a court of equity; as, for the purposes of discovery, account, specific performance, and dissolution; and in connection with some or all of these main objects, and in some instances without reference to any ulterior end, partnership is made the subject of injunction.

§ 2. Inasmuch as the individual members of an indebted partnership may also owe private debts, the liability of partnership property to satisfy such debts, and the conflicting claims of partnership and private creditors, have given rise to many and nice questions both at law and in equity. The general doctrine upon the subject is thus stated by a writer of high authority: "The joint creditors, in case of insolvency, are deemed in equity to have a right of priority of payment before the private creditors of any separate partner. The joint property is deemed a trust fund, primarily to be applied to the discharge of the partnership debts against all persons not having a higher equity. A long series of authorities (as has been truly said) has established this equity of the joint creditors, to be worked out through the medium of the partners, that is to say, the partners have a right, *inter sese*, to have the partnership property first applied to the partnership debts, and no partner has any right, except to his own share of the residue."[1]   The plan of the present work, however, restricts us to a consideration of this point as it has arisen upon applications for injunction.

§ 3. In a leading case upon this subject,[2] it was held that a separate creditor of one partner cannot hold the partnership effects, taken under an execution for his separate debt, against the partnership creditors.   At the time the execution took place the partnership was insolvent; but a commission of bankruptcy had not then issued.   Sir A. Macdonald, Ld. Ch. B., said: "The *corpus* of the partnership effects is joint property; and neither party separately has anything in that *corpus;* but the interest of each is only his share of what remains, after the partnership accounts are taken.—In law there are three relations: first, if a person chooses, for valuable consideration, to sell his interest in the partnership trade; for it comes to that; or if his next of kin or executors take it upon his death; or if a creditor takes it in execution, or the assignee under commission of bankruptcy.   The mode makes no difference; but in all those cases the application takes place of the rule, that the party coming in the right of the partner comes into nothing more than interest in the partnership, which cannot be tangible, cannot be made available, or be delivered, but under an account between the partnership and the partner; and it is an *item* in the account, that enough must be left for the partnership debts. What is the inconvenience?—The individual trusted to the partnership fund in his idea at the time he was lending the money; not that I believe that is very common.   But it may be dangerous in a thousand instances to have anything

[1] 2 Story's Eq. 625, § 1253. See Morrison *v.* Blodgett, 8 N. H. 238 ; Bell *v.* Newman, 5 S. & R. 38 ; 1 Pars. on Contr. 174 ; Somerset, &c., *v.* Minot, 10 Cush. 598 ; Harmon *v.* Clark, 13 Gray, 114 ; Hilliard on Bankruptcy, &c., Chap. 4 ; Merrill *v.* Neill, 8 How. 414 ; Glenn *v.* Gill, 2 Md. 1 ; Douglas *v.* Winslow, 28 Maine, 89.

[2] Taylor *v.* Fields, 4 Ves. 396.

to do with a trader; as for instance to purchase an estate;
for an act of bankruptcy may have been committed.—But
look to the danger on the other side; one partner giving a
bond; and the creditors of the partnership looking to the
stock itself.   It is said—this meritorious creditor has a right
to be preferred on account of his early diligence.   But what
is that, to which he is entitled?   The estate of a partner is
debtor to him.—It, therefore, argues nothing to say, he has
the merit of diligence, till we see upon what that merit can
attach."[1]

§ 4. In late American cases it is held, that equity will enjoin the levy of an execution, against one partner, on property of the firm, in which it is admitted he has no interest
which can pass by a sale; though the bill does not pray for
a dissolution.[2]   And where A. sold out to B., his partner,
retaining, by agreement, a lien upon the property for his
own indemnity; and C., a private creditor of B., was about
to sell on execution B.'s interest, before any account taken:
held, such sale should be enjoined.[3]

§ 5. Contrary to the now prevailing rule upon this subject,
in the case of Moody v. Payne,[4] an injunction was refused,
to stay an execution against the partnership property for the
debt of one partner.   Chancellor Kent remarked, "I do not
know that this court has ever undertaken to stop an execution at law, in such a case, until the partnership accounts
have been taken, and it would be too much for me to assume
it without precedent.   The principle would go to stay executions at law, in every case, against the partnership property
of one partner who owed separate debts, until the disclosure
and liquidation of the concerns of the copartnership.   This
would produce inconceivable delay and much embarrassment

[1] And see Skipp v. Harwood, or
West v. Skipp, 1 Ves. 239; 2 Swanst.
586; Fox v. Hanbury, Cowp. 445;
Young v. Keighly, 15 Ves. 564.

[2] Cropper v. Coburn, 2 Curt. 465.
[3] White v. Parish, 20 Tex. 688.
[4] 2 John. Ch. 548.

in respect to separate creditors."[1] And in a late case it is held, that chancery will not entertain a bill by a creditor of a firm, to restrain an execution creditor of an individual member from enforcing his remedy against the partnership property.[2]

§ 6. In analogy with the general rule upon the subject (§ 5); where a creditor of a firm agreed that he would not press his claims at maturity, if each partner would give his own indorsed note for half the amount; and A., one partner, having complied with the condition, but B., the other, not having done so, a suit was brought against the firm: held, A., was entitled to an injunction to restrain such suit, until his note should be delivered up to him.[3] So one part-owner of a steamboat may enjoin the other from selling his share, and subject it to other claims, for which the complainant is liable, and apprehends that, in consequence of the defendant's insolvency, he will be solely liable.[4] So where, on a dissolution of copartnership between A. and B. it was agreed that A. should take the property, pay off the debts, and indemnify B. against them, an injunction was sustained, to prevent the misapplication of the property by A.[5]

§ 7. Upon a bill to reach property of a debtor, the fact, that certain stock which he had in a canal company was partnership property, in which another person was interested, and that the stockholders were personally liable for the debts of the company, was held no objection to granting an injunction to restrain him from parting with it.[6]

§ 8. By agreement of dissolution between partners, A. and B., A. took the property and agreed to pay the debts. A creditor, having recovered judgment, levied his execution

[1] See also Smith, 16 John. 106 n.; Phillips v. Cook, 24 Wend. 389; Hergman v. Dettleback, 11 How. Pr. 46.
[2] Young v. Frier, 1 Stockt. 465. See Dow v. Saywood, 14 N. H. 9.
[3] Childs v. Horr, 1 Clark, 432.
[4] Thoms v. Southard, 2 Dana, 475.
[5] Deveau v. Fowler, 2 Paige. 400.
[6] Eager v. Price, 2 Paige, 333.

upon the property of both, and afterwards assigned the judgment to C., a relative of A.   A. then assigned part of the property levied on to D., and C., by a sealed instrument, released his interest therein to D., with full notice of the terms of dissolution.   Held, the judgment could not be enforced against B.[1]

§ 9. As we have suggested, application for the process of injunction is often made in connection with the question of *dissolution;* which latter object has been uniformly held to give an unquestionable right of issuing a preliminary injunction, as auxiliary to the ultimate object of the bill.(a)

§ 10. In a late case, a partnership was entered into for a special purpose, the delivery of plank stocks at a certain place.   Subsequently, the partnership was dissolved, the defendant agreeing to pay the plaintiff for his interest in the timber, at certain rates.   A bill was then filed to set aside this contract of dissolution, on the ground of fraud, and praying for an injunction and a receiver.   Upon motion to dissolve the injunction, held, that, where a partnership still subsists, to authorize such bill, there must be great abuse or strong misconduct, if not a prayer for dissolution.   Though after dissolution, the objection to an injunction and the ap-

---

[1] Bell v. Hall, 1 Halst. Ch. 477.

(a) As to the prayer for an injunction without dissolution, see Goodman v. Whitcomb, 1 Jac. & W. 592 ; Kuchell v. White, 2 Y. & Coll. 15 ; Gow, Partn. 111.   It is said, "There are cases where the court will lay injunction or prohibit the dissolution of a partnership."   Coll. Partn. s. 206.   So it is said, " Equity will in case of a partnership, existing during the pleasure of the parties, with no time fixed for its renunciation, interfere (as it should seem) to qualify or restrain that renunciation, unless it is done under fair and reasonable circumstances ; for if a sudden dissolution is about to be made, in ill faith, and will work irreparable injury, courts of equity will, upon their ordinary jurisdiction to prevent irreparable mischief, grant an injunction against such a dissolution."   1 Story Eq. 686, § 668.

pointment of a receiver is not so strong, if there be some urgent and pressing necessity. That, upon the motion to dissolve, the court cannot decide that the contract of dissolution is void. This contract transferred the legal title to the defendant, and the court is always reluctant to interfere in opposition to the legal title, and will only do so in case of fraud clearly proved, and of imminent danger.[1]

§ 11. Another ground of injunction in case of partnership is thus referred to in a late English case.

§ 12. "This court has jurisdiction to prevent one partner from excluding another from, or from so acting as to prevent the continuance of the partnership according to its terms. If two parties agree to devote their whole time to a partnership concern, this court will not permit one of them to exclude the other from the partnership, or to set up a separate business which makes it impossible that he should perform his partnership obligation; and the bill seeking to restrain the violation of such a partnership contract, though it seeks nothing but an injunction, is, in substance, a bill for a specific performance."[2] And in another case it is said, "Where the parties are partners, and one of the partners contracts that he shall exert himself for the benefit of the partnership, though the court cannot compel a specific performance of that part of the agreement, yet, there being a partnership subsisting, the court will restrain that party (if he has covenanted that he will not carry on the same trade with other persons) from breaking that part of the agreement."[3]

§ 13. A. and B. being partners, A. retired from the business, and the amount to be paid him for the good-will was left to arbitration. Upon the verbal understanding that A.

[1] O'Bryan v. Gibbons, 2 Md. Ch. Decis. 9.
[2] Per V. C., Shrewsbury, &c. v. Shrewsbury, &c., 1 Sim. N. 422.
[3] Per Sir L. Shadwell, V. C., Kemble v. Kean, 6 Sim. 333.

would not set up the trade on or near the same street, a certain sum was awarded and paid; nothing being said in the award as to thus continuing the business. A. having afterwards started the business on the same street, held, he should be restrained by injunction.[1] So the plaintiff and defendant, having been partners in stage-coaches, agreed upon dissolution that the business, between Newbury and London, should belong to the plaintiff, and that the defendant should not carry on that business between those places. The defendant afterwards started a coach, beginning its route a few miles from Newbury, but passing through Newbury to London. An injunction was ordered against carrying on the business between Newbury and London.[2] So the plaintiff and defendant, partners, contracted for the mail, each furnishing horses for a certain part of the way. The defendant having improperly horsed the coach, the postmaster had been often obliged to suspend the contract. Held, it being a case of irreparable injury to the partnership, the defendant should be enjoined from interfering with the plaintiff's part of the road.[3]

§ 14. But the distinction is made, that a *temptation* to abuse the partnership property is not sufficient ground of injunction; though it is otherwise, where a partner pursues a course of great impropriety or folly, and it is highly probable that the safety of the firm and the rights of creditors demand such interference.[4] This distinction is illustrated by the following case:—

§ 15. The plaintiff, as one partner in the *Morning Herald* newspaper, filed a bill against the others, praying for an account, and an injunction to restrain them from using the types or partnership effects and the name of the plaintiff in the publication of the *English Chronicle*, of which they, but

[1] Harrison v. Gardner, 2 Madd. 198.

[2] Williams v. Williams, 1 J. Wils. 473, n.

[3] Anderson v. Wallace, 2 Moll. 540.

[4] Coll. Partn. § 185, n. 3.

not he, were proprietors. The bill alleged, that he had for many months been excluded from his rights as a partner in the *Herald*, and that the partnership effects were misapplied, as above stated, intelligence obtained at the expense of the *Herald* having been first used for the *Chronicle* and thus become of no value to the *Herald;* and that his name was used without his consent as publisher of the *Chronicle*.   The answer alleged a failure to account, and indebtedness to the firm, on the part of the plaintiff, in consequence of which they had been compelled to exclude him from interfering in the management of the paper, the defendants being a majority of shares, expressly authorized by agreement to control the minority; that the agreement with the *Chronicle* was beneficial to the *Herald*, on account of the sum paid for the use of the effects, and because the *Herald* had the use of the types composed for new matter in the *Chronicle*, and had also the general use of the types of that paper.   They also relied upon the long acquiescence of the plaintiff.   Sir John Leach, V. C., said : " The right of the majority is confined to matters in the conduct of the partnership.—All newspapers are to some extent rivals.— It might, therefore, have been made a question, whether it would be a due act of management in the partnership concern of a morning paper, to assist—any other newspaper, so as to enable the majority—to bind the minority.   But that question does not arise, because the plaintiff is a party to the practice before his co-partners became the proprietors of the evening paper, and because there is evidence that the proprietors of other morning papers have adopted the same practice—so as to form a sort of usage.   The annual sum paid—outweighs the danger of increased competition.—A considerable part of the expense of a newspaper is occasioned by procuring information ; and if some of the proprietors of a morning paper are also the proprietors of an evening paper, they may have a stronger interest to promote the success of the evening paper than of the morning paper, and a strong temptation to use the information obtained at the expense of the morning paper for the benefit of the evening paper. This temptation forms a powerful objection in all cases to the partner in the concern of one newspaper being permitted to be a partner in the concern of any other.—But it is an objection against which parties may protect themselves by their contracts. In the present case, there is actually a covenant, that the proprietors will not be concerned in any other morning paper," implying "that they might engage in the concern of any evening paper.—Equity would not permit that parties bound to each other by express or implied contract to promote an undertaking for the common benefit, should any of them engage in another concern, which necessarily gave them a direct interest adverse to that undertaking. But the argument here is—that, if their interest be greater in the evening paper than in the morning paper, they are exposed to a temptation to be dishonest.—If they act honestly, it is immaterial to the morning paper whether the defendants are or are not the proprietors of the evening paper." An injunction was allowed, to restrain the defendants from publishing in the *Chronicle* any information obtained at the expense of the *Herald*, till first published in the *Herald*.[1]

§ 15 *a*. In cases of this nature the maxim is applied, that he who seeks equity must do equity. Therefore, when one of two partners in a ferry, who were tenants in common of the land adjacent, died, and his moiety was sold by his administrator, and the purchaser offered to form a partnership with him, and was refused, and afterwards set up an opposition ferry; a court of equity refused to enjoin him.[2] So A. and B. agreed to work a coach from Bristol to London, each furnishing horses for a distinct part of the road. A.'s horses being seized on execution, B. furnished horses for A.'s part of the road, and subsequently persisted in furnishing horses for the whole route, and claimed the whole profits. A.

---

[1] Glassington *v.* Thwaites, 1 Sim. & St. 124; Cond. Eng. Ch. 61.　　　[2] Spann *v.* Nance, 32 Ala. 527.

brings a bill for an injunction, but it was not allowed. Lord Eldon said : "If I enjoin the defendant from bringing horses to convey the coaches between the limits in question, I must enjoin the plaintiff from not bringing horses there. I cannot restrain the defendant unless I have the means of assuring him that he shall find the plaintiff's horses ready. I should otherwise enjoin him from doing that which, if he omits to do, he will be liable to actions by every person whom he has undertaken to convey from Bristol to London."[1]

§ 16. Where one firm have sold out to another, and agreed with them not to resume the same business in the same place, and afterwards do so resume ; a mere prayer for an injunction will be granted on the application of a single member of the injured firm, the injunction being equally for the benefit of his partners; though it would be otherwise where damages are sought.[2]

§ 17. In reference to a mere *breach of covenant*, express or implied, without other grounds of interference, it is said, "Although this court will interfere where there is a breach of covenant in articles of partnership, so important in its consequences as to authorize the party complaining to call for a dissolution—it is a matter of great consideration, whether it will entertain the jurisdiction of pronouncing a decree for a perpetual injunction as to a particular covenant, the partnership not being dissolved by the court. There is one case which is constantly occurring, that of a partner raising money for his private use on the credit of the partnership firm ; and the court interferes then, because there is a ground for dissolving the partnership; but then the danger must be such, there must be that abuse of good faith between the members of the partnership, that the court will try the question whether the partnership should not be dissolved. But

---

[1] Smith v. Fromont, 2 Swanst. 330.   [2] Beard v. Dennis, 6 Ind. 200.

where one party violates a particular covenant, and the other party does not choose to put an end to the partnership, there may be a separate suit, and a perpetual injunction in respect of each covenant; that is a jurisdiction that we have never decidedly entertained."[1]   Conformably with these views, equity will not interfere by injunction on the application of one partner against others, with reference to the names used in the partnership business, on the ground of a breach of covenant, where such breach has not been long continued; no dissolution of the partnership being prayed for.   And it is doubted, whether even in that case an injunction would be granted.[2]   But a surviving partner may enjoin the executor of the deceased partner from using the partnership name in carrying on the business.[3]   So an injunction was granted, to restrain a partner, who had abstracted a firm-book from the counting-house, in violation of a covenant, from continuing such violation.[4]   So, after dissolution, equity will restrain one partner from publishing the letters of another relating to the joint business, unless demanded by civil or criminal justice.[5]   And, in general, it is said: "Courts of equity construe the articles strictly, and do not permit the business to be extended by any of the partners, without the consent of all of them, either express or implied, to any other business or branch of business, of a different nature, extent or kind; and if it is attempted they will interpose by way of injunction."[6]   While, on the other hand, "courts of equity, in interfering by way of injunction in cases of partnership act upon a sound discretion, and will not interfere to waive by any breach of duty, unless they are of such a nature as may produce permanent injury to the partnership, or involve it in serious perils or mischiefs in future.   A mere fugitive temporary breach, involving no serious evils

---

[1] Per Lord Eldon, Marshall v. Colman, 2 Jac. & W. 266.   See 3 Kent, 61.

[2] Marshall v. Colman, 2 Jac. & W. 266.

[3] Lewis v. Landor, 7 Sim. 421.

[4] Taylor v. Davis, 3 Beav. 367, n. e.

[5] Roberts v. M'Kee, 29 Geo 161.

[6] Story, Partn. 289, § 193.

or mischiefs, and not endangering the future success and operations of the partnership, will, therefore, not constitute any case for equitable relief. Equity will not interfere in cases of frivolous vexation, or for mere differences of temper, casual disputes, or other minor grievances."[1]

§ 18. The general positive misconduct of a partner in reference to the partnership business is ground for injunction, more especially in connection with a prayer for other relief. Thus a bill was filed by A. and B., partners in a brewery, charging great misconduct in C., the defendant, another partner, in disobliging and turning away the customers, inducing servants to quit, assaulting and obstructing them, locking up the books, retaining as servants, without consent of the plaintiffs, bruisers and boxers who obstructed the trade, threatening to ruin the business, and refusing to account. The bill prayed for a valuation and division of the stock and utensils, at the end of the partnership, and for an injunction, against any act to obstruct or injure the trade. On motion, after answer, for an injunction, ordered, that the defendant be restrained from using force, either by himself or any other person, to the obstruction of the trade, from obstructing or removing the servants, and removing from the counting-house any books or papers concerning the trade. And the plaintiffs, upon their submission, were enjoined in like manner. So the plaintiff and defendant were bankers, and partners under a parol agreement. The defendant introduced Newnham, a friend of his, to keep cash with them; and contrary to the opinion and desire, and without the consent of the other partner, permitted him to draw upon the partnership; and directed his bills to be paid out of the joint property; by which he became considerably indebted to the partnership. Newnham executed bonds to the defendant only. A balance of above 5,000*l.* remains due from Newnham, with respect to which he referred the plaintiff to the

---

[1] Story, Partn. 328–31, § 225.

defendant; who said, the bank had no demand against Newnham. Bill, praying for an account, dissolution, and that the defendant might be restrained from executing securities in the name of the firm without the plaintiff's consent. A demurrer to so much of the bill as prayed for a dissolution was overruled.[1]

§ 19. It is said, in an approved work, that an injunction may be had against one who has colluded with a partner.[2]

§ 20. We shall hereafter—Chap. XXX.—have occasion to consider the application of injunctions, to restrain the negotiation of bills of exchange and promissory notes, generally. As illustrative of the point of *collusion;* whether an injunction will be granted against the negotiation of a bill or note given by one partner in the name of the firm for his separate debt, seems to depend upon the consideration, whether the party taking such security had reason to suppose that the partner had the right or authority thus to use the name of the firm. Lord Eldon regarded the remedy as applicable, where a partner, indebted to the firm, and unable to pay his separate bill held by his bankers, substitutes for it, by a negotiation with them, a partnership security, made and given without the knowledge or consent of the other partners, the bankers knowing it to be thus executed.[3]   Thus an injunction having been granted against the defendant White, a motion was made for the purpose of continuing the injunction, after the answer came in, and to extend it to the defendant Bolt; who was connected with the other defendant by marriage; and had received from him a bill or note for 5,500*l.* drawn or accepted in the name of the partnership, and, according to the plaintiff's affidavits, negotiated it to Bolt immediately, while the order for the injunction was making, in consideration of a debt, due from White previously to the commence-

---

[1] Master *v.* Kinton, 3 Ves. 74.
[2] Coll. Partn. § 340 n.
[3] Hood *v.* Astor, 1 Russ. 415.

ment of the partnership. Bolt had brought an action and denied notice. The defendants contended that the case should be tried at law; but Lord Eldon overruled the objection, remarking upon the change of practice in regard to sending cases to be tried at law, and also that "the dates and other circumstances, which may be very material, as to the *bona fides* with which Bolt received this bill, are very loosely stated in the answer." Afterwards by a farther answer, put in upon exceptions, Bolt submitted to the relief prayed against him; and by consent the bill, which had been deposited with the Master, was delivered up to the plaintiff to be cancelled; and Bolt was ordered to discontinue his action.[1]

§ 21. More especially, a partner who has involved the firm, or himself become insolvent, will be enjoined from drawing, indorsing, and accepting bills in the firm name, and from receiving the partnership debts.[2]

§ 22. A. and B. entered into partnership, and, A. having advanced the capital, B. gave him his (B.'s) note for his share. The firm afterwards became insolvent, and surrendered the partnership effects to assignees; but A. retained B.'s note, which he afterwards transferred, overdue. Held, the transferree took the note subject to an account between A. and B., and, B. having paid more than his share of the partnership debts, and A. being insolvent, the collection of the note was enjoined.[3]

§ 23. An allegation in a bill in equity, that one defendant claims to have been in partnership with a party deceased, that the other defendant, the administratrix, denies such partnership, and that the complainant himself is ignorant of the state of the case; is not "an averment of partnership" sufficient to authorize orders for an injunction and a receiver.[4]

[1] Jervis v. White, 7 Ves. 412-3-4.
[2] Williams v. Bingley, 2 Vern. 278, Raithby's note.
[3] Peck v. Wakely, 1 McC. Ch. 43.
[4] Guyton v. Flack, 7 Md. 398.

24

So where the representatives of a deceased partner had enjoined the surviving partner from selling the joint property at public sale; it was held that it should be dissolved, there being no charge of fraud, insolvency, or misconduct against the survivor, but a mere allegation of a refusal to account, and no proof that the account had been withheld an unreasonable time.[1]

§ 24. A firm, being indebted to A., agreed that B., one of the firm, should take a lot of land and pay the debt of A. The land was conveyed to A., to hold until B. should pay him; and A. leased it to B. at a rent which would in six years pay the debt. When the first rent fell due, A. distrained slaves of B., on the premises, which B. had before the transaction mortgaged to C., to secure a debt. C. filed a bill against A. and B., to restrain the sale under the distress, and have them applied to his debt, and charging a combination between A. and B. to defraud him of his debt, and also alleging the sufficiency of the land to pay A.'s debt. Pending the bill, the slaves were sold on motion of A., and the money placed in the hands of a receiver. A. then objected to the jurisdiction of the court. Held, the charge of fraud authorized the bill; also the charge that the land was sufficient to pay A.'s debt, on the principle of marshalling assets; and A. had waived objection to the jurisdiction by moving for the sale of the slaves.[2]

§ 25. An injunction was granted, on the application of one partner, against the other's receiving any more of the partnership funds, and a receiver appointed; the latter being in contempt, and not appearing after personal service.[3]

§ 26. The principles, that an injunction should not be granted unless there is danger of irreparable loss, and that

---

[1] Shad v. Fuller, Charl. R. M. 501.

[2] Henley v. Perkins, 6 Gratt. 615.

[3] Read v. Bowers, 4 Bro. Ch. 326, 441.

a prayer for equitable relief comes too late after a judgment at law, have no application to a bill in equity for an account and settlement of a copartnership, brought by one of the partners, who alleges that he was the lessee of the partnership property, and had paid out more than he had received; and that another partner, who held the legal title to the property, which equitably belonged to the company, had recovered judgment in ejectment against the complainant, both for the premises and for mesne profits.[1]

§ 27. Bill, to restrain a suit on a bond, in favor of surviving partners against the representatives of a partner deceased. It appeared, that the articles of partnership provided for an annual settlement, and for payment to the representatives of one deceased of an allowance in lieu of profits since the last annual account, proportioned to the amount of his share of profits during two years next preceding. The suit was brought for repayment of the share of the partner deceased, according to the articles. But it appeared that the parties had omitted for several years to settle the annual accounts, and had engaged in business to which the agreement was not equitably applicable; and an injunction was ordered upon the prosecution of the suit, before settlement of transactions pending at the death of the deceased partner, which resulted in a loss.[2]

§ 28. The plaintiff had received money by bill of exchange which belonged to the defendant, but detained it upon pretence of some accounts between them, and, being sued at law, brings a bill to stay that suit, and on account of the defendant's alleged insolvency the money was brought into court. Prayer for relief, upon an agreement made at the termination of a partnership; for the plaintiff, being at Leghorn, had entered into a partnership with Lee and Canham, in thirds, and being desirous to break off, it was agreed that

[1] Wells v. Strange, 5 Geo. 22.   [2] Jackson v. Sedgwick, 1 Swanst. 460.

27,000 pieces of eight should be paid the plaintiff, which was done; and that the plaintiff should be indemnified from any trouble growing out of the partnership, and in 1664 an instrument was executed accordingly. After this, the plaintiff formed a new partnership with James and John Gold, and was forced by sentence of the court at Florence to pay custom to the Great Duke for goods imported during the former partnership, and is also sued by Mico for a partnership debt. To which the defendant said that there were no customs due after seven years, and that Mico's pretences were groundless, and that there had been a reference of all differences to arbitrators, before whom the matter of the customs was not stood upon. Cur. 1. Let the plaintiff receive back so much of the money brought into court as may be adequate to the sum paid on the sentence for custom, the justice whereof is not examinable here. 2. Let the defendant take the rest, subject to the covenants of saving the plaintiff harmless against Mico, &c.[1]

§ 29. It is ground for injunction that A., one of the defendants, has agreed to do a specific thing, and B., the other defendant, holds a covenant of A., taken in behalf of the plaintiff, according to a prior understanding, and also holds a specific fund, which puts it in the power, and makes it the duty, of one of the defendants to see that the agreement is carried into effect by the other; the plaintiff alleging that B. intends to pay out the fund contrary to the understanding.[2]

§ 80. Equity cannot restrain one joint devisee or one tenant in common from entering upon the land, at the suit of another.[3]

§ 31. One *tenant in common* may enjoin another from cutting saplings and any timber trees or underwood at unseasonable times, which the law regards as *destruction;* but not pure

---

[1] Gold *v.* Canham, 2 Swanst. 343 n.; 1 Cas. in Ch. 311.

[2] Ashe *v.* Johnson, 2 Jones Eq. 149.

[3] Baldwin *v.* Darst, 3 Gratt. 132.

equitable waste, as in the cutting of timber generally. Lord Eldon says: "I never knew an instance of an application to stay waste by one tenant in common against another, one tenant in common having a right to enjoy as he pleases."[1] But in a later case it is held, that, if one co-tenant, while in possession of the whole estate by consent of the others, threaten to commit wilful waste, which would work irremediable mischief, he may be restrained by injunction.[2]

§ 32. After a lease to a railroad company from five out of six tenants in common, at a rent three times as large as the former rent, the company, against the wishes of A., the remaining tenant, who, in the language of the court, "kept the company at arm's length," made a railroad upon the land, which at law was held an ouster. Held, A. should not be enjoined from removing the rails.[3]

§ 33. An injunction lies to restrain the sailing of a ship, until security is given in behalf of one one-part owner against the others, where the respective shares are not apparent and their amount is a subject of dispute, and for this reason the Court of Admiralty would decline to interfere. But the plaintiff must have acted promptly.[4]

---

[1] Hole v. Thomas, 7 Ves. 589.
[2] Twort v. Twort, 16 Ves. 128.
[3] Durham, &c. v. Wawn, 3 Beav. 119.
[4] Haly v. Goodson, 2 Meri. 77; Christie v. Craig, ibid. 137.

CHAPTER XXII.

OFFICERS.

§ 1. EQUITY has undoubted jurisdiction to interfere by injunction, where *public officers* are proceeding illegally and improperly, under a claim of right, to do any act to the injury of the rights of others.[1]   "It is not the mere fact that a public officer is attempting to exercise a void authority which induces a court of equity to restrain him; but, notwithstanding he is a public officer, that he is about, by such exercise, to do an act which brings the case within its peculiar jurisdiction; for example, an act in breach of trust, in derogation of a contract which ought to be specifically performed, or an act of irreparable mischief to the real estate of another."[2]

§ 1 a. "The limits within which this court interferes with the acts of a body of public functionaries are perfectly clear and unambiguous. So long as those functionaries strictly confine themselves within the exercise of those duties which are confided to them by the law, this court will not interfere. The court will not interfere to see whether any alteration or regulation which they may direct is good or bad; but if they are departing from that power which the law has vested in them—if they are assuming to themselves a power over property which the law does not give them—this court no longer considers them as acting under the authority of their commission, but treats them, whether they be a corporation or individuals, merely as persons dealing with property with-

---

[1] Cooper *v.* Alden, Harring. Ch. 72; Mohawk, &c. *v.* Archer, 6 Paige, 83. See Tunstall *v.* Boothby, 10 Sim. 542; Conover *v.* Mayor, &c., 25 Barb. 513.

[2] Per Ames, J., Greene *v.* Mumford, 5 R. I. 475.

out legal authority."[1]   Thus one alleging himself to be a
citizen and resident of the county, and as such interested in
the public welfare, may enjoin a public officer from the commission of a public wrong.[2]   So the magistrates of a county
proposed to cut the timbers supporting the roadway of a
bridge, which timbers and roadway, at the place to be cut,
were within their jurisdiction, but the other extremity in
another county.   Held, a case for injunction, on a bill filed
jointly in favor of the Attorney-General and relators, inhabitants of the county.[3]   So while A. was in possession and exercise of an office, B. ousted him, acting under a commission
from the governor; whereupon A. brought an action of *quo
warranto*, on the ground of the illegality of the commission.
Held, that, pending such action, this court, in view of the
defendant's insolvency, might grant an injunction to prevent
him from receiving the fees and emoluments of the office,
until the decision.[4]   So a court of chancery may restrain,
by injunction, a special commissioner in chancery from
executing a decree of sale.[5]   So where a plan for the drainage of a swamp, under the New York act "for draining
swamps and bog meadows in the counties of Orange and
Dutchess" (Sess. 27, Chap. XCI.), proposed by the inspectors,
exceeded their powers, and would have been to the injury
of the plaintiff's mill, their proceedings were enjoined.[6]

§ 2. But where supervisors have jurisdiction to review
the orders of commissioners of highways on appeal, and
proceed regularly in the exercise of such jurisdiction,
equity will not interfere with their action.[7] So the inclosure
commissioners, under the general inclosure act, 8 and 9 Vict.
c. 118, having made provisional orders, and being about to
confirm the valuer's report, pursuant to a local act, a bill

---

[1] Per Ld. Chanc. Frewin *v.* Lewis,
4 My. & C. 254.
[2] Collins *v.* Ripley, 8 Clarke, 129.
[3] Att'y-Gen. *v.* Forbes, 2 My. &
Cr. 123.
[4] Tappen *v.* Gray, 3 Edw. Ch. 450.

[5] The People *v.* Gilmer, 5 Gilman,
242.
[6] Belknap *v.* Belknap, 2 John. Ch.
463.
[7] Gray *v.* Lott, 18 Ill. 251.

was filed, alleging certain lands in the report to be lands
not subject to inclosure, and praying an injunction. The
lands being commonable, held, the court had no authority
to restrain the commissioners from making their award.[1]

§ 3. An injunction will not issue to eject a clergyman,
once regularly settled, from a church, merely at the wish of
the vestry, there being no conflict, or pretence or expectation of conflict, between him and another claiming the office,
or their adherents.[2] So the only ground of injunction, to
restrain a bishop from passing sentence against a priest is,
that he may affect the civil rights of the priest. Where
such ground exists, the only cognizance which the court
will take of the case is, to inquire whether there is a want of
jurisdiction in the bishop—whether he has power to act, not
whether he is acting rightly; and objections not made at the
trial of the priest will be considered as waived.[3] But in a
suit for specific performance of an agreement for the sale of
the next presentation to a living, the court will restrain the
bishop from taking advantage of a lapse pending the suit.[4]
So an injunction lies, to restrain the Archbishop of Dublin
from collating, by way of lapse, to a deanery, pending a suit
in the consistorial court, respecting the presentment by the
chapter.[5] So where the Archbishop of Canterbury devised
to the defendants and others all options which should fall,
in trust, to present his son, the plaintiff, in the first place;
and, a vacancy having occurred, the defendant procured
himself to be presented for installation and induction; the
plaintiff filed a bill, and on motion obtained an injunction, to
prohibit the bishop from inducting the defendant or any
other person, till answer and further order.[6]

§ 4. An officer of court, who has obtained authority
from it to sue, is not only authorized, but bound, to proceed

[1] Turner v. Blamire, 19 Eng Law
and Eq. 521.
[2] Youngs v. Ransom, 31 Barb. 49.
[3] Walker v. Wainwright, 16 Barb.
486.

[4] Nicholson v. Knapp, 9 Sim. 326.
[5] Daly v. Archbishop, &c., Flan.
& Kel. 263.
[6] Potter v. Chapman, Dick. 146;
Ambl. 98.

with his action, and is not to be restrained by injunction out of another court, or by making him a party to a new action, and obtaining an injunction against him, but by application to the court, whose officer he is, for instructions.[1]

§ 5. A bill in equity will not lie to compel the clerk of the court to issue an execution on a money judgment, as there is a perfect remedy by action on his bond.[2]

§ 6. Pending proceedings in the nature of *quo warranto*, to determine the right of the incumbent of a certain office, an injunction will not be granted to restrain him from discharging its duties during such pendency, and until the validity of the law under which he holds the office is decided.[3]   So. a court of chancery has no jurisdiction to enjoin a flour inspector, who entered upon the discharge of his duties under color of an appointment by the Governor, made during a recess of the senate, or to appoint a receiver of the fees and emoluments, until the rights of the former inspector, who claimed to hold over, and of the defendant, could be determined at law, although the latter is insolvent.[4]   So neither the Supreme Court nor a judge in vacation has any authority, under the statutes of Indiana, to make an order, by way of injunction, requiring the incumbent of an office, although his term has expired and his successor has been duly elected and qualified, to transfer and deliver to his successor the appurtenances of the office.[5]

§ 7. Under (California) Sts. May 1, 1855, and March 26, 1851, the commissioners have, by express terms, no authority as to land outside the boundaries there specified ; therefore their sale of lands outside can give no color of title, and so cannot be enjoined.[6]

[1] Winfield v. Bacon, 24 Barb. 154.
[2] Goodwin v. Glazer, 10 Cal. 333.
[3] People v. Draper, 24 Barb. 265.
[4] Tappan v. Gray, 7 Hill, 259.
[5] Markle v. Wright, 13 Ind. 548.
[6] Kisling v. Johnson, 13 Cal. 56.

§ 8. In case of contest between two sets of trustees as to an election, a temporary injunction should not issue against those in possession, unless they threaten some special injury, beyond their mere incumbency, *pendente lite*.[1]

§ 9. One claimant of a military office cannot have a perpetual injunction against another, until the title of the latter has been directly put in issue and expressly adjudged invalid, thus exempting him from liability for disobedience to superior officers.[2]

§ 10. The plaintiffs belonged to a club, consisting of those who had been parochial overseers of the poor. The society had long been in possession of a silver tobacco-box, inclosed in two large silver cases, all of which were adorned with engravings of public transactions and heads of eminent individuals, affixed, periodically, for a long prior period. These articles were always kept by the overseer for the time, to whom, upon his coming into office, they were delivered by the church-warden, with a charge, under a penalty, to produce them at all meetings, and to deliver them, on leaving office, to the senior church-warden, to be by him delivered to the succeeding overseer. One of the defendants, on becoming overseer, received them in the usual form. On going out of office, he refused to surrender them unless the vestry would pass his accounts, in which they had refused to allow certain payments. A meeting was then called, and it was resolved by the members attending that legal steps should be taken, and, after some negotiation, an action was brought and the defendant arrested. Two of the nominal plaintiffs in that action executed a release to the defendant, who thereupon delivered the box to one of them. A bill in equity was then brought against the parties releasing and the party taking the release to have the articles delivered up. Held, although there was a clear remedy at law, yet, upon the grounds of a

[1] Hartt *v.* Harvey, 32 Barb. 55.   [2] People *v.* Sampson, 25 Barb. 254.

trust, and of the peculiar nature of the property, the bill should be sustained.[1](*a*)

[1] Fells *v.* Read, 3 Ves. 70.

(*a*) In New York, upon the removal, or expiration of the term, of an officer, it is a misdemeanor for him to refuse to deliver to his successor, on demand, all the books and papers of office. 1 R. S. 124. If the title is clear, such delivery may be compelled by law. Otherwise there must be a proceeding in the nature of *quo warranto.* Ibid., 51; Code, ₴ 428; The People *v.* Stevens, 5 Hill, 616.

CHAPTER XXIII.

SUBJECTS OF INJUNCTION.—TRUSTS.

§ 1. HAVING treated of the *grounds* for, and the *parties* to, the process of injunction, we now proceed to consider the *subjects* in reference to which this remedy is ordinarily invoked; remarking, however, that its most distinguishing feature, as part of the flexible and remedial system of equity jurisprudence, is its applicability and adaptation to *any and all* subjects which may happen to give occasion to injuries not susceptible of legal redress.

§ 2. *Trusts* being a peculiar subject of equity jurisdiction, of course no more frequent occasion arises for the process of injunction, than to regulate the disposition of trust property. Thus equity will enjoin a party holding land in trust from parting with his control over it.[1] So where *cestuis que trust* were empowered by the trust deed to change the investment of the trust fund, they were enjoined from making any change in such investment, or interfering with the income or profits, without the sanction of the court on notice to their creditors.[2] So where the trustees of a chapel were proceeding to mortgage it for a small sum without any apparent necessity, the court granted an injunction to the plaintiff, undertaking to abide any order which the court might make as to the payment of the debt proposed to be secured.[3] In the case of Atty.-Gen. *v.* The Mayor, &c., Wood, V. C., said: " You cannot, without previous consent of this court, apply any funds which may be in your hands appropriated by an

[1] Hun *v.* Freeman, 1 Ham. 490.
[2] North Am. Coal Co. *v.* Dyett, 7 Paige, 1.
[3] Rigall *v.* Foster, 23 Eng. Law and Eq. 71.

act of Parliament to the given purposes of that act, for the extension of those purposes, although it is purely and *bonâ fide* an extension of those purposes, or a more enlarged application of it to those purposes.—Considering this money is trust-money applicable to a specific purpose, you, the trustee, must come to this court."[1]   So, A. having conveyed property in trust for the payment of certain judgments which were a lien on such property, B., a *bonâ fide* purchaser from the trustees, files a bill against C., an assignee of some of the judgments, for an injunction, charging that the judgment-creditors had notice of, and assented to the trust, and intended to rely for payment upon the proceeds of the land sold under it.   C. answered that he had no personal knowledge of the plaintiff's equity, and denied, upon information, the facts alleged.   Held, the answer was not sufficient to dissolve the injunction.[2]

§ 3. But the court will enjoin a sale by fiduciary vendors only upon strong grounds, and for irreparable injury or a clear breach of trust.[3]   Thus the court refused to stay a sale by trustees, although to be made the next day, and although the notice was unusually short, it not being a case of irreparable injury, and the trustees being liable to the *cestui* for any damages which might result from a breach of trust.[4]   And a trustee, having a naked title in land, cannot be restrained from asserting or conveying such title, or compelled to convey it to a purchaser from the *cestui*, without proof of a written agreement, or joining the *cestui* in the bill.[5]   So, in Maryland, a party holding a lien on land, based on a conveyance to trustees for his security, is not entitled to an injunction to prevent a judgment creditor of the grantor, whose judgment is subordinate to the lien, from enforcing his judgment by the sale of the lands on execution.   The execution would operate only on the equitable interest of the judgment debtor, and

---

[1] 23 Eng. Law and Eq. 361.
[2] Doub *v.* Barnes, 4 Gill, 1.
[3] Dart on Vend. & P. 38.
[4] Pechel *v.* Fowler, 2 Anstr. 542.
[5] Richards *v.* Richards, 9 Gray, 313.

would leave the prior lien unaffected both at law and in equity.[1] So A. executed a document, attested by two witnesses, giving and granting to B., his wife, a freehold house in which they resided. A. afterwards died intestate, and his heirs at law brought ejectment for the house and premises against B. and obtained a verdict, upon which B. filed this bill. Upon motion to dissolve an injunction, held, the gift was incomplete, the relation of trustee and *cestui que trust* was not created, and the court would not assist either party. but leave them as it found them, and the injunction was dissolved.[2]

§ 4. In reference to the peculiar form of trusts termed *charities*, in the case of Atty.-Gen. *v.* The Foundling Hospital, Lord Commissioner Eyre said, "he had not a doubt that the court had a jurisdiction over charities, and that where they are founded in charters, or by act of Parliament, and a visitor appointed, or where trustees or governors abused their trust, the court could take notice of such abuse; not in the character of a charity, but as an abuse of a trust; but that where the management of a charity was intrusted to governors or guardians by the charter or act of Parliament, such governors had a right to exercise their discretion; and that, as to opinion, although the court should be of a different one from such governors, it would not set up that opinion against the discretion of the trustees." In conformity with these views the court refused to restrain the governors of the Foundling Hospital from building on the charity estates.[3]

[1] Union, &c. *v.* Poultney, 8 Gill & J. 324.

[2] Price *v.* Price, 8 Eng. Law and Eq. 271.

[3] 4 Bro. Ch. 121, 165.

CHAPTER XXIV.

TAXES.

§ 1. AN injunction lies against a *tax* which is illegal, or laid for fraudulent purposes.[1](*a*)　Thus after a decision by the Supreme Court, that certain property is exempt from taxation, injunctions may issue to prevent tax assessments, in order to prevent a multiplicity of suits.　And though tax deeds of the land would be void, yet they would be a cloud on the title, and the issuing them may be restrained.[2] So an injunction may be allowed, to stay a sale for taxes on city lots assessed by a city government.[3]　Or the collection of a special tax levied without authority of law.[4]　Or a sale for taxes by an officer without legal authority.[4]　So upon a bill, alleging that the defendant, who was insolvent, claimed certain lands by a deed under an irregular sale of a tax collector ; that he was threatening and he and others were preparing for waste and trespass ; that the complainants had been disturbed and were likely to be still more seriously in the enjoyment of the land, and deprived of its profits ; the deed appearing in form to be valid, held, an injunction should be granted, and the deed cancelled.[6]　So, in Pennsylvania, the county treasurer may be restrained from

[1] Ottawa *v.* Walker, 21 Ill. 605. See Adams *v.* Castle, 30 Conn. 404.
[3] Morris, &c. *v.* Jersey, &c., 1 Beasl. 227.
[2] Burnet *v.* Cincinnati, 3 Ham. 72.

[4] Culbertson *v.* Cincinnati, 16 Ohio, 574 ; Vanover *v.* Davis, 27 Geo. 354.
[5] Fremont *v.* Boling, 11 Cal. 380.
[6] Lyon *v.* Hunt, 11 Ala. 285.

(*a*) In Massachusetts—Gen. Sts. c. 18, s. 79—the court is authorized on petition of ten taxable inhabitants to enjoin the illegal raising of money by a town or city.

selling unseated land for taxes, where the owners have paid the taxes to the supervisors, and they have been returned to the commissioners.[1] So the collection of a road-tax by suit will be enjoined, where the supervisors have given no notice to non-residents, or opportunity to work out their taxes, by themselves or their tenants; notwithstanding the general rule of non-interference where the right is doubtful, or where the party has a remedy at law.[2] So, in the important case of Mott v. The Pennsylvania Railroad,[3] the remedy of injunction was sustained, to enforce the constitutional principle, that the legislature has no power to alienate any of the rights of sovereignty, such as that of taxation, so as to bind future legislatures; and to avoid a contract made in pursuance of such a legislative act. The specific ground of equitable interposition was, an act of the legislature by which the defendants, in case they should purchase the *Main Line of Public Improvements*, should be thereafter exempted from all except certain enumerated kinds of taxes. On the other hand the State of Ohio, by an act incorporating the Ohio University, vested in it two townships of land for the purposes of the institution, and authorized the University to lease the lands, providing also that they should be forever exempt from taxation. The lands having been leased, a subsequent act was passed, imposing a tax upon them, and such tax was about to be levied. Held, the tax was contrary to the constitutional provision against the violation of contracts; and, to prevent a multiplicity of suits, the plaintiff might for himself and other lessees maintain a bill for an injunction against the treasurer of the county.[4] So a person owning real estate in the city of New York, and paying taxes on it, may by action against the corporation, on behalf of himself and other tax-paying citizens, enjoin them from expending the money to be raised by taxation, in repairing or paving a street in a manner contrary to an express law,

[1] Com. v. Supervisors, &c., 29 Penn. 121.
[2] Miller v. Gorman, 38 Penn. 309.
[3] 30 Penn. 9.
[4] Mattheny v. Golden, 5 Ohio St. 361.

and to add to the taxes of the citizens.[1] So a tax-payer, affected by the illegal payment of claims against the county, may obtain an injunction to restrain the making of such payment.[2] So, in Tash v. Adams,[3] an injunction was granted on the application of twenty-four taxpayers, to restrain a town-treasurer from paying out money in pursuance of a vote to celebrate the surrender of Cornwallis. More especially as the application was made immediately after the vote was passed and before any money was expended, and as the money actually raised and expended for the celebration was furnished by subscription, upon condition that it should be refunded by the town, if the court should sanction its being drawn from the treasury.

§. 2. But on the other hand it is held, that courts of equity ought not, except upon the clearest grounds, to interfere with the speedy collection of public taxes.[4] That a writ of injunction can only be issued, where the complaint makes out a case of equity jurisdiction ; and in all cases involving simply the question of taxation, the issue is strictly one of common law, and courts of equity can take no cognizance thereof.[5] That a party aggrieved by an illegal taxation has ample remedy at law, and need not in any case have recourse to a court of equity ; and a court of equity has no authority to restrain by injunction the collection of such illegal tax.[6] And that the unlawful collecting of a tax is a mere trespass, not to be enjoined, without allegation and proof of irreparable injury therefrom.[7] Thus, in Missouri, the Supreme Court will not interfere by injunction, to prevent a sale of personal property for non-payment of taxes.[8] Nor to restrain a collector from selling the plaintiff's property to satisfy a school

---

[1] De Baun v. The Mayor, 16 Barb. 392.
[2] Foster v. Coleman, 10 Cal. 278.
[3] 10 Cush. 253.
[4] 23 Conn. 232.
[5] Minturn v. Hays, 2 Cal. 590.
[6] Wilson v. Mayor, &c., 4 E. D.

Smith, 675.   See Robinson v. Gaar, 6 Cal. 273.
[7] Ritter v. Patch, 12 Cal. 298; Berri v. Patch, ib. 299 ; Ins. Co. v. New York, 33 Barb. 322.
[8] Lockwood v. St. Louis, 24 Mis. 20.

25

tax assessed by the proper school district.[1]   Nor, where land
was sold for taxes, and purchased by the city of St. Louis,
and the city afterwards proposed to sell it, to restrain such
sale on application of the original owners, on the ground
that the original sale was irregular and void.[2]   Nor to restrain the collection of a tax on the ground that the rate of
taxation is greater than it would have been, had not property
liable to be taxed been improperly omitted from the valuation; this fact not rendering the tax wholly void.[3]   More
especially, equity will not enjoin a tax for mere errors, if
the levy of it is attempted by an officer *de facto* under authority incident to his office; though it is otherwise, in case of
levy by one without pretence of authority, or color of office
to which such right is incident.[4]   Thus equity will not restrain the collection of a school tax, levied by officers *de jure*
or *de facto*, on account of irregularities in their levy or collection.[5]   Nor for irregularities in the assessment.[6]   So it
has been held that equity cannot enjoin the collection of a
tax assessed in the ordinary way, and unaccompanied by
circumstances of peculiar injury, even if the law authorizing
the tax be unconstitutional.[7]   And, in a late case, an application to enjoin an unconstitutional assessment was refused,
the court, as now advised, seeing no ground on which such
assessment conflicts with the Constitution.[8]   So an injunction
cannot be had to restrain the collection of a tax, upon the
ground that the party has paid a previous illegal tax.[9]   So
the Supreme Court of New York has no jurisdiction to restrain, by injunction, the collection of taxes, on the ground
that the returns are insufficient, and show no authority for
the issuing of the warrants of collection.[10]   And, as already
stated, the adequacy of the remedy at law is always held to

---

[1] Sayre v. Tompkins, 23 Mis. 443.
[2] City, &c. v. Goode, 21 Mis. 216.
[3] Exchange, &c. v. Hines, 3 Ohio (N. S.), 1.
[4] Munson v. Minor, 22 Ill. 594.
[5] Merritt v. Farris, 22 Ill. 303.
[6] Chicago, &c. v. Frary, 22 Ill. 34; McBride v. Chicago, ib. 574.

[7] McCoy v. Chillicothe, 3 Ham. 380.
[8] Thompson v. The Treasurer, &c., 11 Ohio, St. 678.
[9] Fremout v. Mariposa, 11 Cal. 361.
[10] Van Rensselaer v. Kidd, 4 Barb. 17; Livingston v. Hollenbeck, 4 Barb. 9.

be ground for denying an injunction. As, to restrain a city corporation from enforcing assessment warrants against personal estate, for the expenses of a public improvement, although the assessment and warrant may be illegal and void.[1] It is said in a late case, "We will not" (stay the collection of an illegal town or city tax) "as against a single tax payer, upon the mere ground that it is illegally assessed upon him, without special equities, and when the law affords a far better and more appropriate remedy, in view of his rights and necessities and those of the public, than any which we can administer."[2] So where the common council of a city have authority by law to make an assessment, chancery will not restrain the collection of such assessment, under a warrant against the goods and chattels of the complainant, but will leave him to his remedy at law.[3] Nor a *distraint* by a treasurer, against the money and property of an incorporated bank, upon the ground that the act imposing the tax is unconstitutional. If so, the treasurer is a trespasser, and is liable at law.[4] Nor, in Rhode Island, the collection of a general, or of a sidewalk tax, of a town or city, on the mere ground that it has been improperly assessed against the complainant, and that his real estate has been levied upon, and is about to be sold for its satisfaction; the remedy at law being sufficiently adequate, and far more consonant with the scope and provisions of the tax act.[5] More especially, equity will not interfere, if there is a statutory remedy.[6] As, to enjoin a city from collecting a tax imposed by its street commissioners, for widening a street, the acts of Assembly and ordinances of the city having given the right of appeal to the city court, which remedy the complainants failed to take.[7] And although the court will, by injunction, restrain the imposition of any illegal tax or burden on the tax-payers of a

---

[1] Dodd v. Hartford, 25 Conn. 232.
[2] Per Ames, C. J., Greene v. Mumford, 5 R. I. 478.
[3] Williams v. Detroit, 2 Mich. 560.
[4] Mechanics', &c. v. Debolt, 1 Ohio, 591.

[5] Greene v. Mumford; Simmons v. Same, 5 R. I. 472.
[6] Hughes v. Kline, 30 Penn. 227.
[7] Methodist, &c. v. The Mayor, &c., 2 Md. Ch. Decis. 78.

city, upon the complaint of any tax-payer, who complains both in his own behalf and in behalf of those who are similarly interested with himself, or on the complaint of any corporator of the city having an interest in the corporate property, such complaint showing an illegal application of any part of the corporate property; yet in such case, in order to a complete determination of all the rights affected by the suit, the plaintiff must aver that he files his complaint as well in behalf of those similarly interested, as in his own.[1] So where a bill in equity was brought by the owner of lots, situated on the plank-road of an incorporated company, to restrain the city government from collecting an assessment for paving the road; held, the company not being a party, the court would not consider whether its rights were infringed, and the complainant alone had no case.[2]

[1] Wood v. Draper, 24 Barb. 187.   [2] Bagg v. Detroit, 5 Mich. 336.

CHAPTER XXV.

CONSTITUTIONAL OR STATUTORY PRIVILEGE — COPYRIGHTS; PATENTS; TRADE-MARKS, ETC.

§ 1. A CONSTITUTIONAL privilege may be protected by injunction. (See *Corporation, Franchise, Bridge.*) Thus, where a county is established by the legislature, in violation of the Constitution, although a writ of *quo warranto* is proper, equity will interfere, by injunction, to stop an organization of the county, on the principle of *quia timet*, to prevent great and irreparable injury; and any person aggrieved may apply for the remedy.[1]

§ 1 a. An injunction will be granted, to secure to a party the enjoyment of a statute privilege, of which he is in actual possession, when the legal title is settled.[2] Or against adverse claims, until their validity has been settled by a trial at law.[3] It is said, "The equity jurisdiction in such a case is extremely benign and salutary. Without it, the party would be exposed to constant and ruinous litigation, as well as to have his right excessively impaired by frauds and evasion. If such a contrivance as this case presents is to be tolerated, all our statute privileges of the like kind, on which millions have been expended, would be rendered of little value, and the moneys have been laid out in vain." Thus, upon a bill by the plaintiff, as lessee of a piece of

[1] Bradley *v.* Commissioners, 2 Humph. 428.
[2] Croton, &c. *v.* Ryder, 1 John. Ch. 611.
[3] Livingston *v.* Van Ingen, 9 John. 507.
[4] Croton, &c. *v.* Ryder, 1 John. Ch. 615.

ground, against the trustees of a turnpike, to stay them from digging gravel; it appeared that the ground in question, three acres and a half, had been added by the plaintiff, a gardener, to seven acres occupied by him as such. Held, the exception of gardens in the turnpike act, under which the defendants justified, was not restricted to gardens annexed to houses, but applied to all fields planted with garden stuff; and an injunction was ordered.[1]

§ 2. By the Constitution of the United States, Congress is empowered to promote the progress of science and the useful arts, by securing, for limited times, to authors and inventors, the exclusive right to their writings and discoveries. And by successive acts of Congress, the power of issuing injunctions in this class of cases is expressly vested in the courts of the United States. "Under the foregoing constitutional and legislative provisions, it has been held by the Court of Appeals of the State of New York, that the jurisdiction in the case of infringements of patents is exclusively in the courts of the United States. The reasoning of the learned judge, in the case of Dudley v. Mayhew, tends to show that the jurisdiction, with respect to literary works and mechanical inventions, stands upon the same ground. It is believed that the jurisdiction to restrain by injunction the infringement of a patent, or the invasion of a copyright, is exclusive in the courts of the United States."[2]

§ 3. An early English case seems to justify this close connection between the two rights of patent and copyright.

§ 4. Bill to restrain the printing of Bibles, the plaintiffs claiming as king's printers, under several *patents* continued down by mesne assignments. In the eighth year of Charles I. such patent was granted to the University of Oxford, and afterwards confirmed. It was observed, that the Bible was

---

[1] Hughes v. Brand, 1 Ambl. 105.
[2] U. S. Const., art. 1, § 8; 6 Laws U. S. 369; U. S. Laws, 1836, 242, § 17; Brightly's U. S. Dig. 193 n. e., 732 n. i.; Dudley v. Mayhew, 3 Comst. 9; Wil. Eq. Juris. 384-5.

translated at the king's own charge, and that printing was brought in by Henry VI. at his own charge. The lord keeper was of opinion that it was never meant by the patent to the University, that they should engross the printing, and prevent the king's farmers of the benefit of their patent; but ordered an action and trial at law, the defendants to admit the printing a competent number of Bibles, and refused an intermediate injunction.[1]

§ 5. Copyrights are a frequent subject of equity jurisdiction and of injunction.(a)   As showing the necessity for the remedy of injunction in the case of copyrights, Judge Story remarks: "The sale of copies by the defendant is not only, in each instance, taking from the author the profit upon the individual book, which he might otherwise have sold; but it may also be injuring him, to an incalculable extent, in regard to the value and disposition of his copyright, which no inquiry for the purpose of damages could fully ascertain. In addition to this consideration, the plaintiff could at law have no preventive remedy, which should restrain the future use of his invention or the future publication of his work. Besides, the bill usually seeks an account, in one case of the books printed, and in the other of the profits which have arisen from the use of the invention."[2](b)

[1] Hills v. University, &c., 1 Vern. 275.

[2] 2 Story's Eq. 246, §§ 932-3 ; Pierpont v. Fowle, 2 W. & M. 23.

(a) Milton's "Paradise Lost" was the subject of four injunctions. Tonson v. Walker, 3 Swanst. 673.   A well-known religious work, "The Whole Duty of Man," was protected in the same way.   Eyre v. Walker, 4 Burr. 2325 ; 3 Swanst. 673.

An author, as well as publisher, may be restrained by injunction. Thus, where an author sold his copyright, and covenanted not to publish any other work to the prejudice of the one sold; he was restrained from such publication by injunction.   Barfield v. Nicholson, 2 Sim. & St. 1.

(b) But a leading case of high authority points out the following limitations of equity jurisdiction, and distinctions between English and American practice.   An injunction, as a preventive remedy, is more

§ 6. It is said: "Formerly courts of equity would not interfere, by way of injunction, to protect copyrights, until the title had been established at law. But the present course is, to exercise jurisdiction in all cases, where there is a clear color of title, founded upon a long possession and assertion of right."[1]

§ 7. An injunction was granted to protect a copyright in an East Indian calendar or directory, it appearing that the work complained of was a mere copy with colorable variations. Lord Chancellor Erskine, in answer to the argument that the work in question was not in its nature a proper subject of copyright, remarked: " In the case of Dr. Trusler's Chronology all the remarkable events, the accounts of eminent persons, every matter of curiosity and interest, were subjects of information past and gone by, which could not be altered. All human events are equally open to all. Dr. Trusler finally had the decision in his favor. The next is the case of a map. How is it possible to have a copyright in a map of the Island of St. Domingo? Must not the mountains have the same position, the rivers the same

[1] 2 Story's Eq. 248, § 935.

---

ample and appropriate than a suit at law ; and hence, when it is asked, and an account and disclosure of facts desired, they will be required, in order to settle the question in controversy. But equity cannot relieve on the ground of a right which the party has failed to redress at law ; but proper matters for the exercise of its jurisdiction must be set out and sustained. Stevens v. Gladding, 17 How. 447; Stevens v. Cady, 2 Curt. 200. If no benefit appears to be gained by proceedings in equity rather than at law ; the bill will be dismissed without prejudice, in order that proceedings may be had at law. In England, where the powers of law and equity are concurrent, equity may in its discretion proceed to act; but in the Circuit Court of the United States it is otherwise, under the judiciary act of 1789, if the remedy at law and in chancery is equally full and perfect; and the objection may sometimes be taken under the answer, and at the hearing, as well as by demurrer. But where the title to the copyright under a contract of sale is also in dispute : this question may be settled in equity, in preference to sending the parties to the law side of the court. Ib.

course? The answer was, that the subject of the plaintiff's claim was a map, made at great expense, from actual surveys. The defendant's map was a servile imitation. In the case of the chart of the English Channel, must not the latitude and longitude of the several points upon the adjoining shores and the soundings, be the same as they were placed by nature? They must be the same, or the chart must destroy the mariner. What room, then, can there be for originality? That may be a reason for not making a new chart, but it is no reason for a servile imitation. In the case of Patterson's Road-Book, the very errors were copied. The charts, representing twenty-five fathoms water, where there was dry land, would have wrecked the mariner. In the Road-Book, where Mr. Justice Grose's beautiful seat, the Priory, is noticed, an error in printing his name was exactly copied."[1]

§ 8. In another leading case upon this subject, the plaintiff had a copyright for six short poems and parts of longer ones, included in a work of the defendant's, which contained an original essay on modern English poetry, biographical sketches of a large number of modern poets, and selections from their poems. The bulk of the defendant's work consisted of the selections, but they were alleged to have been inserted for the purpose of illustrating the essay. Held, the plaintiff was entitled to an injunction.[2]

§ 9. But in Osborne v. Donaldson,[3] Lord Chancellor Henley declined granting an injunction founded upon copyright *at common law*, remarking "that it was a point of so much difficulty and consequence that he should send it to law for the opinion of the judges." So in Baskett v. Cunningham,[4] being a bill brought by the king's printer to restrain the publication of a digest of the Statutes, it appeared that the defendant had contracted with Strahan & Woodfall, proprietors of the patent for printing law books, and the

[1] Matthewson v. Stockdale, 12 Ves. 270, 272.
[2] Campbell v. Scott, 11 Sim. 31.
[3] 2 Ed. 327.
[4] 2 Ibid. 137.

work was printed at their press. The answer disclaimed all property in the work. A general injunction was refused, Lord Chancellor Henley remarking: "I am of opinion that this work is entirely within the patent of the king's printer, and that these notes are merely collusive. But I shall not interfere, but leave them to adjust their rights in a due course of law. The injunction must therefore be to restrain the proprietors from printing at any other than a patent press."[1] And in trifling cases an injunction has been denied. Thus in a periodical work of theatrical criticism, the defendant inserted a few pages of scattering passages from a farce of the plaintiff, forty pages in length. The profits did not amount to £3. Held, a bill for injunction should be dismissed.[2] So an injunction was refused against the copying of tables of calculations, which could be cast anew for less than £8, and in a short time.[3]

§ 10. A bill in equity against three defendants made title on its face in the plaintiff to a copyright, and showed a wrongful and wilful violation of it by all the defendants, and serious injuries inflicted by, and apprehended from such violation, and prayed for an injunction against all the defendants, and for a discovery from all. On general demurrer, held, the relief by injunction was not dependent upon the discovery prayed for, but rested on the equities set forth in the bill, and might be refused or granted irrespective of the discovery, although the bill was bad as a bill of discovery.[4]

§ 11. Neither the bill nor affidavit need specify the parts of the work claimed to be printed, though no copyright is claimed in all the identical passages.[5]

§ 12. Where the injunction is continued, subject to the

[1] Baskett v. Cunningham, 2 Ed. 137-8.
[2] Whittingham v. Wooler, 2 Swanst. 428.
[3] Baily v. Taylor, 1 Russ. & My. 73.
[4] Atwill v. Ferrett, 2 Blatch. Ct. Ct. 39.
[5] Sweet v. Mangham, 11 Sim. 51.

plaintiff's bringing an action, the court will not allow a continuance of the sale, keeping an account, without consent of the plaintiff.[1]

§ 13. In a very late case it is held that the court will hesitate to commit a defendant alleged to have violated an *interim* injunction, if he has endeavored to set himself right with regard to the original charge against him, of infringing the plaintiff's copyright.[2]

§ 14. It is said, "No copyright can exist, consistently with principles of public policy, in any work of a clearly irreligious, immoral, libellous, or obscene description. In the case of an asserted piracy of any such work, if it be not a matter of any real doubt, whether it falls within such a predicament, or not, courts of equity will not interfere by injunction to prevent or to restrain the piracy; but will leave the party to his remedy at law."[3]

§ 15. Judge Story remarks: "In some cases, a court of equity will take upon itself the task of inspection and comparison of books alleged to be a piracy. But the usual practice is, to refer the subject to a master, who then reports, whether the books differ, and in what respects; and, upon such a report, the court usually acts in making its interlocutory, as well as its final decree."[4] And Mr. Curtis says, on the same point: "In general, if the court sees strong ground for supposing that the defendant's work is a violation of the plaintiff's copyright, the course is to grant an injunction *ex parte*, until answer or further order. Then, in order to ascertain the fact of piracy or no piracy, it is referred to a master to examine into the originality of the new book, or the court takes upon itself the inspection of both works. Where the works are long and of a complex character, con-

---

[1] Sweet *v.* Mangham, 11 Sim. 51.
[2] Cornish *v.* Upton, 4 Law Times, N. S. 862.
[3] 2 Story's Eq. 249, § 936.
[4] Ibid. 254, § 941.

taining original matter mixed with much that is common property, they will be referred to a master; but where they are of a class affording facility for the detection of piracy by immediate inspection, the court will examine them."[1]

§ 16. "In cases of the invasion of a copyright by using the same materials in another work, of which a large proportion is original, it constitutes no objection, that an injunction will in effect stop the sale and circulation of the work, which so infringes upon the copyright."[2]

§ 17. The publication of *unpublished manuscripts* has been sometimes made the subject of injunction. It is said, "At common law, an author has a right to his unpublished manuscripts, the same as to any other property he may possess."[3] So it is held, that the writing and sending of a letter does not give the receiver a right to publish it. Although he may own the paper, and have a special property in the contents; the title to a copyright remains in the writer.[4] So it is said, "An injunction restraining the publication of private letters, must stand upon this foundation; that letters, whether of a private nature or upon general subjects, may be considered as the subject of literary property; and it is difficult to conceive, in the abstract, that they may not be so. A very instructive and useful work may be put into that shape, as an inviting mode of publication. In the cases referred to upon the letters of Pope, and Swift, and Lord Chesterfield, the subject derived its right to protection from its character of a literary composition; a character which did not cease, when it was put into the shape of letters."[5] Thus an injunction was granted in favor of the executors of Lord Chesterfield, against the widow and personal representative of his son and the publisher to restrain the

---

[1] Curtis, Copyr. 325.
[2] 2 Story's Eq. 258, § 942.
[3] Per McLean, J., Little v. Hall, 18 How. 170.

[4] Pope v. Curl, 2 Atk. 342.
[5] Per Sir Thos. Plumer, V. C., Perceval v. Phipps, 2 Ves. & B. 24.

publication of letters to his son.[1] So Lord Hardwicke granted an injunction against publication of the letters of Pope, though not of those received by him.[2] And injunctions were granted against publication of the letters of Swift and Burns.[3] So in Queensbury v. Shebheare,[4] an injunction was granted against the printing of the manuscript of Lord Clarendon's History, a copy of which had been given by Henry, Earl of Clarendon, to the father of the defendant, but not for the purpose of publication. So the publication of the manuscript of a work on book-keeping, without consent of the author, may be enjoined, though the system is not a complete one.[5] So an injunction was granted against the publication of letters from an old lady, under a weak attachment to a young man, there having been an agreement not to publish them, but to deliver them up for a valuable consideration, and a sum of money having been actually paid to the defendant.[6]

§ 18. Chancery has jurisdiction to restrain the publication of private correspondence, only on the ground of property, either in the composition, where it is valuable as a literary production, or in the paper on which the letters are written; and it will not interfere merely to prevent an injury to the feelings of the parties.[7] So an injunction against publishing private letters, alleged to have been obtained from an agent, to whom they were sent in confidence, was dissolved, upon the answer, denying confidence, and alleging, as the object of publication in the defendant's newspaper, not profit, but the vindication of his character from the public charge made by the plaintiff of giving false intelligence.[8] Nor, in general,

---

[1] Ambl. 737.
[2] Pope v. Curl, 2 Atk. 342.
[3] Thompson v. Stanhope, Ambl. 737 ; Cadell v. Stewart, 1 Bell, Com. 116 n.
[4] 2 Ed. 329.
[5] Bartlett v. Crittenden, 5 M'L. 32.
[6] ——— v. Eaton, cited in 2 Ves. & B. 22, 26.
[7] Wetmore v. Scovell, 3 Edw. Ch. 515.
[8] Perceval v. Phipps, 2 Ves. & B. 19.

will equity enjoin the publication of commercial or friendly letters; unless the publication would be a breach of trust.[1]

§ 19. It is said that property in a manuscript may be transferred or abandoned. But one who permits pupils to take copies of his manuscripts, for the purpose of instructing themselves and others, does not thereby abandon them to the public; and the publication of them will be restrained by injunction.[2]

§ 20. An injunction lies, to restrain the proprietor of one work from so advertising it as to lead to the belief that it is another, rival work; but not an advertisement in disparagement of the latter; although this might be good ground of action, as a libel.[3]

§ 21. In reference to *patents*, it is said: "If no other remedy could be given in cases of patents and copyrights, than an action at law for damages, the inventor or author might be ruined by the necessity of perpetual litigation, without ever being able to have a final establishment of his rights."[4]

§ 22. Where the right to a temporary injunction does not depend upon any controverted and doubtful facts, but upon the interpretation of a writing, the court is bound to interpret it, and grant or refuse the injunction accordingly.[5] So if, from the various transfers of a patent right, it is doubtful whether an action at law can be effectually brought; equity will take jurisdiction.[6] And where sufficient possession is made out, a doubt as to the validity of the patent will not necessarily prevent an injunction. The court will look to the circumstances, and the comparative inconvenience or loss

---

[1] Perceval *v.* Phipps, 2 Ves. & B. 19; Wetmore *v.* Scovell, 3 Edw. 515; 2 Ves. & B. 27; Granard *v.* Dunkin, 1 Ball & B. 207; Gee *v.* Pritchard, 2 Swanst. 402.

[2] 2 Kent, 378.
[3] Seeley *v.* Fisher, 11 Sim. 581.
[4] 2 Story's Eq. 245, § 931.
[5] Clum *v.* Brewer, 2 Curt. 506.
[6] Bicknell *v.* Todd, 5 McL. 236.

to be occasioned by granting or withholding it.[1]   So where
a court of equity, having heard a case on full proofs, is well
satisfied of the originality of an invention, the regularity of
the patent, and the fact of infringement; it will not send
the case to a jury, prior to granting a perpetual injunction.
Especially if the questions in the case, though questions of
fact, are such as the court can decide upon the testimony of
men of science, as well as, or better than, a jury; and where
a jury trial would be long, costly, or troublesome.[2]

§ 23. No specified time of use is requisite. It depends on
the extent as well as duration of the use or sales, the utility
of the invention, the number of persons interested in questioning the right, and the completeness of acquiescence in it.[3]

§ 24. Where a patent had been in force for twelve years,
and had been the subject of four suits against different persons, all of which terminated favorably to the patentee, and
in two of which verdicts had been given in favor of the
validity of the patent; it was held that, in a fifth case, the
patentee was entitled to an injunction, pending the trial of
the legal right, although a new fact was brought forward,
tending to impeach the novelty of the invention.[4]

§ 25. The distinction is made, that, where a patent is new,
the court considers the proof of the title in the patentee to
be wanting, inasmuch as the public have had no opportunity
of contesting its validity, and therefore refuses to interfere
by injunction until the title has been established at law; but
where there has been a long enjoyment and actual use under
a patent, the public have had an opportunity of contesting
the patent, and the fact of their not having done so successfully is at least *primâ facie* evidence that the title of the

---

[1] Sargent v. Seagrave, 2 Curt. 553.
[2] Goodyear v. Day, 2 Wall. Jr. 283.
See Washburne v. Gould, 3 Story,
122; Githins v. Symes, 28 Eng. Law
and Eq. 380; Sargent v. Larned, 2
Curt. 340; Clum v. Brewer, ib. 506;
Woodworth v. Stone, 3 Story, 749.
[3] Sargent v. Seagrave, 2 Curt. 553.
[4] Newall v. Wilson, 19 Eng. Law
and Eq. 156.

patentee is good; and the court therefore interferes, in such a case, before the right is established at law.[1]

§ 26. A., B., and C., being jointly interested in certain inventions, for which they had severally obtained patents, made A. their agent for selling the rights of using them. A., by fraud and deceit, and the aid of one D., induced E., F., and G. to buy such rights, and they paid therefor a sum of money, and gave their notes for the balance. H. purchased half the share of B. in the avails of such sales, thus becoming equally interested with A. and B. B. having previously, fraudulently, by the aid of I., bought C.'s share of such avails, I., concealing this fraud, persuaded E. to give him one note for $143 87, and another for $1,000; in consideration of which, E. should have the share of I. in the notes given to A. by E., F., and G., a large part of which were the notes of G., who was bankrupt. E. accordingly executed these notes, and the sum of $1,540 was indorsed on the notes given by E. and F. to A., on the sale of the rights, and $300 on the notes of G. G., in consideration of the indorsement on his notes, gave his note to E. for $300. The note for $143 87 was paid, and, suit being brought on the note for $1,000, judgment was rendered in favor of I., before the city court. The action was appealed to the court above, and was pending. I. took out execution, and $550 was paid thereon. E. was ignorant of the fraud practised in obtaining the notes from E., F., and G. to A. E. brought a petition against I., praying for an injunction against the proceedings at law, and for the repayment of the money paid on the execution and the note; and it was held, that he was entitled to the relief sought.[2]

§ 27. Where, on an application for an injunction, it appeared that the machine alleged to be an infringement contained the principle and substance of the plaintiff's invention,

[1] Caldwell v. Van Vlissengen, 9 Eng. Law and Eq. 51.   [2] Sackett v. Hillhouse, 5 Day, 551.

merely carrying it out further in practice than the plaintiff had done when he took out his patent; and that the form of construction of the defendant's machine was in law not even an improvement upon that of the plaintiff, because it was only the result of practical experience in the use of the plaintiff's machine; held, an injunction should be granted, and, the infringement being clear and the right to the injunction manifest, it was not to be stayed upon the defendants' (although they were pecuniarily responsible), giving security.[1]

§ 28. But equity will not enjoin the equitable owner of a patent, on petition of the legal owner.[2] And before a patentee can have an injunction, he must show an exclusive enjoyment, long enough to justify the presumption of a right, or an incontestable right.[3] Upon this subject, the following distinctions, substantially conformable to the cases already cited, are made: " Where a patent has been granted for an invention, it is not a matter of course for courts of equity to interpose by way of injunction. If the patent has been but recently granted, and its validity has not been ascertained by a trial at law, the court will not generally act upon its own notions of the validity or invalidity of the patent, and grant an immediate injunction; but it will require it to be ascertained by a trial in a court of law, if the defendant denies its validity, or puts the matter in doubt. But, if the patent has been granted for some length of time; and the patentee has put the invention into public use; and has had exclusive possession of it under his patent for a period of time, which may fairly create the just presumption of an exclusive right; the court will, in such a case, ordinarily interfere by way of preliminary injunction, pending the proceedings; reserving, of course, until the ultimate decision of the cause, its own final judgment on the merits. And an injunction will be granted not only before, but after

---

[1] Tracy v. Torrey. 2 Blatch. 275; Chamberlain v. Ganson, Ib. 279, note.

[2] Clum v. Brewer. 2 Curt. 506.
[3] Thomas v. Weeks, 2 Paine, 92.

26

the time limited for the expiration of a patent, to restrain
the sale of machines, piratically manufactured in violation of
the patent, while it was in force."[1]

§ 29. A., owning two-thirds of a patent right, filed a bill
against B., to whom he had sold the other third, to compel
the performance of an alleged agreement between them, by
which B. bound himself to discontinue the manufacturing,
under the patent, when he should have made enough to re-
imburse him certain advances, the bill alleging that he had
already made enough. The bill prayed that B. might be
decreed to discontinue; and an injunction restraining him
from manufacturing. B., by answer, which was read as an
affidavit, denied that he had yet reimbursed himself, and
that he was manufacturing under the patent, and claimed,
that the article he was manufacturing was not within the
patent, but a different article. The injunction was denied.[2]

§ 30. The amount of damage, which will follow from restraining the use of a machine held under a patent right, is
a proper consideration upon an application to suspend an
injunction.[3]

§ 31. A bill was filed against K. to restrain him from
violating the plaintiff's patent, and a provisional injunction
granted, and the court afterwards allowed a supplemental
bill, bringing in G. as a new party, and alleging new charges
in regard to K., so as to embrace transactions not covered by
the injunction, but of the same character. Held, the injunction must be extended so as to include them. It appearing
that G. was the clerk of K. from the commencement of the
suit, and knew of the suit and the proceedings, and on the
day the argument closed became the assignee of all K.'s
rights; held, on a motion for a provisional injunction against
G., that he took the subject-matter assigned him with only

---

[1] 2 Story Eq. 246, § 934.
[2] Parkhurst v. Kinsman, 2 Halst.
Ch. 600.
[3] Barnard v. Gibson, 7 How. U. S.
650.

the same rights that K. had, and did not stand before the court as an independent infringer. Held, also, that as G. was merely a volunteer in the controversy, and intermeddled in it after the decision in K.'s case was known, he was the substitute of K., and that an injunction must issue against him.[1]

§ 32. Where a bond was executed by the defendant to the plaintiff, acknowledging the validity of the plaintiff's patent and his right to all that was granted by it, four months before the service of an injunction on the defendant; held, the bond was no evidence of a breach of the injunction, any further than the recital in it, that the defendant had infringed the patent, might have a tendency to establish such breach; but no inference or presumption arising from it could overcome the weight of credible, positive testimony that there was no infringement.[2]

§ 33. Under the common law procedure act of 1854, § 82, the court will grant in the first instance only a rule *nisi* for an injunction; and, upon cause shown, will give such directions as would be given by a court of equity.[3]

§ 34. The plaintiffs obtained an injunction against infringing the patent of a fire-engine of twenty-seven years' standing, in order that there might be a trial at law. They recovered a verdict, but upon a case stated the court were divided. Held, another action must be brought, but the court would not impose terms on the plaintiff, nor dissolve the injunction. Lord Loughborough said: "What has passed does not shake their right; but strongly supports it. The verdict, though it has failed of effect, is not to be disregarded."[4]

§ 35. On motion to dissolve an injunction, upon affidavits,

[1] Parkhurst v. Kinsman, 2 Blatch. 78.
[2] Byam v. Eddy, 2 Blatch. 521.
[3] Gittins v. Symes, 28 Eng. Law and Eq. 380.
[4] Boulton v. Bull, 3 Ves., Jr., 140.

the defendant's proof must overcome the equity of the bill and the evidence in its support.[1]

§ 36. Where the district judge, sitting for the Circuit Court, and being satisfied of an infringement, had granted an interlocutory injunction till trial, and the presiding judge, after hearing the testimony at such trial, differed from the district judge, who upon the same testimony adhered to his former opinion, and the jury failed to agree; held, the full court were not bound either to retain or dissolve the injunction; and they ordered that it be dissolved upon the defendant's giving security to account.[2]

§ 37. Where one of three parties runs a machine, and the other two own it, an injunction is proper against all.[3]

§ 38. If a license to use a patented machine be conditional, the conditions must be performed, in order to justify such use; and an attempt to use it will be an infringement authorizing an injunction, as there is no adequate remedy at law.[4]

§ 39. Circumstances sometimes require an *account* in connection with an injunction. Thus, on a motion for a provisional injunction, the originality of the invention was strongly denied by affidavit, and it appeared that there had been three trials at law on the question of originality, in the first of which the jury found against the patent, in the second did not agree, and in the third found in its favor. The court suspended a decision on the motion, and ordered a trial by jury, directing that in the meantime the defendant keep an account, and report monthly, under oath, to the clerk. The question of infringement was also ordered to be tried by the same jury.[5]

[1] Sparkman v. Higgins, 1 Blatch. 205.   See Orr v. Merrill, W. & M. 376; Woodworth v. Stone, 3 Story, 749.
[2] Wilson v. Barnum, Wall., Jr., 347.
[3] Woodworth v. Edwards, 3 W. & M. 120.
[4] Brooks v. Stolley, 3 McL. 523.
[5] Allen v. Sprague, 1 Blatch. 567. See the Troy, &c. v. Corning, ib. 467.

§ 40. Somewhat analogous to patents and copyrights, and of late even more frequently made the subject-matter of injunction, are *trade-marks*. It is said, "No man has a right to dress himself in colors, or adopt and bear symbols, to which he has no peculiar or exclusive right, and thereby personate another person, for the purpose of inducing the public to suppose either that he is that other person, or that he is connected with, and selling the manufacture of such other person, while he is really selling his own."[1]

§ 40 a. With reference to the interference of equity in enjoining the use of an article not patented, the court in a late case remark, "Different grounds have been assigned for the exercise of that jurisdiction. In some cases it has been referred to property, in others to contract, and in others, again, it has been treated as founded upon trust or confidence."[2] And in another later case it is said : "This right cannot be properly described as a copyright; it is, in fact, a right which can be said to exist only and can be tested only by its violation. Any one, who has adopted a particular mode of designating his particular manufacture, has a right to say, not that other persons shall not sell exactly the same article, better or worse, or an article looking exactly like it, but that they shall not sell it in such a way as to steal (so to call it) his trade-mark, and make purchasers believe that it is the manufacture to which that trade-mark was originally applied."[3]

§ 41. The general rule is, that, where a manufacturer

[1] Per Lord Langdale, Croft *v.* Day, 7 Beav. 88.
[2] Per V. C., Morrison *v.* Moat, 9 Hare, 255.
[3] Per Ld. Cranworth, Farina *v.* Silverlock, 39 Eng. Law and Eq. 516.(*a*)

(*a*) This was the case of Johann Maria Farina, the well-known manufacturer of eau de Cologne. It would appear from a remark of the court, that he claimed to be "descended from a line of ancestors who for a hundred and fifty years have manufactured the article." The label in question was "Johann Maria Farina gegenüber dem Jülichs Platz."

adopts a certain trade-mark, and stamps it upon the article manufactured, he is entitled to the exclusive use of it, and a court of equity will restrain, by injunction, any other person who pirates such trade-mark from using it. It is no defence, that the simulated article is of equal value with the genuine. And an alien manufacturer may maintain a bill for such injunction against a citizen of the United States.[1] In an alleged infringement of a right to trade-marks, the court must ascertain whether the resemblances and the differences are such as naturally arise from the necessity of the case, or whether, on the other hand, the differences are simply colorable, and the resemblances such as are obviously intended to deceive the purchaser.[2] And slight differences, which would not be perceived without strict examination, will not protect the imitation from the injunction.[3] An action to enjoin the use of a trade-mark cannot be resisted, by showing that the names used on the trade-mark are false and fictitious.[4]

§ 42. A manufacturer of steel pens put up his pens for sale in boxes of a gross each, and numbered the boxes. No. 303 denoted extra fine pointed pens, and No. 753 inferior pens, the former being sold by the manufacturer for 75 cents per gross, the latter for 18 cents. The defendant was in the practice of removing the maker's labels from the boxes containing inferior pens, and putting thereon labels made in imitation of the manufacturer's, denoting superior pens. Held, a fraud on the manufacturer and on the public, and productive of damage to both, and the defendant was enjoined from continuing it.[5] So a manufacturer of soap, who has adopted peculiar names, marks, and labels, not before used, in order to designate his own manufacture, which serve to notify purchasers that his peculiar skill in combining the ingredients has been employed, will be protected in equity

[1] Taylor v. Carpenter, 11 Paige, 292.
[2] Taylor v. Taylor, 23 Eng. Eq. 281.
[3] Williams v. Johnson, 2 Bosw. 1.
[4] Stewart v. Smithson, 1 Hilt. 119.
[5] Gillot v. Kettle, 3 Duer, 624.

against fraudulent imitations by others. The court will grant an injunction for that purpose.[1]

§ 48. But the right of a party to the exclusive use of a peculiar label or representation, as, for example, for a medicine which he compounds, must be clear, before he is entitled to an injunction. If the parties were jointly engaged in first getting up the medicine, in view of a contemplated copartnership; though a few other ingredients may have been added to the compound by one of the parties, he will not be entitled to an injunction restraining the other from using marks or labels similar to his, until the matter of right has been determined by an action at law, or otherwise.[2] And in a very late case the distinction is taken, that a person who has appropriated to himself a particular label, sign, or trademark, indicating that a certain article is made or sold by him or his authority, and with which label or trade-mark the article has become indentified, is entitled to the protection of a court of equity, which will enjoin any one who attempts to pirate upon the good-will of his friends or customers by using such label, sign, or trade-mark without his authority. But there must be, between the genuine and fictitious marks, such general similarity or resemblance of form, color, symbols, designs, and such identity of words, and their arrangement, as to have a direct tendency to mislead buyers who exercise the usual amount of prudence and caution; and there must also be such a distinctive individuality in the mark employed by the counterfeiter, as to procure to him the benefit of the deception, resulting from the general resemblance between the genuine and the counterfeit labels or trade-marks.[3] So, after an injunction against the use of trade-marks, a motion to commit the defendant for a breach will not be allowed, if the plaintiff has acquiesced, and indicated a low estimation of the value of the interest in ques-

[1] 2 Bosw. 1.
[2] Coffeen v. Brunton, 5 McLean, 256.
[3] Colladay v. Baird, 7 Upper Canada Law Journal, 132.

tion.[1] So a bill for injunction was held bad on demurrer, which alleged that the defendant manufactured and sold certain medicine under the name of medicine manufactured by the plaintiff, but without assuming the name and character of the plaintiff. The Vice Chancellor remarked : " This bill proceeds upon an erroneous notion of exclusive property now subsisting in this medicine, which Swanson, having purchased, had a right to dispose of by his will ; and, as it is contended, to give the plaintiff the exclusive right of sale. If this claim of monopoly can be maintained, without any limitation of time, it is a much better right than that of a patentee ; but the violation of right, with which the defendant is charged, does not fall within the cases in which the court has restrained a fraudulent attempt by one man to invade another's property ; to appropriate the benefit of a valuable interest in the nature of good-will, consisting in the character of his trade or production, established by individual merit ; the other representing himself to be the same person, and his trade or production the same—combining imposition on the public with injury to the individual.—The bill, stating the defendant's medicine to be spurious, asserts it not to be the same as the plaintiff's.— The defendant merely represents that he sells, not the plaintiff's medicine, but one of as good a quality."[2] So where the plaintiff's trade-mark contained the words " Merrimack Prints. Fast Colors. Lowell, Mass.," but the defendant's was in this form: " English Free Trade. Merrimack Style. Warranted Fast Colors," and the embellishments surrounding both were similar to each other ; it was held, that the resemblance was not sufficient to warrant an injunction, pending a suit at law.[3] So B. had acquired a reputation as a watchmaker, and all watches made by him were stamped with his name. He sold S. the right to stamp his (B.'s) name on

[1] Rogers v. Nowill, 19 Eng. Law and Eq. 83.
[2] Cauham v. Jones, 2 Ves. and B. 218, 221.
[3] Merrimack, &c. v. Garner, 4 E. D. Smith, 387.

watches made by S.   S. assigned to the plaintiffs the right
to stamp B.'s name on watches made by them.   The defendant sold watches made by B. and stamped with his name;
and a motion for an injunction to restrain him from so doing
was denied.[1]   So a bill was filed by a trading company, incorporated by the law of Connecticut, for an injunction to
restrain a manufacturer of Birmingham from continuing the
fraudulent use of the trade-marks of the company, and for
an account of profit.   The answer admitted the use, but relied on a custom, prevalent at Birmingham, for manufacturers
of goods of the kind sold by the company, to affix on the
goods ordered by merchants a particular trade-mark, relying
on the respectability of the merchant, when known to them,
for the fact that those merchants had authority to act as agents
of, or by way of license from, the person entitled to the exclusive use of the trade-marks; and alleged that the defendant
had been informed, that the company themselves had ordered
goods to be manufactured at Birmingham, with their own
trade-mark upon them, for the purpose of sale in foreign
countries.   These statements were not contradicted.   Ordered
that an interim injunction should be continued for a year,
with liberty to the company to bring an action and proceed
to trial within that time, otherwise the bill should stand dismissed with costs.[2]

§ 44. Equity cannot restrain, by injunction, the use of a
trade-mark, which in part consists of the name of one, with
whom a part of the defendants were partners, and which was
invented, adopted, and used by them in his lifetime, without
objection, and has been used by them ever since.   But, under
(Mass.) Gen. Sts., c. 56, § 4, his executors may enjoin the
use of his name in their business and firm, without his
written consent, or that of his executors, and, as the statute
forbids not only the assumption but the continued use of the

---

[1] Samuel v. Berger, 24 Barb. 163.   [2] Collins Company v. Reeves, 28
L. J. Chanc. 56.

name of another person, the injunction may be granted, though it has been used more than six years.[1]

§ 45. A perpetual injunction was ordered, and an account for six years, though the defendant was not aware that the mark was the property of the plaintiff or of any other person.[2] But an injunction to restrain the sale of bottles, stamped with the plaintiff's name and address, followed by the words "genuine superior aerated waters," and containing soda water not manufactured by the plaintiff, was dissolved, the court being of opinion, upon the evidence, that the defendant was not shown to have used the bottles with an intention, or with the effect, of misleading the public, though the latter alone would be sufficient ground of injunction.[3]

§ 46. The plaintiffs and defendants were engaged in similar business. Fifteen months after the lease of the plaintiffs' premises had expired, the defendants procured a lease of the same works, with the exception of mines of clay, and issued a circular and card tending to give the impression that the defendants had succeeded to the business of the plaintiffs, and were working the same material which they had formerly used. Held, though the circular and card might be literally true, they might be restrained by injunction.[4]

§ 47. A plaintiff and another person, who carried on distinct trades at different places of business, had derived from a common predecessor in their respective callings the right to use the name of *Dent* as a trade-mark. The defendant having infringed this right, held, the plaintiff, without averring special damage, might sue alone for an injunction, and for the delivering up of the articles so marked, to have the name erased.[5]

---

[1] Bowman *v.* Floyd, 3 Allen, 76.
[2] Cartier *v.* Carlisle, 8 Jur. N. S. 183.
[3] Welch *v.* Knott, 4 Kay & J. 747.
[4] Harper *v.* Pearson, 3 L. T. N. S. 547.

[5] Dent *v.* Turpin, Tucker *v.* Turpin, 2 Johnson & Hemming, 139 ; 7 Jur. N. S. 673 ; L. J. Chanc. 495 ; 9 W. R. 548 ; 4 L. T. N. S. 637.

§ 48. Declaration, that A., the plaintiff, agreed with B., the defendant, to manufacture for B. fire-bricks, to be marked as B. should direct; that he directed that they should be marked with C.'s name, he well knowing that C. manufactured fire-bricks thus marked to indicate that they were manufactured by him; that A., ignorant of the manufacture of fire-bricks by C., and that marking fire-bricks according to the direction of the defendant would be wrongful, manufactured fire-bricks for the defendant and marked them with the name of C.; that C. filed a bill for an injunction and account against the plaintiff, and that the plaintiff, in order to compromise the suit, paid C. a sum of money. Held, the declaration disclosed two grounds of action : first, because the plaintiff was liable to the injunction, although he used the trade-mark of C. innocently; second, because the natural consequence of the defendant's act was to involve the plaintiff in a chancery suit, even if he had the means of defending it, by reason of his having used the trade-mark of C. innocently.[1]

§ 49. Where A. is ordered by B. to manufacture an article and stamp it with a trade-mark not B.'s, that alone leads to suspicion. A., having caused the article to be manufactured, and admitting having casually heard of the party entitled to use such trade-mark, must submit to a perpetual injunction, and pay costs.[2] So the defendant innocently used the plaintiff's trade-marks, and, on being served with the bill, he removed the labels, and gave an undertaking not to sell any more, but refused to pay the costs. The suit was continued to a hearing, and the account of profits, which were very trifling, was waived. Held, the defendant must pay the whole costs of suit.[3] So a suit was instituted to restrain the use of a trade-mark, and for an account. No application was made to the defendant before suit; and he said he would

[1] Dixon v. Fawous, 7 Jur. N. S. 895, 30 L. J. Q. B. 137.
[3] Collins Company v. Walker, 7 W. R. 222; V. C. K.
[2] Burgess v. Hill, 26 Beav. 244 ; 5 Jur. N. S. 233, 28 L. J. Chanc. 356.

have desisted if applied to.   At the hearing the account was abandoned, but a perpetual injunction was granted.   Held, he must pay the costs.[1]

§ 50. Petition for an injunction against the use of a certain name and mark upon goods, being cutlery, alleged to be made in imitation of the celebrated cutlery of *Rodgers & Company.*   The defendants admitted such use, but claimed that it was their true name, and a right to use it.   The plaintiffs, without moving for the injunction, went into evidence in equity.   At the hearing, the court, being of opinion that the right to an injunction was not established, but that the name and mark were so used as to give the false impression that the goods were manufactured by the plaintiffs, gave the defendants the option, either of a dismissal of the bill without costs, or of having a trial at law.   The bill being retained for a year, with liberty to bring an action, the action was brought, and the plaintiffs recovered a verdict.   Held, an injunction should be granted, with costs at law and in equity, except the costs of the evidence in equity.   In the same case the court refused to require the defendants to make any admissions upon the trial at law.[2]

§ 51. Upon the principle of trade-marks, an injunction lies against *the disclosure of secrets,* communicated to a party in the course of a confidential employment; whether secrets of trade, of title, or otherwise important to the interests of the plaintiff.[3]   And a party may be restrained from using a secret, as for instance that of compounding a medicine not protected by patent, if imparted to him, to his knowledge, in breach of faith or contract.   Thus A., the sole inventor and proprietor of such medicine, upon entering into partnership with B., as manufacturers and vendors of the medicine, for the purposes of the partnership, communicated to the latter the

[1] Burgess *v.* Hately, 26 Beav. 249.
[2] Rodgers *v.* Nowill, 6 Hare, 325. And see Beaufort *v.* Morris, 6 Hare, 340.
[3] Cholmondeley *v.* Clinton, 19 Ves. 261 ; Kvitt *v.* Price, 1 Sim. 483 ; Youatt *v.* Winyard, 1 Jac. & W. 394.

secret. By the partnership deed, either party was empowered to introduce another partner, by deed, to be attested by the other; and, by mutual bonds of even date, A. bound himself not to communicate the secret to any person except a partner so introduced; whilst B. bound himself not to communicate such secret to any person. A. afterwards introduced his sons, the plaintiffs, into the partnership; and B., shortly before his death, in breach of his bond, communicated the secret to the defendant, his son; and then, by deed, duly attested by A., appointed the defendant his successor in the partnership. Shortly after the death of B., the defendant joined A. and the plaintiffs, who were ignorant that he had obtained a knowledge of the secret, in executing a partnership deed, declaring the defendant a sleeping partner, and by which the partners covenanted not to divulge the secret. The defendant also afterwards executed deeds, reciting that the sole property in the secret was in A. A. afterwards died, having bequeathed his property in the secret to the plaintiffs. After the determination of the partnership, the defendant made use of his knowledge of the secret communicated to him by his father, in manufacturing medicine, which he sold as the medicine originally manufactured by A. The court granted an injunction, restraining the defendant from selling, under the title or designation of "Morison's Medicine," any medicine manufactured by the defendant; and also from compounding any medicines according to the secret mentioned in the plaintiff's bill, and from in any way making use of such secret.[1]

§ 52. An injunction will be granted against publishing a magazine in the name of one who no longer authorizes it.[2] Or against assuming the name of a newspaper published by the plaintiff, for the purpose of deceiving the public, and supplanting the good-will of such paper.[3] Or, as has been seen, against the sale, under the name of the plaintiff, with

---

[1] Morison v. Moat, 6 Eng. Law and Eq. 14; 9 Hare, 241.
[2] Hogg v. Kirby, 8 Ves. 215.
[3] Bell v. Locke, 8 Paige, 75.

false labels, of an article of trade by the sale of which he has acquired a reputation.[1] So an injunction lies, against the running of omnibuses, bearing names, words, and devices which colorably imitate those on the omnibuses of the plaintiff.[2]

§ 53. Equity may restrain by injunction a breach of a contract, between two copartners in the practice of medicine and surgery, not to settle in practice, after the expiration of the copartnership, within a certain distance of each other.[3] So, where the plaintiff had sold out to the defendant the lease and good-will of a shop, giving him a bond, with penalty, against selling brandy within a certain place and a certain time; and the defendant brought an action upon the bond, and had a verdict for the penalty: an injunction was granted to the plaintiff, in order that an issue at law might determine the amount of the damage.[4] But the court will not enjoin a judgment recovered for the consideration of the good-will of a trade sold to the plaintiff, with an agreement not to carry on the same business, and to assist the plaintiff in procuring custom, &c. Lord Eldon remarked: "The parties may ascertain for themselves what shall be the damages from time to time; and unless they are so awkward as to put that in the shape of a penalty, instead of liquidated damages, there is a perfect and absolute remedy."[4] And the injuries to the "good-will" of a trade, by the establishment of a rival enterprise, are held to be those in which some deception is practised upon the customers of the prior establishment, or upon the public.[6]

§ 54. A person who had formerly been editor of the "National Advocate," a newspaper published in New York, started another paper, to be published at the same office, entitled the "New York National Advocate," and openly

[1] Motley v. Downman, 3 My. & C. 1; Millington v. Fox, ib. 338.
[2] Knott v. Morgan, 2 Keen, 213.
[3] Butler v. Barleson, 16 Verm. 176.

[4] Hardy v. Martin, 1 Cox, 26.
[5] Shackle v. Baker, 14 Ves. 468.
[6] Snowden v. Noah, Hopk. 347.

appealed to the friends of the "National Advocate," and to the public, to support his paper; and an injunction to restrain the publication of the new paper was refused.[1]

§ 55. A., with two physicians, B. and C., established an insane asylum and an immigrant lazaretto. The parties quarrelled, and A. obtained an injunction to restrain B. and C. from visiting the asylum, and they obtained one to restrain him from disposing of the asylum. Both asked for receivers. Held, that a receiver should be appointed, and, as the good-will of the concern was the most valuable part of it, the receiver should sell the concern with the good-will, and both parties should be restrained from carrying on the same business in New York, where the asylum was situated.[2]

[1] Snowden v. Noah, Hopk. 347.　　　[2] Williams v. Wilson, 4 Sandf. Ch. 379.

CHAPTER XXVI.

ROADS; RAILROADS; CANALS; BRIDGES; FERRIES.

§ 1. INJUNCTIONS are sometimes applied for in reference to public roads.

§ 1 *a*. Where a company, incorporated to construct a plank road, had completed their road, put it in use, and erected a toll-gate opposite the defendant's land, and the defendant opened and worked a road on his own land parallel to, and adjoining the plank road, so that it was passable for travellers, and was used by them to pass the gate, to the prejudice of, and loss of toll to the company; held, the court might restrain the defendant by perpetual injunction from keeping his road open, or permitting it to be kept open, so as to be used for the public travel; and order that it be so closed, as to hinder persons travelling on the plank road from using it as an open road.[1]

§ 2. Equity will not, on the application of trustees of a turnpike road, passing over a hill, who were empowered to lower it when necessary, restrain an adjoining freeholder from making a tunnel under the road, on the ground that it would obstruct the future improvement of the road.[2]

[1] Auburn, &c. *v.* Douglass, 12 Barb. 553.

[2] Cunliffe *v.* Whalley, 17 Eng. Law and Eq. 503.

§ 2 *a*. If a city (in **Massachusetts**), laying out a street so as to compel the removal of buildings, assess to the owner a certain sum in lieu of all damages for such removal; his remedy, if aggrieved, is by petition for a jury, not by injunction.[1]

§ 3. The remedy of injunction, as of other forms of action, is often invoked in reference to *railroads*. Many of the rules of law upon the subject will be found referred to in other connections; more particularly in the chapter—XV.—relating to corporations.[2]

§ 4. In a late case it is remarked, "I think it most essential to the interests of the public, that such jurisdiction should exist, and should be exercised whenever a proper case for it is brought before the court, otherwise the result may be, that, after your house has been pulled down, and a railway substituted in its place, you may have the satisfaction, at a future period, of discovering that the railway company were wrong."[3] And in another case, where, after an injunction against a railroad company, restraining them from so constructing the railway as to obstruct, impede, or render less secure the road in question, the defendants laid permanent rails, on a level, and by order of the commissioners erected gates and opened the line; upon the ground that "their conduct was at once contemptuous and otherwise illegal, wrongful as against the plaintiff, her Majesty's subjects at large, and indeed a bad, almost a scandalous example—a daring invasion of public and private rights;" the court ordered a sequestration.[4]

§ 5. In the State of **Pennsylvania**, the equity power of injunction was disclaimed in reference to a railroad corpora-

[1] Nichols *v*. Salem, 14 Gray, 490.
[2] See Gregg *v*. Baltimore, 14 Md. 479; Spooner *v*. McConnel, 1 McL. 338; M'Arthur *v*. Kelly, 5 Ohio, 139; Mayor, &c. *v*. Curtis, 1 Clarke, 336; Agar *v*. The Regent's, &c., Coop. 77; River, &c. *v*. North, &c., 1 Railw. Cas. 135; Sandford *v*. The Railway Co., 24

Penn. 378; Amelung *v*. Seekamp, 9 Gill & J. 468; Jarden *v*. Philadelphia, &c. 3 Whart. 502; Browning *v*. Camden, &c., 3 Green, 47.
[3] Per Lord Cottingham, River, &c. *v*. North, &c. 1 Railw. C. 135.
[4] The Att'y, &c. *v*. The Great, &c., 3 Eng. Law and Eq. 263.

27

tion, by reason of the restrictive terms of an express statute; but the observations of the eminent judge, who delivered the opinion of the court, indicate the practical value and importance of this summary jurisdiction.

§ 6. In the case of Hays v. The Pennsylvania Railroad,[1] it was held that the equity powers of the Supreme Court, in reference to corporations other than municipal, by the statute of 1836, if not restricted to Philadelphia, are no where any greater than those of a Court of Common Pleas. Hence the Supreme Court, sitting at Harrisburg, cannot control the doings of the Pennsylvania Railroad beyond the county of Dauphin. Gibson, C. J., remarks, " Had the power been conferred upon the Supreme Court alone, it would have enabled us to retain the present bill, but, conferred in the same clause upon the Common Pleas, it leads irresistibly to the conclusion that the design was to give them exactly the same jurisdiction. The Supreme Court, standing on a foundation no broader, and exercising a jurisdiction not more extensive than the foundation and jurisdiction of a Court of Common Pleas, could not supervise or control the proceedings of a corporation whose field of action extends from the Susquehanna to the Ohio.—'Noscitur a Sociis.' It is unnecessary to ask why such jurisdiction has been withheld. It has been the policy of the legislature, from the foundation of the province, to dole out equitable power to the courts with a parsimonious hand. Happily this policy is fast yielding to a more enlightened one. Though the power to issue writs of injunction is a despotic one, which ought to be exercised in the first instance with great caution and only in the clearest and most indisputable cases, it is an invaluable and indispensable one. A writ of quo warranto would lie in a case like the present; but the object of a corporator is not to destroy the charter, but to preserve it. Gigantic corporations may acquire, from combination of capital and the patronage they create, a dangerous influence; and the legislature could curb it only

[1] 17 Penn. 9.

by the instrumentality of the judiciary; but to make the instrument effective, would require it to be invested with an adequate degree of power."[1]

§ 7. The granting of a right of way to a street railroad, by the common council of a city, is not an act of legislation, but a grant upon condition, and may be restrained by injunction.[2] But an injunction has been refused when applied for upon the ground that a railroad charter was unconstitutional.[3]

§ 8. The question of injunction often depends upon the judgment or action of some tribunal other than the court to which the petition is addressed.

§ 9. In New Jersey, though, in the opinion of the chancellor, the Somerville and Easton Railroad Company could not apply for commissioners of valuation and damages until the route of the whole road should be located; yet he refused an injunction to restrain the company from applying for commissioners to value a part located, before a location of the whole route.[4] And it is said an injunction lies to restrain the opening of a road, where the railroad commissioners had ordered a postponement of such opening.[5]

§ 10. Upon the question of arching over a street in connection with a station, an action was ordered before the Barons of the Exchequer to settle the point whether "it was necessary or reasonably convenient." Upon their answering in the affirmative, held, the injunction should be dissolved.[6]

§ 11. Questions of *engineering* are ordinarily referred to an engineer.[7]

[1] Ib. pp. 12, 13.
[2] People v. Sturtevant, 5 Seld. 263.
[3] Deering v. York, &c., 31 Maine, 172.
[4] Doughty v. Somerville, &c., 3 Halst. Ch. 51.
[5] Redf. on Railw., 488.
[6] Att'y, &c. v. The Eastern, &c., 2 Railw. Cas. 823.
[7] Webb v. The Manchester, &c., 4 My. & Cr. 116.

§ 12. A railway company were building an embankment more than five feet above the level, according to the 11th and 12th sections of the railway clauses consolidation act. They had not given the notice required by the 12th section, but had obtained the consent required by the 11th. The court put them on terms to take the opinion of the *board of trade*, submitting to such order as this court should thereafter make; otherwise an injunction would go to restrain the company from proceeding with the embankment.[1]

§ 13. Where a company was authorized to make a direct line of railway, with a branch, and was about to complete and open the direct line, but had abandoned the branch line; held, the attorney-general had no right to file an information to restrain the opening of the direct line, as a means of compelling the completion of the branch, alleging that the abandonment of the branch line was an injury to the public.[2] And it is held that, upon an injunction bill, equity will not decide upon the legal title of two railroad companies to a certain route.[3](a) So A., a railway company, had entered

[1] Pearce v. Wycombe, &c., 19 Eng. Law and Eq. 122.
[2] Attorney-General v. The Birmingham, &c., 8 Eng. Law and Eq. 243.
[3] Morris, &c. v. Blair, 1 Stockt. 635.

(a) It may seem not inappropriate to insert here a newspaper report, probably accurate in substance, of the latest case involving the rights of two railroad corporations :—

"THE GREAT RAILROAD CASE.—The United States Circuit Court, Judges Davis and Treat, yesterday, refused the injunction prayed for by a portion of the stockholders in the Galena and Chicago Railroad Company, to restrain the consolidation of that road with the Northwestern Railroad Company, and for the appointment of a receiver, &c. The court, in refusing the injunction, declined to decide upon the merits of the case; but, nevertheless, the decision is a virtual refusal to set aside the consolidation. One of the strongest points made in the argument was, that the consolidation, which was made over a year ago, was of so gigantic a character that, to overturn and destroy it at this day, was to disturb a system of railways, and overthrow a series of financial and commercial operations, affecting the property and business of thousands

into a contract with B., another company, as to the working of their line. A. now alleged that the contract was void, and proposed to enter into an agreement with the C. company, the effect of which would be a violation of the contract with B. B. moved for an injunction to restrain A. from holding a meeting to sanction the agreement. The court refused to interfere, as it was not clear that the contract with B. was valid, and as the loss of A. from not entering into the agreement with C. might be greater than their loss from violating the contract with B.[1] But, in Pennsylvania, an injunction was granted, in a case turning wholly upon the construction of the charter under which the defendants claimed, and indeed upon the meaning of particular words in that charter; (which however must be read at length, in order to understand the precise points in controversy.) The history of this case, as given in the opinion of the court, is as follows: "In 1837, the legislature incorporated the Sun-

[1] Shrewsbury, &c. v. Shrewsbury, &c., 4 Eng. Law and Eq. 171.

---

of people, who, in no way connected with the consolidation itself, have in good faith acted upon its existence. The court evidently felt the force of this consideration, and therefore refused an injunction, or any other proceedings calculated, however remotely, to disturb the immense interests involved, and the vast works in operation by the consolidated companies. They virtually, if not in fact, decided, that the consolidation was to stand, but that the non-consenting stockholders should be made whole as to the value of their property on the day the consolidation took place. This reduces the question at issue to a mere pecuniary one, viz.: how much the stockholders of the Galena Road are equitably entitled to for their interest? The terms of the consolidation offered them a certain sum; they claimed a greater; the difference between the two valuations is possibly somewhere between fifty and eighty thousand dollars. The great point, however, in which the public are interested is that decided by the court—that the consolidation will not be disturbed or set aside. The amount which the non-consenting stockholders may justly claim is a matter affecting only themselves and the corporation; the public may dismiss their fears that the consolidation which, in its vast scheme, includes so inextricably so many interests, will be broken. That point determined, the other questions involved are of mere personal interest."—*Chicago Republican*, July 9.

bury and Erie Railroad Company, with authority to make a railroad from Sunbury to Erie, but without any authority to extend their work *further south or east than Sunbury.* By this, their original charter, they had no more right to make a road from Sunbury to Harrisburg than if they had never been incorporated at all. Such was the state of things in 1851, when the charter was given to the Susquehanna Company. The act which brought the latter company into being gave them the privilege of constructing their railroad along the Susquehanna River between Harrisburg and Sunbury, by a route to which nobody else had any right or pretence of claim. On the faith of this unequivocal grant of authority to construct their work on a track then entirely open to their enterprise, they raised the capital necessary for the purpose, and prepared to commence it. It is at this stage of their progress that the Sunbury and Erie Company set up their claim as grantees from the state of the same privilege, and assert that they, too, have a legal right to make a road between the same termini, along the same valley, and by the same intermediate points. Did the legislature intend that these two companies should each have equal authority to construct the same identical work? It seems to us extremely improbable. The struggle between two companies, invested with the same privileges, each having an equal right to the ground, would be more likely to end in the ruin of both, than to give either a fair chance of success. Legislation like this would not only be injurious in its effect on the public interest, but it would be a wrong on the company first incorporated—such a violation of justice as no one would expect to see perpetrated by the representatives of a people who love the right and hate the wrong. The improbability that the rival corporations were intended to be clothed with equal power to make the same road along the same route, is infinitely increased when we find that no provision is made for settling the innumerable disputes which must necessarily arise between them. We assume that it is practicable to make both roads, nevertheless the choice of the best location may be of such immense value to the party which gets it that it would be fiercely contended for. How is such a contest to be settled? Shall it be determined by the wager of battle? The struggle would not cease with the survey; and when the building of the two roads would bring thither thousands of excitable men, the probability of violence and bloodshed would be very great. Supposing the road to be made, and the cars and locomotives running side by side, and sometimes crossing each other's track, what hope could be entertained that they would regard each other's convenience and interest in such a manner as to keep the peace and avoid collisions dangerous to property and life?"[1]

§ 14. A very common application for injunction is that made on behalf of some other privilege with which a railroad comes in competition or collision. Thus the defendants, a railroad company, were enjoined, on application of the State, from filling up a part of the State canal, and erecting an arch over it, which would obstruct its use; though this portion of the canal had been for many years abandoned, and without regard to the question of damage.[2]

§ 15. In case of petition for an injunction, restraining the defendants, a railroad company, from crossing the road of the plaintiffs, except by a bridge; the question of right was sent to the Court of Exchequer, who found for the plaintiffs. Held, an injunction should be suspended, in order to give time for building the bridge, the defendants undertaking to build it as speedily as possible.[3]

§ 16. An injunction was granted to prevent an improper mode of carrying a turnpike over a railroad.[4] So where the highway commissioners, on petition of the defendant, had laid out and recorded a private way from his land across the

[1] Per Black, C. J., Packer v. Sunbury, &c., 19 Penn. 216.
[2] Com. v. Pittsburg, &c., 24 Penn. 159. Acc. Hudson, &c. Canal v. New York, &c., 9 Paige, 323.
[3] Northern, &c. v. The London, &c., 1 Railw. Cas. 653.
[4] Atty., &c. v. London, &c., 3 De G. & S. 439.

ropes and fixtures of the inclined plane of a railway.[1] And, on the other hand, an injunction was denied, to restrain the removal by a turnpike road of stone blocks laid across the road by a railroad company, in order to pass from the railroad to a wharf; the charter only authorizing the company to use the turnpike as it was, or requiring a tunnel or bridge if they crossed the road.[2]

§ 17. An injunction has been denied in favor of a toll bridge against a railroad bridge.[3](a)

[1] Mohawk, &c. v. Artober, 6 Paige, 83.

[2] London, &c. v. Cooper, 2 Railw. Cas. 312.

[3] Tucker v. Cheshire, &c., 1 Fost. 29.

(a) See ? 41. In 1790, the legislature authorized A. to build a toll bridge across Harlem River, a navigable river, and provided that no other bridge or ferry should be erected or maintained between the two places connected thereby, except for the private use of the inhabitants of those two places. In 1832, a railroad company was authorized to cross the same river, near A.'s bridge. A bridge having been previously built for the private use of the inhabitants, according to the reservation in the grant to A., the railroad company purchased and used it for their railroad, which use diminished the receipts of A.'s bridge. Held, that the charter to the railroad company, and the use of the bridge for the railroad, were no violation of the grant of a franchise to A., and that he could not restrain them by injunction. Also, that the railroad company, having been authorized to build a bridge for their railroad, were thereby authorized to buy, for the same purpose, a bridge already built. That the owners were also authorized to sell their bridge as they had done. That the railroad company might be restrained by injunction from allowing persons to cross their bridge who were not authorized to cross by law. That the defendants could not object, in a suit to restrain a violation of a franchise which had become vested in the grantee, that the complainants had violated their franchise : there having been no judicial forfeiture of the franchise, it could not be impeached collaterally. That a provision in the grant of the franchise to A., that treble tolls might be recovered before a justice for a violation of his franchise by others, did not preclude a suit in equity for an injunction and account ; and a court of equity had jurisdiction to grant such injunction, but would not enforce the penalty given by the grant. And that in case of a violation by a corporation, who could not be sued before a justice, the necessity of the case would warrant another remedy. Thompson v. New York, &c., 3 Sandf. Ch. 625.

§ 18. Where obstructions to public navigation are about to be erected, and after erection can be removed only at great expense, an injunction may be decreed. Thus a railroad company, authorized to erect a bridge over a navigable stream, in such a way as "to do the least possible injury to navigation," who are about to construct it in a place where the evidence tends to show more injury would be done to navigation than in others, may be restrained until the question whether that is the proper position can be determined.[1]

§ 19. A railroad may be compelled by injunction to build an arch over a mill-race of such dimensions as would secure the mill from injury ; the act requiring compensation for all damage.[2] While, on the other hand, a railroad company, alleging a right of way over a certain strip of land, and that the defendant is about to erect a flouring mill so near their track as not to leave sufficient room for its repair and construction, may have an injunction to restrain the erection of the mill.[3]

§ 19 a. The charter of a railroad provided, that whenever it should be found necessary to cut through, take, or so much injure any part of any quay, wharf, or other communication, as to render it impassable or inconvenient for transporting, &c., any goods ; another, equally convenient, should be constructed. The plaintiff, proprietor of a wharf, brings a bill to enjoin any works that would render the wharf inconvenient, pending an action at law, which involved the question, whether the defendants had not violated their charter by carrying the road in front of the wharf, so as to cut off its general access to the water, and making a jetty between the wharf and the water. It further appeared, that the prosecution of the work would not cause any additional injury. The injunction was granted.[4]

[1] Attorney-General v. Hudson, &c., 1 Stockt. 526.
[2] Coats v. The Clarence, &c., 1 Rus. & My. 181.
[3] Cunningham v. Rome, &c., 27 Geo. 499.
[4] Bell v. Hull, &c., 1 Railw. Cas. 616.

§ 20. The fact, that a railway has been located on some part of the tract, of eighty acres of land, purchased for the use of an institution for educating the deaf and dumb, does not alone authorize the conclusion, that the uses and purposes for which the institution was placed on that particular tract will be so materially interfered with, that the company should be restrained from crossing it.[1]

§ 21. An owner of lots upon a street, upon which a railway is about to be constructed, which will be specially injurious to him, may maintain a suit to enjoin such construction.[2] But, under the New York Statute, incorporating the Auburn and Rochester Railroad Company, where the map, plan, and profile, accompanying the petition of the company, for the appointment of a jury of appraisers, did not show any contemplated viaduct for the use of the owner of lands which were divided by the railroad; held, such owner could not enjoin the company from building their road in such a way as to allow him no viaduct, notwithstanding the counsel for such company may have argued to the jury of appraisers, that the company were bound to make proper crossing places.[3]

§ 22. The taking of land for railroad purposes has given rise to many applications for injunction.[4] (See Appendix.)

§ 23. If a railroad company neglect to pay the owner of land the damages awarded for the right of way; equity will enjoin them from using the land until the damages are paid.[5] So where a railroad company was directed by the charter to locate its road, and deposit a survey in the office of the Secretary of the State, and, when that was done, was permitted to construct the road, subject to compensation for land and

---

[1] Indiana, &c. v. State, 3 Ind. 421.
[2] Milhan v. Sharp, 28 Barb. 228.
[3] Kyle v. Auburn, &c., 2 Barb. Ch. 489.
[4] See Stone v. The Commercial,
&c., 4 My. & Cr. 122; River, &c. v. North, &c., 1 Railw. C. 135; Mouchett v. The Great, &c., 1 ib. 567.
[6] Stewart v. Raymond, &c., 7 S. & M. 568.

materials taken, to be decided on by commissioners appointed by a judge of the Supreme Court on application of the corporation, when the owners could not agree with the corporation; and the corporation proceeded to construct their road through lands of an individual without his assent, and without performing either of the above conditions: held, they should be enjoined until those conditions were complied with.[1] So, in Maryland, under the constitution, Art. 3, § 46, it is sufficient ground to enjoin a railroad from entering upon land, that they have not paid or secured the damages. An averment of irreparable injury is unnecessary.[2] So an injunction may be had against entering upon land, until the opening of a street through which the railroad was required to pass.[3] Or for summoning a jury to appraise a less quantity of land than the corporation had given notice of taking.[4] Or to restrain a railroad from taking land for a warehouse four hundred yards from their track, and making a track to such warehouse.[5] But an injunction has been held not to lie against a *merely void* taking of land.[6] So after the railroad had been built, though the land had been obtained from a tenant of the plaintiff by fraud.[7] And an injunction is sometimes granted, on condition of bringing an action.[8]

§ 24. An injunction does not lie, if the charter provides for an appraisal.[9]

§ 25. An injunction, for non-payment of land damages, was dissolved, on payment of the sum into court, though the charter required a payment into the Bank of England.[10] Or

---

[1] Bonaparte *v.* Camden, &c., Baldw. 205.
[2] Western, &c. *v.* Owings, 15 Md. 199.
[3] Jarden *v.* Philadelphia, &c., 3 Whart. 502.
[4] Stone *v.* The Commercial, &c., 4 My. & C. 122.
[5] Bird *v.* W. & M., &c., 8 Rich. Eq. 46.

[6] Mouchett *v.* The Great, &c., 1 Railw. Cas. 567.
[7] Deere *v.* Guest, 1 My. & Cr. 516.
[8] Kemp *v.* The London, &c., 1 Railw. C. 495; Bell *v.* The Hull, &c., 1 ib. 616.
[9] New, &c. *v.* Connelly, 7 Port. (Ind.), 32.
[10] Hyde *v.* The Great, &c., 1 Railw. Cas. 277.

it may be suspended, upon a stipulation for speedy payment.'(a)

§ 26. In a late case, the Vice-Chancellor, acting on the authority of The London, &c. v. Smith (1 Mac. & Gor. 216), granted an *ex parte* injunction, on the application of a railway company, restraining the land-owner from taking proceedings under the 68th section of the land clauses consolidation act, 1845, for settling the amount of his compensation. His Honor subsequently dissolved the injunction, on the authority of The East, &c. v. Gattke (3 Mac. & Gor. 135, 8 Eng. Rep. 59). In the meanwhile, the time limited for taking proceedings under the 68th section had expired. The company, who had not raised the question before the Vice-Chancellor, appealed from the order dissolving the injunction, on the ground that it ought to have been made on such terms as that their rights to take proceedings under the 68th section might not be affected by the lapse of time. The Lord Chancellor refused the application.[2]

§ 27. A railway company paid for and took a conveyance of a piece of land from A., and B. afterwards claimed the land, and moved to restrain the company from taking it, their compulsory powers having expired; and the evidence of title was conflicting between A. and B. Held, B. had his remedy by ejectment; and the injunction was refused.[3] On the other hand, where a railway had been made across the road leading to a farm, and the landowner served a notice on the company under the land clauses act, claiming 550l.

---

[1] Jones v. The Great, &c., 1 Railw. C. 684.
[2] South, &c. v. Hall, 7 Eng. Law and Eq. 30.
[3] Webster v. Southeastern, &c., 1 Eng. Law and Eq. 204.

(a) As to injunction against the taking of land, where the success of the undertaking is doubtful, see Agar v. The Regent's, &c., Coop. 77; The Mayor, &c. v. Pemberton, 1 Swanst. 244; Salmon v. Randall, 3 My. & Cr. 439; Lee v. Milner, 2 M. & W. 824.

as compensation, or requiring the company to summon a jury to assess the compensation; and the company filed their bill, alleging that the damage complained of was not an injury affecting the land, within the land clauses act, and obtained an *ex parte* injunction to restrain the landowner from taking any other proceedings under that act: held, the injunction could not be maintained.[1]

§ 28. An injunction against taking any more of the plaintiff's land than is necessary, for the purpose of making and maintaining the railway and works authorized by the act, was pronounced by Lord Cottenham "a very objectionable form of order."[2]

§ 29. A railroad may be restrained by injunction from carrying passengers, in a city, from their own station to that of another railroad, without authority in their charter.[3] Or from building a platform and stairs at a place where a station was expressly prohibited.[4] Though not from taking and leaving passengers at such place, or renting rooms in a public house for their accommodation.[5] But that a corporation authorized to construct a railroad from C. to A., with liberty to make a lateral road to B., proposes to construct its main road through B. (no route having been designated between C. and A.), is not sufficient ground for an injunction.[6] And although a railway company may have engaged in an illegal transaction, yet, if they afterwards obtain an act of Parliament to sanction it, the court will not restrain them from proceeding, though the effect of the act may be doubtful.[7] So, upon an application to restrain a railway company from prosecuting certain works, if it appears that

---

[1] South Staffordshire Railway Co. v. Hall, 3 Eng. Law and Eq. 105.
[2] Cother v. Midland, &c., 2 Phill. 469. See Great, &c. v. The Clarence, &c., 1 Coll. 507.
[3] Mayor, &c. v. Macon, &c., 7 Geo. 221.

[4] Lord Petre v. The Eastern, &c., 3 Railw. Cas. 367.
[5] Eton, &c. v. Great, &c., 1 Railw. Cas. 200.
[6] Bonaparte v. Camden, &c., Baldw. 205.
[7] Logan v. Courtown, 5 Eng. Law and Eq. 171.

they intend to abandon the work, the court will not grant the injunction.[1]

§ 30. Injunctions are often applied for by the stockholders of railroads.[2]

§ 31. An injunction will be granted, on the application of a stockholder, to restrain a railroad from making a dividend, contrary to the charter, till completion of the works.[3] Though it is otherwise where the charter makes no provision on the subject.[4] So an injunction will be granted in favor of holders of *preference shares*, to enjoin a general dividend, while the company are liable to a deficit arising from forgeries committed by an officer.[5] And where the directors of a company had entered into a contract, the legality of which was doubtful, to expend money in laying down rails; they were restrained, at the suit of some of the shareholders, from laying down the rails, till the validity of the contract had been decided upon at law.[6] But, in another case, though the acts of the directors of a railway company appeared to have been improper, the court would not restrain the company from enforcing the payment of calls, as it was possible that there were legal obligations to answer, and an injunction was refused, but without costs.[7] Nor will an injunction be granted to a stockholder merely because the construction of authorized branches will diminish his dividends, or the means of the company.[8] So, where the subscription to a railroad does not stipulate that the money shall be expended in the county in which the stockholders reside; the company will not be enjoined from collecting subscriptions, on the ground that the road may be extended beyond that county.

[1] 5 Eng. Law and Eq. 171.
[2] See Bagshaw *v.* The Eastern, &c., 7 Hare, 114.
[3] Allen *v.* Talbot, 30 Law Times, 315.
[4] Brown *v.* Monmouthshire, &c., 4 Eng. Law and Eq. 113.
[5] Henry *v.* Great, &c., 30 Law T. 10, 141.
[6] Beman *v.* Rufford, 6 Eng. Law and Eq. 106.
[7] Logan *v.* Courtown, 5 Eng. Law and Eq. 171.
[8] Newhall *v.* Chicago, &c., 14 Ill. 273.

Such a condition must be clearly and positively alleged, and it must be in writing.[1]

§ 82. A statute provided, that one railroad might aid another by subscription to stock or otherwise, upon consent of two-thirds of the stockholders present at a special meeting. This provision was re-enacted in a subsequent general corporation act, with the further provision that any company might accept the new provisions, and, when a proper certificate of acceptance had been filed, all inconsistent portions of their charter should be repealed. Held, even if the latter repealed the former act (which, it seems, it did not), a stockholder could not maintain a bill to enjoin the fulfilment by the company of contracts for aid, by the indorsement of bonds, the contracts having been unanimously ratified at a special meeting, which amounted to an acceptance, and estopped either party from objecting that no certificate had been filed.[2] So in Ohio it is held, that, admitting that the legislature is constitutionally incompetent to authorize a railroad company to embark in new enterprises, entirely beyond the scope, and outside of the objects contemplated by its charter, at the time the stock was subscribed for, and thus to effectuate a fundamental change in its charter, without the consent of all its stockholders; it is quite clear that, before a stockholder can have an injunction against such proceedings, he must have shown himself prompt and vigilant in the assertion of his rights, and not wait until the mischief of which he complains is accomplished.[3] So, though a shareholder has an equity to enjoin the directors from applying the funds in the completion of a part only of the line, with a view to the abandonment of the remainder; yet where, with knowledge of the intention to abandon the greater part of the line, he remained passive for eighteen months, while the directors

[1] Dill v. Wabash, &c., 21 Ill. 91.
[2] Zabriskie v. Cleveland, &c., 23 How. 381.
[3] Chapman v. Railroads, 6 Ohio (N. S.), 119.

were expending large sums in the completion of the remainder, the court refused to interfere by injunction.[1]

§ 83. The rule, that the majority cannot bind the minority in a joint-stock company as to acts not contemplated by the common contract, has not been applied to corporate companies for a public undertaking, involving public interests and duties under the sanction of Parliament. Thus two shareholders in a railway, suing in behalf of themselves and all others, sought to restrain the company from applying their funds in completing a branch railway, for the construction of which their parliamentary powers had expired. An interlocutory application for an injunction was refused, on the grounds that one of the plaintiffs named had acquiesced in the acts complained of, that the injunction would cause considerable inconvenience, that, as all the land had been purchased, it was not clear that it was illegal to complete the line, and that the suit was not properly framed, being on behalf of all the shareholders, which would include those who had sanctioned the acts.[2] So a company was authorized by three acts of Parliament to make three distinct railways (not forming one line), with separate amount of capital for each. Another company was, by a fourth act of Parliament, authorized to take a lease of the three lines, and did so, and the whole undertaking was placed under the control of a joint committee of directors of all the companies. One of the three lines was sufficiently completed to be, and was, opened, and the directors made calls for the purpose of entirely finishing the opened line, the other two being abandoned. An injunction was granted at the rolls, restraining the application of money and the making of calls for any purpose not authorized by the three acts, excepting only for ordinary repair. Held, on appeal, that, on an interlocutory application, in the absence of the lessee company, the opened

[1] Graham v. Birkenhead, &c., 6 Eng. Law and Eq. 132.

[2] Ffooks v. London, &c., 19 Eng. Law and Eq. 7.

line being worked under the direction of the joint committee, the injunction must be dissolved.[1]

§ 34. When the fundamental contract between two railroads provides that all disputes shall be settled by arbitration, and road A. has illegally misapplied funds or profits of both, with the assent of a majority of road B.; if dissenting stockholders in B. bring a bill in equity for their share of such profits, the court will enjoin both roads, if necessary, from settling or attempting to settle the claims of the complainants by arbitration.[2]

§ 35. Where there were two sets of railroad bondholders secured by separate mortgages, one of the second set was enjoined from collecting his bond by execution, the property being insufficient for all; upon the ground that such sale would interfere with the priority of the other set, and the *pro ratâ* rights of the other members of the second set.[3]

§ 36. In a case of difficulty between a railroad company and a contractor employed in constructing the road, the company claiming that the contract had been violated by him, and a right to discharge him, and collisions occurring between the workmen of the respective parties, and the work being thereby delayed; an injunction was granted against him, forbidding his continuance on the line, and directing an account of what was due him, all questions being reserved for a trial at law.[4]

§ 37. The insolvency of a railroad is no ground of injunction against the collection of subscriptions.[5] But where there are sundry *fi. fas.* against an insolvent railroad, threatening to seize and sell the road, with its equipments, extending one hundred miles in length, through six different counties;

[1] Hodgson v. Powis, 8 Eng. Law and Eq. 257.
[2] March v. Eastern Railroad, 43 N. H. 515.
[3] Pennock v. Coe, 23 How. 117.
[4] The East, &c. v. Hattersley, 8 Hare, 72.
[5] Dill v. Wabash, &c. 21 Ill. 91.

28

equity will take jurisdiction, direct a sale of the entire property for the benefit of all concerned, and distribute the fund according to the practice and usage in chancery, in a creditors' suit against executors and administrators. In such a case, no other court possesses adequate jurisdiction to reach and dispose of the entire merits. Any creditor who has a claim upon the fund, but who is not a nominal party to the suit, may make himself a party thereto in fact, by coming in and presenting his claim under the decree, and submitting himself to the jurisdiction of the court for its settlement and adjustment upon the fund to be distributed. If he neglects or refuses to come in and entitle himself to the benefit of the decree, equity will not assist him to set aside and annul it.[1]

§ 38. There have been some cases of injunction, relating to *canals*.

§ 39. A society, incorporated in 1791, located at the Falls of the Passaic, pulled down a gate and waste-way of the canal of the Morris Canal Co., incorporated in 1824, and discharged the water from the canal into the Passaic, above the falls. The canal company repaired the breach, and filed their bill against the society for an injunction, which was granted. The society filed a cross bill, setting up an agreement, stating breaches thereof, and praying a decree for a specific performance thereof. A demurrer to the bill was overruled.[2]

§ 40. By an act of the Legislature of Illinois passed July 21, 1837, the canal commissioners were authorized to enlarge the natural basin at the junction of the north and south branches of the Chicago River. And, in order to do this, block No. 7, of canal lots in the city of Chicago, was to be reserved for sale, so as to exchange it for block No. 14, which would be removed in the enlargement of the basin. Both blocks were to be appraised at the same time, and the owners

---

[1] Macon, &c. v. Parker. 9 Geo. 377.   &c., 2 Halst. Ch. 252; 1 Halst. Ch.
[2] The Society, &c. v. The Morris,   203.

of block 14 were to take block 7 at its appraised value. In 1843, an act was passed, granting the canal property to trustees, who were required to complete the canal, and afterwards to sell all lands, lots, and water-power granted to them by the act. In 1845 another act was passed, requiring the trustees to proceed forthwith in perfecting the exchange of block No. 14 for block No. 7, as contemplated by the act of 1837. The trustees refused to make the exchange, and advertised block No. 7 for sale, and the owners of block No. 14 filed a bill in chancery against them, to enjoin them from selling, and to compel them to exchange. Held, there was no principle in equity jurisprudence upon which the bill could be sustained; that the complainants had no present interest in block 7, and no right to call upon a court of equity to interfere and prevent the sale, and that, if the trustees had violated their duties, the State alone could complain.[1]

§ 41. In the present connection, it seems proper to refer to one of the most important cases of application for injunction, which have ever arisen in the United States, turning upon the conflicting claims of two *bridge-corporations*.(a) In this case, the nature of the franchise created by a corporate charter for purposes of public travel, as being on the one hand an exclusive privilege, and on the other open to legislative modification and control by a subsequent rival charter, is very learnedly and elaborately discussed both in a State and in the United States courts, and with equal ability, and nearly equal weight of authority, on both sides of the question. It will be seen that the same case involves a view of the franchise of a *public ferry*.

§ 42. By an ancient ordinance, dated 1636, 1640, and

[1] Canal, &c. v. Dewes, 11 Ill. 592.

(a) See Appendix—New Jersey.

1642, the government of the Colony of Massachusetts, having previously established a ferry, between Boston and Charlestown, over Charles River, recite that they have given the *revenue* of the ferry to Harvard College. In 1640, the *ferry* was given to the college, being then leased. In May, 1650, the college was incorporated. In October, 1650, the college having petitioned, in regard to *rectifying the ferry rent*, which belongs to the college, it was ordered that the president, for the college, might lease or otherwise dispose of the ferry. In 1654, an act, imposing a tax for the benefit of the college, spoke of the profit of the ferry, formerly granted. From 1639 to 1785 the college received the profits; since 1650, sometimes managing the ferry themselves, and sometimes leasing it. The college fixed the tolls, but the legislature passed various acts regulating the ferry, and sometimes affecting the tolls. The college was in some instances consulted, in others, not. In 1784, a statute incorporated certain persons, for the purpose of building a bridge in the place where the ferry between Boston and Charlestown is now kept; and authorized them to receive toll for forty years, and double toll on Sunday; they paying the college £200 per annum, which they accordingly paid; the bridge at the end of the time to revert to the State, saving to the college a fair annual compensation for the loss of the ferry. In 1792 an act established the West Boston Bridge Corporation, to build a bridge across the same river from Boston to Cambridge, the legislature having previously resolved that the act of 1784 was not the grant of an exclusive right to build over these waters. The act of 1792 authorized a toll for forty years, required payment of an annuity to the college, and, in consideration of the risk and importance of the work of building the Charles River bridge, and the loss which the plaintiffs would suffer from the new bridge, extended their charter for thirty years, with the exception that the additional toll on Sunday should be relinquished. In 1828, the defendants were incorporated to build another bridge across the river, between Boston and Charlestown, distant from the former, in Charlestown two hundred and sixty feet, and in Boston nine hundred and fifteen feet. The plaintiffs thereby lost two-thirds of their former tolls. A bill in equity for an injunction, brought in the Supreme Court of Massachusetts, was dismissed, the four judges being equally divided in opinion; and in the Supreme Court of the United States the judgment was affirmed, three judges dissenting.[1]

§ 43. Application for injunction by the Mohawk Bridge Company against the Utica, &c. Railroad Company, to restrain the erection of a bridge over the Mohawk River. The plaintiffs owned a toll-bridge across the river, about one hundred rods above the defendants' proposed bridge; and their bill alleged, that the latter would be a damage to them, by diversion of travel from their bridge, and interfere with their chartered exclusive privilege. The plaintiffs' charter prohibited any *ferry* within a certain distance from the bridge. It was held that the plaintiffs' charter, being in derogation of public rights, must be construed strictly, and the injunction was refused.[2]

§ 44. The principle has been applied to a *ferry*, that an exclusive legal right ought to be protected in equity against violations of hourly repetition and interminable duration. Hence equity will sustain a bill for an injunction, where the owner of a public ferry loses part of his rightful profits, by means of a ferry established near his, without right, but cannot procure proof to enforce his claim at law.[3] So, in a leading case relating to ferries, a grantor by deed conveyed his exclusive right to navigate with steamboats from the city of New York to *Elizabethtown Point*. The defendant, to a bill for injunction brought by the grantee, answered, that he

[1] Charles, &c. v. Warren, &c., 7 Pick. 344; 11 Pet. 420.
[2] Mohawk, &c. v. Utica, &c., 6 Paige, 554. See Richmond, &c. v. Louisa, &c., 13 How. 71; Piscataqua, &c. v. New Hampshire, &c., 7 N. H.

59; Newburgh, &c. v. Miller, 5 John. Ch. 101; Nichols v. Gates, 1 Conn. 318; Chesapeake, &c. v. Baltimore, &c., 4 Gill & J. 1.
[3] Long v. Beard, N. C. Term R. 256.

navigated between New York and *Halsted's Point*, which was within the township of Elizabethtown, but separated from Elizabethtown Point by a large and navigable creek, and that his wharf is near Elizabethtown Point. Upon the grounds, that the grant was intended to comprehend the entire benefit of all the travelling and passengers going to and from Elizabethtown and New York; that Elizabethtown Point was used for the landing-place of the town; and that all contiguous and injurious competition was to be excluded; judgment was given for the plaintiff.[1]

§ 45. Where, in a bill to enjoin the usurpation of the complainant's right to a ferry, he describes himself as lessee from certain commissioners, a body corporate to whom the ferry was granted; he must prove their corporate character and the lease, if these facts are put in issue by the answer.[2]

§ 46. A. being the owner of a ferry, and having opened a private way leading from it into the public road on one side of a river, B., who owned a ferry near A.'s, placed an obstruction on the road. A. filed a bill to have it abated, &c. It appearing from the answer of B., that A. had been resorting to unfair means, on the other side of the river, to divert the travel from B.'s ferry; held, the injunction ought to be dissolved.[3]

[1] Ogden *v.* Gibbons, 4 John. Ch. 150.

[2] Carter *v.* Garrett, 13 Ala. 728.
[3] Hill *v.* Averett, 27 Ala. 484.

CHAPTER XXVII.

EASEMENTS.

§ 1. THE remedy of injunction is often invoked in reference to other rights than those considered in the last chapter, belonging to the general class of *easements*. But where a corporation, authorized by law to construct a public improvement, in passing over the land of A. interferes with an easement of B. in the land; B. cannot maintain a bill against A. to compel a restoration of the easement; more especially without making the corporation a party. The court say, it "is an attempt to make an individual in no wise connected with the company restore that which they have taken without question of their right. No argument can support such a claim, and none is needed to answer it. The statement of the claim is the best possible refutation of it."[1]

§ 1 *a.* *Lights* constitute an easement, for the protection of which parties often apply for an injunction.

§ 1 *b.* It is held that there cannot be a perpetual injunction in regard to lights, in case of a disputed title, until the question has been settled at law.[2]

§ 1 *c.* A. applied for an injunction to restrain B. from the erection of his building, setting up in his bill an agreement

---

[1] Per Woodward, J., Mulvany *v.* Kennedy, 26 Penn. 44—15.   [2] Irvin *v.* Dixion, 9 How. 10.

that B. was to sell A. that part of his lot lying in the rear of his own lot, that A. might enjoy light and air over the same. The injunction was granted, and afterwards, on B.'s motion on filing his answer, was dissolved. At the argument of this motion, B.'s counsel, in explaining a diagram of the premises, said that B.'s building did not cover the entire rear of A.'s lot, and, if A. would take down his privy, he could enjoy light and air. A. did take down the privy, and put into the rear of his other buildings a range of fire-proof windows. B. thereupon began the erection of a dead wall along the site of the privy. A. applied for an injunction, restraining such erection. Held, the declaration of B.'s counsel *in facie curiæ*, followed by A.'s acts, constituted a contract with the court and with A., which estopped B. from denying the same and acting in denial of A.'s rights, founded on that declaration; and an injunction was issued restraining the erection of the dead wall.[1]

§ 2. A., who owned a lot of land with buildings thereon, obtained a temporary injunction on filing his bill therefor, restraining B., the owner of an adjacent lot, from erecting a certain building on his lot. This injunction was dissolved on motion, on filing B.'s answer. B. proceeded with his building and also with a dead wall across the rear of A.'s lot, which was not contemplated when the injunction was dissolved. A. moved for an injunction restraining the erection of the dead wall, and filed affidavits in support of his motion, showing new matter since the filing of the bill; and B. also filed in reply new affidavits. Held, that the decision dissolving the injunction was conclusive between the same parties on the same state of facts, or on a new state of facts, without leave to apply anew for a revival of the injunction which was dismissed; but that the judge at the final hearing was not concluded from granting a perpetual injunction or any other relief sought for, an order made on a motion not

[1] Banks v. American, &c., 4 Sandf. Ch. 438.

being *res adjudicata*, nor concluding the court on points of law; and, as the case on the second motion showed that A. was entitled to an injunction, it was granted.[1]

§ 2 *a*. The plaintiff leased to the defendant, for eleven years, a warehouse bounded on vacant land of A., "excepting and reserving unto (the plaintiff) the right to stop up and build against the five windows in said warehouse, which front upon" A.'s land, "and also to build against and put timbers into the wall, on the side of said warehouse in which the said five windows are, at his pleasure." The defendant afterwards took a lease from A. of the vacant land for fifteen years, terminable by himself in ten years, and proceeded to erect a building thereon, in contact with the wall of the warehouse containing the windows. Injunction refused, upon the grounds of a doubtful right; that the injury was trivial, or easily compensated in damages; that the plaintiff was a mere reversioner, having demised the warehouse to the defendant for a long term; and further, that an injunction would be an ineffectual remedy, without a decree compelling a conveyance from A. of the adjacent lot; and that an express statute afforded the plaintiff a simple and economical remedy, for preventing the alleged encroachment from ripening into a right by adverse use.[2]

§ 3. In an action for obstructing ancient lights, with a count for an injunction under the 17 and 18 Vict., c. 125, § 79, after a verdict had passed for the plaintiff, the court granted an injunction, under sect. 82 of that statute, to restrain the defendants from continuing the wrongful acts complained of in the action, and from committing any injury of the kind, relating to the rights and property of the plaintiff, mentioned in the declaration, and from erecting, keeping erected, and continuing the erection of so much of the wall and buildings

[1] Banks *v.* American, &c., 4 Sandf. Ch. 438.   [2] Atkins *v.* Chilson, 7 Met. 398.

as was opposite a certain messuage and premises of the plaintiff mentioned and described in the declaration, and known, &c., so or in such manner as to darken or obstruct any of the ancient lights or windows of the said messuage and premises, and from erecting any other building, and doing any other act whereby the light and air coming to and entering his messuage and premises by means of the said windows might be obstructed, or such messuage and premises might be in any way darkened, and from the repetition or continuance of any act whereby an injury of a like kind might happen to the plaintiff; the writ of injunction to lie in the office till next term, the defendants undertaking to pull down as much of the wall and building as should be sufficient to restore to the plaintiff the full enjoyment of the light and air he had previously, and to do the same to the satisfaction of a surveyor to be agreed on or nominated by one of the judges of the court, the defendants to pay the costs of the rule and of the surveyor.[1]

§ 4. A., the owner of a house, purchased of B. an adjoining strip of land, for the purpose of keeping it open. B. erected a house on the line of this strip, and opened windows which overlooked it. A. thereupon placed blinds upon his land, close upon the windows, and entirely obstructing the view from them. He also erected buildings on the strip of land behind both houses. B. files a bill to compel the removal of the buildings and blinds, alleging that by the contract of sale A. was restrained from building between the houses, and obstructing B.'s light, but by mistake the restriction was omitted from the deed. The agreement was proved, as alleged, and as part of the consideration, but not a reservation of light to B. Held, the averment in the bill applied only to the portion of land between the houses. A. was enjoined from there erecting any building, but not required to remove his buildings in the rear, nor the blinds.[2] (See § 4 c.)

[1] Jessel v. Chaplin, 37 Eng. Law and Eq. 472.

[2] Athey v. McHenry, 6 B. Mon. 50.

§ 4 *a*. *Party-walls* are another easement, which may be protected by injunction.

§ 4 *b*. The owner of one-half of an ancient solid party-wall, long used for the support of buildings erected on each side of it, may be restrained by injunction from cutting away a portion of its face, and erecting a new wall upon his own land, two inches distant from the portion of the old wall which is left standing, and connected with it by occasional projecting bricks and ties.[1]

[1] Phillips *v.* Boardman, 4 Allen, 147.(*a*) See Zugenbhuler *v.* Gilliam, 3 Clarke, 391.

(*a*) An earlier, informal report of this case states it as follows : The parties to a bill for an injunction were owners of adjoining estates in Boston, between which was an ancient party-wall, one foot thick, used by them in common for support of the timbers of their respective buildings. The defendant having taken down his building, and being about to erect a new one, had pared off to a considerable height the face of the wall, on his side of it, to the depth of four inches, and was erecting a new wall, a foot thick, occupying the four inches of the old wall thus removed, and eight inches taken from his own land. In the course of this work, which had reached to the floor of the second story, when an injunction was granted, he had occasionally projected a brick, two inches beyond the face of his new work, so as to reach the centre of the old wall ; partly for support to the remainder, but chiefly to denote the division line as claimed by him, and with the avowed purpose of breaking up the joint character of the old wall, and preventing the plaintiffs from building close to the face of his new wall, if, upon rebuilding, they should desire to do so. It appeared from the report of a master, that the wall was an ancient one, still sufficient for the buildings which it had divided. and for any buildings such as were commonly erected on that street ; that by the paring its capacity for service was materially diminished, and that the new wall was substantially an independent one, affording no material support to the remaining eight inches of the old wall. The injunction restrained the defendant from proceeding to diminish the old wall. Held, upon motion to dissolve the injunction, that, in a case of this nature, neither of the parties could so deal with the wall as to diminish its capacity for service, without consent of the other ; and, in addition to the serious and irreparable mischief, and the difficulty of ascertaining its nature and extent after the work should be

§ 4 c. Equity will not restrain a person from making a reasonable improvement on his own land, upon the ground that he thereby necessarily endangers an adjoining edifice, unless the owner of the latter has special privileges which are thereby violated; derived from the party making the erection, or those under whom he claims, either by prescription or by grant.   Thus the defendant, owning a lot within six feet of Christ's Church, in New York, built more than thirty-eight years before, commenced the erection of a building thereupon, to be six stories high; and was sinking the foundation sixteen feet deep, and ten feet lower than that of the church.   The wall of the church, at the corner opposite to which the excavation had been completed, had so settled as to leave a considerable crack.   The proprietors of the church filed a bill for injunction, stating these facts, and that the church was in great danger if the work should proceed; but not that the defendant was improving his property in an unreasonable or unusual manner, or with any intention to injure the church, or that the plaintiffs had any claim by prescription, or grant from the defendant.   Upon application to dissolve the injunction, which had been granted; it was accordingly dissolved.[1]   And it is remarked in a late work, that the creation of an easement in this class of cases is "confined to cases where the covenant or agreement on the part of the original grantee with the grantor, expressly related to and was for the benefit of the covenantee as owner of another parcel of estate, and it was so made, that the owner of the granted estate, if not himself the covenantor, had notice thereof when he became the purchaser."[2]   And the language claimed to establish an easement of this nature will be construed strictly.   Thus a vendor covenanted that

---

[1] Lasala v. Holbrook, 4 Paige 169.   [2] 2 Washb. R. P. 33.   See Whitney v. Union, &c., 23 Law Rep. 405.

---

covered in, the complainants, by twenty years' use of an independent wall, might, without a multiplicity of suits, wholly lose their title.   Phillips v. Boardman (cited in) 2 Hilliard on Torts (2d ed.), 14.

no building except tombs should be erected on any part of his land, opposite to the land sold. Subsequently, he sold part of the opposite land, and the purchaser built on it without objection from the former purchaser. Afterwards the vendor sold a further part of the opposite land, and the new purchaser commenced building. The original purchaser filed a bill for an injunction, to restrain the defendant from building on any part of the land of the original vendor or the opposite land. Held, the covenant applied only to the lands of the original vendor, exactly opposite to the lands sold to the plaintiff; and the bill was dismissed.[1] (See § 4 b.)

§ 4 d. Another easement is that alleged to grow out of the conveyance or setting apart of real property for certain specified objects, which appropriation is alleged materially to affect the value of adjacent estates.

§ 5. Where, upon a sale of lots in a new town, it was announced that certain pieces were set apart for church lots according to a plan, and a lot was conveyed to a church society by an ordinary deed; held, the lot-owners had no such vested interest in restricting the use of the church lot, as would maintain an injunction against a sale of a portion of it to raise money for building a church on the remainder.[2] But where certain land within the limits of a city is by statute reserved for the use of the State for a court-house, jail, market, public worship, and burial; the public thereby acquire rights and interests in such land as a common or public square, and, although the legal title may be in the city, it holds subject to the trusts above named, and has no power to sell the land for private purposes. Hence the court will grant a perpetual injunction to restrain and prevent the erection of a private dwelling-house on such square, as an

[1] Patching v. Dubbins, 23 Eng. Law and Eq. 609.
[2] Chapman v. Gordon, 29 Geo. 250.

See Maxwell v. East, &c., 3 Bosw. 124.

irreparable public injury. The application may be made by the commonwealth, at the instance of the attorney-general.[1]

§ 6. The right of *common* has also been made the subject of application for an injunction. Thus, in an old case, a man having granted to J. S. common in his down for one hundred sheep and five rams; the bill complained that the grantor overstocked the common, so that the plaintiff, the grantee, could have no benefit of the grant, and prayed the grantor might be enjoined not to overstock, &c. Upon debate, the court dismissed the bill.[2] So an injunction was obtained on affidavits, against cutting, and pasturing cattle, in a wood, the plaintiff claiming as tenant in fee, or as lord of the manor inclosed under the statute. The defendants denied the former title, and as to the latter claimed common of pasture and estovers, and that after the inclosure sufficient common of pasture would not remain. The plaintiff had previously commenced and been nonsuited in an action of trespass, and entered into an agreement with some of the tenants. The injunction was dissolved upon the answer.[3]

§ 7. Continuing *diversion of water* is an irreparable injury, which equity will redress.[4] But, in New York, both by virtue of an express statute, and because the claim is "wholly beneath its dignity," the court will not enjoin a defendant from diverting a stream of water, unless the annual injury to the plaintiff is equal to the interest of $100, or the immediate injury amounts to $100.[5]

§ 8. In a suit to test the question of priority of appropriation of a *mining* stream, a prayer for an injunction to prevent future injury is proper.[6]

[1] Com. v. Rush, 14 Penn. 186.
[2] Fines v. Cobb, 2 Vern. 116. See F. N. B. 125; Robert, &c., 9 Rep. 112.
[3] Hanson v. Gardiner, 7 Ves. 305 b.
[4] Tuolumne Water Co. v. Chapman, 8 Cal. 392.
[5] Smith v. Adams, 6 Paige, 435.

See Pratt v. Lamson, 6 Allen, 457; Binney, 2 Bland, 117; Porter v. Witham, 5 Shepl. 292; Olmstead v. Loomis, 6 Barb. 152; Society, &c. v. Holsman, 1 Halst. Ch. 126.
[6] Marius v. Bicknell, 10 Cal. 217.

§ 9. Bill for an injunction, to protect the plaintiff's coal-mines from injury, by the water flowing to them from the colliery of the defendants. Held, an injunction should be granted against working the defendants' mines in any places which might endanger or injure those of the plaintiff, till answer or further order. Upon evidence and a hearing, a perpetual injunction was refused, but the bill ordered to be retained for a year, with liberty to bring an action, the injunction to remain in the mean time.[1] But upon a verdict found, that the plaintiff was the owner and in possession of land, through which the defendant's ditch was dug, for mining purposes, without the plaintiff's consent, and that the ditch interfered with the comfortable enjoyment of such lot, and injuriously affected it; an abatement of the ditch as a nuisance was ordered.[2]

§ 10. The local board of health, having commenced the construction of a sewer under certain fields, on the banks of the river Avon, belonging to the plaintiffs, who were also entitled to a several *fishery*, and to watering-places for cattle in the river, but were not owners of the water, or of the bed of the river, the outlet to such sewer being intended to open into the river within the limits of the free fishery; were restrained by injunction at the suit of the plaintiffs from prosecuting such works.[3]

§ 11. Equity will not interfere to protect a party claiming the right to flow the land of another, and to maintain a watercourse through it, under a parol license, where the evidence is conflicting and inconclusive, and the agreement on which the license is founded is indefinite and uncertain.[4]

§ 12. Equity will interfere to protect the drainage of surface water over a lot adjoining the plaintiff's, where such

[1] The Duke, &c. v. Morris, 6 Hare, 340.
[2] Weimer v. Lowery, 11 Cal. 104.
[3] Oldaker v. Hunt, 31 Eng. Law and Eq. 503.
[4] Hazelton v. Putnam, 3 Chand. 117.

drainage has continued twenty years; by ordering that the channel be cleared out, and enjoining future obstructions.[1]

§ 13. With more particular reference to *mills*, it is remarked in various cases, in vindication of the remedy of injunction, as follows: "In regulating the rights of mill-owners and all others in the use of a stream, wherein numbers of persons are interested, equity is able, by one decree, to regulate their respective rights, to fix the time and manner in which water may be drawn, and within what limits it shall or shall not be drawn by all parties respectively; and thus it is peculiarly adapted to the relief sought against such alleged nuisance and disturbance, and affords a more complete and adequate remedy than can be afforded by one or many suits at law."[2] "The regulation of the use of water upon the different sides of the stream, for hydraulic purposes, is so essential to the manufacturing interests of our community, and in fact to every branch of domestic industry, that it would be deplorable if any of these important establishments could be destroyed by any individual, or combination of persons, and the owners left to seek an uncertain remedy by an action for damages in a court of law."[3] "If the diversion is a violation of the right of the plaintiffs, and may permanently injure that right, and become, by lapse of time, the foundation of an adverse right in the defendant, I know of no more fit case for the interposition of a court of equity, by way of injunction. If there be a remedy for the plaintiffs at law for damages, still that remedy is inadequate to prevent and redress the mischief. If there be no such remedy at law, then, *à fortiori*, a court of equity ought to give its aid to vindicate and perpetuate the right of the plaintiffs."[4] Thus a bill in equity will lie, to enjoin a mill-owner from keeping up his

[1] Earl v. De Hart, 1 Beasl. 280.
[2] Per Shaw, C. J., Ballou v. Hopkinton, 4 Gray, 328. See Mitchell v. Leavitt, 30 Cow. 587; Lummeny v. Braddy, 8 Clarke, 33; Crittenden v. Field, 8 Gray, 621; Sheldon v. Rockwell, 9 Wis. 166.
[3] Per Walworth, Chanc., Arthur v. Case, 1 Paige, 447.
[4] Per Story, J., Webb v. Portland, &c., 3 Sumn. 189.

dam and flowing the complainant's land, during a portion of the year fixed by a sheriff's jury, under Rev. Sts. c. 116, as the period for which such dam should be kept open, after two judgments at law have conclusively established the plaintiff's right.[1] So where the plaintiffs had for a long time enjoyed the use of the water in a pond, for propelling their mills, upon which use the value of their mills principally depended; an injunction was granted, to protect them in the enjoyment of the privilege, without a prior establishment of their right at law.[2] So equity has jurisdiction of a bill, to restrain the letting off of water from a reservoir established for the benefit of the plaintiff's mill.[3] So an injunction lies, for disturbing the use of land for a *mill-yard.*[4] So where a mill-stream broke the bank, wearing the ground of the defendant, and was making a new channel, with danger of irreparable injury; the court passed an additional order, before appearance, to restrain the defendant from preventing the plaintiff's repairing the bank, or entering the defendant's land for that purpose; also to restrain the defendant from making any channel in his lands, which would divert the water from the plaintiff's mill, unless cause were shown in six days.[5] So, upon a prayer for an injunction against using the water of a stream otherwise than it had been previously used, it appeared that the defendant sometimes withheld the water, and at others discharged it in such quantities as to endanger the plaintiff's mills. The injunction was granted until a pending suit should be decided; which decision being in favor of the plaintiff, it was made perpetual.[6]

§ 13 *a.* The distinction is made, in a recent case, that, where the rights of several owners in the same water-power or privilege are admitted or have been settled at law, equity will regulate the use of the water, and fix the respective

[1] Hill v. Sayles, 12 Cush. 454.
[2] Belknap v. Trimble, 3 Paige, 577.
[3] Ballou v. Hopkinton, 4 Gray, 324.
[4] Gurney v. Ford, 2 Allen, 577.
[5] McSwiney v. Haynes, 1 Ir. Eq. 322.
[6] Robinson v. Byron, 1 Bro. C. 588.

29

rights.   Otherwise, where the object is to settle a disputed
title, which may be settled at law.[1]   But the injunction may
be granted upon the ground of long possession, though the
right has not been established at law.[2]

§ 14. But in case of a bill in equity, alleging that the
plaintiff was lessee of an ancient mill, and that the defendant
had erected flood-gates and other works on the stream, which
obstructed the mill, and praying for their removal; on demurrer, it appearing that the works had been erected for
more than three years, and nothing done to establish the
plaintiff's title at law: held, the bill could not be maintained.[3]
So on application for an injunction, to restrain the defendant
from building a new mill for grinding and sawing for the
public, on the ground that the construction of the dam would
injure the land of the plaintiff and the health of his family;
testimony being heard, the court applied to the case the rule,
that it is not every slight or doubtful injury which will justify
the use of the extraordinary power of injunction to restrain a
man from using his property as his interests may demand,
especially as, if the injury apprehended should result, the
complainant may resort to law for damages.[4]   So where the
complainants owned the water-power on one side of a river,
and one-half of the power on the other, the defendant owning
the other half; he having occasionally used more than his
share of the water, but no suit having been brought against
him therefor, and the complainants having no machinery on
that side of the river propelled by water: held, an injunction
would not be granted, restraining the defendant in the use
of the water.[5]

§ 15. A bill in equity will not lie, on behalf of a mill-
owner, to restrain a riparian proprietor bordering on a pond
above, on the same mill-stream, from cutting ice in such

[1] Bean v. Coleman, 44 N. H. 539.
[2] Bush v. Western, Prec. Ch. 530;
Finch v. Resbridger, 2 Vern. 390.
[3] Weller v. Smeaton, 1 Cox, 102.
[4] Wilder v. Strickland, 2 Jones Eq.
386.
[5] Norris v. Hill, 1 Mann. (Mich.)
202.

pond, the injury, if any, being trifling, the question involved doubtful, and the rights of the parties not having been determined at law.

§ 16. The lessors of certain water-rights agreed by the lease to draw off the water in a certain manner. After drawing the water for some time as agreed, they began an alteration of the works, alleging that the new works would not injure the lessees, and were not inconsistent with their rights under the agreement. An injunction was granted, to keep the works *in statu quo* until the final hearing.[2]

§ 17. The obstruction of the flow of water to a mill, and preventing the party from removing the obstructions, or throwing them again into the stream, were held to afford proper ground for an injunction, as "acts obviously injurious not only to the enjoyment of the right, but prejudicial to its existence. Damages at law would be wholly inadequate.— Successive suits,—instead of redressing the wrong, would in the end be worse than the wrong itself.—Equity will restrain acts of trespass or nuisance, to prevent multiplicity of suits. —So, where wrongful acts might become the foundation of an adverse right."[3]

§ 18. Equity will enjoin *a mill-dam* which may cause irreparable injury.[4] Or restrain the owner of a mill-dam from increasing its height, provided such increase will be the cause of sickness in the family of an adjoining lot.[5] So an injunction will be granted, to restrain the defendant from keeping up a mill-dam, to the nuisance of the plaintiff's privilege above. The court remarked: "It is objected that the plaintiff has an adequate and complete remedy at law, especially in the power given to the court by a late statute,

---

[1] Cummings *v.* Barrett, 10 Cush. 186.
[2] Buller *v.* Society, &c., 1 Beasl. 264.
[3] Per Thompson, J., Scheetz's, &c., 35 Penn. 95.

[4] Lyon *v.* M'Laughlin, 32 Verm. 423. See Sprague *v.* Rhodes, 4 R. I. 301.
[5] Norwood *v.* Dickey, 18 Geo. 528.

authorizing them on motion, after judgment for the plaintiff, in an action on the case for a nuisance, to order such nuisance to be removed and abated, as in case of a common nuisance.   But is this remedy adequate, within the meaning of the statute?   The power given by this statute is obviously discretionary, and the exercise of it will depend upon the circumstances of each particular case; it is to be exercised on motion, all the facts must be proved to the court by affidavit, and besides, it can bind nobody but the party, who must be the actual wrongdoer, and not other parties in interest, claiming rights in the same estate.   Further, such an order and warrant could only be to abate and remove the nuisance. The nuisance or cause of damage is the flowage, and that is occasioned by the dam, sluices, and gates, and the nuisance might be abated by hoisting the gates, or removing the planks from a wasteway.   These might be so easily replaced, that there would be a strong temptation to do it; and I know of no power to enforce the execution of the warrant after it is once executed.   Whereas, a decree in equity can extend to all parties having an interest and bind them, and it may be effectual and perpetual.   Instead of requiring an entire prostration of the nuisance, it may be modified and adapted to the just rights of the parties; it may order an abatement in part, determine the height to which the dam may be kept, the terms on which it may be kept up, the mode of using the water, and other incidents, and thus may be more beneficial for both parties, than a mere and absolute abatement."[1]

§ 19. On a bill to restrain a suit at law against the plaintiff, for overflowing lands by means of a mill-dam, the court, having sustained the plaintiff's right to maintain the dam, retained the suit, for the purpose of settling the rights of the parties in relation to the height of the dam.[2]

[1] Bemis v. Upham, 13 Pick. 169, 170, per Shaw, C. J.   [2] Le Roy v. Platt, 4 Paige, 77.

§ 20. But where different parties, at about the same time, erect mill-dams in a place which admits only of the erection of one, the upper dam being useless, by reason of the one below it; equity will not enjoin the owners of the lower dam from completing it, or compel its removal, before the rights of the parties have been established at law.[1] So where the defendants held adverse possession, for twenty years, of water which had previously flowed into the complainant's pond, and used it by means of an aqueduct, but had disused it for three years, and then had begun to reconstruct the aqueduct; held, they could not be enjoined; it appearing that the defendants had not intended to abandon their right, and that acquiescence by the complainant, or those under whom he claimed, for less than twenty years, would be sufficient to justify the refusal of an injunction.[2] So a party who owns mining claims, but has never worked them, cannot maintain a bill, to prevent an owner lower down from raising a dam, on the ground that the raising will injure him in working his claim, by means of ditches which he has commenced to construct. The plaintiff must wait, until he is damnified in the prosecution of his work by the defendant.[3]

§ 21. Where the complainant in a bill in equity charges that the defendant is placing obstructions in the bed of a navigable river, in front of the complainant's docks, thereby blocking up the channel; he not only shows that he will sustain special damage, quite distinct from what the public will suffer, if the defendant is allowed to complete his erection, but also shows how the injury will be accomplished; and is entitled to an injunction.[4]

§ 22. A. owned lands on the Delaware River, and held and enjoyed a *fishery* appurtenant thereto. After his death,

---

[1] Porter *v.* Witham, 17 Maine, 292. See Society, &c. *v.* Butler, 1 Beasl. 498.
[2] Haight *v.* Proprietors, &c., 4 Wash. C. 601.
[3] Harvey *v.* Chilton, 11 Cal. 114.
[4] Walker *v.* Shepardson, 2 Wis. 384.

his estate was divided, by commissioners, among his heirs. They separated the lands lying contiguous to the river from the fishery, by lines and fixed monuments, and set off the fishery as a separate share, the line of separation being the usual high-water mark. An injunction, which had been granted, restraining the owner from building a wall on such line, was dissolved.[1]

§ 23. A contract was entered into between *a canal company* and the plaintiffs, the owners of paper-mills, as to the mode of enjoyment of the waters by which both were supplied. The company did acts in violation of the contract. Held, it was no answer, upon a bill for perpetual injunction, that the acts proposed would not be injurious, or even to prove that they were beneficial, to the plaintiffs; and the court, although no evidence was given of any actual damage done, made a decree for a perpetual injunction.[2]

§ 25. An injunction lies for one in possession of land, to restrain the threatened appropriation of such land for the purpose of a *highway*,(a) where the proper steps have not been taken to secure a suitable compensation to the plaintiff, or to protect him from an improper appropriation.[3] Or to prevent the laying out and establishing of a road through a farm and improvements, without compliance with the requirements of the law.[4] Or in behalf of a person whose right to the use of a passway, already in existence, has been obstructed; though not where the establishment of a passway is claimed on the mere ground of necessity.[5] So, it seems, an obstruction of a public street, by fencing it, may be restrained by injunction.[6]

[1] Howell *v.* Robb, 3 Halst. Ch. 17.
[2] Dickenson *v.* Grand, &c., 19 Eng. Law and Eq. 287.
[3] Anderson *v.* Commissioners, &c.,
12 Ohio St. 642; M'Arthur *v.* Kelly, 5 Ohio, 140.
[4] Floyd *v.* Turner, 23 Tex. 292.
[5] Hall *v.* McLeod, 2 Met. (Ky.) 98.
[6] Langsdale *v.* Bonton, 12 Ind. 467.

(a) See Chap. XXVI.

§ 26. But, even if a county court has power to lay out a private way over another man's land, yet, to authorize an injunction for removal of impediments placed there by the owner of the land, it must appear, that, in locating the way, the least possible injury that could be, consistently with the end to be attained, is done to the owner of the land.[1] So there is no equity in a bill by an abuttor to prevent a city, in the exercise of its powers, from putting down curb-stones, on the ground that the city is proposing to set them on another than the true line; the matter turns upon a mere question of law, no irreparable injury is threatened, and, it seems, the case is not within equity jurisdiction.[2] So a land-owner in a city, whose property in buildings will be damaged in value by a proposed change in the grade of a street, has no remedy by injunction against the mayor and council, but, if he has any remedy, it must be at law for damages.[3]

§ 27. Where a person sells property lying within the limits of a city, and in the conveyance bounds it by streets, designated as such, in the conveyance, or on a map made by the city or by the owner of the property; such sale necessarily implies a covenant that the purchaser shall have the use of the streets. And any obstruction, by the grantors, which denies the exercise of this particular right of way, as a street, works irreparable mischief, and entitles the purchaser to relief, by injunction. In cases like this, the acts of Maryland, relative to opening streets in Baltimore, do not give the complainant, as matter of right, the redress to which he is entitled; and therefore it cannot be said, that, because of these acts, he is not remediless, except in a court of equity. But, to entitle the complainant to an injunction, the obstruction complained of must work to his great injury, in manifest violation of the obligations of the grantor; and the facts stated in the bill must show this.[4] (See Chap. XXXI.)

[1] Clack v. White, 2 Swan, 540.
[2] Holmes v. Jersey City, 1 Beasl. 299.
[3] Markham v. Mayor, &c., 23 Geo. 402.
[4] White v. Flannigain, 1 Md. 525.

§ 28. A land-owner cannot be compelled by injunction to keep open a way over his land for another's use, unless the right of the latter is clear and undoubted, or established at law.[1]

[1] King v. M'Cully, 38 Penn. 76.

CHAPTER XXVIII.

LANDS; LEASE; MORTGAGE.

§ 1. WE have already—Chapter VI.—considered the application of injunctions *to restrain suits at law*, including, more especially, suits relating to land.(*a*)　It is sufficient to add, in the present connection, a general statement of the rule upon the subject of defences to such suits, in the words of an approved writer and jurist. "If an ejectment is brought to try a right to land in a court of common law, a court of equity will, under proper circumstances, restrain the party in possession from setting up any title, which may prevent the fair trial of the right; as, for example, a term of years or other outstanding interest in a trustee, or lessee, or mortgagee.　But this will not be done in every case; for, as the court proceeds upon the principle, that the party in possession ought not in conscience to use an accidental advantage, to protect his possession against a real right in his adversary, if there is any counter equity in the circumstances of the case,

---

(*a*) See p. 246.　As to injunction against a *conveyance* of land, see Spiller *v.* Spiller, 3 Swanst. 556.

which meets the reasoning upon this principle, the court will not interfere. Thus, it will not interfere with the possessor, who is a *bonâ fide* purchaser for a valuable consideration, without notice of the adverse claim at the time of his purchase."[1]

§ 1 *a*. On the other hand, it is remarked in a late case, in justification of, interference where no suit at law had been brought: "The orator, being in possession,—cannot himself institute any action at law to settle the title, and the defendants, though setting up a claim to the lands, have brought no suit against him, and have shown no intention to do so."[2]

§ 1 *b*. An injunction may be issued to prevent irreparable injury to land, though the title is disputed, if the defendant is irresponsible, or if there is no relief at law.[3] The distinction is taken, that, where there is a privity of estate, as between a reversioner and particular tenant, an injunction may be had, without irreparable injury; otherwise, where the parties are strangers to each other in reference to the estate, or mutually adverse claimants; whether the act be waste or trespass.[4] And, on the other hand, where both the title to, and the possession of, a tract of uninclosed lands were in dispute and spread upon the record, it was held that, while chancery would not undertake to decide which title should prevail at law, there might be a manifest propriety in declaring one of them to be of such a character, as to render it unwise for the court to exercise extraordinary powers, in prohibiting the exercise of acts of ownership under it. And, the title of both adverse claimants being spread upon the record, and the defendants showing that the complainants had controverted, both at law and in equity, in various ways, the title of the defendants, during fifteen years, and that the defendants had always maintained their title, so

---

[1] 2 Story, Eq. 219, § 913.
[2] Per Poland, C. J., Eldridge *v.* Smith, 34 Verm. 487.
[3] Spear *v.* Cutter, 5 Barb. 486.
[4] Georges, &c. *v.* Detmold, 1 Md. Ch. Dec. 371.

far as was necessary for their success, in every controversy; it was held that the defendants showed a title, and possession under it, of such a character, as would preclude a court of equity from enjoining them against acts of ownership under it.[1]

§ 2. And it is said, in a late case, " Where there is a mere dry question of adverse title, a bill filed on that ground, without more, entitles the plaintiff to no relief whatever."[2] Thus the defendants, a railway company, having bought land from A., who appeared by the book of reference to be the owner; the plaintiff, a neighboring owner, whose land was also taken, claimed title to the former lot, and brought a bill to enjoin the possession of, and waste upon it. Injunction refused. The court remarked: "If I were to hold that the plaintiff is entitled to the relief which he asks, and the railway company were to compromise with him, what is there to prevent some other person from filing another bill, showing plausible grounds of title? The consequence of which would be that the company would be stopped again. This is a mere case of adverse title, claimed upon very slight evidence indeed, and without alleging that an action of ejectment or an action of trespass would not give him all the remedy he can possibly be entitled to or wish for."[3]

§ 3. The question of title often arises from the *covenants of warranty* in a deed. (See Chap. XIV.) Thus A. having sold land to B. with the usual covenants, B. brought his action on the covenant of seizin against A.'s widow, having given her notice of a defect only a day or two before. She searched out the defect, and procured conveyances to herself, which perfected the title, and which she tendered B., but he declined them. B. recovered judgment for the purchase-money with interest. The widow then brought her bill in equity, to compel B. to accept the deeds, and to enjoin his judgment, and an in-

---

[1] Cornelius v. Post, 1 Stockt. 196.   [2] Webster v. The South, &c., 1 Sim. N. S. 279.
[3] Ibid. 272, 279.

junction was ordered.[1] So a non-resident, who has not a suffi-ciency of property or effects, within the State, to make good the damages for the breach of a covenant for quiet enjoy-ment, will be enjoined from collecting the purchase-money for land, where the title is defective.[2] But where it was simply alleged in a bill, that the plaintiff had been informed of a superior title to the land, for which the note in question was given, and that a suit was pending between other parties, from which it appeared that such title might be the better one, and that, if so, it was doubtful whether the defendant was in circumstances to make redress, in a suit on the cove-nants; and no ulterior proceeding was suggested as being contemplated, and not even a reference of the title asked: held, it was not proper to allow an injunction.[3]

§ 4. The question of *implied estoppel* is sometimes raised on application for an injunction. (See *Estoppel.*) Thus the plaintiff, proprietor of a colliery, constructed a railway across the lands of several other persons, by agreement, and his solicitor wrote to the defendant, who was one of these per-sons, referring to the powers of a local act of Parliament, supposed to enable him to take lands within certain limits for railways, and offering to pay him at a fair appraisal. The defendant did not reply, and the railway was made. More than a year after, the parties met, but did not agree upon a price; and more than three years after, the defendant brings ejectment for the land. Upon a bill for injunction, held, inasmuch as the dispute had not related to the occupation of the land, but only to the price, the injunction should be granted, upon the plaintiff's giving judgment in the action, and paying into court a sum not less than the amount of the utmost valuation.[4]

§ 5. Bill in equity, alleging that the plaintiffs, believing themselves entitled as devisees to a dwelling-house and shop,

[1] Reese *v.* Smith, 12 Mis. 344.
[2] Richardson *v.* Williams, 3 Jones Eq. 116.
[3] Patterson *v.* Miller, 4 Jones Eq. 451.
[4] Powell *v.* Thomas, 6 Hare, 300.

agreed to lease them, being out of repair, to a tenant, who thereupon expended money in pulling down and rebuilding; that the defendant, who proved to be a part-owner, knew the true state of the title, but had claimed the whole, which claim he repeated a few days before commencement of the improvements; that he also knew of the improvements, and that the plaintiffs and their tenant were acting under a mistake, and yet made no objection. The bill prayed that the defendant might be required to confirm the lease, and enjoined against evicting the tenant. Held, the tenancy in common did not vary the principles applicable to the case; that the original claim of the defendant was sufficient, to protect his title, although it did not state the particulars; and an injunction was refused.[1]

§ 6. "A court of chancery will recognize and enforce agreements concerning the occupation and mode of use of real estate, although they are not expressed with technical accuracy. Nor is it at all material that such stipulations should be binding at law."[2] Thus an injunction lies, against a purchaser with notice, to prevent the use of a house as a family hotel, in violation of covenants, entered into between owners and purchasers of the lot upon a part of which such house is built, not to carry on the business of an innkeeper.[3] So, if the owners of land lay it out into house-lots, and orally agree among themselves that they shall be thus exclusively occupied, and convey the lots with a condition to that effect; any purchaser is bound by such condition, and the owners of other lots may maintain a bill in equity to enjoin him from converting a dwelling-house into a public eating-house.[4]

§ 7. The relation of *landlord and tenant* gives frequent occasion for the remedy of injunction.[5] Thus equity will

[1] Master, &c. v. Harding, 6 Hare, 273.
[2] Per Bigelow, C. J., Parker v. Nightingale, 6 Allen, 344.
[3] Whatman v. Gibson, 9 Sim. 196.
[4] Parker v. Nightingale, 6 Allen, 341.
[5] See Camden v. Morton; Brown v. Quilter, 2 Ed. 219; Brooks v. Diaz, 35 Ala. 599.

aid a tenant in preventing his landlord from breaking a covenant, which will work a forfeiture of his (the tenant's) estate, although not made with the tenant, and even when a suit at law cannot be maintained on such covenant.[1]

§ 8. Equity will restrict a lessee to the specific performance of his covenants.(a) And where a lease restricted the use of the premises to "the regular dry-goods jobbing business," and the lessee commenced selling goods at auction therein; held, although there was no damage or irreparable injury done to the lessor, nor any nuisance at law, yet it was a breach of the covenant, and the lessor could have an injunction.[2] So the defendants obtained from the plaintiffs an agreement for a lease of a house adjoining the plaintiffs' coachmaking establishment, representing, after other and conflicting statements, that they wanted it for a private house. There was also an agreement that the defendants should expend a certain sum in repairs. Immediately upon taking possession, the defendants proceeded to prepare the premises for the business of coachmaking. Held, the plaintiffs were entitled to an injunction.[3] So where A., a lessee, a druggist, with notice that the landlord will not let the premises for a bar-room, agrees to sub-let to B. for that purpose, and himself renews the lease; equity will restrain both A. and B. from using the premises for a bar-room.[4] So the administrator of an insolvent estate, having an undivided interest in a block of stores, may enjoin a lessee of one of them from a use injurious to the income of all.[5] But it is

---

[1] Rogers v. Danforth, 1 Stockt. 289.
[2] Steward v. Winters, 4 Sandf. Ch. 587.
[3] Bonnett v. Sadler, 14 Ves. 526.
[4] Parkman v. Aicardi, 34 Ala. 393.
[5] Ibid.

(a) Where a lessee of alum-works covenanted to leave a certain amount of stock upon the premises; there being reason to fear a breach of the covenant, a decree in equity was made against him. So against a landlord, to restore certain farm stock, taken in violation of his contract. 2 Story Eq. 25, § 710; Nutbrown v. Thornton, 10 Ves. 159.

held that equity will not enjoin the use of leased premises for one purpose, merely because the lease contains a provision that they are to be used for another, unless it is also provided that they shall be used for the latter exclusively.[1]

§ 9. The earlier cases allowed an injunction against an action for rent, where the premises had been accidentally burned. But the later theory is, that the lessee is *pro tanto* a purchaser, and that the loss by fire must fall upon him.[2] But where a clause has been inadvertently omitted from a lease, though verbally agreed on, discharging the rent in case of loss by fire; equity will enjoin a suit for the rent after the premises have been burned.[3]

§ 10. In the case of Buckland v. Hall,[4] an injunction against a landlord, who had brought ejectment against the plaintiff, his tenant, after an agreement for renewal of his lease, on the ground of his having become insolvent, was dissolved; the bill also praying specific performance of the agreement. Lord Eldon remarked:[5] "The court must take care that the tenant is not rashly turned out of possession. With respect to the insolvency, the weight of that objection is more or less in different cases. There is a distinction certainly between a purchase and a lease. In the former instance the bill for specific performance tenders payment of the purchase-money; the latter is very much otherwise; and the court ought not to forget the habit of dealing among mankind with regard to the relation of landlord and tenant. Every man taking a tenant looks to the probability of the rent being paid; that attention is paid to that circumstance through the whole currency of the lease, that introduces a provision not to assign or underlet without license. If the tenant undertakes for nothing but the payment of rent, it

[1] Brugman v. Noyes, 6 Wis. 1.
[2] Fowler v. Bott, 6 Mass. 67; Brown v. Quilter, Ambl. 621; Camden v. Morton, 2 Ed. 219; Steele v. Wright, 1 T. R. 708; Hare v. Graves, 3 Anst. 687; Holtsappfell v. Baker, 18 Ves. 118; 1 Fonb. Eq. 374.
[3] Wood v. Hubbell, 10 N. Y. (6 Seld.) 479.
[4] 8 Ves. 92.
[5] Ib. 93.

(insolvency) must be appreciated accordingly. If beyond that he undertakes for considerable expenditure upon the premises, before he is to be placed in the relation of lessee, that is directly connected as a most important circumstance with the fact of solvency or insolvency. The injunction ought not to be sustained; certainly not without considerable terms imposed; such as bringing no writ of error; giving security for the costs; perhaps for the rent and repairs."

§ 11. In the case of a lease, granted by the defendant and assigned to the plaintiff, for the purpose of erecting mills and other buildings, with covenants for the supply of canals and reservoirs on the defendant's estates, and with certain reservations to the defendant for uses paramount to those of the lease; Lord Eldon expressed doubt, upon a bill for an injunction, whether it was according to the practice of the court to order specifically that the defendant should repair the banks of the canal, stop-gates, and other works; but passed an order, to restrain impeding the plaintiff from navigating, using, and enjoying the premises, by continuing to keep the canals, banks, or works out of repair, by diverting the water, or preventing it by the use of locks from remaining in the canals, or by continuing the removal of a stop-gate; his Lordship somewhat sarcastically remarking: "He will find it difficult, I apprehend, to avoid completely repairing these works."[1]

§ 12. Equity will not enjoin a distress for rent, on account of an agreement under which the landlord owes the tenant more than the amount of such rent. The court say: "The policy of the law does not permit a set-off against a distress, and a court of equity must follow the law, and cannot relieve against the rule of law, where the claim of set-off is founded on a legal demand. It is not necessary to consider how the case might be if the tenant had a counter demand, not at law, but in equity."[2]

[1] Lane v. Newdigate, 10 Ves. 192.   [2] Townson v. Benson, 3 Madd. 110–4.

§ 13. The common injunction to stay proceedings at law does not embrace a distress for rent.   Lord Eldon remarked : "I think I remember a great many special applications to restrain distraining for rent because it does not fall within the strict meaning of a proceeding at law ; it may be stopped by replevying, and is the execution of the party himself; but a proceeding at law is where a party applies for the aid of a court of law."[1]

§ 14. Where a vendor has executed a legal assignment of property to a purchaser, chancery will not, on the application of the latter, enjoin the former from illegally distraining upon the tenants of the property, for alleged arrears of rent accrued since the assignment.[2]

§ 15. Where a tenant gave security to the landlord of the stock on the farm, with an agreement that, whenever the arrears due for advances should exceed a certain sum, the landlord might enter and sell the property ; a bill was restrained in favor of the tenant for restoration of the stock seized, the answer not alleging that more than the specified sum was due at the time of seizure.[3]

§ 16. Lease to A. from B. of a store for a monthly rent. A. afterwards conveyed his stock in trade in the store, in trust, to secure a certain sum to C.   The trustees took possession of the goods, just after B. had induced A. to surrender and cancel the lease, and had substituted another and different one, which was antedated, and under which the rent for the whole term was payable in advance.   Upon this B. brought a suit, attached, levied, and claimed a landlord's lien upon the stock.   C. brings a bill for relief, alleging these facts and the insolvency of A., and tendering the rent actually due.   Held, C. was entitled to the relief prayed for.[4]

[1] Hughes v. Ring, 1 Jac. & W. 392.
[2] Drake v. West, 17 Eng. Law and Eq. 367.
[3] Nutbrown v. Thornton, 10 Ves. 159.
[4] Grey v. Hudson, 5 Clarke, 554.

30

§ 17. To obtain an injunction against a lessee for removing a crop, a part of which is due to the plaintiff as rent, the bill must aver the lessee's insolvency, and that he has no tangible property liable to execution or attachment.[1]

§ 18. A yearly tenant, with the option of purchasing, filed a bill against the landlord for specific performance of the contract of sale. The landlord having proceeded to eject him; held, the tenant was entitled to an injunction, upon undertaking to pay the rent, without prejudice to any question in the cause. But it was afterwards agreed that he should pay the purchase-money into court.[2] So, pending a sale of the estate by the landlord to the tenant, the former will be enjoined from enforcing payment of the rent.[3]

§ 19. The removal of a lessor to another State is no ground for an injunction to stay a suit for the rent, in order to enable the defendant to set off damages caused by an eviction.[4]

§ 20. We have already considered the general subject of injunction to prevent *waste*. (See *Waste*.) As between landlord and tenant, it is sufficient ground of injunction, that a tenant threatens or manifests an intention to commit waste.[5] So it is held that equity will enjoin an act contrary to the covenant of the tenant, or even to an agreement which may be implied from the course of dealing between the parties, though not amounting to waste.[6] So an injunction was granted, where a tenant, in revenge for a distress, threatened to sow the land with mustard-seed, which is very injurious to the soil, and very difficult to eradicate.[7] So where, in a case for waste, the defendant claimed possession by title, but admitted that he was let into possession by the tenant of the plaintiff, in breach of his duty; held, the defendant's

---

[1] Gregory v. Hay, 3 Cal. 332.
[2] Pyke v. Worthwood, 1 Beav. 152.
[3] Daniels v. Davison, 16 Ves. 253.
[4] Tone v. Brace, 8 Paige, 597.
[5] Mayor, &c. v. Hedger, 18 Ves. 355; Caldwell v. Baylis, 2 Meri. 408; Gibson v. Smith, 2 Atk. 182; Kimpton v. Eve, 2 Ves. & B. 349.
[6] Lord Grey v. Saxon, 6 Ves. 106.
[7] Pratt v. Brett, 2 Mod. Ch. 62; Tayl. L. & T. § 691.

title was no better than the tenant's, and an injunction was ordered.[1] But an injunction against waste will not be granted, where the article in question is a mere movable fixture, and not annexed to the freehold; as in case of a *dove-cote*, and the removal of locks from the doors of the house, the chains from the lawn, the statues, images, and fences from the pleasure-ground, or wardrobes, presses, and closets, forming part of the wainscot of the house.[2]

§ 21. A lessee, complainant in a bill in equity, cannot enjoin a third party from removing metals from the premises, if his lease expires before a hearing.[3]

§ 22. Lease from A. to B. of a coal-mine, at the rent of 300*l.* per year, and subject to a royalty of 10*s.* for every *wey* in each year over 600; B. to have the right of determining the lease when the coal should be worked out. B. worked the mine several years, and, when it was nearly exhausted, was prevented, by accidents, and defects in it, from continuing to work it without ruinous cost. B. offered to pay 10*s.* per *wey* for all the remaining coal. Held, a suit for the rent could not be enjoined.[4]

§ 23. Pending an ejectment by a lessor, to recover the premises under a forfeiture for non-payment of rent, he filed a bill, to restrain the lessee from collecting the rents from his sub-tenants, stating that the plaintiff had been informed, and believed, that there was no sufficient distress upon the premises. Held, this allegation was not sufficiently verified, and that the proper course for establishing the fact was by actual distress.[5]

§ 24. The plaintiffs having brought an action against the defendant, who was their tenant of a mill, for breaches of covenant in a lease as to paying rent and repairing, the

[1] Comthope *v.* Maplesden, 10 Ves. 291.
[2] Kimpton *v.* Eve, 2 Ves. & B. 349.
[3] Boyle *v.* Laird, 2 Wis. 431.
[4] Phillips *v.* Jones, 9 Sim. 519.
[5] Styvesant *v.* Davis, 9 Paige, 427.

defendant proposed to plead, as an equitable defence, that it was agreed between the parties, that the defendant should surrender by yielding the premises in his occupation, and permitting the plaintiffs to receive the rent, and the tenants of the other portions to attorn, and that the defendant should pay the sum of 250*l.* and give up a quantity of machinery to the plaintiffs, in consideration of the tenancy being put an end to, and in discharge of all claims under the lease. That the defendant accordingly paid such sum of money and delivered up the lease, and withdrew from possession of the premises occupied by him, and permitted the plaintiffs to receive the rents of the tenants who were willing to attorn, and that the defendant relinquished also the machinery, and had done all conditions precedent, and had been ready and willing to do all other things necessary on his part for putting an end to the tenancy, and by way of satisfaction as aforesaid; and that this action was brought in fraud and breach of the agreement, and that it was entirely the fault of the plaintiffs that such surrender was not completed. Held, such plea did not constitute an equitable defence, within the 17 and 18 Vict. c. 125, §§ 83, 86 (the common-law procedure act, 1854), as a court of equity would not either compel performance of the agreement, or restrain the plaintiffs from executing their judgment, without at the same time compelling the defendant to execute a surrender in writing, pursuant to the statute of frauds; and that this court had no power to compel the defendant to execute such surrender. That the power of the court to act, under the above sections, is confined to cases where they are empowered to grant an injunction absolute and without terms.[1]

§ 25. The service of an injunction, at the suit of a stranger, asserting a title to a ferry in the possession of a lessee, and restraining him from interfering in the use of the ferry, is not an eviction, and therefore will not prevent the lessor from recovering rent when the bill is dismissed. But although a

[1] Mines, &c. *v.* Magnay, 28 Eng. Law and Eq. 447.

sheriff, serving an injunction, may have no authority to expel one from the possession of a ferry, or put another in, yet, if he does so, the lessee may consider it a lawful expulsion, if the plaintiff in the suit is invested with a title paramount to that of his lessor.[1]

§ 26. It is held that a *mortgagee* will be restrained by injunction from proceeding at law to sell the equity of redemption.[2](a)   So where property was under mortgage to its full value, a subsequent judgment creditor was restrained by injunction from selling the premises, and the mortgagees were ordered to foreclose with all possible despatch.[3]

§ 27. Where a mortgage of personal property, given to secure a bond payable in three years, with interest annually, and containing a provision, that, on default of payment of the principal sum, or of the interest, at any time when the same should become due, it should be lawful for the mortgagee to grant, sell, &c., was foreclosed for the first instalment of interest; held, the mortgagee had a right to foreclose and collect the whole debt.   But on the coming in of the mortgagee's answer, with application to dissolve an injunction obtained by the mortgagor, it appearing that two of the negroes, for whom the debt was incurred, were so diseased as to greatly impair their value; held, the injunction should be continued, until there could be a hearing on the merits.[4]

§ 28. Where a purchaser of mining lands, machinery, and slaves, gave a mortgage on the property to secure the purchase-money, and, on account of difficulties arising in the

---

[1] Ricketts v. Garrett, 11 Ala. 806.
[2] Severns v. Woolston, 3 Green Ch. 220.
[3] Duncan v. Edwards, 2 Desau. 369.
[4] Shellman v. Scott, Charl. R. M. 380.

(a) See, as to mortgage, Long, &c. v. Mallery, 1 Beasl. 93; McIntier v. Shaw, 6 Allen, 83.

title to portions of the property, it was agreed, in writing, on certain conditions as to paying interest and a sum down, that the payment of the residue of the purchase-money should be postponed until certain suits about the slaves should be settled; it appearing that such conditions had been complied with, held, an injunction to restrain the mortgagee from selling for the purchase-money due ought not to have been dissolved on the coming in of the answer, but it should be continued until further order.[1]

§ 29. In Iowa, in a proceeding in equity to enjoin a summary foreclosure, under Code, c. 118, the court has power, under § 2084, to decree a foreclosure in favor of the respondent, without a cross-bill or anything praying a foreclosure.[2]

§ 30. Equity will not enjoin an action of ejectment by a mortgagee, to recover the mortgaged premises, where no discovery is prayed, and a performance of the condition is insisted upon by the mortgagor as his ground of relief.[3]

§ 31. An injunction will not be granted to restrain a mortgagee, where he advertises the mortgaged property for sale, "to the full extent of the powers derived to or by him under and by virtue of" the mortgage deed, "and not otherwise."[4]

§ 31 a. A suit for the mortgage note will not be enjoined, upon the ground that the mortgagee, having a power of sale, has contracted to sell part of the estate for a sum exceeding the amount due on the note.[5]

§ 32. Where a mortgage is made for the purchase-money of land, equity will not enjoin a foreclosure for want of title

---

[1] High, &c. Co. v. Grier, 4 Jones Eq. 132.
[2] Westfall v. Lee, 7 Clarke, 12.
[3] Henry v. Tupper, 1 Williams, 518.
[4] York, &c. v. Myers, 41 Maine, 109.
[5] Willes v. Levett, 1 De G. & S. 392.

in the mortgagee, who conveyed with warranty, without an allegation of fraud, mistake, or irreparable injury. Otherwise, the remedy is on the covenants.[1]

§ 33. Where a corporation, holding a mortgage to secure money loaned at seven per cent., the money having been advanced in the shape of certificates of deposit payable in twenty years at five per cent., was proceeded against and enjoined from foreclosing the mortgage, because it appeared doubtful whether the transaction was legal; the court refused to dissolve the injunction on the coming in of the answer, but allowed the corporation to file a cross bill to compel a sale of the property.[2]

§ 33 a. Where an injunction, against selling the mortgaged premises under a decree in a foreclosure suit, is dissolved, the damages should include the interest upon the whole sum, the collection of which was either suspended or defeated, the counsel fees for obtaining the dissolution, the taxable costs of so much of the proceedings in the suits as were necessary to obtain such dissolution, and the costs of the reference to a master to ascertain the amount of the damages. And, the purchaser, upon foreclosure and sale, being entitled to the growing crops or emblements, as against the mortgagor; the value of such crops taken off by the mortgagor, during the time in which the sale was suspended, should be allowed as a part of the defendant's damages.[3]

§ 34. Doubts have been sometimes expressed, whether an injunction would be granted against the commission of *waste* by a mortgagor, as, for example, by the cutting of timber; the mortgagee being held in fault for leaving him in possession.[4] So it has been held that the court would not thus interfere, unless first satisfied that the security was defective.[5]

[1] Crocker v. Robertson, 8 Clarke, 404; Young v. Butler, 1 Head, 640; Stipe v. Stipe, 2 ib. 169.
[2] Stoney v. American, &c., 4 Edw. Ch. 332.
[3] Aldrich v. Reynolds, 1 Barb. Ch. 613.
[4] Usborne v. Usborne, 1 Dick. 75.
[5] King v. Smith, 2 Hare, 239.

But it is now the prevailing doctrine, that the mortgagee may have an injunction, though the debt is not due, if the mortgagor in possession commits waste, or in any way attempts to diminish the value of the property; or, if it consists of personalty, where he is about to remove it beyond the reach of his creditor.[1] An injunction lies more especially, where the land is scanty security for the debt. So it will be granted for the destruction of underwood, if contrary to the usual course of husbandry; though not of underwood generally, even though the mortgagor is insolvent or a bankrupt.[2]

§ 35. If the interest of the estate require that the wood be cut, chancery may make provision for the cutting of it upon the mortgagor's giving security. Thus, where a large proportion, in value, of pine woodland was burned over, and it was proper, in order to save the burned wood from rotting, and for the permanent benefit of the estate in reference to the new growth, that the burned wood should be cut off, the land without the wood being of small value, and the mortgagor was proceeding to cut it, when the mortgagee obtained an injunction; held, the value of the wood should be ascertained by a reference, in order that the mortgagor might give security.[3]

§ 36. A purchaser of part of a mortgaged estate may have an injunction, against waste by an assignee, for benefit of creditors, of the mortgagor of another part; standing in the light of a surety for the mortgage debt.[4]

§ 37. A mortgagor in possession, after a sale under decree and execution, will be restrained from waste.[5]

§ 38. An injunction against a mortgagor, restraining him

[1] Salmon v. Clagett, 8 Bland, 180; 5 G. & John. 314; Murdock, 2 Bland, 461.

[2] 1 Pow. 165; Humphreys v. Harrison, 1 Jac. & W. 581; Hampton v. Hodges, 8 Ves. 105; Brown v. Stewart, 1 Md. Ch. 87; Ensign v. Colburn, 11 Paige, 503.

[3] Brick v. Getzinger, 1 Halst. Ch. 391.

[4] Johnson v. White, 11 Barb. 194.

[5] Phœnix v. Clark, 2 Halst. Ch. 447.

from quarrying on a quarry lot, the half of which was conveyed as such to him by the mortgagee, and to secure the consideration for which conveyance the mortgage was given; was dissolved, on an answer denying the charges in the bill, from which it might be inferred that the defendant was improperly impairing the value of the mortgaged premises and endangering the complainant's security.[1] And a mortgagor will not be compelled to repair, where the estate has been injured without his fault; as, to rebuild in case of destruction by fire.[2]

§ 39. An injunction may be granted against the mortgagor, where the mortgage is for years.[3](a)

§ 40. If after a decree for foreclosure the mortgagor begin to commit waste, he will be restrained by injunction, though no injunction is prayed in the bill.[4]

§ 41. Where a mortgagee in fee in possession commits waste by cutting down timber, and the money arising from the sale of the timber is not applied in sinking the interest and principal of his mortgage, the court, on a bill brought by the mortgagor to stay waste, and a certificate thereof, will grant an injunction.[5]

§ 42. On a sale of mortgaged premises, in a suit to foreclose, if the tenant in possession refuses to deliver them up, the court will grant an order to deliver possession, and, in default thereof, an injunction will issue.[6]

[1] Vervalen v. Older, 4 Halst. Ch. 98.
[2] Campbell v. Macomb, 4 John. Ch. 534; Reid v. Bank, &c., 1 Sneed, 262.
[3] Farrant v. Lovel, 3 Atk. 723.
[4] Goodman v. Kine, 8 Beav. 379.
[5] Farrant v. Lovel, 3 Atk. 723.
[6] Ludlow v. Lansing, Hopk. 231.

(a) In Massachusetts, where a mortgagee has brought a suit for foreclosure or possession, the court or any justice thereof, in term-time or vacation, may issue an injunction against waste, done or threatened by the mortgagor, or any person claiming under him, or by his permission. Sts. 1852, 892; Gen. Sts.

§ 43. Where a mortgagee has a judgment at law, there need be no decree *in personam* against the mortgagor praying to be permitted to redeem, but the amount to be paid should be fixed by the decree, and, if paid by a certain day, the injunction perpetuated, and the defendant's claim released, and, if not paid, the property should be sold; and where the property was in the mortgagor's hands, if not surrendered to be sold, and the money could not be got from the complainant, the bill should be dismissed, and the injunction dissolved.[1]

§ 43 *a*. Where mortgaged personal property is delivered to the mortgagee, and there is a continued change of possession, the mortgagee is not entitled to an injunction to restrain a subsequent execution against the mortgagor, as he has a perfect remedy at law.[2]

§ 43 *b*. So an injunction will not be granted, to restrain a party from selling, on an execution against a mortgagor, personal property mortgaged to the complainant to secure an antecedent debt, where the execution was issued, although not actually levied, prior to the execution of the mortgage.[3]

§ 44. Where a conveyance of land is obtained without deception, but upon a verbal promise subsequently to secure the purchase-money by a mortgage, which the grantee afterwards refuses to do; this will not constitute a sufficient ground for enjoining him from selling the land.[4]

§ 45. A. indorsed for B. certain notes given by B. in part payment of a steamboat, and B., to secure A., mortgaged the boat, and agreed to insure and assign the policy to A. B. afterwards, being in failing circumstances, assigned all his estate, including the boat, to C. A. filed a bill in chancery against B. and C., alleging the assignment, the insolvency of

---

[1] Chaney *v.* Cooke, 5 Monr. 248.
[2] Warner *v.* Paine, 3 Barb. Ch. 630.
[3] Warner *v.* Paine, 3 Barb. Ch. 630.
[4] Ellsworth *v.* Starbird, 32 Maine, 176.

B., and that he had neglected to insure the boat and assign the policy; that C. denied the right of A. as mortgagee, claimed an exclusive right to the boat, to enable him to execute his trust, and avowed his purpose to employ and sell it irrespective of A.'s lien, and that C. was unable to make good a loss resulting from the destruction of the boat, or its condemnation, to satisfy the demands of persons furnishing supplies, &c. Held, although neither of the notes was due, chancery would interpose, so as to make the boat subservient to A.'s lien, upon the principle *quia timet*.[1]

§ 46. A., in Mississippi, having made a second mortgage, covering all his property, which was fraudulent on its face, in conveying perishable property to secure a debt on long time, with liberty to A. to use a portion of it, and fearing lest his equity of redemption might be sold on execution, sent to Kentucky for his brother-in-law, and sold to him the entire property, amounting to about $200,000, for the consideration that B. would pay the incumbrances, nearly equal to the value of the property. Bill in equity by B., to enjoin an execution afterwards levied on the property. A. had retained the property for two years after his conveyance, and B. knew his situation, although it was the opinion of a witness, familiar with the parties, that the sale was fair and honest. Held, B. stood in no better situation than A., and the bill should be dismissed; and this, although B. had subsequently executed his notes to the assignees of the creditors preferred by the mortgages, payable in instalments, for the amount of their respective debts, the assignees retaining the original mortgages for their security.[2]

§ 47. A bill, setting out a promise by the defendant to give a mortgage of all his stock in trade, and charging that he now refuses to fulfil his promise, and is selling his stock, and the complainant, being a large creditor, fears to lose his

[1] Walker v. Miller, 11 Ala. 1067.　　[2] Farmers', &c. v. Douglass, 11 S. & M. 469.

security, shows an equitable lien, and will authorize an injunction.[1]

§ 48. The questions, whether after foreclosure of a mortgage, insufficient in value to satisfy the debt, the mortgagee may maintain an action at law for the balance of the debt, with a deduction of the value of the estate; and whether by the bringing of such action the foreclosure is opened and the right of redemption revived; have given rise to many applications for the process of injunction. Thus the bill in the original cause by the mortgagee was, that the defendant, the mortgagor, might redeem or stand foreclosed, and there was the common decree of foreclosure; the defendant not paying the money reported due by the time appointed, he was absolutely foreclosed. The plaintiff, the mortgagee, afterwards sold the estate so foreclosed, and the money produced by the sale not amounting to what was reported on the mortgage, he brought his action against the mortgagor to recover the deficiency. The plaintiff in this suit thereupon brought his bill for an injunction, to stay the defendant's proceeding at law, upon the ground that having got his pledge, he could have no more, and obtained an injunction till answer and further order. Upon showing cause for continuance of the injunction, his lordship (Lord Thurlow) was clear, that the defendant, the mortgagee, under the mortgagor's covenant in the mortgage deed, was entitled to be paid what was due on the mortgage; that so long as he kept the estate, he must take the pledge as a satisfaction, because, by not knowing what it would produce, he would not say anything was due, but if he sold the estate fairly, and without collusion, and for the best price, it would then appear whether it produced the amount of the money reported due; and to the extent of what it did not, the mortgagee had a right, and so it was now established, to bring an action against the mortgagor to recover the deficiency. Injunction dissolved.[2]

[1] Trieber v. Burgess, 11 Md. 452.   [2] Tooke v. Hartley, 2 Dick. 785.

§ 49. In the case of Perry *v.* Barker,[1] Lord Eldon intimated an opinion, that a suit would not lie upon the debt after a sale of the land, because the mortgagee no longer had power to reconvey the estate; but at the same time remarked, that Lord Thurlow had decided that the action might be maintained, either before or after a sale. In a subsequent hearing of the same case, Lord Erskine held, that an action would lie upon the bond after foreclosure; but the right of redemption was thereby revived, and, if the mortgagee had sold the land, he should be allowed time to get it back. But where this could not be done, that the suit would be restrained by a perpetual injunction.[2]

§ 50. A mortgagee for a long term obtained a decree of foreclosure, took possession, sold the estate at auction, and afterwards called upon the mortgagor for the balance of the debt, with interest from completion of the sale, and brought an action upon the mortgage bond. The plaintiff files a bill praying for redemption and injunction, or that the defendant may be decreed to have elected to take the premises in satisfaction of his debt, to deliver up the bond, and be forever restrained from proceeding against the plaintiff. Lord Eldon said: "No case has been produced, previous to 1786, in which, after a foreclosure, the mortgagee has brought the estate to sale, and afterwards brought an action for the money. That circumstance has some weight. The action in that case must have been for the whole money, for it was an action upon the bond. But consider how it would be if the action was upon the covenant, laying the damages for the remainder of the money. It is not very consistent to say, you open the foreclosure, desiring him to bring in only the remainder of the money; for the consequence of opening the foreclosure would be, that a new account should be taken of the principal and interest; and the money to be brought in upon that footing should be all that is due, or nothing. The case of Tooke *v.* Hartley certainly does not decide this;

[1] 8 Ves. 527.   [2] 13 Ves. 197.

for the estate, in fact, sold or not, was in the possession of the mortgagee; and if placed in the same situation as if there had been no foreclosure, the estate being in his possession, what was required by justice as to the reconveyance might be done by the court. But where it is sold to a stranger, that cannot be. The power of reconveyance is gone, and the mortgagor cannot have the right, if it is to be considered opened. At the same time, I certainly understood Lord Thurlow's opinion to have been, that, whether the estate was sold to a stranger, or remained in the possession of the mortgagee, there was no distinction; but an action might be brought for the difference. That opinion of Lord Thurlow, and the circumstance that this particular case was never decided, make it proper at present to grant the injunction, extending it to stay trial, the plaintiff paying the money into court."[1]

§ 51. In the case of Lockhart v. Hardy,[2] the Master of the Rolls expressed an opinion, that equity would enjoin a suit upon the personal obligation for which a mortgage had been given as security, after foreclosure of the mortgage; and refused to let the mortgagee come in under an administration suit, and prove for the deficiency.

§ 52. In Hatch v. White,[3] Judge Story expresses doubts whether a suit upon the mortgage debt should be enjoined in chancery, until the debt has been fully paid; and also whether the foreclosure is opened by bringing an action for the debt. He remarks, that a foreclosure may properly be regarded as a *purchase*, at the full value of the land, if less than the debt, and, if greater, at the amount of the debt. Where the debt is much less than the value of the land, the mortgage will seldom be foreclosed; hence foreclosure is *primâ facie* evidence that the land is insufficient to pay the debt. By taking the land, the creditor suffers an inconve-

[1] Perry v. Barker, 8 Ves. 528, 531.   [3] 2 Galli. 159.
[2] 9 Beav. 349.

nience. He must lose by any depreciation of value, and therefore he ought to have the benefit of any rise in value. If after foreclosure the mortgagee should go into a court of equity for further relief, he might be held to the rule of reciprocal equity; but this does not justify an injunction against the enforcement of *legal rights*. And even if such injunction should be granted where the estate remains unsold, it would seem that after a sale he ought to recover the balance due. Whatever may be the practice in equity, all the decisions concur in the principle that *at law* foreclosure of a mortgage is no bar to a suit for the balance of the debt. Judge Story further holds, that whatever rule upon this subject a court of chancery, acting upon its own peculiar principles, may adopt, it will not authorize the opening of a foreclosure, in consequence of a suit upon the bond, where the right of redemption is by statute limited to a certain time after possession taken by the mortgagee.

§ 53. Upon the same subject it is remarked by the court in Maryland: "The mortgaged estate is considered as a pledge sufficient for the satisfaction of the debt, and as having been so taken by the parties themselves by the nature of their contract. Therefore if the creditor, on his bill in equity, has a decree to foreclose, and nothing more, he is held to have obtained that kind of satisfaction of his claim for which he stipulated; and if after such a decree he sues upon the bond, he thereby opens the decree, and admits the right of the mortgagor to redeem; because by the institution of the suit he disclaims the satisfaction he had obtained by the decree. And if he has placed it out of the mortgagor's power to redeem, by aliening the estate after the decree, he will be perpetually enjoined from proceeding upon the bond. But if the creditor on his bill in equity, instead of a decree to foreclose, obtains a decree for a sale, and the mortgaged estate sells for less than the debt, the balance may be recovered in an action on the covenant or bond, without opening or affecting such a decree for a sale, by which the pledge itself is not taken as a satisfaction, as by a decree to fore-close."[1]

§ 54. After an injunction has been obtained against a mortgagor who is bankrupt, and his assignee and a receiver have been appointed, it is too late to raise any objection to the injunction or receiver on a motion to apply the rents in the hands of the receiver.[2]

§ 55. A. purchased land of B., and gave his note for the price, payable in instalments, to meet payments to be made on a mortgage upon the land. A. failed to pay the note, and the mortgage was foreclosed, and A. purchased at the fore-closure sale. B. recovered judgment on his note. Held, A. was not entitled to relief in equity against the judgment.[3]

§ 56. An injunction will not be granted to restrain the statute foreclosure of a mortgage, on the ground that an appeal is pending from a decision of the vice-chancellor, dis-missing a bill filed by the mortgagor to correct an alleged error in the amount of the mortgage.[4]

§ 57. An injunction to stay sale, under a power in a mortgage, was granted a few days before the expiration of the notice of sale, on a bill by the mortgagor, charging a parol agreement, enlarging the time of payment, and that payments had been made on the mortgage, which were not credited. After answer admitting some of the payments, but denying the agreement charged, the injunction was dis-

[1] Per Bland, Chancellor, Andrews v. Scotton, 2 Bland, 666. See fur-ther, upon the same general subject, though not directly involving the remedy of *injunction*, Omalby v. Swan, 3 Mas. 474; West v. Chamberlin, 8 Pick. 336; Lawrence v. Fletcher, 8 Met. 165; Leland v. Loring, 10 Met. 125; Capen v. Richardson, 7 Gray, 364; Daniels v. Mowry, 1 R. I. 151; Bassett v. Mason, 18 Conn. 131; Coit v. Fitch, Kirby, 254; McEwen v. Welles, 1 Root, 202; Southard v. Wilson, 29 Maine, 56; Porter v. Pills-bury, 36 ib. 278; Paris v. Hulett, 26 Verm. 308; Langdon v. Paul, 20 ib. 217; Hunt v. Stiles, 10 N. H. 469; The Globe, &c. v. Lansing, 5 Cow. 380; Osborne v. Tunis, 1 Dutch. 633; Hubbel v. Broadwell, 8 Ham. 120; Wilson v. Wilson, 4 Iowa, 309.

[2] Post v. Dorr, 4 Edw. Ch. 412.

[3] Clark v. Condit, 13 Mis. 222.

[4] Outtrin v. Graves, 1 Barb. 49.

solved, on the terms of giving six weeks' further notice of the sale, and a reference to a master was ordered, to ascertain the sum due.[1]

§ 58. Where, at a sale, under an order of the probate court, of mortgaged property, in behalf of the mortgagee, a third party gave notice that the title was in the deceased only in trust for him, and, after it was bid off to the mortgagee and another, obtained an injunction restraining further proceedings, which was served on the chief-justice before the confirmation of the sale; the injunction was perpetuated on payment of the mortgage by the plaintiff.[2]

[1] Nichols v. Wilson, 4 John. Ch. 115.　　　[2] Fisk v. Wilson, 15 Tex. 430.

31

CHAPTER XXIX.

CONTRACTS.

§ 1. EQUITY sometimes interferes by injunction in case of contracts. Thus where a contract contains mutual stipulations, and one party performs his part, equity may by injunction prevent the other from violating the contract, although it has not been actually violated, if the danger of violation is imminent and actually impending. And although such contract may be somewhat obscure, the court will struggle hard for its meaning, according to the probable intent of the parties.[1]

§ 2. Applications are sometimes made, to enjoin the violation of contracts against following some particular trade or calling.(a) Thus an injunction was granted, to restrain a solicitor, who had sold his business to the plaintiff for valuable consideration, with an agreement not to practise in Great Britain for twenty years, from thus practising, or seeking to induce clients to cease employing the plaintiff. (In this case Lord Langdale, M. R., carefully analyzes some of the leading cases and approved principles, relating to agree-

[1] Casey *v.* Holmes, 10 Ala. 776.

(a) With regard to the validity of contracts in restraint of trade, see Alger *v.* Thacher, 19 Pick. 51 ; Chappel *v.* Brockway, 21 Wend. 157 ; 2 Pars. on Contr. 254 and notes.

ments in restraint of trade.)[1] But an injunction will not be granted in aid of a right claimed under an agreement, unless such right is free from doubt, and its violation would be an irreparable injury.[2] And where the rights of parties are founded upon an agreement between them, before a decree establishing their rights, equity will not grant an injunction, the effect of which will be to restore the complainant to the possession of premises in the occupation of the defendant.[3]

§ 3. In Whittaker v. Howe,[4] Lord Langdale, M. R., said : " I do not think that this court can refuse to grant an injunction to restrain the violation of a contract or covenant, because there may be some part of the agreement which the court could not compel the defendant specifically to perform." Thus where a contract contains covenants to do certain acts, and also to abstain from doing certain other acts, the court has jurisdiction to restrain the breach of the negative covenants, though there may be no jurisdiction to specifically perform the affirmative covenants. But in such cases the court will decline to interfere, where the jurisdiction cannot be beneficially exercised, or where its exercise would work injustice, as in a case where the consideration for the negative covenant of the one party is the affirmative covenant of the other party, which latter the court cannot specifically perform.[5]

§ 4. This general rule, with the modifications growing out of special circumstances, has been several times illustrated by cases arising between *dramatic managers and performers.* The extravagant prices commanded by popular actors, and the large profits from crowded houses still remaining to their employers after successful engagements, seem to have held out a temptation too strong to be resisted, to violate and procure the violation of the most formal and positive engage-

---

[1] Whittaker v. Howe, 3 Beav. 395.
[2] Morris, &c. v. Socy. &c., 1 Halst. Ch. 203.
[3] Akrill v. Selden, 1 Barb. 316.
[4] 3 Beav. 395.
[5] Kemble v. Kean, 6 Sim. 333 ; Kimberley v. Jennings, Ibid. 340. See 5 Law J. Rep. (N. s.) Chanc. 115 ; Collins v. Plumb, 16 Ves. 454 ; Hills v. Croll, 2 Phil. 60 ; 14 Law J. Rep. (N. s.) Chanc. 444.

ments, to perform for a specified time at one theatre, and not to perform at any other.

§ 5. In a case often cited, A. agreed in writing with B., that, for certain considerations therein expressed, she would sing and perform at his theatre for a specified period ; and that during her engagement with B. she would not sing elsewhere without his license in writing. Afterwards A. contracted with C., to sing and perform at his theatre during this period. Upon bill by B., praying simply that A. might be restrained from singing and performing elsewhere than at his theatre during the period specified, the court granted an injunction accordingly. In this case[1] it was contended, that the court ought never to grant an injunction, except in cases connected with specific performance, or where, if forbearance to do an act is the object, the injunction will execute the whole of the agreement or all that remains to be performed. After commenting at length upon the leading cases cited, the Lord Chancellor remarks :[2] " What is the principle of the jurisdiction of the court? That principle is to bind men's consciences to a fair and liberal performance of their agreements.——It enforces, where it can, the literal performance of the contract. It is objected that if I refuse this application, I exclude this lady from performing at Covent Garden, when I cannot compel her to perform at the Queen's Theatre. I cannot compel her to perform, of course.——But what cause of complaint is it that I should prevent from doing an act which may compel her to do what she ought to do? Though that is not the object the court has in view ; for the court cannot indirectly do a thing, and I disclaim doing a thing indirectly which I cannot do directly.——Though I cannot compel the execution of the whole of the contract, I leave nothing unaccomplished by my order which I hold it is in the power of the court to accomplish. She will be committed to prison by this court if she does any act in breach of this injunction ; and it will have this effect : by preventing her

[1] 13 Eng. Law and Eq. 255.   [2] Page 257.

from doing the act, there will be no case, in an action by Mr. Lumley against her, for such an amount of vindictive damages as a jury might probably be disposed to give if she exercised her talents in the rival theatre.   I shall merely carry out, as far as I can, the whole power of the court on one subject, which fortunately has a bearing upon another subject which I cannot directly touch."[1]

§ 6. It was agreed, in February, 1828, between the plaintiffs, proprietors of Covent Garden Theatre, and the defendant, a celebrated actor, that he should act for twenty-four nights, at a salary of 50*l.* for each night; beginning the 1st of October, and concluding before Christmas; that he should give them the preference in the renewal of an engagement, and during his engagement should not perform at any other theatre in London.   He acted sixteen nights, but, in consequence of an accident to the gas-works in the theatre, could not complete his engagement before Christmas. The parties then agreed for twelve nights after Christmas, instead of the remaining eight, upon the same terms.   He acted on two nights, and was to have acted on a third, but was unable to appear.   Soon afterwards, he having expressed a wish to suspend his performance in London and retire into the country to recruit his health and study some new parts; the plaintiff, Kemble, informed him by letter, dated January 21, 1829, that they consented, it being understood, that he would be ready, at the commencement of the season 1830—1, to return, when required, to his engagement—ten nights still remaining—and that in the mean time he was not to act in London.   January 22, he, by letter, accepted these proposals. In November, 1830, he returned to London, and soon afterwards engaged to act at Drury Lane Theatre.   Whereupon the plaintiffs file a bill for specific performance and for injunction.   Lord Lyndhurst granted an injunction, restraining the defendant from acting in London, till he should have acted ten nights at Covent Garden.   But, on motion, the

_____
[1] Lumley v. Wagner, 13 Eng. Law and Eq. 252—5.

injunction was dissolved. Sir J. Chadwell, V. C., says: "Independently of the difficulty of compelling a man to act, there is no time stated, and it is not stated in what characters he shall act; and the thing is, altogether, so loose that it is perfectly impossible for the court to determine upon what scheme of things Mr. Kean shall perform his agreement. There can be no prospective declaration or direction of the court, as to the performance of the agreement; and, supposing Mr. Kean should resist, how is such an agreement to be performed by the court? Sequestration is out of the question, and can it be said that a man can be compelled to perform an agreement to act at a theatre by this court, sending him to the Fleet for refusing to act at all? There is no method of arriving at that which is the substance of the contract between the parties, by means of any process which this court is enabled to issue; and, therefore (unless there is some positive authority to the contrary), my opinion is that, where the agreement is mainly and substantially of an active nature, and is so undetermined that it is impossible to have performance of it in this court, and it is only guarded by a negative provision, this court will leave the parties, altogether, to a court of law, and will not give partial relief by enforcing only a negative stipulation." The Vice-Chancellor proceeds to distinguish between this case and one of *partnership*, in which, under similar circumstances, the court would interfere by injunction. He refers particularly to the case of Morris v. Colman,[1] and the following account of it, given by Lord Eldon in a subsequent case: "Morris, Colman, and other persons were engaged in a partnership in the Haymarket Theatre, which was to have continuance for a very long period, as long, indeed, as the theatre should exist. Colman had entered into an agreement which I was very unwilling to enforce, not that he would write for the Haymarket Theatre, but that he would not write for any other theatre. It appeared to me that the court could enforce that agreement by restraining him from writing for any other theatre.

[1] 18 Ves. 437.

The court could not compel him to write for the Haymarket Theatre; but it did the only thing in its power, it induced him, indirectly, to do one thing by prohibiting him from doing another. There was an express covenant on his part contained in the *articles of partnership.*"[1]

§ 7. In a case in Maryland, where the defendant contracted, that his wife should perform at the theatre of a certain manager, for a specific time and salary; held, a court of equity would not enjoin the wife from performing elsewhere during that time; nor the husband from permitting her to change her abode; nor another manager from employing her; more especially pending a suit at law upon the contract.[2] And the same rule was adopted in another case, in New York, where a person contracted to sing at operas, &c., and not to make other engagements for the same purpose; that an injunction will not be granted to restrain the contractor from making such other engagements; the party was left to his remedy at law.[3]

§ 8. Contracts relating to *railroads* have sometimes been the subjects of application for injunction.

§ 9. Where there is an agreement between two railway companies, which is beyond the powers of both, and against the policy of their acts of Parliament, a shareholder in one of the companies may file a bill on behalf of himself and all the other shareholders therein, against his own company and the other company, for an injunction to restrain the execution of the agreement, and without making either the directors of the former company, or the shareholders therein who promoted the agreement, or any of them, defendants to the suit.[4]

§ 10. In the case of the Great Western, &c. v. The Bir-

---

[1] Kemble v. Kean, 6 Sim. 333.
[2] Burton v. Marshall, 4 Gill, 487.
[3] Sanquirico v. Benedetti, 1 Barb. 315.

[4] Winch v. The Birkenhead, &c., 13 Eng. Law and Eq. 506.

mingham, &c. (Railways), the defendants had entered into a contract to sell their railway to the plaintiffs, and the bill was filed for specific performance.   And it alleged that the plaintiffs were obliged to take such proceeding, because the defendants, contending for the invalidity of their contract with the plaintiffs, were proceeding to contract for a sale to the Northwestern Company; and the bill prayed for an injunction against such contract, or any proceedings inconsistent with the rights of the plaintiffs, without their consent. Injunction granted.[1]   But notwithstanding this case, in The Shrewsbury, &c. v. The Shrewsbury, &c., the vice-chancellor declined to interfere by injunction under circumstances thus stated: "They (the defendants) are proposing to enter into a contract with the London and Northwestern Company, under which the latter bind themselves to pay to them a sum which amounts to 40,000l. or 50,000l. a year for twenty-one years. Supposing it were to turn out, in the result, if I were to issue this injunction, that the defendants are right, and that the agreement which the plaintiffs have entered into is invalid *in toto*, and therefore there was no legal bar to the defendants entering into this contract, in what predicament would this court then find itself, if it should have issued an injunction restraining the defendants from entering into a contract *ex hypothesi* a valid contract, which there was no legal ground to prevent them from entering into, and then afterwards they should be unable to enter into it, and so lose 50,000l. a year for twenty-one years."[2]

§ 11. In the same case, the vice-chancellor made the following general remarks.

§ 12. "I do not mean to say that this court will not, under some circumstances, prevent parties, pending litigation, from alienating, or even entering into contracts relating to sub-

---

[1] (Cited in) The Shrewsbury, &c.   [2] 1 Sim. 430.
v. The Shrewsbury, &c., 1 Sim. N. S.
428.

ject-matters of litigation.   By such alienations or contracts no eventual injury can, in general, result to the plaintiff; but they may impose on him the necessity of making additional parties, and may delay and embarrass him in the assertion of his rights.   In some cases they might even tend to destroy the subject-matter in dispute.—But this interference is by no means a matter of course.—There are, I apprehend, two points on which the court must satisfy itself. First—not that the plaintiff has, certainly, a right, but that he has a fair question to raise as to the existence of such a right.—There is a further question, namely, whether interim interference, or a balance of convenience and inconvenience to the one party and to the other, is or is not expedient. Where the alternative is interference or probable destruction of the property, there, of course, the court will be very ready to lend its immediate assistance, even at considerable risk that it may be encroaching on what may eventually turn out to be a legal right of the defendant.   But where, on the other hand, the only evil tó result from non-interference is, that the plaintiff may, by the contracts or deeds of the defendants, be retarded or embarrassed by his litigation, there the court will be far more ready to listen to any suggestion of the defendant, showing that interference during litigation will prejudice his rights."[1]

§ 13. Injunction is often applied for, in connection with contracts for the sale and purchase of real estate.   In case of a mere agreement to convey, defect of title is ground for injunction in favor of the purchaser.[2]   And though the sale is under a decree, equity cannot make a man take a title which he is to support by a bill for an injunction.[3]

§ 14. The remedy of injunction is more especially invoked in connection with the claim for *specific performance.*   Upon

[1] Per Vice-Chanc., The Shrewsbury, &c. *v.* The Shrewsbury, &c., 1 Sim. N. S. 424, 426.

[2] Buchanan *v.* Alwell, 8 Humph. 516; Buchanan *v.* Lorman, 3 Gill, 51.
[3] Per Lord Rosslyn, Shaw *v.* Wright, 3 Ves. 22.

this subject, a writer of high authority lays down the following general propositions.

§ 15. "If a bill be filed for a specific performance, the court will enjoin either party not to do any act to the injury of the other. Therefore, if the purchaser is in possession, and has not paid the money, the court will grant an injunction against his cutting timber. So, on the other hand, the vendor will be restrained from conveying away the legal estate in the property, because such a measure might put the purchaser to the expense of making another party to the suit; and à *fortiori* he will be restrained from selling the estate to a third person. But in Spiller *v.* Spiller the lord chancellor expressly laid it down, that, upon a bill filed for specific performance, he wished it to be understood, that the court would not take from a seller the disposition of his property. So injunctions may be granted against the agents of the parties. But an injunction will not be granted against a person who is not a party to the suit; and in a late case, upon a bill filed by a seller for a specific performance, and an injunction against the purchaser's proceeding at law to recover the deposit from the seller's attorney, to whom it was paid, Sir John Leach, V. C., refused the motion, with costs, because the attorney was not a party to the suit. But in a later case, the same judge granted an injunction to restrain the purchaser from proceeding in an action against the auctioneer, although he (the auctioneer) was not a party to the suit; the seller offering to bring the deposit into court. Pending a suit by a purchaser for a specific performance of an agreement to sell a presentation to a living, the seller may be restrained by injunction from presenting, and the bishop from instituting, or in the case of a lapse from collating to the living any clerk not named by the purchaser."[1]

§ 15. Where a bill has been brought for specific performance, and a decree made and complied with, and the plaintiff

[1] 1 Sugd. on Vend. and P. 289.

in such bill brings an action at law for damages caused by delay in performing the contract; the defendant cannot have an injunction in the original cause, though he might in a new suit.[1]

§ 16. Pending a suit by the vendor for specific performance, equity will not enjoin an action of the purchaser for the deposit, unless the former consent to its being brought into court.[2] Excepting, however, the case where the vendor retains the estate from the fault of the purchaser; as where the former is able to make a good title, and the latter refuses to complete the purchase.[3]

§ 16 a. After a decree for specific performance, the defendant cannot proceed by action at law on the contract for damages. The vice-chancellor says: "My decree proceeds upon the ground that the defendant has dispensed with the time stated in the contract. If the plaintiff in equity had before the decree applied for an injunction to restrain the defendant from proceeding in an action at law to recover damages, I should, upon the same principle, have then granted the injunction; and à fortiori, I must grant it now. The proceeding at law is inconsistent with the decree in equity."[4]

§ 16 b. Where a bill by a seller for specific performance is dismissed, and without the proviso that it shall not prejudice the plaintiff's remedy at law; equity will in a proper case restrain the seller from afterwards bringing an action for damages; for example, where the bill was dismissed because the seller had no title.[5]

§ 17. If objections arise to the title, and the vendee brings an action at law for non-performance of the agreement, and

---

[1] Ford v. Compton, 1 Cox, 296.
[2] Tanner v. Smith, 4 Jur. 310; Annesley v. Muggridge, 1 Madd. 593.
[3] Wynne v. Griffith, 1 Sim. & St. 147.
[4] Reynolds v. Nelson, Madd. & Geld. 290.
[5] McNamara v. Arthur, 2 Ball & B. 349; 1 Sugd. Vend. and P. 497.

the vendor files his bill for a performance in specie, and an injunction is granted; the court will not dissolve it without the Master's report as to the title, where the action is brought on the ground of want of title.[1]

§ 18. In case of sale by auction, if both parties claim the deposit, the auctioneer may file a bill of interpleader, and pray for an injunction, which will be granted upon payment of the deposit into court.[2]

§ 19. An injunction lies to restrain the vendor of real property, defendant in a bill for specific performance, from conveying the estate, upon the ground that the plaintiff might be thereby subjected to the expense of making an additional party, when the cause might be just ready for a hearing.[3]

§ 20. Equity will enjoin the cutting of timber by one who has got possession under articles to purchase.[4] So a purchaser, under a decree of the court of equity, by the purchase submits himself to the jurisdiction of the court, and, therefore, if he obtain possession before completion of the contract, he may be enjoined from the commission of waste.[5]

§ 21. In case of a covenant by a purchaser, restricting the mode of enjoyment of the purchased estate, equity will not enjoin a breach of such covenant by a second purchaser without notice; nor where no real injury is likely to arise; or there has been a change of circumstances. And an injunction against the erection of buildings was refused, where the plaintiff had himself erected buildings, which defeated the object of the covenant.[6] In a case where the plaintiff had

[1] 1 Sugd. on Vend. and P. 490.
[2] Farebrother v. Prattent, 5 Price, 303.
[3] Echliff v. Baldwin, 16 Ves. 267.
[4] Crockford v. Alexander, 15 Ves.
138; Baldwin v. Belcher, 1 J. and Lat. 18.
[5] Cassamajor v. Strode, 1 Sim. & St. 381.
[6] Bedford v. British, &c., 2 My. 552.

contributed to a fund, on condition that a literary and theological seminary should be permanently located at a specified place, which was accordingly done; an injunction was granted against an unauthorized and illegal removal.[1]

§ 22. An injunction will lie against a purchaser, on behalf of creditors, to restrain payment to the heir.[2]

§ 23. Where the defendant is in Maryland, but the land in controversy in Virginia, and it is sought to vacate a decree in Virginia, though this cannot be done, yet the defendant, seeking to enforce such decree, may be enjoined from accepting a conveyance of lands purchased by him under it, or, if he has inequitably obtained title, may be decreed to reconvey.[3]

[1] Hascall v. The Madison, &c., 8 Barb. 174.
[2] Green v. Lowes, 3 Bro. C. 217.
[3] Buchanan v. Lorman, 3 Gill, 52.

CHAPTER XXX.

NEGOTIABLE INSTRUMENTS.

§ 1. IN reference to the remedy of injunction as applied to written instruments, Judge Story remarks: "A question has often occurred, whether, if the instrument be void, and ought not to be enforced, the more appropriate remedy in a court of equity would not be, to order a perpetual injunction to restrain the use of the instrument rather than to compel a delivery up and cancellation of the instrument."[1]   And it is said by the same eminent jurist in a case which came before him as a judge: "Thirty years ago, it seems to have been thought by Lord Eldon, that an injunction to restrain the negotiation of a negotiable instrument was an extraordinary interference of the court, and that, upon the coming in of the answer, the case stood exactly as if the case had been upon the common injunction to stay proceedings at law.[2] But this doctrine has been since completely abandoned; and in Hood v. Astor,[3] Lord Eldon himself, adverting to the supposed practice, not to interfere in cases of negotiable securities to prevent their negotiation said: 'I do not recollect such a doctrine to have been at any time in my experience the law of this court.' This last doctrine has been in the fullest manner recognized and acted upon by the Supreme Court of the United States."[4]   Thus an injunction lies, to restrain the holder of a note made in connection with a marriage brocage contract from putting it in circulation, and thus depriving the maker of the right of making such de-

---

[1] 2 Story, Eq. 10, § 698.
[2] Berkeley v. Breymer, 9 Ves. R. 355, 356.
[3] 1 Russ. R. 412.
[4] Per Story, J., Poor v. Carleton, 3 Sumn. 76.

fence against an indorser.[1]   So A. and B. purchased from C.
a plantation and slaves, and executed to him their notes, and
a deed of trust on the property, to secure them.   C. assigned
a part of the notes to D., in trust, to secure certain debts to
sundry creditors. C. became the *bonâ fide* holder of a portion of
the debts, to secure which, the notes were assigned by C. to
D.   D. sued A. and B. on the notes.   Held, a court of chancery,
on a bill, filed by A. and B. against D., would restrain him
from collecting out of them such portion of the notes, as,
when collected, D. would have to pay over to A.[2]   So when
a party, liable over as transferrer of a note, is notified of a
plea of failure of consideration filed by the maker, in a suit
brought by the transferree thereon ; the transferrer is a privy
in law to the judgment rendered against the plaintiff on such
a plea, and is concluded thereby ; and if afterwards the transferrer is proceeding at law to enforce security against the
transferree, taken in payment for the note, equity will relieve
the transferree to the extent of such failure of consideration,
by injunction and decree.[3]   Though equity will not restrain
an action on a note or bill, where the failure of consideration
is unliquidated.[4]   So equity will interfere by injunction,
to prevent the transfer of a specific thing, which, if transferred, will be irretrievably lost, as negotiable securities and
stocks.[5]   So where a person has negotiable securities in his
possession, under a void contract, and is not of sufficient
responsibility to answer for the value thereof, the negotiation
of them may be restrained by injunction.[6]   So a State court
of chancery has jurisdiction to grant an injunction, at the
suit of another State, to restrain the transfer, within the
former State, of negotiable securities issued by the latter.[7]
So if a note be given by a person immediately on his coming of age, for extravagant supplies made to him during his
infancy ; the negotiation may be restrained by injunction.[8]

[1] Smith v. Haytwell, Ambl. 67.
[2] Nelson v. Dunn, 15 Ala. 501.
[3] Bullock v. Winter, 10 Geo. 214.
[4] Glennie v. Imri, 3 Y. and Coll.
Exc. 436.

[5] Osborn v. Bank, &c. 9 Wheat.
738.
[6] Delafield v. Illinois, 2 Hill, 159.
[7] Delafield v. Illinois, 26 Wend.
192.
[8] Brook v. Galby, 2 Atk. 34.

So when a bill or note has been obtained fraudulently, or upon an illegal transaction, as at play, upon a bill filed charging these facts, supported by an affidavit, an injunction to prevent the negotiating or parting with the bill or note will be granted immediately upon filing the bill, and even before the service of the subpœna to appear.[1] So, in Louisiana, if the plaintiff came improperly into possession of a note, which was left conditionally with a third person, the defendant's remedy is by injunction, not by an appeal from the order of seizure and sale.[2]

§ 2. The orators, with their father, executed a promissory note to the defendant, the orators signing as "sureties," under an agreement that the note should not be delivered, nor become operative, until certain conditions were performed by the defendant. The father mortgaged certain premises to secure the note; but the defendant, without the consent of the orators, obtained the note and mortgage, and then refused to perform the conditions. Held, the defendant should be enjoined from negotiating or enforcing the note as against the orators. But, the father having deceased, and his personal representative not being a party to the bill; held further, the court could not, upon this bill, interfere, to set aside the note and mortgage, as against his estate.[3] So if one, to whom negotiable paper has been confided for a special use or limited purpose, should attempt, in breach of the confidence reposed in him, to pervert the paper to a different use or purpose, equity will, upon proper application, enjoin him from doing any act, though it be the carrying on of a suit at law, which he may make the means or instrument of his bad faith; and indorsees of the paper, after it is overdue, though for value, are subject to the same equities, and may be prevented in the same mode from misapplying it. And where one of several notes, on demand, with interest, given

---

[1] 4 Bouv. Inst. 128.
[2] Weems v. Ventress, 14 La. An. 267.
[3] Chase v. Torrey, 20 Vt. 395.

by a corporation before it had issued stock certificates to its stockholders, in evidence of their proportionate interest in certain of its own stock held by it in trust for them, and upon which no money was to be paid, was negotiated for value by a stockholder, thirteen months after its date; held, such note was overdue at the time it was taken by the holder, so as to entitle the corporation to enjoin a suit at law commenced by him to recover the amount of the note from them, upon the ground of the equities subsisting between them and the payee of the note.[1]

§ 3. The plaintiff, a member of a corporation in Oregon, agreed to make a loan to the company, who agreed, upon his request, to give their note therefor, secured by mortgage of their whole property. The plaintiff, then in Oregon, thereupon drew sundry drafts on A., his agent in Connecticut, for about half the amount of the loan, and delivered them to the company. The drafts were forwarded to Connecticut, and accepted by A. A part were paid by A., when due, but one was protested for non-payment, A. having been unable to dispose of certain property of the plaintiff in his hands in season to meet it, and it was returned to the president of the company. The company soon after failed, and could not give the promised security; and the plaintiff made no further advance. He also notified A. not to pay the draft, and demanded it of the company, but the directors refused to surrender it. Afterwards, while the draft was in the hands of the president, B., a creditor, member, and director of the company, knowing all the facts, attached the draft, with other corporate property, and the president thereupon, on his demand, delivered it to him. B. sent the draft to C., whom he owed, to collect and apply the proceeds on his account, and C. brought a suit upon it in Connecticut against A. A. then had funds of the plaintiff, with which he intended to pay any judgment which C. might recover. The plaintiff brings a bill in equity against C. for an injunction

---

[1] Atlantic, &c. v. Tredick, 5 R. I. 171.

of the suit, and cancellation of the draft.   Held, even if the plaintiff would have a good defence at law, he was entitled to a cancellation of the draft, because other suits might be brought upon it.   Also, that, as the company had become unable to give the stipulated security, the plaintiff was not bound to complete the loan, or demand the security.   Injunction granted.[1]

§ 4. An injunction in force against the negotiation of a note does not destroy its negotiability.[2]

§ 4 *a*. A. accepted a bill for 150*l*., drawn by and for the accommodation of B.   B. indorsed the bill, and, to facilitate its being discounted, procured the indorsement of C.   Before maturity, B. delivered the bill to D., as security for 100*l*. When the bill fell due, D. demanded the sum loaned, and, some weeks afterwards, C. took up the bill and gave a new one for 160*l*., upon a further advance of 50*l*.   C. then brings an action against A. upon the bill, and A. files a bill for injunction, and to have the bill delivered up.   Held, the case was one exclusively for a court of law, and a common injunction, obtained by the plaintiff, should be dissolved.[3] So where a person has lent his name as maker of a note, to enable the borrower to keep up a false credit by using the paper as business paper, he cannot come into court for relief against the consequences.[4]

§ 5. Bill for a perpetual injunction of judgments, obtained on bills of exchange drawn by the complainant, and passed by the respondent into the hands of third persons, by whom the judgments were obtained.   Held, the injunction ought not to be decreed, until the answers of the third parties had come in, although the bill stated, and the respondent admitted, that he paid the judgments, and was the only person

---

[1] Ferguson *v.* Fisk, 28 Conn. 501.
[2] Winston *v.* Westfeldt, 22 Ala. 760.
[3] Hammon *v.* Sedgwick, 6 Hare, 256.
[4] Davenport *v.* City Bank, 9 Paige, 12.

interested in them, because such statements and admissions might be made by collusion.[1]

§ 6. Judgment was recovered by the holders of a bill of exchange against an indorser, who filed a bill to enjoin it, alleging that the bill had been paid by a subsequent indorser, which payment was not known to the complainant until after the judgment was recovered; that it was paid out of funds furnished by the drawer; and that the suit was brought in the name of the holders, fraudulently, to deprive the complainant of a good defence against the indorser, who paid the bill. Held, on demurrer, that the indorser, who paid the money, was not a necessary party to the bill; that it was not necessary to set out particularly the nature or amount of the funds furnished by the drawer, or whether any or what part were applied to the payment of the bill.[2]

§ 7. Two notes, given for the purchase-money of two distinct tracts of land, but bearing date and executed on the same day, do not thereby become parts of the same transaction, nor so blended together, that an eviction from one of the tracts will enable the vendee to enjoin the collection of the note given for the other.[3]

§ 8. A. and B. gave a bond for title to land to C., who paid a part of the purchase-money, and gave his notes for the balance, three to A. and three to B. C. being unable to pay, it was agreed between the parties, that the contract should be rescinded, and the bond was surrendered, and A. and B. delivered to C. his notes, except one which A. had assigned to D. On this note D. afterwards recovered judgment against C., who filed a bill to enjoin its collection, making A. and D. parties. Held, B. was not a necessary party; that C. was not entitled to an injunction against D.; and, the contract having been rescinded, A. would be liable

---

[1] Marshall v. Beverley, 5 Wheat. 313.

[2] Atkins v. Dicks, 14 Pet. 114.
[3] Wray v. Furniss, 27 Ala. 471.

to C. for the note he had assigned, whenever C. should pay the judgment, or A. should be otherwise released from his liability to D.[1]

§ 9. Chancery will take jurisdiction and grant relief where a promissory note has been lost or destroyed, if the complainant tenders adequate security against loss to the defendant; otherwise he will be turned over to the courts of law.[2]

§ 10. An assignee of a note brought trover, in the name of the assignor, husband of the payee, for a conversion prior to the assignment. On a bill by the payee against the assignor, her husband, claiming the notes, and for a stay of the suit at law, it was held, that the assignee need not be made a party, as he had no right to commence such suit.[3]

§ 11. The drawer of a bill cannot enjoin an innocent holder from collecting it of an accommodation acceptor, on the ground of fraud in the payee.[4]

§ 12. The orators, with their father as principal, executed a note to the defendant, the orators signing as "sureties," under an agreement that the note should not be delivered, nor become operative, until certain specified conditions were performed by the defendant. The father mortgaged certain premises to secure the note; but the defendant, without the consent of the orators, obtained possession of the note and mortgage, and then refused to perform the conditions. Held, the defendant should be enjoined from negotiating the note, or enforcing its collection, as against the orators. But also, the father having deceased, and his personal representative not being a party to the bill; that the court could not upon this bill interfere, to set aside the note and mortgage, as against his estate.[5]

[1] Drake v. Lyons, 9 Gratt. 54.
[2] Ross v. Wright, 12 Geo. 507.
[3] Chase v. Chase, 1 Paige, 198.
[4] Winn v. Wilkins, 35 Miss. 186.
[5] Chase v. Torrey, 20 Vt. 395.

§ 13. Affidavits are not admissible in support of an injunction against the negotiation of a bill. Lord Eldon makes the distinction, that "in the case of waste the irreparable mischief is not with reference to the circumstance whether the man can or cannot pay, but in this respect, that the timber cannot be set up again."[1](a)

[1] Berkeley v. Brymer, 9 Ves. 354, 355.

(a) As to the delivering up of papers to be cancelled; see Minshaw v. Jordon, 3 Bro. 18, n.; Hamilton v. Cumming, 1 John. Ch. 521; Bromley v. Holland, 7 Ves. 3; Apthorpe v. Comstock, 8 Cow. 386; 2 Paige, 482; Loomis v. Cline, 4 Barb. 453; Harrington v. Bigelow, 11 Paige, 349.

CHAPTER XXXI.

MISCELLANEOUS CASES OF INJUNCTION.

§ 1. THE following rather leading English and American cases have not seemed strictly to belong to the subject-matters of any of the foregoing chapters, though illustrative of many of the points already considered in the present work. Partly from the fact that they are somewhat *abnormal* and individual, and partly from their intrinsic authority and importance, they are perhaps of more than ordinary interest.

§ 2. In the case of the Attorney-General *v.* Cleaver,[1] Lord Eldon remarked : "This court has originally no jurisdiction whatsoever either to enjoin or regulate the proceedings upon an indictment, but circumstances may give that jurisdiction : where, for instance, the relators are the persons prosecuting the indictment, I should have a control by order personally affecting them ; but I am not satisfied that I have the same control over these defendants, who have not come in. There is one case of a bill, and a cross-bill, and also an indictment between the plaintiffs and defendants. Lord Hardwicke held that he would deal with the subject with reference to what was civilly in question between them, though also the subject of a criminal prosecution ; but I do not find that he thought himself justified in that with regard to persons who had not themselves resorted to him."

§ 3. The plaintiffs claim the sole right of fishing in the river *Ouse;* the defendant claims a right likewise ; a bill and

[1] 18 Ves. 219.

cross-bill were brought, to establish their several rights. While these suits were depending, the plaintiffs caused the agent of the defendant to be indicted at *York* sessions, where they themselves are judges, for a breach of the peace, in fishing in their liberty. A motion was made on behalf of the defendant, to stop the prosecution. Lord Chancellor (Hardwicke). " This court has not originally and strictly any restraining power over criminal prosecutions; and, in this case, if the defendant had applied to the attorney-general, he would have granted a *noli prosequi*. For when a complaint is grounded on a civil right, for which an action of trespass would lie, the attorney-general of course grants a *noli prosequi*. This is a complaint merely for fishing in the river, without any actual breach of the peace, which the mayor and corporation say is a trespass upon them. If it could be made appear at law, that the plaintiffs were both judges and parties, it might come out to be *coram non judice*, but it might be difficult to make out this. If actions of trespass had been brought *vi et armis*, this court would have stopped them; but though I cannot grant an injunction, yet I may certainly make an order upon the prosecutors to prevent the proceeding on the indictment. Where parties submit their right to the court, they have certainly a jurisdiction, and may interpose. Therefore I will make an order to restrain the plaintiffs from proceeding at the sessions, till the hearing of the cause and further order."[1] (See pp. 1 and note, 274.)

§ 4. A bill charged that the plaintiff, as lord of a borough, was entitled to a heriot on the death of any tenant, and that conveyances were made to the defendants in trust, to defraud him; and prayed a discovery of the deeds, and an injunction or equivalent order to stay proceedings on a mandamus to compel the plaintiff to hold a court, and admit the defendants as tenants. A demurrer to the bill was allowed. Hardwicke, Lord Chanc., said: "If I should overrule this demurrer, I should open a new door of jurisdiction to this court, which,

[1] The Mayor, &c. *v.* Sir Lionel, &c., 2 Atk. 302.

I believe, would afford a scene of very great inconvenience and mischief, and bring all the corporation and borough causes in this kingdom in some shape or other on the footing of discovery or relief. This court has no jurisdiction to grant an injunction to stay proceedings on a *mandamus;* nor to an indictment; nor to any information; nor to a writ of prohibition, that I know of. The reason is, that a *mandamus* is not a writ remedial, but mandatory. It is vested in the king's superior court of common law to compel inferior courts to do something relative to the public. That court has a great latitude and discretion in cases of that kind, can judge of all the circumstances, and is not bound by such strict rules as in cases of private rights. I will go by Littleton's rule, that it is a good argument, an action lies not, because one was never brought. I never knew a bill of this kind, and therefore will not make the precedent."[1]

§ 5. By act of Parliament, the Commissioners of Woods and Forests were authorized to make certain new streets, according to a certain plan, and to lease and agree to lease the ground in the lines of the streets. They leased two plots, upon which the lessees built two houses in the line of one of the streets. Each lease described the plot leased, as "on the north side of a new street then forming there, called," &c., and "fronting towards the south on said new street." The plan referred to exhibited an open space in front of the sites of these houses, but neither lease mentioned the plan. The streets were finished, and the space in front of the houses left open. The commissioners and the paving committee of the parish afterwards authorized certain persons to erect an *equestrian statue* in the open space; which they accordingly did, but not interfering with the line of the carriage-way of the new street in which the houses stood. The lessees thereupon filed a bill for an injunction, alleging that, upon the treaty for the leases, they were shown the plan of the proposed new street and parts adjacent, indicating that the space

[1] Lord Montague *v.* Dudman, 1 Ves. 396-7-8.

was to be open and unobstructed, and that it was stated that opposite the two houses a free passage would be left of certain dimensions, which passage would be contracted by the erection of the statue; that it would diminish the value of their property, and be a public and private nuisance. An injunction, granted by the vice-chancellor, was dissolved by the chancellor (Lord Cottingham). His lordship remarked: "If contract be the ground for the interference of the court, it is as applicable to the statue at the top of Portland Place as the statue now in question, although the plaintiffs may not have so much interest in that distant part of the property delineated on the plan. This proposition would evidently lead to the most absurd consequences. A man who is about to sell a corner of an estate may exhibit a plan of the whole estate, in order to show the relative position of that part which he is about to sell; but is he, on that account, to have his hands forever tied up from the enjoyment and use of all other parts of the estate, and is he to preserve it in exactly its present state? If, however, the right to the injunction is to be put upon the ground of contract, it is necessary to consider how, in point of law, it is to be supported. Such a contract must be looked for *dehors* the deed. The case assumes that the contract has been carried into effect, and that the estate contracted for has been created by the lease. New agreements, by way of covenant, are entered into, to secure the objects of the grant, but the contract for the lease exists no longer. The plaintiff's case is not that a provision has been omitted out of the lease, by fraud, misapprehension, or mistake, but that a separate and distinct contract arose from the mere exhibition of the plan.—The parol agreement was merged in the written contract, if there was one, and both were merged in the deed.—It is said that the statue will be a public nuisance. This it can only be by obstructing the carriage-way; but I am clearly of opinion that the erection of the statue will, upon the whole, be a great benefit to the public, as contradistinguished from the occupiers of the adjoining houses. It is quite immaterial whether a majority of the inhabitants of the neighboring houses do or do not object, and I give no opinion as to whether it is likely to depreciate the value of the property of the plaintiffs; but the injury and inconvenience, if any, do not constitute such a description of private nuisance as would justify the interference of this court."[1]   In the course of his elaborate and learned opinion, Lord Cottenham cites several leading cases, among others The Feoffees of Heriot's, &c. v. Gibson,[2] carried from the Scotch Court of Session to the House of Lords, in which the following piquant remarks are attributed to Lord Eldon: "There was a reference to one case, the Prince's street case, Deas v. The Magistrates of Edinburgh, House of Lords, April 10th, 1772, referred to,[3] where the magistrates exhibited a plan, with a beautiful view of the disposition of the grounds in front of the new buildings to be erected, a thing which was done here every day without any idea that the proprietors were to be prevented from erecting other houses merely by having exhibited a different disposition of the grounds in a picture, unless it were so stipulated in the contracts between the parties.   The magistrates, the ground being their own, began to erect houses where they had exhibited terraces and walks.   An action of declarator was brought, to have it declared that the magistrates were not entitled to erect these new buildings, without consent of the fenars, and a process of suspension was also instituted to stop the progress of the work in the mean time.   The court refused to pass the bill, and the question came to this house, where Lord Mansfield, who would be remembered as long as the law of England or Scotland existed, made a very eloquent speech.   But after all that he had *said*, what he *did* was merely to give an opportunity of examining the question of right.   He could easily conceive that deference to his opinion had put an end to further proceedings in that case, the corporation having been, perhaps, almost frightened out

---

[1] Squire v. Campbell, 1 My. & Cr. 459; 13 Eng. Ch. R. 468.

[2] 2 Dow. 301.

[3] Ib. 304.

of their senses by his speech; but still this was no judgment upon the question of right."[1] (See Chap. XXVII., *Estoppel*, *Easement*.)

§ 6. A bill was brought against the defendants, the church-wardens, and against the parson and overseers of the town of Hammersmith, to stay the ringing of the five o'clock bell of the town, which had usually been rung at five o'clock A. M. from Michaelmas to Candlemas, except upon holy days, and the twelve days at Christmas. The plaintiffs, husband and wife, had a house near the church, and she, being an invalid, was much disturbed by the bell, and about to remove. An agreement was then made, that the plaintiffs should build a cupola to the church, and erect a clock and new bell, provided that during their respective lives the five o'clock bell should not be rung. The plaintiffs thereupon made the agreed erections, and the five o'clock bell was silenced for about two years. But the defendant, Watkin, an ale-house keeper, being since chosen church-warden, a new order of vestry was obtained for the ringing again of the five o'clock bell. Held, an injunction should be granted for the lives of the plaintiffs, "for here was a meritorious consideration; the church-wardens were a corporation, and might sell the bells or silence them, and make a reasonable agreement, and thereby bind the parishoners and their successors as also the succeeding church-wardens; that the ringing did not seem to be of any use to the parish, though of very ill consequence to the plaintiff, the Lady Howard, and ample recompense had been made, both in the expense of the *cupola*, &c., and also of 1,500*l.* in improving the plaintiffs' own house, which otherwise they would have left; and it, moreover, appearing that the majority and better part of the parish continued willing to abide by this agreement and protested against the new order."[2] (See p. 270.)

§ 7. The following case, as stated, in substance, by Judge

[1] Squire *v.* Campbell, 1 My. & Cr. 480.

[2] Martin *v.* Nutkin, 2 P. Wms. 266.

Story, in his animated and eloquent judgment, was determined in the Supreme Court of the United States.

§ 8. "The bill was brought by the original plaintiffs, alleging themselves to be trustees and agents for the German Lutheran Church composed of the members of the German Lutheran Church of Georgetown, in behalf of themselves and the members of the said church. It charges the laying out of the lot in question for the sole use and benefit of the Lutheran Church, to be held by them for religious purposes. That soon afterwards the lot was taken possession of by the said German Lutherans; who organized themselves into a church, and erected a church or house of worship thereon; and hath been kept and held by them during a period of fifty years; and hath been used as a burying-ground, with the avowed intention of building thereon another church, the first building being decayed, whenever their funds would enable them so to do. That their possession has never been questioned, and the lot has been exempted from taxation as property set apart for a religious purpose. That a committee and trustees were appointed to take care of the said church," the plaintiffs being so appointed. "That Charles Beatty" (former owner of the land) "died about sixteen years ago without having made any conveyance, and that Charles A. Beatty, the defendant, is his heir. That Ritchie, the other defendant, has unwarrantably disputed their title; and has entered upon the lot and removed some of the tombstones, and means to dispossess the plaintiff and to remove the tombstones and graves. The bill therefore prays that a writ of injunction may issue. The material allegations are established. Shortly after the appropriation, and more than fifty years ago, the Lutherans of Georgetown proceeded to erect a log house on the lot, which was used as a church, and was also occasionally, and at different times since, used as a school-house under their direction. That at a much later period, a steeple and bell were added; that the land was used as a churchyard; that more than one-half the lot is covered with graves; that the possession was never questioned by Charles Beatty, or in any manner disturbed until a short period before the commencement of the present suit.   The house, in consequence of inevitable decay, fell down some time ago; it seems to have been more than forty years after its first erection.   Efforts have since been made to rebuild it, but hitherto they have not been successful. The defendant, Beatty, has, since the decease of his father, repeatedly admitted the claim of the Lutherans to the lot, and his willingness that it should remain for them, as it had been originally appropriated."   Upon these facts the court held, that, at the time of the appropriation of the lot, there was no grantee capable of taking, nor could any presumption of a grant arise from lapse of time, there never having been any incorporated church, and the town not being a corporation at the time.   But that the appropriation should be sustained, as a dedication of the lot to public and pious uses, rendered valid by the bill of rights of Maryland, which recognized the doctrines of the statute of Elizabeth, relating to charities.   Judge Story closes his opinion, in favor of an injunction, as follows: "No action at law would afford an adequate and complete remedy.   This is not the case of a mere private trespass; but a public nuisance, going to the irreparable injury of the Georgetown congregation of Lutherans.   The property consecrated to their use by a perpetual servitude or easement, is to be taken from them; the sepulchres of the dead are to be violated; the feelings of religion, and the sentiment of natural affection of the kindred and friends of the deceased are to be wounded; and the memorials erected by piety or love, to the memory of the good, are to be removed, so as to leave no trace of the last home of their ancestry to those who may visit the spot in future generations.   It cannot be that such acts are to be redressed by the ordinary process of law.   The remedy must be sought, if at all, in the protecting power of a court of chancery; operating by its injunction to preserve the repose of the ashes of the dead, and the religious sensibilities of the living.[1]" (See p. 318.)

§ 9. The following case, as stated in the opinion of Lord Eldon, is often cited. "The bill was filed by an elder brother against his younger brother. The former had in his possession, at the time of the death of their father, certain indentures, conveying an estate to the latter, and the purpose for which they were executed was stated to be that, in case any information should be exhibited against him for sporting without a qualification, he might go to the chest of his father, and, by producing them, defeat any such information. The father died with these deeds in his own possession. They had been delivered, in the technical sense of the word, but not to the younger son, and the younger son in his answer states that his father had been in the habit of making him certain allowances, as one of his sons, and that he retained the rents of these lands by way of reimbursing himself of the advances he so made. The bill alleged that the father made his will by which he left the estates to his eldest son, and that some time after the death of the father, the younger son came to his elder brother, and told him that he had made a bet with A. B. that he was a man qualified to sport, and he desired him, in order to win that wager, to put into his hands these indentures that he might show them to A. B. If the father executed these deeds for the purpose which the plaintiff alleges, it might have become a considerable question, if the younger son had got possession of these deeds, whether a court of equity would have done anything to relieve the father. The deeds were left in the possession of the father till his death, and the eldest son then obtains possession of them. He states in his bill that he thought it necessary to show them to his brother, to enable him to win this bet, intimating that he was very wrong in so doing, and contending that he had no qualification; but he lends himself to the purpose of imposing upon A. B.

[1] Beatty v. Kurtz, 2 Pet. 566, 579, 581, 584.

That having been done, and whether or not the younger son was looking to any purpose beyond that which the elder son says was his pretence, he turns round, as the plaintiff alleges, and says, now I have got these deeds, I shall give notice to the tenants not to pay their rents to you any longer, but to pay them to me as owner of the estate; and he brings an ejectment to get into possession. *Prima facie*, with these deeds in his hands, there was nothing to impede that ejectment; and the plaintiff accordingly files his bill for an injunction and the delivery of the deeds.—The court directed the defendant to try an ejectment.—The defendant at law sets up an old outstanding estate, and defeats the ejectment; and application is afterwards made to the court which ordered the trial, and it directs that no outstanding estate should be set up. My opinion about that is, that, in a case such as this is, that order ought not to have been made.—If it was right to let the ejectment decide the matter under the circumstances in which these parties stood, it was right to let it decide the matter, as it would have been decided in the actual circumstances in which they stood before the order was made; and it is a very different thing to say, there may be an equity arising out of circumstances, to prevent an individual setting up a term to defeat an ejectment, and to say, merely, because an ejectment is brought, it shall not be set up. I shall, therefore, discharge the order for not setting up the outstanding estate, but without prejudice to the defendant's filing any bill for that purpose.—If the defendant chooses to file a bill to put the term out of the way, the court, if a proper case were made, might, perhaps, be able to relieve him; but it cannot be done on motion."[1]

§ 10. The plaintiff and those under whom he claimed had been in quiet and uninterrupted possession of land for twenty-five years. The defendants, the corporation of the city of New York, under pretence that the buildings and

[1] Brackenbury *v.* Brackenbury, 2 Jac. & W. 392.

fence upon such land stood or encroached upon the highway, entered and disturbed the plaintiff in the enjoyment of the lot. Held, he was entitled to an injunction to restrain the defendants from entering upon, digging, throwing down, or destroying "the ground so possessed" by him, and that the injunction should be perpetual, or until the defendants should have established their title by due course of law. But further, that such injunction did not interfere with their right of digging down the street close to his line, though the necessary consequence was the falling of his soil into the excavation.[1]

§ 11. Under an act for draining swamps and bog meadows, in the counties of Orange and Dutchess (New York), it was held that the inspectors, appointed by the court, for draining the great swamp or bog meadow near Newburgh, must strictly observe the limits prescribed in the act, and could only continue the main ditch dug for that purpose at the north end of the *great pond*, through lands adjoining the swamp. That they could not dig down the outlet, at the southeast end of the pond, and thus destroy or injure valuable mills, &c., on the outlet, and on land not adjoining the great swamp, or break up ancient and useful streams by draining the natural reservoirs which fed them, and that they should be perpetually enjoined from all proceedings touching the outlet of the pond, and the plaintiffs quieted in the enjoyment of the water for their mills, &c. Chancellor Kent remarked: "The project of draining this little lake, and thereby destroying one mill, and affecting, more or less, all the others which are supplied by its water, is a stretch of power never within the contemplation of the act. It would be an unreasonable and dangerous construction. The power given was supposed to be harmless. It was never intended to touch and materially injure valuable improvements on adjoining lands; much less to break up useful ancient streams, and the natural and capacious reservoirs which fed

[1] Varick v. The Mayor, &c., 4 John. Ch. 53.

them. It is most fit, therefore, that this power should be kept within the words of the act. This is not a case of an ordinary trespass impending, but one great and special, leading to lasting mischief, and to the destruction of the estate, and tending to multiplicity of suits. There is no fact in this case to be ascertained. The whole case turns upon the construction of the act."[1] (See Chap. XXVII.)

§ 12. In the late case of Burr v. Duryee[2] (doubtless an application for injunction, though the report does not so expressly find) in the Supreme Court of the United States, it is said (p. 532 n.), "The whole business of making hats from the disintegrating of the fur to the production of a hat body, was actually carried on and exhibited in the court room. No similar argument, perhaps, was ever made in any court of law; nor could a case be explained in a manner more satisfactory. This 'clinical' style of argument illustrated perfectly the poet's truth—

> 'Segnius irritant animos demissa per aurem
> Quam quæ sunt *oculis* subjecta fidelibus et quæ
> Ipse sibi tradit spectator.' "

[1] Belknap v. Belknap, 2 John. Ch. 463, 472–3. S. C. p. 377. [2] 1 Wallace, U. S. 531.

33

APPENDIX—STATUTES.

THE following are the leading statutory provisions in the United States, on the subject of *Injunction*. There may be others which have escaped notice. Inasmuch as the present work is designed for *general* use, and the statutes of one State can have no practical application in another, this addition is made to the body of the book, not as an absolutely complete statement of the various legislative enactments, but solely for two different purposes. First, a decided case, referred to in the foregoing pages, may sometimes be usefully explained by reference to some statute on which it is founded, when it might otherwise seem erroneous or anomalous. Secondly, it is highly desirable, by way of precedent, that the course of legislation on this as well as all other legal subjects, in each of the States of the Union, should be *generally* and *comprehensively* understood by the profession in all the other States. Nothing more effectually encourages useful legislation for the supply of defects, or the correction of evils, than a good example actually set by a neighboring and associated commonwealth. The course of statutory law in the United States has been from the beginning noticeably *contagious;* and all practicable facilities should be afforded for the continuance and increase of so desirable a tendency in the jurisprudence of a united, and yet separated, nation.

By act of Congress, March 2, 1793, § 5, no injunction can be granted to stay proceedings in a State court, nor in any case without reasonable notice.[1]

[1] See Brightly's U. S. Dig. 256, § 3.

By act of Feb. 13, 1807, the same power is given to judges of the District Courts to grant injunctions as is exercised by judges of the Supreme Court, subject to the rules prescribed by the judiciary acts. But no injunction, unless so ordered by the Circuit Court, shall continue beyond the next circuit. And a district judge shall not grant an injunction, where there has been reasonable time to apply to the Circuit Court.[1]

By act of March 3, 1820, the district judge may enjoin proceedings by warrant and distress against a debtor to the government or his sureties.[2]

In Massachusetts, the Supreme Court, or a justice thereof, may, either in term time or vacation, after the filing of the bill or other commencement of a suit concerning waste, issue a writ of injunction to stay waste, and issue such other writs and processes, and make such orders and decrees, according to the course of proceedings in equity, as justice and equity may require. The injunction may be dissolved, in term time or vacation, by the court or by a judge thereof.

When a person whose real estate is attached commits waste thereon, or threatens or prepares so to do, or when a real action is brought to foreclose or for possession under a mortgage, or for recovery of land, and waste has been committed or threatened by the defendant or any one claiming under him or acting by his permission ; an injunction may issue (as above). But the petitioner may be required to give bond for all damages. And the court may arrest and commit the defendant for a violation of such injunction, and issue such other process as may be necessary or proper to enforce obedience, in like manner as the Supreme Court may do upon a suit in equity. The injunction may be dissolved (as above).[3]

When leave is granted to file an information in the nature of a *quo warranto*, or at any time before final judgment, the court may by writ of injunction restrain the defendant cor-

---

[1] See Brightly's U. S. Dig. 256 § 5.

[2] Ibid. 19, § 15.

[3] Mass. Gen. Sts. 710.

poration, its managers, servants, and agents, from exercising the franchise in question till further order of court.[1]

In New Hampshire, the Superior Court may grant writs of injunction, whenever necessary to prevent injustice; and any justice of said court may issue writs of injunction to stay proceedings or waste until the end of the next term of the court in any county, unless sooner dissolved.[2]

Where the bank commissioners deem it unsafe for a bank to continue the issuing or circulation of its bills or notes, or where a bank refuses an examination by them; they may obtain an injunction from a justice of the Superior Court.[3]

Such commissioners may also restrain by injunction any creditor of a bank from proceeding at law against such bank, where its affairs are in process of liquidation.[4]

Upon non-compliance on the part of a railroad corporation with any order relative to the construction of bridges, passes, or gates; a judge of the Superior Court may by injunction prohibit the use of the road till compliance with the order.[5]

The same provisions, substantially, are made for injunction against insurance companies, as in the case of banks.[6]

When the levy of an execution is stayed by injunction, the lien and interest of the attaching creditor shall continue for thirty days after dissolution of the injunction. The levy shall be suspended during the injunction, and may be resumed within thirty days after dissolution, though the return day have passed. If notice of sale has been given at the time of the injunction; upon dissolution, notice may be given as in the case of the sale of personal property.[7]

In Maine, writs of injunction may be issued in cases of equity jurisdiction, and when specially authorized by statute. A justice of the Supreme Court may issue them in term time or vacation, to continue in force through the next term

---

[1] Mass. Gen. Sts. 744.
[2] N. H. Comp. Sts. 434.
[3] Ib. 324.
[4] Ib. 326.
[5] Ib. 349.
[6] Ib. 373.
[7] Ib. 504.

unless sooner dissolved, after notice to the adverse party, or upon bond with sureties for damages and costs.[1]

The bank commissioners may apply to a justice of the Supreme Court for injunction against a bank which has made over-issues, without paying the forfeiture of ten per cent. provided by law. And such bank shall be enjoined till payment of the forfeiture and costs; and, unless paid within the time fixed, perpetually enjoined. The commissioners may also obtain an injunction against a bank which is insolvent, or has exceeded its powers, or failed to comply with the requirements of law; and upon a hearing the injunction may be dissolved, modified, or made perpetual.[2]

Any court of record, before which an indictment, complaint, or action for a nuisance is pending, may in any county issue an injunction to stay or prevent such nuisance, and make such orders and decrees for enforcing or dissolving it as justice and equity require.[3]

In case of a railroad, when land damages remain unpaid for thirty days after demand, a judge of the court may, after notice, without bond, enjoin the use or occupation of the land till payment of damages and costs. If payment has not been made at the second term after the injunction, it may be made absolute, and all title to the land and what has been placed on it shall cease. In case of violation of the injunction, provision is made for the individual liability of the parties guilty of such violation.[4]

An injunction may be granted by a justice of the Supreme Court against waste by the defendant in an action to recover real estate, or whose real estate is attached. Either notice or a bond is required.[5]

In Connecticut, a judge of the Supreme Court of Errors may on motion grant and enforce writs of injunction, according to the course of proceeding in courts of equity,

[1] Maine Rev. Sts. 469.
[2] Ib. 342.
[3] Ib. 214.
[4] Ib. 364.
[5] Ib. 584.

in all cases within the jurisdiction of the Superior Court, arising in any county, when such court is not in session, which writs shall be returnable to the next Superior Court in that county. So also the judges of the county courts, in all causes within their jurisdiction, when the court is not in session. So the judge of the county court in any county, in all causes within the jurisdiction of the Superior Court when not in session, returnable to the next Superior Court.

The facts must be verified by the oath of the petitioner or a witness. The injunction may be issued with or without previous notice. The judge who issues the injunction may hear and decide upon a motion to dissolve it. In case of injunction by the judge of a county court, upon petition returnable to the Superior Court, a petition to dissolve may be presented either to him or a judge of the Supreme Court of Errors. Provision is also made for the sickness or other disability of a judge of the Supreme Court.

Upon injunction of the sale of personal property on execution, the judge or court may order an adjournment of the sale. If there be no such order, the officer may adjourn it, and the lien shall still continue.[1]

An injunction is authorized in case of the attachment of partnership property by a creditor of a partner.[2]

Also, after notice, on application of the county attorney or the bank commissioners, against any bank whose charter in their opinion is forfeited, or by which the public are in danger of being defrauded.[3]

Also on the application of a creditor to an amount exceeding one hundred dollars.[4]

A judge of the Superior Court, on application of the commissioners, may issue an injunction against any railroad corporation, where its rails, bridges, switches, engines, or cars are in such condition, or its affairs so conducted, as to endanger the safety of the public, or where such corporation has in any material respect violated the law, or refused to obey the

[1] Conn. Sts. 1854, p. 473.
[2] Ib. 479.
[3] Ib. 241.
[4] Ib. 250.

lawful directions of the commissioners, or unlawfully suffered any person to hold or exercise the duties of any office in the corporation.[1]

In Vermont, no injunction issues till a bill is filed. The issuing of a subpœna attached to a bill is deemed the filing.

No injunction shall issue to stay the trial of a personal action at issue in a court of law, until the applicant gives bond with surety, conditioned for the payment of all intervening damages caused by delay, with additional costs in the action, if the plaintiff finally recovers. So also an injunction after verdict or judgment. But in case of actual fraud, a bond may be dispensed with. So an injunction, after verdict, against an action of ejectment. In this case, the damages, upon dissolution, shall be settled by a master, and include the reasonable rents and profits and all waste committed after the injunction. The sufficiency of the surety shall be ascertained by the Chancellor or by a Master. The bond shall be filed before the injunction issues. Upon dissolution of an injunction staying execution of a judgment, the court may require the respondent to give security to the complainant for all such damages and costs as shall be finally awarded him by the court. Upon breach of a bond, the court shall order its delivery to the party entitled to the benefit of it, for prosecution, if circumstances so require.[2]

When the commencement of a suit is stayed by injunction, the time during which such injunction shall be in force shall not be included in the statute of limitations.[3]

The bank commissioner may obtain an injunction, after notice, against any banking corporation which is insolvent or has proceeded in violation of law; and a receiver shall thereupon be appointed.[4]

Similar provision is made in regard to savings banks.[5]

[1] Conn. Sts. 1854, p. 761.
[2] Verm. Gen. Sts. 253.
[3] Ibid. 444.
[4] Ib. 575.
[5] Ib. 548-9.

In Rhode Island, the Supreme Court, or in vacation a justice thereof, may, upon notice and for cause, enjoin any railroad or turnpike corporation from using any Rhode Island franchises, in violation of law or of its charter.[1]

The Supreme Court, or, in vacation, a justice thereof, on complaint of the bank commissioners, that in their opinion any bank or institution for savings has forfeited its charter, or is so conducting that the public or those having funds in its custody are in danger of being defrauded, or has become insolvent, shall issue notice to show cause why an injunction should not be granted; and after a hearing may enjoin the corporation from further proceeding with its business, and appoint a receiver. During such injunction all proceedings for the collection of debts against the corporation shall be stayed. A limited and temporary injunction may be granted, without the appointment of a receiver. Heavy penalties are imposed, for refusal to deliver the property to the receivers.[2]

"In New York, the *writ* of injunction, as a provisional remedy, is abolished by *the Code of Procedure*, and an injunction by *order* substituted.(a) The order may be made by the court in which the action is brought, or by a judge thereof, or by a county judge, and when made by a judge, may be enforced as the order of the court."[3]

[1] Rhode Island Rev. Sts. 389.   [3] Will. Eq. 342.
[2] Ib. 290.

(a) For elaborate comments upon the New York system, by which jurisdiction at law and jurisdiction in equity are combined or blended, see Knowles *v.* Gee, 4 How. Pr. 317; Millikin *v.* Cary, 5 Ib. 272; Williams *v.* Hayes, Ib. 470; Wooden *v.* Waffle, 6 Ib. 145. It is said, "a bitter controversy, at one time, existed in New York, between the Supreme Court and the Court of Chancery, with respect to the power of the former to commit for contempt. And there has always been, while the two courts were kept separate, a strong party adverse to the existence of the Court of Chancery as a distinct tribunal. Nevertheless, the Supreme Court held that an existing injunction, although operating only on the parties, their attorneys and agents, would be noticed by the court for the purpose of promoting the ends of justice, and of preserving harmony between the two courts." Will. Eq. Juris. 346.

An injunction may be had to restrain the commission or continuance of some injurious act during the litigation; or when the defendant, during the litigation, threatens or prepares to do some act in reference to the subject of suit, which will render a judgment ineffectual. Also to prevent a threatened disposition of property, pending an action, in fraud of creditors.[1]

No personal action at issue in a court of law shall be enjoined, without a bond with surety, conditioned for the payment of all moneys which may be recovered, or the collection of which may be thereby stayed; and of the costs in equity. In case of application for an injunction after verdict and before judgment, either the amount of the verdict and costs must be deposited, or a bond given, as afterwards prescribed; and a subsequent section of the statute provides, that, after judgment, such bond shall be given, conditioned for the payment of such damages and costs as may be awarded at the first hearing, or the amount of the judgment deposited. The money may be paid over to the plaintiff at law, on his giving security to refund it, when ordered by the court. In actions for the recovery of lands or the possession thereof, after verdict, a bond must be given for the damages and costs that may be recovered therein. Where actual fraud in the verdict or judgment is alleged, the security above stated may be dispensed with. By the Code, when there is no statutory provision for security, the court or judge shall require a written engagement to pay all damages, not exceeding a certain sum, which may be caused by the injunction.[2]

Upon a civil action being commenced by the Attorney-General in the Supreme Court, it may enjoin any corporation from assuming or exercising any franchise, &c., or transacting any business, not allowed by the charter. Also any individuals from exercising any corporate rights, &c., not granted them by a law of the State. Such injunction may be issued before answer, if the defendants have usurped, &c., any fran-

[1] Code, § 219.
[2] 2 N. Y. Rev. Sts. 188, § 139; 190, § 147; Sts. 1847, 323, § 16; Code, § 222; Will. Eq. 348–50.

chise, &c., not granted to them; and after answer it may be continued till judgment at law.[1]

The Supreme Court may restrain all alienations of property threatened or reasonably apprehended by the officers of a corporation, contrary to law, or for unauthorized purposes, known to the party receiving it.[2]

When a corporation with banking powers, or to loan on pledges or deposits, or to make insurances, becomes insolvent or violates the law; the Supreme Court, upon application of the Attorney-General, may issue an injunction against it.[3]

Where the collection of taxes is stayed by injunction, provision is made as to the duty of the collector.[4]

When an execution is returned unsatisfied, the creditor may by bill in chancery prevent the transfer of any property, money, or thing in action, or the payment or delivery thereof to the defendant, with the exception of trusts not executed by the defendant himself.[5]

Further provision is made to forbid the transfer of, or interference with, property of a judgment debtor, not exempt from execution.[6]

When commencement of an action is stayed by injunction, the time shall not be included in the statute of limitations.[7]

A similar provision is made in regard to the lien of judgments stayed by injunction, if a notice thereof is filed with the clerk within ten years of the docketing.[8]

A few decided cases are subjoined, turning, to some extent, upon the statutory law, and not cited in the body of this work.

The judgment of a justice without jurisdiction, on its face regular, may be perpetually enjoined by the Supreme Court.[9]

The plaintiff must show a case in which he will be entitled to final relief, and must pray for final judgment.[10]

[1] 3 N. Y. Rev. Sts. 5th ed. 762. See Ib. 531.
[2] Ib. 762–3.
[3] Ib. 764.
[4] 1 N. Y. Rev. Sts. 5th ed. 921.
[5] 3 N. Y. Rev. Sts. 5th ed. 264.
[6] Ib. 550.
[7] 3 N. Y. Rev. Sts., 5th ed., 507.
[8] Ib. 637.
[9] Codper v. Ball, 14 How. 275.
[10] Corning v. Troy, &c., 6 How. 89.; Hulce v. Thompson, 8, 475; Hovey v. M'Crea, 4, 31.

(With regard to the change effected by the Code in the nature of the remedy of injunction, see Linden v. Fritz.[1])

It is still held to be *discretionary*.[2]

The Code is held not to create new rights of action or remedies.[3]

(As to the circumstances justifying an injunction, see Androvette v. Bowne.[4])

A distinction is made between an injunction granted in an action as a provisional remedy, and the prohibition of the transfer of the property of a judgment debtor.[5]

Injunction may be moved for at a general term.[6]

An injunction order may be vacated or modified without notice; but it is held to be very objectionable, without urgent cause.[7]

(In reference to the dissolving or modifying of injunctions, see Newbury v. Newbury.[8])

No State officer or board, or person employed by them, shall be enjoined in the performance of any official duty, except by the Supreme Court sitting in the district where such board is located or such duty required, at a general term; after prescribed notice.[9]

An alderman cannot be enjoined from unlawfully voting by a tax-payer.[10] Nor can the doings of commissioners of highways be enjoined.[11] Nor the exercise of an office, pending a *quo warranto* to test the title of such office.[12]

---

[1] 3 Code R. 165; 5 How. 188.

[2] Crooker v. Baker, 3 Abb. 183; Minor v. Terry, 6, 210; M'Cafferty v. Glazier, 10 ib. 475.

[3] Wordsworth v. Lyon, 1 Code R. N. S. 163.

[4] 4 Abb. 440; also 15 How. 75; Gallatin v. Oriental, &c., 16 How. 253; Lewis v. Oliver, 4 Abb. 121.

[5] Green v. Bullard, 8 How. 316.

[6] Drake v. Hudson, &c., 2 Code R. 67.

[7] Bruce v. Delaware, &c., 8 How. 440.

[8] 1 Code R. N. S. 409; also Minor v. Terry, 6 How. 210; Malcomb v. Miller, 6 How. 456; Smith v. Austin, 1 Code R. 135; Bruce v. Delaware, &c., 8 How. 440.

[9] Sts. 1851, c. 488, § 1. See Fitzpatrick v. Flagg, 4 Abb. 213; Mace v. Trustees, &c., 15 How. 161; Fuller v. Allen, 7 Abb. 12: also Chap. XXII.

[10] Lewis v. Oliver, 4 Abb. 121.

[11] Thatcher v. Dusenbury, 9 How. 32.

[12] The People v. Draper, 4 Abb. 333; 14 How. 233.

(As to injunctions against proceedings in the same or other courts, see Arndt *v.* Williams.[1])

A party enjoined from the prosecution of a suit is bound to communicate the prohibition to all parties employed by him.[2]

(As to the injunction of proceedings relating to land, see Wordsworth *v.* Tyon.[3]

As to the injunction of acts pending litigation, see Olsen *v.* Smith.[4])

In an action by a wife for a divorce *a mensâ*, the defendant may be enjoined from disposing of his property and leaving the State without provision for her.[5]

(As to injunction in cases of fraud and insolvency, see Malcomb *v.* Miller.[6])

A stockholder may enjoin the declaration of a dividend by the corporation, but not the payment of it, after it has been declared.[7]

As stated in the text of this work, injunctions have been granted to restrain the imposition of an illegal tax.[8] The violation of an agreement for exclusive service.[9] Or against carrying on a trade; though not where a penalty is provided.[10] To give possession.[11] To restrain the fraudulent transfer of stock by the company.[12]

(As to injunction in case of mortgage, see Tarrant *v.* Quackenboss.[13]

In reference to trade-marks, see Christy *v.* Murphy.[14]

[1] 16 How. 244; Hunt *v.* Farmers', &c., 8 How. 416; Chappel *v.* Potter, 11, 365; Bennett *v.* LeRoy, 14 How. 178; Field *v.* Holbrook, 3 Abb. 377.

[2] Mayor, &c., *v.* Conover, 5 Abb. 244.

[3] 1 Code R. N. S. 63; also 4 How. 463; Cure *v.* Crawford, 1 Code R. N. S. 18; Hyatt *v.* Burr, 8 How. 168; Capet *v.* Parker, 1 Code R. N. S. 90; Bokee *v.* Hamersley, 16 How. 461.

[4] 7 How. 481; also Sebring *v.* Lant, 9, 347; Reubens *v.* Joel, 3 Kern. 488.

[5] Vermilyea *v.* Vermilyea, 14 How. 470.

[6] 6 How. 467; also Pomeroy *v.* Hindmarsh, 5, 437; Brewster *v.* Hodges, 1 Duer, 609.

[7] Carpenter *v.* New Haven, &c., 5 Abb. 277.

[8] Wood *v.* Draper, 4 Abb. 322; 14 How. 233.

[9] Fredericks *v.* Meyer, 13 How. 566.

[10] Vincent *v.* King, 13 How. 234.

[11] Erpstein *v.* Berg, 13 How. 92.

[12] The People *v.* The Parker, &c., 10 How. 140.

[13] 10 How. 244; also Van Wagemen *v.* La Farge, 13 ib. 16.

[14] 12 How. 77; also Samuel *v.* Berger, 4 Abb. 83; Fetridge *v.* Wells, 4 Abb. 144.

In reference to the security by bond or otherwise, see Hutchinson *v.* Central, &c.[1]

As to the determination of the damages, see Shearman *v.* N. Y., &c.[2]

As to the effect of dismissal and an appeal, see Guilford *v.* Cornell.

In reference to the admissibility and effect of affidavits, see Millikin *v.* Carey.[4])

In New Jersey, the Court of Chancery shall be considered as always open for the granting of injunctions.[4]

No injunction shall issue to stay proceedings at law in any personal action after verdict or judgment, on application of the defendant, unless the amount, with costs, is deposited with the clerk, or unless a bond satisfactory to the Chancellor is given, with condition to abide any order or decree of the Chancellor. A similar provision is made, in reference to security, in case of any mixed action after verdict or judgment.

Provision is made for subsequently inquiring into the sufficiency of the bond, ordering further security, or, in default thereof, dissolving the injunction.

No injunction shall be granted to stay proceedings before verdict or judgment, unless the Chancellor is satisfied of the complainant's equity, by affidavit or otherwise.

In case of injunction against waste, if the injunction is violated, an attachment of contempt may issue, and the party may be committed.[6]

An injunction staying proceedings in ejectment was granted

---

[1] 2 Abb. 394; also O'Donnell *v.* Murn, 3 Abb. 391; Higgins *v.* Allen, 6 How. 30; Willett *v.* Stringer, 15, 310.

[2] 11 How. 269; also Hope *v.* Acker, 7 Abb. 308; Wilde *v.* Joel, 15 How. 320; Griffin *v.* State, 5 How. 205; Quilford *v.* Cornell, 4 Abb. 220.

[3] 4 Abb. 220; also Hope *v.* Acker, 7 ib. 508; Hoyt *v.* Carter, 7 How. 140.

[4] 3 Code R. 250; also Levy *v.* Levy, 6 Abb. 89; Badger *v.* Wagstaff, 11 How. 562; Roome *v.* Webb, 1 Code R. 114; Florence *v.* Bates, 2 ib. 110; Blatchford *v.* New Haven, &c., 7 Abb. 322; Schoonmaker *v.* Reformed, &c., 5 How. 267; Jaques *v.* Areson, 4 Abb. 282; Powell *v.* Clark, 5 Abb. 70.

[5] Nix. Dig. 97.

[6] Ib. 97, 98.

for the loss of title deeds, but dissolved upon answer fully denying all knowledge of them.[1]

An injunction will not be dissolved as of course for a mere formal or technical denial of the charges in the bill.[2] (See Chap. III.)

The objection of a *stale* claim applies only to the demand of the *complainant.* An injunction will not be continued, upon the ground that a claim which the defendant is seeking to enforce at law is stale.[3]

(As to an injunction and the dissolving thereof in case of a mine, see Boston, &c. *v.* New Jersey, &c., 2 Beasl. 215; New Jersey, &c. *v.* New Jersey, &c., 2 Beasl. 322.)

An individual can enjoin a public nuisance, preventively, only where he apprehends an injury distinct from that to the public.[4]

Equity will not enjoin the building of a bridge within certain limits, upon the claim of a bridge company to an exclusive right within those limits; the answer showing that the bridge of the complainants has been so far appropriated to the uses of a railroad, as to render it inconvenient and dangerous for ordinary travel.[5]

Where a bridge was technically a nuisance, but built in good faith and for the public benefit, under claim of lawful authority; it was held that the court would not restrain it by injunction upon an information of the attorney-general.[6]

In 1790, the complainants were incorporated with authority to build a bridge over the Hackensack River, to take tolls from man and beast. It was also provided that it should not be lawful for any person to erect any other bridge over the river for a hundred years. In 1860, the legislature gave to the defendants power to build a railway from Hoboken to Newark, with the necessary viaduct over this river. The defendants built such viaduct, thus described in their answer: "A structure, so as to lay iron rails thereon,

[1] Horner *v.* Jobs, 2 Beasl. 19.
[2] Ib.
[3] Ib.
[4] Allen *v.* Board, &c., 2 Beasl. 67.

Acc. Jersey, &c. *v.* Hudson, &c., ib. 420.
[5] Trenton, &c. *v.* City, &c., 2 Beasl. 46.
[6] Allen *v.* Board, &c., 2 Beasl. 67.

upon which engines and cars may be moved and propelled by steam, not to be connected with the shore on either side of said river, except by a piece of timber under each rail, and in such a manner, as near as may be, so as to make it impossible for man or beast to cross said river upon said structure, except in the cars of the defendants; that the only roadway between said shores and said structure will be two or more iron rails, two and a quarter inches wide, four and a half inches high, laid and fastened upon said timber four feet ten inches asunder." It was held (in a learned and ingeniously critical and illustrative opinion), that the proposed structure was no *bridge*, within the meaning of the plaintiffs' charter; having no footway for man or beast, and it being provided that the plaintiffs might collect tolls from men walking over their bridge, and for animals walking over it, drawing their burthens, while the defendants could not collect tolls for such use; the franchises therefore being different: and the bill was accordingly dismissed.[1]

(As to service and violation of an injunction, see Haring *v.* Kauffman, 2 Beasl. 397.)

In Pennsylvania, the Supreme Court have chancery power and jurisdiction, for the prevention or restraint of the commission or continuance of acts contrary to law and prejudicial to the interests of the community or the rights of individuals.

No injunction shall be issued, except where the commonwealth or a city or county is complainant, until the applicant gives bond with sureties for all damages thereby caused. In the case excepted, the court shall expedite the cause by such orders as they deem expedient.

No courts within the city and county of Philadelphia shall grant or continue injunctions against the erection or use of public works erected or in progress of erection, under authority of the legislature, until the questions of title and damages shall be submitted and finally decided by a common law court.

[1] Proprs., &c. *v.* Hoboken, &c., 2 Beasl. 503.

Special provision is made for security, in case of appeal from any order for the assignment or delivery of securities, documents, chattels, or things in action.[1]

Any bank, against which the auditor-general has proceeded for alleged insolvency, if it denies the allegation, may apply for an injunction; which, after notice, and the finding of a jury that the bank has at all times redeemed its notes in specie, shall be granted.

If that officer fails to proceed according to law against any bank, a creditor of the bank may obtain an order upon him thus to proceed.

If any bank neglect or refuse to comply with a legal order of the auditor-general to do any act deemed necessary for the security of its creditors; the court, upon his petition, may enjoin such bank from pursuing its banking business, and place its property in the hands of a receiver.[2]

Provision is made for an injunction in certain cases against the erection of buildings in the city of Philadelphia.[3]

In case of ouster and exclusion by *quo warranto*, execution shall be had by a writ of injunction; reciting the judgment and enjoining the exercise of the office, &c., referred to; to be enforced by attachment and sequestration.[4]

In Delaware, upon petition of one holding a lien upon real estate, the Chancellor may award an injunction against waste.[5]

In Maryland, where an injunction has issued against waste, if the party commits or authorizes waste, the court may issue an attachment for contempt, and punish by fine or imprisonment, or both. On complaint, the court, either before or after attachment and imprisonment, may ascertain the value

---

[1] Purd. Dig. 404. (As to the rules of *practice* in this State, see "Rules of Practice, adopted by the Supreme Court of Pennsylvania, May 27th, 1865." See also Brightl. Equ. 240; Fowle *v.* Spear, 7 Penn. L. J. 176; Stephen Girard, 4 Am. L. J. 101; Cooper *v.* Mattheys, 5 Penn. L. J. 40.)

[2] Purd. Dig. 83.
[3] Ib. 781.
[4] Ib. 833.
[5] Laws of Delaware, 294.

34

of the waste, and require payment of double the amount, and enforce it by attachment for contempt or *fieri facias.*

Upon application by an executor or administrator to stay proceedings at law, the court may prescribe the penalty of a bond, with security, to perform the order or decree; and may decree against him according to equity and good conscience.

Where an officer is prevented by injunction from selling personal property taken in execution; he shall restore it, and not be answerable to the execution plaintiff.[1]

Each of the circuit judges may grant injunctions in his circuit.

Clerks may approve injunction bonds.[3]

No injunction shall be granted to stay any sale, or proceedings after any sale, of mortgaged premises (under a power of sale), unless the applicant therefor is party to the mortgage, or claims a right under a party accruing since the recording of the mortgage, nor without an allegation on oath of full or partial payment, for which the mortgagee refuses to give credit, or fraud, particularly set forth, in obtaining the mortgage. If such injunction is granted, the court or judge may, after ten days' notice, hear and decide on a motion to dissolve it; and, if obtained by misrepresentation and for delay, shall award ten per cent. interest on the mortgage debt from the granting to the dissolving of the injunction; to be enforced like other decrees. The complainant or some person in his behalf shall give bond, with at least two good securities, to perform the decree; upon which bond the mortgagee or his assigns may recover all the debt, damages, interest, and costs decreed on dissolving the injunction.[4]

In Ohio, the injunction provided by the Code is a command to refrain from a particular act. It may be the final judgment in an action, or may be allowed as a provisional remedy; and shall be by order. The writ of injunction is

[1] 1 Md. Laws, 81.
[2] Ib. 82.
[3] Ib. 109.
[4] Ib. 447.

abolished. Injunction may be had, when the petition shows
a title to relief, consisting in the restraint of the commission
or continuance of some act, the commission or continuance
of which, during the litigation, would produce great or irreparable injury, or when, during the litigation, the defendant
is doing or threatens, or is about to do, or is procuring or
suffering, some act in violation of the plaintiff's rights, and
tending to render the judgment ineffectual.

Very liberal provision is made as to the courts which may
grant the injunction. Notice is authorized to be given. A
party who has answered shall not be enjoined without notice;
but may be restrained until the application for an injunction
is decided. A bond shall be given, with sufficient surety,
for all damages. Provision is made in regard to the service.
The injunction is binding from the time the party has notice,
and the required undertaking is executed. No injunction
shall be granted by a judge, after a motion therefor has
been overruled on the merits by his court, and, if refused by
the court in which the action is brought or a judge thereof,
it shall not be granted to the same applicant by an inferior
court or a judge thereof.

Injunction from a judge may be enforced as the act of the
court. Disobedience may be punished as a contempt by the
court or a judge who might have issued it in vacation. An
attachment may be issued, and the party required to pay a
fine not exceeding two hundred dollars, make immediate
restitution, and give further security, or else committed.

Where a surety has left the State or is insufficient, the
court may vacate the injunction, unless a new security is
given.

Affidavits may be used. If the injunction is granted
without notice, the defendant, at any time before trial, may
apply to have it vacated or modified. The application may
be made upon the petition and accompanying affidavits, or
upon affidavits for the defendant, with or without answer.
If made upon affidavits for the defendant, the plaintiff may
offer affidavits and new evidence.

A defendant may have an injunction upon an answer in the nature of a counterclaim. He shall proceed as above.[1]

No security is required from the attorney-general, when he proceeds by injunction on behalf of the State.[2]

In Michigan, provision is made for the security to be given in case of injunctions restraining proceedings to enforce judgments. So also, with special reference to suits brought for the recovery of lands. Also for determining the damages upon dissolution of the injunction. In case of alleged actual fraud, the above provisions may be dispensed with.[3]

Provision is made for restraining proceedings against corporations or its officers in certain cases.[4]

An appeal lies from an order adjudging a party guilty of contempt in violating an injunction, and awarding a sum of money as indemnity.[5]

An injunction bill, strictly, is one asking no other relief. If other relief is asked, the injunction is auxiliary, and falls with the bill.[6]

Though a party in possession be enjoined from committing trespasses, interfering with the possession, or entering; he cannot be punished as for contempt, for maintaining his possession by force. Even a wrongdoer cannot be turned out of possession by an *ex parte* preliminary order or process.[7]

In Wisconsin, the Supreme Court may grant writs of injunction.[8]

So also the Circuit Courts.[9]

The writ of injunction is abolished. The injunction provided for by law is a command to refrain from a particular act. It may be the final judgment in an action, or may be

---

[1] Curwen's Laws of Ohio, 1200.
[2] Ib. 1108.
[3] 2 Michigan Comp. L. 1021.
[4] Ib. 1299.
[5] People *v.* Messler, 9 Mich. 492.
[6] Blackwood *v.* Van Vleet, 11 Mich. 252.
[7] People *v.* Simonson, 10 Mich. 335.
[8] Wisc. Rev. Sts. 639.
[9] Ib. 644.

allowed as a provisional remedy. The order may be made by the court in which the action is brought, or a judge thereof, or a county judge, or court commissioner; and when made may be enforced as the order of the court.

When the complainant appears by his complaint entitled to relief by restraining the commission or continuance of some act, which during the litigation would be injurious to him, or when, during the litigation, the defendant is doing, or threatens, or is about to do, or procuring or suffering some act in violation of the plaintiff's rights, respecting the subject of the action, and tending to render the judgment ineffectual; such act may be temporarily enjoined. So when, pending an action, it appears by affidavit that the defendant threatens or is about to remove or dispose of his property in fraud of creditors.

The injunction may be granted at the commencement of the action, or any time after, before judgment. A copy of the affidavit must be served with the injunction.

An injunction is not allowed after answer, unless upon notice or an order to show cause. But in such case the defendant may be restrained, until the decision of the court or judge, granting or refusing the injunction.

In the absence of express provision by statute, the plaintiff shall give a written undertaking, with or without securities, to pay damages, not exceeding a certain sum, if the injunction be refused; the amount to be ascertained by reference or otherwise, as the court shall direct.

The defendant may be allowed a hearing, if thought proper, and restrained in the mean time.

An injunction to suspend the general and ordinary business of a corporation shall not be granted except by the court or a judge thereof; nor without notice, unless the people are a party, until the plaintiff give security to pay all damages (settled, as above).[1]

A railroad company, which neglects for six months after

<hr />

[1] Wisc. Rev. Sts. 735.

taking or appropriating land, to pay therefor, may be en-joined from the use thereof till payment.[1]

The time, during which an action is restrained by injunction, is excepted from the statute of limitations.[2]

Appeals in case of injunction are regulated.[3]

No injunction shall be dissolved at chambers but by a circuit judge.[4]

Provision is made for injunction against waste.[5] Also in case of a meandered river.[6]

The Circuit Court, upon complaint under direction of the attorney-general, may enjoin a corporation from assuming or exercising any franchise, &c., or transacting any business, not authorized by the charter. It may also enjoin an individual from unlawfully exercising any corporate rights, &c.[7]

In Missouri, injunctions may be granted by the Circuit Court or a judge in vacation, or, in cases specified, by the county court or any two justices in vacation.

A temporary injunction lies, when the petition shows ground for restraining the commission or continuance of some act, which during the litigation would be injurious, or when during the litigation the defendant is doing, or threatens, or is about to do some act in relation to the plaintiff's rights respecting the subject of action, and tending to render the judgment ineffectual.

Before injunction to stay proceedings, notice is required.

No injunction shall be granted to stay any judgment or proceeding, except so much of the recovery or cause of action as the plaintiff shall show himself equitably entitled to be relieved against, and so much as will cover costs.

The injunction operates as a release of errors.

No injunction, unless on final hearing or judgment, shall issue, without a bond with security for the amount or other matter to be enjoined and all damages; to abide the decision

[1] Wisc. Rev. Sts. 737.
[2] Ib. 823.
[3] Ib. 826.
[4] Ib. 826.
[5] Ib. 855.
[6] Ib. 857.
[7] Ib. 874.

thereon, and pay all damages and costs adjudged, in case of dissolution.

Upon dissolution, in whole or in part, damages shall be assessed by a jury, if demanded; otherwise by the court; not to exceed ten per cent., exclusive of legal interest and costs, where money or proceedings for collection of any money or demand have been enjoined. The court shall enter judgment upon the bond, and issue execution or proceed otherwise, according to rules and practice.

When a court is applied to for injunction upon its own proceedings, no notice is required, unless prescribed by rules of court.

Successive injunctions are provided against.

Violation of an injunction is punishable by commitment as a contempt.

After answer, a motion may be made to dissolve. Testimony may be introduced, and the court shall decide thereupon, without being bound by the answer.

Provision is made for postponement, for the purpose of disproving the bill or answer. Also in reference to affidavits, depositions, and notice.

A married woman may have an injunction against her husband, when from habitual interference or other cause he is about to squander and waste her separate property, or fraudulently convert it to his own use.

Special provision is made for proceedings in the county of St. Louis.[1]

Upon dissolution of an injunction against a judgment, it is erroneous to enter judgment upon the bond.[2]

The State has no interest in the matter of restraining a county court from issuing its bonds or levying a tax to pay for a subscription to the stock of a railroad; and cannot therefore be properly made plaintiff in a bill for injunction, at the relation of an individual.[3]

An officer upon an execution against A. seized personal

---

[1] 2 Miss. Rev. Sts. 1247.
[2] Roach v. Burnes, 33 Mis. 319.
[3] State v. Parkvitte, 32 Mis. 496.

property, which was replevied by B. In the replevin suit, the officer had judgment against B. and his securities in the bond for the value of the property, and A. afterwards assigned to B. the surplus over the execution and costs. Held, B. could not enjoin the officer from collecting the full amount of the judgment.[1]

In Tennessee,[2] injunctions are granted by the chancellors and circuit judges, and judges of special courts. The party must state in his bill or petition that it is the first application. If an application is made and refused, no other shall be granted, except by the court in which the bill is filed.

The clerk and master shall take, besides the usual bond for prosecution of the suit, a bond conditioned, according to the object of the bill, as follows:—

In case of judgment, to pay the amount of it with interest, damages, and costs, or to perform the decree of the court if the injunction is dissolved, and also to pay all damages caused by the wrongful suing out of the attachment. If before judgment at law the investigation of the questions has been drawn by injunction into the Court of Chancery, as having concurrent jurisdiction, the condition shall be to pay costs and damages awarded by the chancery court on dismissing the bill.

If the object is to enjoin a money demand after judgment, the penalty shall be in double the judgment or sum sought to be enjoined. In all other cases, such sum as the court shall order. If no order, in the sum of five hundred dollars.

The damages may be ascertained by the court in which the cause is heard and injunction dissolved, upon reference to the clerk and master, and proof, or upon an issue of fact before a jury.

If the defendant evade or attempt to evade service of the injunction, leaving a copy at his residence shall be sufficient service.

A defendant may move to modify or dissolve an injunc-

---

[1] Hobenthal v. Watson. 34 Mis. 183.　　[2] Sts. of Tennessee—Injunction.

tion in vacation, before the Chancellor of the division in which the bill is filed, either for want of equity in the bill, or upon the coming in of the answer, to be heard upon certified copies.

A motion to dissolve may be made at any time, upon answer, or for want of equity on the face of the bill.

Pending exceptions to the answer, a motion to dissolve upon the answer does not lie, unless the motion would not be affected by such exceptions.

Upon dissolution of an injunction to stay proceedings upon a judgment for money, in whole or in part, the decree interlocutory or final shall be entered against the complainant and sureties for such amount as the court may order; and execution may issue thereon.

In case of the dissolving of an interlocutory injunction upon a judgment for money, the defendant shall give a refunding bond, in double the sum to be collected, conditioned to refund it, if so ordered on final hearing; upon which bond the court may render a decree.

(There are some other provisions, not requiring to be stated.)

In Kentucky, when an injunction is dissolved, the plaintiff shall be decreed to pay the costs occasioned thereby.[1]

A judge of the Court of Appeals may reinstate injunctions.[2]

The presiding judge of the County Court may grant injunctions .

In Illinois, the Supreme and Circuit Courts, and any judge thereof in vacation, may grant writs of injunction. But not to stay proceedings under a judgment of a justice of the peace, for a sum not exceeding twenty dollars, besides costs.

An injunction from the Supreme Court or a judge thereof shall be returnable into the circuit of the proper county.

An injunction to stay a suit or judgment at law shall be

[1] 1 Ky. Rev. Sts. 291.
[2] Ib. 304.
[2] Ib. 325.

in the same county, and the writ of subpœna may be sent into any county where the defendant resides.

Injunction of a judgment shall be only for such sum as the party is not equitably bound to pay, and costs. An injunction shall operate as a release of errors. A bond is given, with surety, for all money and costs due or to be due to the plaintiff at law, and all costs and damages awarded in case of dissolution. If dissolved, wholly or in part, the complainant shall pay, exclusive of legal interest and costs, such damages as the court shall award, not exceeding ten per cent., and the clerk shall issue execution thereof, with execution on the judgment.

For disobedience and breach of an injunction, an attachment for contempt may issue, from the judge who granted it, or, if granted in open court, from any judge of that court, in vacation. Unless disproved or purged, the party may be committed till the sitting of the court in which the injunction is pending, or bail taken for his appearance.

Upon filing an answer, a dissolution may at any time be moved for. Testimony is admissible, and the answer need not be taken as true. For the purpose of meeting the answer, alleged to be untrue, by testimony to be subsequently procured, the case may be continued. The testimony shall be by depositions, except the affidavits filed with the bill or answer. The depositions may be read on the final hearing of the cause.[1]

Proceedings upon an execution, issued on a judgment by confession or warrant of attorney on a demand not due, may be enjoined by the Circuit Court for the county. A bond is required, as in other cases.[2]

Bills for injunctions of proceedings at law shall be filed in the office of the Circuit Court of the county where the record of the proceedings is made.[3]

Injunctions by masters in chancery are authorized, in the absence of a judge.[4]

[1] 1 Statutes of Illinois, 147.
[2] Ib. 164.
[3] Ib. 138.
[4] Ib. 145.

Provision is made for motions to dissolve in vacation.[1]

Upon application of bank commissioners, for violation of the provisions of the act relating to them, by any bank, corporation, broker, banker, dealer in money, produce or foreign merchandise, or their officer, clerk, agent or employé; an injunction may be issued, to be enforced according to the proceedings in chancery. And a bank may thereupon be put into liquidation.[2]

Where a town collector is enjoined from the collection of taxes for wrongful assessment, the board of supervisors may order a re-assessment.[3]

Injunctions may issue in behalf of the State.[4]

Writs of injunction may be issued by judges of the circuit courts.

A perpetual injunction will be granted against a sale on mortgage, where the mortgagor, wholly under the control of the mortgagee, is made imbecile by habitual intemperance, and nearly insane; no consideration being proved.[6]

A bill to enjoin a judgment will be dismissed, unless it not only show why the evidence was not saved by exceptions, but what the evidence was which authorized the judgment, and the grounds of defence, the reason why it was not made, and other necessary facts.[7]

An injunction may be had against the collection of the obligations originally given for the support of a railroad, if the company discontinue the work, or attempt to misapply its funds, or radically to change the character of the enterprise.

One in quiet possession as owner may have an injunction against dispossession by process in a litigation to which he was no party.[9]

[1] 1 Statutes of Illinois, 149.
[2] Ib. 123.
[3] Ib. 361.
[4] Ib. 643 ; 2 Ib. 1168.
[5] 1 Ib. 125.
[6] Van Horn v. Keenan, 28 Ill. 445.
[7] Buntain v. Blackburn, 27 Ill. 406.
[8] Illinois, &c. v. Cook, 29 Ill. 237.
[9] Goodnough v. Sheppard, 28 Ill. 81.

An injunction bond includes costs, if awarded on dissolution.[1]

Damages may be recovered upon the bond, whether awarded on dissolution, or afterwards, or in a different proceeding.[2]

In Indiana, injunctions may be granted, to stay waste; to stay all proceedings on judgments at law; to stay and suspend proceedings on suits pending before the Circuit Court or court of inferior jurisdiction; to exercise all powers usual and necessary for courts of chancery, in granting and enforcing restraining orders and injunctions; and to issue all requisite and usual (in chancery) process.

No injunction lies, except in case of emergency, till ten days' previous notice, unless applied for in open court, in relation to a suit pending therein.

A judgment in a personal action shall not be enjoined, without a bond with surety for its amount, interest, and costs, and the damages and costs of the injunction, if dissolved. And the complainant shall also indorse and sign on his bill a release of errors, when required.

Injunction shall be limited to the amount of the judgment not equitably due.

No injunction shall issue to stay proceedings at law after judgment in an action for lands, without a bond with surety for all damages and costs.

In other cases, a bond shall be given for damages and costs.

Ten per cent. damages upon dissolution of injunction to stay proceedings after judgment.

In case of injunction against a suit for land after verdict or judgment, the damages, upon dissolution, shall include the rents and profits, and all waste subsequent to the injunction.

Upon the granting or continuance of an injunction, the

---

[1] Hibbard v. McKindley, 28 Ill. 240.   [2] Ib.

court may impose equitable terms and conditions on the party obtaining it.

When an injunction is allowed after judgment, all officers of the court, the party, his agent and attorney shall suspend proceedings, and any process issued shall be stayed.

A writ of injunction is not necessary.

Provision is made for repayment of money collected on execution by the sheriff.

Also for an attachment for contempt, upon violation of an injunction against waste.

Particular provision is also made as to motions for dissolution.

Jurisdiction is given to the probate courts.[1]

As to the authority of one court over another, see the Indiana, &c. v. Williams.[2]

The collection of illegal taxes may be enjoined.[3]

An injunction will not be granted, upon the principle of marshalling securities, where a judgment is recovered against A. and B., and the property of A. has been conveyed under a junior lien to C., and the property of B. to D., and the judgment creditor seeks and enforces payment in the first instance from the property of A.[4]

Land was conveyed to the defendants, trustees of a religious society, of which the plaintiffs were members, for its use, according to the discipline of the General Conference. The society having erected a church, with a basement for a prayer-room, the trustees leased the latter to a teacher of a common day school, with leave to adapt it to his business. Held, an injunction should be granted.[5]

An injunction or temporary restraining order is rightly dissolved, unless the complaint allege sufficient ground therefor.[6]

An injunction cannot be granted by a master commissioner.[7]

---

[1] Indiana Rev. Sts. 851. See p. 543.
[2] 22 Ind. 198.
[3] The Toledo, &c. v. Lafayette, 22 Ind. 262.
[4] Sanders v. Cook, 22 Ind. 436.
[5] Perry v. McEwen, 22 Ind. 440.
[6] Sutherland v. The Lagro, &c., 19 Ind. 192.
[7] Glass v. The Board, &c., 16 Ind. 113.

A judge of the Circuit Court granted an injunction in vacation without notice. At the next term, the defendants appeared and demurred, and, pending the demurrer, prayed an appeal from the original order. Held, allowable, and that the order, without notice, was erroneous.[1]

But a temporary restraining order of the court or a judge is not appealable to the Supreme Court.[2]

In Minnesota, the District Court or a judge thereof may grant writs of injunction in all civil actions, on complaint, and, when a counterclaim or equities in the nature of one are set up in an answer, then on such answer affidavits are allowed. Such writs may be granted in the progress of any action, either by petition duly verified, or on affidavits, or both. But no injunction shall issue to stay proceedings in any civil action, before final decision.[3]

Provision is made for injunction against corporations, and individuals claiming corporate powers.[4] Also against insolvent corporations.[5] For appeal.[6] And in reference to the general course of proceeding, security, &c.[7]

In Oregon, no writ of injunction shall be issued, but upon bill or petition, filed, and verified by oath. It may be issued by the court or a judge in vacation. A bond shall be given, with surety, to abide the decision, and pay all damages and costs adjudged in case of dissolution. In case of proceedings at law, the bond shall be for payment of all moneys and costs due or to become due from the complainant, and all decreed against him upon dissolution.

In case of injunction to stay proceedings at law for recovery of money, upon dissolution, and dismissal of the bill, the court shall render a decree for the debt or damages, interest and costs accruing in chancery, with five per cent. on the debt and interest. When an officer has received money

---

[1] Flagg v. Sloan, 16 Ind. 432.
[2] Cincinnati, &c. v. Huncheon, 16 Ind. 436.
[5] Sts. of Minnes. 480.
[4] Ib. 606.
[5] Ib. 607.
[6] Ib. 621.
[7] 670-1.

on an execution which is enjoined, the officer shall repay the money, retaining costs of collection ; if it has not been paid over.[1]   (The same provision is made in Indiana.)

In Kansas, injunctions may be dissolved or modified in vacation.[2]

An injunction is a command to refrain from a particular act. It may be final or provisional—the latter by order. The writ of injunction is abolished.   (The circumstances under which injunction is allowed are substantially the same as in other western States, and similar to those in New York. Also the provisions as to security and notice.)   The order of injunction is addressed to the party enjoined, states the injunction, and is issued by the clerk.   When allowed at the commencement of the action, the clerk indorses upon the summons "injunction allowed," and no order is necessary ; nor in case of notice of the application.   An injunction is binding from notice.   Provision is made against successive injunctions.   An injunction granted by a judge may be enforced as the act of the court.   Disobedience may be punished as a contempt.   The party may be fined not exceeding two hundred dollars, required to make immediate restitution, and give security—or committed.   Further security is provided for in case of removal or insufficiency. Affidavits are allowed.   Provision is made for modifying or dissolving the injunction.[3]

Provision is made for enjoining the transfer of or interference with property by a judgment debtor.[4]

In Iowa,[5] an injunction may be granted as an independent means of relief or as auxiliary to other proceedings, in accordance with the rules heretofore observed, except as herein modified.

When applied for as an independent means of relief, the

[1] Oregon Sts. 202.
[2] Comp. Laws of Kansas, 454.
[3] Ib. 164.

[4] Ib. 208.
[5] Iowa Code, Chapters 112, 114, 126, 141.

petition must be sworn to and presented to the District Court, if in session in the county, for an allowance of the injunction. If not in session, application for that purpose may be made to any judge of the Supreme Court or District Court, or to the judge of the County Court of the proper county.

If the order of allowance is made by the court in session, the clerk shall make an entry thereof in the court record, and issue the writ accordingly. If made in vacation, the judge must indorse the said order upon the petition.

When it is a mere auxiliary measure resorted to during the trial of the principal cause, the terms on which it is allowed, as well as the kind of notice to be given to the opposite party, shall be such as the court prescribes.

In both the cases contemplated in the last section, the order of allowance must direct the writ to issue only after the filing of a bond in the office of the Clerk of the District Court, in a penalty to be therein fixed, with sureties to be approved by said clerk (unless the court or judge granting the said order has previously approved said sureties), and conditioned for the payment of all the damages which may be adjudged against the petitioner by reason of such injunction.

When proceedings in a civil action are sought to be enjoined, the suit must be brought in the county wherein such proceedings are pending. The bond must also in that case be further conditioned to pay any judgment that may be ultimately recovered against the party who seeks the injunction, for the cause of action on which the suit sought to be enjoined is founded.

The penalty of the bond must be fixed by the court or judge who makes the order, and must be doubly sufficient to cover any probable amount of liability to be thereby incurred.

Upon the filing of the bond as required, the clerk must issue the writ of injunction as directed by the order of allowance.

The court or judge before granting the writ may, if

deemed advisable, allow the defendant an opportunity to show cause why such order should not be granted.

If the writ is granted without allowing the defendant to show cause, he may at any time before the next term of the court apply to the judge who made the order to vacate or modify the same.

Such application must be with notice to the plaintiff, and may rest upon the ground that the order was improperly granted, or it may be founded upon affidavits on the part of the defendant. In the latter case the plaintiff may fortify his application by counter-affidavits and have reasonable time therefor.

The judge may thereupon decide the matter at once, unless some good cause for delay be shown. But the vacation of the order shall not prevent the cause from proceeding, if anything be left to proceed upon.

Any judge of the Supreme or District Court, being furnished with an authenticated copy of the writ of injunction, and also with satisfactory proof that such injunction has been violated, shall issue his precept to the sheriff of the county where the violation of the injunction occurred, or to any other sheriff (naming him) more convenient to all parties concerned, directing him to attach said defendant and bring him forthwith before the same or some other judge, at a place to be stated in said precept.

If, when thus produced, he files his affidavit denying or sufficiently excusing the contempt charged, he shall be released, and the affidavit shall be filed with the clerk of the court for preservation.

But if he failed to do so, the judge may require him to give bond, with surety, for his appearance at the next term of the court, and also for his future obedience to the injunction, which bond shall be filed with the clerk.

If he fail to give such security, he may be committed to the jail of the county where the proceedings are pending, until the next term of the court.

35

If the security be given, the court at the next term shall act upon the case, and punish the contempt in the usual mode.

The defendant may move to dissolve the injunction, either before or after the filing of the answer.

Issue may be joined on the defendant's answer, and a trial had as in other cases.

When practicable, the whole matter connected with the injunction shall be disposed of on such trial, and complete justice administered to all parties.

Only one motion, to dissolve or modify an injunction upon the whole case, shall be allowed.

Upon the dissolution, in whole or in part, of an injunction to stay proceedings upon a judgment or final order, the damages shall be assessed by the court, which may hear the evidence and decide in a summary way, or may, on the request of either party, cause a jury to be empanelled to find the damages. Where money is enjoined, the damages may be any rate per cent. on the amount released by the dissolution, which, in the discretion of the court, may be proper, not exceeding ten per cent. And where the delivery of property has been delayed by the injunction, the value of the use, hire, or rent thereof shall be assessed. Judgment shall be rendered against the party who obtained the injunction, for the damages assessed, and against the surety of such party.

For good cause shown, a judge's order may issue in vacation, directing any of the officers of the court in relation to the discharge of their duties.

Such order shall be in force only during the vacation in which it is granted, and for the first two days of the ensuing term.

The judge granting it may require the filing of a bond, as in case of an injunction, unless, from the nature of the case, such requirement would be clearly unnecessary and improper.

In all cases of breach of contract or other injury, where the party injured is entitled to maintain, and has brought an action by ordinary proceedings, he may, in the same cause, pray and have a writ of injunction against the repetition or continuance of such breach of contract or other injury, or the committal of any breach of contract or injury of a like kind, arising out of the same contract, or action, and he may also, in the same action, include a claim for damages or other redress.

In such action, judgment may be given for other relief, and also that the writ of injunction do or do not issue, as justice may require; and in case of disobedience, such writ of injunction may be enforced by attachment by the court, or when such court shall not be sitting, by a judge thereof.

It shall be lawful for the plaintiff, at any time after the commencement of the action, and whether before or after judgment, to apply *ex parte* to the court or a judge for a writ of injunction to restrain the defendant in such action from a repetition or continuance of the wrongful act, or breach of contract complained of, or the committal of any breach of contract or injury of a like kind, arising out of the same contract, or relating to the same property or right; and such writ may be granted or denied by the court or judge, upon such terms as to the duration of the writ, keeping an account, giving security, or otherwise, as to such court or judge shall seem reasonable and just, and in case of disobedience, such writ may be enforced by attachment by the court, or, when such court shall not be sitting, by the judge thereof: *Provided always*, that any order for a writ of injunction, made by a judge, or any writ issued by virtue thereof, may be discharged or varied, or set aside by the court, on application thereto by any party dissatisfied with such order.

The party seeking to vacate or modify a judgment or order made in the District Court, or by a judge thereof, may obtain an injunction suspending proceedings on the whole or part thereof, which injunction may be granted by the court or the judge thereof, upon its being rendered probable, by affidavit or petition sworn to, or by exhibition of the record, that the party is entitled to have such judgment or order vacated or modified.[1]

(As to injunctions by courts of law; and that the application need only conform substantially to the statute, see Hall v. Crouse.)[2]

A motion for injunction must specify the grounds.[3]

A perpetual injunction will not be reversed by the court alone, unless it appears that the record embraces all the evidence.[4]

A tax sale will not be enjoined upon the ground of a vague and indefinite description of the property.[5]

A purchase under a false impression as to the article purchased, but without fraud or warranty, is no ground for injunction.[6]

Under the code of 1851, damages might be awarded on the bond, upon dissolution. A subsequent award upon notice and motion would be irregular, but not reversed unless in case of appearance and objection.[7]

A petition for injunction in a proceeding to cancel a mortgage sale must allege a tender of the amount admitted to be due.[8]

After a mandamus to a county judge, requiring him and the other members of the board of canvassers to canvass the returns of an election on a proposition to remove the county seat from one town to another; an injunction may still be granted against such removal. The object of the latter process is to determine the validity of the returns; of the former, to compel ministerial officers to perform their duty by a canvass.[9]

In California, an injunction is a writ or order, requiring a person to refrain from a particular act.

It may be granted—

[1] See Way v. Lamb, 15 Iowa, 79; Taylor v. Dickinson, ib. 484; Davis v. Bonar, ib. 171.
[2] 14 Iowa, 487.
[3] Hall v. Crouse, 14 Iowa, 487.
[4] Hayden v. Wittze, 13 ib. 604.
[5] The Burlington, &c. v. Spearman, 12 ib. 113.
[6] Street v. Rider, 14 Iowa, 506.
[7] Woods v. Irish, ib. 427.
[8] Sloan v. Coolbaugh, 10 ib. 31.
[9] Dishon v. Smith, ib. 221.

1. When the complaint shows that the plaintiff is entitled to the relief demanded, and such relief or any part thereof consists in restraining the commission or continuance of the act complained of, either for a limited time or perpetually.

2. When it appears by the complaint or affidavit that the commission or continuance of some act during the litigation would produce great or irreparable injury to the plaintiff.

8. When it appears during the litigation that the defendant is doing, or threatens, or is about to do, or is procuring or suffering to be done, some act in violation of the plaintiff's rights, respecting the subject of the action, and tending to render the judgment ineffectual.

The injunction may be granted at the time of issuing the summons upon the complaint; and at any time afterwards, before judgment, upon affidavits. The complaints or affidavits must show sufficient grounds. The complaint must be sworn to by the plaintiff or some one in his behalf. The oath must declare, that the party has read or heard the complaint, and knows the contents, and that it is true of his own knowledge, except matters stated on information, &c., as to which he believes it to be true. When granted on the complaint, a copy of the complaint and verification shall be served with the injunction; if upon affidavit, a copy thereof.

An injunction is not allowed after answer but upon notice or order to show cause. But the defendant may be restrained until the decision upon the application for injunction.

A written undertaking shall be given, except by the people, to pay all damages.

Notice may be required, and the defendant restrained in the mean time.

An injunction to suspend the general and ordinary business of a corporation shall not be granted except by the court; nor without notice to the officers, unless the people are a party.

A party may apply upon reasonable notice to the court or the judge who granted an injunction, without notice, for a dissolution; either upon the complaint and affidavit, or affidavit on the part of the defendant, with or without answer. If upon affidavits for the defendant, not otherwise, the plaintiff may offer affidavits, or new evidence.

The injunction may be dissolved or modified.[1]

Dissolution of an injunction was ordered upon answer, denying equities.[2]

(As to the effect of *laches*, see Real, &c. v. Pond.[3]

As to the dissolving of an injunction by the judge who granted it, see Creavor v. Nelson.[4]

As to the rules of practice, affidavits, and appeal, see Gagliardo v. Crippen.[5])

Upon denial of equities by affidavits, *pendente lite*, an injunction was refused.[6]

So in case of denial in the answer, the cause being heard on the pleadings.

(As to notice, see Johnson v. Wide, &c.[7])

An injunction was granted in case of a right of way.[9]

A perpetual injunction will be granted, where the statute under which proceedings are had for condemnation of land for road purposes is unconstitutional; or for want of notice, or compensation.[10]

Such injunction does not prevent a future opening upon correct proceedings.[11]

In case of disputed title, the question of injunction during litigation depends materially upon the pecuniary ability of the creditors.[12]

(As to the injunction of executions, see Spencer v. Vigneaux.[13])

A grantee may enjoin a sale of real estate on an execution against the grantor; such sale, though passing no title, being sufficient to throw a cloud over the title.[14]

---

[1] California Laws, 537.
[2] Real, &c. v. Pond, &c., 23 Cal. 82.
[3] 23 Cal. 82.
[4] Ib. 464.
[5] 22 Cal. 362.
[6] Gagliardo v. Crippen, 22 Cal. 362.
[7] Ibid.
[8] 22 Cal. 479.
[9] Kittle v. Pfeiffer, 22 Cal. 484.
[10] Curran v. Shattuck, 24 Cal. 431.
[11] Ibid.
[12] Real, &c. v. Pond, &c., 23 Cal. 82.
[13] 20 Cal. 442; also Comstock v. Clemens, ib. 77.
[14] England v. Lewis, 25 Cal. 357.

An owner of land, in possession, cannot enjoin a sheriff from executing a writ of restitution issued on a judgment rendered against third parties, to which he is a stranger.[1]

No injunction lies to protect property, during litigation, where the complainant shows that he has no interest or claim to relief.[2]

(As to injunction in case of mining, see Logan v. Driscoll.[3])

A claimant of public lands, for fruit trees or crops, cannot enjoin mining thereon, unless the trees were planted or crops sown before location for mining.[4]

In an action for trespass upon a mining claim, the plaintiffs alleged that the defendants were working and extracting from the mine, which was admitted by the answer, but the title denied. The jury found a verdict for the plaintiffs, and an injunction was granted.[5]

An injunction was refused in the case of rival bridges.[6]

Where land has been condemned according to law for a highway, and damages assessed, and an official warrant for the amount tendered and refused; equity will not enjoin the road overseer from tearing down the fences and opening the highway.[7]

An injunction lies against using the name of a hotel. Thus the complainant kept a hotel under the name of "The What Cheer House," upon leased land. He afterwards purchased the adjacent lot, and erected a larger building, continuing to occupy both, but having the principal sign on the latter. He then surrendered the former estate, continuing the business upon the latter. The defendant purchased the former estate, and exhibited the same sign, with the prefix of the word "original" in smaller letters. Held, a case for injunction.[8]

A mortgagee may have an injunction against material waste, in case of insolvency.[9]

[1] Ferris v. Ellis, 25 Cal. 516.
[2] State v. M'Glynn, 20 Cal. 233.
[3] 19 Cal. 4.
[4] Ensminger v. M'Intire, 23 Cal. 593.
[5] Laughlin v. Kelly, 22 Cal. 211.
[6] Hall v. County, &c.,
[7] Creanor v. Nelson, 23 Cal. 464.
[8] Woodward v. Lazar, 21 Cal. 448.
[9] Robinson v. Russell, 24 Cal. 473.

Judgment was rendered against a mortgagor, constituting a lien. The mortgagee foreclosed, making the mortgagor alone a party. The land was sold under the decree to him, and a deed made to him. The creditor takes out execution, and advertises for sale. Held, such sale could not be enjoined by the holder of the title under the sheriff's deed, the creditor having a right to sell any interest of his debtor at the time of the judgment or execution.[1]

(As to the amount of injury to water rights required for an injunction, see Phœnix, &c. v. Fletcher.[2]

As to parties and general practice, see Trinity v. M'Cammon.[3])

In Louisiana, the clerks of the District Courts, except those of the parish of Orleans, may grant orders of injunctions in the absence of the judge from the parish, or when he is interested; and when for a specific sum, shall require bond in an amount one-half over the sum enjoined. But when the sale of specific property is enjoined, the bond shall be for one-half over the estimated value, as certified by the seizing officers. Injunctions may be issued by the clerk, on the oath of the party or his attorney of the absence or interest of the judge.

Injunctions may be granted on application of any purchaser, whose property is seized for the price, whenever suit has been brought for the property.

Injunctions may be granted to stay execution, when payment after judgment is alleged, when compensation is pleaded against the judgment, or when the sheriff is illegally proceeding on the execution, upon affidavit of the facts, and compliance with the legal requisitions.

No judgment or execution shall be enjoined on an allegation of compensation, set-off, or subsequent payment, except for the amount of such sum plead in compensation, &c., as shall be legally established by the defendant. And the

---

[1] Alexander v. Greenwood, 24 Cal. 511.

[2] 23 Cal. 481.

[3] 25 Cal. 119.

judgment shall be executed for the surplus, as if no injunction were granted. Bond and security shall be required in double the sum alleged to be paid, conditioned for payment of damages, if the injunction were wrongful.

The clerks of the District Courts, in case of injunction shall take from the party a bond, with one or more good securities in the amount fixed by the judge, conditioned according to law.

On the trial of injunctions, the surety in the bond shall be considered a plaintiff; and upon dissolution the court shall condemn the plaintiff and surety, jointly and severally to pay to the defendant interest at the rate of eight per cent. on the judgment, and not over twenty per cent. damages unless more be found. And the sureties shall not avail themselves of the plea of discussion. The same provisions shall apply, where a third person enjoins the execution of a judgment.[1]

In Alabama, injunctions shall be granted only by the judges of the Supreme and Circuit Courts and chancellors.

An injunction to a judgment operates as a release of errors.

Proceedings after judgment shall not be enjoined, without bond, conditioned to pay the amount of the judgment with interest, and such damages and costs as may be decreed against the party.

In actions for the recovery of lands, the bond shall be for payment of the damages in the judgment if enjoined, and all damage and costs which the judgment plaintiff sustains by the injunction, if dissolved.

In other cases, the bond shall be conditioned to pay all damages which any person may sustain by the injunction, if dissolved.

After refusal of an injunction by one circuit judge, no other one can act upon the application, but application may be made to a chancellor or judge of the Supreme Court. If refused by a chancellor, it may be renewed to a judge of the

[1] Laws of Louisiana, 1855, 324, No. 262.

Supreme Court, but no other officer; and if refused by him, cannot be renewed.

No application shall be made to a judge of the Supreme Court for an injunction which may be granted by any other judge or officer, unless made to and refused by the latter. A refusal must be indorsed on the bill, and a heavy penalty is provided for erasing it.

When an injunction to stay proceedings in an action is dissolved, on final hearing, the Chancellor may decree six per cent. damages on the amount of money for which such judgment was enjoined, if obtained for delay.

A bond to enjoin proceedings at law on a judgment for money, upon dissolution, in whole or in part, either upon an interlocutory or final decree, has the force and effect of a judgment, and being certified by the register to the clerk of the court in which the judgment was rendered, execution may issue for the amount enjoined, interest, and the damages decreed. The register may also issue execution for costs, if decreed.

In case of an interlocutory decree dissolving an injunction of a judgment, a refunding bond shall be given, payable to the register, conditioned to refund the money and interest he may collect on the judgment, if on final hearing perpetually enjoined; and the court may render a final decree on such bond.

A defendant may move to dissolve an injunction in vacation, before the Chancellor of the division in which the bill is filed, either for want of equity or on the coming in of the answer.

An appeal lies to the Supreme Court on all interlocutory orders, dissolving injunctions.

Notices, in case of suits and judgments, may be served upon the attorney.[1]

When money is paid or collected on an execution, the whole or any part of which is enjoined in chancery, it shall

[1] Code of Alabama, 531.

be refunded on demand, if not paid over to the plaintiff, without notice of the injunction.[1]

In North Carolina, writs of injunction may be issued by the judges of the Courts of Equity and Supreme Court.[2]

No injunction commanding the stay of an execution shall be issued, except on judgments in actions of detinue, for more than the complainant shall make oath to be just.

And he shall give bond for the payment into office, upon dissolution, of the sum complained of and all costs.[3]

After four months from recovery of judgment, he shall also deposit the amount of the judgment and costs with the master; unless he make oath that the delay arose from the fraud or false promises of the other party; or that he was out of the State when judgment was recovered.

If in case of injunction the complainant deposits the sum enjoined, it may be paid upon an order of court to the plaintiff at law upon his giving bond.[4]

(There are some other provisions not requiring to be stated.)

In Mississippi, an injunction to stay judgment or execution shall not be granted without notice, and the opportunity of answering.[5]

In Georgia, no injunction shall be sanctioned or granted by a judge of the Superior Courts, until the applicant has given to the adverse party, by application to the clerk of the Superior Court, a bond with good security for the eventual condemnation money, with future costs.

Provisions are made upon divers points of practice.

The dilatory practice of granting bills of injunction a second time, after dissolution of the first bill or bills, shall not be admissible or allowed in any case.[6]

[1] Code of Alabama, 451.
[2] N. C. Rev. C. 190.
[3] Ibid. 191.
[4] Ibid. 191–2.
[5] Laws of Miss. 74.
[6] 1 Cobb's Sts. 524.

By a later act, injunctions may be granted on terms discretionary with the judge.

A second injunction may be granted, where a previous one has been dismissed, for cause not connected with the merits, and when the judge is satisfied that a second injunction should issue.[1]

In Texas, provision is made as to injunction of judgments and executions; for security, and for the assessment of damages and an interlocutory decree on the bond on dissolution, where the collection of money has been enjoined; in other cases, the damages to be assessed by jury if required.[2]

In Florida, no writ of injunction, or *ne exeat*, shall be granted until a bill be filed praying for such writ, except in the special cases, and for the special causes in which such writs are authorized by the practice of the courts of the United States, exercising equity jurisdiction, and no writ of injunction to stay proceedings at law shall issue, except on motion to the court or judge, and reasonable notice of such motion previously served on the opposite party or his attorney; and the defendant, after injunction granted, may either before or after answer filed, on due notice being previously given to the opposite party, or his solicitor, move the court or the judge for the dissolution of any injunction which may have been granted.[3]

All injunction bonds executed in this State shall be conditioned to pay the debt and interest enjoined, and such damages as may be occasioned by the wrongful issuing of said injunction, instead of the condition now required by law, to wit, to pay the debt and interest, and ten per cent. damages thereon.[4]

---

[1] 1 Cobb's Sts 524.
[2] Oldh. & White, Dig. of Laws of Texas, 240.
[3] Laws of Florida, Tit. 7, Chap. 1.
[4] Florida Sts., 1852, Chap. 526.

INDEX.

A.

37

E ,

in case of injunction, 48, 531, 533, 534, 535, 540, 542, 249, 550, 554.
dissolution for want of, 81.
of motion to dissolve, 110.
in connection with dissolution, 124.
of injunction, in connection with the question of violation, 142, 149, 150.
injunction of judgment for want of. 169, 170, 176.
in case of injunction against corporation, 307.
in case of injunction against bank, 320.
to agent, of injunction, 341 n.

NOVELTY OF PATENT,
whether injunction requires, 399, 400.

NUISANCE,
remedy at law for, prevents injunction, 16.
injunction of, 269, 518, 527.
general jurisdiction of chancery, 269.
restrictions, 270.
public nuisance, 273.
abatement and injunction, 278.
case of equestrian statute, 505.
information against, 527.

O.

OATH
of plaintiff in case of injunction, 26, 29.
in connection with dissolution, 112.
of corporation, in reference to dissolution, 324 n.

OBSTRUCTION OF NAVIGATION,
injunction of, 425.

OFFICER,
sale by, after injunction, 143.
injunction against, violation of, 151.
suit against, injunction of, 258.

OFFICERS
of corporation, answers of, 325 n.
injunction in case of, 374, 524, 548.

OHIO,
injunction in, 36, 39, 162 n.

OMISSION
in allegations for injunction, 39.

OPENING
of foreclosure, by action for debt, 476.

Vida De Napoleon Bonaparte
by Walter Scott

Check Out More Titles From HardPress Classics Series In this collection we are offering thousands of classic and hard to find books. This series spans a vast array of subjects – so you are bound to find something of interest to enjoy reading and learning about.

Subjects:
Architecture
Art
Biography & Autobiography
Body, Mind &Spirit
Children & Young Adult
Dramas
Education
Fiction
History
Language Arts & Disciplines
Law
Literary Collections
Music
Poetry
Psychology
Science
…and many more.

Visit us at www.hardpress.net

CPSIA information can be obtained
at www.ICGtesting.com
Printed in the USA
BVHW071757190819
556220BV00014B/817/P